D1564871

The Tax System in Industrialized Countries

The Tax System in Industrialized Countries

Edited by

Ken Messere

OXFORD UNIVERSITY PRESS

1998

336.2
T23595

Oxford University Press, Great Clarendon Street, Oxford OX2 6DP
Oxford New York
Athens Auckland Bangkok Bogotá Buenos Aires Calcutta
Cape Town Dar es Salaam Delhi Florence Hong Kong Istanbul
Karachi Kuala Lumpur Madrid Melbourne Mexico City Mumbai
Nairobi Paris São Paolo Singapore Taipei Tokyo Toronto Warsaw
and associated companies in
Berlin Ibadan

Oxford is a registered trade mark of Oxford University Press

Published in the United States by
Oxford University Press Inc., New York

© Oxford University Press 1998

All rights reserved. No part of this publication may be reproduced,
stored in a retrieval system, or transmitted, in any form or by any means,
without the prior permission in writing of Oxford University Press.
Within the UK, exceptions are allowed in respect of any fair dealing for the
purpose of research or private study, or criticism or review, as permitted
under the Copyright, Designs and Patents Act, 1988, or in the case of
reprographic reproduction in accordance with the terms of the licences
issued by the Copyright Licensing Agency. Enquiries concerning
reproduction outside these terms and in other countries should be
sent to the Rights Department, Oxford University Press,
at the address above

British Library Cataloguing in Publication Data
Data Available

Library of Congress Cataloging in Publication Data
The tax system in industrialized countries/edited by
Ken Messere.
p.   cm.
Includes bibliographical references (p.)
1. Taxation–Europe.   2. Taxation–North America.
3. Taxation–Japan.   I. Messere, Ken.
HJ2599.5.T28   1998
336.2–dc21   98-35493

ISBN 0–19–829331–3

1 3 5 7 9 10 8 6 4 2

Typeset by J&L Composition Ltd,
Filey, North Yorkshire
Printed in Great Britain
on acid-free paper by
Bookcraft (Bath) Ltd,
Midsomer Norton, Somerset

Dedicated to the memory of
Joseph A. Pechman,
the pioneer of internationally
comparable tax analysis

University Libraries
Carnegie Mellon University
Pittsburgh PA 15213-3890

Note on Structure

Authors of the chapters were asked to conform to a standardized format to facilitate comparison between the ten countries. In essence this has been done, but there are some differences in approach to the various subsections, particularly in Sections C3, C4, C5, and C6 due to varying availability and reliability of data (See Chapter 1, Section A1, for further discussion of this point).

Standardized format for country chapters:

A   Introduction or overview

B   The Tax System
B1 Individual Income Tax
B2 Corporate Income Tax
B3 Social Security Contributions and/or Payroll Taxes
B4 Value-Added and/or Sales Tax
B5 Excises and other Consumption Taxes
B6 Capital Taxes
B7 The Local Tax System

C   Economic and Social Aspects
C1 The Fiscal Deficit
C2 Savings and Investment Incentives
C3 Distribution of the Tax Burden
C4 The Hidden Economy
C5 Administrative and Compliance Costs
C6 Taxes and Labour Supply

D   Tax Reforms
D1 Main tax reforms, mid-1980s to mid-1990s
D2 Recent and prospective tax reforms

University Libraries
Carnegie Mellon University
Pittsburgh PA 15213-3890

Contents

5. Italy

Laura Castellucci

6. Japan

Hiromitsu Ishi

8. Spain

Miguel A. Lasheras and Isabel Menendez

Contributors

Krister Anderson is Chief Economist and Head of Reasearch at Skandanivska Enskilda Bank

Richard M. Bird is Professor of Economics and Director of the International Centre for Tax Studies at the University of Toronto.

Laurence Blotniki is a member of the research centre at the University of Paris I and teaches at the Institute of European Studies affiliated with the University of Chicago.

Wolfgang Büttner was an economist in the OECD Fiscal Affairs Division. He is now at the German Ministry of Finance.

Laura Castellucci is Professor of Economic Policy at the University of Rome 'Tor Vergata'.

Andrew Dilnot is Director of the Institute for Fiscal Studies in London.

Ulrich von Essen is an economist in the German Ministry of Finance.

Christophe Heckly teaches economic policy at the Institute for Public Administration in the University of Paris X.

Hiromitsu Ishi is Professor of Economics at Hitatsubashu University, Tokyo.

Flip de Kam is Professor in the Department of Economics and Tax Law at Groningen University and is presently a member of the OECD Fiscal Affairs Division.

Miguel A. Lasheras is Commissioner of the regulatory body for utilities of the electricity industry. He was previously General Director of the Economics Department of the Prime Minister's Staff and General Director of the Institute for Tax Studies in Madrid.

Willi Leibfritz was Head of the Public Economics Division in the Economics Department of OECD. He is now Head of the Department for Macroeconomic Analysis and Public Finance at the Institute for Economic Research (IFO) in Munich.

Isabel Menendez is a tax auditor in Spain.

Ken Messere was head of the Fiscal Affairs Division of OECD from 1971 to 1991. Since then he has been a freelance writer on tax matters and occasional consultant for OECD, IMF, and the World Bank.

Leif Mutén is Professor Emeritus of International Tax Law at the Stockholm School of Economics, Rector of the Stockholm School of Economics in Riga and a Member of the Tax Notes International Advisory Board.

David B. Perry is Research Associate at the Canadian Tax Foundation.

Gregory Stears was a Research Officer at the Institute for Fiscal Studies, and is now an economist with the Association of British Insurers.

Janet G. Stotsky is a senior economist in the Fiscal Affairs Department of the International Monetary Fund (IMF).

Emil M. Sunley is an Assistant Director in the Fiscal Affairs Department of the IMF.

Thomas A. Wilson is Professor of Economics and Director of the Policy and Economic Analysis Programme at the University of Toronto.

1 An Overview

KEN MESSERE

A. Preliminary Remarks

A1 Structure and Objectives of the Book

This book derives from a series of articles written mostly in 1993 and published in various numbers of *Tax Notes International* during 1994 and 1995. To facilitate comparisons between countries, articles were written in a standardized form based largely on the framework established by Joseph Pechman in his book *Comparative Tax Systems: Europe, Canada and Japan* (Tax Analysts, 1987). To accommodate new tax policy preoccupations additional sections were added on fiscal deficits, administrative and compliance costs, and the effect of taxation on labour supply. The standardized format is reproduced in the skeleton provided before the list of contents. These articles were substantially revised by the authors in the light of a number of comments received and they were updated as far as time and space constraints permitted.

The primary aim of the book is to examine tax developments between the mid-1980s and mid-1990s in ten industrialized countries, noting what has changed and what has remained the same, as well as the nature and likelihood of tax reforms in these countries over the next few years. This overview makes comparisons between the ten countries and between the situation in the mid-1980s and mid-1990s, concentrating in particular on how far common trends and attitudes have emerged, how far countries have gone their own way and seem likely to continue to do so over the next few years. In the overview there are some references to fourteen other OECD countries, but not to recently joined Korea, Mexico and Eastern European countries for which comparative data are lacking.

It follows from the aim of the book that the contents of Sections C and D of the skeleton are the most important part of the country chapters, with Sect. A providing a general overview and Sect. B the necessary background on tax systems. Sect. B usually reflects the main tax provisions in 1994 to 1996, but

Ken Messere thanks Richard Bird, Sijbren Cnossen, Flip de Kam, and anonymous reviewers for comments on earlier versions of this chapter, as well as all contributors to this book for their cooperation. Also in his capacity as editor of the book he would like to express his gratitude for the valuable work of the assistant editor and copy-editor of the Oxford University Press.

where possible, brief reference is made to the most important changes occuring up until early 1998. The problem with Sect. C, especially Sects. C3 to C6 is that these are areas where different types of methodology have been employed, each giving different results, and in a few countries, little or no research has been carried out in some of these areas. Consequently, it had to be left to the authors of the country chapters to provide what they regarded as the most reliable data. For these reasons comparisons between countries of the data shown in Sects. C3, C4, C5, and C6 have to be made with care and nothing is said about the data in this overview.

I am aware that the country chapters vary considerably in length and detail (from around 25 to 50 pages). I can only plead that, as editor, I have done my best to reduce differences between the length of the original articles, which reflect the fact that tax reforms have been a much more important topic in some countries than others. For example, tax reform has been high on the political agenda of Canada, Italy, Japan, The Netherlands, and USA (long chapters), and less so in Spain and the UK (short chapters).

A2 Developments Since 1985

The main trend between the mid-1980s and mid-1990s is that nearly all the ten countries have reduced the rates and broadened the base of the individual and corporate income tax, a move largely influenced by the 1986 US Tax Reform Act. France provides the main exception to this trend while in Japan the lowering of the corporate income tax was not accompanied by a broadening of its base and in Italy and Spain there were no reductions to corporate tax rates. A more recent trend is that between 1990 and 1998 there has been an almost universal increase in the standard rate of value-added tax (see Table 1.10 and the conclusion of Sect. B4).

The tax policy climate in the mid-1990s is very different from that of the mid-1980s. Following the radical changes of the late 1980s and early 1990s, reforms have increasingly shifted to administrative matters, for most governments accept (Italy being the exception) that business requires stability in tax laws. Recent changes typically concentrate on reducing administrative and compliance costs, and improving the quality of the tax administrations as well as relationships between the tax authorities and taxpayers.

Another striking difference between the mid-1980s and the mid-1990s is that in the earlier period a major issue was how to offset the arbitrary effects of high rates of inflation on increasing tax bills through bracket creep (i.e. taxpayers with the same income in real terms paid higher marginal rates of tax because their nominal income had increased) and erosion of the real value of family allowances. Bracket creep under the then prevailing highly progressive rate schedules added to progressivity, while the erosion of allowances reduced it. Some thought bracket creep should be offset, others that allowances should be adjusted for inflation. In virtually all countries, there was a debate about whether offsetting should be done by indexation or discretionary changes, and governments frequently changed their minds. Nowadays, with inflation falling to low levels in most of the ten countries reviewed, and tax schedules having been flattened, how to deal with the effect of inflation on tax yields is no longer a major issue.

In more recent years fiscal consolidation has become the main tax policy concern in most countries. The period 1985 to 1993 may be divided into two parts: between 1985 and 1989, economies were usually buoyant (average growth in real GDP of 3 and 4 per cent), whereas between 1989 and 1993 average growth in GDP was usually well under 2 per cent. Also the average OECD deficit declined from 3.5 per cent of nominal GDP in 1985 to 1.2 per cent in 1989, after which fiscal deficits increased sometimes to unprecedented degrees. By 1993 all OECD countries were in deficit and all save Norway were expected at the end of 1996 to remain so in 1996 and 1997 (see Table 1.11). However, as at mid-1998, budget balancing has ceased to be a constraint in Canada, Sweden, and USA.

While most governments aimed at reducing the deficit by cutting government expenditure, they have had limited success during the recent recession when unemployment was increasing almost everywhere—and in the longer term, demographic trends also are going to make cuts in government expenditure difficult. So a reduction in fiscal deficits to 3 per cent of GDP as required under the Maastricht treaty (see Sect. D3) as well as under sound fiscal policy has entailed tax increases in nearly all the ten countries (see Fig. 1.1) and is likely to continue to do so in the future despite the popularity of tax reduction in most of these countries.[1]

Another theme that has attracted government attention in recent years, but less so ten years ago, is to level the playing field in respect of the tax treatment of savings. In the mid-1980s, progressive expenditure taxes plus cash-flow corporation taxes were widely advocated (and still receive some support in the USA), whereas nowadays governments generally recognize that such a radical departure from present tax structures would present too many practical problems. Currently favoured solutions aim at allowing deduction of all kinds of savings from the income tax base, which, of course, will have the effect of reversing recent base-widening trends as well as resulting in a regressive rather than progressive expenditure tax. It is generally believed that such deductions will have little effect on the level of savings, although most certainly they will affect the form that savings take, and could also simplify the tax system as well as removing opportunities for tax evasion.

---

[1] Of relevance here is an article in OECD *Economic Outlook*, 59: 33–41, on the experience of eighteen countries (including the ten surveyed in this book) with fiscal consolidation between 1974 and 1996. It noted that significant and fiscal consolidation, defined as a positive change in the general government structural financial balance equivalent to at least 3 percentage points of GDP which takes place continuously over consecutive years occurred on fifteen occasions. In all but one of these fifteen cases, fiscal consolidation included at least some increase in the proportion of total revenue to GDP.

Another recent trend reversal from the 1985 personal income tax scene is the retreat from global taxation. This takes various forms:

- introduction of alternative minimum taxes (Canada and USA);
- supplementary taxes on gross income (Denmark and Norway);
- anti-shelter provisions (USA); and
- most recently, a two-rate schedule that combines a progressive rate on earned income and a low flat rate on capital income sometimes equal both to the corporate tax rate and the lowest marginal rate on labour income (most of the Nordic countries).

A last difference between the mid-1980s and mid-1990s is the greater emphasis on green or environmental taxes in recent years. However, this emphasis is of more relevance to environmental policy than tax policy, since the few environmental excises in Italy, the Netherlands, and Sweden bring in little revenue. Important revenues would result only from a heavy tax on carbon emissions as recommended by the European Commission, but international considerations render the introduction of such a tax unlikely in the near future. It is true, however, that most countries now impose lower rates of tax on unleaded petrol and cars equipped with catalytic converters. Another recent trend is the end of the relative decline of the traditional excises on smoking, drinking, and motoring. However, although these taxes may have favourable environmental effects, their main purpose is to raise large amounts of revenue.

B. Tax Revenue Developments Between 1985 and 1995

B1 Methodology

A number of chapters have used national revenue statistics or national accounts data. There are good reasons for this, including the fact that more recent data are available and even projections for future years on the basis of national statistics, whereas, at the time of writing (end 1997), the standardized OECD data stop at 1995, with 1996 estimates for most countries. For a comparative

Table 1.1   Unweighted OECD average percentage of total tax receipts

	1985	1990	1995
1. Personal income tax	30	29	27
2. Corporate income tax	8	8	8
3. Social security contributions	22	23	25
4. VAT and sales taxes	16	17	18
5. Excises and other specific taxes on goods and services	16	13	13
6. Property and capital taxes	5	6	5
Total of above taxes	97	96	96

Source: Revenue Statistics, 1965–1996 (OECD, 1997).

overview, however, it is necessary to use the standardized OECD data published annually by the OECD under the title *Revenue Statistics*. This is why data in this chapter sometimes differ from those provided in other chapters.

Since over 95 per cent of revenues come from six levies, little is said here about the remaining kinds of tax. These six sources are shown in Table 1.1.

The only other methodological issue necessary to mention here is that, domestically, some countries do and some countries do not regard social security contributions as taxes. The OECD classification of taxes includes them. Also, following OECD practice, if contributions are levied on an income tax base, as in some Nordic countries, they are treated as personal income taxes, not as contributions, in the tables of this overview.[2]

B2 Tax-level Developments

Tax levels are generally measured by the ratio of total tax receipts to GDP or what may be called total tax ratios (TTR). Table 1.2 indicates how TTRs have changed between 1985 and 1995 in the ten countries and it may be noted that developments are very different among them (i.e. continuous increases in Canada and Italy and decreases until recently in the UK, little change in France, Germany, and the USA except in Germany after unification, and increases followed by decreases in Japan, the Netherlands, Spain, and Sweden).

Fig. 1.1 illustrates developments in the ten countries included in the present study. It covers only the years 1985, 1990, and 1995, the period 1985–90 being mostly boom years and 1990–5 slump years.

This figure suggests or illustrates, first, that it is easier to get a consensus for high taxation (including social security contributions) in small rather than large countries, Sweden and the Netherlands having the highest and Japan and the USA the lowest TTR throughout the period. (This is confirmed by the fact that the other OECD countries with the highest TTRs are Denmark, Luxembourg, Finland, Norway, Belgium, and Austria.) The figure also shows that for most countries ranking orders do not change over the period, but the UK moved from fifth to seventh place and Italy from sixth to fourth.

Table 1.3 provides information on the levels of receipts from some of the main sources of revenue for the ten countries covered in 1985 and 1995. The average of the ten indicates that the (modest) increases in TTRs between the two years is mainly due to increases in personal income tax, social security, and VAT receipts as a percentage of GDP. There also was a slight decline in the percentage of receipts from corporation taxes and specific taxes raised on goods and services.

---

[2] As from 1990. the Netherlands has levied contributions to finance the general social insurance on the basis of taxable income (with a ceiling), applying the personal exemptions of the personal income tax, and should accordingly be classified as taxes on income. However, the Revenue Statistics continue to report the payments concerned as contributions. This should be kept in mind when interpreting Tables 1.3 and 1.4.

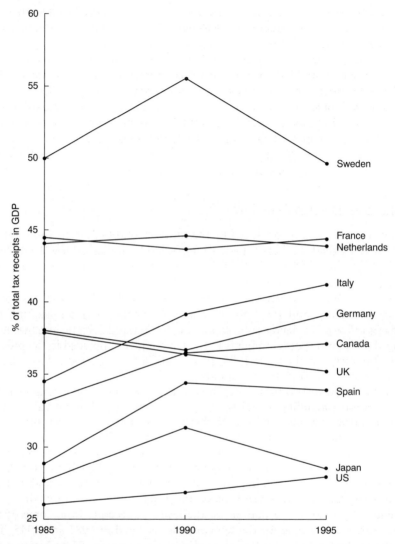

Fig. 1.1   Total tax ratios in 1985, 1990, and 1995[a]

[a] Intervening years are not covered. For Germany only the 1995 figure includes East Germany.

Source: Revenue Statistics, 1965–1996 (Paris, 1997).

B3 Changing the Tax Mix

Table 1.4 shows how tax structures have changed in the ten countries between 1985 and 1995. It indicates that between 1985 and 1995 the personal income tax share substantially increased in Spain and substantially declined in Sweden. There was a major change in the Netherlands between income tax

Table 1.2   Total tax revenues as a percentage of GDP, 1985–1995

	1985	1986	1987	1988	1989	1990	1991	1992	1993	1994	1995
Canada	33.1	33.7	34.7	34.0	35.1	36.5	36.7	36.4	35.9	36.4	37.2
France	44.5	44.0	44.5	43.8	43.7	43.7	43.9	43.7	43.9	44.1	44.5
Germany[a]	38.1	37.1	38.0	37.7	38.2	36.7	38.2	39.0	39.0	39.2	39.2
Italy	34.5	36.0	36.1	36.8	37.9	39.2	39.7	42.1	43.8	41.7	41.3
Japan	27.6	28.4	29.7	30.3	30.7	31.3	30.8	29.2	29.1	27.8	28.5
Netherlands	44.1	44.9	47.5	47.6	44.9	44.6	47.2	46.8	47.5	45.3	44.0
Spain	28.8	30.6	32.5	32.8	34.6	34.4	34.7	35.9	34.9	35.0	34.0
Sweden	50.0	52.5	55.4	54.8	55.5	55.6	53.7	51.0	50.1	50.8	49.7
UK	37.9	37.6	37.2	37.1	36.2	36.4	35.7	35.1	33.5	34.2	35.3
USA	26.0	25.8	27.1	26.9	27.0	26.7	26.8	26.7	27.0	27.5	27.9

[a] United Germany from 1991.

Source: See Table 1.1.

Table 1.3   Percentage of certain tax receipts to GDP 1985 and 1995

	Personal income tax		Corporation income tax		Social security contributions		VAT and sales taxes		Specific tax on goods and services	
	1985	1995	1985	1995	1985	1995	1985	1995	1985	1995
Canada	11.6	13.9	2.7	3.0	4.5	6.2	4.4	5.6	4.3	3.1
France	5.7	6.2	2.0	1.6	19.3	19.3	8.9	7.8	3.9	4.0
Germany	10.9	10.7	2.3	1.1	13.9	15.4	6.0	6.8	3.3	3.7
Italy	9.2	10.8	3.2	3.6	12.0	13.1	5.0	5.7	3.2	4.6
Japan	6.8	6.1	5.8	4.3	8.4	10.4	0	1.5	3.3	2.3
Netherlands	8.6	8.3	3.1	3.3	19.5	18.4	7.1	6.9	3.2	4.0
Spain	5.7	8.1	1.5	1.9	11.9	12.3	4.2	5.5	3.7	3.5
Sweden	19.4	17.5	1.7	3.1	12.5	14.5	7.0	7.5	5.8	4.3
UK	10.3	9.7	4.7	3.3	6.8	6.3	5.8	6.7	5.2	5.0
USA	9.9	10.1	2.0	2.6	6.6	7.0	2.1	2.2	2.2	2.1

Source: See Table 1.1.

and social security contributions, as described in Chapter 7 Sects B3 and D1. The corporation tax share has substantially declined in Japan and in the UK. The very high reliance on social security contributions in Italy, the Netherlands, and Spain has decreased, but has remained stable in France, while such reliance increased in Canada, Germany, Japan, and Sweden. There has been little change in the VAT share except in the UK, where it substantially increased and in Canada and Japan where VAT was introduced. The excise share has declined greatly in Japan, somewhat in Canada,

Spain, and Sweden, and has remained more or less the same in the other six countries.

Various pressure groups have been arguing, for the most part unsuccessfully, for three kinds of changes in the tax mix.

First, in many countries there is advocation for a move from income to consumption taxation. There are many well-known reasons for making such a shift, but between 1985 and 1995 (compare columns 1 plus 3 with 7 plus 9 to columns 2 plus 4 and 8 plus 10 of Table 1.4) it has occurred only in the UK. The introduction of VAT in Canada and Japan and recent increased rates of VAT in a number of countries may modify the picture a little in the next years, but due to the greater automatic elasticity of even the new flatter rates of income tax, the effect is likely to be slight.

Second, in a few countries (France, Italy, and Spain where employers' contributions are extremely high) a switch from payroll taxes to VAT has been suggested partly to move some of the initial burden from labour input to consumption as a whole thus reducing a disincentive to taking on especially unskilled and part-time labour and partly to improve international trade balances, since VAT but not payroll taxes are rebated when goods cross frontiers. In the long term tax shifting of payroll taxes into lower wages and exchange rate adjustments may invalidate these two arguments. But in the short run increases in payroll taxes may be reflected in both lower profits and higher prices and in the European Union there are constraints on exchange rate adjustments. There have been many representations from employers in France, Italy, and Spain, who regard payroll taxes as a non-wage labour cost, claiming that they are at a competitive disadvantage with other countries due to these high payroll taxes.

Third, in a few countries, a move from the employees' social security contributions base towards an income tax base has been advocated even though the proceeds may remain earmarked for social welfare benefits. Here the argument is between those who regard contributions as social insurance contributions rather than taxes and those who regard them as a regressive form of taxation, with flat rates, no thresholds, low ceilings, and no allowances for family circumstances. The Nordic countries earlier and the Netherlands recently have largely integrated the two levies and other countries have relaxed the regressivity of contributions (see Sect. C3 below).

It may be relevant for future relative reliance on income, payroll, and consumption taxation that four of the ten countries have recently introduced small surcharges to the personal income tax for specific expenditures: in France for social welfare, in Germany for unification costs, and in Sweden for defence. More recently Italy has introduced a one-off personal income tax with a separate schedule (Eurotax) to meet the Maastricht criterion—see Sect. D.

Table 1.4 Percentage of certain tax receipts in total tax receipts, 1985 and 1995[a]

	Personal income tax		Corporation income tax		Social security contributions		VAT and sales taxes		Specific tax on goods and services	
	1985	1995	1985	1995	1985	1995	1985	1995	1985	1995
Canada	35	37	8	8	13	17	13	15	13	8
France	13	14	4	4	43	43	20	17	9	9
Germany	29	27	6	3	36	39	16	17	9	9
Italy	27	26	9	9	35	32	14	14	9	11
Japan	25	21	21	15	30	36	0	5	12	8
Netherlands	19	19	7	7	44	42	16	16	7	9
Spain	20	24	5	5	41	36	15	16	13	10
Sweden	39	35	3	6	25	29	14	15	12	9
UK	27	27	12	9	18	18	15	19	14	14
USA	38	36	7	9	25	25	8	8	8	8

[a] To nearest percentage point.

Source: See Table 1.1.

B4 Revenues of Subordinate Levels of Government[3]

It is not possible to make valid comparisons in a short space between federal countries with large state and local governments, such as Canada and the USA, with small unitary countries. Nor are data available to disaggregate revenues of subordinate levels of government in unitary countries. Subject to these limitations, Table 1.5 shows the following.

First, the share allocated to social security agencies increased between 1985 and 1992 in most of the ten countries, with Italy and Spain moving in the opposite direction.

Second, despite the political cries for decentralization in many countries, there has been no big shift from federal/central to state and local levels of government except in Sweden. The UK represents the other extreme, where the share of local government own revenues fell by more than 50 per cent between 1985 and 1995 due to the shift from a classical property tax (rates) to a 'poll tax'. (see Sect. B2.7 of Chapter 10 for a brief description of UK local taxation over the last decade).

Third, among the three federal countries, the share of receipts of state and local governments is quite high; among unitary governments, it is relatively

---

[3] It should also be noted there is an ambiguity on what counts as 'local taxes'. The source of Table 1.5 follows the principle that taxes are allocated according to which levels the revenues accrue, irrespective of whether subordinate levels of government have any right to fix (always within strict limits) the rate and base of such taxes.

Table 1.5   Shares of tax revenues to different levels of government 1985 and 1995[a]

Federal Countries	European Union		Federal		State		Local		Social Security	
	1985	1995	1985	1995	1985	1995	1985	1995	1985	1995
Canada			41	40	36	34	10	9	13	17
Germany	1.0	0.6	32	31	22	21	9	9	36	39
USA			45	42	20	20	13	13	20	25

Unitary Countries	European Union		Central				Local		Social Security	
	1985	1995	1985	1995			1985	1995	1985	1995
France	0.6	0.4	47	46			9	10	43	43
Italy	0.6	0.4	62	63			2	5	35	32
Japan			44	39			26	24	30	36
Netherlands	1.5	1.4	52	67			2	3	44	42
Spain		0.6	43	51			11	13	41	36
Sweden			54	45			30	32	16	23
UK	1.1	1.0	71	77			10	4	17	18

[a] To nearest percentage point, except for contributions to the European Union. EU contributions do not include VAT own resources, which are not considered to be a tax.

Source: See Table 1.1.

high in Japan and Sweden, moderate in France and Spain, and extremely low in Italy, the Netherlands, and the UK.

Also, while most of the ten countries finance subcentral levels of local government by a variety of taxes—including income taxes, property taxes, use and permission taxes, and in the case of Canada and the USA, consumption taxes, in Italy until very recently, the Netherlands, and the UK, local revenue resources are very limited, which explains their low share.

C. Main Developments in the Major Taxes Between 1985 and 1995

C1 Personal Income Tax[4]

It is not feasible in an overview of this size to comment on the enormous diversity in the treatment of the tax base (which comprises both income included (capital gains, fringe benefits, etc.) as well as expenses excluded or reduced (such as interest payments on home mortgages and other expendi-

---

[4] Personal income tax (PIT) and individual income tax are used interchangeably in this book since different authors have different preferences.

tures, insurance premiums, private health insurance, employees' social security contributions, and state and local taxes)), except to say that the base has widened in all OECD countries.[5] Accordingly, this section and Table 1.6 focus on three more manageable issues: developments in nominal tax rates, the tax unit, and indexation of rate schedules and allowances. It may also be mentioned that there has been a trend to move away from what are called 'tax allowances' in Europe and 'tax deductions' in the USA (i.e. deductions from income subject to tax) towards tax credits (i.e. deduction from the tax itself). This increases the progressivity of the tax, since the value of the tax allowance is a function of the marginal rate of tax. The imposition of ceilings on certain expense-related tax allowances and tax credits has also increased progressivity.

C1.1 Nominal Tax Rates

In all ten countries, there was a sharp decline in top tax rates between 1985 and 1994, together with a reduction in the number of rates. This does not, however, entail a loss of overall progressivity of income tax systems among most of the ten countries, because of the offsetting progressivity of the base-widening as well as increases in tax thresholds, and the movement from tax allowances to tax credits, referred to in the previous paragraph.

The changes in lowest positive rates shown in Table 1.6 can easily be misinterpreted because they do not provide details about thresholds and zero-rated bands—something too complicated to do on a comparative basis. But it is generally accepted that despite the increase in lowest nominal rates in a number of countries, progressivity was usually increased for low-income taxpayers because of increases in thresholds, which were especially large in the reforms of Spain and the USA.

In fourteen other OECD countries between 1985 and 1993:

- the flattening or reduction of the number of brackets occurred in all countries except Austria and Luxembourg (increase) and Denmark, Ireland, and Turkey (no change);
- top rates declined in all countries, except Denmark, Switzerland, and Turkey, where they remained the same; and
- those other countries were more or less equally divided among those where the lowest positive rate increased and where it decreased.

C1.2 The Tax Unit

In the 1970s and early 1980s, the appropriate tax unit for earnings of married couples was a major policy issue, when there was much ideological conflict

---

[5] See K. Messere (1993: 41 and ch. 10 *passim*). Pp. 264–5 and 274–81 provide some information about what is included in and what is excluded from the income tax base in OECD countries during recent years.

between traditional family values in favour of joint taxation on the one hand, and incentives to wives to enter the labour force as part of the female emancipation phenomenon in favour of separate taxation on the other. In practice, ideology took precedence over reality, first because in most countries the tax unit was less important than the rate schedule and the structure of tax reliefs in determining relative tax payments among different family units, and second because separate taxation, insofar as it did affect relative tax liabilities, benefited high-earning wives and penalized low-paid working-class wives. A choice between the two could be seen as a rational compromise, but this did not occur in many countries. During the 1970s and the early 1980s, there was an almost one-way move from joint to individual taxation.

Income-sharing under joint tax systems and transferable allowances under separate systems, plus the flattening of tax schedules, reduced even further the influence of the tax unit on different tax bills. This is reflected in the relative absence of change between 1985 and 1994, which occurred only in Spain and the UK (see Table 1.6). Probably the tax unit for earned income will increasingly become a non-issue.

On the contrary, the tax unit treatment of investment income has been changed greatly since 1985. Until quite recently, most countries with separate taxation for earned income required joint taxation for dividend and interest income to prevent tax avoidance by couples artificially splitting their investment income. One consequence of the flattening of the rate schedules is that this is no longer regarded as a problem, so countries with separate taxation for earned income nowadays usually extend it to unearned income as well.

C1.3 Adjusting Rates and Reliefs for Inflation

Although no longer a priority topic with present low inflation rates in most OECD countries, it remains interesting why some governments fully index, then partially index, and then cease to index, while others go in the reverse direction. This is especially so in view of a 1986 OECD study concentrating on the late 1970s, when inflation was much higher, which suggested that there was not much difference in the amount by which fiscal drag was offset as between countries applying an index to convert nominal income to real income in respect of the rate schedule and reliefs, and countries taking discretionary measures.

It may be concluded that governments are especially influenced by political and sociological considerations in changing their attitudes to indexation. Governments (especially right-wing governments as under Reagan and Thatcher) wish to reassure taxpayers; others, not necessarily right wing, such as Australia, Canada, and the Netherlands, chose either partial or some form of optional indexation (i.e. no indexation when inflation is below a certain level (Canada) or when the government needed money (Australia) and partial indexation (Netherlands)). Germany, under both CDU and SDP governments, regarded macroeconomic control as more important than being bound by indexation, a view also taken by Spain and, until recently, Italy and Sweden. The latter two countries suggest that governments consider that their taxpayers require the reassurance of indexation when income taxes have greatly increased—as happened in Denmark in the early 1970s. Finally, France has frequently used indexation for redistributional purposes by not indexing the highest bracket but indexing the others.

Since automatic indexing provisions frequently are either offset or accentuated by separate discretionary measures, it is a game in OECD countries that some governments like to play and others do not. Of course, different considerations apply to the Third World and some OECD countries with very high inflation rates, when indexation may be more serious than a game.

Although during the high inflation years of the 1970s and early 1980s there were frequent changes in many countries between indexation, non-indexation, partial indexation, and even irregular indexation, Table 1.6 shows that changes since 1985 occurred only in Italy, from non-indexation to indexation in 1990, and in Sweden, where indexation was reintroduced in 1990, having been introduced in 1979 and abandoned in 1983. (Of other

Table 1.6 Personal income tax in 1985 and 1994 (federal/central government)[a]

| | Rates on earned income | | | | | | Tax unit[b] | | Indexation | | | |
| | Top rate | | Lowest positive rate | | No. of brackets | | | | Of schedule | | Of allowances | |
	1985	1994	1985	1994	1985	1994	1985	1994	1985	1994	1985	1994
Canada	34	29	6	17	10	3	Individual	Individual	yes	yes[e]	yes	yes[e]
France	65	56.8	5	12	13	7	Family	Family	yes	yes	no	no
Germany[h]	56	53	22	19	n/a	n/a	Optional	Optional	no	no	no	no
Italy[c]	62	51	18	10	15	7	Individual	Individual	no	no[i]	no	yes
Japan	70	50	10	10	9	3	Individual	Individual	no	no	no	no
Netherlands	72	60	16	7	9	3	Individual	Individual	yes[f]	yes[f]	yes[f]	yes[f]
Spain	66	53	16	20	34	16	Family	Optional	no	no	no	no
Sweden	54	20	3	0	15	7	Individual	Individual	no	no	yes	yes
UK	60	40	30	20	6	3	Optional	Individual	yes[f]	yes[f]	yes[f]	yes[f]
USA[d]	50	39.6	11	15	14	5	Joint	Joint	yes[g]	yes[g]	yes[g]	yes[g]

n/a = not applicable (see Chapter 4, Section B1.2)
[a] It is recalled that there are very important personal income taxes at subordinate levels of government at flat rates in Canada (17% though progressive from 16 to 24% in Quebec) and Sweden (31%) as well as less important progressive taxes in Japan (around 5 to 11%) and the USA (around 2 to 4%).
[b] As regards earned income.
[c] 1986 and 1993.
[d] Some variations between joint and separate filing.
[e] Sometimes partial.
[f] Sometimes not applied.
[g] But not before 1985. Applies to some but not all state income taxes.
[h] 47% on business income as from 1993.
[i] Yes between 1990 and 1992.

OECD countries, indexation was recently introduced in Belgium and Greece.)

C2 Corporation Income Tax

Provisions relating to the tax base (definition and scope of taxable income, depreciation rules, valuation of stocks, inflation adjustment, etc.) are too varied and complex to make comparisons possible in an overview of this size, but it is noted that the general widening of the tax base over the last decade has usually taken the form of reducing and abolishing particular tax incentives. Table 1.7 provides some information on developments in the two other main components of the corporate tax: nominal tax rates and the tax treatment of distributed profits relative to that of retained profits.

C2.1 Nominal Rates

In the corporate tax area, following the seminal King and Fullerton (1984) study, government and academic research has concentrated on establishing marginal effective tax rates (METR) on capital income, with a view to drawing policy recommendations for reducing tax distortions within and between countries. By demonstrating that tax systems are generally not neutral as between the taxation of different assets, towards financing sources or different sectors in the economy, METR studies have had some influence on national legislations during this period (see OECD, 1991: 174–5 for some examples including moving tax depreciation nearer to economic depreciation and reducing differences in average effective tax rates between different sectors of the economy). Also the base broadening referred to earlier, undertaken for other reasons, has generally reduced differences in METRs, even if the reduction of nominal rates within countries has intentionally increased METRs as between countries, in certain circumstances to attract capital investment (see Ruding, 1992). However, there is little reference to METR studies in the country chapters and for a variety of reasons they are not further discussed here: first the methodology is complex and cannot be summarized briefly; second, the METR rests upon a number of assumptions about the firms considered (manufacturing, service, financial, etc., established or new, rate of growth, asset structure, etc.) and the effects on direct and portfolio investment have to be treated separately; third, while the larger MNEs may have a good idea of their own METRs and how to reduce them, there is evidence (e.g. written submissions to the Ruding Committee) that the more numerous smaller firms and hence governments are concerned with nominal rates of corporate tax compared to those of their competitors in other countries, however misleading nominal rates may be as a guide to effective rates.

Table 1.7 shows that nominal rates fell—often sharply—in eight of the ten countries, but remained unchanged in Spain while increasing slightly in

Italy. That nominal rates are higher in Germany and Italy than in other countries is probably due to the fact that tax on distributed profits are fully deductible from the shareholders' income tax base. (Between 1986 and 1991, the nominal rates also declined in all other OECD countries except Norway and Switzerland, where they remained unchanged, and Turkey, where they slightly increased.)

Table 1.7 also shows that, leaving aside special provisions for small enterprises, most of the ten countries have a single corporate rate. Exceptions are the UK and the USA, which have 'progressive' rates, the Netherlands, which until 1998 had a 'regressive' rate—although it is doubtful if it makes much sense to use the words 'regressive' and 'progressive' in the context of a corporation tax—and Canada, which has various rates depending on the activity of the enterprise and its size. (Of other OECD countries, only Switzerland has a 'progressive' rate schedule and Austria recently substituted one rate for a multi-rate schedule.)

C2.2 Taxation of Distributed Profits

The choice between the various ways of taxing distributed profits in relation to how retained profits are taxed has been much discussed over the last three decades. Not only have different countries chosen different systems since the mid-1960s, but they have changed them in different ways, and official and unofficial reports of the EC/European Union have recommended three different systems, the latest pronouncement of the 1992 Ruding Committee considering that there was no need for a harmonized EU system, at least for the time being.

The first basic issue is whether measures should be taken to offset the increased tax burden on distributed profits over retained profits, because the former are also subject to personal income tax in the hands of the shareholder, whereas the latter are not. If the answer is that there is no need to take offsetting measures, the personal and corporate tax remain separate, the so-called 'classical system'. If, on the other hand, offsetting measures are chosen, they can be taken either by reducing or abolishing personal income tax on shareholders' dividends or by reducing or abolishing corporation tax on distributed profits.

There are two fundamentally different ways of going about the first course. One is to exempt or reduce tax on dividends paid by resident companies to resident individuals and are here described as 'shareholder dividend schemes'. The other way of exempting or reducing shareholders' tax on dividends is to make the relief a function of corporate tax paid on the distributions. 'Imputation' is reserved for this system, 'full imputation' indicating that credit is given for all corporation tax on distributed profits, and 'partial imputation' indicating that credit is given for some proportion of it.

If it is preferred to offset the tax disadvantage of distributed as compared to retained profits at the company level, there are again two ways of going about it, although the differences seem to be more of administrative than of policy importance. These options are (i) to apply a lower rate to distributed profits (the split-rate system) or (ii) to deduct a proportion of all distributed profits from the tax base (the dividend deduction system). At the limit, a zero-rate system would be identical to a deduction of all distributed profits from the tax base.

Table 1.7 shows that there are many different systems among the ten countries and that there have been few changes over the last decade. To change systems radically imposes enormous costs to both government and business. There are also a number of other possible systems such as ACE, CBIT, and DEP which so far have not been adopted in OECD countries (see US Treasury, 1992).

Table 1.7 Corporation tax rates and treatment of distributed profits*, 1985 and 1994

	Central government rates on undistributed profits		Tax treatment as of 1994	Changes between 1985 and 1994
	1985	1994		
Canada[a]	36	28.84	Partial shareholder dividend relief	None
France	45	33.33	Full imputation	From partial imputation
Germany[a,b]	56	45	Full imputation plus split rate	None
Italy[a]	36 (10)	36 (16.2)	Full imputation	None
Japan[a]	43 (19)	37.5 (19)	Partial shareholder dividend relief	From split rate in 1990
Netherlands	42	35–40[c]	Classical	None
Spain	35	35	Dividend deduction	None
Sweden	52	28	Full shareholder dividend relief	From dividend deduction in December 1993
UK	35	25–35[d]	Partial imputation	None
USA[a]	From 15 to 46	From 15 to 39[e]	Classical	None

* This table deals only with main provisions and does not, for example, cover special rates on profits of manufacturing and of small enterprises.
[a] Countries with local corporation taxes. Local rates are shown for Italy and Japan in parentheses. In Germany there is rate-sharing. In Canada there are lower rates for manufacturing and small enterprises. In Canada federal and provincial rates are integrated. In the USA rates at state corporation tax vary and are not shown here.
[b] 30% for distributed profits, but 36% until 1992. As from 1995 there will be a surcharge of 7.5% to contribute to the costs of financing German unification.
[c] Regressive rate of 40% on the first Dutch Dfl. 250,000 to limit the incentive for the self-employed to incorporate.
[d] Progressive until £1$\frac{1}{2}$m. profits after which the rate is reduced to 33$\frac{1}{3}$.
[e] Progressive' but after a certain sum of profits the 38 and 39 rates are reduced to 35.

Table 1.8   Corporate tax treatment of distributed profits in thirteen other OECD countries, 1985 and 1994

	Tax treatment as of 1994	Changes between 1985 and 1994
Australia	Full imputation	1987 from classical
Austria	Shareholder dividend relief (partial)	1989 abolition of split rate
Belgium	Shareholder dividend relief (partial)	1989 form of relief changed
Denmark	Shareholder dividend relief (partial)	1991 form of relief changed
Finland	Full imputation	1989 from dividend deduction
Greece	Zero rate	no change
Iceland	Shareholder dividend relief (partial)	no change
Ireland	Partial imputation	no change
Luxembourg	Classical	no change
New Zealand	Full imputation	1988 from classical
Norway	Shareholder dividend relief (full)	from zero rate
Portugal	Shareholder dividend relief (partial)	1989 abolition of split rate
Switzerland	Classical	no change

To emphasize the diversity of country practices, Table 1.8 indicates the practices of other OECD countries. In view of this diversity it seems unlikely that there will be any convergence, even in EU countries, in the foreseeable future. Further work in the European Union is more likely to concentrate on how to iron out non-neutralities flowing from the different systems of different countries.

C3 Social Security Contributions

Table 1.9 shows that contributions are perceived very differently among the ten countries as well among other OECD countries. Here there is space only to indicate some of these main differences.

A basic difference is between the income support approach, which regards contributions as just another way of financing pensions, health care, unemployment etc, and the compulsory social insurance approach, which sometimes holds, especially in France and Germany and especially in the case of pension contributions, that they should not be regarded as taxes at all. Some countries regard contributions as taxes, but of a special kind, perhaps because they are perceived as more acceptable since some quid pro quo is usually provided. Table 1.9 provides a classification of country attitudes.

The income support approach suggests there is no need for different rates for different benefits while the social insurance approach suggests the reverse. Table 1.9 indicates this is in fact what happens in practice, as countries adopting the insurance approach have different rates of contribution for pension and death, health and maternity, unemployment and work insurance.

Table 1.9 Some comparisons of social security contributions, 1985 and 1995

	Perceived as primarily insurance	Perceived as primarily to finance government expenditure	Intermediate	Global schedular, or intermediate	Receipts from employees' contributions as percentage of total tax receipts		Receipts from employers' contributions as percentage of total tax receipts	
					1985	1995	1985	1995
Canada			x	Schedular	5	5	9	11
France	x			Schedular	12	13	28	27
Germany	x			Schedular	16	17	19	20
Italy	x			Schedular	7	7	25	21
Japan			x	Schedular	11	14	15	18
Netherlands			x	Intermediate	20	27	18	7
Spain		x		Global	7	6	31	25
Sweden		x		Global	0	3	24	25
UK			x	Global	8	7	9	10
USA			x	Schedular	11	11	9	13

Table 1.9 shows for the same years the relative shares of employees and employer contributions. Except in the Netherlands, where the employee paid more, and in Germany and the UK, where there is little difference, employer contributions are generally the greater and usually very much so. Of the major shifts during the period, the decline in the employers' share in Italy and Spain reflects the decline in the reliance on social security contributions as a whole, while the increase in Sweden resulted from a partial switch in 1986 from an unearmarked to the earmarked payroll tax. A radical change in the Netherlands was part of the 1990 reform described in Chapter 7.

Typically, both employers' and employees' contributions are levied on something like gross income at a flat rate, often up to a ceiling and with no (or a very small) threshold. There are, however, exceptions among the ten: for example, the Netherlands uses an income tax base rather than gross earnings; in the UK, there is a mild progression for low-paid workers; and in France, Italy, and Spain, lower rates have been applied to encourage the development of certain regions, labour-intensive industries, and employment of females and the young.

Over recent years, the general increase in contributions seems to be due to rate increases combined with raising or sometimes abolishing ceilings.

C4 Consumption Taxes

Excises and other specific taxes on goods and services are far too varied to compare between countries and over time, so this section deals only with VAT—which entails omitting the USA, the only OECD country without a general consumption tax at the federal/central level of government. The special problems of having VAT at the federal level when there exist retail sales taxes at the state/provincial level are well discussed in Sect. D of the chapters on Canada and the USA.

To avoid repetition in the country chapters the main characteristics of the value-added taxes (VAT) are summarized here. With the exception of Japan (see Chapter 6, Sect. D1.4 and D2.2) VAT follows what is variously known as the European Union type, the invoice type, the credit type with an indirect substraction method. Under this method of charging VAT, traders collect tax on their individual sales (outputs) and tax paid on purchases, including those of their commercial inputs, then pay to the tax authorities the difference between the tax collected and the tax paid for each tax accounting period.

In most countries VAT applies to nearly all domestically produced and imported goods and services other than financial services which are usually exempt from VAT. Typically exempt are small businesses and farmers, for whom there may also be special regimes. Exemption from VAT entails the obligation to pay VAT on all inputs without refund of tax paid on purchases. Exports of goods and services are invariably zero-rated. Under zero-rating in contrast to exemptions, traders are reimbursed VAT paid on their inputs.

Imports by traders within the VAT network may be charged either at the time of importation or on first domestic sale. Practices vary on this point. Transactions between countries of the European Union where the concept of 'importation' and 'exportation' is no longer applicable are not charged VAT when goods cross frontiers, though future practices are still under discussion. The following are the more important European Union decisions already accepted by member countries.

- The standard rate of VAT should be at least 15 per cent of the tax-exclusive value of the goods;
- there should be no rates higher than the standard rate;
- one or more lower rates of between 4 and 9 per cent may apply to a narrow range of specified goods and services;
- exports apart, zero-rating is not permitted, but countries with zero-rating are allowed an (unspecified) transitional period to abolish it. (Only Ireland and the UK are seriously concerned);
- member countries have the option to tax or exempt certain specified financial and other services;
- finally, special regimes or exclusion from VAT altogether or lower rates are

Table 1.10   Standard rates of value added tax, 1986–1998[a]

	Standard rate as at 1986[b,c]	Standard rate at Dec. 1995[c]	Other main changes since 1986
Canada	n/a	7	
France	18.6	20.6	Abolition of higher than standard rate[d]
Germany	14	15	Increase to 16% in 1998
Italy	18	19	Abolition of higher than standard rate[d]
Japan	n/a	3	Increase to 5% in 1998
Netherlands	19	17.5	Increase to 19% planned for 1999
Spain	12	16	Abolition of higher than standard rate[d]
Sweden	23.5	25	Extension of base and introduction of reduced rates
UK	15	17.5	Introduction of lower rate on fuel

[a] The USA has no VAT or general consumption tax at federal level but many different rates of retail sales taxes at state and local level and is not included in this table. The retail sales taxes, also at different rates in Canada, are also excluded. Some details are provided in the country chapters.

[b] For Canada (1991) and Japan (1989) when VAT was first introduced, rates were respectively 7 and 3%. For the other countries when VAT was first introduced the rates were France 20% (1968), Germany 10%(1968), Italy 12%(1973), Netherlands 12%(1968), Spain 12%(1986), Sweden 11.1%(1969), and UK 10%(1973).

[c] As percentage of retail price of goods exclusive of the tax.

[d] In conformity with EU Directive.

applied to certain regions of some countries (e.g. see the last sentence of sect. B5 of Chapter 8).

Table 1.10 shows that over the last decade, in contrast to personal and corporate tax rates, standard VAT rates tended to increase. They did so in eight of the nine countries (from zero to positive in Canada and Japan) but there was a reduction in the Netherlands. Standard rates apply to the vast majority of goods and services in all countries and are the only positive rate in Canada and Japan; also in the UK, except for the recent introduction of a lower VAT rate on fuel. (The standard rate is also the only positive rate in Denmark, Finland, New Zealand, and Norway. In other OECD countries there were increases in the standard rate in Belgium, Denmark, Finland, Greece, Iceland, Luxembourg, New Zealand, Norway, and Turkey of between 1 and 3 percentage points.)

Table 1.10 (note b) shows that over the longer term, the standard rates of all countries that introduced VAT prior to the mid-1980s have increased and in most cases substantially.

Sweden is the only country with what was almost a single-rate VAT to introduce lower rates, the details of which are provided in section B4 of the chapter on Sweden.

C5 Capital Taxes

These include local property taxes on buildings and land, and net wealth taxes and capital transfer (gifts and death) taxes, both of which generally accrue to federal/central levels of government. The revenue importance of local property taxes is usually greater than that of other capital taxes: in 1989 they represented around 8 to 10 per cent of tax receipts in Canada, the UK, and the USA, and 5 per cent in Japan, 2 per cent in France, and much less in the other five countries. The range of net wealth taxes was from 0.3 to 0.6 of tax receipts. Capital transfer taxes are relatively important in Japan at 1.6 per cent of total receipts; they range from 0.5 to 0.9 per cent in France, the Netherlands, the UK, and the USA, and around 0.2 per cent in Germany, Italy, Spain, and Sweden. They do not exist in Canada and Australia, both countries abolishing them in the late 1970s when introducing a capital gains tax.

OECD (1983) noted that apart from France, Ireland, and Spain, net wealth taxes were generally around fifty to 100 years old, that 50 per cent of OECD countries with them had never seriously considered abandoning them, and that 50 per cent of OECD countries without them had never seriously considered adopting them. Things have changed recently. In addition to the trend to reduce or abolish these taxes reported in the chapters on the Netherlands and Sweden, similar developments have occurred in Austria, Denmark, and Norway. This recent trend is probably due primarily to the increasing mobility of capital, with the fear of capital flights, which has taken precedence over vertical and horizontal equity concerns.

The other main change during the period was the restoration in France in 1989 by the Socialist government of a net wealth tax, having some differences from the 1982 tax which was abolished by the right-wing coalition in 1987. Among the ten countries there has never been a net wealth tax in Canada, Italy, UK, or USA, and it existed only for a short time in Japan.

The other major capital taxes on households are those on death and gifts, which are prominent in discussions on tax policy for they are one of the few ways of substantially reducing capital inequalities through the tax system, although some believe that legacies should not be taxed. Most of the ten country chapters have little to say on these taxes, for, except in Italy, there has been little change since the mid-1980s. Most OECD countries have inheritance taxes based upon the amount received by the donee, the rate depending on the relationship between deceased and donee, backed up by gift taxes to avoid tax avoidance. A few (e.g. the USA and UK, the latter without a back-up gift tax) have an estate tax based on the amount left by the deceased. Italy and Japan have both kinds of death tax.

They also are capital taxes on enterprises in Canada, Germany, and the Netherlands, which have been much criticized, and also in most countries taxes on capital and financial transactions, often collected by stamp duties. They are mostly small, and vary considerably in coverage and rates as between countries.

D. Fiscal Deficits and Gross Public Debt

Table 1.11 suggests that after the enormous increase in fiscal deficits in the early 1990s, there will be a decrease in most countries as a result of government fiscal consolidation measures, including greater control of public expenditure. Table 1.11 predicts that by 1998 the limit of 3 per cent deficit of GDP (the 1991 'Maastricht criteria' set by the EU as a precondition of economic and monetary union, to be realised by 1999) will be met in all EU countries except Austria, Greece, and Italy. Since then, forecasts have varied both about which countries will meet this target, and the rigidity with which it will be applied to EU countries wishing to adopt the single currency. Later estimates suggest that all EC countries except Greece will meet the target, and that Sweden (alone of EC countries) will be in surplus (see Annexe Table 31 of *Economic Outlook*, 62, December 1997). Of the non-EC countries, Canada is also expected to be in surplus, and USA to have balanced its budget by 1998, though Japan will remain in deficit.

Table 1.12 shows that the Maastricht condition that total gross debt at nominal values should not exceed 60 per cent of GDP is unlikely to be achieved by 1998 in any European Union country except France and the UK. Little concern has been expressed about the general failure to meet this target in contrast to the worry expressed about the size of fiscal deficits.

Table 1.11 General government financial balances (surplus (+) or deficit (−) as a percentage of nominal GDP)

	1980	1981	1982	1983	1984	1985	1986	1987	1988	1989	1990	1991	1992	1993	1994	1995	Estimates and projections 1996	1997	1998
USA	−1.4	−1.1	−3.5	−4.1	−3.0	−3.2	−3.5	−2.6	−2.1	−1.7	−2.7	−3.3	−4.4	−3.6	−2.3	−2.0	−1.6	−1.8	−1.8
Japan	−4.4	−3.8	−3.6	−3.6	−2.1	−0.8	−0.9	0.5	1.5	2.5	2.9	2.9	1.4	−1.6	−2.1	−3.3	−4.1	−2.6	−2.3
Germany[a]	−2.9	−3.7	−3.3	−2.6	−1.9	−1.2	−1.3	−1.9	−2.2	0.1	−2.1	−3.3	−2.8	−3.5	−2.4	−3.5	−4.1	−3.4	−2.6
France[b]	−0.0	−1.9	−2.8	−3.2	−2.8	−2.9	−2.7	−1.9	−1.7	−1.2	−1.6	−2.0	−3.8	−5.6	−5.6	−4.8	−4.1	−3.2	−3.0
Italy	−8.6	−11.5	−11.4	−10.7	−11.7	−12.6	−11.7	−11.0	−10.7	−9.9	−11.0	−10.2	−9.5	−9.6	−9.0	−7.1	−6.7	−3.7	−3.4
UK	−3.4	−2.6	−2.5	−3.3	−3.9	−2.8	−2.4	−1.4	1.0	0.9	−1.2	−2.5	−6.3	−7.8	−6.8	−5.7	−4.8	−3.7	−3.0
Canada	−2.8	−1.5	−5.9	−6.9	−6.5	−6.8	−5.4	−3.8	−2.5	−2.9	−4.1	−6.6	−7.4	−7.3	−5.3	−4.1	−2.7	−1.5	−0.6
Total of above countries	−2.7	−2.8	−4.0	−4.4	−3.6	−3.4	−3.3	−2.5	−1.8	−1.2	−2.1	−2.7	−3.8	−4.3	−3.5	−3.3	−3.2	−2.5	−2.2
Australia	−1.7	−0.7	−0.5	−3.9	−3.3	−2.8	−3.0	−0.3	1.0	1.0	0.6	−2.7	−4.0	−3.7	−4.0	−2.2	−1.7	−1.1	−0.1
Austria	−1.7	−1.8	−3.4	−4.0	−2.6	−2.5	−3.7	−4.3	−3.0	−2.8	−2.2	−2.7	−1.9	−4.2	−4.4	−5.9	−4.3	−3.0	−3.4
Belgium	−8.9	−13.1	−11.1	−11.6	−9.4	−9.0	−9.5	−7.7	−7.0	−6.4	−5.6	−6.5	−7.2	−7.5	−5.1	−4.1	−3.2	−2.9	−2.7
Denmark	−3.3	−6.9	−9.1	−7.2	−4.1	−2.0	3.4	2.4	0.6	−0.5	−1.5	−2.1	−2.9	−3.9	−3.5	−1.6	−1.5	−0.4	0.3
Finland	2.9	3.6	2.0	0.6	3.0	3.0	3.5	1.1	4.1	6.3	5.4	−1.5	−5.8	−8.0	−6.2	−5.4	−2.9	−1.7	−0.7
Greece	−2.6	−8.3	−6.3	−7.1	−8.4	−11.5	−10.3	−9.5	−11.5	−14.4	−16.1	−11.5	−12.3	−14.2	−12.1	−9.1	−8.2	−5.7	−5.1
Iceland	1.3	1.3	1.7	−2.0	2.2	−1.7	−4.1	−0.9	−2.0	−4.6	−3.3	−2.9	−2.8	−4.5	−4.7	−3.1	−2.1	−1.0	−0.8
Ireland	−12.1	−12.8	−13.2	−11.2	−9.4	−10.7	−10.6	−8.5	−4.4	−1.8	−2.3	−2.4	−2.5	−2.5	−2.0	−2.3	−1.5	−1.1	−0.5
Netherlands	−4.3	−5.4	−6.6	−5.8	−5.5	−3.6	−5.1	−5.9	−4.6	−4.7	−5.1	−2.9	−3.9	−3.6	−3.4	−4.0	−2.6	−2.3	−2.1
Norway	5.2	4.3	4.0	3.8	6.8	9.3	5.3	4.3	2.6	1.8	2.6	0.2	−1.7	−1.5	0.3	3.0	5.4	5.0	4.1
Portugal	−5.6	−10.8	−7.7	−10.3	−7.1	−7.5	−6.5	−5.6	−3.6	−2.3	−5.5	−6.4	−3.3	−6.9	−5.7	−4.9	−3.8	−2.9	−2.9
Spain	−2.2	−3.7	−5.4	−4.6	−5.2	−6.9	−6.0	−3.1	−3.3	−2.8	−4.1	−4.9	−3.6	−6.8	−6.3	−6.6	−4.8	−3.4	−2.9
Sweden	−4.0	−5.3	−7.0	−5.0	−2.9	−3.8	−1.2	4.2	3.5	5.4	4.2	−1.1	−7.8	−12.3	−10.3	−7.9	−3.8	−2.5	−0.5
Total of above smaller countries	−2.5	−4.6	−5.2	−5.4	−4.5	−4.6	−4.3	−2.9	−2.4	−2.1	−2.8	−3.9	−4.6	−6.2	−5.4	−4.8	−3.3	−2.3	−1.8
Total of above OECD countries	−2.7	−3.0	−4.2	−4.5	−3.7	−3.5	−3.5	−2.5	−1.9	−1.3	−2.2	−2.9	−3.9	−4.5	−3.7	−3.5	−3.2	−2.5	−2.2

Memorandum item

Total of above European Union countries	−3.4	−5.1	−5.3	−5.1	−4.9	−4.9	−4.5	−3.8	−3.3	−2.5	−3.8	−4.4	−5.2	−6.5	−5.7	−5.2	−4.6	−3.3	−2.8
General government financial balances excluding social security																			
USA[c]	−1.3	−0.9	−3.3	−4.1	−3.1	−3.5	−3.8	−3.1	−2.9	−2.7	−3.7	−4.2	−5.2	−4.4	−3.2	−2.8	−2.5	−2.7	−2.8
Japan	−7.0	−6.6	−6.3	−6.3	−4.8	−3.9	−4.1	−2.4	−1.6	−0.8	−0.7	−0.8	−2.0	−4.8	−5.0	−6.2	−7.0	−5.3	−4.7

[a] Includes balances of the German Railways Fund from 1994 onwards and of the Inherited Debt Fund from 1995 onwards.

[b] As of 1992, due to several accounting changes, the above deficits calculated using the 'Maastricht' definition, are smaller than those published by INSEE, the national statistical agency.

[c] OECD Secretariat estimates, derived from fiscal year data converted to a calendar year basis. The coverage of the social security systems is not the same in the USA and Japan.

Note: Fiscal policy assumptions are based on announced measures and stated policy intentions, where they are embodied in well-defined programmes. Detailed assumptions for individual countries are provided in special boxes in the country notes. There may be large margins of error around the 'point forecasts' of fiscal positions, reflecting uncertainties about: economic growth rates and inflation rates; income elasticities of tax revenues, especially in the event of tax reforms; impacts of new structural measures (e.g. in the labour market) on spending propensities; future measures, notably those which should contribute to the achievement of the declared intents by European Union governments planning to meet the Maastricht fiscal criteria in 1997, but are as yet not concrete or not known; and calendar year estimates for countries whose fiscal year does not start on 1 January.

Source: *Economic Outlook*, 60, Annexe Table 30 (OECD, Paris, Dec. 1996).

Table 1.12 Maastricht definition of general government gross public debt[a] (As a percentage of nominal GDP)

| | 1990 | 1991 | 1992 | 1993 | 1994 | 1995 | Estimates and projections | | |
							1996	1997	1998
Austria	58.3	58.7	58.3	62.8	65.1	69.0	71.8	73.3	74.7
Belgium	129.7	129.4	130.7	137.0	135.0	133.7	129.9	127.2	124.6
Denmark	59.6	64.6	68.7	80.1	76.0	71.9	71.9	70.4	68.0
Finland	14.5	23.0	41.5	57.3	59.5	59.2	60.1	60.2	60.2
France	35.4	35.8	39.6	45.6	48.4	52.8	55.1	56.6	57.7
Germany	43.8	41.5	44.1	48.2	50.4	58.1	61.3	63.2	64.0
Greece	90.2	92.4	99.3	111.8	110.4	111.8	108.5	104.5	100.7
Ireland	96.3	96.6	94.0	97.1	91.0	84.8	80.2	76.0	71.0
Italy	98.0	101.5	108.4	119.3	125.5	124.9	124.4	122.9	120.4
Luxembourg	4.8	4.2	5.2	6.2	5.74	6.1	—	—	—
Netherlands	78.8	78.8	79.5	80.8	77.6	80.0	78.0	76.0	75.7
Portugal	65.5	70.2	62.4	67.3	69.6	71.7	70.3	67.6	66.3
Spain	45.1	45.8	48.3	60.5	63.0	65.8	68.0	68.9	69.2
Sweden	43.5	53.0	67.1	76.0	79.0	79.4	78.7	78.5	75.8
UK	n.a.	35.5	41.6	48.3	50.3	53.9	56.1	56.5	56.3

[a] General government gross debt according to the definition applied under the Maastricht Treaty is based on estimates in national currencies provided by the Commission of the European Communities for 1990 to 1995 and projected forward in line with the OECD Secretariat's projections for general government financial balances and GDP. These data may differ from the gross financial liabilities figures shown in Annexe, table 34. For further details see *OECD Economic Outlook*, 55, p. 17.

Source: *Economic Outlook*, Annexe table 61 (OECD, Paris, Dec. 1996)

E. Rational Tax Policy and Prospects for International Convergence

It is a truism that where you might go depends on where you start from, and Tables 1.2 to 1.4 have already illustrated the diversity of individual tax levels and structures as well as the changes in them among the ten countries between 1985 and 1995. The great diversity of tax systems raises the question: were deliberate choices made or did they happen largely by accident? For example, consider the two smallest of these ten countries, the Netherlands and Sweden, which have in common the highest TTR. Why is it that the local government share of tax revenues is 2 per cent in the Netherlands and 34 per cent in Sweden and that social security contributions are paid almost exclusively by employees in the Netherlands and by employers in Sweden?

The extent of government intervention in the economy, very roughly reflected by the TTR, is evidently a political choice and is not discussed here, nor is the extent to which tax policy should aim at neutrality or at improving equity and economic efficiency, e.g. in changing income distribution or influencing savings behaviour. But governments' different approaches to tax policy as such is the theme of this and the next section. Over the past twenty-five years, each country—until recently—appears to have gone its own way, without regard to what other countries did. Between 1965 and 1985, country divergences increased considerably, especially with regard to social security contributions, with those countries relying most on them increasing their reliance and those relying least on them reducing their reliance.

Over recent years, this isolationist trend has been largely, but by no means entirely reversed, most likely as a consequence of the increasing globalization of national economies, international tax competition, and the influence of the European Union. Also, it is increasingly accepted that while there is no absolute truth in taxation and that in a number of cases opinions continue to differ on what is the best approach, majority opinion has converged on a number of issues: for example, that broad-based, low-rate income taxes are an improvement on high-rate income taxes with a narrow base; that VAT is the best kind of general consumption tax; that having net wealth taxes may induce capital flight; that donee-based death taxes are superior to donor-based taxes; and that subordinate levels of unitary governments are best financed by a mixture of local income and property tax, with some, but not too much, discretion at the subordinate level of government to vary rates and base.

Evidently, in the real world, moves towards what may be seen as fiscal rationality may have to take second place to political, economic, and constitutional constraints prevailing in each country. The authors of the chapters that follow have taken this into account in assessing what is likely to happen in their own country.

Of relevance also to fiscal policy is that differences in effective tax rates and tax compliance among countries distort international capital flows, but the question of how independent States and international groupings such as the European Union and OECD have dealt and might continue to deal with these anomalies is outside the scope of this book. Nevertheless, the question arises whether international tax laws combined with the growing economic interdependence of countries and consensus on certain aspects of tax policy is likely to lead to greater tax convergence. Despite the examples of 15 per cent minimum VAT among European Union countries, modifications to net wealth taxes, and the introduction of relatively low flat rates on capital income, the empirical evidence provided in Tables 1.2 to 1.10, the profiles in the next section, and in Chapters 2 to 11, as well as discussions in parliaments and the media, all suggest that international considerations are likely to have little or no effect on most national tax policy choices. The rejection of the Ruding Committee's proposal for a minimum corporation tax rate to prevent unfair international competition provides one example of countries' preference to remain free from international pressures to fix their total ratios and their relative reliance on different kinds of tax. Also there remain considerable differences among the ten as regards, for example, personal income tax schedules (thresholds, brackets, and progressivity), corporate tax rates, base, and system, rates and coverage of social security contributions, and excises on alcoholic drinks, cigarettes, petroleum, and automobiles. All these decisions seem to be influenced primarily by pre-existing tax systems and by govern-ments' perceived preferences of voters in obtaining the amount of revenue considered necessary to finance their spending requirements, as modified by the size of their fiscal deficit and/or their balance of payments, and sometimes by the importance they give to reducing it or them at any particular period.

There are also forces against any radical tax reform which, apart from the recent waves of income tax reform and the move to VAT, have rarely occurred; business requires stability, radical reform usually implies winners and losers and it has been considered that the latter are more likely to be active at the ballot box. Harmonization of excise rates which vary considerably between countries provides a concrete example of the difficulties involved. Voters in low-excise countries will not take kindly to large increases and governments in high-rate countries will be unable to afford the revenue loss resulting from large rate reductions. In addition, governments may wish to increase or decrease rates for environmental or budgetary reasons. These rate differentials distort trade, which is particularly important in countries attempting eco-nomic union. The European Commission has made some, if limited progress in reducing rate differentials on most excises, if none at all on wine. As noted in Sect. C4 above, the Commission has had an even greater influence on the base and rates of VAT and recently has made radical new proposals for convergence of VAT rates and the treatment of VAT on goods crossing EU frontiers. For the reasons given in Messere (1994, 1997), I believe it very unlikely that EU countries will accept these proposals.

Taking all the above factors into account it seems likely that national preferences will continue to have a much greater influence on most tax policy decisions than will the forces making for international convergence.[6]

F. Country Profiles

This final section attempts to identify in what major respects and for what reasons the tax provisions of each of the ten countries differ from the consensus and to evaluate how far such divergences from what is usually practised are justified; in other words, how far they seem arbitrary and irrational from the point of view of sensible tax policy. It is relevant that although some authors find tax reform is high on the agenda of a number of governments (e.g. Germany, Japan, and the Netherlands) most (e.g. France, Italy, and Spain) see little prospects for major tax reform in the near future, either because of various constraints or lack of political will or because they consider enough (or too much?) unsettling tax reform has recently occurred, and that any necessary increases in generating revenues should be achieved by improved tax administration rather than changes in the tax law. Meanwhile,

---

[6] International convergence is used in the sense of countries' tax levels, structures, and rates coming closer together and not in the sense of countries having common trends such as increases in VAT rates and decreases in income tax rates. The latter but not the former has generally occurred over the last decade (see Messere, 1997).

Table 1.13 Some particular characteristics of the tax system and main recent changes

	Personal income tax	Corporation income tax	Social security contributions	Consumption taxes	Capital taxes	Unusual local taxes
Canada	Non-wastable tax credits			Federal VAT combined with provincial retail sales tax	Absence of tax on bequests	
France	Low yield and archaic collection		Highest reliance, especially on employers' contribution	Many 'nuisance' excises	Reintroduction of net wealth tax	*Taxe professionelle*
Germany	Formula instead of tax brackets	Highest nominal rate and lowest yield		Low VAT rate and low excises on alcoholic drinks		*Gerwebesteur*
Italy	Recent heavy increases. Introduction of new Eurotax		High reliance on employers. Reductions followed by 1993 increase			
Japan		Highest yield, though recently decreased		Very low yield. Recent slight increase with introduction of VAT		
Netherlands	No capital gains tax		Paid mainly by employees		New form of net wealth tax	
Spain	Recent heavy increases		High reliance on employers, but recent reductions			
Sweden		Changes to corporate tax system	Paid almost entirely by employers, including government	Retreat from single rate VAT		
UK		Large decrease in yield		Narrowest VAT base but rate increased	A donor-based tax without back-up gift tax	Poll and council taxes
USA	Narrow tax base			No federal general consumption tax. Lowest gasoline tax		

Table 1.13 summarizes what seem to be the main tax 'eccentricities' of the ten countries and their main tax changes over the last ten years.

F1 Canada

Unlike any other OECD country, Canada has VAT at the federal level and retail sales tax (RST) at the provincial level. The Canadian chapter comments on the reasons for the unpopularity of the federal VAT, as well as the reasons for the coexistence of these two separate taxes. How much the separation increases administrative and compliance costs remains unclear but it is the price of disagreement between federal and provincial governments.

Canada's other main difference from OECD countries is the absence of a tax on bequests—shared only by Australia. Death and gift taxes bring in little revenue, but are one of the few ways that taxation can reduce inequalities in wealth.

One special feature of the Canadian system is the widespread use of the non-wastable tax credits described in Sect. B1 of the Canadian chapter. It seems that both Canadian academics and civil servants are quite impressed with it as a way of offsetting the regressivity of, for example, introducing a wide-based VAT. How far it would easily transplant to other countries it is difficult to know, but both in targeting and take-up it does seem to have advantages over the more usual ways of providing benefits for low-income groups, though there remains the important problem of fraudulent take-up.

F2 France

As part of my contribution to the French chapter in Pechman's *Comparative Tax Systems*, I wrote over ten years ago:

France has been a pioneer in European taxation in its adoption of VAT, the imputation system with halfway credit to shareholders on distributed profits, and indexation of the income tax schedule. Otherwise, France appears neither to have greatly influenced nor been influenced by tax trends in other industrialized countries. For example, at a time when reform proposals in other countries (USA, Scandinavia, Australia, New Zealand) took the form of widening the base to achieve greater neutrality, France has been increasingly using the individual and corporate income tax system to promote economic and social objectives. With its high payroll taxes and tough rules for claiming VAT credit on input, together with low personal income taxes and excise, the formal tax burden on enterprises in relation to households is higher than in other industrialized countries.

Little has changed since then. The rules for claiming VAT input tax have been relaxed, but France remains with by far the lowest personal income tax receipts and by far the highest employer social security contribution receipts of all OECD countries. The high threshold which means that half of the French households do not pay income tax and the fact that France is still the only OECD country (save Switzerland) to use the archaic method of collecting income tax on wages and salaries in the year after they are earned instead of requiring employers to withhold them at source are the main reasons that income tax receipts are so low. The high threshold entails a progressive schedule, around half the tax receipts being paid by 5 per cent of taxpayers, and the archaic collection method leads to the worst of both worlds, since the government loses interest because of the delayed collection and taxpayers are traumatized by the large amounts they have to pay when the bill arrives every four months.[7]

The authors of the chapter on France do not find reform of this method on the agenda perhaps because of fears of annoying employers over the compliance costs required by the pay-as-you-earn collection technique, especially as French employers remain resentful of their heavy social security contributions, which they regard as non-wage labour costs, even if in practice they may be shifted into lower wages. It would seem sensible to follow the Italian example of the late 1970s to swap a withholding of income tax on wages and salaries for a substantial reduction in employer contributions.

Nuisance excises (i.e. other than those products related to drinking, driving, and smoking) raise little revenue, are expensive to administer, easy to avoid if worth avoiding, and distort competition. Helped by the influence of the European Commission nuisance excises have been disappearing in nearly all industrialized countries except France, where they remain on numerous products. However, because of its relatively lenient treatment of drinking and smoking, France remains a low excise country.

Another criticism frequently made of the French tax system is that it is particularly severe on enterprises, even if the costs are shifted to the consumer in the long run. Another unpopular business tax is the mixed-based *taxe professionnelle* to finance local government. Like most mixed-based taxes, it is generally considered to be a bad tax and may well be replaced by a business property or income tax in due course.

F3 Germany

Analogous considerations apply to the German local business tax as to the French *taxe professionnelle*, and as with other federal States, problems arise with respect to the allocation of taxing rights of the federal government, the Länder, and the local authorities. Most of the Länder revenues derive from a share of the receipts from income taxes and VAT, whereas revenues from the German local business tax accrue exclusively to local governments, which probably is the reason that this tax has not been abolished. (For more detailed criticism of this local business tax, see Sect. B7 and D2 of Chapter 4.)

---

[7] Although an option exists to pay by monthly instalments, only 45% of taxpayers use it, even though 53% of taxpayers are reported to prefer a pay-as-you-earn system (see Sect. B1 and D of Ch. 3.). Paying later and gaining interest under the present system has obvious advantages for the high-income earners who pay a larger proportion of the income tax than in most other countries.

A traditional characteristic of the German system, until recent revenue increases resulting from the reunion of East and West Germany, was to maintain stability with regard both to tax levels and tax structures, as happened between 1978 and 1991. To contribute towards unification taxes were increased in a somewhat chaotic way: a one-year only income tax surcharge in 1991 followed by a pause, and then another income tax surcharge of indefinite duration in 1995 (see Sect. D1 of Chapter 4). Despite its increase from 15 to 16 per cent in April 1998, the German VAT rate is among the lowest of all European countries, even if more VAT revenue is collected in Germany than in Italy or the UK with higher nominal rates because of evasion in Italy and the narrow UK VAT base. A further increase of VAT by one or two percentage points would accordingly be an alternative to on-off-on increases in income tax surcharges as a means of financing unification costs. Finally, another respect in which Germany differs from non-Mediterranean European countries is in its low taxation of alcoholic beverages.

F4 Italy

The most interesting final section of the chapter on Italy, where the author gives her personal views, suggests a general consensus that from the mid-1970s, Italy moved in a very rational way from a typical Third World to an industrialized country tax structure, while left with a primitive tax administration, both at central and local government levels. It is difficult to disagree with her conclusion that Italy should now give priority to improving the tax administration, rather than introducing further tax reforms with the sole purpose of raising revenues. In this context the 1997 eurotax—a one-off income tax with a different rate schedule and base from the main income tax—is perhaps the most bizarre innovation since the British poll tax.

The existence of fifty-five Italian governments in under fifty years is doubtless partly responsible for what is generally regarded as an inefficient tax administration where tax evasion and avoidance are probably far higher than in any of the other nine countries covered here. Over the last decade, tax administrations in many OECD countries have increased tax revenues without changes in tax law by improving tax compliance techniques and methods of recruiting, training, and retaining skilled tax administrators. This seems the priority route for Italy as well. An article in *The Economist* (28 January, 1995, p. 57) describes one example of the advantages of concentrating on tax evasion:

In theory, with social security contributions supposedly adding 37 per cent to every workers' pay, Italy boasts one of the most taxed labour markets in the world. In practice, Italian businesses have managed to make this environment a little more friendly through the same ancient management technique they have applied to other taxes: not paying them. By one unofficial estimate, social security tax evasion amounts to 35 trillion lire ($22 billion) a year. Now, with a cash-strapped government taking a firmer line, these previously mythical taxes are hurting.

In the past employees were often willing conspirators in social security fraud. Because their pensions were based on only their final five years' salary, employees cared about full contributions only at the very end of their careers. Now the government has extended that period to ten years. The latest ruse is for companies to treat some employees (particularly computer staff and accountants) as outside 'consultants' who invoice the company for services. But a new law is forcing companies to make social security contributions to 15 per cent of such invoices. And the inspectors now comb through withholding tax returns, which list payments to all non-payroll people.

For corporate Italy, this clampdown could not have come at a worse time. Many businesses have stayed afloat largely thanks to tax evasion. Notorious non-paying industries include farming, construction, and clothing and footwear manufacturing. Small and medium-sized businesses are the main offenders, but one INPS official says that 'even the largest corporations' have broken the law. In 1994, 190,000 businesses took advantage of an amnesty that allowed them to pay only a quarter of the usual penalties. That yielded around 2 trillion lire in extra revenues. This has presented the government with a novel dilemma: now that Italian businessmen are actually paying taxes, should it lower the taxes to a more reasonable level?

F5 Japan

Along with the USA, Japan has by far the lowest TTR of the ten countries, and as with the USA, this follows primarily from low taxes on consumption. There are other deviations from what happens in most other OECD countries.

First, Japan has by far the highest reliance on corporation taxes (see Tables 1.3 and 1.4) for the reasons, given at the beginning of Sect. 6B2.[8] In 1989, the corporation tax accounted for nearly 25 per cent of total tax revenues (OECD, 1995, Table 13), with only Luxembourg anywhere near, at around 17 per cent. Despite a decline in corporate tax receipts through rate lowering and insufficient base broadening they still accounted for around 15 per cent of total tax revenues in 1995, higher than any other OECD country (except Luxembourg).

Second, anecdotal evidence suggests that tax evasion and avoidance assume Mediterranean proportions among small Japanese traders and were the main cause of the massive resistance to VAT and the absence of the invoice method, as well as the government's failure to win acceptance of a tax identification number as generally required in other OECD countries.[9]

Third, pressure-group resistance to fundamental tax reform has been stronger in Japan than in other OECD countries and, hence, the pace of reform has been slower. Nevertheless, such reform has occurred over the last few years, culminating in a proposal to introduce a more modern-style VAT, albeit at only 5 per cent, far below that in other OECD countries. One can only concur with the conclusions of Professor Ishi's chapter as regards what would constitute future rational tax reform. This chapter was completed

---

[8] See also K. Kaizuka in Pechman (1988: 163).
[9] See H. Ishi (1993: 380–1) on recent developments.

before the recent downturn in Japan, for which the VAT increase from 3 to 5 per cent was implausibly held to be one cause. Tax reform is now high on the political agenda, and as at mid-1998, it is expected that this will take the form of further reductions to the personal income tax. However, not for the first time, action seems paralysed by political indecision.

F6 The Netherlands

The three main differences between the Netherlands and typical OECD tax profiles are: (i) it is the only country, except New Zealand, never having had a capital gains tax on individuals; (ii) the percentage of taxes directly collected by local governments is exceptionally low (only Greece is lower), although local governments are entitled to around 12 per cent of nearly all taxes levied by the central government; and (iii) it uses environmental taxes more than most other OECD countries.

I agree entirely with Professor de Kam's view that it would be rational to get rid of these first two eccentricities (see Sect. D2 of the chapter on the Netherlands). Environmental taxes account for less than 1 per cent of total tax receipts and, accordingly, are more relevant to environmental policy than tax policy.

F7 Spain

To a large extent the history of Spanish tax policy over the last two decades parallels that of Italy: a move from heavy social security contributions on employers to personal income taxes with a more recent focus on modernizing administration. Also like Italy, but unlike most OECD countries, the Spanish TTR has increased considerably since 1985 (see Fig. 1.1).

Employers' social security charges remain extremely high in Spain (exceeded only by those in Belgium, Finland, France, Italy, and Sweden, all of which have much higher TTRs than Spain).[10]

Apart from the high employer social security contributions, the Spanish tax structure differs little from the OECD average, except for the gentle way it taxes smokers and drinkers, as is the case in other Mediterranean countries.

F8 Sweden

According to OECD statistics, Sweden has had the highest TTR of all OECD countries since 1976. However, if employer payroll taxes paid by the government to itself were not considered as taxes, Sweden would not have invariably or even usually the highest TTR.[11] This draws attention to one Swedish

[10] See table 18 of *Revenue Statistics, 1965–96* (Paris, OECD, 1997).
[11] OECD statistics, unlike IMF statistics, include such payments as taxes. If they were excluded, the Netherlands and the other Scandinavian countries would probably be shown as having a higher TTR than Sweden. Their inclusion gives a better measure of the size of the public sector, their exclusion of the tax burden on the private sector.

deviation from a normal OECD profile: throughout the last decade, and for many years before, Sweden has had higher employer social security contributions than any OECD country except France, Italy, and Spain, a large portion being government contributions as employers,[12] and Sweden also has had a higher unearmarked payroll tax on employers than any other OECD country except Australia and Austria.

Another unusual feature about Sweden is that nearly 100 per cent of local government revenues (actually 99.6 per cent) are derived from local income taxes, so that it is not surprising that personal income tax receipts represent only 4.4 per cent of central government revenues—less than one-third of any other OECD country and less than an eighth of most of them. Presumably it is the absence of income tax revenues at the central government level that requires such high payroll taxes.

As noted earlier, Sweden is the only OECD country with an almost one-rate VAT system to introduce lower rates for food and tourist services. (For details, see Sect. B4 of Chapter 9.) It seems very doubtful if any economic advantages outweigh the resulting administrative complications and loss of revenue, especially given Sweden's large fiscal deficit. Abolition of these changes would accordingly seem rational.

It would appear that the traditional consensual Swedish attitude toward tax reform prevailed until the 1990 tax reform, but since then ideological considerations prevalent in many countries has taken over, with changes depending on whether the anti-socialist coalition or the social democrats were in power.

F9   United Kingdom

Over the last decade, the then British government introduced three unique (and regressive) features into the tax system. In addition, the UK is the only OECD country substantially to reduce the TTR between 1985 and 1993, even if there were subsequent increases.

The UK is the only industrialized country ever to introduce either a poll tax or a council tax (see Sect. B2.7 of the UK chapter for details of these taxes). The regressive poll tax was introduced in 1989–90 to be replaced a few years later by the somewhat less regressive but more complicated council tax. Although the poll tax and council tax were justified on the grounds of increasing local accountability, the UK is the only OECD country to reduce substantially the taxing and spending powers of local governments during the last decade.

The UK is one of the few countries with an estate tax based on the amount left by the deceased rather than an inheritance tax based on the amount the

---

[12] In 1982 government social security payments represented nearly 5 per cent of GDP, far higher than any other countries considered (see OECD (1987)).

beneficiary receives and is the only country not to back this up with an effective gift tax, which was removed when the misnamed 1986 Inheritance Tax was introduced.

Before the June 1997 election, the UK Conservative government were proposing another rare and regressive measure, the abolition of capital gains and capital transfer tax. However, the election was won by the Labour party, who enacted their own unique tax—an earmarked windfall tax on the profits of privatized utilities (for other measures taken by the new government during 1997 and 1998, see Section 10D2).

Leaving aside those OECD countries introducing VAT during the last decade, the UK is the only country to substantially increase reliance on VAT over that period, despite the fact that it has the narrowest VAT base of any OECD country, with only Ireland remotely approaching it in the extent of zero-rating. (For details of zero-rating, see Table 10.10 of the UK chapter.)

Bringing goods such as basic foodstuffs, printed matter, drugs and medicines, and so-called 'essential' goods into the VAT base is known to be politically unpopular and both the Labour and Conservative parties have implied they will not do it, even though it would probably be the most efficient way of raising large sums of revenue. For a number of reasons, the European Commission disapproves of zero-rating and permits it only as a transitional measure. Possibly the European Commission could do a future British (and Irish) government a favour by announcing the end of the transition period so that the European Union would get the blame, while the government could get voter credit for introducing some new form of offsetting relief for the poor, such as the Canadian non-wastable credit.[13]

F10 United States of America

As with Canada, one of the main problems in the US tax system follows from competition for revenues between federal and state governments, which is possibly why the USA is the only OECD country without a general consumption tax at the national (federal) level. As well as its far greater population, the USA may have far more serious problems than Canada in arriving at a consensus on tax policy solutions, because of the separation of taxing powers not only between the Administration and Congress, but also between the Senate and the House, all three often producing very different proposals. Unlike Canada, general consumption tax revenues have always accrued to the states, and the current US trend in favour of decentralization of federal taxing powers renders the introduction of a federal VAT unlikely over the next few years.

---

[13] The Commission Directive to make 15% the minimum standard rate was probably welcomed by Germany and Spain, both of which had lower rates and were looking for ways of reducing their deficits.

Apart from the absence of a federal general consumption tax, the tax component in petrol prices is excessively low by OECD standards,[14] and despite the 1986 base-broadening reform, the US personal income tax base probably remains much narrower than that of most OECD countries.[15]

These are the reasons why the USA has the lowest TTR among the ten countries. Now that the budget is for the time being in balance and there are so many differences in the views on tax reform of the Administration and Congress, there seems little prospect of major change in the US tax system for the rest of this century.

G. Relevant Non-Fiscal Data

One feature influencing different tax profiles, relates to non-fiscal differences between countries. Table 1.14 provides details of some of them.

---

[14] e.g., percentage of taxes in the price of premium (regular in Japan) petrol during 1993–4 was as follows: Canada, 46; France, 78; Germany, 75; Italy, 74; Japan, 48; Netherlands, 70; Spain, 65; Sweden, 71; UK, 69; USA, 28 (Source: tables 2 and 3, pp. 294 and 295 of *Energy Prices and Taxes*, 3rd quarter 1994.)

[15] These include allowances or reductions for mortgage interest on secondary residences, medical expenses, charity donations, state taxes, imputed rent, more generous treatment of fringe benefits and pension and life insurance contributions than in most OECD countries.

Table 1.14 Some non-tax comparative data, 1985–1995

		Canada	France	Germany	Italy	Japan	Netherlands	Spain	Sweden	UK	USA	Source in OECD, in Economic Outlook, 60
Area (sq. km)		9,976	549	357	301	378	41	505	450	245	9,373	
Population (millions)		26.5	56.1	81.3	57.1	123.5	15	39	8.7	58	249	
Real GDP % change over previous year	1985	4.8	1.9	2.0	2.8	4.4	3.1	2.6	1.9	3.8	3.7	Annexe Table 1
	1990	-0.2	2.5	5.7	2.1	4.8	4.1	3.7	1.4	0.4	1.2	
	1995	2.3	2.2	1.9	3.0	0.9	2.1	2.8	3.6	2.4	3.0	
Consumer prices % change from previous period	1985	4.8	5.8	2.1	8.6	2.0	2.3	8.8	7.4	6.1	3.5	Annexe Table 16
	1990	4.8	3.4	2.7	6.1	3.1	2.5	6.7	10.5	9.5	5.4	
	1995	2.2	1.7	1.8	5.4	-0.1	1.9	4.7	2.9	3.4	2.8	
Standardized unemployment rates, as % of total labour force	1985	10.5	10.2	7.1	9.6	2.6	10.6	21.1	3.0	11.2	7.1	Annexe Table 22
	1990	8.1	8.9	4.8	10.3	2.1	7.5	15.9	1.8	6.9	5.6	
	1995	9.5	11.6	8.2	12.2	3.1	6.5	23.7	9.2	8.7	5.5	
Gross national savings, as % of nominal GDP	1985	19.6	18.9	22.0	21.6	31.7	24.3	20.6	17.5	17.6	17.6	Annexe Table 27 [* = 1994]
	1990	16.4	21.5	24.1	19.5	33.6	26.1	21.7	17.7	14.3	15.6	
	1995	17.1	19.7	21.4	20.5	31.4	24.6	21.5	13.8*	13.5*	16.2*	
General government total outlays as % of nominal GDP	1985	45.3	52.1	47.0	51.2	32.6	57.1	41.2	63.3	44.0	32.9	Annexe Table 28
	1990	46.0	49.8	45.1	53.2	31.7	54.1	42.0	59.1	39.9	33.3	
	1995	46.5	53.7	48.1	51.8	35.4	52.3	44.8	66.0	43.3	33.2	
Short-term interest rates	1985	9.6	9.9	5.4	15.3	6.6	6.3	12.2	14.2	12.2	7.5	Annexe Table 36
	1990	13.0	10.3	8.5	12.0	7.7	8.7	15.2	13.7	14.8	7.5	
	1995	7.0	6.6	4.5	10.3	1.2	4.4	9.4	8.7	6.7	5.5	
Long-term interest rates	1985	11.1	11.9	7.2	13.7	6.5	7.3	13.4	13.2	11.1	10.6	Annexe Table 36
	1990	10.8	10.4	8.8	13.5	7.0	8.9	14.6	13.2	11.8	8.6	
	1995	8.4	7.7	6.9	11.8	3.4	6.9	11.3	10.2	8.2	6.6	
Nominal exchange rates vis-à-vis US dollar (average of daily rates)	1985	1.366	8.984	2.994	1909	238.6	3.222	170.1	8.602	0.779	1.000	Annexe Table 37
	1990	1.167	5.446	1.616	1148	144.8	1.678	101.9	5.918	0.563	1.000	
	1995	1.372	4.991	1.423	1629	94.1	1.605	124.7	7.134	0.634	1.000	
Current account balances, as % of GDP	1985	-1.3	-0.1	2.4	-0.1	3.6	3.1	1.6	-1.4	0.6	-3.0	Annexe Table 51
	1990	-3.8	-0.8	3.3	-1.6	1.2	3.5	-3.4	-2.8	-3.5	-1.7	
	1995	-1.5	1.1	-0.7	1.1	2.2	4.4	0.2	2.0	-0.4	-2.0	

Source: OECD, *Economic Outlook*, 60

References

European Commission, *Report of the Committee of Independent Experts on Company Taxation* chaired by O. Ruding (Brussels, 1992).

Ishi, H., *The Japanese Tax System* (Oxford University Press, 1993).

King, M., and Fullerton, D., *The Treatment of Income from Capital: A Comparative Study of the United States, the United Kingdom, Sweden and Germany* (Chicago, 1984).

Messere, K., *Tax Policy in OECD Countries: Choices and Conflicts* (IBFD, Amsterdam 1993).

—— 'International Consumption Tax Rules' (*IBFD Bulletin*, Amsterdam, Dec. 1994).

—— 'OECD Tax Developments in the 1990s' (*IBFD Bulletin*, Amsterdam, July 1997).

—— and Owens, J., *International Comparisons of Tax Levels, Pitfalls and Insights* (OECD Economic Studies, Paris, 1987).

OECD, *Income Tax Schedules: Distribution of Taxpayers and Revenues* (Paris, 1981).

—— *Personal Income Tax Systems under Changing Economic Conditions* (Paris, 1986).

—— *Taxation of Net Wealth, Capital Transfers and Capital Gains of Individuals* (Paris, 1988).

—— *Taxpayers' Rights and Obligations* (Paris, 1990).

—— *The Personal Income Tax Base* (Paris, 1990).

—— *Taxing Profits in a Global Economy* (Paris, 1991).

—— *Taxation and Household Savings* (Paris, 1994).

—— *Energy Prices and Taxes* (Paris, 1994).

—— *Economic Outlook*, 59 and 60 (Paris, June and Dec. 1996).

—— *Revenue Statistics of OECD 1965–1996* (OECD, 1997).

Pechman, J. (ed.), *Comparative Tax Systems: Europe, Canada and Japan* (Tax Analysts, Arlington, 1988).

—— (ed.) *World Tax Reform: A Progress Report* (Brookings Institution, Washington, DC, 1988).

US Treasury, *Integration of the Individual and Corporate Tax System: Taxing Business Income Once* (Washington, DC, 1992).

2 Canada

RICHARD M. BIRD, DAVID B. PERRY, AND
THOMAS A. WILSON

A. Overview

Over the last decade, the Canadian tax system has undergone its most drastic change since the income tax reform of 1971—the mundane reality that emerged from the political process following the classic statement of the 'comprehensive tax base' approach in the Carter Commission Report of 1966.[1] Apart from a series of changes attempting to adapt to the inflationary environment of the late 1970s and early 1980s—most of which were later reversed—and continued recourse to tax incentives for a variety of policy reasons, no fundamental changes were made in federal income taxes until the mid-1980s, when Canada joined the worldwide move towards lower rates and broader bases.[2] This second wave of major tax reform culminated—at least temporarily—in 1991 with the introduction of Canada's version of a VAT, the Goods and Services Tax (GST), to replace a federal manufacturer's sales tax that had been in place since 1923.[3]

With respect to both income taxes and sales taxes, Canada's recent reform appears to be more or less in line with worldwide trends. Such features of recent tax changes as the lowering of corporate taxes, the substantial reductions in tax incentives, and the introduction of a VAT are common to many countries. Appearances, however, may be deceptive. In fact, there are a number of interesting twists to the Canadian tax story, and the story is by no means yet concluded. In the first place, Canada was the first industrial country to drop all attempts to tax personal wealth directly.[4] Second, despite all the recent tax reforms the version of (partial) shareholder relief for

The authors are grateful to Robert D. Brown, Wolfe Goodman, Leif Mutén, Ken Messere, and an anonymous reviewer for helpful comments on earlier versions of this chapter.
[1] The history of the Carter reforms is set out in Bucovetsky and Bird (1972), their effects are evaluated in Thirsk and Whalley (1982), and the process of reform is reviewed in St Hilaire and Whalley (1985). For detailed accounts of the Canadian tax system before the major reforms of the last few years, see Kitchen (1987) and Boadway and Kitchen (1984).
[2] See Dodge and Sargent (1988), Dodge (1989), Bossons (1988), Whalley (1990), and Mintz and Whalley (1989) for extensive discussions of what Canada did, how it related to what other countries did, and what its effects were.
[3] See Gillis (1985) and Whalley and Fretz (1990) for the background to this change.
[4] This story is told in Bird (1978). For recent discussion of wealth taxes, see Smith (1993) and Mintz and Pesando (1991).

dividend income introduced in the early 1970s remains largely unchanged. Third, at the same time as personal income tax rates were being lowered and simplified, various partial moves towards 'integrating' parts of the transfer system with the tax system have resulted in a complex and irrational effective rate structure. Fourth, and in many ways most important, Canada is among the most decentralized of OECD countries, and its provinces have substantially influenced both income and sales tax policy. As federal personal income tax rates came down, for example, provincial income tax rates have gone up, with the result that effective marginal tax rates have actually increased for many Canadians over the last decade. Similarly, the continued existence of visible provincial retail sales taxes in many ways lies at the heart of the continuing agitation to replace, or at least hide, the GST.[5]

The central importance in Canada of federal–provincial relations is evident in the revenue figures shown in Tables 2.1 and 2.2. Both levels of government obtain substantial revenues from income and sales taxes, with about 60 per cent of income taxes (mainly personal income taxes) and 46 per cent of consumption taxes going to the federal government and the balance to the provinces. Only the municipal governments, which are essentially the creatures of the provinces, are dependent upon a single tax, the real property tax, for almost all their tax revenue (and about half their total revenue).[6]

In international terms, the most outstanding feature of Canadian tax policy in the last decade has undoubtedly been the extent to which Canada, almost alone among OECD countries, has attacked its deficit problem by substantially increasing the share of personal income tax (PIT) relative to GDP, as shown in Table 2.3. Though Canadians are sensitive to comparisons with the traditionally much lower taxing USA,[7] until very recently there has been little evidence of any desire on the domestic political scene to bring income taxes back into internationally comparable lines. Indeed, in 1994 the federal government at one point proposed to replace the GST in part by introducing a flat-rate tax on gross income, thus moving the Canadian tax system even further away from taxing consumption and towards taxing income. Only in mid-1995, with the election of a new Conservative government in the largest province (Ontario) committed to a 30 per cent cut in provincial income taxes did US-style anti-income tax rhetoric begin to receive much media attention in Canada.

---

[5] See House of Commons (1994) and Bird (1994a) for two recent studies of the GST and possible replacements.

[6] See Kitchen (1992) for the most recent treatment of this tax. (The small provincial property tax shown in Table 2.1 reflects different provincial–municipal financial arrangements in a few small provinces.) The other half of municipal revenues comes from provincial transfers Kitchen (1984) which in total are just about equal to the transfers the provinces themselves receive, under various heads, from the federal government (Boadway and Hobson, 1993).

[7] See the extensive comparative studies in Shoven and Whalley (1992).

Table 2.1 Taxes in 1994 ($m.): National accounts basis

	Federal	Provincial	Local	CPP/QPP[a]	Total
Personal income tax	58,877	45,400			104,277
Corporate income tax	11,804	5,252			17,056
Taxes on non-residents[b]	1,690				1,690
Sales taxes	20,199	20,784			40,983
Taxes on motive fuel	3,662	6,227			9,889
Taxes on alcohol and tobacco	3,010	1,858			4,868
Real property taxes		2,744	25,852		28,596
Social security levies					
Pension plans				12,931	12,931
Unemployment insurance	19,940				19,940
Workers' compensation		4,290			4,290
Other taxes	6,269	13,407	4,430		24,106
Total taxes	125,451	99,962	30,282	12,931	268,626

[a] The Canada and Quebec pension plans are considered a separate subsector in Canadian national income and expenditure accounts.
[b] Withholding taxes on payments to non-residents.

Source: Statistics Canada, CANSIM.

Table 2.2 Taxes in 1994 as a percentage of gross domestic product

	Federal	Provincial	Local	CPP/QPP[a]	Total
Personal income tax	8.2	6.0			14.2
Corporate income tax	1.5	0.7			2.2
Taxes on non-residents[b]	0.2				0.2
Sales taxes	2.7	3.1			5.8
Taxes on motive fuel	0.6	0.8			1.4
Taxes on alcohol and tobacco	0.3	0.4			0.6
Real property taxes		0.3	3.6		3.9
Social security levies					
Pension plans				1.7	1.7
Unemployment insurance	2.6				2.6
Workers' compensation		0.7			0.7
Other taxes	1.3	1.3	0.6		3.2
Total taxes	17.7	13.3	4.2	1.7	36.5

[a] The Canada and Quebec pension plans are considered a separate subsector in Canadian national income and expenditure accounts.
[b] Withholding taxes on payments to non-residents.

Source: See Table 2.1.

Table 2.3 Personal income taxes as a percentage of GDP

	Canada	USA	OECD average
1965	5.9	7.9	7.1
1970	10.1	10.3	8.6
1975	10.6	9.5	10.5
1980	10.8	10.8	11.3
1985	11.6	10.2	11.3
1988	12.8	10.3	11.9
1991	15.0	10.3	11.3
1992	14.2	10.1	11.4
1993	13.5	10.2	11.3

Source: *Revenue Statistics of OECD Member Countries, 1965–1994.*

B. The Tax System

It should be noted that this section and most of the chapter as whole, reflect the situation in 1996 (three budgets ago as at mid-1998). However, there is little new to report, other than the change from budget deficict to surplus referred to in Sect. C and modifications to the GST described in Sect. D1.

B1 The Personal Income Tax

Both personal and corporate income taxes may be levied by federal and provincial governments. During the Second World War the federal government predominated, but the main trend in the post-war period has been the gradual build-up of provincial access and autonomy.

B1.1 Tax Base

The base of the tax includes all earned income, most forms of investment income, and some transfer payments, such as benefits from the Canada and Quebec Pension Plans (CPP/QPP) and unemployment insurance (UI), renamed employment insurance (EI) in 1996. Most income-tested transfers from federal, provincial, and local governments are, however, exempted including social assistance (which is provincially designed, partly federally financed, and, in some provinces, locally administered). Basic government transfers to those over 65 years of age (old-age security (OAS) pensions financed from general revenues) are included in the base, but supplements (the 'guaranteed income system' (GIS)) for low-income individuals are not,[8]

---

[8] The Guaranteed Income System (GIS) is in effect a 'negative income tax' for the elderly which (in 1993) insured a minimum annual income of $10,896 for a single person over 65 and $14,208 for a couple both over 65. The GIS is paid out monthly with the OAS payment, with the amount paid being based entirely on information in the previous year's income tax return: about 40% of pensioners get such supplementary payments. Although GIS payments are not subject to income tax, they are taxed implicitly because GIS is reduced by 50 cents for each dollar of income in excess of the OAS/GIS minimum level.

Workers' compensation payments are excluded, as is strike pay—although deductions are allowed for union dues. Because the income tax system is used to deliver a number of tax credits unrelated to the income tax, all these non-taxable transfers are first taken into income to determine total income and then deducted to arrive at taxable income.

Some fringe benefits, such as employer-financed group life insurance and company automobiles, are included in the tax base but others, notably employer contributions to pension plans and employer-financed health insurance premiums, are excluded. A special 'northern allowance' is granted for persons residing in certain remote parts of the country.[9]

Since the Income Tax Act and regulations define both personal and corporate income taxes, the definition of income from a business is the same for self-employed individuals, partnerships, and corporations. While the law does not explicitly mention generally accepted accounting principles as defined by accounting bodies, the general test of 'reasonableness' is applied to all income and expense items. Certain income and expense items are specifically defined and given special treatment. In general accrual accounting is used, although certain taxpayers—mainly in farming and fishing—are on a cash basis. Inventories are taxed on a FIFO (first-in, first-out) basis.

Depreciation (called 'capital cost allowance') is defined for thirty-two different classes of assets, with a specific rate on a diminishing balance basis being allowed for each class. In most cases, the rates established by regulation are more generous than those used in accounting records, leading to significant deferral of tax in the early years of asset life. Only 50 per cent of expenses on meals and entertainment may now be deducted. Among the few remaining tax incentives are deductions for the exploration and development of Canadian natural resource properties,[10] investment credits for scientific research and development, and certain limited partnership arrangements.

The tax treatment of capital gains has changed rather dramatically over the past decade. In 1984, half of capital gains realized were taxed as personal income. In 1985, a controversial lifetime exemption for capital gains was phased in over a three year period. The lifetime limits were $500,000 for farms and small corporations and $100,000 for other assets. The 1987 income tax reform increased the tax burden on capital gains (outside the lifetime exemption) by increasing the inclusion rate to two-thirds for 1988–9 and to three-quarters for 1990 and subsequent years. The $100,000 lifetime capital gains exemption was terminated for real estate in 1992 and for other assets in the 1994 budget, although those who had not claimed some or all of the exemption prior to the budget date were in effect allowed to do so, to the extent they had accrued gains, when filing their 1995 income tax return.[11]

---

[9] See Bird and Slack (1983) for a discussion. This allowance was recently reviewed by an official committee (Canada, 1989) but it was—properly (Bird, 1991)—decided to leave it in place.

[10] Some of these incentives take the form of so-called 'flow-through shares' which in effect pass the benefit of the deduction on to equity investors and hence lower the cost of finance in the favoured industries. A recent official evaluation found that this incentive mechanism probably had some limited effect in encouraging the aided activities (Dept. of Finance, 1994c).

[11] See Mintz and Richardson (1995) for an assessment of the lifetime capital gains exemption.

The remaining $500,000 exemption for farms and small corporations is under review. At death, or the fiscal equivalent of emigration, an individual's capital assets are deemed to be disposed of at current value and 75 per cent of the net proceeds taken into income in the year of death (or emigration).[12] Some provisions allow roll-overs to immediate relatives. Gains realized from the sale of principal residences are fully exempt, as are gains from certain personal property selling for less than $1,000—an amount which has not been changed since 1971.

A key feature of the Canadian income tax system is partial tax relief for dividend income. Since 1971, dividend income from Canadian corporations has been subject to a gross-up and credit under the personal income tax.[13] The gross-up and credit system has been adjusted as needed from time to time to achieve approximate equivalence of taxes for small corporations and unincorporated businesses. Under the 1987 income tax reform, for example, the lowering of corporate rates was accompanied by reduced gross-ups and credits in order to preserve this equivalence. At present, dividends are grossed up by 25 per cent—regardless of whether any tax has been paid at the corporate level[14]—and the grossed-up amount taken into taxable income. After calculation of the federal 'basic tax' (a term explained later), the federal tax is reduced by a credit equal to 13.33 per cent of the grossed-up dividend. After provincial taxes are taken into account, the net result is to offset on dividend income roughly 50 per cent of corporate taxes for public companies and about 100 per cent for 'Canadian-controlled private corporations', which are usually taken to be roughly equivalent to small businesses.[15]

All pension income is taxable, but all contributions to such plans are given preferential, though varied, treatment. Employee contributions to the government plans—the CPP and QPP—are converted into tax credits at the lowest rate in the personal tax rate schedule and deducted from tax otherwise payable.[16] In contrast, contributions to employer–sponsored pension plans (RPPs) and individual retirement savings plans—registered retirement savings plans (RRSPs)—are *deductible* from taxable earned income. Deductible individual contributions are limited to 18 per cent of earned income up to about $75,000 per year. Special provisions equate the benefits of an employer-sponsored pension plan with those available to individuals under the individual plans. Any 'excess' room available to employees may be used for investment in individual plans, and until 1996 at least $1,000 of RRSP

---

[12] Canadian real property and private businesses are basically exempt from this so-called 'departure tax' on the accrued capital gains of emigrants.

[13] Prior to 1971, a flat credit of 20% had existed for dividend income.

[14] Note that this feature makes the Canadian dividend tax credit quite different in both intent and effect from the 'imputation' systems found in a number of European countries.

[15] The precise percentages vary from province to province and also to some extent with the nature of the business owing to the different corporate rates on manufacturing (see Table 2.8).

[16] Payroll taxes levied to finance UI are treated similarly.

deduction was allowed in most cases. Income accruing to pension funds and RRSPs is exempt.

Non-refundable credits, at the lowest marginal rate, are provided for medical expenses, charitable donations (donations over $200 are creditable at the top marginal rate), and post-secondary education expenses including both tuition and an education allowance of $80 per month. (These amounts are not indexed, but have been adjusted occasionally.) Union dues, expenses of self-employment, alimony and child support, and certain childcare expenses are also deductible.

A unique aspect of the Canadian system is the use by the federal and all provincial governments of a single income allocation formula for both personal and corporate income taxes. Individual taxpayers pay provincial tax to the province where they were resident on 31 December, unless they were self-employed and doing business in more than one province, in which case their business income is allocated according to the corporate formula, as discussed below. As a rule, there is neither any double taxation by provinces nor any reported income that escapes the provincial tax net.

B1.2 Tax Rates

The rate structure of the personal income tax is confusing. Because nine provinces and the two territories have their personal income taxes collected by the federal government under long-standing collection agreements, they express their rates as a percentage of 'federal basic tax'—a term of art that describes the result of applying the rate schedule to taxable income and then allowing for certain adjustments.[17] Federal surtaxes and foreign tax credits are then applied to arrive at federal tax payable. Provincial or territorial taxes, expressed as a per cent of federal basic tax (at rates ranging from 45.5 to 69 per cent in 1993), produce 'basic provincial tax', to which are applied in most provinces various surtaxes and low-income tax reductions. Finally, a few provinces apply a flat tax expressed as a percentage of either taxable or assessed income.

The province of Quebec applies its own rate schedule to its own definition of taxable income and has its own non-refundable credits.[18] Table 2.4 shows the federal and Quebec rate schedules. Owing to special arrangements instituted in 1966 to compensate the province for opting out of certain federal–provincial cost-sharing programmes, the federal basic tax applicable to Quebec residents is reduced by 16.5 per cent, with the result that Quebec

---

[17] Federal basic tax—the base for provincial taxes—is calculated by applying the federal rate schedule of 17, 26, and 29% to taxable income, and then deducting the non-refundable credits for dependants, medical, charitable, education, CPP or QPP and UI premiums (payroll taxes), and the dividend tax credit.

[18] The definitions of total and taxable income are similar to those in the federal law, but the treatment of dependants differs from the federal system described below. Additional credits are provided in the Quebec system for such incentive programmes as investment in domestic firms and retraining programmes.

Table 2.4 Federal and Quebec rate schedules for 1995 (excluding surtaxes)

	Taxable income brackets ($)
Federal rates (%)	
17	up to 29,590
26	29,591 to 59,180
29	over 59,180
Quebec rates (%)	
16	up to 7,000
19	7,001 to 14,000
21	14,001 to 23,000
23	23,001 to 33,492
24	over 33,492

Sources: Treff and Cook (1995).

residents pay less federal tax and more provincial tax than their counterparts in other provinces. Tables 2.5 to 2.7 should be read with this factor in mind.

Effective personal income tax rates are also influenced by other programmes delivered in whole or part through the income tax system. In a major reform introduced in 1993, all tax deductions and credits for dependent children (as well as a taxable 'family allowance' paid to parents of all children under 18) were replaced by a 'child tax benefit' based on family income. These refundable credits[19] are targeted to provide assistance to low- and lower-middle-income families and hence taper down to zero at specified thresholds depending on the number of children and the family income.[20] No tax relief is available to families with children and income above certain limits.

Additional refundable credits are provided to roughly the same groups to compensate for the effect of the federal value-added tax (the GST). The effect of these two vanishing credits is to increase marginal tax rates in selected income ranges by up to 10 per cent. Some provinces provide similar refundable credits to offset the effects of their retail sales taxes and property taxes, adding another 1–2 per cent to the marginal rates. Moreover, the federal government also 'claws back' old-age security (OAS) pensions at a rate of 15 per cent—though above a much higher threshold than in the case of the child tax benefit—and unemployment insurance at 30 per cent above yet

---

[19] 'Refundable credit' is the expression generally used in Canada even if nothing is actually refunded. The OECD calls these 'non-wastable credits' to denote that if the credit exceeds any tax liability the excess is paid out ('refunded') in contrast to most tax credits, which are 'wasted' to the extent they exceed tax liability.

[20] See Kesselman (1993) for a detailed analysis and critique of this system.

Table 2.5 Federal and provincial marginal tax rates on a single taxpayer in 1995

Taxable income	Federal rates		Provincial rates									
	Quebec	Other provinces	Nfld.	PEI	NS	NB	Que.	Ont.	Man.	Sask.	Alta.	BC
7,500	11.9	14.5	11.1	9.6		10.3				10.0		8.4
10,000	11.9	14.5	11.1	9.6	9.6	10.3	21.0	27.9	13.3	15.0	11.7	8.4
12,500	13.9	16.5	11.1	9.6	9.6	10.3	18.2	9.3	13.3	15.0	11.7	8.4
15,000	13.9	16.5	11.1	9.6	14.6	10.3	20.2	9.3	13.3	11.0	11.7	10.4
17,500	13.9	16.5	11.1	9.6	14.6	10.3	20.2	9.3	13.3	11.0	7.8	8.4
20,000	13.9	16.5	11.1	9.6	9.6	10.3	20.2	9.3	12.3	11.0	7.8	8.4
22,500	13.9	16.5	11.1	9.6	9.6	10.3	20.2	9.3	10.3	11.0	7.8	8.4
25,000	13.9	16.5	11.1	9.6	9.6	10.3	22.3	9.3	10.3	11.0	7.8	8.4
27,500	18.9	21.5	11.1	9.6	9.6	10.3	22.3	9.3	10.3	11.0	7.8	8.4
30,000	26.7	30.8	17.3	14.9	14.9	16.0	22.2	14.5	17.0	15.9	11.9	13.1
35,000	22.0	26.2	17.6	15.2	15.2	16.4	24.0	14.8	17.3	16.3	12.2	13.4
40,000	22.0	26.2	17.6	15.2	15.2	16.4	14.8	17.3	16.3	12.2	13.4	
						24.0						
50,000	22.0	26.8	17.9	15.4	15.4	16.6	26.2	15.1	17.5	18.7	13.3	13.6
75,000	26.5	31.3	20.0	17.3	17.3	18.6	26.4	21.9	19.1	20.6	14.8	19.8
100,000	26.5	31.3	20.0	19.0	19.0	20.1	26.4	21.9	19.1	20.6	14.8	22.9

Source: See Table 2.4.

Table 2.6 Federal and provincial marginal tax rates on a married taxpayer[a] in 1995

Taxable income	Federal rates		Provincial rates									
	Quebec	Other provinces	Nfld.	PEI	NS	NB	Que.	Ont.	Man.	Sask.	Alta.	BC
7,500	11.9	14.5	11.1	9.6		10.3				10.0		8.4
10,000	11.9	14.5	11.1	9.6	9.6	10.3	18.2	27.9	12.3	15.0	11.7	8.4
12,500	13.9	16.5	11.1	9.6	9.6	10.3	21.0	9.3	12.3	15.0	11.7	8.4
15,000	13.9	16.5	11.1	9.6	14.6	10.3	20.2	9.3	12.3	11.0	11.7	10.4
17,500	13.9	16.5	11.1	9.6	9.6	10.3	20.2	9.3	12.3	11.0	7.8	8.4
20,000	13.9	16.5	11.1	9.6	9.6	10.3	20.2	9.3	12.3	11.0	7.8	8.4
22,500	13.9	16.5	11.1	9.6	9.6	10.3	20.2	9.3	10.3	11.0	7.8	8.4
25,000	13.9	16.5	11.1	9.6	9.6	10.3	22.3	9.3	10.3	11.0	7.8	8.4
27,500	23.9	26.5	11.1	9.6	9.6	10.3	22.3	9.3	10.3	11.0	7.8	8.4
30,000	31.7	35.8	17.3	14.9	14.9	16.0	22.2	14.5	17.0	15.9	11.9	13.1
35,000	27.0	31.2	17.6	15.2	15.2	16.4	24.0	14.8	17.3	16.3	12.2	13.4
40,000	27.0	31.2	17.6	15.2	15.2	16.4	24.0	14.8	17.3	16.3	12.2	13.4
50,000	22.0	26.8	17.9	15.4	15.4	16.6	26.2	15.1	17.5	18.7	13.3	13.6
75,000	26.5	31.3	20.0	17.3	17.3	18.6	26.4	21.9	19.1	20.6	14.8	19.8
100,000	26.5	31.3	20.0	19.0	19.0	20.1	26.4	21.9	19.1	20.6	14.8	22.9

[a] Assumes dependent spouse and two children under 18

Source: See Table 2.4.

Table 2.7 Federal and provincial marginal tax rates on a single taxpayer aged 65 in 1995

Taxable income	Federal rates		Provincial rates									
	Quebec	Other provinces	Nfld.	PEI	NS	NB	Que.	Ont.	Man.	Sask.	Alta.	BC
7,500	11.9	14.5	11.1	9.6	9.6	10.3	21.0	27.9	13.3	10.0	11.7	8.4
10,000	11.9	14.5	11.1	9.6	9.6	10.3	18.2	9.3	13.3	15.0	11.7	8.4
12,500	13.9	16.5	11.1	9.6	9.6	10.3	20.2	9.3	13.3	15.0	11.7	8.4
15,000	13.9	16.5	11.1	9.6	14.5	10.3	20.2	9.3	13.3	11.0	7.8	10.4
17,500	13.9	16.5	11.1	9.6	9.6	10.3	20.2	9.3	13.3	11.0	7.8	8.4
20,000	13.9	16.5	11.1	9.6	9.6	10.3	20.2	9.3	10.3	11.0	7.8	8.4
22,500	13.9	16.5	11.1	9.6	9.6	10.3	22.3	9.3	10.3	11.0	7.8	8.4
25,000	13.9	16.5	11.1	9.6	9.6	10.3	22.3	9.3	10.3	11.0	7.8	8.4
27,500	18.9	21.5	11.1	9.6	9.6	10.3	22.3	9.3	10.3	11.0	7.8	8.4
30,000	26.7	30.8	17.3	14.9	14.9	16.0	22.3	14.5	17.0	15.9	11.9	13.1
35,000	22.0	26.2	17.6	15.2	15.2	16.4	24.0	14.8	17.3	16.2	12.2	13.4
40,000	22.0	26.2	17.6	15.2	15.2	16.4	24.0	14.8	17.3	16.3	12.2	13.4
50,000	27.0	31.8	17.9	15.4	15.4	16.6	26.2	15.1	17.5	18.7	13.3	13.6
75,000	26.5	31.3	20.0	17.3	17.3	18.6	26.4	21.9	19.1	20.6	14.8	19.8
100,000	26.5	31.3	20.0	19.0	19.0	20.1	26.4	21.9	19.1	20.6	14.8	22.9

another threshold.[21] Finally, both the federal and the Quebec systems introduced 'minimum tax' provisions in 1986, though very few taxpayers are
affected by these provisions.[22]

Tables 2.5–2.7 reflect the child tax benefit, the GST credit, and the old-age
security clawback, but too many assumptions would be required to incorporate the other federal and provincial provisions mentioned.

B1.3 The Family Unit

The personal income tax system in Canada is based on individual taxation.
Some recognition of the existence of families is contained in the tax credits
available for non-working spouses, certain dependants (except children under
18, as noted above), and the deduction for childcare expenses. Income
attribution rules prevent income splitting between family members, at least
in theory. On the other hand, allowable deductions and credits are in most
cases transferable between spouses and from dependants. Similarly, the
refundable credits mentioned earlier for child benefits and the GST are determined by family income. The clawback system for OAS and unemployment
insurance benefits described above is not based on family income, however.
Since 1991, spouses include common-law spouses.

The treatment of divorced and separated couples is currently contentious.
The existing law provides for deductibility of maintenance and alimony payments from the income of the payor, and inclusion in the income of the
recipient. A recent court case[23] ruled that inclusion was discriminatory
against previously married women, but was silent on the treatment of the
payor. It is under appeal, and a task force of Parliament is reviewing the issue.

B1.4 Indexation for Inflation

Although full indexation of the personal exemptions and the rate schedule
existed from 1974 to 1982, since 1985 the federal system has been indexed
only for inflation in excess of 3 per cent per year.[24] Over the 1985–93 period,
less than one-third of the cumulative inflation was indexed under this system.
Since 1991, inflation has been less than 3 per cent, so there has been no

---

[21] Canadians over 65 years of age receive an old-age security pension of $4,579.20 (in 1993) per
year. This pension is subject both to the normal income tax and to a special tax (deductible from
taxable income) equal to 15% of net income in excess of $53,215 (in 1993), up to a maximum of
the benefits received. A similar 'clawback' at a rate of 30% of income in excess of a threshold of
$58,110 (in 1993) is applied to recipients of unemployment insurance benefits, up to a maximum
of benefits received.   [22] See Larin and Jacques (1994).

[23] Thibodeau vs. MNR Tax Court of Canada, 1994, currently under appeal by the federal
government. For an extensive discussion of the issues, see Durnford and Toope (1994).

[24] Despite the articulate and convincing argument initially put forward by federal officials to
the effect that indexation is an essential feature of an equitable income tax: see Allan *et al.* (1974).
The province of Quebec never introduced automatic indexation, choosing instead to have the
government set the indexation factor annually. In most instances, the result was indexation below
the rate of inflation. In recent years, Quebec's performance has been close to that of the federal
government—that is, no indexation.

indexation. 'Bracket creep' is thus one factor explaining the marked growth of personal income tax revenues in Canada in recent years.

B2 The Corporate Income Tax

B2.1 Tax Base

As noted above, the rules for determination of taxable income are set out in general terms for all businesses, whether incorporated or not. Special reliefs apply to certain types of corporate bodies such as charitable organizations, trusts, or foundations, and certain cooperatives.

While financial institutions are subject to the general rules for the calculation of taxable income, they are allowed special treatment to reflect the need to provide for loan losses and policy claims (for insurance companies), and, in the case of investment and mutual fund companies, to flow through capital gains free of tax to individual investors who can then take advantage of the preferential treatment available for these gains described above.

B2.2 Tax Rates

The federal statutory rates, shown in Table 2.8, reflect the general abatement available in respect of corporate income that is also subject to provincial tax.[25] Seven of the provinces (and the two territories) have empowered the federal government to collect corporate income tax on their behalf.[26] As in the case of the individual income tax, all provinces accept the corporate income allocation rules agreed to in the 1950s, which are based on a weighted average of payroll (wages and salaries) and gross sales.[27] Special rules apply to specified companies—such as transportation companies—where the general rules are considered inadequate. Not all provinces have been happy with the allocation rules, however, and some have adjusted their income and capital, payroll, or property tax systems to try to compensate. The federal and provincial corporate income tax rates shown in Table 2.8 do not reflect these additional taxes. The low rates in Quebec, for example, must be considered in the context of relatively high payroll taxes in that province.

There is no special treatment for dividends paid out by Canadian corporations, but dividends received by Canadian corporations from other Canadian corporations are excluded from taxable income (unless classed as dividends on certain preferred shares). This provision, like the dividend tax credit for individuals, applies irrespective of whether any tax has been paid by the

---

[25] The rates shown in Table 2.8 include a 3% surtax imposed on federal corporate income tax payable before taking any deductions for small business or 'manufacturing and processing' profits.
[26] In 1994, Alberta, which had introduced its own corporate income tax in 1981, began negotiations to re-enter the federal–provincial tax collection agreement, but so far no agreement has been reached. Although Ontario and Quebec have had their own corporate income taxes since 1947, the basic structure of all the separate provincial taxes closely follows the design of the federal tax.   [27] See Smith (1976).

Table 2.8 Combined federal and provincial corporate income tax rates, 1995

	Nfld.	PEI	NS	NB	Que.	Ont.	Man.	Sask.	Alta.	BC
Federal corporate income tax rates (%)										
General business	29.12									
Manufacturing and processing profits	22.12									
General small business	13.12									
Combined federal and provincial rates (%)										
General business	43.12	44.12	45.12	46.12	45.37	44.62	46.12	46.12	44.62	45.62
Manufacturing and processing profits	27.12	29.62	38.12	39.12	31.02	35.62	39.12	39.12	36.62	38.62
General small business	18.12	20.62	18.12	20.12	18.87	22.62	22.12	21.12	19.12	23.12

[a] The statutory federal rate has been reduced by 10 percentage points to reflect the tax room, or abatement, provided for provincial taxes.

Source: See Table 2.4.

company issuing the dividend and hence differs significantly from European 'imputation' systems.

Canadian-controlled private corporations (generally small and medium-sized incorporated business) qualify for preferential rates on the first $200,000 of taxable income under both federal and provincial tax regimes. Additional deductions lower the rate for profits from manufacturing and processing activities, as shown in Table 2.8.[28]

There is no minimum corporate income tax in the federal system. The province of Ontario, however, has recently (1994) introduced a relatively modest minimum corporate income tax system despite the clear recommendation of a provincially appointed tax commission against it.[29] It is not yet clear whether the Conservative government elected in 1995 will continue with this initiative of its New Democratic Party predecessor. Like several other provinces, and the federal government, Ontario also levies special taxes on corporate capital, as discussed below.

B3   Payroll Taxes

B3.1   Earmarked for Social Security Expenditures

The Canada Pension Plan (CPP) provides an earnings-related pension and death and survivor benefits, to both employed and self-employed persons. In Quebec, a comparable programme—the Quebec Pension Plan (QPP)—is run by the provincial government. Neither plan was designed to be fully funded, and the income from early funding has proven inadequate to finance pay-outs. The rates of contribution are therefore to be raised from the 1994 level of 2.6 per cent of the first $34,400 of employment earnings (the average industrial wage) now levied on each of employers and employees, with double that amount for the self-employed, to 2.9 per cent by 1997.[30] Contributions are creditable for individuals and deductible for employers.

Unemployment insurance (UI) is a federal responsibility, financed in 1994 by contributions from employees of 3.07 per cent of wages and salary up to about $38,000; employer contributions are 1.4 times employee contributions (or 4.298 per cent of insurable earnings). As with the CPP and QPP, contributions are creditable for employees and deductible for employers. Revenues are separately identified within government accounts, although the operations of the unemployment insurance account (unlike those of the CPP and QPP) form part of budgetary revenues and expenditures. The legislation provides that employee/employer contributions must meet the cost of

---

[28] The origin of these favourable rates was as a response to the US DISC programme of the 1960s. Note that the definition of 'processing' can be rather broad: reportedly, half the income of restaurants has been so classified.   [29] Ontario Fair Tax Commission (1993).

[30] The first 10% of the taxable wage base is exempted, and there is a maximum annual contribution of $894 for employees, or $1,788 in total.

providing basic benefits. In recent years, however, the federal government has exercised its power to hold rates below that break-even point. As a result, the UI account has an accumulated deficit.

At the provincial level, payroll taxes are levied on employers on an 'experience-rating' basis to finance workers' compensation plans.[31]

B3.2 Other

Payroll taxes other than those for workers' compensation are levied by four provinces, with exemptions or low rates for small employers. Nominally, these taxes are related to the financing of public health insurance programmes. There is, however no earmarking of these taxes, nor any specific provisions that the tax must meet a specified share of the total programme cost.[32] The rates range from less than 1 per cent to 3.25 per cent.

B4 Value-Added and Sales Taxes

Canada has two general consumption tax systems—the federal value-added tax (GST) and provincial retail sales taxes (RSTs) in all provinces except Alberta, where there is none, and Quebec, which has a value-added tax.

B4.1 The Goods and Services Tax

Since 1 January 1991, the federal government has levied the GST on the sales of most goods and services.[33] Certain purchases are exempted or zero-rated in whole or in part: among those to whom such special rules apply are provincial governments, representatives of foreign governments and international organizations, charitable organizations, municipalities, universities, schools, and hospitals, and Canada's native peoples.

The tax is applied to a broad range of goods and services (including most of the 'fringe benefits' subject to income tax), but basic groceries and prescription drugs are zero-rated. Financial services, medical services, and residential rents are exempt. Partial rebates are available for most purchases of new homes.[34] Input tax credits on meals and entertainment are limited (as under the income tax) to 50 per cent. As noted earlier, a system of refundable tax credits is administered through the personal income tax to alleviate the regressive effects of the tax on low- and lower-middle-income families.

---

[31] For a recent discussion, see Vaillancourt (1994*b*).

[32] Such 'notional' earmarking is common in Canada: see Thirsk and Bird (1993). For a full discussion of provincial payroll taxes, see Kesselman (1994).

[33] As noted earlier, the GST replaced a long-existing federal sales tax levied at the manufacturing level. The rationale for, and effects of, this tax substitution are discussed later.

[34] As is often the case with GST, this simple sentence conceals a host of complexities: for a careful review of the treatment of real property under the GST, see Arkin (1994).

B4.2 *Provincial Retail Sales Taxes*

Retail sales taxes have been the domain of the provinces for the post-Second World War period.[35] The rates range from 7 per cent to 12 per cent on a tax-exclusive basis on final selling price and are applied to a narrower base of goods than the GST plus a few services. Each of the nine provinces imposing retail sales taxes provides a wide range of exemptions. In general, food is exempt, as are low-priced meals. Some goods taxed under other statutes, such as gasoline, are also exempt. Building materials are taxable, but the sale of land and buildings is exempt. Production equipment and consumables are usually exempt, but goods not directly related to the production process are taxable. It has been estimated that from one-third to one-half of retail sales taxes are actually collected on business inputs.[36]

B5 Excises

The federal government imposes excise taxes or duties on tobacco and alcoholic beverages, motor vehicle fuel, and certain minor items such as automobile air-conditioners. All provincial governments levy special excise taxes on motor vehicle fuel and tobacco. The provincial rates on motor vehicle fuel are higher than the federal rates and are collected from distributors. Few provinces levy special excise taxes on alcoholic beverages, however, because in most cases they are the sole retail vendors of distilled spirits so their 'tax' takes the form of a large mark-up in the selling price. Sales by independent stores selling beer or wine, however, are taxed to provide a comparable return to the province.[37]

Tobacco taxation has recently become a vexatious matter in Canada. Combined federal and provincial taxes were, until recently, equal to or higher than those prevailing in Europe, and therefore much higher than those imposed in bordering states in the USA. The relatively open border (especially through Indian reserves) led to the development of an extensive smuggling network that supplied a black market in which prices were less than half the legal retail price. Such illegal sales came to account for over one-half of all sales in some provinces (notably Quebec). In early 1994 the federal and Quebec governments substantially reduced their tobacco taxes in order to eliminate the differential between legal and black-market prices. The resulting pronounced price differential between Quebec and neighbouring provinces (such as Ontario) soon resulted in similar tax cuts in Canada's five eastern provinces. Most recently, greatly increased mail order sales of cigarettes in western provinces have begun to put pressure on their taxes also.

[35] For an extended discussion, see Robinson (1986)

[36] See Kuo, *et al.* (1988) and Dean (1989).

[37] Alberta—which is much more of a fiscal 'out-lier' in Canada than Quebec—has recently privatized the sales of alcoholic beverages, imposing flat excise taxes on beer, wine, and spirits at levels intended to maintain provincial revenues from alcohol.

B6 Capital Taxes

Canada has no direct taxes on personal wealth. Following the abolition of the federal estate tax in 1972, all the provinces abolished their inheritance taxes, with the last such tax, in Quebec, vanishing in 1985. Since then, the most significant tax on wealth in Canada has been the real property tax, which in most provinces is levied entirely by municipalities, although as a rule on a base assessed by provincial authorities.[38] Taxes based on the gross value of a particular class of asset are of course only crudely, if at all, related to personal wealth and income, especially since as a rule the effective rate of tax is higher on business than on residential property and half or more of property tax yields come from business property.[39]

In addition, in recent years increasing use has been made by both federal and provincial governments of various forms of taxes on corporate capital. The federal government now levies an annual tax of 0.2 per cent of the paid-up capital in excess of $10 million of all corporations. This tax is not deductible for income tax purposes but is instead creditable against the federal surtax on corporate income tax (see n. 25), with generous carry-forward and carry-back provisions. Banks, trust companies, and life insurance companies are subject to additional capital taxes ranging from 0.5 per cent to 1.5 per cent. Capital taxes are also levied by most provinces, with higher rates charged to financial institutions. In some industries, such taxes—like the business real property tax—often constitute a higher tax burden than the corporate income tax.

B7 The Local Tax System

As described above, federal and provincial taxes on income are closely related in a number of ways. Although the other main source of revenue at the provincial level, the retail sales tax, is as yet formally related to the federal GST only in Quebec, it is likely (as noted below) that this second pillar of the federal–provincial tax system will also become more interdependent over time. Even in the case of such minor levies as the tobacco tax, as already mentioned, federal and provincial tax decisions are interdependent to a considerable degree. Somewhat curiously perhaps, the very fiscal importance of the provincial governments in Canada has meant that their tax systems are so closely related to that of the federal government that it sometimes seems to make little sense to talk of a separate provincial tax system, or systems. Nonetheless, there are interesting differences in provincial taxes—most strikingly, the absence of sales taxes and the lower income taxes in Alberta owing to the great importance of royalties in the revenues of that province—and numerous minor

---

[38] Since capital gains are not indexed, the deemed realization of capital gains at death is also in part a crude form of wealth taxation.

[39] For a view of the property tax as a tax on personal wealth, see Kitchen (1992).

variations (e.g. in sales tax exemptions and motor vehicle and fuel taxes) that have been little studied.[40]

Similarly, taxation at the local level in Canada is superficially the same everywhere, but in fact on closer examination turns out to differ significantly across provinces. As noted earlier, throughout the country the major source of local tax revenues is the property tax, but there are considerable variations in the weight placed on this tax, and on its residential and non-residential components, in different parts of the country, in part reflecting the different roles taken by local and provincial governments in providing services in different provinces.[41] In some areas, these roles are in the process of change. In Ontario, for example, a recent provincial tax commission recommended a substantial shift from local property tax finance of (about half of) the costs of primary and secondary education to provincial income tax finance.[42] While this recommendation was not adopted by the newly elected provincial government, which is committed to reducing rather than increasing provincial income taxes, some major changes in the present system of financing regional and local governments in the province did take place in response to the argument that some 'hollowing-out' of the core of the greater Toronto region is occurring as a result of differentials in local business property taxes. Since 1998 the provincial government in Ontario has been financing an increased share of educational costs, but through a provincial takeover of non-residential property taxation not an increase in income taxes.

C. Economic and Social Aspects

C1 The Fiscal Deficit

When the Conservative government took office in the autumn of 1984, the federal deficit for fiscal year 1984–5 was running at an annual rate of $39.4 billion, or 8.7 per cent of GDP. Deficit control and fiscal constraints were the watchwords of the new Minister of Finance, and over the next six years, the government did reduce the deficit relative to GDP: by 1989–90 the deficit was down to $29.0 billion, or 4.4 per cent of GDP, as shown in Table 2.9.

Since 1990, however, the government has repeatedly failed to achieve the medium-term deficit targets set out in successive budgets: see Table 2.10. With the recession of 1990–1 and the subsequent slow recovery period, the fiscal plan was thrown off-track. The deficit rose to $30.6 billion in 1990–1, and continued rising to $42.0 billion in 1993–4, before finally declining in 1994–5.

---

[40] The most complete account of provincial public finances may be found in a two-volume study edited by McMillan (1991). One volume of this study contains a province by province analysis and the other contains a variety of comparative studies across provinces.

[41] For more detailed discussion, see Kitchen (1984, 1992) and Bird and Slack (1993).

[42] Ontario Fair Tax Commission (1993).

Table 2.9 Budget deficits as a percentage of GDP

	Public accounts deficit[a] ($m.)	Nominal GDP ($m.)	Deficit as a % of GDP
1982–3	29,430	379,193	7.76
1983–4	35,146	416,385	8.44
1984–5	39,412	452,992	8.70
1985–6	34,628	486,173	7.12
1986–7	30,783	513,956	5.99
1987–8	28,251	565,909	4.99
1988–9	28,981	618,101	4.69
1989–90	29,106	658,619	4.42
1990–1	32,088	668,948	4.80
1991–2	34,463	678,765	5.08
1992–3	41,021	694,063	5.91
1993–4	42,012	720,534	5.83
1994–5	37,462	760,791	4.92

[a] Public accounts deficit is adjusted to include UI for 1982–3 to 1984–5, in order to be comparable to subsequent years.

Source: Finance Canada, Budget Documents (various years).

Table 2.10 Budgetary deficit ($m.)[a]

Fiscal year	3-year forecast	2-year forecast	1-year forecast	Actual
1982–3			22,649	29,430
1983–4		22,907	34,435	35,146
1984–5		30,629	31,418	39,412
1985–6	27,121	28,108	34,047	34,628
1986–7	25,619	32,508	29,465	30,783
1987–8	33,607	25,940	29,330	28,251
1988–9	25,045	29,710	28,946	28,981
1989–90	28,130	28,590	30,500	29,106
1990–1	26,095	28,000	28,525	32,088
1991–2	24,400	26,850	30,500	34,463
1992–3	20,832	24,000	27,500	41,021
1993–4	16,600	22,500	32,600	42,012
1994–5	14,500	29,000	39,700	37,462

[a] includes UI in 1982–3 to 1984–5 (see note to Table 2.9).

Source: See Table 2.9.

Moreover, the federal deficit alone does not reveal the full impact of the recession on Canada's public finances since in its attempts to limit the rise in the deficit, the federal government has cut back on transfer payments to the provinces, targeting most of the cuts to the three wealthiest provinces—Ontario, British Columbia, and Alberta.

In November 1984, the Department of Finance released a major policy paper which identified the large deficit and growing debt as the main macroeconomic obstacles to growth, and proposed fiscal restraints to be concentrated on the spending side. Nevertheless, two of the three major initiatives in the first budget of the new government exacerbated the deficit problem, namely significant tax reductions for the energy sector and a lifetime exemption for capital gains. Only the limitation of the indexing adjustments for the personal income tax (and for certain transfer payments) to the rate of inflation in excess of 3 per cent generated an increasing stream of future revenues. In addition, the budget imposed increases in sales and excise taxes and surtaxes on higher-income individuals and large corporations. The latter were announced to be temporary; in the event, as so often happens, they became permanent and were extended in future budgets.

The 1986 budget continued this pattern of tax increases and expenditure restraints. On the tax side, the manufacturers' sales tax was increased by another percentage point, and two new income tax surcharges were introduced. The major income tax reform introduced in 1987–8 was designed to be revenue-neutral after the transition period. However, the timing of the implementation of the income tax reform measures actually generated a transitory increase in the deficit of up to \$2 billion in fiscal year 1989–90.[43] The GST implemented on 1 January 1991 was also designed to be revenue-neutral, with increased PIT surtaxes and expenditure restraints implemented to round out the package. However, the sales tax reform package included generous transitional provisions to small businesses, which, combined with the adverse macroeconomic transitional effects, may have generated a transitory increase in the deficit.[44]

Since 1991, the GST has been little changed. In the 1992 budget, however, the general PIT surtax was reduced from 5 per cent to 3 per cent in two stages. The 1992 budget also partially reversed the corporate tax reforms of 1987 by restoring the favouritism to manufacturing characteristic of post-war Canadian tax policy: the tax depreciation (capital cost allowance, or CCA) rate for manufacturing and processing was increased from 25 per cent to 30 per cent, and the statutory tax rate for manufacturing was reduced by 2 percentage points.

Despite these various tax changes, on the whole federal budgets in the early 1990s typically emphasized expenditure restraints as the key deficit-reduction strategy. Among the expenditures cut were transfers to the provinces—a move

---

[43] Wilson and Dungan (1993: 120, 122).   [44] Wilson and Dungan (1993, Table 72: 142–3).

that has led to accusations that the federal government has 'down-loaded' its deficit to the provinces. Such accusations became particularly marked in 1995 when the second budget of the new Liberal government announced the impending bundling of the last major 'open-ended' federal matching transfer—the Canada Assistance Plan, under which the federal government financed (with some recently imposed limits in the richer provinces) 50 per cent of welfare costs—together with the so-called Established Program Financing grant which finances the (diminishing) federal share of provincial spending on health and post-education into a new 'Canada Health and Social Transfer'.[45] The new transfer system will have the great merit from the federal point of view of setting a clear limit of federal financing of provincial spending: what the reaction of provincial governments will be remains to be seen.

Despite such measures, the federal deficit has remained high in recent years, as shown in Table 2.9, in part owing to the continued rise in interest payments on the growing public debt and in part owing to the effects of the recession on both sides of the federal budget. However, since early 1996 Canada has run an operating surplus, which federal politicians are eagerly trying to distribute.

C2 Savings and Investment Incentives

A decade ago, the Canadian income tax system contained a number of savings and investment incentives, albeit reduced in magnitude and scope from earlier periods.[46] In addition to specific incentives, the treatment of dividends and capital gains provided additional incentives for equity investments outside registered plans.

C2.1 Savings Incentives

In 1985, as now, the most important income tax savings incentive was the deductibility of contributions to Registered Pension Plans (RPPs) and Registered Retirement Savings Plans (RRSPs), combined with the sheltering of investment income within these plans.[47] In addition, however, other general tax incentives to savings were provided by an investment income deduction, which allowed individuals to deduct up to $1,000 of investment income, by provisions which permitted deferral of taxes on interest income for three years, and by the deductibility of the first $1,000 of pension annuity income.

[45] This is not the place to describe Canada's complex federal–provincial transfer arrangments, which are in any case in the process of change: see Boadway and Hobson (1993).

[46] Prior to the November 1981 budget, for example, individuals could defer tax from certain income sources (the most important of which was capital gains) by buying income averaging annuity contracts (IAACs). Interest on borrowed funds to purchase RRSPs was deductible. The 1981 budget eliminated these provisions and also reduced the first year deduction for capital cost allowance (CCA) by one-half.

[47] As noted above, employer as well as employee contributions are deductible within prescribed limits. Further, employer contributions to deferred profit-sharing plans (DPSPs) are deductible, and income accrued within these plans is also sheltered from tax.

Moreover, savings for the first-time purchase of a residence could be deducted and sheltered under a Registered Home Ownership Plan (RHOSP).[48]

The Conservative government elected in 1984 soon eliminated or modified several of these provisions. In their first (1985) budget the RHOSPs were abolished. As part of the major income tax reform in 1987, the deduction for investment income was eliminated, and the deduction for pension annuity income was replaced by a tax credit at the lowest marginal rate. Subsequently, the deferral for accrued interest income was eliminated: interest income must now be reported on an annual basis. These changes effectively eliminated most incentives to savings under the PIT, except for the most important one: the deductibility of contributions to, and the sheltering of income within, RPPs and RRSPs.

The limits to contributions to Retirement Savings Plans since 1979 are shown in Table 2.11. Two events stand out. In 1986, the contribution limit for RRSP contributions was raised to $7,500. In 1991, a major reform of the income tax treatment of pensions was put into effect. Under the new system, RPPs and RRSP are more effectively integrated, and the contribution limits for higher-income and individuals increased significantly. For individuals with incomes below $37,500, however, the new system actually *reduced* RRSP contribution limits because the maximum percentage contribution was lowered to 18 per cent of eligible income from the previous 20 per cent.

The initial increase in the maximum contribution limit was $4,000, bringing the limit to $11,500 in 1991. Under the initial pension reform proposal announced in 1991, this limit was to increase by $1,000 per year until it reached $15,500 in 1995, after which date the limit would be indexed. However, in fact the limit was frozen in 1993 for one year at $12,500, delaying the end of the phase-in period until 1996. This freeze was extended in the 1995 budget.

Table 2.11 also shows RRSP limits in constant 1993 dollars. Inflation clearly substantially eroded the real value of the contribution limits during the 1980s until the large increase in the RRSP limit in 1991.[49]

Another traditional theme in Canadian tax policy—even though Canada is one of the few countries to allow no deduction for mortgage interest—is solicitude for housing. The 1992 federal budget introduced a temporary provision for the withdrawal of up to $20,000 tax free from RRSP for the purchase of a residence.[50] Originally scheduled to expire in 1993, this measure

---

[48] As now, taxpayers could also contribute to a Registered Education Savings Plan (RESP) for their children (or other individuals). Although contributions to RESPs are not deductible, investment income earned within these plans is sheltered from tax. Amounts distributed from these plans for educational purposes are taxed in the hands of the beneficiaries.

[49] Burbidge and Davies (1994) evaluate RRSP limits back to 1970 and show that the peak value of the limit in real terms was actually attained in 1972.

[50] Under this provision, the $20,000 withdrawn from the RRSP must be repaid in equal instalments over 15 years. Hence the measure allows, in effect, an interest free loan from an RRSP to buy a residence.

Table 2.11   RRSP contribution limits 1979–1995

Year	% of income limits	Absolute $ limit		Absolute limit in constant 1993 dollars (not in RPP)
		Not in RPP	In RPP[b]	
1979	20	5,500	3,500	10,233
1980	20	5,500	3,500	9,153
1981	20	5,500	3,500	8,544
1982	20	5,500	3,500	8,092
1983	20	5,500	3,500	7,777
1984	20	5,500	3,500	7,597
1985	20	5,500	3,500	7,394
1986	20	7,500	3,500	9,810
1987	20	7,500	3,500	9,415
1988	20	7,500	3,500	8,951
1989	20	7,500	3,500	8,598
1990	20	7,500	3,500	8,363
1991	18[a]	11,500	11,500-PA[c]	11,715
1992	18[a]	12,500	12,500-PA[c]	12,625
1993	18[a]	12,500	12,500-PA[c]	12,500
1994	18[a]	13,500	13,500-PA[c]	13,479
1995	18[a]	14,500	14,500-PA[c]	14,195[d]

[a] After 1990, the limit of 18% relates to the previous year's income.
[b] 'In RPP' prior to 1991 relates to an individual who is a member of an RPP to which his/her employer contributes. After 1991 it refers to an individual who is a member of an RPP.
[c] PA refers to the 'Pension Adjustment', which is the dollar amount contributed to money purchase plan RPPs and an equivalent amount for defined benefit RPPs based on a complex formula. The PA is adjusted so that members of an RPP have at least $1,000 of contribution room for RRSPs.
[d] Estimated.

Source: Canadian Tax Foundation, National Finances (various years).

was subsequently extended for a year to 1994 and then extended indefinitely for 'first-time' buyers in the 1994 budget by the newly elected Liberal government.

The distribution of RRSP/RPP contributions by income and age has been analysed in detail by Burbidge and Davies (1994). Their results indicate that participation in, and amounts contributed to, these plans increased with age (up to normal retirement age) and with income. Participation has also been increasing over time.

With higher-income individuals accounting for a significant fraction of total contributions to registered savings plans, the increases in the absolute dollar limit following on the 1991 reform should dominate the smaller relative reduction in the percentage of income limit. Combined with the increased flexibility of the carry-forward rules for unused RRSP contribution 'room' (now seven years), it seems reasonable to conclude that the recent pension reforms should stimulate an increase in net contributions to these plans.

RRSP contributions for 1991 increased by 26 per cent over the previous year. In 1992, they increased by an additional 10.6 per cent. Since contributions in 1990 and 1991 may have been affected by the recession, it may be more useful to compare the contribution rates for 1991–3 with the average for the 1986–90 period when the $7,500/20 per cent limit was in effect. The results are shown in Table 2.12. It is clear that contributions for 1991–3 were higher both in absolute terms and relative to income than in any of the previous years shown. On average, RRSP contributions relative to income were slightly higher after pension reform and have been rising.

It therefore appears reasonable to conclude that the new system has generated greater contributions to RRSPs. Whether these contributions represent increased savings or asset reallocations cannot be readily determined, however. Published studies of the impact of the RPP/RRSP system on savings show diverse results.[51]

C2.2 Investment Incentives

Canada has for many years had an accelerated capital cost allowance (CCA) system with assets written off on a declining balance basis at favourable rates. Furthermore, the CCA system permits considerable flexibility—firms can choose how much CCA to claim up to the limit for an asset class, thereby enabling firms to average income over time more effectively.[52]

In the early 1970s additional provisions were introduced to stimulate investment, with particular emphasis on manufacturing and processing and primary industries (agriculture, mining, and forestry). An investment credit was introduced, initially at the rate of 5 per cent, but later increased to 7 per cent. This credit was applicable to investment in machinery and equipment and non-residential construction in primary industries, manufacturing, and processing. Over time, enriched credits were provided for investment in designated 'slow-growth' areas and for research and development (R&D). In addition, special accelerated CCA was introduced. Manufacturing and processing firms were permitted to write off investments in machinery and equipment over two years. Other favourable CCA measures were introduced for mining, and for investment in energy conservation and pollution abatement equipment.[53]

During the 1980s, however, most of these special investment measures were weakened or eliminated. As noted above, the allowable CCA rate for the first

---

[51] See e.g. Ragan (1994), Ingerman and Rowley (1993), and, for analysis of a similar earlier plan intended to finance home ownership (RHOSP), Engelhardt (1994).

[52] Within the limits on loss carry-backs (3 years) and carry-forwards (7 years), this CCA discretion permits firms to manage tax liabilities over time to some extent.

[53] See Bird (1980*a*) for a description and evaluation of investment incentives in the 1970s, and Rushton (1992) for similarly sceptical review of the literature in the 1980s.

Table 2.12 RRSP contributions 1985–1993 ($m.)

Year	Total income	RRSP deductions		RRSP limits[a]
		Amount	As % of income	
1985	307,552	6,672	2.17	5,500 (20%)
1986	327,712	7,920	2.42	7,500 (20%)
1987	353,261	9,024	2.55	7,500 (20%)
1988	393,389	10,600	2.69	7,500 (20%)
1989	431,845	11,938	2.76	7,500 (20%)
1990	455,074	10,626	2.34	7,500 (20%)
Average 1986–90		10,022	2.55	
1991	465,694	13,371	2.87	11,500 (18%)
1992[b]	473,434	14,784	3.12	11,500 (18%)
1993[b]	484,068	17,500	3.62	12,500 (18%)
Average 1991–3		15,218	3.21	

[a] Absolute dollar limits with per cent of income limitation in parentheses. Note that, after 1990, the per cent of income limitation is based on the previous year's income.
[b] 'Total income' in 1992 and 1993 is adjusted to exclude 'tax exempt income' in order to be comparable to data for prior years.

Source: *Taxation Statistics for 1985–1993*, table 2, Canada, Dept. of National Revenue.

year of an asset's life was cut in half in 1981. In 1985, a White Paper on corporate tax reform recommended lower corporate tax rates coupled with reduced investment incentives. The 1986 budget began this process by phasing out the general investment credit over a three-year period. Only the special regional and R&D credits survived this pruning. The income tax reform of 1987 completed the process. The special two-year write-off for manufacturing was replaced by a 25 per cent declining balance CCA category (raised to 30 per cent in 1992), and other CCA rates were reduced.

Although corporate tax rates were lowered significantly in the reform, the combination of lower investment tax credits and reduced CCA more than offset the lower statutory rate for new capital. As a result, effective tax rates on investment were increased.[54] One study, using a CGE model, found that the adverse dynamic effects of the reduction in investment incentives effectively wiped out the efficiency gains from the reduction of inter-industry and inter-asset distribution of effective tax rates.[55] A macroeconomic study similarly found that when fully implemented the corporate tax changes would reduce aggregate investment, unless offset by an easing of monetary policy.[56]

While the pre-reform income tax system provided favourable incentives to

[54] See Daly and Mercier (1988) and Grady (1989).
[55] Hamilton and Whalley (1989, table 4: 390).　　　[56] Wilson and Dungan (1993).

business investment, the pre-reform sales tax system did the opposite. Many capital goods were not exempt from the federal sales tax (FST), and virtually all capital goods bore an indirect sales tax burden because a significant fraction of the FST fell on business inputs rather than final consumer products. The sales tax reform implemented in 1991 had as one objective eliminating (most of) the tax burden on business inputs and capital goods by replacing the FST with the GST.[57] One study found that this sales tax reform should have had favourable effects on investment in machinery and equipment and non-residential construction and that, for investment in the aggregate, it should have roughly offset the adverse effect of the income tax reform.[58]

C2.3 Tax Treatment of Income From Equities

The gross-up and credit system for dividend income provides partial relief for equity owners from the 'double taxation' of corporate source income. Since the gross-up and credit is only applicable to Canadian residents who receive dividends from Canadian corporations, in principle it should provide some incentive for Canadian investors to shift their portfolios in favour of Canadian equities although there do not appear to have been any empirical studies of this effect.

C3 Distribution of the Tax Burden

Two recent studies of tax incidence in Canada neatly sum up the present state of knowledge on this subject. Although both studies employ a similar database and methodology—based on an extensive microdatabase maintained at Statistics Canada[59]—one concluded that the tax system was slightly progressive up to the median level and was thereafter more or less proportional, while the other concluded that the system was significantly progressive and substantially redistributive to lower-income groups. Both agreed, however, that the federal tax system was more progressive than those at the provincial or local levels and also that the personal income tax was the main progressive element in the tax system as a whole. Of course, these particular results reflect

---

[57] Since, like most VATs, Canada's GST does not apply to most financial sector activities, some input tax remains.

[58] See Wilson and Dungan (1993). Hamilton and Whalley (1989) analysed the overall effect of the sales tax reform using a CGE model and found a small increase in consumer welfare owing to the reduction of inter-industry price distortions resulting from the replacement of the FST by the GST.

[59] As described in Bordt *et al.* (1990). The studies cited here are Vermaeten, *et al.* (1994) and Ruggeri *et al.* (1994*a*). Other noteworthy incidence studies that have appeared in last decade include Meng and Gillespie (1986) and Kitchen (1992) on the property tax; Grady (1990*b*, 1991), Gillespie (1991*a*), and Ruggeri and Bluck (1990) on sales taxes; Dalhby (1992) on payroll taxes; and Dahlby (1985), Davies (1992), and Grady (1990*a*) in general.

differing income concepts and shifting assumptions—but then so do all incidence studies.[60]

The point may be illustrated by considering the most discussed recent tax question in Canada—the introduction of the GST. It is commonly assumed, for example, that just as the burden of personal income taxes remains with those who pay them,[61] so sales taxes like the GST are often assumed to be paid by the final consumer—the public—although this is by no means either accepted by all analysts or necessarily correct.[62] Even if consumers do pay the GST, what does this imply about the incidence of the tax? Again, the answer is by no means clear. Several analyses of GST incidence have been published, but, as always, the results of such studies depend to a considerable extent upon the specific assumptions made by the author.[63] Contrary to what many seem to think, no one can really *know* who pays any tax, where 'pays' is defined in the economic sense of whose real income is reduced as a result of the imposition of the tax. Tax incidence is studied by applying a series of assumptions based on economic theory to facts on incomes and expenditures collected by statisticians: the results essentially display the assumptions in quantitative dress and need bear no relation to the unknown, and perhaps unknowable, reality. Nonetheless, such studies are the only means we have of determining who pays what tax and, if carefully done, their results can be interesting and useful.

The most recent such study of the incidence of the GST, for example, suggests that the GST falls most heavily on the 'middle' income group. Those in the top 25 per cent of income recipients are definitely better off with the GST than they would be if the same amount were collected in income tax, while for those in the lowest 25 per cent the adverse effects of the GST are largely offset by the GST credit.[64]

C4 The Hidden Economy

Recently, there has been a considerable revival of interest in the hidden economy—that part of economic activity not recorded by government statisticians—as well as in the 'underground' economy—that (larger) part of economic activity not known to the taxing authorities. One recent study in Canada, for example, attributed much of the alleged recent growth in the size of such unreported activities to the introduction of the GST.[65] More

---

[60] For the classic demonstration of the sensitivity of incidence studies to such assumptions, see Whalley (1984); an earlier account may be found in Bird (1980b).

[61] See, however, an interesting study by Schaafsma (1992) which indicates that self-employed dentists in Canada appear to shift forward 100% of their personal income tax burden!

[62] Disagreement on this point, for example, is one reason for the different results noted above. For a useful overview of alternative approaches to this question, see Whalley (1984).

[63] For a clear demonstration of this point, see the exchange of views in Grady (1990b), Gillespie (1991a) and Grady (1991).   [64] Ruggeri *et al.* (1994b).

[65] See Spiro (1993).

broadly, although, as usual, different methods have produced very different estimates of the size of such activities in Canada—ranging from a low of 3 per cent of GDP for the 'hidden' part to a high of around 20 per cent for the broader 'underground' concept, with perhaps the most plausible figures being in the range of 5–10 per cent—there appears to be a growing consensus that (i) there has been some growth in the size of the 'underground' sector of the economy in recent years and (ii) this growth is associated with the increase in tax rates.[66] Certainly, there is growing evidence that Canada's traditionally rather placid taxpaying population seems to be undergoing a sea-change.

A 1994 survey, for example, was conducted specifically to provide a statistically reliable picture of Canadian opinion of taxation and tax evasion, especially with respect to the GST.[67] The survey questionnaire included ten belief statements to which people were asked to respond using categories ranging from 'Agree a lot' to 'Disagree a lot'. Factor analysis suggested that each respondent's position could be defined within a three-dimensional space formed by three factors—broadly characterized as (i) high taxation and wasteful government, (ii) catching tax cheaters, and (iii) are honest taxpayers fools?—and then segmented using cluster analysis. The results of this analysis suggests that Canadians may be divided into four groups with respect to their attitudes to the tax system, as follows:

Group 1. Upset and Envious = 34 per cent of the population.
These people think that the tax system is unfair and that the money is squandered by government. They also think that most people cheat, and that much stronger action should be taken to stop it.
Group 2. Model Citizens = 22 per cent of population.
Model citizens tend to think that Canadians get good value for their taxes, that the present tax system is fair, and that people who pay all their taxes are not fools. This group has the highest proportion of post-secondary graduates and higher-income households.
Group 3. Honest but Resentful = 28 per cent of the population.
These people think that most people are honest and would not cheat. But they also think that the tax system is unfair, that taxes are squandered, and that they do not get good value for their money.
Group 4. Tax Anarchists = 16 per cent of the population.
These people agree with Group 1—the 'Upset and Envious'—in terms of fairness, waste, and value. But they also think that people are foolish to pay taxes, and they are against increased tax-enforcement effort and increased penalties for evaders.

---

[66] See Vaillancourt (1994*a*), Mirus *et al.* (1994), Spiro (1994), and Gervais (1994) for recent estimates.
[67] This discussion follows closely that in Bird (1994*a*). A similar survey in late 1995 produced broadly similar results, according to newspaper reports.

Governments at all levels in Canada presumably already knew the bad news reported in this survey: most people don't trust them, don't think they are doing a good job, and consider the tax system to be unfair. Some of them (especially the young) are so disaffected that they think cheating is fine and are against increased tax enforcement. At the other extreme, a few think all is more or less well with the fiscal world. Unfortunately, most people seem closer to the former than the latter in many of their attitudes. The GST experience has no doubt played a role in producing this unhappy state of affairs. The same survey reported that 51 per cent of the population thought there was a significant amount of tax evasion in Canada, and 63 per cent thought tax evasion had increased over the last five years.

When asked to say what proportion of the population evaded tax in four specific ways, significant proportions of those surveyed said that half or more of the population evaded in the following ways: (i) by failing to report income—21 per cent; (ii) by buying smuggled liquor or tobacco—33 per cent; (iii) by failing to declare goods bought abroad—37 per cent; and (iv) by avoiding the GST by having work done for cash—33 per cent.

More tellingly, when asked how likely they personally would be to evade tax in these ways, the answers were as follows: (i) 19 per cent said they might not report income; (ii) 26 per cent said they might buy smuggled liquor or tobacco; (iii) 32 per cent said they might fail to declare goods bought abroad; and (iv) 49 per cent said they might avoid the GST by having work done for cash.

This last number speaks for itself. It is reinforced by another question on the survey, which asked about the acceptability of evasion of income tax and GST. Only 19 per cent found income tax evasion even mildly acceptable, compared to 32 per cent for GST evasion. Whatever the experience elsewhere with value-added taxes, it seems clear that Canada's GST has not made it easier to collect, let alone to raise, taxes.

If so, this result is surprising. The conventional argument is that not only is VAT probably more difficult to evade than the RST but that its existence may also make it a bit more difficult to evade the income tax.

Of course, the GST is not, as some have claimed, 'self-enforcing'. Nonetheless, the trail of invoices it creates provides a stronger basis for tax enforcement than exists with an RST. Auditors working down the invoice trail can, and in many countries have, uncovered not only VAT but also income tax evasion, since the two usually go hand in hand. Despite Canadian myth, there is no reason to think that the VAT system of collecting sales taxes somehow lost its potential administrative virtues when implemented in the form of the GST.[68]

---

[68] Of course, there is no silver lining without a cloud. The GST gives rise to its own new form of potential fraud because of the possibility of claiming input tax credits in excess of those to which a taxpayer may be legally entitled. Any tax which operates by paying out almost as much money as it takes in net requires constant vigilance against such fraud.

What seems to have happened is something quite different. For the first time in Canada sales taxes were extended to a wide range of services. Services are special in several respects. Many of them are supplied by small businesses, for whom the cost of compliance was high (see below) and where enforcement of any tax is always most difficult and most costly per dollar of revenue collected. Moreover, many services are 'retail' in nature and involve few inputs other than labour: if the tax on the final transaction is evaded, the whole GST is lost.

In addition, the GST was implemented at a time of economic recession, when more people engage in full- or part-time service activities 'off the books' to supplement or replace their incomes. Some people may have shifted from visible and fully taxed payrolls of large enterprises to a mix of small business service activities that were not very visible to the tax authorities.

Whether or not the GST itself increased tax evasion, the result of the widespread failure to comply in the small business sector was that, for the first time, as the survey reported above suggests, almost every Canadian not only knew someone who was openly evading taxes but was also likely to be a tax evader himself or herself: it takes two, a buyer and a seller, to evade the GST. Within a short time, for example, it became common practice in the home renovation business for many firms to quote a lower 'no GST' price for cash transactions—and if they did not do so initially, their customers often asked them to do so. Tax evasion became almost respectable and, it would appear, seldom punished.

Another important phenomenon bringing the GST into disrepute and fostering tax evasion was a marked increase in cross-border shopping in 1991. Encouraged by a favourable exchange rate, Canadians flocked across the US border to stock up on goods and services that were free not only of GST but of Canada's high excise taxes. When they came home, many of them probably, as the survey suggests, also evaded customs duties by failing to declare their purchases. It became a weekend ritual for some in cities such as Toronto to take the one-hour drive across the border, stock up with alcohol, tobacco, chickens, and clothing, fill up the car with cheap US petrol, drive home, and brag to the neighbours about all the money they had saved by breaking the law.[69]

Initially, the border-control system simply could not cope with the increased flow without unduly hampering legitimate trade. As the Canadian dollar fell relative to the US dollar in 1993, however, much of this cross-border shopping died a natural death. Still, its legacy remained. As in the case of the home renovation industry, some Canadians had, for the first time, entered the fiscal paradise of tax evasion and had enjoyed its fruits without paying any penalty. The resulting impact on taxpayer morale and voluntary

---

[69] For an interesting analysis of the effects of differential access to cross-border shopping on the incidence of the GST, see Boisvert and Thirsk (1994).

compliance in general was not beneficial. There seems little doubt that the introduction of the GST in Canada resulted in a marked decline in taxpayer morale and an increase in the respectability of tax evasion.

C5 Administrative and Compliance Costs

The costs of taxation have been studied in detail in Canada in recent years. The administrative cost of the personal income tax system (with the associated federal payroll taxes) has been estimated at 1 per cent of revenues, and the compliance cost at a relatively high 6 per cent.[70] The cost to employers was found to be particularly high, at 3.5 per cent on average—though decreasing with size—owing in part to the joint administration of the CPP/QPP and UI systems with the PIT. A similar inverse relationship between firm size and compliance costs was found in a study of the costs of sales taxes prior to the introduction of the GST. The estimated compliance cost of the former federal sales tax, for example, ranged from 0.7 per cent of revenues for very large firms to as high as 32 per cent for the smallest firms, and the cost of the Ontario retail sales tax, which was estimated at 6 per cent of revenues on average, similarly ranged up to as high as 26 per cent for the smallest firms.[71]

More recently, considerable attention has been paid to the compliance costs of the GST. One study made shortly after the tax was introduced suggested that such costs might be as high as 25 per cent of revenues, but this figure is clearly inflated for a number of reasons. A later and better-conceived estimate from another study suggested that in fact GST compliance costs were probably lower than 1 per cent of revenues on average and less than 6 per cent even for small firms (though this figure is undoubtedly too low for the smallest firms),[72] On the whole, it seems not implausible that the compliance costs of the GST may be roughly comparable to those of the provincial RSTs, despite the much greater public fuss about the former.

Nonetheless, Canada's GST statute may be the most complex VAT law in the world. The original law was exceptionally long and involved owing to the many special treatments provided for small businesses, non-profit organizations, charities, the 'MUSH' (municipality-university-school-hospital) sector, real estate, financial institutions, and so-called 'basic groceries'.[73] Numerous subsequent amendments in total exceeded in length the original, already complex, law. Even the attempt to provide simplicity for small businesses, like the attempts to provide equity and competitiveness and conceptual purity, resulted in complexity. Each of the decisions made in drafting the GST law

---

[70] See Vaillancourt (1989).   [71] See Vaillancourt (1992).

[72] The two studies cited are, respectively, Cleroux (1992) and Plamondon *et al.* (1993). As Cnossen (1994) notes, the figures from the latter almost certainly underestimate the costs for the smallest firms.

[73] While extensive citations could be provided on every one of these issues, the previously cited treatment of real property (Arkin, 1994) will serve to illustrate the point.

clearly had its own rationale. Taken together, however, the result was an amazingly complex law. When this complex structure was applied to almost two million firms, many of which had not previously been subject to retail sales taxes, the initial costs of setting up and complying with the GST were, unsurprisingly, very high, especially for the many small firms that encountered the federal sales tax administration for the first time. With time and experience, these costs have of course declined, as noted above.

C6 Taxes and Labour Supply

Most research in Canada on the relation between taxation and labour supply has focused on payroll taxes, even though such taxes are, in international terms, relatively low. A recent survey of this literature concluded that, although reasonable estimates of the elasticity of supply of labour in Ontario were close to zero (−0.10 to 0.10) the demand for labour was relatively elastic (−1.35 to −4.50), with the result that increases in payroll taxes over the last decade have almost certainly reduced employment and raised the rate of unemployment, perhaps by as much as 1 percentage point or more.[74] Taking a broader perspective on the effect of taxes on human capital formation, another recent survey concluded that increases in income tax—such as those which have occurred in Canada in the last few years (see Table 2.3)—have probably decreased labour supply, although only by a small amount.[75] Nonetheless, the study just cited found that there was a strong case for more generous tax treatment of human capital acquired through on-the-job training, for example, through the institution of some form of training tax credit for employers. Actually, such a scheme has existed in Quebec since 1991, although as yet there appears to have been no systematic evaluation of its effects. For the most part, neither theory nor the scanty empirical evidence available permits very clear conclusions on these matters.[76]

D. The Past and Future of Tax Reform

D1 Future Tax Reform

In 1986–7, Canada's federal government introduced a substantial tax reform that lowered tax rates and broadened tax bases. The combined federal and provincial corporate income tax rate was reduced from 50 per cent to 43 per cent (with lower rates for manufacturing and small businesses), and the base

---

[74] See Dahlby (1993) and sources cited there; also Thirsk and Moore (1991).

[75] Specifically, a tax change that reduces net wages by 1% was estimated to reduce hours of labour supplied by, on average, one-quarter of 1%: see Gunderson and Thirsk (1994).

[76] A study of interregional migration in response to fiscal differences found little effect from taxation differences, although regional differences in UI benefits did have a significant impact (Day and Winer, 1994).

was broadened by cutting back such tax preferences as investment tax credits, accelerated depreciation allowances, and earned depletion.

Personal income tax rates were similarly reduced from a top rate of over 50 per cent to about 45 per cent, although since 1987, the provinces have taken up the slack, pushing the top marginal rates to well over 50 per cent again for most provinces. Most personal income tax deductions—intended to compensate for the costs of childrearing, disability, medical treatment, and so on—were converted into tax credits.

In 1991, this major tax reform was completed when the federal manufacturers' sales tax, which in 1989 was levied at a rate of 13.5 per cent on manufactured goods, was replaced by the GST at a 7 per cent rate on a base that included most goods and services. Still further changes seem likely in the future. Most immediately, the recently elected Liberal federal government has publically and repeatedly committed itself to replace the GST.

D1.1 The future of the GST[77]

The GST was initially introduced for two reasons. The first reason was that the previous federal sales tax (FST) was considered to be so bad that it had to be replaced. The second reason was that the GST was considered to be the best possible replacement. Those few Canadians who realized that the FST existed had long been unhappy with it. Economists disliked its effects on both resource allocation and income distribution; lawyers disliked the fact that it was largely operated by administrative fiat; and manufacturers, of course, disliked the fact that it picked on them. These complaints had been known for years and extensively documented in many academic papers and official reports.[78]

For decades, however, no significant changes were made in response to such complaints. Indeed, perhaps it was unrealistic to expect any government to make major changes in a tax that year after year produced 15 to 20 per cent of federal revenues with no adverse political reaction from a largely unsuspecting public. As concern about the deficit and the debt rose in the 1980s, however, the government decided to reform the sales tax both to help cope with the deficit and to make Canadian industry more competitive internationally.

The base of the federal sales tax—essentially the manufacturers' sales price of goods—amounted to perhaps one-third of total consumption. As the years passed, this tax base had been whittled away as the many deficiencies in the 1923 FST law were increasingly exploited by astute taxpayers. In the face of this attack, sales tax revenue was maintained in the 1980s only by repeated legislative changes both to broaden the tax base in various ways and especially by repeated rate increases (in 1984, 1986, 1987, and 1989) which raised the general rate of the FST by 50 per cent, from 9 to 13.5 per cent. Something

---

[77] Much of this section follows Bird (1994a).
[78] See Gillis (1985) and Whalley and Fretz (1990) on the background to GST reform.

drastic had to be done to halt the erosion of the sales tax base if rates were to be kept from going through the roof.

Moreover, about half of the revenue collected from the FST came from taxes on such business inputs as the purchase of computers and office supplies and equipment. This substantial part of the tax was 'cascaded' through the system and incorporated as part of the price of even such nominally exempt items as food and sales for export. Taxing investment and exports seldom makes sense in any country, and increasing worries about Canada's vulnerable and, many argued, weakening international competitive position made this aspect of the FST look especially ripe for reform as the 1980s drew to a close.

The desire to eliminate the taxation of business inputs and capital goods (and hence, indirectly, of exports) led to the decision to replace the FST by a value-added tax (VAT). Not only would a VAT deal with these problems, but it was also clearly the fiscal flavour of the decade. The value-added tax was the fastest-rising star on the international fiscal horizon. Its rate of adoption was so rapid, and its apparent success so great, that VAT looked like the only acceptable face for a modern indirect tax system. VAT did the job; and everyone was doing it. Why not VAT for Canada?

Not all signals were 'Go', however. Canada differed from every other OECD country that had adopted VAT in several important ways. First, and most important, nine of the ten provinces already had long-established, important, and relatively high-rate retail sales taxes (RSTs). Although many intergovernmental discussions were held in an attempt to work out some kind of national or joint federal–provincial sales tax, in the end the federal government chose to go it alone. One result of this decision was that most retailers naturally decided to treat the new GST as much like the existing RST as possible, that is, by adding it on to the price at the cash register.[79]

Second, as noted above, most Canadians did not realize they already had a national sales tax in the FST. Now, however, they got the bad news every time they had to dig in their pockets to pay the highly visible GST. Moreover, because most provincial RSTs taxed few services, and the essence of the GST compared to the FST was to 'untax' investment and to make up the revenue loss by extending the tax base to most services, people now had to pay a 'new' federal sales tax not only on the goods they bought but also on the services: dry-cleaning, hairdressers, auto repairs—wherever you looked, there was the GST. How to sell this apparently new tax at a time when real incomes were stagnant and unemployment rising was not obvious.

Third, although some people in the USA were talking about adopting a VAT, nothing happened. The USA did not have a national sales tax of any sort, and it still does not. No other country which had adopted a VAT had

[79] One of the few clear statements about taxation in Canada's constitution is that provinces are restricted to levying 'direct' taxation within the province. For the retail sales tax to be considered 'direct', it must be expressed as a tax on purchasers—a legal technicality reinforced by the separate quotation of the RST.

such a large neighbour that dominated its trade, that most of its population could drive to within a few hours (and often did), and that had no equivalent tax. The 'world's longest undefended border' was thus put under new fiscal stress as a result of the GST.

And, finally, since the Conservative government was reeling at the end of the 1980s from the concerted attack that had been made on it by much of the articulate public in the course of the debate on the US–Canada Free Trade Area (since subsumed in NAFTA), it was concerned to defend itself against the chorus of complaints heard from most of the same quarters against a fiscal measure that seemed to many to fall with special weight on the poor.

The form the GST took was shaped by all these factors. The FST had to go for its many defects, and VAT was the best way to deal with the 'cascading' and competitiveness problems. The type of VAT adopted—the so-called 'invoice-credit' form—was the VAT of choice in most of the world and was alleged to have special administrative advantages as well. Some even said it was 'self-enforcing' and would reduce tax evasion. The regressivity issue was dealt with both by freeing most food from tax and by providing a new 'GST credit' calculated to free most lower-income Canadians completely from any additional indirect tax burden and in fact to make them relatively better off than they were under the FST. Indeed, Canada went further than any other country had done in its efforts to ensure that the introduction of a VAT did not worsen the distribution of income.

The inevitable complaints of the millions of small businessmen who for the first time had to deal with the federal as well as the provincial sales tax administration—or just with the former—were dealt with by providing several simplified systems for small business. Again, Canada did more than any other VAT country had done in this respect.[80] Moreover, negotiations continued with a number of provinces on ways of 'harmonizing' federal and provincial sales tax administration. Although for a time several provinces seemed to be hopping on the GST bandwagon, in the end a form of harmonization agreement was reached only with Quebec.[81] Finally, although no one seems to have anticipated the need to tighten border controls in general, elaborate arrangements were established to deal with cross-border shopping by mail.

None of these ways of dealing with the problems mentioned was perfect, but on the whole they seemed satisfactory at the time. The difficult job of selling to the public what most of them would inevitably see as a new tax was initially supposed to be facilitated by coupling the imposition of the GST with

---

[80] Compare the treatments in different countries discussed in e.g. Tait (1988) and OECD (1988).

[81] The Quebec Sales Tax (QST) is 'harmonized' with the GST in the sense that both taxes are collected by the provincial government and that the base of the two taxes is broadly the same. There were some substantial differences, however: e.g. the QST was initially applied at a lower rate on services; financial services are zero-rated (rather than exempted as under the GST); and a number of input tax credits that are granted for business purchases under the GST are not granted under the QST. However, with changes to the QST in 1996, it has now become virtually identical to the GST.

significant cuts in the federal personal income tax (PIT) in 1987. Unfortunately, the timing slipped in part because of the free trade debate and the 1988 election. By the time the GST came into force in 1991 most Canadians had not only forgotten about the PIT cuts but for many no cuts remained, in part owing to offsetting income tax increases by both the federal and provincial governments. A promised reduction in income tax rates on middle-income groups was dropped in the last stages of the GST process when 'basic groceries' were zero-rated and the 7 per cent rate adopted.

Still, despite these and other complications, and despite continued objections by some academic critics who preferred to replace the federal sales tax by such alternatives as increased income taxes, payroll taxes, or some new (and untried) form of direct consumption tax, no great problems were anticipated by the government with respect to either the implementation or the acceptance of the GST.[82] Canada had, it seemed, simply become another member of the well-established international VAT community.

Something went wrong, however. In the eyes of many Canadians, the results of the GST have been all bad. The governing party not only lost the next election but was virtually wiped out. The visibility of the tax and its attempt to sweep into the sales tax net millions of small service activities have not only increased public resentment and compliance costs but have also, as noted above, arguably led to a considerable expansion of the 'underground' (tax–evading) economy. Revenues have not expanded; the deficit has not shrunk. In short, the GST yields too little, costs too much, and has had a pernicious effect on the level of tax morality in Canadian society. In addition, some have argued that it is both inefficient and inequitable. All in all, no tax in recent Canadian history has been as maligned as the GST.

The GST may have simply replaced an existing tax, and it did not increase government revenues. But it looked like a new tax, it affected a broad range of activities that had not previously been (visibly) taxed, and it was applied in an environment in which many people were under economic stress. Avenues of escape were soon found—the underground economy, cross-border shopping— and when those who took them were not visibly penalized, some of those who were initially reluctant to cheat felt like fools. Regardless of the theoretical merits of the VAT approach to sales taxation in general, there seems little question that the introduction of the GST in Canada resulted in a marked decline in taxpayer morale and an increase in the respectability of tax evasion.

Finally, in some ways the root of the GST problem lies in the simple fact that all of Canada's provinces except Alberta already levied retail sales taxes, at rates ranging from 7 per cent in several provinces to a high of 12 per cent in Newfoundland. As far as most Canadians are concerned, the GST was just an additional 'new' RST levied on a much wider base.

Nonetheless, there are important structural differences between the two

---

[82] Not everyone was so sanguine: see Dungan and Wilson (1989).

taxes. The GST is a very different tax from the RST in the way it operates, so it looks quite different (and more complex) to taxpaying firms.[83] The main economic merit of the GST is that it frees most business inputs from tax, compensating for the revenue thus lost by taxing a broad range of consumer services. In contrast, as noted earlier, from a third to a half of all provincial RST revenue comes from taxes on business inputs such as vehicles and computers, and only a few services are subject to tax. To the extent the RST is, in the first instance, a tax on business inputs, its impact on consumers, like that of the old FST, cascades unevenly into the prices of goods and services (whether subject to the RST or not) and is hidden from the consumer. Such taxes may not be particularly desirable from an economic perspective, but they are clearly more palatable politically than visible taxes on consumers. Or at least so many provincial politicians seem to think, judging by their cool reaction to recent federal proposals to replace their RSTs by a share of a new national VAT.

At present, Canada has two partially overlapping but distinct sales taxes. Consumers see both, and consider the GST the worse of the two because it is new and extends to such a broad range of services. Businesses may in principle prefer the GST because it relieves them of tax on many purchases, but for many of them, especially small and service firms, the GST also constitutes an unwanted additional or new compliance burden. The federal government received no additional revenue from the GST and has taken a lot of political flak. The provincial governments see the federal GST as squeezing their fiscal possibilities at a time when they felt sufficiently pressed already. Municipalities, schools and universities, hospitals, and a wide variety of charitable and non-profit organizations that had previously escaped the toils of both the income tax and the RST must all now, willy-nilly, cope with the intricacies of a tax that in some respects is coming to mirror the complexities of income taxation.

In short, nobody is happy with the GST. The public sees it as an additional, highly visible, and highly irritating tax imposed by an unpopular government that has now been thoroughly rejected at the polls. Canadians were told that the GST would help relieve the deficit problem; it has not done so. They were told it would help reduce tax evasion; most of them think it has increased it, and it has certainly made evasion more acceptable to a broader range of people. The poor think they pay the tax; the middle class know they do; and no one sees any good reason why this new levy was imposed on them in the middle of a major economic recession. Even after five years, when the initial costs of adapting to the new system have largely been incurred, some small businesses continue to complain about the cost and complexity of complying with the tax, despite various simplifications—amounting to some extent to a move towards a gross receipts tax—that have been introduced in

---

[83] For further discussion of this point, see Bird (1994*b*) and sources cited there.

response to their complaints. Finally, the main economic advantage of the GST, the extent to which it has freed business inputs and hence investment and exports from tax, is neither visible nor considered an advantage by a population that largely thinks that if 'business' pays a tax, then that means they do not.

Europeans, who seem to have accepted the adoption and expansion of the VAT with little fuss, may find it hard to understand Canada's continuing problems with this tax. Japanese and those in other federal States with sales taxes at two levels of government (Brazil, Argentina, India) may have less difficulty.

Given this background, it is not surprising that the Liberal government elected in 1994 committed itself to replace the GST. Canada has not had a good experience with the GST. The tax could have been better designed: it is an uneasy compromise between political expediency (basic groceries, special small business rules) and conceptual perfectionism (fringe benefits, non-resident sales, etc.). It could have been better implemented, with a serious initial effort to enforce it visibly and effectively. And even though it suffered from 'guilt by association' with a very unpopular government, it could probably have been better sold. The GST was either implemented too late (it should have been packaged with the 1987 income tax cuts) or too soon (it should have been delayed, if necessary for a decade, until a coherent federal–provincial sales tax could be worked out). All this may be true: but it provides no clear guide for the future.

Many alternatives to the GST have been canvassed[84] but as yet it is quite unclear which, if any, will be chosen: most tax experts appear to prefer a 'cleaned-up' VAT, some academic economists want to try out new ideas, businesses would like to recast federal–provincial relations and end up with a single tax system, and the public just wishes it would all go away.

Despite the new federal government's promise when elected in 1994 to replace the GST by 1996 and, it initially appeared, to announce the nature of that replacement by the end of September 1994, the total lack of agreement between federal and provincial governments has so far precluded action. Following prolonged public hearings by a House of Commons committee and a well-argued Committee report issued in June 1994, the federal Department of Finance proposed that a single national VAT, levied on more or less the same base as the GST but at a rate of up to 11 per cent, should replace both the GST and the provincial RSTs, with about 40 per cent of the revenue going to the federal government and the balance to the provinces.[85] The resulting shortfall in federal revenue would, under this proposal, be made

---

[84] See the reviews in Bird (1994a), Mintz *et al.* (1994), and House of Commons (1994).

[85] This account is based largely on the unpublished report of a symposium held under the auspices of the Canadian Tax Foundation in August 1994 and on various unverifiable news reports of the subsequent confidential meetings between federal and provincial officials. Deciding important tax policy issues 'behind closed doors' (McQuaig, 1987) is, unfortunately, an old Canadian tradition: see also Good (1980).

up by a flat tax of up to 1.5 per cent on individual income and any shortfalls in provincial revenue would be offset by additional capital and payroll taxes on business, and/or perhaps similar flat gross income taxes. Intensive discussions were held (in virtual secrecy) between federal and provincial governments on this and several alternative proposals from different provinces, but no agreement was reached, and all parties concerned seem to have moved GST replacement to the back burner for a time.

Tax policy changes in Canada, as elsewhere, depend to some extent on who is in charge. The Conservative party, which took power at the federal level in 1984, was virtually eliminated as a political force in the election of 1993, in part in reaction to their introduction of the much-hated GST. It is thus not suprising that the newly-elected Liberals, who had promised to replace the GST, were under substantial pressure to do so. In the end, however, they did not—and indeed, probably could not. Instead, in 1997 they introduced a new combined federal–provincial GST, called the HST (harmonized sales tax), persuading three small fiscally-dependent eastern provinces to sign up for the new scheme, in part in exchange for an additional federal transfer of up to a billion dollars. Since by that time the controversy had largely died down, this strategy seems to have been successful in political terms. However, it did not succeed in dealing with the basic problems that arise when two levels of government impose sales taxes, partly due to the new Conservative government elected in the key province of Ontario in 1994—by the same voters who had just elected the Liberals at a federal level—which quickly decided that there was no advantage in joining the HST scheme. The relation between federal and provincial sales taxes thus continues to be a somewhat unresolved issue in Canada.

D1.2 The Further Future[86]

Whatever happens with the GST, tax policy in Canada will no doubt continue to evolve in varied and sometimes surprising directions. Only a few years ago, the future direction of tax policy seemed clear. The rhetoric, and to some extent the reality, of tax policy was dominated by the image of levelling the playing field, and the much-touted phenomenon of globalization was taken to mean that the field was likely to be levelled to a low common denominator. Governments were no longer growing, the welfare state was increasingly seen as obsolete, and only the occasional out-of-touch crank seemed at all concerned about the redistributive consequences of reducing taxes on wealth and high incomes.

In some ways, the tax reform of the late 1980s clearly reflected the market-oriented variety of politics and economics of Ronald Reagan, Margaret Thatcher, and in Canada, Brian Mulroney. Under this philosophy, most government expenditure, regulatory, and tax policies are considered in their very nature to constitute obstacles to economic growth. As the initial

---

[86] This section largely follows Bird and Mintz (1994).

economic policy statement of the newly elected Conservative government put it in 1984, reducing government intervention in the economy would result in increased job creation by the private sector, and free Canada to maximize its economic potential.[87]

At first, these policies seemed to work well as Canada experienced significant growth in the latter part of the 1980s. Subsequently, however, the economic recession of the early 1990s, the failure of governments to reduce deficits, and one of the more severe cases of 'restructuring' in any industrialized country in recent years have all contributed to growing doubts by many about the relevance of the almost *laissez-faire* policies of the 1980s Governments in Canada in the 1990s are looking intensively for means by which they can, in partnership with the private sector, spur sufficient economic growth to preserve the 'social safety net' for the economically disadvantaged while still reducing the government deficits that now dominate fiscal policy.[88] It is not yet clear how this perspective will be affected by the re-emergence of Reagan-like conservative views at the provincial level in the important provinces of Alberta and Ontario.

In any case, even if critical attitudes to government have, at least in part, softened in recent years in Canada—certainly much more so than in the USA—they have by no means reverted to the euphoric post-war view that all things were possible for the well-intentioned policy-maker—as it were, that the road to heaven is paved with good intentions. On the contrary, one lesson that has been well and properly learned almost everywhere is the limits of government intervention. Even those who wish to bring about in their own country the next 'Asian miracle' are, for the most part, properly sceptical about the extent to which government possesses the needed economic wisdom. What will, can, and should happen depends as much or more on the economic and political environment faced by governments as on what those governments do.

For the immediate future—the next five years—it seems unlikely that any grand plan for tax reform will be developed in Canada, although recent statements by the Finance Minister suggest that some efforts may soon be forthcoming to reform business taxation in some unspecified way. Nonetheless, as in the past, there are likely to be continuing incremental changes in taxation driven both by the need to deal with deficits without imposing new taxes and by increased public concern for equity as compared to economic efficiency.

Such piecemeal reforms may, for example, occur with respect to continuing problems as the treatment of the family, the confused interrelation of tax and transfer systems, the treatment of interest expenses, tax assistance for retirement, the taxation of foreign-source income, and the taxation of capital gains received by trusts. The taxation of tobacco products was, as mentioned earlier, recently changed drastically in an attempt to counter widespread smuggling,

---

[87] See Dept. of Finance (1984*a*).

[88] The latest official pronouncements along these lines are Dept. of Finance (1994*a*, 1994*b*), parts of which could equally well have appeared in Dept. of Finance (1984).

but long-term policy in this area remains unclear. Similar problems may soon arise with respect to distilled spirits—and perhaps a similar tax-cutting solution adopted—but again the appropriate long-term solution is not obvious. Another area where change may soon take place concerns local property taxes. In some provinces, such taxes are relatively low because local governments do not have to finance much of the cost of education; in others, they are high, because they do. As mentioned earlier, a recent tax commission in Ontario recommended shifting more of the cost of education finance to the province, along with responsibility for the taxation of non-residential property. Similar changes in provincial–local financial relations have taken place, or are being discussed, all over the country: this area remains one of considerable unrest.[89]

D2 Deficits, Social Policy, and Taxation

Large public-sector deficits require governments to make difficult choices. Given continuing high unemployment, governments in Canada have responded in two ways. One approach is exemplified by the provincial government of Alberta: since 1993, it has slashed its budget deficit by over one-half, and has promised to eliminate the deficit altogether within three years.[90] The other approach, taken by the federal government and most other provinces, is to condition deficit reduction in part on employment prospects. Expenditures must still be reduced but less painfully in the sense that the pace of deficit is to be related to growth: the faster the economy, and tax revenue, grows, the more quickly the deficit will decline.

Regardless of the approach taken, expenditure restraint is clearly the order of the day for all governments in Canada, as in most countries these days. Taxes, as a percentage of GDP, have increased from about 32 per cent in 1980 to almost 38 per cent in 1993: voters are unhappy, and governments are wary of further tax increases. The only feasible way to reduce the deficit further, in the absence of a marked (and unlikely) jump in the growth rate is thus through expenditure restraint. In Canada, as in most Western countries, the most important public expenditures are on the components of the 'welfare state'—health, education, and social assistance. Expenditure restraint thus implies changes in social policy.

The aim of such social policy reform is both to control costs and to target assistance more accurately to lower-income individuals. Tax policy has a potentially important role to play in this reform exercise.[91] For example, as noted

[89] It appears that Smith (1990) may have been a bit too optimistic on this subject.
[90] This approach is presumably more feasible politically in oil-rich Alberta, which had the highest expenditure levels and lowest taxes in Canada.
[91] Unfortunately, the important connection between tax and transfer policies is hardly mentioned in the recent federal social policy paper (Human Resources Development, 1994). Perhaps more curiously, this connection was also not very well developed in the report of the Ontario Fair Tax Commission (1993), although one would have thought it should have been at the head of the fiscal agenda for the then socialist government of the province. For a more recent survey of the problems involved, see Bird (1997).

earlier, cost control and targeting objectives have already resulted in Canada in the introduction of clawbacks of general old-age security benefits and unemployment insurance under the income tax. Such provisions might be extended to include other benefits such as health care and post-secondary education, and some proposals in these directions have already emerged. The existing clawbacks have, as described earlier, already resulted in the introduction of a mishmash of family concepts and rate scales in the income tax. In addition, high marginal tax rates are imposed on recipients of welfare who, by working, may lose benefits that are more than the amount of income earned.

Ideally, the need to be more efficient in expenditure and to restore some integrity to the fundamental concepts of the tax system should result in a better integration of the tax and transfer systems than at present exists. Indeed, some version of the so-called negative income tax—already familiar in Canada in the form of the GIS for the elderly—may, under the pressure of deficits, come to pass, not so much to eliminate targeted transfer programmes as to implement them more effectively in the face of deficit restraint.[92]

An additional possible trend is the design of tax policies to encourage self-reliance so that individuals will be less dependent on government largesse. For example, tax-assisted savings for retirement—already more important in Canada than in most countries—might be extended to allow taxpayers to save for expenditures on training and education. Moreover, contrary to the Canadian reforms of the 1980s, in which tax deductions were turned into tax credits and hence made less remunerative for middle- and upper-income taxpayers, the future may see a return to deductions for non-discretionary expenditures related to such items as disability and medical costs which are in part subsidized under universal programmes.[93]

As social policy becomes more concerned with targeting benefits to the poor, rather than making them universally available to all, there may even be more interest in providing some tax relief for middle-income taxpayers who incur what the Carter Commission of the 1960s called 'non-discretionary expenditures'. Unless this is done, the tax-transfer system may come increasingly to be perceived as unfair in the sense that those individuals who incur special living costs—for example, owing to physical disability—are worse off than those with similar incomes who do not incur these costs.[94] Moreover, a similar development may well occur with respect to such educational costs as tuition, as education comes to be an ever more important ingredient of a productive life in this evolving world.[95]

Those concerned with maintaining the integrity of the welfare state often argue against tax relief for such particular expenditures as creating a 'two-class' system and hence violating the equality maxim many supporters of such

---

[92] But see Hum (1988) for a sceptical view of this possibility.

[93] On the other hand, a different perspective on what is fair may lead to still further moves to e.g. convert the RRSP deductions also into credits or even in some way to penalize those who have saved for their futures in such government-assisted schemes.

[94] For an example of this line of argument, see Krashinsky (1981: 28).

[95] Although Gunderson and Thirsk (1994) are sceptical of the merits of this approach.

policies hold dear. Given the ability to administer such targeting through impersonal, and largely invisible, accounting systems, however, the old argument against the stigma of singling out the poor as second-class citizens has probably lost most of its force. More important, perhaps, targeted social policy reforms may prove to be neither popular nor even feasible unless the majority—the taxpaying middle class—who now benefit from universal programmes in most developed countries, are also given some immediate and visible benefits such as tax relief for the private provision of social insurance.

The choice may thus not be 'all' (universality) or 'nothing' (nothing) but 'targeting' or 'nothing'—and to make even targeted social programmes possible, some sops (tax reliefs) to the middle class may well prove politically necessary. Moreover, as suggested above, in at least some instances a good efficiency and equity case can be made for tax relief (partial subsidy) for some private substitutes for publicly subsidized services. Further twists in the tangled tale of tax and transfer policy are likely to emerge in the course of the ongoing debate on deficits and social expenditures.

D3 Economic Integration

What tax structure is appropriate for Canada in the face of increased globalization and, more specifically, NAFTA? This question raises a fundamental question about the mix of taxes to be used in the future. With growing economic integration, mobile tax bases are likely to become more difficult to tax since they can either leave the country or avoid payment of taxes altogether.[96] Not only capital income but also certain highly skilled individuals are highly mobile. Even the consumption of goods and services is increasingly transborder in nature, as Canada's recent experience with the GST and tobacco taxes demonstrates.[97]

No taxing jurisdiction is an island unto itself; each is a part of the global whole and especially of its immediate region, and hence its freedom of fiscal action is to some extent inevitably constrained. In particular, it seems likely that corporate tax rates may have to conform to some extent to an international norm that will be set by the dominant economies. Similarly, at least in some countries, tax progressivity may have to be limited to retain highly skilled labour,[98] and even

[96] See Bird and McLure (1991).

[97] The case of tobacco taxes—Canada cut its taxes substantially in early 1994 to reduce the price to closer to US levels—perhaps reflects mainly political reluctance to enforce laws on the native reserves where most of the smuggling took place. Nonetheless, the close relation in the minds of many, including policy-makers, between consumption tax levels in Canada and in the USA is undeniable.

[98] This argument is not new in Canada: see Gillespie (1991 *b*: 50) for an interesting discussion of this factor in pre-First World War Canadian tax policy. The Carter Commission used a similar argument in the mid-1960s to justify lowering income tax rates on upper middle-income professionals. As it happened, the passage of a new immigration law in the USA in 1966 made it much more difficult than before for Canadians to move south of the border and removed this constraint on rate policy. The new ease of cross-border professional moves under the North American Free Trade Agreement (NAFTA), however, has again made this point salient, although one should note that Day and Winer (1994) found little effect of tax differentials in inducing migration even within Canada.

consumption taxes have to be kept 'reasonable' relative to those in neighbour-ing markets. Such factors are commonly perceived as strong and influential in Canada, located as it is next to the dominant, and low-tax, USA.

What does this suggest for the tax mix in Canada? One view is that the tax mix will tend to shift so that businesses can compete better internationally. In the case of Canada, this would imply a reduction in taxes on business inputs (such as the provincial retail sales taxes, which obtain, on average, a third of their yield from this source) and on capital (the corporate income tax, property taxes, and capital taxes). But of course any reduction in such taxes when governments need revenue implies that other taxes must increase. Yet significant increases in personal taxes on labour income and general sales taxes such as the VAT seem equally unlikely in the absence of radical changes in the US tax structure. As tax rates increase on any base, taxpayers will increase political resistance, try to avoid payments, resort to evasion, or move activities abroad, legally or illegally.

One reason for utilizing a variety of taxes is so that no one tax will be too much out of line with international norms. From this perspective, the taxes most likely to be increased in any country in the future may perhaps be forecast to some extent simply by looking at international comparisons. In Canada, for example, payroll taxes, low by international standards, have been increasing rapidly in recent years. The current concern about unemployment has slowed down the trend, but this obstacle might perhaps be overcome by a redesign of payroll taxes to broaden the base (e.g. eliminating the present earnings limits and exclusion of certain forms of labour compensation).[99] Governments at all levels may also come to rely more on benefit taxes and user fees—although this may be slowed down by the common (and often incorrect) perception that such charges are inherently regressive taxes and hence unfair.[100] Environmental or 'green' taxes may also, as has been long predicted, become more popular, although (largely unwarranted) concern about competitiveness may continue to constrain their use in many countries for some time to come, and the revenue yield of such measures is not likely to be great.[101]

Some taxes seem unlikely to grow much in the future—in particular, taxes on companies. Not only is the cost (in terms of lost tax base) of being different

[99] Kesselman (1994) makes a strong argument for relying more on payroll than on sales taxes; but see Dahlby (1993) for an equally strong argument preferring sales taxes.

[100] For an early discussion of this point, see Bird (1976); the evidence on distributive effects is reviewed in Bird and Miller (1989).

[101] To the extent such taxes cause decision-makers to take real social costs into account, their economic effects are obviously beneficial; and the fact that other countries ignore such costs is their loss—although such arguments are as unlikely to prove politically persuasive as arguments against mercantilistic export promotion policies. Of course, if the country to which the polluting firm moves is so situated that the pollution blows back into the country from which it came, the analysis may be quite different (e.g. reducing power-generation in Canadian plants may lead to expansion of coal-fired power plants in Ohio, which may then pollute 'virtuous' Canada more than their immediate neighbourhood).

increasing as capital becomes more internationally mobile, but investment incentives, for example, are not as some think, dead: they are at most dormant, and over time there may again be increasing use of corporate tax incentives to encourage investment, growth, and restructuring of industry. Recently, in contrast to earlier literature, some academic arguments have again emphasized how incentives favouring, for example, research and development or machinery and investment may, in certain circumstances, accelerate growth. Although there is no necessary implication in these arguments that increased growth results in increased welfare, policy-makers looking for a rationale for doing something they want to do in any case have never worried about such refinements in the past, and they seem unlikely to do so in the future. For this and other reasons, corporate tax incentives seem likely to creep back into most tax systems as time goes on.

Governments in all countries face increasing problems as the voting public becomes increasingly irritated with complexity which imposes costs on the economy. Federal countries such as Canada seem likely to face particular problems in this respect since the number of taxes depends in part upon the number of governments levying them. Governments can obviously reduce the compliance and administrative costs of taxes by harmonizing taxes so that there is only one collector and auditor. Alternatively, governments could pursue 'disentanglement' by allocating taxes to each level (for example, the corporate income tax to the federal government and excise taxes to provincial governments).[102] Either solution means that governments will lose some autonomy in taxing powers. Global economic integration has the same impact: governments are constrained in what they can do. Central governments in countries such as Canada are thus doubly pressured: on one hand, from below to decentralize and, on the other hand, from international competition to cut the costs of taxation and to harmonize.

In addition to globalization, the world is now undergoing what may prove to be the most important economic revolution since the Industrial Revolution: the Computer Revolution. The adoption of computer-related technologies may, over time, have a dramatic impact on the structure of taxation. Industrial restructuring in many countries has, for example, resulted in many former middle-level managers becoming self-employed consultants. Computerization also makes it easier for businesses to use the services of people who are working at home. The income and sales revenue of self-employed taxpayers are always and everywhere difficult to determine for taxation purposes. The rise of the personal income tax was historically accompanied by two important institutional changes: the creation of effectively controlled international borders and the move of the working population into the premises of large employers. Both of these constraints on tax evasion are now weakening, as the growth of the

---

[102]   For recent proposals along these lines in Canada, see Ip and Mintz (1992) and Ruggeri *et al.* (1993). For discussion, see Bird (1993).

underground economy and the increasing difficulty of cross-border tax enforcement in many countries demonstrate.

On the other hand, as a consequence of computerization, it is easier than before in some ways for government to enforce tax laws. In principle, the information governments can use to trace unreported amounts of income or revenues has become much easier to follow. As the rapidly spreading use of electronic filing of tax information has demonstrated, computerization also reduces compliance and administrative costs in the tax system. Even from this perspective, however, not all signs are good for tax collectors. Government's ability to follow the flow of information stops at the national border. When millions of dollars can move from one country to another as a result of an electronic impulse received by a satellite high above the globe, what price national fiscal sovereignty? Reliance on increased international cooperation seems a weak tool with which to cope with the implications of these trends, and the long-run prognosis for the ability of governments to track down cross-border manipulations seems dim.[103]

D4 Conclusion

Other factors that seem likely to result in continuing and potentially substantial reforms of the tax system adopted in the 1980s to even the playing field amongst taxpayers include changing demographic trends—which will impact both on social security systems and, perhaps, on the operational tax unit concept—and currently rather dormant but probably resurgent environmental concerns.[104] Tax policy in the 1990s seems likely to be used selectively in response to evolving economic and political issues reflecting these and other factors. Tax neutrality, which for several decades had been the Holy Grail of tax reformers, may well fade away in favour of an approach that sees taxation as just one of a broad set of public policies attempting to secure particular objectives and constraints.

What does this line of argument suggest for the future development of tax policy in Canada over the next decade or so?

As the experience of the 1980s has already demonstrated, there is unlikely to be any significant shift to consumption taxation from income taxation—although the increasing difficulty in enforcing taxes on capital income in an open economy may well reduce the distinction between the two tax bases in any case.[105]

The taxes most likely to increase in importance are those that are most

---

[103] For a recent discussion of these and related matters, see McCracken (1995).

[104] For extensive discussions of these subjects in the Canadian context, see Bird and Mintz (1992).

[105] The pace of financial innovation and the resulting difficulty of taxing 'arbitrage' would seem to reinforce this somewhat bleak view of the future of progressive taxes on income from capital.

difficult to avoid and those that are not large by international standards. In Canada, the most prominent example of such a tax is undoubtedly the payroll tax—although the growth of self-employment limits the extent to which this base can be exploited.[106]

The personal income tax may perhaps be revised to encourage training and education by allowing more deduction of monetary outlays for these purposes. The personal income tax may also be increasingly integrated with the transfer system and used to deliver targeted social assistance. There may also be increased pressure for, as it were, 'compensatory' recognition of the costs incurred by taxpayers to earn income or to support themselves.

Progressivity may creep back into the tax system to some extent, despite the difficulty of subjecting some forms of capital income to a progressive tax. An essential part of the deficit reduction package in Canada has turned out to be effective increases in income tax rates on high-income taxpayers through surtaxes, minimum taxes, and a variety of devices. Maintenance of a certain level of perceived fairness in fiscal affairs appears to be an essential element of a democratic fiscal constitution.

Political manoeuvring may sometimes require short-term increases in business taxes to make personal tax changes palatable. Nonetheless, over time corporate taxes will almost certainly decline in importance as a source of revenue in part as governments turn again to tax incentives to encourage the adoption of new technologies, the expansion of investment, and the international competitiveness of enterprises.

Finally, governments will face continuing pressure to reduce tax complexity. Reconciling such pressures with the need for decentralization on the one hand and globalization on the other will provide a continuing challenge for tax policy, particularly in federal countries like Canada. In principle, new technologies should permit governments to reduce both administrative and compliance costs as well to improve the enforcement of the tax system domestically, but no one as yet has worked out any viable system (short of world government) for enforcing taxes across borders. The 'final frontier' for tax policy is, in a way, the frontier itself, and exploring ways of grappling with this problem will undoubtedly occupy tax experts in the years to come. From this perspective, the fiscal dimensions of NAFTA may in time come to loom as large in the minds of Canadian tax policy-makers as the European Union does in the smaller countries of the EU: nothing in the NAFTA agreement determines precisely what can or should be done in terms of tax policy, but, as always in Canada, no significant tax changes are likely to be made without considering how they relate to the big neighbour to the south.[107]

---

[106] Of course, one of us predicted a long time ago that Canada would 'soon' turn to more use of payroll taxes: see Bird (1970). It did, but much more slowly than suggested. The same may be true of many of the conclusions suggested here: directions are often easier to forecast than timing.

[107] For further development of this thought, see Bird (1995); the historical precedents are discussed in Gillespie (1991a).

References

Allan, J. R. Dodge, D. A., and Poddar, S. N. (1974), 'Indexing the Personal Income Tax: A Federal Perspective', *Canadian Tax Journal*, 22: 355–69.

Arkin P. R. (1994), 'The Application of the Goods and Service Tax to Real Property Transactions', *Canadian Tax Journal*, 42: 1175–235.

Bird, R. M. (1970), 'The Tax Kaleidoscope: Perspectives on Tax Reform in Canada', *Canadian Tax Journal*, 18: 444–78.

—— (1976), *Charging for Public Services: A New Look at an Old Idea* Toronto: Canadian Tax Foundation.

—— (1978), 'Canada's Vanishing Death Taxes', *Osgoode Hall Law Journal*, 16: 133–45.

—— (1980a), *Tax Incentives for Investment: The State of the Art*, Toronto: Canadian Tax Foundation.

—— (1980b), 'Income Redistribution through the Fiscal System: The Limits of Knowledge', *American Economic Review, Papers and Proceedings*, 90 (May): 77–81.

—— (1991), 'Time, Space, and the Income Tax', *Osaka Economic Papers*, 40: 107–14.

—— (1993), 'Federal–Provincial Tax Policy in Turbulent Times', *Canadian Public Administration*, 36: 479–96.

—— (1994a), *Where Do We Go From Here? Alternatives to the GST*, Tortonto: KPMG Centre for Government.

—— (1994b), 'The Cost and Complexity of Canada's VAT: The GST in International Perspective', *Tax Notes International*, 8 (3 Jan.): 37–47.

—— (1995), 'A View from the North', *Tax Law Review.*

—— (1997), *Taxation and Social Policy*, University of Alberta.

—— and McLure, Jr., C. E.(1991), 'The Personal Income Tax in an Interdependent World', in Cnossen and Bird (eds.) (1991).

—— and Miller, B. D. (1989), 'Taxes, Pricing and the Urban Poor', in Bird and Horton (eds.), *Government Policy and the Poor in Developing Countries*, Toronto: University of Toronto Press.

—— and Mintz, J. M. (eds.), (1992), *Taxation to 2000 and Beyond*, Toronto: Canadian Tax Foundation.

—— —— (1994), 'Future Developments in Tax Policy', *Federal Law Journal* (Canberra), 22: 402–13.

—— and Slack, E. (1983), 'The Taxation of Northern Allowances', *Canadian Tax Journal*, 31: 783–97.

—— —— (1993), *Urban Public Finance in Canada*, 2nd edn.; Toronto: Wiley & Sons.

Boadway, R., and Hobson, P. (1993), *Intergovernmental Fiscal Relations in Canada*, Toronto: Canadian Tax Foundation.

—— and Kitchen, H. (1984), *Canadian Tax Policy*, 2nd edn.; Toronto: Canadian Tax Foundation.

Boisvert, M. and Thirsk, W. R. (1994), 'Border Taxes, Cross-Border Shopping, and the Differential Incidence of the GST', *Canadian Tax Journal*, 42: 1276–93.

Bordt, M., Cameron, G. J., Gribble, S. F., Murphy, B. D., Rowe, G. T., and Wolfson, M. C. (1990), 'The Social Policy Simulation Database and Model: An Integrated Tool for Tax/Transfer Policy Analysis', *Canadian Tax Journal*, 38: 48–65.

Bossons, J. (1988), 'Comment', in J. Pechman (ed.), *World Tax Reform: A Progress Report*, Washington, DC: Brookings Institution.

Bucovetsky, M., and Bird, R. M. (1972), 'Tax Reform in Canada: A Progress Report', *National Tax Journal*, 25: 15–41.

Burbidge, J., and Davies, J. (1994), 'Government Incentives and Household Savings in Canada', in J. M. Poterba (ed.), *Public Policies and Household Saving*, Chicago: University of Chicago Press: 19–56.

Canada (1989), *Report of the Task Force on Tax Benefits for Northern and Isolated Areas*, Ottawa: Ministry of Supply and Services.

Canadian Tax Foundation (1993*a*), *The National Finances 1993*, Toronto.

—— (1993*b*), *Provincial and Municipal Finances 1993*, Toronto.

Cleroux, P. (1992), 'The GST and Compliance Costs: A Small Business Perspective', in Canadian Tax Foundation, *Symposium on the Simplification of the Federal/Provincial Sales Tax System*, Toronto.

Cnossen, S. (1994), 'Administrative and Compliance Costs of the VAT: A Review of the Evidence', *Tax Notes International*, 8: 1649–68.

—— and Bird, R. M. (1991), *The Personal Income Tax: Phoenix from the Ashes?* Amsterdam: North Holland.

Dahlby, B. (1985), 'The Incidence of Expenditures and Taxes in Canada: A Survey', in F. Vaillancourt (ed.), *Income Distribution and Economic Security in Canada*, Toronto: University of Toronto Press.

—— (1992), 'Taxation and Social Insurance', in Bird and Mintz (1992).

—— (1993), 'Payroll Taxes', in A. M. Maslove (ed.), *Business Taxation in Ontario*, Toronto: University of Toronto Press.

Daly, M. J., and Mercier, P. (1988), 'The Impact of Tax Reform on the Taxation of Income from Investment in the Corporate Sector', *Canadian Tax Journal*, 36: 345–68.

Davies, J. B. (1992), 'Tax Incidence: Annual and Lifetime Perspectives in the United States and Canada', in Shoven and Whalley (1992).

Day, K. M., and Winer, S. L. (1994), 'Internal Migration and Public Policy: An Introduction to the Issues and a Review of Empirical Research on Canada', in A. M. Maslove (ed.), *Issues in the Taxation of Individuals*, Toronto: University of Toronto Press.

Dean, J. M. (1989), 'A Note on Interprovincial Variations in the Base for the Retail Sales Tax', *Canadian Tax Journal*, 37: 1017–19.

Dept. of Finance (1984), *A New Direction for Canada: An Agenda for Economic Renewal*, Ottawa.

—— (1994*a*), *A New Framework for Government Policy*, Ottawa.

—— (1994*b*), *Creating a Healthy Fiscal Climate*, Ottawa.

—— (1994*c*), *Flow-Through Shares: An Evaluation Report*, Ottawa.

Dodge, D. A. (1989), 'Economic Objectives of Tax Reform', in Mintz and Whalley (1989).

—— and Sargent, J. J. (1988), 'Canada', in J. Pechman, (ed.), *World Tax Reform: A Progress Report*, Washington, DC: Brookings Institution.

Dungan, P. D., and Wilson, T. A. (1989), 'The Proposed Goods and Services Tax: Its Economic Effects under Alternative Labour Market and Monetary Conditions', *Canadian Tax Journal*, 37: 341–67.

Durnford, J. W., and Toope, S. J. (1994), 'Spousal Support in Family Law and Alimony in the Law of Taxation', *Canadian Tax Journal*, 42: 1–107.

Engelhardt, G. V. (1994), 'Tax Subsidies to Saving for Home Purchase: Evidence from Canadian RHOSPs', *National Tax Journal*, 17: 363–88.

Gervais, G. (1994), 'La economie souterraine', *Policy Options*, 15: 29–33.

Gillespie, W. I. (1991*a*), 'How to Create a Tax Burden Where No Tax Burden Exists: A Critical Examination of Grady', *Canadian Tax Journal*, 39: 925–36.

—— (1991*b*), *Tax, Borrow and Spend: Financing Federal Spending in Canada 1867–1990*, Ottawa: Carleton University Press.

Gillis, M. (1985), 'Federal Sales Taxation: A Survey of Six Decades of Experience, Critiques, and Reform Proposals', *Canadian Tax Journal*, 33: 68–98.

Good, D. A. (1980), *The Politics of Anticipation: Making Canadian Federal Tax Policy*, Ottawa: School of Public Administration, Carleton University.

Grady, P. (1989), 'Real Effective Corporate Tax Rates in Canada and the United States after Tax Reform', *Canadian Tax Journal*, 37: 674–92.

—— (1990*a*), 'The Distributional Impact of the Federal Tax and Transfer Changes Introduced since 1984', *Canadian Tax Journal*, 38: 286–97.

—— (1990*b*), 'An Analysis of the Distributional Impact of the Goods and Services Tax', *Canadian Tax Journal*, 38: 632–43.

—— (1991), 'The Distributional Impact of the Goods and Services Tax: A Reply', *Canadian Tax Journal*, 39: 937–46.

Gunderson, M., and Thirsk, W. R. (1994), 'Tax Treatment of Human Capital', in A. M. Maslove (ed.), *Taxes as Instruments of Public Policy*, Toronto: University of Toronto Press.

Hamilton, B., and Whalley, J. (1989), 'Efficiency and Distributional Effects of the Tax Reform Package', in Mintz and Whalley (1989).

House of Commons (1994), *Replacing the GST: Options for Canada*, Finance Committee, CCH Special Report, North York: CCH Canadian Limited.

Hum, D., (1988), 'On Integrating Taxes and Transfers', *Canadian Tax Journal*, 36: 671–90.

Human Resources Development (1994), *Improving Social Security in Canada*, Ottawa.

Ingerman, S., and Rowley, R. (1993), 'Tax Expenditures for Retirement Savings: An Appraisal', McGill Working Papers in Economics 11/93.

Ip, I., and Mintz, J. M. (1992), *Dividing the Spoils: The Federal-Provincial Allocation of Taxing Powers*, Toronto: C. D. Howe Institute.

Kesselman, J. (1993), 'The Child Tax Benefit: Simple, Fair, Responsive?' *Canadian Public Policy*, 19: 109–32.

—— (1994), 'Canadian Provincial Payroll Taxation: A Structural and Policy Analysis', *Canadian Tax Journal*, 42: 150–200.

Kitchen, H. (1984), *Local Government Finance in Canada*, Toronto: Canadian Tax Foundation.

—— (1987) 'Canada', in J. Pechman, (ed.), *Comparative Tax Systems: Europe, Canada, and Japan*, Arlington, Va.: Tax Analysts.

—— (1992), *Property Taxation in Canada*, Toronto: Canadian Tax Foundation.

Krashinsky, M. (1981), *User Charges in the Social Services: An Economic Theory of Need and Inability*, Toronto: University of Toronto Press for Ontario Economic Council.

Kuo, C-Y., McGirr, T. C., and Poddar, S. N. (1988), 'Measuring the Non-neutralities of Sales and Excise Taxes in Canada', *Canadian Tax Journal*, 36: 655–70.

Larin, G. M., and Jacques, M. N. (1994), 'Is the Alternative Minimum Tax a Paper Tiger?' *Canadian Tax Journal*, 42: 804–42.

McCracken, M. (ed.) (1995), *The Search for New Tax Bases for the 21st Century*, Ottawa: Informetrica Ltd.

McMillan, M. (ed.) (1991), *Provincial Public Finances* (2 vols, Toronto: Canadian Tax Foundation.

McQuaig, L. (1987), *Behind Closed Doors*, Markham, Ont., Viking.

Meng, R., and Gillespie, W. I. (1986), 'The Regressivity of Property Taxes in Canada: Another Look', *Canadian Tax Journal*, 34: 1417–30.

Mintz, J. M., and Pesando, J. E. (eds.) (1991), 'The Role of Wealth Taxes in Canada', *Canadian Public Policy*, suppl.

—— and Richardson, S. R. (1995), *The Lifetime Capital Gains Exemption: An Evaluation*, Ottawa: Dept. of Finance

—— and Whalley, J. (eds.) (1989), *The Economic Impacts of Tax Reform*, Toronto: Canadian Tax Foundation.

——, Wilson, T. A., and Gendron, P. P. (1994), 'Canada's GST: Sales Tax Harmonization is the Key to Simplification', *Tax Notes International*, 8: 661–78.

Mirus, R., Smith, R. S., and Karoleff, V. (1994), 'Canada's Underground Economy Revisited: Update and Critique', *Canadian Public Policy*, 20: 235–57.

Ontario Fair Tax Commission (1993), *Fair Taxation in a Changing World*, Toronto: University of Toronto Press.

Organization for Economic Co-operation and Development (1988), *Taxing Consumption*, Paris: OECD.

Plamondon *et al.* (1993), *GST Compliance Costs for Small Business in Canada*. A Study for the Dept. of Finance.

Ragan, C. (1994), 'Progressive Income Taxes and the Substitution Effect of RRSPs', *Canadian Journal of Economics*, 27: 43–57.

Robinson, A. J. (1986), *The Retail Sales Tax in Canada*, Toronto: Canadian Tax Foundation.

Ruggeri, G. C., and Bluck, K. (1990), 'On the Incidence of the Manufacturers' Sales Tax and the Goods and Services Tax', *Canadian Public Policy*, 16: 359–73.

Ruggeri, G. C. *et al.* (1993), 'Vertical Fiscal Imbalance and the Reallocation of Tax Fields in Canada', *Canadian Public Policy*, 19: 194–215.

—— Van Wart, D., and Howard, R. (1994*a*), 'The Redistributional Impact of Taxation in Canada', *Canadian Tax Journal*, 42: 417–51.

—— —— —— (1994*b*), 'Equity Aspects of Sales Taxes and Income Taxes', *Canadian Tax Journal*, 42: 1263–74.

Rushton, M. (1992), 'Tax Policy and Business Investment: What Have We Learned in the Last Dozen Years?' *Canadian Tax Journal*, 40: 639–65.

Schaafsma, J. (1992), 'Forward Shifting of the Personal Income Tax by Self-employed Canadian Dentists', *Canadian Journal of Economics*, 25: 636–51.

Shoven, J. B., and Whalley, J. (eds.) (1992), *Canada–US Tax Comparisons*, Chicago: University of Chicago Press.

Smith, E. H. (1976), 'Allocating to Provinces the Taxable Income of Corporations: How the Federal-Provincial Allocation Rules Evolved', *Canadian Tax Journal*, 24: 545–71.

Smith, R. S. (1990), 'Why the Canadian Property Tax(payer) is Not Revolting', *Canadian Tax Journal*, 38: 298–327.

—— (1993), *Personal Wealth Taxation: Canadian Tax Policy in a Historical and an International Setting*, Toronto: Canadian Tax Foundation.

Spiro, P. S. (1993), 'Evidence of a Post-GST Increase in the Underground Economy', *Canadian Tax Journal*, 41: 247–58.

—— (1994), 'Estimating the Underground Economy: A Critical Evaluation of the Monetary Approach', *Canadian Tax Journal*, 42: 1059–81.

St. Hilaire, F., and Whalley, J. (1985), 'Reforming Taxes: Some Problems of Implementation', in D. Laidler (ed.), *Approaches to Well-Being*, Toronto: University of Toronto Press.

Tait, A. A. (1988), *Value Added Tax: Practices and Problems*, Washington, DC.: International Monetary Fund.

Thirsk, W. R., and Bird, R. M. (1993), 'Earmarked Revenues in Ontario', in A. Maslove (ed.), *Taxing and Spending*, Toronto: University of Toronto Press for Ontario Fair Tax Commission.

—— and Moore, J. (1991), 'The Social Cost of Canadian Labour Taxes', *Canadian Tax Journal*, 39: 554–66.

—— and Whalley, J. (eds.) (1982), *The Economic Impact of Tax Reform*, Toronto: Canadian Tax Foundation.

Treff, Karin, and Cook, Ted (1995), *Finances of the Nation 1995*, Toronto: Canadian Tax Foundation, 1995.

Vaillancourt, F. (1989), *The Administrative and Compliance Costs of the Personal Income Tax and Payroll Tax System in Canada, 1986*, Toronto: Canadian Tax Foundation.

—— (1992), 'The Compliance Costs of Sales Taxes in Canada: Evidence from the Eighties, Prospects for the Nineties', in *Symposium of the Simplification of the Federal/Provincial Sales Tax System*, Toronto: Canadian Tax Foundation.

—— (1994*a*), 'Public Policy, Taxation, and the Underground Economy', Centre de recherche et développement en économique, Université de Montreal.

—— (1994*b*), *The Financing of Workers' Compensation Boards in Canada, 1960–1990*, Toronto: Canadian Tax Foundation.

Vermaeten, F., Gillespie, W. I., and Vermaeten, A. (1994), 'Tax Incidence in Canada', *Canadian Tax Journal*, 42: 348–416.

Whalley, J. (1984), 'Regression or Progression: The Taxing Question of Incidence Analysis', *Canadian Journal of Economics*, 17: 654–82.

—— (1990), 'Recent Tax Reform in Canada: Policy Responses to Global and Domestic Pressures', in M. J. Boskin and C. E. McLure, (eds.), *World Tax Reform*, San Francisco: ICS Press.

—— and Fretz, D. (1990), *The Economics of the Goods and Services Tax*, Toronto: Canadian Tax Foundation.

Wilson, T. A., and Dungan, D. P. (1993), *Fiscal Policy in Canada: An Appraisal*, Toronto: Canadian Tax Foundation.

3 France

LAURENCE BLOTNICKI AND CHRISTOPHE HECKLY

A. Overview

The French tax system remains very different from those of other developed countries. The top marginal income tax rate is among the highest in developed countries, but the average rate of this tax is one of the lowest. This paradox is one example of the uniqueness of the French tax system.

While the proportion of French total tax receipts to GDP is appreciably above the average OECD ratio (44 percent for France against an average level of 39 percent for OECD countries in 1991), it is above all reliance on revenue sources that is so different in France (see Tables 3.1 and 3.2 for details).

Social security contributions as a whole represent a higher proportion of GDP in France than in any other industrialized country. About two-thirds of these taxes are paid by employers. There are also a number of taxes on businesses based largely or entirely on payroll. On the other hand, personal income taxes represent a much lower proportion of GDP than in any other industrialized country.

The French tax system applies a heavier burden on production costs than those of other OECD countries. In fact, social security contributions, the apprenticeship tax, the employee training tax, or the business tax are all based on wages. This distinctive feature of the French tax system inevitably affects the capital/labour ratio and the level of employment. Thus, in the short term, an increase in an employer's contributions has the same effect as an increase in wages and gives rise to a loss of competitiveness of the firms, even if in the longer run it is generally believed to be reflected in lower wages than would otherwise be paid.

This imbalance between the income and payroll tax was slightly redressed by the introduction in February 1991 of a new flat-rate tax on income known as the Generalized Social Contribution ('Contribution Sociale Généralisée') henceforth referred to as GSC, the proceeds of which are earmarked for social welfare benefits. It applies to labour income as well as capital gains, dividend, and interest. The rate was originally 1.2 percent but was raised to 2.4 percent as from 1 January 1994. In addition, during this period there was a social security surcharge of 1 percent on approximately the same kinds of revenue as the GSC which was introduced in 1983, earmarked for the financing of old-age insurance. An additional surcharge was introduced in 1997 which applied

Table 3.1 Tax revenue of main headings as percent of GDP and of total taxation, France and OECD, 1991 (per cent)

	Income and profits	Social security	Payroll	Property	Goods and services	Other
To GDP						
France	8.0	19.4	0.8	2.5	12.0	1.4
EEC	14.1	11.9	0.2	1.8	12.9	0.3
OECD	14.6	9.5	0.4	2.0	11.8	0.4
To total tax receipts						
France	18.0	43.8	1.9	5.8	27.1	3.4
EEC	33.9	28.9	0.4	4.4	31.7	0.7
OECD	37.9	24.0	1.0	5.4	30.4	1.2

Source: *Revenue Statistics of OECD Member Countries, 1965–1992* (OECD, 1993).

Table 3.2 Tax revenues (per cent of GDP)

	1980	1985	1989	1990	1991	1992
Personal income tax	5.4	5.7	5.1	5.2	6.0	5.9
Corporate taxes	2.1	2.0	2.4	2.3	2.0	1.5
Social security contributions	17.8	19.3	19.2	19.3	19.4	19.5
Consumption taxes	12.7	13.2	12.6	12.4	12.0	11.7
of which Value-added tax	8.7	8.7	8.3	8.1	7.7	7.5
Total	41.7	44.5	43.7	43.8	44.2	43.6

Source: *Tableau de l'économie française* (INSEE, 1993).

only to capital income. Since the introduction of the GSC, the first surcharge was applied only to capital income.

B. The Tax System

B1 Personal Income Tax

Unlike other OECD countries, France does not use withholding as a collection technique for employed persons. The tax payments are spread over the year after the income is earned. The personal income tax is paid in three instalments: two equal instalments on provisional assessment are paid in February and May, the third within two months after receiving notice (usually in September). A 10 percent penalty based on the tax liability is levied in the case of late payment. An option exists, however, for monthly payments based on income earned two years previously (year n−2), with an adjustment at the end year n−1 to take into account differences between n−1 and n−2 income. This option is taken by only 45 percent of taxpayers, however.

The personal income tax generates a minor portion of revenue for the budget, about half the average level in OECD countries. In addition, it affects a small number of households. In 1993, only 48 percent of them paid personal income tax. The main reason is that the tax threshold is particularly high in France.

B1.1   Tax Base

In spite of some changes introduced in the early 1980s (see below), the personal income tax has retained its main characteristics of sharp progressivity, a narrow base, and complexity, given the many rebates and deductions (about 100).

The personal income tax applies to the person, individually or jointly, including those enterprises not liable to corporate income tax (partnerships, for example). Income subject to tax is the sum of annual incomes actually received, of which the most important are salaries, wages, and capital gains.

B1.2 Tax Rates

Some changes to the rates were introduced in the 1994 Finance Act (see Table 3.3). First, the tax system has become less complicated—some tax reliefs were eliminated and the number of tax brackets was reduced. Secondly, there was a downward trend of the rate and a widening of the tax base.

Under the 1994 Finance Act, the number of tax brackets was reduced from 13 to 7, with rates ranging between 5 and 56.8 percent, the top rate remaining unchanged compared to 1992. The rate schedule for a person without dependants for the years 1992 and 1993 is presented in Table 3.3.

Between the income declared and the tax assessed, there were many technical measures aimed at taxing the household according to its ability to pay. First, all taxpayers may opt for a standard deduction of 10 percent of wages and salaries, with minimum (FF2,160) and maximum (FF72,250) amounts, or, alternatively, a deduction of actual work-related expenses (giving justification). In addition to the 10 percent deduction for expenses, there is a standard deduction of 20 percent from taxable income. For income and pensions earned in 1993, this deduction was subject to a maximum income limit of FF657,000.

Deductions from taxable income are also provided for the following:

- interest paid in acquiring and repairing a primary residence; in this case, the relief is equal to 25 percent of the total interest, subject to a ceiling that varies according to the date of the mortgage agreement and the age of the building being acquired;
- life insurance premiums; this relief is equal to 25 percent of the part of the premium that represents saving, with a ceiling of FF4,000 plus FF1,000 per dependent child in 1993. The ceiling applies to the premium and not to the tax credit. Further, interest income is not taxed as it accrues on a life insurance policy;

- union subscription (30 percent);
- donations to charities; the relief varies according to the beneficiaries;
- school fees;
- childcare expenses; and
- alimony payments.

Finally, some additional standard allowances are granted for specific professions (journalists—30 percent; artists—25 percent; sales representatives—30 percent; etc.).

B1.3 Treatment of Different Kinds of Income

(i) *Taxes on capital gains.* Capital gains are subject to tax under various provisions. In some cases, they are included in taxable income, either wholly or partially. In other cases, they are subject to a separate flat-rate tax and excluded from the tax base. Capital losses from the disposal of assets may be offset only against gains from the same category. Losses from the disposal of immovable property may not be offset against any income category. The flat-rate capital gains tax is 16 percent. In addition, a social surtax of 1 percent and the GSC of 2.4 percent are also imposed.

Capital gains on real property owned for fewer than two years are treated as normal income. Gains on real property owned for more than five years receive an abatement of 5 percent for each year of ownership (becoming exempt if held for twenty-two years). Gains made on a second home owned for five years or less receive a one-off reduction of FF20,000

Table 3.3 Tax rates for persons without dependants

Bracket	Taxable income 1993 (on 1992 income) (FF)	Rates	Brackets	Taxable income 1994 (on 1993 income) (FF)	Rates
1	0–19,220	0	1	0–21,900	0
2	19,220–20,080	5.0	2	21,901–47,900	12
3	20,080–23,800	9.6	3	47,901–84,300	25
4	23,800–37,620	14.4	4	84,301–136,500	35
5	37,620–48,350	19.2	5	136,501–222,100	45
6	48,350–60,690	24.0	6	222,101–273,900	50
7	60,690–73,450	28.8	7	Over 273,900	56.8
8	73,450–84,740	33.6			
9	84,740–141,190	38.4			
10	141,190–194,190	43.2			
11	194,190–229,710	49.0			
12	229,710–261,290	53.9			
13	Over 261,290	56.6			

Source: Ministry of Finance.

for each spouse, FF30,000 for individuals, and FF10,000 for each dependent child. The capital gain (sale price net of cost price and various expenses) is subject to the taxpayer's income tax rate, adjusted to reduce the level of progression through a 'quotient' system according to which the taxable income is divided by a figure that varies with the number of members and the family status of the household (see Table 3.4 and Sect. B1.4 below).

Any capital gains realized on the sale of the taxpayer's principal residence are tax-exempt. Capital gains realized on the sale of the second home and housing that is let, subject to a flat relief of FF6,000, are exempt from tax in the following cases:

- gains from the first transfer of a building by people who do not own their main home are exempt (under certain conditions); and
- gains on the transfer by a taxpayer of the immovable property worth less than FF400,000 (increased by FF100,000 for each dependent child beyond the second) are exempt.

(ii) *Dividends.* Dividends paid by French companies carry a tax credit (*avoir fiscal*) to which French shareholders are entitled. The tax credit is 50 percent of the net amount of dividends received. It is added to dividend receipts in order to calculate the tax liability and then credited against individual income tax, or refunded in cash if no tax is due. When the corporate rate was 50 percent, the tax credit of 50 percent of cash dividends eliminated half the double taxation; when the corporate rate of 33.3 percent was eventually reached (see Sect. B2.2 below), the tax credit of 50 percent completely eliminated double taxation. In addition, dividends are subject to the GSC of 2.4 percent and two social surtaxes of 1 percent each.

(iii) *Interest.* Interest on current or fixed-term deposits is treated as income from movable property and taxed under the progressive system. For certain types of securities taxpayers may opt to have their tax on interest income withheld as the final tax. The rate of the *prélèvement libératoire* on interest is normally 19.4 percent for bonds and other negotiable instruments (this rate includes the two social surcharges of 1 and 2.4 percent for the GSC), but rates ranging from 35 to 50 percent (for anonymous bonds), plus the social surcharge and the GSC, apply to interest from Treasury bills and cash certificates (*bons de caisse*). The withholding tax is final for interest on:

- non-indexed bonds;
- cash certificates (paper issued by a banker or a financial company against a loan which is being made to it whereby it undertakes to repay it at a fixed date); and
- other loan securities where neither the capital nor the interest is indexed and when the debtor is resident or has a permanent establishment in France.

There is a tax exemption on interest received on sums paid into the first savings deposit account (Livret A), on repayment on sums deposited in a popular savings account (CEP), on interest on sums deposited in an account for industrial development (CODEVI), on interest and savings premiums paid to holders of housing savings accounts or housing savings plans, on lump-sum payments, annuities and life insurance premiums paid beyond the eighth year after the opening of a popular savings plan (PEP); and under certain conditions, on the income (and capital gains) that relate to investments made in an equity savings plan (*Plan d'épargne en actions*), the tax credits for shareholders and other tax credits refunded upon payment, beyond the eighth year, of a life annuity.

Withholding tax is automatically levied on Treasury bonds and other similar securities. Finally, withholding tax is obligatory for income from cash certificates for non-residents.

(iv) *Immovable property.* There is a standard allowance fixed at 13 percent on gross revenue for urban property and to 10 percent for rural property in order to take into account some expenses (insurance, management, and amortizations) that cannot be deducted.

(v) *Pensions.* Under the French social security system, all employees must belong to a basic (social security) pension scheme and to a complementary scheme. Employees may also find themselves obliged to contribute to a supplementary pension scheme, either with regard to their employer or their profession. Employee contributions made to compulsory schemes are deductible from the income tax base. However, for complementary and supplementary schemes, the deduction is only allowed up to a certain limit, defined as a function of the total annual employee and employer contributions, paid for each employee into basic, complementary, and supplementary pensions schemes. The limit for 1992 was FF219,062.

Employee contributions to optional pension schemes are not deductible. The treatment of employer contributions is integrated with the regime for employee contributions. If membership in a private scheme is compulsory for an employee, the employer contributions are not added to the employee's taxable income. However, if the sum of employer and employee contributions exceed a certain ceiling (FF219,062 for 1992), the surplus contributions to complementary and supplementary schemes are added to the employee's taxable income.

If membership of the scheme is optional, employer contributions are considered to be a supplement of salary and are included in employee's taxable income.

(vi) *Housing.* Interest on a mortgage can be deducted from taxable income for the first five annual instalments. The deduction is equal to 25 percent of the total interest, subject to a ceiling that varies according to the date of the mortgage agreement and the age of the building being acquired.

For contracts signed since 1 January 1987 for the purchase of new housing, the ceiling for interest deduction is FF15,000 (FF30,000 for a married couple, with additional allowances for dependent children). The ceiling applies to the amount of interest and not to the tax deduction.

For contracts signed since 18 September 1991 for the purchase of new housing, the ceiling is FF20,000 (FF40,000 for a married couple).

Interest on a mortgage contracted to purchase a second home is not deductible.

Proprietors can deduct interest from mortgages incurred to purchase or construct housing to let, under the general rule that charges incurred in respect of the purchase of a part of taxable income are deductible from the tax base. There is no ceiling on this allowance. The interest is only deductible from property income, however.

A tax relief is available to all taxpayers who acquire or build new housing in France and rent it unfurnished as a principal residence for a minimum of six years. For housing construction that began prior to 15 March 1992, this relief is spread over two tax years and is equivalent to 10 percent of the purchase or market price, subject to a ceiling of FF300,000 (FF600,000 for a married couple). For housing construction registered to begin after 15 March 1992, the rate of relief is increased to 15 percent and the ceiling to FF400,000 (FF800,000 for a married couple) when the rent and resources of the tenant do not exceed certain ceilings. The relief is spread over four tax years and may only be received once.

Imputed income from owner occupation is not subject to income tax. Actual income from housing is included in taxable income and taxed according to the progressive schedule.

(vii) *Equities.* The acquisition of equities is not deductible from personal income tax liability, except where the taxpayer is subscribing to the capital of a new company or to a company that specializes in high-risk investments. In this case, tax relief equal to 25 percent of the investment applies, subject to an annual ceiling of FF10,000 (FF20,000 for married couples). The ceiling applies to the sum of such investment and subscription to certain other investments (i.e. qualifying investments in the French overseas territories, purchase or partnership of new ships, and financing of cinematic or audio-visual projects).

(viii) *Investment funds.* In general, to avoid double taxation of portfolio income, distributions from investment trusts and communal investment funds are allocated to the shareholders and taxed according to the rules for that type of income. In the case of funds specializing in high-risk investments that have at least 50 percent of their assets invested in unquoted securities, any distributions that constitute a net capital gain on their portfolio are subject to a tax of 18.1 percent. Insurance companies and banks are subject to the normal corporate tax rate of 33.3 percent on any profits or capital gains arising from management of their portfolio.

(ix) *Life insurance*. Life insurance contracts are subject to income tax when the policy matures on the difference between the amount paid to the beneficiary and the premiums paid. The beneficiary can choose to designate the withholding tax as the final tax paid. The rate of the tax varies according to the length of the contract: those of fewer than four years are taxed at 35 percent, those between four and eight years at 15 percent; and those contracts for eight years or more are subject to a zero rate. French residents are liable to extra taxes of 3.1 percent and anonymous beneficiaries are subject to a rate of 50 percent.

B1.4 Treatment of the Family

Husbands and wives are jointly assessed for the purposes of income tax. However, there are separate assessments if the spouses have divided their property and do not live together.

To adjust the tax to the resources of each household, the progressive personal income tax takes into account the taxpayer's marital status and the number of dependants. This system of *'quotient familial'* is applied only in France and Luxembourg. The taxable income is divided by a certain coefficient that varies according to the number of members and the family status of the household (see Table 3.4). Under this quotient system, the income of husband, wife, and unmarried children is aggregated and then divided by the coefficient shown in Table 3.4. The tax rate is then applied to the resulting income and the tax so computed is subsequently multiplied by the same coefficient. However, the benefit of this relief is subject to a ceiling of FF15,400 applied to the tax due for each coefficient of 0.5 in excess of 2. This ceiling is increased to FF19,060 for the coefficient of 1 for the first children if the taxpayer is either single, divorced, or separated.

Unmarried children of 18 years or older are taxed separately. However, they

Table 3.4   Income-splitting coefficient

No. of dependent children	Married persons or became widow persons in 1993	Single, divorced, or separated persons	Widowed persons
0	2	1	1
1	2.5	2	2.5
2	3	2.5	3
3	4	3.5	4
4	5	4.5	5
5	6	5.5	6
+1	+1	+1	+1

Source: Ministry of Finance.

may opt to be taxed under the above coefficient provided that they belong to the following categories:

- they are under age 21;
- they are students and under the age of 25; and
- they are fulfilling their military obligations.

Married children, irrespective of age, are taxed separately. However, they may elect to have their income added to that of their parents if they fall under one of the above categories. This opportunity is also offered if children with family commitments are single, divorced, or widowed and fall within one of the above categories.

B1.5 Indexation for Inflation

In 1968, France was one of the first industralized countries to adjust income tax brackets for inflation. This measure still applies, but is now less important with the slowing down of inflation. With the decreasing rate of inflation, the income tax burden of most taxpayers tends to be reduced because they pay the tax with their current income, whereas the brackets are indexed according to the inflation rate of the previous year.

B2 Corporate Income Tax

In 1993, the corporate income tax accounted for nearly 5 percent of total tax receipts and 2 percent of GDP.

Since the early 1980s, the corporate income tax has undergone important changes. These changes were brought about by the need to bring the French tax system into line with those of the other developed countries, taking into account the opening of economies, and by the need to stimulate the activity of firms. In general, measures aiming at increasing firms' after-tax profitability appear to be more effective in encouraging investment than fiscal incentives focused on investment, according to surveys on company managers' opinions.

B2.1 Tax Base

Income subject to tax for a resident company is based on the profit earned through business operations in France, whatever the nationality of the corporation. On the other hand, the profits of a French corporation obtained abroad are not taxable. Taxable firms include corporations (*sociétés à responsabilité limitée*), silent partners of limited partnerships, limited partnerships with shares (*sociétés en commandite par actions*), and subsidiaries of foreign corporations.

The taxable profits of the company are the net profits, obtained by subtracting from gross profits general expenditures, amortizations, and provisions.

For tax purposes, land, goodwill, trademarks, and leasehold rights cannot be depreciated. For machinery, the general method of depreciation is straight-line, although taxpayers may opt to use the declining-balance method for new assets with a useful life of at least three years. The rate of depreciation depends on the estimated lifetime of assets according to the rules in force for the business sector (see Table 3.5). For energy-efficient or raw-materials-saving machinery, the rates of 1.5, 2, and 2.5 are increased to 2, 2.5, and 3. For buildings with a useful life of less than fifteen years, the declining-balance method may not be used, except for hotel buildings and certain light construction buildings.

Taxpayers may switch at the optimum point from the declining-balance to straight-line method with respect to equipment, but not vice versa. (Declining-balance rates appear in Table 3.6.)

Companies subject to the corporate tax are liable to an annual lump-sum tax (i.e. a minimum tax) even if they obtain no profits. The lump-sum tax varies according to the corporation's turnover as shown in the Table 3.7.

Inventory is valued at cost price (purchase price). If the market value is lower, a deduction can be taken. Cost price can be determined by using FIFO. The LIFO method is not permitted, unless it approximates actual physical flows.

Table 3.5   Rate of depreciation

Assets	Straight-line rates (%)
Commercial building	2–5
Industrial building	5
Machinery	10–20
Plant (tools and office equipment)	10–15
Automobiles	20–25
Patents	25

Source: *Taxing Profits in a Global Economy* (OECD, 1991).

Table 3.6   Rate for declining balance

Normal useful life	Declining balance rates
3–4 years	1.5 straight-line rate
5–6 years	2.0 straight-line rate
over 6 years	2.5 straight-line rate

Source: See Table 3.5.

Table 3.7   Corporate lump-sum tax

Turnover (FF)	Tax
less than 1,000,000	5,000
1,000,000–2,000,000	7,500
2,000,000–5,000,000	10,500
5,000,000–10,000,000	14,500
in excess of 10,000,000	21,000

Source: *Taxation and Small Businesses* (OECD, 1994).

B2.2 Tax Rates

Since the mid-1980s, the most important measures adopted concern the general reduction of corporate taxes and its corollary the tax credit (*avoir fiscal*). Specifically, the tax rate gradually came down from 50 percent in 1986 to 33.3 percent in 1993. The first rate reduction occurred in 1986, when the rate on retained profits fell to 45 percent; then in 1988, the rate on both retained and distributed profits was reduced to 42 percent. Rate changes were made in each subsequent year, until the rate on both retained and distributed profits reached 33.3 percent in 1993 (see Table 3.8).

In 1988, the rules on group taxation were brought into line with those of foreign countries. A French firm may choose to be taxable on the whole profit of the group, which consists of a head office and the subsidiaries it controls in France and abroad by owning at least 95 percent of their capital. The only difference between France's rules and those of other countries is the requisite ownership percentage: in the USA, it is 80 percent, in the UK, 75 percent, and in Germany, 50 percent.

B2.3 Investment Incentives

(i) *Investment tax credits.* Special regional incentives are available.

(ii) *Business expenses.* All research and development expenses, other than

Table 3.8   Main changes in corporate tax rates (%)

Since 1 January	Rates
1986	45 only for retained profits
1988	42 for both retained and distributed profits
1989	42 for distributed profits
	39 for retained profits
1990	42 for distributed profits
	37 for retained profits
1991	42 for distributed profits
	34 for retained profits
1992	34 for both retained and distributed profits
1993	33.3 for both retained and distributed profits

for depreciable assets, are deductible in the year they occur. Buildings related to research and development expenses may be depreciated in the first year up to 50 percent. A tax credit for research expenses also is available. The credit corresponds to the difference between the amount of research and development expenses for the year in question and those incurred in the preceding year, and is limited to FF40,000,000 annually, as of 1991. Firms in deficit can only obtain the tax credit if it cannot be imputed on the year of the investment or on the five following years.

(iii) *Reserves.* Since 1988, companies have been entitled to set up a tax-free reserve for investment in commercial establishments abroad. The investment must be in the form of the creation or acquisition of subsidiaries whose principal activities are the marketing of products made in France by the enterprise. No special government approval is necessary if certain conditions are met. Banks and other enterprises participating in foreign commercial or industrial ventures in support of a French company investing abroad are also entitled to this reserve. The reserve must be added back to taxable income in annual instalments as of the sixth year.

B2.4 Small and Medium-sized Enterprises

No special rate of tax applies to small and medium-sized enterprises. Unincorporated enterprises are liable to the rates of the personal income tax (0–56.8 percent); incorporated enterprises are taxed at 33.3 percent.

However, as in most OECD countries, France does apply specific measures aimed at improving the economic and technological environment of small and medium-sized enterprises. For instance, unincorporated small and medium-sized enterprises are liable to a lump-sum tax (*forfaitaire*) when their turnover is less than FF500,000 for the sale of goods, and FF150,000 from other activities (mostly services).[1] The amount of the lump-sum tax is assessed by the tax officials according to standards that vary with the turnover of the firm and the type of industry. With respect to capital gains, no tax is due if the activity was exercised for five years before sale where turnover is less than FF1,000,000 (FF300,000 for services).

B3 Payroll Taxes

Payroll taxes are very high in France, over 45 percent of its total revenues (see Table 3.1) and nearly 48 percent of its welfare system is funded through direct contributions by employees and employers (see Table 3.9).

B3.1 Earmarked for Social Security

Taxes earmarked for social security cover industrial injuries insurance, unemployment insurance, sickness insurance, pensions, and widowhood.

---

[1] OECD, *Taxation and Small Business*, Paris, 1994: 51.

Table 3.9 Social security contributions and payroll taxes (FF billion)

Type of levy	1970	1975	1980	1985	1990	1991
Social security contributions	100,991	219,799	500,068	905,143	1,253,142	1,305,687
Paid by employees	19,248	46,591	130,216	246,399	376,695	387,420
Paid by employers	73,942	158,976	332,845	585,915	773,348	808,581
Paid by self-employed	7,801	14,232	37,007	72,829	103,081	109,686
Other payroll taxes	3,338	10,499	25,811	42,980	54,021	56,679
of which:						
Salary tax	3,162	6,923	15,831	26,413	34,165	34,785
Tax for apprenticeship	176	234	1,129	827	661	678
Tax for professional training	—	250	1,550	668	195	178

Source: See Table 3.1.

Table 3.10 Distribution of CSG by kind of revenue

	FF Billion	Per cent
Earned income	31.1	77.3
Transfer income	6.7	16.8
Capital income	2.4	5.9

Source: *Problèmes économiques*, 2380, 8 June 1993.

French policy concerning social protection has been influenced by three major constraints: the slowdown of economic growth, the persistence of a high unemployment level, and the necessity to reduce the budget deficit. France has had to find new resources, mainly by increasing contribution rates, particularly unemployment insurance rates by abolishing the ceiling for the assessment of contributions. At the same time, new kinds of contributions have been introduced to widen the base of financing. The main new tax is the GSC, referred to in the introduction. In 1993, the GSC yielded FF41.5 billion (see Table 3.10). Its increase of 1.3 percentage point as from 1 January 1994, has been earmarked to the solidarity fund for old age.

During the last four decades, the share of payroll taxes paid between employees and employers has changed, to the detriment of employees. In 1950, employers paid more than 75 percent of payroll taxes, while by the early 1990s, they paid 60 percent.

B3.2 Other Payroll Taxes

Employers also have to pay some other payroll taxes in addition to social security levies. The wages paid by employers constitute the base of four taxes:

- the salary tax (*taxe sur les salaires*) the rate of which has been 4.25 percent since the early 1980s: according to the law of 29 November 1968, this tax is payable only by employers who are not subject to VAT;
- the apprenticeship tax, the rate of which is 0.60 percent on total annual gross wages and salaries;
- training taxes, with a minimum amount equal to 1.20 percent of total annual wages and salaries; and
- the transportation tax, which applies to employers who have more than nine employees; this tax varies among departments, and according to the size of the city.

B4 Value-Added Tax

France was the first country to introduce the value-added tax; it introduced its VAT in 1954, thirteen years before any other developed country. The VAT is the main tax applicable to spending. In 1993, VAT accounted for FF521.5 billion, and represented just over 17 percent of total tax receipts.

B4.1 Tax Base

The tax base is broadly the same as in other countries of the European Community.

Under the Law of 29 December 1978, transactions that correspond to any economic activity, and not only an industrial or commercial activity, are liable to VAT. The scope of this tax has been extended to every economic activity, particularly agricultural activities, liberal professions, and research activities. Only activities concerning administration, health, financial services, banks, and insurance are outside its scope. The VAT on some inputs (private cars, fuel, travelling expenses) cannot be paid back to taxpayers.

B4.2 Tax Rate

The number of VAT rates and the rates themselves have varied over the years. Between 1982 and 1989, there were four official rates:

- the super-reduced rate of 5.5 percent, introduced in 1982, which applied to food products (excluding drinks), products used in agriculture (fertilizers, etc.), drugs, books, and newspapers;
- another reduced rate of 7 percent, which applied to certain services (tourism, passenger transportation, and entertainment);
- a higher rate of 33 percent, which applied to motor cars, audio-visual equipment, tobacco, luxury goods (jewels, furs, etc.); and
- a standard rate of 18.6 percent which applied to all taxable transactions

liable neither to the reduced rate nor to the higher rate; this was the case for most consumer goods, manufactured products, construction, and services.

Since 1 January 1989, there have been changes in the rate structure. The number of rates was reduced to three, the two reduced rates being merged into only one rate of 5.5 percent. The higher rate had been reduced to 22 percent and then abolished on 14 January 1992. Now there are two rates of 5.5 and 20.6 percent, the standard rate having been increased in August 1995 from 18.6 percent.

B4.3 The One-month Lag Rule

Until June 1993, firms were obliged to pay VAT in advance on their current purchases. They also played the role of the State's banker, since they lent to the Treasury the amount of taxes that were paid to them and had to wait for one month before being reimbursed for the taxes they had paid to their suppliers. This rule dates back to 1948 when firms obtained the right to deduct from their production tax (*taxe à la production*) the tax they had paid to their suppliers. This one-month lag rule was maintained in 1954 when VAT was adopted and was only removed on 1 July 1993. This rule put firms at a disadvantage, for the lag gave rise to cash-flow problems and reduced their equity capital and their ability to borrow. In addition, it distorted the conditions under which they competed with other European firms, which were not liable to this rule.

The tax on goods and services is now deductible from the tax due in the same month that the right to deduction arises. Thus the paying back of the firms' claims has been accelerated. For claims under FF150,000, 100 percent of the amount due is paid back immediately. For claims over FF150,000, 25 percent of the amount is paid back immediately, with a minimum amount of FF150,000, the remainder being paid back over a period that cannot exceed twenty years. The government was obliged to reimburse firms gradually because of the heavy cost of this reform, which was more than FF90 billion, for the budget of the State.

B5 Excises and Other Consumption Taxes

The development of direct taxation and VAT has brought a relative decline of the share of excises in budgetary resources. In 1993, the consumption taxes other than VAT represented FF269 billion or 8.7 percent of budgetary resources. This percentage has scarcely changed in France since 1985, and remains one of the lowest in OECD.

Excises are frequently divided into two classes: major revenue raisers such as those on motoring (especially oil products), drinking and smoking, and 'nuisance excises' which bring in little revenue and may be expensive to administer. Of the first kind, France has relatively high excises on oil and motor vehicles but relatively low excises on cigarettes and alcoholic drinks; but while most OECD countries have phased out nearly all their 'nuisance excises', France remains with such excises on a large range of products including soft drinks, sugar, clocks and watches, jewellery, matches, mechanical lighters, toilet goods and perfumery, meat, furnitures, clothing, textiles, and forestry products.

B6   Net Wealth and Capital Transfer Taxes

B6.1   Inheritance and Gift Taxes

Since 1942, inheritances and gifts have been treated in the same way. However, the granting of gifts is encouraged by tax reductions that depend on the age of the donor. The personal allowance, which is free of tax, amounts to FF300,000 for gifts to individuals in the giver's direct line and to gifts between spouses. The taxes are paid on the share of each heir according to a progressive schedule. The taxes are much higher on gifts to individuals in the giver's collateral line than to individuals in the direct line: in the first case, the allowance is only FF10,000.

For children or spouses, the marginal rate of tax is between 5 and 40 percent. A 20 percent rate applies to gifts above FF200,000, a 30 percent rate applies to gifts above FF3.4 million, and a 40 percent rate applies to gifts above FF11.2 million. A single 60 percent applies to gifts to individuals in the collateral line.

Some goods are exempt from inheritance and gift tax. Examples of exempt goods are: the capital paid to beneficiaries of a life insurance if the insurance contract was taken out before a given age; agricultural property if it has been leased out for a long period; and a given part of the value of woods and forest under certain limits.

B6.2   Net Wealth Tax

A net wealth tax on large properties was introduced in 1981 and was abolished in 1987. Since 1 January 1989, the *impôt de solidarité sur la fortune* (ISF) replaced the *impôt sur les grandes fortunes*. Under the Finance Act for 1994, the net wealth tax applies to individuals whose assets exceed FF4.47 million. The rate of progressive, varying between 0.5 and 1.5 percent. Tax brackets are indexed for inflation.

The base is the net value of all assets liable to tax, assessed on their market value. However, there are exemptions for antiques, works of art, literary and artistic property rights, and productive assets, including machinery and equipment, plants and buildings. In 1993, the ISF was paid by 163,125 taxpayers and its yield amounted to FF7.2 billion or 0.59 percent of total net tax receipts (FF1,211 billion in 1993).[2]

---

[2] *Les notes bleues de Bercy*, 40 (1994).

B6.3 Financial Transactions

Various taxes apply to financial transactions. Financial transactions concerning residential buildings are subject to a registration tax. The rate of this tax varies between departments from 4.2 to 6.5 percent, plus regional tax of up to 1.6 percent, a communal tax of up to 1.2 percent, and a surcharge of 2.5 percent for collection costs that is assessed on the departmental tax itself and not on the basis of this tax. The maximum rate of 6.5 percent was reduced to 6 percent from 1 June 1993, to 5.5 percent from 1 June 1994, and will be reduced to 5 percent from 1 June 1995.

Each transfer transaction on the French stock exchange carried out by financial intermediaries is subject to a specific stamp duty; the duty does not apply to bonds (with some exceptions). The rate of this tax is 0.3 percent for transactions of less than FF1,000,000 and 0.15 percent for other transactions.

The transfers of movable property (shares, bonds, units in investments funds) are taxed as capital gains above a specified threshold. For transfers made in 1992, this threshold was FF332,000. For transfers made in 1993 and beyond, the threshold is reduced by half for units in OPCVM (UCITS or Undertakings for Collective Investments in Transferable Securities) and commercial bonds. The tax rate is 16 percent of the capital gains. To this rate is added a social surtax of 1 percent and the GSC of 2.4 percent for French residents. Since 1 January 1996, the thresholds have been abolished and the capital gains are fully taxable.

B7 Local Taxes

In 1993, local authorities collected about FF232 billion of direct local taxes, including the land tax (*impôt foncier non bâti*), the property tax (*impôt foncier bâti*), the tax on occupied housing (*taxe d'habitation*), and the business tax (*taxe professionnelle*). Each of these four taxes is described in more detail below.

The local tax yield in 1993 was 10 percent or FF21 billion higher than in 1992, while the central government tax yield was 2 percent lower. The local tax bases went on increasing in 1993. They were 7.7 percent higher than in 1992 for the business tax, 7.4 percent for the property tax, and 4.9 percent higher for the tax on occupied housing. These increases resulted from the Ministry of Finance's decision to revalue the bases and from the increasing number of buildings.

The decentralization measures taken in the early 1980s had a considerable impact on the structure of public expenditure and revenue. Since 1982, local government spending has risen at an average rate of 3.4 percent a year in real terms (11 percent a year in the case of regions), while central government spending has only increased by about 1.3 percent per year. Capital spending has been especially buoyant, mostly since 1985, as local authorities took over responsibility for school buildings and transportation infrastructure investment. The debt burden of local authorities also increased steeply, from 7.6 to 9.7 percent of their spending between 1980 and 1990, due to the removal of subsidized loans, and the rise in real interest rates. A consequence of the sharp increase in local government spending was a corresponding rise in local taxes, up from 3.2 percent of GDP in 1981 to 4 percent in 1990, and an increase in transfers of tax revenues from the central government to local authorities, which represented 2.1 percent of GDP in 1990 as compared to 1.7 percent in 1981.

Due to the increased role of local authorities in the economy, public finance management became more difficult. In 1990, it was decided to link increases in the block operating grant (*dotation globale de fonctionnement*) to a fixed percentage of real GDP growth, whereas between 1979 and 1990, it had been tied to VAT receipts. The aim of this measure was to ease somewhat the upward momentum of central government transfers to local authorities, which had increased by 9 percent in 1989. The block operating grant, which amounts to 40 percent of state grants to local authorities and 14 percent of their total budget, is the keystone of local finance. By taking this measure, Budget Minister Charasse imposed on local authorities a loss of FF5 billion a year. This measure was probably not enough to convince the local authorities to pursue a sufficiently stringent tax policy nor to keep their expenditure under tight control. Thus, the efforts made to reduce central government expenditure were partly cancelled out by the policies of local authorities. The widening of the local authorities' role has also given rise to problems of equity, as some areas are richer than others. The block operating grant is apportioned between local authorities according to very complicated criteria, among which are population and a comparison between local and national fiscal capacity.

The local fiscal system lacks autonomy. The national authorities are involved in the assessment and collection of local taxes. The National Tax Directorate sets tax bases, leaving only the tax rates to the local representatives. Their freedom to manoeuvre is thus very narrow. The Treasury collects the tax at the end of the year and lends it to local authorities by twelfths. In return, the latter must deposit their liquid assets in a Treasury account without interest. The central government finances an important part of the reliefs applicable to the tax on occupied housing *(taxe d'habitation)* and business tax *(taxe professionnelle)* which amounted to nearly FF37 billion in 1989. The central government bears 28 percent of the costs of the business tax. With respect to the tax on occupied housing, there is a ceiling of 4 percent of the households' taxable incomes for purposes of the tax, which, while reducing inequalities obliges the central government to increase its share by another FF1.8 billion in the financing of tax relief. The share of the central government in financing of direct local taxation was 22 percent in 1989, compared to 14.4 percent in 1980. These reliefs reduce the number of persons liable to tax and result in an ever smaller number of taxpayers bearing the cost of each additional measure.

In 1994, the central government set an upper limit of FF252 million on its grants to municipalities, departments, and regions. Between 1985 and 1993, those grants had increased from FF180 billion to more than FF250 billion.

Among local governments' sources of indirect tax revenue of local authorities are the road tax(*vignette*), the car registration tax (*taxes sur les cartes grises*), the taxes on property transactions (*taxes sur les transactions immobilières*), and transfer taxes (*droits de mutation*). In 1993, the regions and departments increased the tax burden. The regions raised the rates of property tax by 17.5 percent, the rates of the tax on occupied housing by 17.1 percent, and the rates of the business tax by 15 percent, while the departments raised these rates by 5.5, 4.9, and 4.3 percent respectively.[3]

B7.1 Land Tax

The land tax is paid by landowners. It mainly concerns rural municipalities. To facilitate the reform of the Common Agricultural Policy and alleviate the tax burden on farmers, in July 1992 the government announced the gradual elimination of the departmental and regional shares of this land tax. The central government would share the costs of this measure.

B7.2 Property Tax

The property tax is paid by the owners of buildings. The yield of this tax (which is equivalent to one-tenth of the yield of the income tax) is very concentrated: 10 percent of households, the largest taxpayers, pay half of this tax, while 58 percent of them together pay only 10 percent of it. However, the link between the property tax base and the income seems relatively loose, and the property tax burden is approximately evenly distributed among the different income brackets, which alleviates the distributional impact of direct taxation. Half of the French population own their principal residence and one French resident out of five is exempted from tax because of his/her low level of income. As a whole, 42 percent of households are liable to the property tax for their main residence. Firms pay the property tax if they are owners of their plants or office buildings. Less than 8 percent of households pay the tax as lessors, but their share amounts to nearly one-third of the total tax yield. Tax rates are, on average, lower in rural areas than in towns, but in Paris *intra muros*, the rate is very low: 3.4 percent of the rental value, compared to 11.2 percent in the country as a whole. Accordingly, notwithstanding higher rental values in the capital, the average property tax paid by each taxpayer in Paris is not much more than half that paid by each taxpayer in the suburbs.[4]

---

[3] J.-P. Coulange, 'Les édiles lâchés par les quatre vieilles', *Le Nouvel Economiste*, 915 (1993).
[4] *Le Monde*, 28 Nov. 1989.

B7.3 *Tax on Occupied Housing*

The tax on occupied housing is due by dwelling occupants, whether they are tenants or owners. It is composed of three parts: the municipal part, the departmental part, and the regional part. The three shares are based on the rental value of the dwelling, multiplied by a rate which is set every year by the different local authorities. There is a tax allowance for dependent persons and old people, while widows or invalids who were not liable to the personal income tax during the previous year are totally exempt. About 16 million French people (28 percent of a total population of 57,372,000) are now liable to the tax on occupied housing. This tax has many drawbacks, but it does not systematically put poor people at a disadvantage—they are often exempt—compared to rich owners or occupants; rather, there is discrimination between departments or municipalities.

B7.4 *Business Tax*

The business tax is due from individuals or legal entities that carry out an occupational activity but are not wage earners: for instance, firms, tradesmen, craftsmen, and professionals. Farmers and social entities are exempt. The business tax is based on the rental value of equipment and a part of the wage bill. The amount of tax cannot exceed 3.5 percent of the value added.

In 1993, the business tax yielded FF129 billion, which is comparable to the yield of the corporate tax. Among the four local direct taxes, the business tax has the most rapidly growing yield: between 1989 and 1993, it increased from 44 to 49 percent of the total yield of these four taxes.

Taking into account equipment and wages, the business tax puts at a disadvantage firms that invest in machines (it amounts to 10.9 percent of the cost of an investment) and firms with a skilled workforce (it amounts to 2.7 percent of the cost of a job). The business tax is also heavier for industrial firms. The industrial sector pays 45.8 percent of the tax, while its share in the national value added is only 36 percent. In contrast, banks and insurance companies pay 5 percent of the business tax for a value added of 11 percent.

The richest local authorities, which have many firms on their territory, can apply low rates. In Ile-de-France, the average tax base is FF12,633, compared to FF5,151 in Corsica, for a national average of FF8,514.[5] Inside the Paris region itself, disparities are important and the tax rates vary between 4.62 percent in Courbevoie and 24.38 percent in Villejuif. Equalizations were set up between rich and poor localities, but they concern only 4 percent of the total amount of tax.

To alleviate the adverse effects of the business tax and avoid excessive increases, particularly for small and medium-sized enterprises, the national

[5] 'L'essentiel sur la réforme de la taxe professionnelle', *l'Expansion*, 5–18 May, 1994.

authorities set up ceilings and relief mechanisms, the central government setting off the financial losses of the local authorities. Thus, the real tax burden of the firms amounts only to two-thirds of the funds received by local authorities. Further, 0.7 percent of firms pay 64.5 percent of the tax, whereas nearly 75 percent of them pay less than 6 percent of it.

C. Economic and Social Aspects

C1 The Fiscal Deficit

Due to the slow growth and to some measures taken by the government to revive activity, there was a doubling of general government net borrowing from 1991 to 3.9 percent of GDP in 1992. General government revenue growth slowed to below 3 percent and expenditure growth accelerated to more than 6 percent, far above the GDP growth rate of 3.7 percent. The deterioration in public finances was strongest in the central government accounts (Table 3.11).

The considerable growth of the central government's fiscal deficit was largely unforeseen. On the basis of a projection of real growth of 2.2 percent, the deficit was budgeted to remain at 1991 level, a little below FF100 billion

Table 3.11 Receipts and expenditure by level of government (%)

	1990	1991	1992	1993	1994	1995
General government						
Receipts	6.7	4.3	2.8	2.2	4.2	3.9
Expenditure	7.3	5.5	6.3	5.9	4.2	3.0
Net lending	−1.5	−2.1	−3.9	−5.8	−5.8	−5.3
State						
Receipts	4.7	2.8	−1.1	−1.2	—	—
Expenditure	5.7	2.5	6.9	5.8	—	—
Net lending	−1.9	−1.8	−3.3	−4.4	—	—
Local authorities						
Receipts	7.6	5.8	4.4	4.5	—	—
Expenditure	6.4	6.3	6.0	6.4	—	—
Net lending	−0.0	−0.1	−0.2	−0.4	—	—
Social security						
Receipts	−5.3	5.6	5.2	4.4	—	—
Expenditure	6.5	7.2	6.6	6.2	—	—
Net lending	0.2	0.1	−0.4	−0.9	—	—
Memorandum item						
Nominal GDP growth	5.6	3.7	3.7	1.8	3.0	4.1

Source: *Economic Surveys, France* (OECD, 1994).

(1.25 percent of GDP). Expenditures and revenues increases were both expected to remain below nominal GDP growth. However, revenues fell short even of their 1991 level. Only a small part of this weakness can be explained by tax measures announced in the budget (mainly cuts in the top VAT and corporate tax rates). Other factors contributed to the fall: the base was over-estimated in 1991 (leading to a revenue shortfall of FF40 billion) and nominal GDP growth was much lower than expected. In addition, receipts from taxes on profits fell sharply and increased spending on lower-taxed items dragged VAT receipts down.

On the other hand, expenditures increased rapidly. Interest payments rose by 15 percent, due to the sharp increases in the deficit. In addition, spending initiatives during the fiscal year, for instance on labour market measures, were not offset by cuts elsewhere.

The deficit of local governments hardly increased, as their revenues are less cyclically sensitive (Table 3.11). Likewise, the deficit of the social security system showed only a minor increase, due to the full-year effect of the growth in the health insurance contribution rate in mid-1991 and various measures to improve the financial position of the unemployment insurance scheme.

The 1993 budget was based again on improving economic conditions, with falling interest rates from mid-1992 onward and real growth of 2.6 percent for 1993. Under these assumptions, the general government deficit should have been limited to 2.7 percent of GDP, slightly below the Maastricht target. This budget contained only minor tax measures, spending priorities for the Ministries of Education, Research, Employment, and Justice, and the announcement of further partial privatizations, yielding FF16 billion.

With the deepening of the recession by late 1992, the revenue base for the budget again proved to be overly optimistic. In April 1993, the new government, headed by Édouard Balladur, appointed a commission to assess the position of public finances. The commission estimated that revenue shortfalls would reach FF124 billion and spending overruns at FF44 billion, resulting in a deficit of 4.6 percent of GDP—nearly twice more than the initial deficit estimate. The commission also foresaw a fast rise in social deficit, about FF60 billion, i.e. slightly above the June estimate of the social security accounting commission (FF55.6 billion).

The new government proposed amendments to the 1993 budget that were based on two conflicting considerations. On the one hand, there was consensus that deficits had reached an unsustainable level, but, on the other hand, the recession and gloomy outlook for the rest of the year made it very difficult to resist mounting pressures for more spending. The amendments resulted in a planned deficit of FF318 billion (4.4 percent of GDP) a figure somewhat below the commission's estimate, as the authorities believed that reallocation of expenditure would support activity.

Enterprises benefited greatly from the budget amendments (FF61 billion) as VAT refunding was accelerated and contributions to the family allowances schemes were reduced for low-income earners. Spending initiatives included various measures to help agriculture, small and medium-sized enterprises, and the construction industry; capital increases for state-owned enterprises; and higher spending on infrastructure.

On the other hand, excise taxes were increased and the GSC was raised from 1.1 to 2.4 percent to finance a newly created Solidarity Fund. In addition, the privatization of twenty-one state-owned enterprises was announced with receipts in 1993 amounting to FF27 billion.

The spending initiatives were to be partly financed by the 'emprunt Balladur', which would be repaid later by privatization receipts. However, the 'emprunt Balladur' yielded FF110 billion, FF70 billion more than initially planned. The additional receipts were allocated to financing a further acceleration in VAT refunds (FF35 billion), training and school renovation by local governments (FF15 billion), and a quadrupling of the school-start allowance (FF5 billion), while the rest was held in reserve. Only a small part of these measures are actual expenditure for the central government, so that the deficit estimate for 1993 was not much affected.

The 1994 budget aimed at unprecedented expenditure restraint (see Table 3.12). Growth in 1994 turned out to be significantly stronger than expected and fiscal receipts were higher than 1.5 percent. In addition, receipts from privatization were larger than projected (FF63.7 billion against FF55 billion forecast). Nevertheless, additional tax revenues were not used to reduce the deficit but to finance an increase of outlays, which rose by 3.1 percent above budgeted spending. The deficit of FF300 billion was close to the budget forecast.

The 1995 budget also aimed at expenditure restraint and a fall in the deficit. Expenditures were estimated to rise by about 2 percent, and the deficit to fall from 4.1 percent of GDP in 1994 to 3.6 percent in 1995. Expenditures restraint concerned mainly capital expenditures, and transfers to local authorities and the European Union.

The budget amendments, introduced in June 1995 by Juppe's government established by President Chirac, included several spending initiatives in favour of employment, the housing sector, and small and medium-sized enterprises. There was also a cut in employers' social security contributions for low-income earners.

As well as these new spending initiatives, overspending and revenue short-fall (FF49 billion) in the first half of 1995 also needed to be covered. Over-spending was highest on interest payments, employment programmes, and income support, giving an overall total of FF23 billion.

Direct and indirect tax increases (close to 1 percent of GDP on the full-year basis) should have covered these initiatives as well as overspending and revenues shortfall. The rise in taxation included a raising of the standard VAT rate from 18.6 to 20.6 percent and a temporary increase in corporate and wealth taxes.

Table 3.12 Budget and out-turns (FF billion)

	1991	1992		1993		1994		1995	Budget amendments 1995
	Outcome	Budget	Outcome	Budget	Outcome	Budget	Outcome	Budget	
Direct taxes	562.9	591.6	549.1	585.5	546.8	535.3	545.6	566.1	576.7
Indirect taxes	890.0	969.4	904.5	974.3	882.9	922.3	919.9	960.1	974.3
Repayments	−224.6	−231.3	−238.2	−238.7	−220.5	−221.0	−211.1	−220.4	−224.1
Fiscal net receipts	1,228.3	1,329.7	1,215.4	1,321.1	1,209.1	1,236.6	1,254.4	1,305.9	1,326.9
Other receipts	158.1	141.9	164.9	153.7	189.0	181.4	204.8	179.5	183.5
Transfers to local authorities and EC	−215.4	−225.1	−219.8	−237.5	−232.6	−244.1	−236.8	−245.2	−240.2
Receipts	1,171.0	1,246.5	1,160.5	1,237.3	1,165.5	1,173.9	1,222.4	1,240.2	1,270.2
Compensation	477.7	479.7	481.7	510.1	509.1	525.5	531.8	542.4	549.9
Public debt	149.5	152.7	172.6	169.9	190.0	209.0	208.3	216.1	232.9
Other current expenditure	484.7	510.9	535.0	530.8	596.6	556.7	601.3	575.6	635.0
Capital expenditure	190.9	192.6	197.5	191.9	185.5	184.0	180.2	181.1	174.5
Expenditure	1,302.8	1,335.9	1,386.8	1,402.7	1,481.2	1,475.3	1,521.6	1,515.3	1,592.2
Deficit	−131.8	−89.4	−226.3	−165.4	−315.6	−301.4	−299.1	−275.1	−322.0[a]
Memorandum item									
Deficit (per cent of GDP)	2.0	1.2	3.2	2.2	4.4	4.1	4.1	3.6	4.1
Nominal GDP growth	3.7	5.1	3.7	5.5	1.0	3.4	4.1	5.3	5.3

[a] The budget does not include privatization receipts

Sources: Economic Surveys, France (OECD, 1994, 1995).

The initial budget aimed at a deficit of FF275 billion (including FF47 billion in privatization receipts) but in order to bring budgeting procedures closer to the Maastrich definition, privatization receipts may no longer be used to finance current expenditures. According to this definition, the target was to bring the deficit below FF322 billion (excluding net privatization receipts). This target was achieved thanks to the cancellation of lower-priority outlays. On the basis of the amended budgetary statements, general government borrowing could be 5 percent of GDP in 1995.

The previous Balladur government aimed to meet the Maastricht target by cutting the general government deficit to 3 percent of GDP by 1996. According to the convergence programme, the general government deficit should have been reduced to 5.1 percent of GDP in 1994 and 4.2 percent in 1995. Juppe's new government set a revised deficit reduction path: 5 percent in GDP in 1995, 4 percent in 1996, and 3 percent in 1997. The Maastricht criterion in 1997 could be achieved only through large expenditure cuts. These could be found only by strongly reducing two important items: the government wage bill and social spending. However, the very acute social trouble at the end of 1995 has shown that such measures are very difficult to implement.

C2 Savings and Investment Incentives

During the 1980s, France increased its reliance on tax expenditures to encourage saving and investment. The tax incentives take various forms (see Section B). The main incentives to household saving are provided in the personal income tax system, but the other taxes also play a role in this regard.

The French tax system is not neutral towards savings as is shown by all these fiscal incentives. Moreover, the fiscal structure itself is rather favourable to savings because of the importance of consumption taxes and of the low progressivity of the total tax burden. If one admits that the propensity to save is greater for high-income earners, the importance of social contributions and their regressivity can be considered as favourable to global savings. However, the level of the top marginal income tax rate can be seen as a disincentive. Likewise, the existence of a wealth tax can discourage people whose assets value is just below the tax threshold to save more, and so to become liable to this tax. It can even induce taxable people to sell their assets, and so to use their wealth to finance their current consumption, or even to emigrate. But those concerned are very few. For 'upper-middle-income' taxpayers, it can be said that the fiscal system is rather favourable to savings.

Some French economists, like Maurice Allais, advocate the complete removal of income tax as a measure to encourage savings. A socialist economist, Pierre Uri, was concerned by the fact that tax incentives mostly benefited high-income earners. He proposed, in the late 1970s, a system of tax exemptions for savings that would have been proportionally greater for low-income earners. This system was to be completed by a wealth tax.

The Socialist governments (1981–6 and 1988–93) did not directly apply Pierre Uri's proposals, but they were influenced by them, and they enacted measures to encourage savings by low-income earners (e.g. by creating the *Livret d'épargne populaire*) and reduced tax concessions deemed unduly favourable to high-income taxpayers.

The French tax system also is not neutral towards the distribution of savings between movable and immovable property. The government admits that immovable property is too heavily taxed, and intends to alleviate gradually the tax burden applicable to this kind of asset. One of the reasons for the weakness of the construction sector is the excessive lowering of the standard deduction on rents. The authorities also intend to reduce taxes on the transfer of buildings, particularly office buildings.

But all these measures are costly and have a limited effect on public opinion. The French government considers that total neutrality of taxation between income from immovable and movable property is not possible and probably not in the interest of property owners. The main benefit of the present system of taxation of income from immovable property is the deductibility of interest expenses and maintenance and repair expenses. If property owners should want a standard rate of 19.4 percent, as for bond interest income, the tax authorities consider that the tax should be calculated on gross rents.

The tax system is also not neutral towards investment decisions. There are many tax incentives, even though it is widely recognized that tax incentives are only one of many other factors affecting business decisions. Besides the measures mentioned above that concern the corporate tax, the value-added tax constitutes also an incentive to invest, and even to substitute capital for labour. A firm that invests can obtain a reimbursement of the value-added tax it has paid. On the other hand, if it hires labour, it must pay very heavy social security contributions and never obtains reimbursement of them.

C3 Distribution of Burden

As with most countries, the French system of taxes and contributions appears almost proportional.[6] We have seen above that the corporate tax is proportional to the profits of the companies, and that the other important taxes, like VAT, the property tax, and the business tax, are not linked to the income of the taxpayer. The only progressive levies are the personal income tax, the gift and inheritance taxes, and the wealth tax, but the share of the latter taxes in total tax receipts is too low and their bases too narrow to allow them to play a significant role in the redistribution of income and wealth.

[6] G. Malabouche, 'L'impôt sur le revenu, un mécanisme complexe', *Economie et statistique*, 241 (1991).

The most important of these progressive taxes, the personal income tax, yields a low return to the State, about FF300 billion in 1993, compared to FF630 billion for the sum of VAT and the tax on oil products. The personal income tax represents hardly a fifth of total tax receipts, or 4 percent of GDP. The weight of personal income tax in France is about half the average level of developed countries. Moreover, this tax applies only to half of the 28 million tax units, and it has tended to be even more concentrated during the past decade. According to the 1990 Report of the Tax Council (*Conseil des impôts*), the income subject to tax corresponds only to half the economic income of households. The average tax rate amounts to 8.5 percent of total declared income, but if only taxable households are taken into account, this rate becomes 11.5 percent.[7]

The personal income tax threshold is particularly high in France, compared to most other large countries. In 1993, the tax applied to net income of FF56,900 for a single person, FF85,500 for a couple without children, and FF117,800 for a couple with two children. In 1992, this threshold corresponded to 98.2 percent of the guaranteed minimum wage (the SMIC), 46.4 percent of the average net wage in the private sector, and 57 percent of the medium net wage in the private sector.

The richest 5 percent of households (i.e. hardly 1.4 million taxpayers, out of 28 million), who receive 24.5 percent of total incomes before taxes, pay 55 percent of the total personal income tax, while the 14 million poorest households, who receive only 22 percent of total incomes, pay 3.6 percent of the total income tax.

The tax schedule is very progressive, and the number of brackets (thirteen until 1993, reduced to seven in the 1994 Finance Act) is higher than in most other countries. However, the vertical distributional impact (from higher-income households to lower-income households) is comparable to what can be observed in other countries.

In addition, the horizontal redistribution through the family quotient mechanism is more favourable to families in France, especially if they are affluent. In all countries, a single person pays, for the same level of income, more taxes than a family with two children. However, the discrepancy between the two situations varies between 1 and 7 from one country to another, with France and Germany being the most generous towards families, and Spain, Italy and the UK being the least generous. Moreover, the French tax system is peculiar in that the advantages offered increase with income, while the reverse situation can be observed in other countries. This effect has been reduced, however, since the application of a ceiling to high-income families in 1982.

---

[7] J. Bensaid and E. Desquesses, 'La réforme de l'impôt sur le revenu: une mise en perpective', *Economie et prévision*, 110–11 (1993).

As wages increase, the respective shares of social security contributions and income tax change: for a worker whose income is the minimum wage, the whole levy consists of the social security contributions; for a junior executive, social security contributions represent 76 percent of the levy and income tax 24 percent; for a senior manager, social security contributions represent only 48 percent of the levy and income tax 52 percent.

For all high-income earners, France is one of the countries where the rate of levies is the highest. This is notably due to the fact that the different allowances cease to apply beyond a certain level of income (about FF710,000 of net wages) so that the maximum marginal rate (56.8 percent) applies to gross wages and gives rise to a strong increase of the average personal tax rate.

For a married couple with children, the rate of levies applicable to income of FF800,000 is 45 percent in France, compared to 42 percent in Germany, 41 percent in Italy, and 37 percent in the USA. For single persons, the French tax system appears much more progressive than for families.

However, the progressivity remains relatively low for families with low and medium incomes: for a couple with two children, the rate of levies applicable to a household whose income level is that of a junior executive is only 2 percentage points higher than the rate applicable to a household getting the minimum guaranteed wage. The difference is 5 percentage points in Germany and 12.5 points in the UK.

The other progressive taxes—the inheritance and net wealth taxes—have an even narrower base than the income tax. With respect to inheritance taxes, in 1984, 267,000 statements were registered, out of 530,000 deaths.[8] The same year, 763,000 people received a legacy, the average of which was FF122,000. Half of these legacies had a value below FF50,000, while 5 percent of them were worth more than FF425,000. Only 5 percent of heirs received 36 percent of the total value of legacies, while half of them shared 91 percent of this value. The values of most estates, therefore, are below the tax threshold, or are taxed at rates below 20 percent. The highest rates, 30 and 40 percent, apply to a very small proportion of estates, but for these estates it can be said that inheritance taxes have a distributional impact that is not insignificant.

As regards the net wealth tax (ISF), 163,125 statements corresponding to taxable estates were registered in 1993, compared to 157,666 in 1992. The total yield of this tax was FF7.2 billion in 1993.

The net wealth tax is also very highly concentrated. According to the report of the Finance Commission of the National Assembly on the Finance Bill for 1990, the 2,158 richest taxpayers (whose taxable wealth is beyond FF20 million) together paid FF1,644 billion for that tax, which corresponds to an average tax of FF761,816 per taxpayer. On the other hand, almost half of net wealth taxpayers (58,000) belonged to the least-taxed bracket (the value of their estate being between FF4 million and FF6.5 million in 1989). They

---

[8] A. Laferrère, *Economie et statistique*, 214 (1988).

paid only 7.5 percent of the total yield of this tax, with an average share of FF5,750.

C4 The Hidden Economy

The value of the 'underground economy' was estimated to be about FF250 billion, or 4 percent of GDP in 1988, according to a study of INSEE.[9] It results from tax evasion, of which FF135 billion consist of concealment or omission of receipts, and FF35.5 billion of not paying VAT, with the total representing 3 percent of GDP. For example, in the retail trade, hotels, pubs, restaurants, and services to households, more than 15 percent of the value added corresponded to undeclared activities that were estimated by national accountants.

Another aspect of the underground economy, 'moonlighting', corresponds to a value added estimated at FF63 billion, or 1 percent of GDP, with one-third of the amount attributable to the construction sector. There are all sorts of other unreported activities, however, from neighbourhood services consisting of babysitting, housework, private lessons, or house repairs, to the concealed activities of craftsmen, wage earners with two jobs, unemployed persons, and retired people.

Tax evasion devices have become more and more complex and international. The removal of exchange controls since 1 January 1990 has allowed French-resident individuals to open accounts abroad. Measures have been taken to prevent this liberalization from becoming a new device for tax evasion: residents and non-residents are obliged to declare transfers of funds worth more than FF50,000, and residents must declare the accounts they open abroad.[10]

The main forms of tax evasion discovered in tax audits and the sectors involved are shown in Tables 3.13 and 3.14.

Some have stated that the establishment of the European internal market on 1 January 1993 facilitated all sorts of dealings and fraud, because it removed border controls. The customs administration had to adjust its activities by establishing mobile controls on the roads near the borders, and also within the whole national territory.

In 1993, seizures of heroin and cannabis increased significantly. Seizures of cocaine have not changed much, but the quantities involved are important (1,284 kilograms). France is frequently used as a transit country for drug trafficking towards European countries. Cannabis is thus channelled from Morocco through Spain towards the Netherlands or the French market. As regards synthetic drugs (ecstasy, LSD, and amphetamines), their production and distribution come mostly from the Netherlands and supply the European

---

[9] *Economie et statistique*, 206 (1989).
[10] 'Le contrôle fiscal en France', *Les notes bleues de Bercy*, 564 (1991).

Table 3.13   Forms of offences giving rise to proceedings in 1990

	No.	Per cent
Undeclared or hidden activity	493	66.60
Concealment of receipts	225	30.40
Fictitious transactions	15	2.10
Other devices	7	0.90
Total	740	100.00

Source: *Les notes bleues de Bercy*, 1992.

Table 3.14   Socio-professional distribution of proceedings in 1990

	No.	Back taxes paid	
		Total	Average
Agriculture	6	4,009,584	668,264
Industry	56	69,670,064	1,244,119
Construction	98	129,677,422	1,323,239
Trade	189	206,421,453	1,092,177
Services	149	199,629,008	1,339,792
Professions	131	104,636,643	798,753
Managers and wage earners	111	181,290,861	1,633,251
Total	740	895,335,035	1,209,912

Source: See Table 3.13.

markets through French territory, where they are introduced by road and railroad.

C5 Administrative and Compliance Costs

The French tax system is very complex, which gives rise to high costs, both for the tax administration and for taxpayers. Compared to VAT, whose high yield is due to its broad base and relatively high compliance rate, other types of taxes, particularly local taxes but also income tax and net wealth tax, have a double drawback in that they are difficult to administer and have a narrow base.

C5.1 Administrative costs

Local taxes are received by the local authorities, but they are assessed and collected by national civil servants. According to some sources,[11] 30,000

---

[11] *Le Monde*, 28 Sept. 1992.

national civil servants or 37 percent of a total of 80,000 are involved in local taxes management. These taxes are often misunderstood by taxpayers, and they give rise to three million complaints every year.

In 1990, the government began a reassessment of real properties for purposes of the land and property taxes. These properties had not been assessed since 1961 for land tax purposes and 1970 for property tax purposes. In the intervening years, the tax bases were simply adjusted by a fixed amount every year, which resulted in tax bases that were far from market value. During the first stage of the reassessment, from 1990 to 1992, 2,000 civil servants were sent out to assess 37 million premises and 90 million plots, at a cost of nearly FF1 billion, according to the Ministry of Finance.[12]

Personal income tax and corporate income tax also have high administrative costs due to the numerous tax incentives and preferences that have been enacted over the years and to difficulties in the auditing of tax returns. In 1990, the total amount of taxes recovered after audits reached FF33 billion, or 3.5 percent of the central government's total tax revenues, which amounted to FF900 billion.[13]

Audits of large firms—those whose turnover exceeded FF400 million— resulted in the highest collections: 2.5 percent of audits account for 40 percent of the amount of tax adjustments, the average amount of adjustments after tax audits being FF700,000.

Only 6,500 officials of the Tax Directorate (*Direction Générale des Impôts*) have tax-auditing responsibilities. Some of these perform both tax audits and assessment tasks, while others (about 3,500) specialize in auditing. According to the importance and the complexity of cases, tax auditors audit between eight and twelve firms or individuals every year. The duration of audits is limited by administrative regulations to three months for small firms. For the larger ones, this duration is not limited. Because of the lack of auditors, whose number decreased after 1984, many small firms are not likely to be audited.

Some sectors or regions, where small and medium-sized enterprises are audited on average only once every twenty or even forty years, look like real tax havens. This extremely low audit rate is attributable to the fact that the fiscal authorities have wanted to focus on larger cases, which are more efficient in terms of costs versus collections, and their desire to avoid exacerbating the economic difficulties of many small firms.

The net wealth tax also has a low yield for its high administrative costs. In a 1979 report, the commission set up to study the feasibility of this tax *Commission d'étude d'un prélèvement sur les fortunes)* estimated that 1,000 agents should have been recruited to manage this tax. This number can be

---

[12] D. Seux, 'Valeurs locatives: le marathon de la révision', *Le Nouvel Economiste*, 22 Sept. 1990.
[13] See n. 11.

compared with the number of tax returns sent in 1990: 142,000, which gave rise to 22,000 audits and more than 3,000 adjustments.

In an effort to cope with its expanding workload and declining workforce, the tax administration made an important effort to computerize its operations, and particularly to buy laptop computers. The cost of this programme has been estimated at nearly FF100 million a year. However, equipment and training did not go together and in 1991 only 4,500 jobs were computerized. Nevertheless, the French tax administration is more advanced than in many other European countries as regards use of new technologies. The OCEANS system *(Operations de Contrôle Externe Assistees de Nouveaux Systèmes)*, introduced in 1990, brings technical assistance to tax auditors by way of microcomputers, laptop computers, and a series of software.

C5.2 Compliance Costs

The self-assessment system that is applied in France gives rise to costs, not only for the administration, which has to control returns, but also for taxpayers, who have to file sometimes complicated documents to comply with the tax laws.

With respect to personal income tax, it is difficult, even for a household of wage earners, to assess their income tax bill rapidly. Nevertheless, the proportion of individuals who turn to tax advisers remains very low, contrary to what can be observed in some foreign countries.

It is obvious that compliance costs are all the more substantial for taxpayers receiving large capital incomes, and costs are still greater for the taxpayers who are liable to the net wealth tax and who must take stock of their wealth every year, which gives rise to assessment problems, particularly for immovable property.

Firms bear the highest compliance costs. They complain about having to play the role of tax collectors. This is particularly the case for VAT, since they collect the tax before turning it over to the tax administration.

Firms also play the role of tax collector for social security contributions, which makes them bear a high cost, in terms of contributions assessment and various formalities. This is one of the reasons why businesses oppose a 'pay-as-you-earn' system of income tax collection. They already act as tax collectors for nearly two-thirds of revenues, and they do not want to have this role increased.

The tax administration endeavoured to alleviate the compliance costs of taxpayers. Firms are now obliged to keep necessary information in a computerized form, but they can also be exempted, if they so wish, and produce the information on paper. The tax officials can, if the taxpayer agrees, use the firm's computers. In 1991, the Tax Directorate created seven teams for computerized accounts auditing. Those brigades are under the control of the Directorate for National and International Auditing *(Direction des vérifications nationales et internationales).* Over the last three years, the resources of these teams have been progressively reinforced.

D. Tax Reform

The tax reforms introduced between 1986 and 1993 are far from being the first reform package affecting the French tax system. The willingness to enact tax reforms has been a constant feature of French economic policy, in response to both internal and external pressures that have arisen during the last two decades. Internal pressures result from the economic crisis confronting France, like many other industrialized countries. The slowdown in economic growth and the increase in unemployment have, in fact, induced left-wing as well as right-wing governments to take measures aiming at stimulating the activities of enterprises and so boost employment.

Tax policy has endeavoured to promote a more efficient channelling of funds towards the industrial sector. Thus, within the scope of strong efforts to maintain self-financing within firms and to improve their equity ratios, the corporate tax rate has been gradually reduced from 50 to 33.3 percent in recent years. Now, the French corporate tax rate is close to the average level of other European countries. France followed, but to a lesser extent, the reform movement that began in the 1980s in the OECD area which in other countries involved more base broadening. Nevertheless, French firms claim that they bear one of the heaviest tax burdens due to the social security system, which relies heavily on employers' contributions.

Internal pressures result also from the difficult problem posed by the social security system, whose financing relies mostly on wages. This method of financing, which was adopted after the Second World War, is no longer appropriate in the present situation. In fact, the surge of unemployment has considerably reduced the number of contributors and the base itself, for unemployment exerts a downward pressure on wages. At the same time, due to the opening up of the economy, a way of financing that increases the costs of French products without affecting those of imports has many drawbacks, all the more as the French authorities generally tried to maintain a policy of strong currency (*politique du franc fort*).

The reform of the French tax system was made urgent by the setting up of the European single market. The birth on 1 January 1993 of a Europe without boundaries is an important event with numerous economic effects. Besides removing boundaries, the treaty establishing the single market prescribed the dismantling of regulatory and tax barriers.

The harmonization of securities taxation has been necessary to avoid the risk of tax avoidance (enterprises issuing their stocks and bonds on the most active and the least-taxed stock exchanges) and capital outflows. To this end, beginning with the Finance Act of 1990, France has been gradually adjusting

Table 3.15   Summary of reforms introduced between 1986 and 1993

Personal income tax: Reduction of the number of brackets from 13 to 7 (1994)

Corporate tax: Gradual reduction of the rate of tax from 50% to 33.3% between 1986 and 1993 (see Table 3.14)

Payroll taxes: Introduction of the general social contribution (CSG) in 1991 at a rate of 1.1%. The rate was raised to 2.4% in 1994.

Value-added tax: Reduction of the number of rates from four to three in 1989: a reduced rate: 5.5%, a standard rate of 18.6%, and a higher rate of 22%. Higher rate eliminated in 1992. One-month lag rule abolished in 1993.

Wealth tax: Introduced in 1981; abolished in 1986; restored in 1989.

Local taxes: Introduction of an income tax at the level of 'Departments' (1992); however, a law adopted a few months later postponed the application of this reform.

---

its tax rates downward (for instance, it lowered by 10 points the rate of the withholding applicable to fixed-income investments to 15 percent).

As a whole, the reforms just summarized were limited to adjustments of the traditional system and most of them were ineffective, according to the various governments who followed one another. On the other hand, radical reforms, which appear more and more essential, are still awaited.

The new GSC, established in 1991 to help finance social welfare expenditures through the income tax rather than through social security contributions, constituted a first step towards a reducing reliance on the latter, even if the GSC is a flat rate rather than a progressive income tax. The Ducamin Report released by the government in August 1995 advocates a broadening of the base of the GSC by including, for example, family benefits, interest on housing savings plans, or popular saving accounts that are now tax-exempt.

However, the most important reforms are still to be made, particularly as regards income tax, which, because of the assessment mechanisms it uses, remains very unequal, exceptionally complex, and with a low yield. The setting up of a 'pay-as-you-earn' system, while it was often suggested, in particular by the Tax Council in its report of 1990, is not at present on the agenda. However, according to the results of a poll published by the newspaper *Les Echos* in 1990, 53 percent of taxpayers would favour such a system.

Some progress nevertheless has been made towards lowering the tax rates, broadening the tax base, and reducing the number of brackets (from thirteen to seven), the final objective being to apply only four or five brackets. In the end, though, these measures are not radical enough. The base of the tax remains too narrow, and the top marginal tax rate is still one of the highest among developed countries. The right-wing government in power from 1993 did not want to reduce it, however, for fear that such a measure would be unpopular. Balladur remembered his previous experience of 1986, when the rapid removal of the wealth tax was much criticized. While it was proposed in the programme of his party to exempt the main home from the wealth tax, this measure was not applied.

The difficulties encountered by the previous left-wing majority to adopt tax reforms are also illustrative. The GSC introduced by the Rocard government in 1990 gave rise to many criticisms, even among his own majority: the communists were against this reform, and even some socialists disapproved of it. A few months later, another proposal to reform the local system by introducing an income tax at the level of department gave rise to still stronger opposition from many socialists. Some journalists have compared the difficulties encountered by the French government with those faced by the British government following the introduction of a poll tax. This tax was finally adopted by Parliament at the end of 1991, but so far it has not been implemented. The socialist majority has often been reproached for introducing too many new taxes, and they took this criticism into account.

As regards the business tax (*taxe professionnelle*) Balladur's government intended to replace its present base by the value added generated by the firm. Such a reform would have been consistent with the proposals made by the Tax Council in its report of 1989, but it would have given rise to many shifts of the tax burden between enterprises. It is not yet known whether this measure will be included in the global tax reform planned by Balladur's successor for 1996 but postponed, taking into account the very difficult social climate. In fact, there were many attempts to reform this tax in the past, but they were always very difficult to apply.

In conclusion, while the most important problems remain and the radical reforms are always postponed, the French tax system has undergone important changes in tax rate and base over the last eight years, as indicated in Table 3.16.

Table 3.16 Summary to reforms introduced since 1993

Personal income tax: Top rate was to be reduced from 54% to 52 % in 1997 with the intention of reducing it to 47% in 2001. However, the Socialist government elected in June 1997 set the top rate at 54%. There was some widening of the base.
Capital gains taxes: There were increases in 1998.
Corporation tax: The rate was increased in 1995 to 36% and in 1998 for large firms only to 41.6%.
Payroll tax: In 1995, the GSC was raised from 2.4% to 3.4% and in 1997 to 7.5%, its base being widened. There was a reduction in employees' health contributions from 4.75% to 0.75%.
Value-added tax: Standard rate increased from 18.6% to 20.6% in 1995

4 Germany

WILLI LEIBFRITZ, WOLFGANG BÜTTNER, AND
ULRICH VAN ESSEN

A. Overview

A1 History of German Tax Policy

The basic structure of the present German tax system emerged at the end of
the First World War. Taxes on income and net wealth, which before this time
had been the principal sources of revenue for the States (*Länder*), came under
federal control in 1920. Since then, legislation in the field of taxation has been
primarily a federal matter, although the states have continued to play an
important role in the administration of the tax system.

Changes in tax policy that have occurred since the Second World War have
been due partly to historical circumstances—the allied occupation, the needs
of reconstruction, and the prolonged recession of the mid-1970s and the early
1980s—and partly to changes in the objectives of public policy. It is
convenient to divide the post-war years into six distinct periods:

First, immediately after the war, the allied Control Council introduced high
personal income tax rates (up to 90 percent) and corporation tax rates (50
percent, raised to 60 percent in 1951). Favourable depreciation allowances,
however, reduced the effective tax burden.

Second, during reconstruction there were successive reductions in personal
tax rates (1948, 1953, 1954). In 1958 a new rate structure was introduced that
despite subsequent modification has been largely maintained. This structure
comprised a low-exemption level, a bracket with a constant marginal tax rate,
a second bracket with progressive rates, and a final bracket with a constant
marginal tax rate. During this period the major change in the corporation tax
was the introduction of a 'split-rate system' in 1953. Tax rates on retained
earnings and dividends were changed repeatedly (1953, 1955, 1958). Along
with the general reduction in tax rates, depreciation allowances were reduced,
apparently in the hope of forcing firms to seek external finance for new
investments by restricting cash flows.

Third, with the end of the reconstruction period (mid-1960s) governments
showed increased concern with demand management and the existing pattern
of income distribution. It was often stated (especially by the advisory board of
the Ministry of Finance) that tax policy towards investment should be

employed to smooth cyclical fluctuations or to assist certain types of activity (regional development, R&D, etc.). Moreover, as in the case of grants, the instruments applied should attempt to be as neutral as possible among firms of different size. Hence, surcharges on income and corporate taxes (in 1970–1, 1973–4), an investment tax (1973), and a temporary tax-free investment grant (1974–5) were introduced at different times. Investment grants were provided for regional development, research, environmental protection, and energy saving.

Fourth, since the mid-1970s, there has been a change of climate in favour of establishing a 'better general framework' for investment. In 1977, the new corporate tax system was introduced that abolished (for residents) double

Table 4.1 Sources of tax revenue, 1970–1992

Revenue source	1970	1980	1990	1991	1992
	Share in GDP (%)				
Social security contributions	10.0	13.0	13.8	14.9	15.2
Taxes	22.9	25.2	23.0	23.7	24.4
Total receipts	32.9	38.2	36.8	38.6	39.6
	Share of total taxes (%)				
Social security contributions	30.3	34.4	37.5	38.6	38.4
Taxes on personal incomes	26.7	29.8	27.6	27.3	28.0
Taxes on wages and salaries	15.7	19.9	19.9	19.6	20.6
Assessed income tax	7.2	6.6	4.1	3.8	3.5
Withholding except wages and salaries	0.9	0.7	1.2	1.0	0.9
Enterprise tax	2.4	2.5	2.3	2.0	2.0
Other	0.4	0.0	0.0	0.8	1.0
Taxes on corporate incomes	5.6	5.5	4.8	4.3	4.0
Corporation tax	3.9	3.8	3.4	2.9	2.6
Enterprise tax	1.7	1.6	1.4	1.2	1.3
Other	0.1	0.0	0.0	0.1	0.1
Payroll taxes of enterprises	0.6	0.1	0.0	0.0	0.0
Property taxes	4.9	3.3	3.4	2.8	2.7
General taxes on goods and services	17.1	16.7	16.5	16.5	16.5
Taxes on specific goods and services	12.9	9.3	9.2	9.3	9.3
Alcohol	1.0	0.7	0.5	0.5	0.5
Tobacco	2.9	2.0	1.9	1.8	1.6
Petroleum	5.2	3.8	3.9	4.4	4.6
Other	3.8	2.8	2.9	2.7	2.6
Miscellaneous taxes	1.7	1.2	1.0	1.0	1.1
Total taxes	100.0	100.0	100.0	100.0	100.0

Sources: OECD, *Revenue Statistics 1965–93* (Paris, 1994), authors' calculations. Tax revenue refers to West Germany until 1990 and to all Germany beginning in 1991.

taxation of distributed earnings by introducing a system with full imputation of corporate tax payments at the recipient level. Wealth tax rates were reduced in 1978 after they had been increased in 1975. Exemption limits were raised for the local business tax, and in 1980 one component of the local business tax—the local payroll tax—was abolished. Furthermore, depreciation allowances were increased in 1977 and 1981, which seemed to indicate a departure from previous attitudes towards the tax treatment of investment. There was a major income tax cut in 1975 and further smaller cuts by the end of the 1970s and the beginning of the 1980s.

Fifth, after the rapidly rising government debt had become a major policy issue during the recession in the early 1980s, the new government made big efforts to restrain spending in order to reduce the deficit and to make room for tax cuts. This policy was successful and during 1986–90 income tax was gradually reduced.

Sixth, since unification, the main task of German economic policy has been to restructure the East German economy. After unification industrial production in East Germany broke down. The main reasons were the low productivity and the poor competitiveness of East German firms. This was aggravated by the fact that currency union brought a strong effective revaluation for East German exporters. In addition, the traditional trade with Eastern Europe, including the former Soviet Union, declined sharply. A variety of tax and subsidy measures has been taken to promote investment in Eastern Germany and to restructure that region's whole economy. With the unexpectedly high cost of unification and the cyclical shortfall of tax revenues during the recession in 1993, government debt has again increased sharply. Therefore, the government felt compelled to increase taxes again, especially VAT, mineral oil tax, and other indirect taxes, thus adding to the shift from direct to indirect taxes. Furthermore, a surcharge on income tax was put into effect from mid-1991 to mid-1992 and was reintroduced (although with the intention to abolish after the budgetary position has been improved) in 1995. As in the 1980s, efforts have been made to restrain public spending to reduce the deficit and to make room for future tax cuts. Also in response to concern that Germany's relatively high rates of business taxes would weaken its international competitiveness and attractiveness as a business location, the government reduced business taxes in 1994. However, the scale of the reform was rather limited given the budgetary constraints.

A2 Main Features of the Tax Revenue System

Over the last thirty years, the tax/GDP ratio (including social security contributions) increased from about 31 percent to almost 40 percent. This increase was mainly due to social security contributions while the other taxes fluctuated between 23 and 25 percent; in East Germany they amount, at present, to less than 15 percent of GDP.

As shown in Table 4.1, the most important revenue source is social security contributions (38.4 percent of the total tax yield in 1992). Other important sources are the personal income tax (28 percent) and VAT (16.5 percent). Taxes on corporate income (including the local business tax on corporations) yielded only 4 percent in 1992. The reason for the relatively low share of corporate income tax revenues does not lie in a low effective tax rate but rather in the fact that unincorporated companies have a relatively high share in the German economy.

Given the federal structure of Germany there is a distinct system of revenue sharing among the various government levels. The Federal Government and the States share tax revenues obtained from VAT, corporate income tax, and individual income tax. The revenues from the latter are also shared with local authorities. The distribution of tax revenue generally is fixed, but in the case of VAT is periodically renegotiated.

At present about 94 percent of total tax revenue (excluding social security contributions) is almost equally shared by the Federal Government on one hand and the States and the local governments on the other hand. Approximately 6 percent of total revenue (excluding social security contributions) is given to the EU. Some taxes, however, are attributed to only one level of government. Federal Government sources are excise duties, monopolies (e.g. the spirit monopoly), and various consumer and transfer taxes. The States receive, among others, the motor vehicle, net wealth, inheritance, and beer taxes. The local authorities obtain the revenue from business, real estate, and local consumption taxes. As the revenue share of local authorities is only 12–13 percent, which is much less than their share in total government spending (about 20 percent of total government spending, excluding social security), the States have established a vertical revenue-sharing system that allocates part of their tax revenues to the local authorities (*kommunaler Finanzausgleich*). There also exists a horizontal redistribution system among the States that reallocates revenues from States with above-average revenues to financially weaker ones (*Länderfinanzausgleich*). These transfers are supplemented by transfers from the Federal Government (*Bundesergänzungzuweisungen*). After unification a so-called 'German Unity Fund' was set up to provide financial support for the eastern States and their local authorities. This fund, which was fed jointly by the Federal Government and the western States, was a substitute for a nationwide financial equalization system among the federal States until the end of 1994. As from 1995 a new redistribution system among States including the eastern States became effective and the German Unity Fund ended.

B. The Tax System

B1 Individual Income Tax

B1.1 Tax Base

All resident individuals in Germany are taxed on their worldwide income. Individuals who do not have their residence or customary place of domicile in Germany are subject to tax liability only on income from domestic sources. The base of the individual income tax generally includes income from all sources.

Capital gains or losses from the sale of private property are taxable only if they derive from short-term speculative transactions or from the sale of a significant interest (25 percent or more) in the shares of a company. These short-term or speculative transaction gains are taxed if they exceed DM1,000 per annum and if the private property is sold within two years of acquisition in the case of real property, or within six months in the case of securities or other assets. Speculative losses may be offset only against speculative gains in the year in which they have occurred. Gains and losses from the sale of assets related to a trade or business (including farming and professional services) are, as a rule, fully included in the tax base and taxed at ordinary tax rates. They are taxed when realized. However, business capital gains are tax free if they are earmarked to cover the purchase or production costs of certain recently acquired assets. They carry other tax privileges, such as high limits of tax exemption or the application of a reduced tax rate, if they derive from the sale of certain production plants or parts thereof, business shares in the form of substantial interests, or assets that serve professional activities. Capital gains not in excess of DM30 million and deriving from the sale of a whole business or division, or the sale of a partnership interest, are taxed at half of the ordinary tax rates after allowing for specific tax-free amounts.

B1.2 Tax Rates

Germany's tax schedule is based on a formula and does not have brackets. Individuals pay taxes according to an arithmetic progression at rates between 25.9 and 53 percent. As of 1994 the top marginal tax rate on business income was reduced from 53 percent to 47 percent. Table 4.2 shows the scale of income tax rates:

- A basic personal exemption of DM12,095 is granted on taxable income of a single person (DM24,191 of a married couple);
- the excess of taxable income up to DM55,257 of a single person (DM110,515 of a married couple) is subject to marginal tax rates increasing linear from 25.9 to 33.5 percent;
- in the next zone, from DM55,258/110,516 (single person/married couple) to DM120,041/240,083, marginal tax rates rise in steady and linear

progression from 33.5 to 53 percent. Taxable income above DM120,041/ 240,083 is subject to a flat marginal rate of 53 percent; and
• income from trade or business exceeding DM120,278 is subject to a maximum tax rate of 47 percent.

Members of Catholic and Protestant churches pay an 8 or 9 percent surcharge on their income tax (church tax), which qualifies as an itemized deduction. To raise additional revenue to further cope with financial needs stemming from reunification, in 1995 a solidarity surcharge of 7.5 percent on the income and corporate income taxes was (re)introduced. Wages and salaries below a certain threshold (DM23,977 for a single person and DM45,523 for a married couple) are free of the surcharge.

The tax table used for withholding taxes on wages and salaries is derived from the income tax rates, after allowing for the tax-free amounts for employees and their families and a 'standard employee deduction' of DM2,000. The solidarity surcharge of 7.5 percent is levied on the withholding tax.

Table 4.2   Income tax and income tax rates (1996)

Taxable income[a] DM	Joint return			Single return		
	Tax on DM	Average %	Marginal %	Tax on DM	Average %	Marginal %
12,100	0	0	0	13	0.1	25.9
16,000	0	0	0	1,034	6.5	26.6
20,000	0	0	0	2,110	10.6	27.3
24,000	0	0	0	3,214	13.4	28.0
28,000	1,012	3.6	26.2	4,345	15.5	28.7
35,000	2,876	8.2	26.8	6,400	18.3	29.9
40,000	4,220	10.6	27.3	7,905	19.8	30.7
45,000	5,586	12.4	27.7	9,471	21.1	31.6
60,000	9,842	16.4	29.0	14,422	24.0	34.8
80,000	15,810	19.8	30.7	21,976	27.5	40.8
100,000	22,126	22.2	32.5	30,743	30.8	46.9
120,000	28,844	24.0	34.8	40,751	34.0	53.0
140,000	36,096	25.8	37.8	51,341	36.7	53.0
160,000	43,952	27.5	40.8	61,930	38.7	53.0
200,000	61,486	30.8	46.9	83,137	41.6	53.0
240,000	81,502	34.0	53.0	104,345	43.5	53.0
260,000	92,092	35.4	53.0	114,934	44.2	53.0

Note: For income over DM260,000, the tax payable amounts to 53% less DM22,842 (single returns); and, for joint returns, 53% of one-half of DM22,842 multiplied by two.

[a] Total income subject to tax minus losses and standard tax reliefs, e.g. social security contributions, childcare allowances, and income- and non-income-related expenses.

Source: Ministry of Finance.

The following are credited against the assessed tax:

- Any income tax prepayments made for the current year, which are assessed by the tax office based on the estimated tax liability for the year;
- any income tax withheld at source (e.g. tax on wages and salaries or interest and dividend withholding tax); German corporate income tax on dividends received from a German corporation; and
- foreign income taxes paid, up to the amount of the corresponding German tax.

B1.3 Treatment of Different Kinds of Income

The German individual income tax law lists the following seven sources of income:

- agriculture and forestry;
- trade or business enterprises;
- professional and certain other independent personal services;
- employment (wages and salaries);
- capital investments (interest and dividends);
- rentals and royalties;
- certain other sources of income designated in the income tax act (e.g. speculative gains).

Unemployment and sickness benefits are not subject to tax. (However, the progressive tax rates applied take these benefits into account, leading to a possible increase in the taxation of other income.)

Not only monetary income, but also income in kind is subject to tax. For example, taxable employment income comprises all forms of remuneration, including allowances and benefits in cash and in kind. Benefits in kind are valued, in principle, at cost to the employer, although there are some global allocations (e.g. cars), mostly for administrative simplicity.

In response to a decision by the German Federal Constitutional Court (which declared the existing tax collection on interest income to be non-constitutional on the grounds that it did not affect all persons equally, because of widespread evasion), a withholding tax of 30 percent (35 percent for over-the-counter sellings) on interest income and dividends paid to resident taxpayers was introduced as of 1 January 1993. The savers' tax-free amount of DM600/1,200 was increased to DM6,000/12,000.

Expenditures to acquire, secure, and/or maintain revenue (so-called operational expenses and costs incurred in earning income), certain annuities, church tax, and tax consulting fees are fully deducted from income, but interest payments on consumer loans are not deductible. In addition, there are, among other things, deductions and allowances for disability, dependent children, and business expenses, as well as special expenses, such as standard social security contributions and specific insurance premiums. Donations for certain ecclesiastical, religious, and public benefit purposes are generally deductible up to a ceiling of 5 percent of the donor's gross income, or in the case of scientific, charitable, and specified cultural purposes, up to 10 percent of gross income. Membership dues and donations to political parties attract a tax deduction of 50 percent of the expense, subject to a ceiling of DM3,000/DM6,000 of the expense. Contributions to political parties are deductible up to a total of DM60,000 per annum (DM120,000 for married couples).

B1.4 Treatment of Family

Married couples may elect to be assessed either jointly or separately. In the case of joint assessment, the net income accruing to each spouse is aggregated and the couple treated as a single taxpayer. Income tax is then determined by a joint income-splitting system, with tax being computed according to the basic table on one-half of the joint income and the result being doubled. Tax computed in this way mitigates the effect of the progressive increase in the tax rates provided for by the basic table and, therefore, is invariably lower than if the couple had filed separate returns. Couples also benefit from higher allowances and deductions of expenditures, as most deductible allowances and expenses that are not related to income are graduated according to marital status. The income-splitting method has been criticized as providing disproportionate relief to higher-income couples, but no ceiling has been put on this relief so far.

The system of child relief has been restructured completely in 1996. The former child benefits were raised to DM200 per month for the first and the second child, DM300 per month for the third child, and DM350 per month for the fourth and subsequent children and transformed into a tax credit. This tax credit is taken into account in computing the withholding tax on wages. In the income tax assessment a child allowance of DM6,264 replaces the tax credit if it leads to higher relief.

The child allowance for each dependent child amounts to DM4,104, and additional educational allowances in the case of children attending school away from home range from DM1,800 per child under 18 years of age to DM4,200 per child over 18 years of age. For children attending school who are over 18 years of age and living in the taxpayer's home in Germany, an educational allowance of DM2,400 per child is deductible. Any income and earnings accruing to a child in excess of DM3,600 a year must be set off against the educational allowance, as must be any grants from public funds connected with the child's education or vocational training.

Children with their own income are taxed separately. Single persons with children are entitled to a household allowance of DM5,616. In addition, unmarried persons, who are employed or physically or mentally handicapped can deduct from the tax base the cost incurred in the care of children up to a maximum amount of DM4,000 for the first child, plus DM2,000 for each

Table 4.3 The imputation system

At corporation level	Distribution of retained earnings (DM)	Corporate income and capital yields tax (DM)
Pretax income	100.0	
Corporate income tax on retained earnings (45%)	(45.00)	45.00
Corporate income tax reduction upon distribution (in order to arrive at 30% tax rate for distributed earnings)	15.00	(15.00)
Net dividend distributed	70.00	
Capital yields withholding tax (25%)	(17.50)	17.50
Cash dividend paid	52.50	
Taxes paid		47.50

At resident shareholder level	Dividend income (DM)	Tax credits (DM)
Cash dividend received	52.50	
+Capital yields withholding tax	17.50	17.50
Net dividend	70.00	
+Creditable corporate income tax (30/70 of net dividend)	30.00	30.00
Taxable income subject to individual income or corporate income tax	100.0	47.50

additional child. The same applies to a married couple if one spouse is handicapped or ill.

B1.5 Payment System

The individual income tax is collected either by withholding tax at source or by self-assessment. The former method is applied to wages and salaries and income from capital investment. In the case of self-assessment, the taxpayer sends his or her tax return to the local tax office. The tax payable is determined by the issue of a formal notice of assessment. During the year, quarterly instalments are payable, with a final settlement when the assessment is issued. The quarterly instalments are based on the estimated ultimate income tax liability, which is usually the total tax due as shown by the last assessment issued. Employees from whose earnings tax on wages and salaries is withheld will be assessed for income tax only in certain circumstances, for instance, if their income exceeds DM27,000, or DM54,000 in the case of married couples, if they have additional income other than wages or salaries of more than DM800 or if they claim specific tax reliefs.

B1.6 Indexation for Inflation

German income tax law is strictly based on the nominal-value principle and, therefore, does not provide for indexation, with the effect that the average tax rate on real income increases constantly with inflation. This problem has only been slightly alleviated by adjustments to the basic personal exemption, the tax rates, and, in 1990, by cutting the marginal tax rates in the progressive zone of the income tax schedule, thereby lowering the average tax burden.

B1.7 Penalties and Interests

A penalty of up to 10 percent of the tax due or DM10,000, whichever is lower, can be levied on a taxpayer for late filing. No penalties or fines may be assessed for under-reporting of income, except in the case of tax evasion. A surcharge of 1 percent per month based on the tax liability is assessed if there is late payment. Back taxes and tax refunds, which for any reason are assessed more than 15 months after the end of the relevant tax year, are subject to 0.5-percent interest per month up to a maximum period of 48 months.

B2 Corporate Income Tax

B2.1 Tax Base

The German corporate income tax provides for a full imputation for dividends paid to resident taxpayers (see Table 4.3). Corporations, limited partnerships, and other entities of a similar standing, such as branches of foreign corporations, whose registered domicile or place of management is in Germany, are liable to corporate income tax on their worldwide income irrespective of its source, except where a double tax treaty provides for specific exclusions.

For tax purposes, losses up to a maximum of DM10 million may be carried back to offset profits earned in the preceding two years. Remaining losses can be carried forward indefinitely and offset against the first available taxable

Table 4.4 Depreciation allowances, 1994

Kind of investment	Method	Rate
Equipment	Declining balance	2.5 times the straight-line rate maximum 25%
Construction	Straight line or	4%
	5 years	7%
	6 years	5%
	14 years	2.5%
Inventories	last in, first out	—

income of the following years. Losses incurred in foreign operations through a branch may be set off against domestic profits under specific conditions only and the set-offs will be recovered to the extent the branch subsequently makes a profit. However, in certain circumstances losses from foreign permanent establishments, which normally would be excluded from the tax base under the provisions of a double tax treaty, may be deducted.

Dividend income from a participation in a foreign corporation of 10 percent or more and capital gains derived by a resident corporation from the alienation of shares in a foreign subsidiary or affiliate are exempt from corporate income tax. Foreign corporations conducting business activities in Germany through a permanent establishment are subject to limited tax liability and are taxable only on certain income from sources within Germany (primarily farming and forestry, business income from a permanent establishment or permanent agent, capital investments, rents and royalties from real estate and registered patents, and profits from the sale of real estate sold within two years of purchase).

Net profits are calculated on the basis of historical cost. All expected losses and liabilities and impairments in asset values must be provided for in the form of write-downs or accruals. Unrealized profits, however, may not be included in the tax base until their realization (imparity principle). Inventories are valued at the lower of acquisition cost or cost of production or market value. Costs are allocated if possible on a direct item-by-item basis. The LIFO (last in, first out) method and a moving-average or standard-cost method are approved for the purpose of simplifying the valuation process. The LIFO method has been allowed since 1990, which makes the German business sector less vulnerable to inflation. The FIFO (first in, first out) method is generally accepted only if it can be shown that the method reflects the physical movement of the goods.

Capital gains are taxed on company level as ordinary income at regular tax rates. However, gains resulting from the disposal of land or buildings, or up to 50 percent of the gains from the disposal of assets that for tax purposes have a period of depreciation of more than twenty-five years, or a substantial interest in a corporation or limited liability company may be allocated to a tax-free reserve. This reserve may be deducted from the acquisition cost or cost of production of new land and building or other specific assets within six years of disposal.

Depreciation allowances were increased during the 1970s and the 1980s to bring them closer to international standards, but recently they were reduced slightly. These allowances are shown in Table 4.4.

B2.2 Non-deductible Expenses

The main expenses that are not deductible when computing income for corporate income tax purposes are:

- corporate income tax itself;
- the net worth tax;
- one-half of fees paid to members of the Supervisory Board;
- business gifts in excess of DM75 per recipient per annum;
- 80 percent of expenses incurred in business entertainment;
- fines and other penalties of a punitive nature levied by a court of law; and
- charitable donations and contributions to political parties in excess of the amounts described under Sect. B1.3 above.

Table 4.5 Corporation tax calculation

Assumptions
1. Entity's taxable income after charging all expenditure and all taxes, except taxes on income, amounts to DM1,000,000. The entity has earned none of its profits in West Berlin or Eastern Germany.
2. Except for net assets tax of DM40,000, there are no disallowable charges for corporation tax purposes. For purposes of the income element of the municipal trade tax, DM60,000, representing one-half of the interest on long-term loans, must also be added back.
3. The effective rate of municipal trade tax on income is 15%.
4. The corporation tax charge is to be computed on the basis that a distribution of DM400,000 will be resolved by stockholders.

Income element of municipal trade tax (DM)		
Profit before taxes on income		1,000,000
Add disallowable items:		
Net assets tax	40,000	
Long-term interest (Total: DM120,000)	60,000	100,000
Profits subject to municipal trade tax on income		1,100,000
Tax thereon at the rate of 15%		165,000
Corporation tax (DM)		
Profit before taxes on income		1,000,000
Add net assets tax disallowable		40,000
Profits subject to corporation tax before charging income element of municipal trade tax		1,040,000
Less income element of municipal trade tax as computed above		165,000
Profits subject to corporation tax		875,000
Corporation tax payable 875,000 at 45%		393,750
Tax reduction on distributed profits 400,000 at 15/70 (see note)		(85,714)
Net corporation profits tax payable		308,036

Note: Distribution of a dividend out of profits that have been taxed at 45% always gives rise to a reduction of corporation profits tax of 15. The dividend (which includes the tax refund element) will then have been taxed at 30%, leaving 70% of income before taxes.

Source: Price Waterhouse.

In addition, interest payments under the thin capitalization rules are not deductible. These provisions generally characterize as constructive dividend distribution any interest paid to foreign-related parties where the loan exceeds a debt/equity ratio of 3/1 for operating companies. A safe haven debt/equity ratio of 9/1 applies to German holding companies with respect to non-hybrid debt instruments. More restrictive provisions apply to interest based on profits.

B2.3 Tax Consolidation (Organschaft)

A German corporation can be financially, economically, and organizationally integrated into another resident business enterprise or into a foreign business enterprise that operates a registered branch in Germany, i.e. the parent company (*Organträger*) controls one or more German subsidiaries (*Organgesellschaften*). In that case the entities can conclude a profit-and-loss pooling agreement for a period of at least five years. Under this system profits and losses generated during the term of the agreement of all relevant companies are consolidated.

B2.4 Tax Rates

Corporate tax is levied at a flat rate of 45 percent, which is subsequently reduced to 30 percent for distributed profits. A solidarity surcharge of 7.5 percent of the corporate income tax payable is levied as from 1995 to contribute to the financing of German unification.

Foreign companies subject to limited taxation are taxed at a flat rate of 42 percent regardless of whether or not the income is repatriated. As a branch is legally unable to distribute profits in the form of dividends, remittances of branch income to foreign head offices are not subject to withholding tax. Despite the most recent reductions in tax rates in 1994, Germany's corporate tax rate is still considerably higher than the current average standard rate of roughly 35 percent in the other EU countries, 37.5 percent in Japan, and 35 percent in the USA. Taking into account the German enterprise tax (see Sect. B7 below) and, as of 1995 the 7.5 percent solidarity surcharge, the average tax burden of German corporations is relatively high in relation to other countries (see Tables 4.4 and 4.5).

B2.5 Treatment of Distributed Profits

Taxation of resident shareholders.   Dividend distributions are subject to a 25-percent dividend withholding tax. Gross dividends, including German and foreign withholding taxes and the prepaid corporate income tax on distributed profits are added to taxable income. Under the imputation method, a tax credit (including the solidarity surcharge) is granted to the shareholder, so that the shareholder in the end pays only its individual income or corporate income tax (see Table 4.3). In the event that the shareholder's income tax is lower than the tax credit, a refund is payable. Dividends received by a German

Table 4.6 Corporate taxes—Rates (1994)

Corporation tax (Körperschaftsteuer)

Tax basis—taxable income
Resident corporation: %
   Undistributed profits 45
   Distributed profits 30
Branches of foreign corporations 42
A surcharge of 7.5% of the corporation tax payable will be levied from 1995.

Trade tax (Gewerbesteuer)
Tax basis—Trade income and trade capital
Trade tax: %[a]
   On income 13–21
   On capital[b] 0.6–1.0

Net wealth tax (Vermögensteuer)[c]
Tax basis—Assessed valuation of business net assets or business property over
DM500,000 × 0.75 per annum.
Tax rate—0.6%

Value-added tax (Umsatzsteuer-Mehrwertsteuer)
Tax basis—Proceeds from domestic sales and services; taxable imports; acquisitions
from EU countries.
Tax rates—Generally 15%, with a reduced rate of 7% for some items.

Real estate acquisition tax (Grunderwerbsteuer)
Tax basis—Purchase price or value of consideration received in exchange; if no
purchase price or consideration received in exchange or if all the shares in a real estate-
owning company are acquired, the assessed value of real estate (*Einheitswert*).
Tax rate—2%.

---

[a] Approximate per annum.
[b] This element of the trade is not levied in eastern Germany.
[c] The net assets tax is currently not levied in eastern Germany.
Source: See Table 4.5.

shareholder corporation remain tax-exempt to the extent the dividends were
distributed out of foreign treaty-exempt income. However, the further distribution of such income to the ultimate German individual shareholder will
remain taxable to the recipient. There also is no relief for any foreign tax paid
on the relevant income underlying the distribution.

Taxation of non-resident shareholders. The following specific provisions are
applicable to non-resident shareholders:

- the 25 percent dividend withholding tax may be reduced by a double tax
  treaty (from 1 January 1996, withholding tax on most intercorporate
  dividends within the EU have been abolished); and

● non-residents are not entitled to the 30 percent corporate income tax credit.

B2.6 Small and Medium-Size Enterprises (SMEs) and Tax Incentives.

SMEs may claim accelerated depreciation (see below). Apart from that, there are no special tax rates or tax holidays as investment incentives. There are only few investment concessions or allowances in Germany and most of them are restricted to the five new *Länder* or are aimed at subsidizing specific projects, in particular those related to research and development, environmental protection, etc. Most of the tax concessions may be claimed in the form of accelerated depreciation or untaxed reserves.

B3 Social Security Contributions

The social security system for workers and their families is, to a large extent, financed by compulsory social security contributions from employers and employees. By paying contributions, employees become entitled to receive benefits. These payments are not regarded as government transfers but as insurance benefits. There are five separate branches of the social security system: pension insurance, health insurance, unemployment insurance, work injury insurance, and—beginning in 1995—care insurance for the elderly.

Work injury insurance is distinct from the other systems in that it is financed exclusively by employer's contributions. These contributions are differentiated according to the enterprises' risk categories. Benefits are provided in case of occupational accidents, accidents on the way to work, and occupational diseases. In the remaining branches of social security, contributions are split evenly between employers and employees (the main exception being contributions to the pension system for miners, where the employers' share is larger than the employees' share). The contribution rate is proportional to gross wage up to an insurable ceiling.

Employee's contributions are withheld by the employer from the wage or salary bill and paid together with the employer's share to the relevant health insurance organization. The health insurance organization is responsible for further distribution among the different branches of the social insurance system.

The pension insurance system is characterized by a linkage between contributions and pension payments, although there are some redistributional features in the system. In addition to old-age pensions, there are pensions to survivors and disabled persons. The pension payment is determined by the number of years during which contributions have been paid and by the income position of the worker relative to the average. There are special rules for widows' pensions and pensions to disabled persons. Pensions in West Germany are adjusted annually according to the change in net wages in the two preceding years. Due to the rapid increase in wages and prices since unification, pensions are adjusted twice a year in East Germany according to a special procedure.

It is generally not possible for workers to opt out of the pension system. The contribution rate (employee's share) is 9.6 percent in 1996, up to a taxable ceiling per year of DM96,000 in West Germany and DM81,600 in East Germany. Taxable ceilings are raised each year in accordance with the average increase in wages and salaries.

The pension insurance works on a pay-as-you-go basis. Current contributions are earmarked for current pension payments. Apart from a liquidity reserve, there is no accumulation of assets in the pension insurance system. It is obvious that with population ageing during the first half of the next century, this system will come under pressure and contribution rates will have to be raised considerably and/or benefits cut. Another solution is to raise the retirement age. It is currently 63 for men (under certain conditions it is 65) and 60 for women and it will be raised gradually to 65 for men and women during the first two decades of the next century. Furthermore early retirement which has been used extensively will be reduced.

In case of unemployment, the unemployment insurance pays benefits amounting to 67 percent of the last net wage for insured workers with children and 60 percent for workers without children. The contribution rate (employee's share) is 3.25 percent up to the same insurable ceiling that applies for pension insurance.

The main objective of health insurance is to protect workers against a decline in income as a result of sickness. Health insurance generally covers all costs of medical care and services in case of sickness. As opposed to the pension system, there is a large redistribution in the health insurance: while contributions are proportional to gross wages, benefits are uniform. In addition, children and spouses who are not gainfully employed are insured without paying additional contributions. So there is a redistribution from single persons to families. Another difference compared with pension insurance is that workers can opt out of the system if their earnings are higher than the insurable ceiling, which is 75 percent of the ceiling applied for pension insurance. Contribution rates to health insurance are not uniform as there exist several institutions with a different structure of insured persons. The average contribution rate for 1996 is estimated to be 6.75 percent. The taxable ceiling is DM72,000 in West Germany and DM61,200 in East Germany.

After a controvrsial debate a pay-as-you-go-financed care insurance for the elderly (*Pflegeversicherung*) was finally enacted in 1994. In the first phase, starting in January 1995, only home care is financed. The contribution rate (employee's share) is 0.5 percent of gross wages up to the taxable ceiling applied for health insurance. In the second phase, care in institutions will be covered and the contribution rate (employee's share) will rise to 0.85 percent beginning in July 1996. The care insurance system is operated by health insurance institutions, but financed separately. As in the case of health insurance, workers with gross wages above the taxable ceiling may opt out of the system.

B4 Value-Added Tax

B4.1 Introduction

VAT was introduced in 1968 as a replacement for the previous cascade tax. It is intended to be non-discriminatory, both with regard to imports, compared with products and services of domestic suppliers, and with regard to the number of business entities taking part in the manufacturing and distribution process. VAT is a tax on the net value added at every stage of the production, with a deduction for prepaid VAT on purchases. In practice, suppliers of goods and services must add VAT to the net prices of their sales and pay VAT to the tax offices, with an entitlement to credit for VAT paid on their input. Chapter 1 provides general details of VAT systems, so this section refers only to exemption and rates specific to Germany.

B4.2 Exemptions

The most significant exemptions from VAT are for the following transactions or institutions:

- banking and insurance business;
- sales of land and buildings;
- services of hospitals and medical doctors; and
- most cultural institutions.

B4.3 Tax Rates

As from 1993, the standard VAT rate was raised from 14 to 15 percent, with a reduced rate of 7 percent on sales of specific goods, e.g. certain basic food items, books, newspapers, and antiques, and specific services remaining unchanged. The tax rate of 15 percent is the minimum standard value-added tax rate within the EU. Special tax rates and flat-rate input tax deductions apply to farming and forestry businesses.

B4.4 Assessment System

Taxpayers are required to file monthly tax returns and an annual tax return, which theoretically is a summary of the previous twelve monthly returns, but in practice differs in that adjusting entries and corrections made in the financial statements have to be taken into account. In calculating the monthly or annual VAT liability, any import VAT and input VAT paid upfront on goods and services supplied to the taxpayer may be offset against the VAT that has been charged to customers. The difference is due immediately and a credit will be refunded by the local tax office.

B5 Main Excises

There are a number of excises but two of them—the duty on hydrocarbon oils and the duty on tobacco—are the most important. In 1992, the duty on hydrocarbon oils yielded DM55.1 billion (4.6 percent of total tax revenues, or 7.5 percent of tax receipts excluding social security contributions) and the duty on tobacco yielded DM19.2 billion (1.6 percent of total tax receipts, or 2.6 percent of tax receipts excluding social security contributions). The hydrocarbon oil tax is levied on motor fuel and furnace fuel. The tax on cigarettes is made up of a price-related and a volume-related element. Both the tobacco tax and the hydrocarbon oil tax are harmonized within the EU. Among the other excises, the most important ones are those on alcohol, beer, coffee, and champagne, but their yield amounts to only between about DM1 billion (from the duty on champagne) and DM6 billion (from the duty on alcohol).

B6 Capital Taxes

B6.1 Net Wealth Tax

Federal taxes on net wealth have long been a feature of the German tax system although the yield is relatively small. In 1992, revenues from the net wealth tax amounted to DM12.8 billion (1.1 percent of total tax revenues). Only a quarter of this amount was paid by individuals; the remaining three-fourths was paid by corporations. In addition, the inheritance and gift taxes yielded DM3 billion (0.3 percent of total taxes).

In assessing the wealth tax, all assets are valued according to a set of rules incorporated in the Fiscal Code. Buildings and land are assessed separately from other assets on special dates and with reference to definite periods of time. These 'standard' or 'ratable' values (*Einheitswert*), which have not been regularly computed in recent years, and buildings and land are widely believed to be considerably undervalued. The valuation of the equipment is based on the so-called *Teilwert*, which the tax law defines as the value a potential buyer of the enterprise would place on the individual piece of equipment. For individuals, an amount of DM120,000 (before 1995, DM70,000) is tax-free. The general wealth tax rate for individuals is 1 percent (before 1995, 0.5 percent) and a tax rate of 0.5 percent applies to agricultural and forestry property, business property, and shares in corporations. For corporations the wealth tax rate is 0.6 percent.

B6.2 Capital Transfer Tax

Since 1923 Germany has had an inheritance tax on gifts and at death, the rate varying according to the relationship between donor and donee.

B7 The Local Tax System

The German Constitution guarantees the autonomy of local governments. Following the principle of subsidiarity, communities are responsible for all

Table 4.7   Structure of local public finance in Germany (1992) (% of total receipts)

	West Germany	East Germany
Taxes	38	9
Fees	14	8
Unconditional grants	23	44
Investment grants	6	21
Other receipts	19	18

Source: *Gemeindefinanzbenicht* 1993, authors' calculations.

government functions that can be executed best on the local level. These include, for example, the payment of social assistance. In this case it is argued that means-testing is easier for nearby local authorities than for remote federal or regional agencies. To satisfy the principle of subsidiarity, the yield of certain taxes is assigned to local governments and communities have some discretion in defining tax rates. Giving full financial autonomy to local governments would, however, lead to major differences in tax rates and in the level of public goods and services. 'Wealthy' communities (with a large tax base) could have lower tax rates and nevertheless provide more public goods than 'poor' communities. To achieve a certain uniformity of living conditions, State governments provide differentiated general and specific grants to communities.

Obviously, there is a trade-off between the goals of 'uniformity of living conditions' and 'local autonomy'. As a compromise, local budgets are financed by local revenue as well as by state grants. As shown in Table 4.7, the structure of local public finance differs substantially between communities in former West Germany and East Germany.

While taxes and fees amount to more than half of total receipts in former West Germany communities in East Germany have to rely heavily on state grants. The share of the communities in total tax receipts (excluding social security contributions) was 12.8 percent, or DM96 billion in 1993. The local governments share in the personal income tax (DM45 billion) and the local business tax constitute the lion's share of local tax receipts. A third major source of tax revenue is the real estate tax (DM11.7 billion). The rest is made up by the real property transfer tax (DM0.3 billion) and local consumption and excise taxes (DM1.1 billion). Local governments as a whole receive 15 percent of total personal income tax receipts and 12 percent of the withholding tax on interest. The receipts of each community are linked with the income tax paid by its citizens. The basic idea of the local business tax and the real estate tax is to levy taxes according to the equivalence principle, where profits, capital, and size of property serve as proxies for the amount of local services consumed by local businesses and citizens.

The local business tax is a tax on profits and capital of businesses located in the community. If a business has plants in several communities, the local business tax is divided among them generally according to the share of wage payments in each community. The federal base rate for the local business tax on profits is 5 percent (graduated rates apply for small unincorporated businesses). The corresponding rate for the local business tax on capital (not levied in East Germany) is 0.2 percent. Local governments are allowed (within certain limits) to levy a multiple of the basic tax. There is considerable variation between communities, the average of this multiple being close to 400 percent. The local business tax is deductible from the base for itself and for personal and corporate income taxes.

The local business tax is criticized for several reasons. First, the receipts vary strongly between communities of different size. In 1990, the share in total tax receipts was 54.4 percent in communities with more than 500,000 inhabitants, while it was only 32.5 percent in communities with less than 10,000 inhabitants.

Second, the receipts of the tax on profits varies considerably with the business cycle. To stabilize local government finance, communities were granted a share of the less volatile personal income tax in 1970. In exchange, a (varying) part of the local business tax receipts (10 percent of gross receipts in 1993) has to be transferred to federal and state governments.

Third, the tax on business capital (like the net wealth tax) has to be paid even when businesses incur losses.

The local business tax on profits constitutes a special burden for taxpayers receiving income from business activity, as income from self-employment, agriculture, and forestry is exempt from local business tax. As a remedy, a special tax concession for income from business (limitation of marginal tax rate to 47 percent) was introduced in the personal income tax code in 1993. This is generally regarded as an element of schedular taxation that should be removed as soon as possible.

The local real estate tax applies to real estate of farming and forestry enterprises, as well as to land and buildings. As in the case of the local business tax, a basic federal rate is applied to the standard value of the real estate to achieve the basic real property tax, to which local authorities apply their own multipliers. Thus, the actual rate paid thus varies across the country. Furthermore, there are local consumption and excise taxes, which include, for example, entertainment taxes, beverage taxes, dog taxes, and hunting and fishing taxes.

C. Economic and Social Aspects

C1 The Fiscal Deficit

In the past, the general government deficit (National Accounts basis) fluctuated between 1.5 to 2.5 percent of GDP. This range was only exceeded during the recessions in the mid-1970s and the early 1980s, and after these events the government made major efforts to restrain spending to reduce the

deficit and to stabilize the debt/GDP ratio. This policy was especially successful during the second half of the 1980s and by 1989, the general government
budget was in small surplus.

At the beginning of the 1990s various factors contributed to a sharp
deterioration of the budget: the income tax cut in 1990; higher government
spending in West Germany, especially at the local level, in the aftermath of the
economic boom; the beginning of the reconstruction of East German public
infrastructure; and the current transfers to East Germany (including transfers
to the social security sector). The flow of transfers from the west to the east
amounts to about 5 percent of GDP per year, and during the five-year period
1991 to 1995, these transfers amounted to about DM760 billion. If the deficit
of the privatization agency (*Treuhandanstalt*) is included, transfers from the
west to the east during 1991 to 1995 amounted to almost DM900 billion for
East Germany, or more than DM50,000 per East German citizen.

Since unification, the share of government outlays in GDP increased by
about 5 percentage points. While in 1989, West Germany had a (gross) debt/
GDP ratio of 43 percent, it increased to almost 60 percent by the mid-1990s,
which is equal to the Maastricht Treaty's upper limit. This increase reflects the
takeover of old and new Eastern German debt, as well as high government
deficits in West Germany that are to some extent related to the cyclical
weakness of the economy during 1993.

As with the situation in the aftermath of the recession in the early 1980s,
the government took various measures to restrain spending in order to
reduce the deficit and to make room for future tax cuts after the recent
tax increases. The central government plans to reduce its deficit from DM70
billion in 1993 to DM25 billion by 1998. General government spending
(excluding social security) is projected to increase by not more than 3 percent
per year in the years ahead, which would reduce the share of public spending
in GDP significantly. Although the task of fiscal consolidation appears to be
more difficult now given the cost of unification and higher structural unemployment in Germany, it is expected that the general government deficit
(amounting to 3.6 percent of GDP in 1995 and still above the Maastricht
Treaty's upper limit of 3 per cent) will decline steadily to 1.5 to 2.5 percent of
GDP in the coming years.

C2 Incentives

C2.1 Savings Incentives

From the view of the comprehensive income tax concept, all features of a tax
system that allow for a deduction of income saved and/or do not tax interest
income at normal rates can be regarded as savings incentives. Taking this
traditional view, there are many important savings incentives in Germany. The
most important perhaps is the savings allowance of DM6,000/12,000 (singles/

married couples) that exempts about 80 percent of taxpayers from paying tax on interest and dividend income.

Another major tax relief concerns old-age pensions and life insurance. Employee contributions to public pension insurance are deductible from the income tax base, subject to a ceiling of DM2,610/5,220. Half of the remaining expenses can be deducted up to a limit of DM1,305/2,610. These ceilings apply, however, to the sum of contributions to pension, health, and un-employment insurance, the new care insurance for the elderly, and private providence expenses. Mainly for the self-employed, an additional allowance of up to DM6,000 (DM12,000 for married couples) is granted. In addition, there is a very favourable tax treatment of pension payments exempting nearly all pensioners from income tax.

Employer contributions are tax-exempt when made to a statutory pension scheme. In addition, taxable employer contributions to company pension schemes are liable to a flat-rate wage tax of 15 percent, leading to a tax expenditure of DM2.2 billion in 1994. Premia for life insurance are deductible within the limits mentioned above if the policy is taken out for at least twelve years or does not contain a savings component (revenue loss: DM 3.7 billion in 1994). Interest occurring in life insurance is not taxed. So life insurance saving is heavily subsidized by tax policy. It is often argued that this preferential treatment channels savings into less productive investments.

Another important part of household savings that enjoys preferential tax treatment is owner-occupied housing. There are several provisions in the income tax law:

- tax credit DM5,000 for eight years for new constructed buildings;
- tax credit of DM2,500 for eight years for purchasing existing houses or flats;
- additional tax credit of DM1,500 per child for eight years;
- lump-sum allowance of DM3,500 for financing costs in advance of construction/acquisition.

Savings are not only promoted by tax incentives but also by savings premia. Under the law for Promoting Capital Formation by Employees, a bonus of 10 percent is paid if part of the employee's wages, up to a ceiling of DM936 per annum, is invested in the company's assets (shares especially) or in a building and loan association. Employees are eligible for the bonus if their taxable income is not higher than DM27,000 (DM54,000 for married couples). Under the Law on the Payment of Premiums for Financing the Construction of Residential Properties, a housing bonus is paid for contributions to building and loan associations, of 10 percent for annual ceiling of DM1,000 (DM2,000 for married couples). This bonus applies where payments made are not 'capital-creative' under the Law for Promoting Capital Formation by Employees. In order to be eligible, taxable income must not exceed DM50,000/100,000 (singles/married couples). It is not possible to claim both the housing bonus and the partial deduction of contributions to Building and Loan Associations from the income tax base.

C2.2 Investment Incentives

Since German unification investment incentives for West Berlin and the border area are being phased out and promotion of investment is concentrated on East Germany. The most important measures are the introduction of an investment tax credit and of accelerated depreciation allowances for investment in the new *Länder*.

The investment tax credit is confined to investment in equipment. In order to reduce investment promotion as the economic situation improves, the investment tax credit is reduced from 12 percent (for investment completed between January 1991 and July 1992), over 8 percent (for investment begun before January 1993 and completed between July 1992 and January 1995), and to 5 percent (for investments begun after January 1993 and completed before January 1997). Some sectors, such as banks and insurances, electricity and gas supply, and trade are excluded from the tax credit.

To promote capital formation by native East German citizens, an increased investment tax credit of 20 percent was introduced in 1993 for investment of enterprises owned by persons who lived in former GDR on 9 November 1989. This tax credit was confined to manufacturing and crafts and limited to investment volumes up to DM1 million annually. However, this special tax credit proved to be out of line with EC law because it discriminated against investors from EU countries. As a consequence, recent legislation abolished this special measure for investment after 1 January 1995, and introduced a new special tax credit of 10 percent that is available for all investors in manufacturing and crafts under the following conditions: (i) the maximum investment amount that can benefit from the increased rate is DM5 million (for investment in excess of this amount, the normal rate of 5 percent can be claimed) and (ii) only businesses with less than 250 employees may claim the increased tax credit. The basic idea behind this special investment incentive is to channel investment into the manufacturing sector, where economic development (in contrast to services and construction) has been slow and where it has proved most difficult to generate small and medium-sized enterprises. The loss of income tax revenue due to the investment tax credit in East Germany is estimated to be DM5.5 billion in 1994.

An accelerated depreciation allowance is granted for investment in the new states. In contrast to the investment tax credit, this measure applies not only to movable assets but also to buildings. The maximum depreciation rate is 50 percent of construction/acquisition cost; corresponding tax expenditures are estimated to be DM2.4 billion in 1994.

Claiming the investment tax credit and the accelerated depreciation allowance is not mutually exclusive. Additional incentives for investment in housing in the new States is provided by special depreciation allowances and partial

Table 4.8 Income tax distribution (1993)

Upper per cent of taxpayers	Income subject to tax above (DM)	Share (%) of	
		Taxable income	Income tax
5	125,800	25.1	39.6
10	100,000	35.9	50.5
15	86,300	44.7	58.7
20	76,700	52.2	65.4
25	68,900	58.9	71.1
30	62,600	64.8	76.0
35	57,400	70.0	80.2
40	52,500	74.8	84.1
45	48,200	79.2	87.5
50	43,800	83.2	90.5

Source: Ministry of Finance.

deductibility of expenses (revenue loss: DM0.7 billion in 1994). In addition, the fact that neither the local business tax on capital nor the wealth tax is levied in East Germany can be regarded as an incentive to invest.

Besides these measures targeted at investment in East Germany, there are several nationwide incentives to invest in housing and in small and medium-sized enterprises. The incentives to invest in housing (in addition to the already described measures to promote owner-occupied housing) include special depreciation for investment in: (i) the creation of new flats in existing houses, (ii) modernization and reconditioning of old houses in reconstruction areas, (iii) preservation of historical buildings, and (iv) flats for tenants with low income (with a limit on rents) (total revenue loss: DM0.7 billion in 1994). A special depreciation allowance for investment in energy-saving measures (installation of new boilers, use of alternative energy sources, etc.) is ending, but still leads to a revenue loss of DM0.4 billion in 1994.

Tax concessions for small and medium-sized enterprises are twofold. Small businesses are entitled to claim an extra depreciation allowance of 20 percent on equipment investment. This leads to a revenue loss of DM1 billion in 1994. A second concession, which will come into effect on 1 January 1995, allows these businesses to build up tax-free reserves for future investment. This reserve can amount to up to half of the costs of acquisition/construction. If the investment does not occur until the end of the second year, the reserve has to be dissolved. Tax expenditures resulting from this investment incentive are estimated to be DM0.9 billion in 1995. New measures in order to promote energy-saving investments in housing were introduced recently (estimated revenue loss: DM50 million).

C3 Distribution of Tax Burden

Although no statistical data are available for the total tax burden, there are estimates by the Federal Ministry of Finance for the distribution of the personal income tax burden in 1993. These estimates are based on the income tax statistics provided by the Federal Statistical Office for West Germany and survey data provided by a major German research institute (DIW) for East Germany. The tax burden is simulated using a microsimulation model on income taxation assuming formal incidence. Table 4.8 stresses the progressive nature of the German income tax schedule:

According to these estimates, the upper half of taxpayers bears about 90 percent of the income tax burden, while their share in taxable income is 83 percent. The 5 percent of taxpayers with the highest incomes have one-quarter of taxable income but pay almost 40 percent of the income tax.

C4 The Hidden Economy

From the public finance point of view, the hidden economy causes two major problems: first, there is tax fraud (especially with wage tax, social security contributions, VAT), and second, there is unwarranted payment of social benefits (unemployment insurance and social assistance) due to fraudulent claims. Both problems become most severe in times of economic recession, when public budgets are exposed to declining tax receipts and rising social security expenditures. So it is not by chance that the German government started an initiative to reduce the amount of illicit work in 1993.

Two main species of illicit work can be distinguished.

First, enterprises that employ workers without delivering wage taxes and social security benefits to the authorities. This has become an increasing problem in Germany mainly in the construction sector. Since the borders to eastern Europe were opened some years ago, it is very tempting to employ workers from these countries at low wages (by western, not by eastern standards!) and without paying taxes for these workers. Recent efforts by the Federal Ministry of Labour and Social Affairs have concentrated, there-fore, on controls of building sites. In many cases, illegal workers unlawfully receive unemployment benefits or social assistance.

Second, there are craftsmen with regular employment who work during their spare time without paying VAT and income tax. While illegal employ-ment—if discovered—is generally undeniable, this second kind of illegal work is often not as easy to prove. The borderline between such work to help within the family and to help neighbours and friends is sometimes not easy to distinguish.

To restrain illicit employment, a social security card for all employees was introduced in July 1991. This card contains the name of the employee and his or her social security number. In sectors where offences against social security and tax laws are most widespread, the card also shows a photo of the employee. Employees in these sectors (especially construction and room cleaning) are obliged to carry the social security card with them at work, thus alleviating controls. The increased control effort of the labour authorities led to additional tax revenue and a decline in expenditures on social benefits.

For part-time work, social security and tax laws provide incentives to stay in the 'official' economy by reducing the tax burden: if working time is less than 15 hours a week and monthly wages do not exceed DM560/440 (old states/new states) in 1994, wages are exempt from social security contributions (employer's and employee's shares). If these wage limits are not exceeded and monthly working hours are less than 86, the employer can take over the payment of the wage tax at a lump-sum rate of 15 percent. This rate is even reduced to 3 percent for part-time employees in agriculture and forestry.

The problems of transition from social assistance to legal employment are currently being discussed intensively in Germany. As social assistance is means-tested and additional wage income reduces social assistance by the full amount (withdrawal rate of 100 percent), the incentive to take up regular employment is low. Instead, social assistance payments are quite often supplemented by wage income from illicit work. The concept of a negative income tax with marginal tax rates substantially below 100 percent in the negative branch has been discussed, but at present it is not likely to be introduced. As taxation would start at relatively high-income levels, it would lead to high revenue losses.

Reliable data for the size of the hidden economy in Germany are not available. While more recent estimates based on microdata conclude that the product of the hidden economy amounts to only about 1 percent of GDP, earlier macroeconomic studies arrive at values up to 10 percent.

C5 Administrative and Compliance Costs

In recent years, tax laws have been complicated by a large number of new tax provisions, which have increased the administrative burden on the fiscal authorities and compliance costs for taxpayers. The point has been reached where tax inspectors are hardly able to apply all regulations properly. Recent tax legislation therefore aimed at simplification and some progress was made:

- the system of child relief was simplified by replacing a complicated system with child allowance, income-related child benefits, and additional child benefits for taxpayers with low income by a tax credit not related to income and an option to choose a child allowance in the tax assessment (the latter will be relevant only for about 5 percent of families and the comparison of the relief of child benefits and child allowance is done automatically by the tax administration);

- the system of tax relief for owner-occupied housing was simplified with respect to eligibility;
- the number of lump-sum allowances for additional expenditures on food during official journeys has been reduced drastically;
- the fringe benefit from private use of business cars has been quantified as 1 percent of the cars purchase-price per month;
- a lump-sum deduction for costs related to income from letting and leasing was introduced; and
- the exemption level for VAT for small enterprises was raised from DM25,000 to DM32,500.

This progress is, however, only partial and efforts have to be increased to achieve a further simplification of tax laws and a reduction of compliance costs.

D. Tax Reforms

D1 Main Tax Reforms 1987–96

Tax reforms in the years between 1987 and 1993 can be divided into two phases, the watershed being German unification in 1990. The first phase was dominated by a major income tax reform carried out in three steps in 1986, 1988, and 1990. The basic idea of this reform was, as in several other industrial countries during the 1980s, to broaden the tax base and reduce tax rates. In total the reform led to a net tax reduction in revenues of about DM50 billion.

The first step (net relief: DM10.9 billion) was to reintroduce a child allowance, to increase the basic allowance, and to reduce tax rates slightly. The second step, in 1988 (net relief: DM13.7 billion) saw a major reduction in tax rates and a further increase in the basic allowance. The special depreciation allowance for small and medium-sized enterprises was enlarged.

Most important was, however, the third reform step in 1990 that brought a net tax relief of DM24.7 billion. At the core of this reform was the introduction of a so-called linear-progressive tax schedule with linear increases in marginal tax rates in an income range covering the bulk of taxpayers. The top rate was reduced from 56 to 53 percent, and the lowest rate from 22 to 19 percent. At the same time, the corporate income tax rate for retained earnings was reduced from 56 to 50 percent. The child allowance was increased from DM2,284 to DM3,024 in this final reform step. Deductibility of insurance contributions was increased mainly for the self-employed. While there was no base broadening in the first two steps, some tax concessions were curtailed in 1990.

The 10 percent withholding tax on interest income that had been introduced in January 1989 was abolished already in June 1989 after massive outflows of capital had occurred during the year. At the same time, the savings exemption was doubled. The year 1989 also saw a major increase in the excises on hydrocarbon oil and tobacco and in the insurance tax, amounting to a total of DM8.8 billion.

To sum up, tax reforms between 1987 and 1990 brought a shift of tax burden from direct to indirect taxes. There was, however, a considerable net relief. This is reflected in the reduction of total tax revenue as percentage of GDP from 38 percent in 1987 to 36.8 percent in 1990.

Immediately after German unification in 1990, it became clear that the huge transfer payments to East Germany required increases in tax receipts. The first straightforward step was to phase out tax concessions for West Berlin and border areas beginning in July 1991. The additional revenue amounted to DM9.9 billion. Part of these receipts was immediately used to promote investment in East Germany through special depreciation allowances (DM1.9 billion) and investment tax credits (DM2.2 billion). These investment incentives were extended to 1996 in 1992–3.

Tax revenue was further increased by the so-called 'solidarity law' enacted in 1991. It introduced a 7.5 percent surcharge on taxpayers' personal and corporate income tax liability for one year (July 1991 to June 1992), yielding DM22 billion in total. In addition, taxes on hydrocarbon oil (additional revenue: DM13.1 billion), insurance premia (additional revenue: DM1.9 billion), and tobacco (additional revenue: DM0.9 billion) were raised substantially.

Another major tax reform package was enacted in 1992. It reduced several tax concessions, but it also increased child benefits and allowances amounting to a total of DM6.7 billion. The normal VAT rate was raised from 14 percent to 15 percent, yielding DM12.3 billion. On the other hand, revenue from local business tax was reduced by DM2.3 billion due to the introduction of several new concessions, mainly for small unincorporated businesses. In total, the package brought an additional tax yield of DM4.8 billion.

Besides fiscal pressures caused by unification, several judgments of the Constitutional Court were a major driving force for tax changes since 1990. In 1990, the court decided that the child allowance had been too low because the minimum costs of childraising were not exempt from income taxation. This led to the already mentioned increase in child allowances and child benefits (serving as a partial substitute for tax allowances) in 1992. Following the same line of reasoning, the court decided in 1992 that the basic allowance was much too low because the subsistence level (measured by the level of social assistance payments) was not free of income tax. Legislation on this issue was finalized in 1995 (see below).

A third important decision of the Constitutional Court dealt with taxation of interest income. The judgment here was that it is not sufficient to state in the tax code that interest income is taxable: compliance has to be enforced. In reaction to this judgment, a 30-percent withholding tax on interest was introduced in 1993. At the same time, the savings exemption was raised from DM600/1,200 (singles/couples) to DM6,000/12,000, relieving about 80 percent of taxpayers from paying tax on interest. Another important feature of this tax act was an expansion in the deduction of insurance contributions and an increase in the exemption for pensions (total revenue loss: DM5.2 billion).

As in 1989, there was a massive outflow of capital in 1993, mainly to Luxembourg. But in contrast to the short-lived withholding tax of 1989, the new withholding tax exempts foreigners. Therefore, capital flowed back into Germany via 'foreign' investment funds. So this time, the introduction of the withholding tax on interest did not result in problems for the German capital market but 'only' in tax evasion.

Three major tax reform packages were enacted in 1993. The first aimed at improving tax conditions for businesses. Due to fiscal constraints, the reform was designed to be roughly revenue-neutral. Corporate income tax rates on retained and distributed profits were reduced from 50 percent to 45 percent and from 36 to 30 percent, respectively. The marginal personal income tax rate on income from business was limited to 47 percent. A special balance reserve scheme was introduced from small and medium-sized enterprises. These measures were mainly financed by less generous depreciation allowances.

The second act contained further major tax increases, mainly coming into effect in January 1995. The solidarity surcharge of 7.5 percent on the personal and corporate income tax was reintroduced (this time without time limitation, although with the intention to abolish it after the fiscal situation has improved) with a prospective annual yield of DM30 billion. Net wealth tax rates were doubled from 0.5 percent to 1 percent, while the personal allowance was raised from DM70,000 to DM120,000 (additional yield: DM1 billion). Insurance tax rates were raised in two steps (July 1993 and January 1995), finally reaching the VAT tax rate of 15 percent (as insurance premia are free of VAT, insurance tax can be thought of as a substitute). In addition, the act further limited several tax concessions. Finally, in December 1993, another attempt was made to cut back tax concessions and to fight tax fraud. As a result of this tax law, an additional yield of DM3.6 billion was expected.

In the context of the privatization of the German railway companies (take-over of debts by the federal government), the tax on hydrocarbon oil was increased again at the end of 1993, yielding additional revenue of DM8.5 billion in 1994.

Due to new legislation over a short time-period, tax laws have been seriously complicated. On the other hand, there have been some simplifications as well. Seven taxes were completely abolished: the stock exchange transactions tax (1991), the company tax (1992), the bills of exchange tax (1992), and the excises on salt, sugar, tea, and lamps (1993). Another important simplification was the introduction of a lump-sum allowance of DM2,000 for work-related expenses in 1990, relieving most workers from listing their expenses in the income tax assessment. Net wealth-tax and local business tax on capital have not been introduced in East Germany, which can be thought of as a first step towards abolishing these taxes altogether.

While the total tax burden increased substantially between 1990 and 1993, not all groups of taxpayers were hit equally. The additional burden on single persons was higher than the additional burden for families. Tax concessions for families rose—in spite of fiscal constraints—from DM14 billion in 1990 to DM22.1 billion in 1993.

The most urgent problem to be solved by tax legislation in 1995 was to exempt subsistence income from income tax. As noted above, in 1992, the German Constitutional Court declared the basic allowance (or better: the zero-rated range in the tax schedule) unconstitutional because it was so low that low-wage earners, although taxed, might have to apply for social assistance.

The court demanded to solve the problem immediately for low-wage earners and that a new tax schedule be introduced beginning in 1996. Parliament reacted by creating a transitionary provision for 1993–5, exempting taxpayers earning less than DM10,500/21,000 (singles/married couples) in 1993, DM11,000/22,000 in 1994, and DM11,500/23,000 in 1995 from paying income tax. For other taxpayers, the normal tax schedule still applied. 'Earnings' in this case were defined much more comprehensively than 'taxable income'. So, for example, the full amount of old-age pensions, which generally were only partially taxed, was regarded as 'earnings', and special allowances, such as for housing, were added to 'taxable income' to arrive at 'earnings'. These provisions made the transitionary solution quite 'cheap' (income tax revenue was reduced by DM2.2 billion in 1993, DM3.1 billion in 1994, and DM3.8 billion in 1995). The major drawback was, however, that effective marginal tax rates were about 60 percent (1993 and 1994) and 50 percent (1995) respectively, in a very narrow income range above the exemption level, in order to return to the 'normal' tax schedule.

A straightforward solution for 1996 would, of course, have been to increase the basic allowance from current DM5,616 to about DM12,000, but this solution would have led to losses in tax receipts of more than DM40 billion. Another solution, which was explicitly offered by the Constitutional Court would have been to limit tax losses by increasing marginal tax rates, thus phasing out the effect of the increased basic allowance.

The Minister of Finance had asked a group of independent experts for advice in this matter. The expert group recommended increasing the basic allowance from DM5,616/11,232 to DM13,000/26,000, increasing the starting flat rate from 19 percent to 22 percent, and significantly broadening the tax base. The latter would imply full taxation of most income transfers. Legislation did, however, not follow the experts' proposals as they were thought to be 'too radical'.

The system of child relief was restructured completely beginning in 1996. During the year all families receive tax credits (DM200 per month for the first and second child, DM300 per month for the third child, and DM360 per month for the fourth and subsequent children), that either reduce the withholding tax on wages (for the great majority of employees) or are paid out in cash. In the income tax assessment the tax administration checks if the deduction of a child allowance of DM6,264—the estimated subsistence level of a child—leads to higher relief. This is, however, only the case for a small minority of taxpayers with very high marginal tax rates. The latter provision makes sure that the subsistence level of children is in effect exempted from income tax in all cases without having to raise the child tax credits further.

A reform of the tax provisions for owner-occupied housing was enacted in 1995. The most important feature is the revenue-neutral replacement of the partial deduction of the cost of construction/acquisition by a system of tax credits. This leads to a shift in tax expenditures from higher-income taxpayers to taxpayers with average or lower income. The additional tax credit for children was increased from DM1,000 to DM1,500 per child. Contributions to building and loan associations are no longer tax-deductible, but on the other hand the income ceilings and the maximum saving amounts for the housing bonus were raised considerably.

In 1995 the Constitutional Court decided that the very different valuation of assets for the purpose of net wealth tax and inheritance and gift tax was unconstitutional. While e.g. shares and bonds were included at market value, the valuation of immobile assets was much lower than market value. As a consequence, the net wealth tax will be abolished altogether in 1997. The resulting revenue loss of DM9.3 billion for the *Länder* will be, however, to a large extent compensated by increases in other tax revenue. The inheritance and gift tax was modified with a higher valuation of immobile assets leading to additional revenue of DM2.1 billion. The tax rate of the real property transfer tax was raised from 2 to 3.5 percent yielding additional revenue of DM5.3 billion. In total, the compensation amounts to DM8.1 billion.

D2 Prospective Tax Reforms

There is general agreement among the major political parties that the local business tax on business capital should be abolished and that the communities should get a share of VAT instead.

Furthermore, a fundamental tax reform was planned for 1999. It was envisaged to reduce income tax rates significantly (top marginal rate from 53 per cent to 39 per cent and lowest marginal rate from 25.9 per cent to 15 per cent) and also to reduce corporate income tax rates to 35 per cent (retained profits) and 32 per cent (distributed profits). The solidarity surcharge was planned to be phased out. Reductions in tax rates would have led to a total tax relief of about DM100 billion but it was also planned to broaden the income tax base and to raise indirect taxes which would limit revenue losses. However, this tax reform plan of the Kohl government was rejected by opposition parties and did not pass the Bundestat. Nevertheless, there is general agreement that fundamental tax reform remains on the political agenda.

5 Italy

LAURA CASTELLUCCI

A. Overview

After the enactment of the basic tax reform of 1973–4, and through the 1980s until the beginning of the 1990s, the Italian tax system underwent a process of rationalization, simplification, and, to some degree, of convergence towards something like a typical 'European tax system', whatever that may be. During this period direct taxes grew more than indirect ones and became the most important source of revenue. Among direct taxes the personal income tax consolidated its position as the pillar of the system (in 1989 revenue from direct taxes was for the first time higher than that of social security contributions). The number of personal income tax rates was reduced and to a level that now corresponds more to that of other European countries. The average tax burden reached that generally prevailing in Europe, while in the 1990s the increase in tax revenue was unusual in the context of OECD Europe, being around 4.5 percentage points over the period 1990–3, of which 3.5 percentage points were reached in the last two years. From the point of view of tax collection no one can deny (and no one does) the 'success' of the basic reform of the 1970s and of the subsequent adjustments. From the conventional equity and efficiency points of view, evaluations can diverge as indicated later in the presentation of specific topics.

This chapter refers mainly to what has happened since 1986, which was the year of reference of the previous chapter on Italy in the volume *Comparative Tax Systems: Europe, Canada, and Japan*, ed. by J. A. Pechman (Tax Analysts, Arlington, 1987). Two possible scenarios may be envisaged in the period from 1987 to 1997 according to two different attitudes towards the tax system. From the beginning of the period until the 1990s the aim was to continue the rationalization and modernization of the system along certain commonly shared lines with their roots in the basic reform of the 1970s and having equity considerations as the main focus. In the 1990s, and especailly since 1992, it has become quite difficult to identify any rationale behind the fragmented interventions, too often disrupting what was built over many years, apart from getting more revenue in the short term. This might prove to be dangerous both in terms of revenue in the longer run and of equity (not to

I wish to thank Ken Messere for his expert comments on successive drafts of this chapter.

mention efficiency). In practice the 1990s have been characterized by the introduction of new tax provisions followed shortly by their temporary or permanent repeal. This was the case with the capital gains tax, enacted in 1991 and 'temporarily' suspended since 1993. This was also the case with the so-called 'minimum tax' enacted in 1992 and which practically vanished in 1994, and so on. Worse than this, most recently a harmful tax amnesty for 'building laws violations' (*abusi edilizi*) was introduced in December 1994. The expected revenue of L7,000 billion was the only motivation for the provision, which may prove to further impair compliance and to increase offences against environment and building regulations. Even a building built totally without building licence, which under the current 'urban and land planning' legislation (*legislazione urbanistica*) would have to be demolished, may now be legalized simply by making the appropriate payment under the new provision.[1]

B. The Tax System

B1 Individual Income Tax

B.1.1 Tax Base and Tax Rates

The individual income tax (IRPEF, *Imposta sul reddito delle persone fisiche*) is, but only in principle, a comprehensive income tax (see below). Total taxable income (TTI) is obtained by subtracting from total gross income (a concept approximately equivalent to the US 'adjusted gross income') a number of income (or non-personal) deductions. Tax rates from the rate schedule are then applied to get gross tax liability (GTL). From GTL a number of tax (or personal) credits or deductions are subtracted to get net tax liability (NTL), which is the amount finally due by the taxpayer. Tax rates and income brackets were revised several times and reduced in number (Table 5.1). Adjustments for inflation took both the form of changes in tax deductions, which was the usual form in Italy and one which complicated an already complicated system of deductions and corrupts its logic, and a new and more proper form of indexation enacted in 1990 (see Section B1.6 below).

Italy has two types of tax relief: deductions from taxable income (Table 5.2) and from tax due (Table 5.3) The latter play a particularly important role in the individual income tax and vary with the source and level of income.[2] With regard to the source of income a distinction is made between income from

---

[1] Such payments are indeed taxes (albeit extraordinary or *una tantum*) because they are introduced precisely as a new source of revenue by transforming the breaking of building and environment laws into a special tax base.

[2] It could be argued that the practical complications caused by this double system of deductions are not worth while, but no change in present policies is anticipated. On the contrary there has always been a great deal of discussion in Italy about these different types of deductions and about their different consequences in terms of equity, as Tables 5.2 and 5.3 indicate.

Table 5.1 Taxable income brackets (million) and tax rates (%) under personal income tax (IRPEF) (various years)

1986		1987–8		1989		1993–1996	
Income brackets	Tax rates	Income brackets	Tax rates	Income brackets	Tax rates	Income brackets	Tax rates
up to 6	12	up to 6	12	up to 6	10	up to 7.2	10
6–12	22	6–11	22	6–12	22	7.2–14.4	22
12–30	27	11–28	27	12–30	26	14.4–30	27
30–50	34	28–50	34	30–60	33	30–60	34
50–100	41	50–100	41	60–150	40	60–150	41
100–150	48	100–150	48	150–300	45	150–300	46
150–300	53	150–300	53	over 300	50	over 300	51
300–600	58	300–600	58				
over 600	62	over 600	62				

dependent employment and pensions on the one hand, and income from self-employment and unincorporated business on the other. Originally the underlying idea was to adhere to a principle called the 'qualitative discrimination of incomes', which has a long tradition in the history of the Italian tax system. Although its reasons (the traditional ones for taxing capital income more than labour income) are now widely regarded as much weaker than decades ago, it still has some validity. Changes in tax deductions have been made in order to adjust for the tax rate escalation due to inflation, but they have openly favoured pension and dependent employment income. More recently such preferential treatment has been more justified on the ground that there is much more evasion among the self-employed and small entrepreneurs than among employees and pensioners.[3] As Table 5.3 indicates, tax deductions for self-employed are *much* lower than ones for dependent wages and salaries, and have been further reduced especially since 1985, and more narrowly concentrated on really low incomes. Such substantial source discrimination at low-income levels seems to me to be somewhat irrational.

B1.2 Treatment of Capital Gains

One of the reasons why the individual income tax is only in principle a comprehensive income tax is the treatment of capital gains in particular

[3] This seems to be the case in all countries: there are categories which are inherently 'difficult to tax' (this was one of the topics addressed by the IIPF Conference on *Public Finance and Irregular Activities*, Berlin, 23–6 Aug. 1993. See e.g. A. Das-Gupta, 'A Theory of Hard-to-Tax Groups'). Nonetheless I do believe that such preferential treatment of wage earners only hurts the honest non-wage income taxpayer and certainly does not solve the problem of tax evasion. The real reason, at least in Italy, is more likely to be the government's wish to please the unions, which are generally opposed to non-wage earners.

Table 5.2   Main deductions from taxable income under personal income tax (IRPEF)

1993[a]

1. Compulsory health contributions
2. L85,000 (compulsory lump-sum medicare contribution, per head)
3. Voluntary contributions to various religious institutions (subject to different limitations in amount and destination)
4. 25% of certain energy-saving expenses made by property owners (the deductible expenses are fixed by a law of 15.2.1992)
5. Voluntary contributions to LDCs (up to a maximum of 2% of total income)
6. Alimony
7. Certain health expenses for the handicapped
8. Other

1986

1. Local income tax (ILOR)
2. Interest paid on mortgage loans, up to L4 million
3. Interest paid on agricultural loans
4. Medical expenses (specialist care, surgical, dental, etc.)
5. Funeral expenses, up to L1 million
6. Fees for private high school and college (up to the fees of corresponding state schools and colleges)
7. Compulsory social security contributions
8. Non-compulsory social security contributions and life insurance premia (up to L2.5 million)
9. Maintenance and restoration expenses for 'historical and artistic' building (when necessary and certified)
10. Alimony
11. Other

---

[a] Deductions from taxable income were severely restricted in 1993. On equity grounds it has been chosen not to favour high-income taxpayers with income deductions. Some deductions from taxable income allowed in the past were changed into deductions, by an amount equal to 27% of the deductible expense, from gross tax liability. By 1996 items 2, 4, and 6 above had been abolished.

and of financial capital income in general. In the area of capital gains the general logic of the 1973–4 tax reform was (i) to restrict taxation to capital gains on physical assets, and (ii) to require the existence of a speculative motive in the transaction giving rise to the capital gain. To tax the capital gain earned on a physical asset the revenue authorities must prove the existence of a speculative motive, except when it is presumed *de jure* (in which case the taxpayer cannot object). The *de jure* presumption is based on the length of time between the acquisition and disposition of the physical asset. In the case of land and real estate it is five years, for works of art and antiquities it is two years. The tax base is the difference between the sale and purchase

Table 5.3 Main deductions from gross tax liability under personal income tax (IRPEF), 1993, 1986, and 1985

	Item		Credit (L)
1993			
Family composition	Spouse (at home, with income less than L5.1 million)		757,000
	Dependent children (each)		87,500
	When taxpayer is a widow/er: first child		757,000
	every other child		175,000
	Other dependent relatives (each)		121,000
Other credits (slightly changed in 1996)	Dependent workers (wages, salaries and pensions):	up to 13.90m.	994,000
		up to 14.00m.	955,000
		up to 14.10m.	877,000
		up to 60.00m.	797,000
		up to 60.06m.	777,000
		up to 60.12m.	747,000
		over 60.12m.	727,000
	Self-employed and unincorporated	up to 7.60m.	189,000
		up to 7.70m.	155,000
		up to 7.80m.	72,000
		over 7.80m.	0
Deductions by an amount equal to 27% of the deductible expense (22% since 1996)	1. Medical expenses (specialist care, surgery, dental, etc.) 2. Interest paid on mortgage loans, up to L4 million (with different provisions for mortgages stipulated before and after 1993) 3. Interest paid on agricultural loans (up to the income of the piece of land concerned). Abolished in 1996 4. Funeral expenses, up to L1 million 5. Fees for private high school and college (up to the fees of corresponding state schools and colleges 6. Non-compulsory social security contributions and life insurance premia (up to L2.5 million) 7. Other		
1986			
Family composition	Spouse (at home, with income less than L3 million)		360,000
	Dependent children (each)		48,000
	When taxpayer is a widow(er): first child		360,000
	every other child		96,000
	Other dependent relatives (each)		96,000
Other credits	Dependent workers (wages, salaries, and pensions)		492,000
	Self-employed and unincorporate business (up to L6 million)		150,000
Extra deductions	Dependent workers (wages, salaries, and pensions), up to L11 million		156,000

Table 5.3   Continued

Item		Credit (L)
1985		
Standard exemptions	Individual income up to L10m.	96,000
	More than L10m.	36,000
Family composition	Spouse (at home)	282,000
	Up to 4 children	21,000
	5th child	36,000
	6th and 7th child	49,000
	8th child	106,000
	9th child or more	134,000
Other credits	Wages, salaries, and pensions, up to L5m.	180,000
	For the cost of producing income (wages, salaries, and pensions only)	296,000
	Lump-sum tax credit in place of income deductions (wages and salaries only)	18,000
Extra deductions	Wages, salaries and pensions:	
	Up to 10.6m.	381,000
	10.6–11.8m.	325,000
	11.8–14.0m.	183,000
	14.0–17.7m.	99,000
	17.7–18.8m.	71,000
	Self-employed and unincorporated business:	
	Up to L7m.	235,000
	L7–14m.	117,000

prices. In practice, with the exception of such *de jure* cases, no personal income tax is paid on capital gains.

The tax system that emerged from the 1973–4 reform did tax (progressively) capital gains on land and real estate, but through the introduction of a separate, general local tax, namely the 'Tax on the Increments of Value of Real Estate' (INVIM, *Imposta sugli incrementi di valore degli immobili*). Such tax was to be subtracted from the capital gains tax liability as determined under the individual income tax. It was then abolished with the introduction of the local wealth tax ICI in 1992 (see below the section on local taxation).

The 1973–4 system did not substitute capital gains tax on financial assets, either through the individual income tax or through some separate tax. Only in 1988 (law no. 67/88) certain transfers were subjected to the individual income tax. The speculative motive was again a necessary requirement, but it was presumed *de jure* when two conditions were simultaneously met, first, the sale of the shares took place within a five-year span and second, the value of the transaction was not less than 2, 10, or 25 per cent of the entire company's or business's capital, depending on whether the transaction was made in the stock market, in the over-the-counter market, or in other settings (as in the case of participations in unincorporated businesses). If equities were acquired through gift or inheritance, no tax was due. This provision was marginal from the point of view of the individual income tax, but it can be seen as a first step towards the extension, in the early 1990s, of the tax base to capital gains on financial assets. After an intensive debate, in 1991 a law (no. 102/91) was eventually passed intended to tax financial capital gains received by individual taxpayers pending a general revision of capital income taxation. Such general revision, scheduled for 1992, had not materialized by 1997. The 'story' of this most expected tax is really short having been suspended in 1992 (starting from the 1993 fiscal year, i.e. it has been applied for two years only; see also below, Sect. D1.5), but it is an interesting story.

B1.3 Tax Treatment of the Family

The taxpaying unit is the individual earner (earner-unit approach) as it was in the past. The splitting of an individual's income among family members is not allowed, except in the case of a family business. The profits of a family business can be split among members of the family in proportion to their respective shares in them. This splitting licence, unlimited in the 1970s and early 1980s, was reduced in 1988 by a tax provision stipulating that no more than 49 per cent of an unincorporated business's income can be attributed to the members of the entrepreneur's family.[4]

Parliament empowered the government to revise this regime in 1992 along the lines of the French splitting system. The taxpayer would have been given the choice of remaining with the old taxpaying unit or to adopting the new 'family ratio'. But no action followed on the part of the government (see Sect. D. for further comments) and by 1997 the idea seemed to have been abandoned.

Tax assessment is separate, but separate or joint-filing are both possible.[5] In fact, joint-filing may be profitable in two instances: first, when tax deductions to which one spouse is entitled exceed his or her tax liability; and second, when one spouse's taxable income turns out to be negative. In the first case, the other spouse may use the excess deductions; in the second, the negative taxable income may be offset against the positive income of the other spouse.

---

[4] This provision can be seen as a sign of the non-splitting view prevailing in the past. The mood has since changed in favour of some 'partial splitting', but no changes have as yet been introduced. Under the above 49 per cent rule, and due to the tax rates progressivity, a family's business income may escape a substantial part of its tax liability through the fictitious participation in the business of members of the entrepreneur's family not actually contributing to it.

[5] If husband and wife each earn income, they can either file separate returns or a joint return, but in either case the assessment of the tax is separate. In other words, each of them calculates his/her tax liability on his/her income, and the joint or separate filing is only a question of practical convenience.

B1.4　Current Payment System

The bulk of tax collection is currently carried out through two types of withholding. The first is an 'advance payment' (*acconto*). The second is a final payment. The first type, which applies to all wages, salaries, and pensions is by far the most important. Since withholding is net of most tax deductions and credits, if the wage earner or pensioner has no other income his tax liability would be completely settled. In this case no return is filed by the taxpayer (see the following paragraph), and only a copy of the employer's withholdng certificate has to be sent to the Internal Revenue Authority.

The most important withholding of the second type is made by banks and postal authorities interest paid to individuals on their deposits.[6] Such interest receipts are not lumped together with other types of income in the individual income tax base. They do, however, enter into the corporate income tax base.

Final payments of the most important income taxes, such as IRPEF, IRPEG, and ILOR, relative to a given fiscal year are due around May–June of the following year. But since 1978 in November of each year every taxpayer has to pay a substantial percentage of his assessed tax liability for the current year. The percentage has been rising steadily, from 75 per cent in 1978 to 98 per cent in 1991, and remained so in 1997.

There were two main reasons for this advancing of tax collection. The first was the need for financing increasing deficits, the second was to shorten the time interval between income-earning (producing) and tax payment, thereby reducing the discrimination against taxpayers subject to substantial withholding (basically wage earners and pensioners *vis-à-vis* the self-employed).

B1.5　Requirements for Filing Tax Returns

Until May 1994 all citizens with the exception of those having wage or pension income only had to file tax returns. Since then, in an effort to simplify tax administration both for tax authorities and taxpayers, exemptions from the obligation of filing tax returns have been further extended. For many taxpayers, particularly those who are old or less educated or live in backward areas, the self-assessment of their income tax may be quite difficult. In fact a very large number of taxpayers have only one wage or pension income, but also own a small flat with imputed income (when owner-occupied),[7] which puts them under the obligation of filing a tax return. In 1994 the obligation was

---

[6] In Italy all types of deposits pay interest.

[7] For tax purposes, imputed income from land and real estate is a conventional income established in the registry of land property and in the registry of real estate for every physical unit. Until 1992 the incomes in such registries were those determined, in 1939 and in 1962 respectively, with the revenue authorities periodically issuing revaluation coefficients. It was generally thought that even with such revaluations the resulting imputed income underestimated actual (potential) market income. The ensuing preferential treatment of those occupying their own home was especially argued by those in favour of a wealth tax. But eventually in 1992 a radical revision of incomes inscribed in the registries was completed, while a local wealth tax (ICI) was also introduced in 1993.

cancelled for those taxpayers whose tax liability left over after withholding can be presumed to be very small. Such were those (just mentioned) with one wage or pension income plus a (owner-occupied) small flat, when imputed income does not exceed a given level; those with more than one dependent income, or with income from land and buildings only, provided the total income doesn't exceed certain levels, and the like. Of course everyone *can* file the tax return, and will do so if this results in crediting extra deductions which reduce his tax bill. On filing a return, the taxpayer calculates his tax liability net of all deductions and credits and then subtracts from the tax due the amount which has already been withheld, and that which has already been paid in the relevant fiscal year as advance payment.

B1.6 Adjustments for Inflation

As already mentioned, adjustments for inflation were usually made by increasing tax deductions and occasionally revising tax rates (Table 5.1). During the three years 1989–91 the individual income tax was indexed, but since 1992 indexation has been confined to deductions.

B2 Corporation Income Tax

B2.1 Tax Base and Tax Rates

Corporations are subject to two taxes: the corporate income tax (IRPEG) and the local income tax (ILOR). The combined rate is now 53.2 per cent, the highest in Europe.[8] In 1992 an extra tax on the net wealth of corporations was introduced (with a rate of 0.75 per cent).

The tax base is total net business income as it results from the profit and loss account as required by the legal discipline of business bookkeeping (conventional economic accounting), adjusted according to certain special provisions imposed or allowed by the law for tax purposes. The definition of business income for tax purposes, whether corporate or non-corporate, departs in certain respects from the conventional economic profit and loss definition. Special rules apply among other things to inventory evaluations and depreciation accounting, and in general to the evaluation of outstanding physical and financial assets, and to interest charges. To determine the tax base certain extra deductions from general business income are allowed. They concern, in particular, maintenance and preservation expenses for objects of historical and artistic value, charities and gifts to government and non-profit institutions, and expenses for carrying out or promoting research. Deductions are also allowed for the ordinary and decennial tax on the increments of the

---

[8] In 1997 the rate of IRPEG was 37% and the rate of ILOR was 16.2%. In 1977 ILOR was made deductible from IRPEG. In 1991 the deductibility was reduced to 75% and in 1993 totally abolished.

value of land and real estate (INVIM), and for losses in previous years up to the last five years.

When the corporation income tax was introduced it was conceived as a tax on a distinct entity, separate from the shareholders (absolutist view). The tax is now regarded as a partial payment of the individual income tax and the two taxes are integrated (see Section B2.3 below).

B2.2 Treatment of Small Firms

Small firms are allowed to adopt a simplified system of accounts under which taxable income is determined as the difference between all revenues less a specified list of certified expenses, and given percentages of gross revenues for the non-certified ones. In the case of very small firms the tax base is determined on a lump-sum basis by applying profitability coefficients to gross receipts. In 1989 the favourable treatment of small firms was restricted in that the maximum turnover required to be eligible as a small firm was reduced from L780 million to 360, while a maximum turnover of L18 million[9] is required to be elibigle as 'very small'.

Fiscal experts were generally opposed to such favourable treatment of precisely those categories believed to be most evading taxes. New ways of assessment have consequently been enacted in the last two years. The first is represented by the so called 'presumed coefficients' and the second by a sort of 'mimimum tax'. For self-employed and firms in the service sector with turnover less than 360 million, the tax authority can assess 'by induction' a firm's revenue when revenues calculated according to predetermined co-efficients (which vary with sector, location, etc.) appear to be greater than declared. With the same aim of reducing evasion a sort of a minimum tax was introduced by law 438/92. But there was so much opposition that it was substantially revised in 1993, and virtually disappeared in 1994.

B2.3 Treatment of Dividends

Dividends must be included by taxpayers in their tax returns. To avoid double taxation, a tax credit is allowed for taxes paid by corporations. In outline, the 'dividend tax credit' or 'relief' works as follows. The tax rate on a company's income is 36 per cent. Suppose a shareholder receives a dividend of L64. If there had been no corporate tax, he would have received a dividend of L100. The shareholder calculates his tax credit by multiplying the dividend received by $^9/_{16}$ ($0.36/0.64 = t(1 - t)$). Both the dividend (64) and the tax credit (36 = 64 × (0.36/0.64)) are included in the shareholder's taxable income. The shareholder calculates his tax liability on his total income under the progressive personal income tax rates and then subtracts the tax credit (36) from such tax liability. When ILOR was fully deductible from IRPEG the $^9/_{16}$ tax credit was

---

[9] And belonging to particular trading sectors, such as retail trade, handicrafts, grocery stores, and the like.

equal to tax paid by corporation. A 1992 law has made ILOR non-deductible from IRPEG thereby causing the dividend tax credit to be less than the tax paid at the corporate stage.

A provision intended to avoid a tax subsidy to dividend recipients was added in 1983 and is still in operation. Since the dividend tax credit applies to all dividends received and since there are numerous corporate tax favours (such as reduced rates on incomes originating in the South), to the extent that dividends come from such favoured sources the $^9/_{16}$ tax credit implies a tax subsidy to the shareholder. As it would be impossible in practice to trace the source of dividend income, an additional corporate tax was introduced, called 'balancing tax' (*Imposta di conguaglio*). This tax is paid by a company in proportion to the amount of distributed income which exceeds the (net) income subject to full taxation, and therefore comes by definition from tax-favoured income. As a result of integration, the corporation income tax as such is really a tax on undistributed taxable profits.[10]

B3 Payroll Taxes

Social security contributions are generally proportional (but sometimes regressive) taxes on wages and salaries. The tax base includes wages and salaries, professional income of the self-employed, and income of unincorporated businesses (handicrafts, trade, and agriculture). Several different rates, whose rationale goes back to the type of risk they were intended to cover, contribute to make up the final rates. The rates depend on the: (i) type of job and self-employment; (ii) sector; (iii) blue- or white-collar job; (iv) handicraft industry, trade, and agriculture; (v) location in the national territory; and (vi) sex.

Table 5.4 gives the tax rates for several sectors in 1994. They range from a comparatively low (!) 48.5 per cent for agriculture to a high 59.45 per cent in industry. Social security contributions are a significant part of total tax revenues and of GDP, as shown in Table 5.5. Just after 1973–4 reform they were by far the largest part of total tax collection, with 44.8 per cent as opposed to the 21.8 per cent of direct taxes and the 33.4 per cent of indirect taxes, and only in 1989 they became the second largest source, with 36.1, 37.3, and 26.6 per cent respectively (see below D1.8 for a discussion of the issues).

[10] Until 1993 it was possible for high-income taxpayers with marginal tax rates higher than the corporate rate to partially avoid the individual income tax by transferring their assets to a legal entity established precisely for that purpose and kept under the majority control of family members. By keeping such income undistributed it remained subject only to the proportional IRPEG and not to the progressive (marginal) IRPEF. But since 1993 the corporate income tax rate (53.2%) has become higher than the highest personal income tax rate (51%).

Table 5.4   Rates of social security contributions on wages and salaries, by sector,[a] 1994 (%)

		Industry		Handicrafts	Trade	Financial	Agriculture
		Non-building	Building				
Blue-collar workers	*rate on employer*	45.96	49.46	40.81	42.86	40.31	39.16
	rate on employee	9.99	9.99	9.69	9.69	9.69	9.34
	total rate	55.95	59.45	50.50	52.55	50.00	48.50
White-collar workers	*rate on employer*	42.54	47.24	38.59	42.56	40.31	39.16
	rate on employee	9.69	9.99	9.69	9.69	9.69	9.34
	total rate	52.23	57.23	48.28	52.25	50.00	48.50

[a] Rates also vary with firm dimension and among subsectors.

Table 5.5   Social security contributions: % of total revenues (taxes + s.s.contr.) and of GDP, 1987–1996

	1987	1988	1989	1990	1991	1992	1993	1994	1995	1996
% of total revenues	37.7	36.8	36.1	36.5	36.3	35.1	34.8	34.5	35.8	35.7
% of GDP	13.8	13.7	14.0	14.4	14.7	15.0	15.3	15.3	14.9	15.0

Source: Own calculations on Banca d'Italia data.

B4   Value-added Tax (IVA)

B4.1   Tax Rates and Exemptions

The value-added tax (IVA, *Imposta sul valore aggiunto*) is a tax on domestic consumption, but it is paid at every transaction stage (in other words, it is a multistage consumption-type tax). IVA is by far the most important indirect tax in Italy. The tax was eventually introduced in 1973, after having been deferred beyond the extension granted by the EEC. It was introduced as a substitute for the previous general turnover tax (IGE, *Imposta generale sull'entrata*). Multiple rates were adopted to avoid weakening the progressivity of the system, but although progressivity is a desirable tax property, the structure of IVA is excessively cumbersome. First, the very definition of 'transactions of goods and services' for IVA purposes is a complicated one. Second, a distinction is made among types of transactions, which may be taxable, non-taxable (taxed at zero rate), excluded and exempt.[11] Third, a

---

[11] *Non-taxable* transactions include exports, international transportation, and necessities. *Excluded* transactions are those made by subjects who are as such not liable to IVA. They include

special treatment is provided for agriculture.[12] Fourth, while the number of taxpayers is large, too many of them are small. As in the case of income tax there exists also for IVA a simplified regime for small businesses in the service sector and for self-employed, with a turnover of less than L360 million (one billion for businesses outside the service sector). Conformity with EU decisions is now a major concern in handling this tax.

Rates have been reduced in number and chosen in accordance with EU decisions. In 1996 they were 20, 10, and 4 per cent.[13] According to several studies IVA appears to be a mildly progressive tax. In 1995 the estimated average rate for a family belonging to the first decile of income was 8.9 per cent, while for the last one it was 10.8 per cent. A recent study provides a general quantitative view of the structure of IVA (and its variations) through the calculation of average rates for groups of goods weighted with the weights they have in the consumption basket of families. As appears from Table 5.6 the overall average rate has increased during the ten years studied (1981–91) although at different rates.[14]

Tax liability is determined by subtracting the IVA paid on inputs from the IVA due on sales. Differential rates combined with exemptions and exclusions create a great deal of room for manipulating one's tax liability. However, this was neither the only nor the worst problem. The main problem was the handling of refunds by the revenue authority. When the difference between IVA on sales and IVA on purchases is negative, the revenue authority has to refund the difference. Given the tax structure, refunds are to be expected, but their amount is huge and very costly. In the 1980s it was estimated that about 26 to 30 per cent of gross annual IVA revenue gave rise to new 'credits' and the total amount of credits was increasing at a faster rate than gross revenue. An important source of IVA credits has always been exports.[15]

Apart from these aspects, the problem with IVA is that it is evaded to a substantial degree. Indeed, by comparing GDP figures with those of IVA returns the degree of evasion was estimated to be at least around 30 per cent in the 1980s, and, according to more pessimistic estimates, around 40 per cent.[16] When the tax was introduced, the revenue authorities were confident that compliance was going to be good thanks to the conflicting

---

credit, financial and insurance transactions. Non-taxable transactions are regarded as taxable at zero rate, and enter into the final calculation of IVA, while *exempted* transactions do not. A special mechanism of 'tax suspension' on domestic purchases, less than or equal to the amount of a firm's exports and other non-taxable transactions, is also established.

[12] The argicultural sector was, and still is, subject to an especially favourable method of IVA assessment called the 'agricultural system'.

[13] To give an idea of the changes that occurred during the twenty years since the tax's introduction, rates were: six in 1974, namely 1, 3, 6, 12, 18, and 30%; nine in 1979, namely 1, 3, 6, 8, 9, 12, 14, and 18%; seven in 1983, namely 2, 8, 10, 15, 18, 20, and 38%; four in 1991, namely 4,9,19, and 38%; three in 1993, namely 4, 9, 12, and 19%.   [14] Rossi (1993).

[15] But no longer under the current EU deferred payment system. Also the 'origin' and 'destination' principles are highly ambiguous.   [16] Vitaletti, *et al.* (1988).

Table 5.6   Average rates (%) of VAT for categories of goods

	1981–3	1984–8	1989	1990	1991
Food, beverages, tobacco	8.05	8.59	8.55	9.95	9.95
Clothes, shoes	9.67	10.70	10.82	9.36	12.21
Housing	9.17	10.29	10.34	10.84	10.70
Transport, commerce	15.15	15.56	15.53	16.34	15.86
Other goods and services	9.58	10.56	10.71	11.23	11.23
Average	9.83	10.77	10.71	10.77	11.50

Source: N. Rossi (ed), *La crescita ineguale, 1981–1991. Primo rapporto CNEL sulla distribuzione e redistribuzione del reddito in Italia*, Il Mulino, 1993.

interests of taxpayers, who are simultaneously debtors and creditors of IVA, and would therefore cross-check each other to the benefit of revenue authorities. But in practice compliance has been very low.

For agriculture a favourable treatment is still in operation in that the determination of tax liability is made on an *à forfait* basis, but its abolition has been announced.

B4.2 Administrative Costs

The administrative and compliance costs of IVA are high both for the taxpayer and for the revenue authority. Since the time of its introduction the opposition to IVA by business, especially small business, was based on the high costs involved in order to satisfy the demanding bookkeeping requirements. The recognition of this may have been responsible for the introduction of a *'forfaitaire* system' of assessment for small businesses. The story of this system is instructive because it was introduced, eliminated, and then restored, showing the current state of indecision and uncertainty on the part of tax authorities dealing with a tax whose performance in terms of revenue is highly unsatisfactory.

The *forfaitaire* system requires only sales records, the deduction of IVA paid on inputs being determined by applying given coefficients to taxable sales. The system has been widely criticized because it was thought to be largely responsible for tax evasion. The abolition of the system on the other hand was equally criticized because it implied additional costs for the taxpayers with no certain benefits for the revenue authorities. Tax consultants would have become the true beneficiaries. We still have the two systems (standard and simplified). Indeed, it was an arduous task for the revenue authorities to manage and check the 5.2 million returns in 1993.[17] On top of these already strained administrative conditions, one must add the claims for reimburse-

---

[17] To get an idea of the dimensions of the problem, consider that the number of returns in France is little more than half of those filed in Italy.

ment, which were getting out of hand.[18] Fear of a further decrease in revenue following the abolition of customs is now also widespread.

B4.3 Effects of VAT on the Price Level

It is generally thought either that IVA does not raise the price level or, if it does, it raises it only slightly. Pedone (1981) reported an average price increase of about two to six percentage points, assuming an average IVA rate of 10 per cent. Ceriani (1981) concluded that inflation would be reduced by substituting IVA for social security payroll taxes (as was done once in 1977). The same position can be found in other studies by the Bank of Italy in the same period.

The administrative mess and the huge evasion, which go hand in hand, are currently the main problems of the Italian IVA.

B5 Excise Taxes

Indirect taxes have being losing their importance since the early 1970s and this is due to many causes. Most of the excise taxes left by the basic reform were not *ad valorem* but specific. They therefore did not grow automatically, while the high inflation of the 1980s provided a reason not to raise them because of their likely effect on prices. On top of these two reasons, concern for vertical equity was prevailing during the period. The reduction of the relative importance of indirect taxes in tax collection was indeed a desired target, and thought to enhance the progressivity of the system. But in more recent years the huge and increasing deficit combined with the dramatic increase experienced in the personal income tax (see above) have forced a revision of this attitude. From 1985 to 1990 the revenue from indirect taxes grew by 2.6 percentage point of GDP as a result of tax provisions relating to (IVA and) some excises. The most important excises are on hydrocarbon oils such as petrol and diesel oil. Rates are higher for gasoline than for diesel oil in accordance with the aim of avoiding increases in the transportation costs of goods (i.e. as an anti-inflation device). This caused the government to grant tax credits to carriers (in terms of both direct taxes and IVA) when raising tax rates, as in 1989 and in 1993.

By and large from 1988 the taxation of energy products in general has undergone a process of revision due to two reasons: the need for more tax revenue and for environmental protection.

Other excises fall on spirits, spirit beverages, and tobacco. Another important indirect tax, which is really on wealth, is the registry tax (see Sect. B6).

It is at the moment generally argued that only increases in indirect taxes are possible.

---

[18] The *forfaitaire* system in France, while inexpensive for the administration, seems to yield a considerable amount of tax revenues. Thus the problem must lie more with the type of the system used rather than with the *forfaitaire* as such.

B6   Net Wealth Tax and Capital Transfer Taxes

B6.1   General

The taxation of wealth has represented the most controversial area of debate since the basic reform of 1973–4. The opposition to an ordinary wealth tax has always been very strong in the country and one can trace it back to the idea that wealth should be regarded only as an 'extraordinary' source of taxation. Probably the four 1992 tax provisions on wealth might have found strong support precisely because of the particularly serious financial difficulties of the government that year.

Until 1992 there was, strictly speaking, only one tax on wealth, called the 'tax on inheritance and gifts'. This was the only (direct[19]) tax whose amount was (and is, since the tax is still there) determined by applying given tax rates to the current value of wealth. But other taxes (then partially abolished in 1993) burdened wealth. The main ones are the two local taxes, namely the 'tax on the increments of value of land and real estate' (INVIM, *Imposta sugli incrementi di valore degli immobili*) and the 'local income tax' (ILOR, *Imposta locale sui redditi*).[20]

The 1992 provisions have introduced extraordinary taxes on wealth: (i) on bank and postal deposits (only for that year); (ii) on some durable luxury goods; (iii) on net wealth of firms; and (iv) on immovable property (ISI, *Imposta straordinaria sugli immobili*). The first is not worth mentioning, the second is almost irrelevant in practice, while the third and the fourth require some comments.

The tax on net wealth of firms was introduced in principle for three years, but in 1997 it was still in existence. The value of net wealth is that recorded in the firm's books, and there are two ways of calculating it, applying to firms with ordinary and simplified bookkeeping, respectively. The rate is 0.75 per cent and the tax is not deductible from IRPEG (or IRPEF, for unincorporated businesses).

The extraordinary tax on immovable property (ISI) gave rise to the 'ordinary' one (ICI, *Imposta comunale sugli immobili*) introduced in 1993. This 1993 tax is a local tax, and with its introduction two problems of the Italian tax system appear to have been addressed: the straightforward adoption of wealth as a tax base, and the decentralization of tax revenues. The introduction of ICI has brought with it exclusion of immovable property owned by individuals from ILOR and the abolition of INVIM.[21] Rates can vary between 0.4

---

[19]   There was (and is) also a special type of indirect wealth tax, called 'registration tax' (*imposta di registro*), which is the oldest Italian tax on transactions of property *inter vivos*. Its survival in the present tax system is doubtful.

[20]   Although ILOR is an income tax, its (introduction and) scope is to tax wealth through the income it generates: when income comes from wealth ILOR is added to the ordinary income tax.

[21]   ILOR is now levied practically only on corporations' income. Business income produced by labour is excluded. The exclusion holds also under the minimum tax law, in those cases in which business income is considered *de jure* as produced by labour. INVIM is completely abolished but for corporations it will continue to exist for the next ten years, the increment of value being represented by the difference between the value at the end of 1992 and acquisition value.

and 0.7 per cent according to the discretion of the municipal authority. Some deductions for owner-occupied housing are allowed as well as special provisions for the agricultural sector. Exemptions for certain government, religious, and other buildings are established. ICI is not deductible from IRPEF.

B6.2 The 'Older' Wealth Taxes, Capital Transfer Taxes, and Registration Taxes

Bequests and gifts are subject to the same tax. The tax due at the moment of death cannot be avoided by making gifts during lifetime, because both transfers are taxed equally. The tax is progressive and is determined in two stages, with the exclusion of spouses and direct-line relatives (for whom only the first stage applies). In the first stage progressive rates are applied to the value of the whole net wealth transferred. Receivables and other rights to wealth are included, while liabilities are deducted. Also included are the goods and rights alienated by the deceased in the last six months of life. In the second stage, progressive rates are applied to the separate amounts received by the different heirs or beneficiaries. The rates in the two stages are different. In the second stage the rates vary depending on the closeness of kinship,[22] but this does not hold for spouses and direct-line kinship. The assessment of the tax base and tax liability is made by the revenue authority on the basis of the heirs' or beneficiaries' return. In doing so the revenue authority enjoys large discretionary power. This is thought to be responsible for a large tax evasion. The tax is not an important one in terms of revenue.

More important in terms of revenue is the other old wealth tax, called the 'registration tax' (*Imposta di registro*). This is generally considered a bad tax, costly and burdened by legal disputes. It is also considered anachronistic and confusing, because its tax base is difficult to define. There are two main categories of taxable 'items': (i) all 'written acts', civil and commercial, which must be officially registered in order to be legally valid, and (ii) all other non-written contracts, when they are required for court decisions. The written acts under (i) are listed in the tax law. The most important ones from the revenue point of view are all transfers and renting of property (real estate) and of certain 'registered' durables (such as cars, boats, and the like), and all business takeovers. Assessment is based on market value or selling price. Economically it is in essence a wealth tax, paid whenever assets are transferred, rented, or otherwise negotiated. The tax may be quite heavy, especially on real estate transfers where the seller is not the construction firm 'producing' the asset, in which case the tax due is IVA (the Tax Reform Act of 1973–4 has in fact envisaged the registration tax as an alternative and not a complement to IVA).

---

[22] Thus at the second stage, siblings and direct-line relatives are taxed at a lower rate than more distant relatives who in turn are taxed at a lower rate than non-relatives.

B6.3 Revenue Yield and Methods of Avoidance

The revenue from the tax on inheritance and gifts is remarkably low both in absolute value and as a percentage of total direct tax revenues or of GDP. The natural explanation for such low revenues is the coexistence of widespread legal and illegal tax avoidance. The general method of (legal) avoidance is the under-reporting of the value of assets and transactions subject to the wealth taxes. Such values, as reported in the taxpayers' returns, are generally significantly lower than the market value of the assets or the actual value of the taxable transaction. Another common legal method is to make fictitious sales instead of, or before, gifts and inheritance, sales being less heavily taxed. In such cases great legal expertise and (costly) professional advice may be required, because the revenue authority may presume that certain sales between close relatives are fictitious substitutes for gifts, and the beneficiaries must prove the contrary. As to illegal avoidance, it is generally understood that this is made possible by exploiting the large discretionary power of tax administrators in the tax assessment, to the advantage of both taxpayers and civil servants themselves.

In Italy, there are no other legal ways of avoiding inheritance taxation, such as the establishment of controlled non-profit foundations in the USA or discretionary trusts in the UK. Finally, it must be noted that the actual tax burden for a given amount of wealth depends on its composition, because such assets as money, treasury bonds, jewellry, and antiques can change ownership without registration and therefore without paying any tax, while real estate cannot. But real estate and other registered assets are usually the largest part of inheritance transfers. A further explanation of the low yield of the gift and inheritance tax probably lies with tax on land-value increments (now abolished). This tax is deductible from the inheritance and gift taxes, and thus absorbs part of its potential revenue.

As far as the revenues from the 'new' wealth taxes are concerned, official figures are not yet available.

B7 The Local Tax System

B7.1 Major Features of Fiscal Federalism

Until 1993 fiscal federalism in Italy was based almost entirely on a system of transfers from central government to lower jurisdictions. Before the Tax Reform Act of 1973–4 the situation was different, especially for municipalities (*comuni*), whose finances were largely based on their own taxes, abolished by the 1973–4 Act. Since then a 'new' reform of the local tax system has been announced almost every year. The choice of a fiscal federalism based primarily on transfers from a central to lower levels of government rested on the 'dualistic' structure of the Italian economy. It was thought that, instead of gradually disappearing, duality would have been accentuated by a territorially decentralized and autonomous local tax system. The rich areas would have become richer and the poor ones poorer, as a result of insufficient services provided through the limited budgets of the poorer local administrations.

The granting of greater autonomy and independence at the local level, now widely requested, rests on two main reasons. First, in order to reduce local government deficits it is necessary, even if not sufficient, to link expenditure responsibility to taxation responsibility; second, although the 'dualism' argument has not died out, in the recent past the idea of taxation based on the benefit principle has gained ground.

B7.2 Major Taxes Used and Relationship to National Taxes

While abolishing most existing local taxes,the 1973–4 Act introduced what were meant to be the main new local taxes, namely the 'local income tax' (ILOR) and the 'tax on the increments of value of land and real estate' (INVIM). ILOR is an *in rem* tax, whose tax base is essentially all non-labour income, and is now (1997) restricted to corporate income and is in course of being abolished. It has a 16.2 per cent rate, is self-assessed according to the same basic rules of national income taxes, and is filed with the same income tax returns.

Although it was originally conceived as a local tax, with its revenues going to the jurisdictions where income was produced, this never really happened. It has become evident that the true purpose of ILOR has never been, not even marginally, to finance local governments, but rather to impose 'qualitative discrimination', i.e. a comparatively heavier overall tax burden on non-labour income.[23] The revenue of INVIM did instead actually go to local governments until 1992. From 1993 it goes (though not entirely) to the central government, and has been phased out (see Sect. B6).

B7.3 System of Political Decentralization

There are three decreasing levels of territorial decentralization: *regions, provinces,* and *municipalities*. Regions are the most recent local government institutions, having been established in the 1970s. In 1989 93 per cent of their revenues were central government transfers, 86 per cent of which were conditional ones (63 per cent for health). In 1993 the National Health Service Tax was attributed to them. The rest is supplied by the annual driving licence tax (road fund tax) and other minor levies for the use of public land and goods. Regions in turn transfer 91 per cent of their revenues to provinces and municipalities. Thus, the main economic function of the regions is either to 'plan' the economic activity of lower-level jurisdictions, or simply to pass on, passively, any transfers received from central government.

Regions receive transfers from central government through the formation of funds. One of these, called the 'common fund' is built up from certain

---

[23] It is worth while remembering that the original 1973–4 Act distinguished between wages and salaries, and income from self-employment, with only the former being exempted from the tax. In 1980, the Supreme Court (*Corte Costituzionale*) declared such discrimination as unconstitutional.

indirect tax revenues (such as those on tobacco, spirits, and the production of mineral oil) and other contributions. The fund is allocated among regions by applying certain coefficients to their population, unemployment rate, and tax burden. This fund is intended to finance the normal activities of regions. The other funds are tied to specific purposes. They are the 'development fund' (mainly for agriculture), the 'national health fund', the 'national transportation fund', and others. The total amount of each fund is annually determined in the national budget. In 1997 the fund system was under revision.

Provinces have been progressively stripped of their original functions. Presently their revenues are less than 1 per cent of GDP, and there are recurrent proposals to abolish them.

Municipalities are the oldest type of local government. Their functions are of two types: (i) their own original functions, attributed to them by the national law, and (ii) delegated functions, which are functions attributed by the Constitution to regions, and in turn delegated by regions to municipalities. In practice the functions of municipalities cover a large area, including metropolitan and rural police, housing and urban planning, health, social welfare and school assistance, trade licences, control over retail prices, road maintenance, and others. Municipalities provide their services either directly or by establishing 'municipal public enterprises'. They are financed by transfers from central government and regions, supplemented by their own local taxes. They are the only type of local government whose own local tax revenues are not trivial (at least until 1990 when tax revenues of regions also reached 12.72 per cent of their current revenue; see Table 5.7). Before the introduction of ICI in 1993, by far their most important local tax was INVIM, which provided about 15 per cent of total municipal revenues. Other municipal taxes are directly tied to specific services. In 1983, and for that year only, municipalities were allowed to levy a special surtax on real estate (called SOCOF), and 80 per cent of municipalities elected to do so. This was a relatively minor tax, but it was widely regarded as a tentative step towards new forms of local wealth taxation. Table 5.7 shows the past and present situation concerning the composition of revenues for regions, provincies, and municipalities.

The local tax system is currently a main subject of debate. In part, things have already been settled by giving to municipalities a wealth tax (ICI). Things are still unsettled in other important respects regarding the role of regions and provinces. While municipalities retain their prevailing importance, proposals to enlarge the role of regions are gaining momentum, while no substantial changes in attitude towards provinces are in sight. The present situation is as follows.

(1) Municipalities have eight own taxes. The most important are ICI (already described), ICIAP,[24] a tax on advertising, one on the occupation of

---

[24] A 'municipal tax on the performing of business, arts, and professions' (ICIAP) was introduced in 1989. The tax liability is calculated on the extent of the space utilized for the activity. In 1990 income was added for the calculation of tax liability.

Table 5.7 Local revenues by source type, % ratios (cash data)

	Regions				Provinces					Municipalities				
	1987	1988	1989	1990	1987	1988	1989	1990	1991	1987	1988	1989	1990	1991
Current transfers/current revenues	89.93	89.04	87.75	81.86	89.46	87.80	86.79	85.27	86.02	77.74	73.49	68.60	66.60	63.87
Tax revenues/current revenues	4.94	5.63	7.03	12.72	6.95	8.57	9.37	8.87	8.65	11.49	13.39	17.86	19.47	19.35

Source: Own calculations on ISTAT data, *Annuario statistico*, various years.

public spaces, one on refuse collection, and some others. They also have supplementary charge on national taxes, such as the one on electricity consumption (by households and non-households).

(2) Provinces have something resembling an autonomous tax, the so called 'tax for environmental protection'. It is actually a surtax on the municipality tax on refuse collection, and has little to do with environmental protection since it depends on the physical size of the buildings subject to the tax. They also have a supplementary charge on the inscription in the Public Automobile Registry, and a tax on household provision of gas and electricity. Both municipalities and provinces receive transfers from the central government through the formation of funds.

(3) Regions have a motor tax, tax on the use of State property, and the National Health Service Tax. Regions receive revenue coming from income on immovable property located within their borders. They also have an 'additional' on the national tax on registration in the Public Automobile Registry. A new regional tax on local value added, was expected to be introduced in 1997.

C. Economic and Social Aspects

C1   The Fiscal Deficit

Deficit financing has occurred in nearly all of OECD countries during the last fifteen years but whereas the OECD average has mostly varied between 2 and 4 per cent of nominal GNP over this period, in Italy it has been around 9 to 13 per cent. Italian deficit financing[25] generated an accumulated debt almost equal to GNP in 1990 and to 125.2 per cent of GNP in 1996. The interest bill represents a serious government concern in many respects. Since interest on public bonds must make their subscription 'attractive' to the public, an unhealthy competition for finance with the private sector has developed. A considerable amount of income redistribution takes place (within the country and, to a smaller extent, abroad). The height of debt stock and obligations caused the search for practicable offsetting methods to become one of the priorities of economic policies in the 1990s. The Maastrict prescriptions have only added pressures to pursue this medium-term objective. The sustainability of public debt has monopolized the theoretical and economic policy debate in recent years. Indeed, the present situation appears to be a truly difficult one.

(1) A further substantial increase in taxation cannot be expected. Although the direct tax burden has never been higher, a parallel personal income tax has been introduced, in principle for one year on 1996 income. This is known as the Euro tax. It has the same base, but different rates, thresholds, and reliefs

---

[25] See *Economic Outlook 4*, OECD June 1997: Table 34.

for family and the self-employed from the IRPEF, the main income tax. It appears unjust and even unconstitutional.

(2) Expenditure reductions may threaten the very existence of the welfare state, the major areas of expenditure being pensions and health care (besides interest on public debt).

(3) The requirements of public debt sustainability (even apart from the Maastrict agreements) make the continuation of deficit financing through the market really dangerous, while monetary financing is ruled out by the current unanimous anti-inflation consensus.

A composite solution will probably emerge, made up of small increases in indirect taxes, some expenditure rationalizations (reform of pensions, health, public employment) combined with small cuts, and a much expected economic recovery.

Fig. 5.1 shows the recent trends (1981–96) in public debt, nominal and real total deficits, and primary deficit. Notwithstanding strong measures to reduce deficits, public debt has continued to grow, really threatening the performance of the entire economy. The efforts to increase taxes and to decrease, at least to some extent, expenditure, did succeed in bringing up the primary balance, first to zero in 1991 and then to positive values in 1992 and after. Nevertheless the enormous amount of interest matured on the stock of cumulated debt causes a growth of the debt itself. The Bank of Italy's recommendation to further increase by about 3 percentage points tax receipts to GNP ratio seems to many an impossible dream, unless its likely effects on the supply of labour and saving are disregarded.

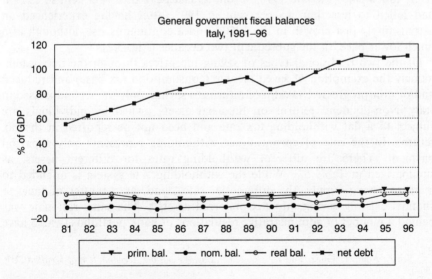

General government fiscal balances
Italy, 1981–96

Real balance = nominal balance less inflation tax
Net debt: break in the series starting 1990.

Fig. 5.1 Government debt and fiscal balances, 1981–1994

Source: Own calculation on OECD *Economic Outlook* data.

C2 Savings and Investment Incentives

C2.1 General

In principle, all income sources are included in the personal income tax base
(*IRPEF*). The sources are classified as (i) land, (ii) capital, (iii) labour, (iv)
unincorporated business, and (v) others (such as speculative capital gains).
However, within category (ii) only dividends on shares are included in the
personal income tax base, while interest on bank and postal deposits and on
private and public bonds, as well as capital gains (as already explained), are
all excluded. On the other hand, interest received by corporations, including
interest on bank deposits and the like, is subject to the corporation income
tax, and the bank's withholding represents only a partial tax payment.

In addition, the flat-tax rate on income from financial capital (except
dividends), varying with respect to financial instruments and categories of
taxpayers, indicates the unfairness and distortions of Italy's capital income
taxation. Its general revision was scheduled for 1992 but it has been postponed several times.

C2.2 Savings Incentives Through the Tax System

The well-known exceptionally high-saving propensity of households in Italy
has been shrinking in recent years. Under all its definitions, namely the rough
one taken straight out of the national accounts or the more worked-out
economic one, it appears clearly that private saving propensity has progressively fallen since the late 1970s. From its last peak of 25 per cent in 1979 it
had fallen to less than 15 per cent in 1993, after having experienced an
astonishingly fast growth in the 1950s, and a continuous rise, although at a
much lower pace, in the subsequent two decades (Fig. 5.2).[26]

Of the two traditional types of saving incentives through the tax system,
namely the exemption of saved income (consumption tax base) and reduced
and/or non-progressive taxatin of returns to saving, only the second is used in
Italy. Non-dividend returns on financial assets owned by individuals are
subject to a flat withholding tax rate and need not be reported in the tax
returns. In the case of corporations, withholding represents only a partial
payment. There are different withholding rates for different assets, as
summarized in Table 5.8. While the withholding rate system is intended to
increase saving supply, the differential rates tend, as a matter of fact, to
channel existing saving into tax-preferred assets.[27] The same rationale was
behind a number of administrative regulations of bank portfolios (which have

---

[26] See A. Audo, L. Guiso, and I. Visco (eds.), *Savings and the Accumulation of Wealth* (CUP,
1994).

[27] It is perhaps worth while to notice that the Italian financial market is characterized by a
comparatively high degree of liquidity, a dominating position of the banks in absorbing short-
term assets, combined with an increasingly large market share occupied, at least since 1975, by
short-term treasury bonds.

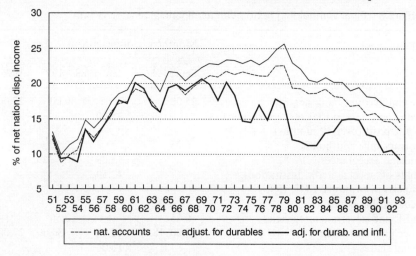

Fig. 5.2 Net private saving rate, 1951–1993

Source: A. Ando, L. Guiso, and I. Visco (eds), *Saving and the Accumulation of Wealth*, Cambridge, Cambridge University Press, 1994, Statistical Appendix.

been regarded as a form of 'hidden taxation' like inflation) ensuring a large subscription by the banking system of Treasury bond issues in the 1970s and early half of the 1980s. With the new banking law of 1993 (and the 1992 law enforcing the second CEE directive of 1989) many of these regulations have formally vanished, but moral persuasion has taken their place. The term-structure of interest rates also has an important effect on the allocation of saving. Higher interest rates are not associated with longer asset maturities and assets with longer maturities are not taxed at reduced rates. Such facts may help to explain the Italian saver's strong preference for liquid assets.[28]

An important type of compulsory saving, whose taxation regime is currently under revision on various grounds, is represented by the *Trattamento di fine rapporto* ('severance payment'). Every employee when leaving his job receives a sum (*liquidazione*) obtained by capitalizing some given amount over the time-span of his working years. Every month some fraction of his wage is 'lent' to the employer who will return the cumulated capitalized sum to the employee at the moment of his leaving. The fraction to be set aside, determined by law, varied between sectors and between white- and blue-collar workers. In the private sector it was $^1/_{13.5}$ of the monthly wage for the former,

---

[28] The level and structure of interest rates have long since been the subject of debate. It is even questioned whether it is the official discount rate that performs the pivotal role in determining bank interest rates or the interest on short-term Treasury bonds. According to the latter view, most common in the banking community, high-interest rates on Treasury bonds would be acompanied by high-interest rates on deposits and therefore on bank loans. The government cannot expect banks to charge a lower interest on their loans, thereby favouring private investment, as long as interest on Treasury bonds remains high.

Table 5.8 Final withholding tax on various financial assets % rate

Type of asset	Month/year of enactment			
	Sept. 1986	Jan. 1988	1992	1996
Current account bank deposits	25.00		30.00	27.00
Saving accounts, postal savings, certificates of deposit (over 12 months)		25.00		
Treasury bills and bonds	6.25		12.50	
Bankers' acceptances		15.00		
Bonds of 'special credit' institutions, financial institutions, ENI, IRI, convertible bonds		12.50		
ENEL and government agencies	6.25		12.50	
Other financial assets	15.00–18.00	18.00	30.00	27.00
Saving shares		15.00		
Investment funds	A *wealth* tax on funds of (i) public and private bonds, (ii) mixed domestic assets (bonds and shares), (iii) others, of 0.05, 0.1, 0.25% respectively			

while different fractions applied to the latter (in 1993 the treatments were equalized). In the public sector the fraction is $^1/_{12}$. The capitalization rate is also determined by law and is much lower than the market rates of interest. As a way of partially compensating the employee for this lower capitalization rate, the severance sum he receives is not subject to *IRPEF* but to the same sort of substitute levy applied to financial assets.[29] The revision of this institution has in recent years been much debated. It is linked to 'voluntary' saving through life insurance, to the reform of pensions, and to the tax incentives required to promote some sort of 'supplementary pension schemes'. Moreover since it constitutes a 'cheap' source of finance for firms, its reform cannot disregard the firms' financial conditions.

C2.3 Effects of Dividend Relief on Equity Financing

There are two basic types of distorting effects usually attributed to the corporate income tax. The first, concerning a company's dividend policy, has been eliminated through the imputation system; the second, concerning a company's choice of equity versus debt financing, still operates since debt interest on borrowed capital is a cost deductible from taxable income while no deduction of imputed interest on equity capital is permitted. It may be argued in principle that this arrangement provides an incentive to debt finance. As a

---

[29] The tax base is the total amount less L500,000 multiplied by the number of years of work, while the tax rate is an average applicable to a normalized income.

matter of fact, however, the volume of transactions in the Italian stock exchange has been small and share ownership is not widespread among average households. In the middle 1980s there was a boom in the stock market resulting mainly from an increased flow of private saving into investment funds. The limited size of the Italian stock exchange has generally been imputed, among other causes, to Italy's comparatively recent industrialization, and to the 'unfair' competition of government in absorbing private savings. Interests on government securities, tax-free until 1986, are now subject to a 12.5 per cent flat-rate final withholding tax, and they don't have to be reported in the tax return.

Dividends are not only subject to progressive taxation (they must be reported in the tax return), but in addition stocks are, in theory, registered assets,[30] a fact which arouses the utmost distrust in Italian taxpayers. Also the competition from interest-bearing bank deposits is unfair, because their interest is subject only to a flat-final withholding tax, and bank deposits are protected by bank secrecy (which can only be lifted by a court order). The relative boom of the 1980s in the stock market through investment funds, accompanied by a decline in public bonds' subscriptions, could be explained in part by the growing fear that sooner or later interest on public bonds was going to be taxed (as indeed happened in 1986). The unequal taxation of returns on financial assets; the undercapitalization of the corporate sector, with its excessive level of bank indebtedness; and the strong preference of savers for liquid assets, which in turn boosted the so-called 'double inter-mediation',[31] are widely regarded as responsible for the poor state of the equity market. On the other hand, there is no evidence of the dividend relief (implemented to some extent four months after the enactment of the 1973–4 reform, and then replaced in 1977 by the full tax credit) having induced an increase in equity finance. It seems instead likely that the introduction in 1991 of a capital gains tax (later suspended) has contributed to further depress the equity market. The government was empowered to legislate during 1997 on the taxation of financial capital income.

C2.4 General Investment Incentives

Government intervention for stimulating investment is pervasive in the Italian economy, but it is also so chaotic that it is hard to get a clear picture of what is going on, let alone to assess its effects. Four points may be singled out. First, a consistently designed and implemented industrial policy does not exist. There are several regulations and provisions, enforced and expiring at different

[30] Stocks are registered assets but only at company level. There exists no 'general register', and therefore the revenue authorities would need to cross-check every company's list of shareholders against individual returns, which is impracticable. A 'general register' of shareowners has often been announced but never implemented.

[31] Double intermediation refers to the fact that savers don't invest directly in the stock market, but leave it to the banks to channel their savings.

dates, for different durations, and favouring different sectors and subsectors, depending on the type and location of the investment, the year in which it is made, and so on. Second, interventions to promote economic development in the South are made and administered primarily through a special government agency, called the National Agency for the Development of the South (which has replaced in 1984 the *Cassa per il Mezzogiorno*). Third, the favoured method of intervention is through transfers or grants. Fourth, there is a considerable amount of lending under special terms to promote small and medium-size businesses,[32] exports, and of course investments in the South. Many regard such transfers and subsidized loans as excessive, misdirected, or unnecessary interferences in the ordinary working of the credit system. The government acts as a sort of a 'hidden banker,' less efficient than the private banking system in the allocation of credit.

There are three main types of tax incentives: (1) repeal of payroll taxes on wages and salaries, (2) tax credits for reinvested profits and job creation, and (3) accelerated depreciation.

(1) *Repeal of payroll taxes*. The government has at different times temporarily repealed payroll taxes, recovering the lost revenue through other types of general taxation or the value-added tax (the first such repeal was introduced in 1968 in favour of businesses in the South).[33]

(2) *Tax credits for reinvested profits and for job creation* (provisions introduced in July 1994). (i) 50 per cent of reinvested profits are tax free. Moreover, as for the past, firms can set aside funds, called 'funds under tax suspension', which are tax free if reinvested within two years; (ii) a tax credit up to L7.5 million per worker newly hired is granted. Also, to encourage young people to start new businesses, in July 1994 a *forfait tax* was established for the first three years (2, 3, and 4 million for the first, the second, and the third year respectively).

(3) *Depreciation*. Allowances for depreciation have undergone tightening all the way through the 1990s. Standard and accelerated depreciations are provided for. *Standard depreciation* refers to the proper economic (physical and technological) depreciation of real assets used in business, including structures, plants, and equipment. Straight-line charges reflecting economic depreciation, calculated by applying coefficients listed in the law to the purchase price, plus all supplementary maintenance expenses, are deductible as costs from business income, beginning in the year of its first utilization (instead of in the year of its purchase, as was the case until 1989). Moreover in

[32] The definition of small business for such subsidized loans does not coincide with the definition for special treatment under the corporation income tax. The basic criterion here is the number of employees.

[33] Since 1977 there have been 'temporary' national repeals, each lasting generally eight months. Therefore, since that date there have been two repeals a year, from January to June and from June to December. The repeals cover only a part of social security contributions and, although they apply to the whole national territory, they are neither uniform nor equal for every category of worker (they distinguish, for instance, between male and female workers).

the first year the charges are reduced to one-half of the coefficients listed. Additional deductions for 'anticipated depreciation' are still allowed but reduced in amount. In 1989 the standard charges could be raised by up to two and half times, while from 1990 they may only be doubled in the first three years. These larger deductions (*accelerated depreciation*) are allowed when the asset is used up more intensively.[34] If an asset is scrapped before depreciation is fully recovered, the residual value is deductible (but if sold, the residual value becomes taxable income).

The crucial question about depreciation concerns the adjustment of the value of assets for inflation. As mentioned, the asset values for depreciation purposes are still based on historical cost. The debate over proper accounting for inflation has not led to the adoption of the qualitatively different concepts of replacement costs or present value in place of the historical cost concept. Occasionally, particular provisions have been introduced from time to time, until more general revaluations of listed assets were allowed in 1975 and 1983, and again more recently in 1990 (law 408/90). While the former provisions did actually aim at recuperating the effects of inflation on the value of assets, the latter combines this aim with that of revenue maintenance. The former provisions allowed even for the revaluation of already fully amortized assets (provided they appeared in the firm's accounts). Basically two types of revaluations were allowed. A 'direct' revaluation, consisting of the application of given coefficients to the purchase price of each asset (20, 30, or 40 per cent, depending on the date of purchase), and an 'indirect' revaluation, allowed for corporations only, consisting of a global revaluation of all physical assets up to a maximum of 50 per cent of the value of the firm's equity capital. The 1990 provisions also allowed for revaluations, but the taxpayer must both pay a 'substitute tax' and wait three years before utilizing the increased depreciations charges. It is not surprising to find out that very few firms revalued their assets according to this law. And indeed in 1991 (law 413/91) revaluations were made compulsory.[35]

In addition to standard depreciation, a so-called *financial depreciation* can

---

[34] No particular rules hold for 'accelerated' depreciation. The law says that accelerated depreciation is allowed when the firm 'uses more intensively' its assets, but no proof of this is required. The fiscal authority may question this procedure a posteriori, but it does so very rarely, if ever. Depreciation allowances are in a sense left to the firm's discretion, within the established general rules and magnitudes.

[35] When inflation is high, as was the case until recently in Italy, depreciation charges calculated at the purchase price do not enable the firm to replace its physical assets at the end of their lives. The 'present value' is the current value faced by the firm wanting to buy the new asset, while the purchase price is the 'historical cost', i.e. the price at which the asset was originally acquired. Pressures from business to have depreciation charges calculated on a present-value basis (instead of historical cost) in order to be able to replace worn-out assets with the charges set aside, were met in the years of high inflation by the revaluation provisions introduced in 1975 and 1983. A different provision, with similar aims and results, was introduced in 1977. This provision, known as *scorporo*, allowed firms to break up single chunks of investment. The singled-out capital equipment could then be allocated to a new branch of the company at its current price. Depreciation charges would thereafter depend on that price.

be deducted from taxable income when the holder of a temporary (although usually very long) licence or concession to utilize a public good or facility for a business purpose, or to organize and run a public service, hands over free to the authority issuing the concession (municipality, regional government, or other) the physical capital assets acquired for running the business when the concession expires. These supplementary annual financial charges are determined by dividing the original acquisition cost of the physical assets by the number of concession years. The rationale would seem to be to exempt from taxation that part of profits which would have to be set aside to repay the value of the assets to be turned over free to the authority at the end of the concession.

Provisions also exist for a so-called *economic depreciation*, consisting in the spreading out of operating losses over a number of years and in depreciation charges for certain expenses for intangibles such as research and development and the acquisition of patent rights. R&D expenses may be amortized over a maximum period of five years, but on the condition of giving a positive result. Expenses for patent rights may be amortized at constant annual rates over the period of utilization established in the contract. Other amortizable expenses are those incurred for the establishment of a new business and for increasing equity capital. Amortization of such expenses is allowed over a maximum period of five years, but the yearly deduction cannot exceed 50 per cent of the total expense.

C2.5 Incentives for Housing and Some Particular Industries

In the 1980s incentives to the housing sector were a main concern. In 1982 an Act was passed granting temporary benefits to boost housing, whose main provisions were the following. For businesses, capital gains enjoyed through the sale of buildings utilized for running the business were exempted from corporate and individual income taxes, provided they were reinvested in the acquisition of other buildings, through the setting aside of a fund tied up for that particular purpose (if they were not so reinvested, a penalty of 75 per cent was due). If an individual bought a flat or a house, new or old, to live in or to rent at the legally determined *equo canone* ('just rent'), the upper limit of mortgage interest and related expenses deductible from taxable income was raised (in contrast, tax increases were introduced for flats or houses held vacant by the owners). Transfers of flats or houses between individuals, which are, as a rule, heavily burdened by indirect taxation, were granted a tax reduction on a temporary basis. In the 1990s these tax expenditures were abolished, and although the construction sector remained sluggish, even the standard deductions for mortgage interest have been reduced. Only the softening of the 'just rent' regulations during the 1990s, by helping to eliminate distortions in the housing market, could produce some beneficial effects.

This evolution is consistent with the declared tax policy aims of the 1990s, namely the gradual elimination of all or most tax expenditures. A quantitative estimate of the revenue costs of tax expenditures was made by a commission of the Ministry of Finance in the 1990s (law 408/90, modified by law 413/91). The enquiry identified 825 tax expenditures concerning direct taxes, VAT, *imposta di fabbricazione* ('production tax'), local taxes, customs, registration taxes, and stamp duties.[36] This widespread and chaotic system of tax incentives to the production sector creates too many distortions, especially because it causes the effective tax rates to be quite different from the statutory ones. In this respect, firms which are ineligible for tax expenditure are twice discriminated against. The aim of gradually eliminating the great majority of tax expenditures enjoys great verbal support, but it has proved to be very difficult to put into practice. However, in line with the general philosophy, the tax expenditures of the 1990s (in the form of tax credits) concern few cases, namely small and medium firms (law 317/91), mining and *imprese distributrici di carburanti* (law 75/93), and *imprese rivenditrici di prodotti audiovisivi e cinefotoottici* (law 42/93).

C3 Distribution of the Tax Burden

C3.1 Effective Income Tax Rates by Income Classes

Recently effective income tax rates have been calculated on the basis of both the 1989 data as the most recent ones provided by the Ministry of Finance and those of 1982 as the year of comparison. During this period revisions of number of brakets, of rates, and deductions took place making the comparison quite interesting. The study divides the 27.7 million taxpayers of 1989 (23 millions in 1983) in five quintiles, every one containing 20 per cent of the total (taxpayers) population. The following emerges from the study:[37]

(1) Total average income increased from L9.97 million in 1982 to L19.16 million in 1989. The average effective rate changed very little, being 17.3 in 1982 and 18.5 in 1989.

(2) For the second quintile a reduction of 0.2 per cent was registered in the effective rate. For all the other quintiles increases in the effective rates were instead registered. The smallest of them concerned the first quintile (see Fig. 5.3).

(3) Concentration of ratio of net tax liability increased from 56 to 59 per cent, showing an equitative capacity of the income tax during the period.

(4) Notwithstanding point (3), the checking for the intensity of the equitative capacity through the redistribution index, led to the discovery of a reduced capacity as measured by the decline in the value of the index, from

---

[36] Many of the 825 tax expenditures are irrelevant in terms of revenue loss. In fact 72% of the estimated revenue loss comes from 35% of the provisions. The revenue loss associated with the 190 most important of them has been estimated to be L76,861 billion.   [37] Rossi (1993).

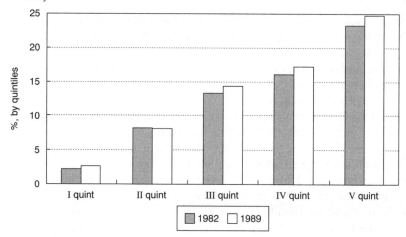

Fig. 5.3 Average effective IRPEF rates, 1982 and 1989

Source: Reproduction of Fig. 3.1 in N. Rossi (ed.), *La crescita ineguale, 1981–1991*, Primo rapporto CNEL sulla distribuzione e redistribuzione del reddito in Italia, Il Mulino, 1993.

10.2 to 9.5 per cent. This result is confirmed by the use of the Lorenz curve: the 1982's one totally dominates that of 1989.

C3.2 Overall Tax Burden by Income Tax Classes

It is generally believed that the Italian tax system is roughly proportional, and there is wide agreement on the following propositions.

(1) The progressive income tax is not really a global tax, but rather a discriminating one on some incomes, with a high level of evasion (illegal) by certain categories of income earners and an extensive avoidance (legal) of the tax base. Only wages, salaries, and pensions are fully taxed.

(2) VAT has been believed to be slightly progressive, thanks to its multiple rates, but it is known to suffer from extensive evasion, and the need to conform to EU common rules has further impaired its nominal progressivity through the abolition of higher than standard rates.

(3) The tax on inheritance and gifts is supposed to contribute substantially to the progressivity of the system, both because the tax base is wealth and because its nominal rates are themselves highly progressive. The philosophy underlying this tax has always been that of redistributing unearned wealth among individuals, and this is the main reason for its high nominal progressivity. As a wealth-redistributing tax, it has been widely considered superior to other taxes on the (questionable) assumption that it doesn't discourage work and saving. Nevertheless, since its revenue is unrealistically low the tax is thought to be largely evaded, legally and illegally, and its actual role in the redistribution of wealth and in contributing to the system's progressivity seems to have been a minor one so far. On the other hand the system's

progressivity is expected to increase following the recent introduction of a proper (progressive) wealth tax (first ISI and then ICI, see above).

There is no general agreement regarding the economic incidence of payroll taxes. Views range from the belief that they are fully shifted into prices or lower wages to the assertion, especially by the business community, that at least in the short run they squeeze profits. The persistent request by the business community for fiscal relief from social security contributions is a sign that to some extent the latter view may be valid. With respect to exports, the non-shifting hypothesis seems to be the most likely.

Quantitatively, in the recent past microsimulation tax models have entered the Italian scene.[38] In a recent model of this type (Bernardi *et al.* 1992) the distribution of the tax burden by income classes has been calculated with reference to the following taxes: IRPEF, ILOR, withholding taxes on bank, postal deposits and Treasury bonds, and social security contributions. As is always the case in this type of model, the assumptions concerning tax shifting are crucial for the results. In the B et al. model the no-shifting hypothesis holds for all mentioned taxes, except for social security contributions on employers, which are assumed to be fully shifted forward. Under these assumptions, using Bank of Italy data on households, consumption, and with 1987 as the reference year for the fiscal data, a high progressive impact for low-average income classes emerges from the model. This high progressive impact quickly slows down as household income grows. This particular fact is quite common to many tax systems although the level of income at which progressivity slows down may vary. The result obtained by a microsimulation exercise that replaces the withholding taxes on financial incomes (except dividends) with the income tax is a peculiar and interesting one. Apparently the resulting distributional impact would be little modified. If this were true, the widely held view in the Italian debate, that the withholding system of taxing financial incomes significantly impairs progressivity, would be contradicted.

C4 The Hidden Economy

C4.1 The Parallel Economy Explanation
The most widely accepted explanation for the existence of a hidden economy in Italy, given by Contini[39] at the end of the 1970s, and known as the 'parallel economy' explanation, is probably still valid today. Of course the hidden economy of the 1990s is in many respects quite different from that of the 1980s, which in turn is different from that of the 1970s, basically because it first appeared as a typical phenomenon in the less skilled and less remunerated sectors (backward and labour-intensive sectors), but it is now widespread also

[38] Bernardi (1990); and Bernardi *et al.*, (1992).
[39] Contini (1979; 1981: 33; 1992).

in the technologically advanced sectors.[40] The parallel economy explanation is that the hidden economy is an anticyclical phenomenon: the hidden activity grows when the economy slackens. The hidden economy is a solution to the rigidities of the economy with respect not only to wages but also to all other regulations brought by union power into industrial relations. Such rigidities—the most important being the immobility of labour and the practical impossibility of activating part-time jobs (only very recently some timid proposals to allow for part-time jobs have appeared)—were overcome by moonlight jobs which escaped payroll taxation. Moonlight jobs escaped income tax as well, but this was not as important a motivation as the avoidance of payroll taxes. Proof of the primary role of payroll taxes is the persistent request by businesses for their 'fiscalization' (i.e. transformation into general taxation), and the persistent tendency to switch to more capital-intensive techniques as soon as the government allows businesses to release employees.

Other aspects of the social security system are also responsible for the hidden economy. If high payroll taxes are the main cause on the employers' (demand) side, the receipt of social security benefits is an important cause on the workers' (supply) side. A major part of concealed legal employment comes from pensioners, pre-pensioners,[41] recipients of unemployment benefits, and housewives, who don't want to lose their social security benefits.[42] On the labour supply side, not losing social security benefits seems to be a more important motive than escaping income tax.

As far as VAT is concerned, the level of evasion is high. It is quite common, especially in the small business sector, to under-report revenues by simply not issuing invoices, or issuing greatly underpriced ones. Very often home repairs, as well as services by physicians, lawyers, and the like, are paid by the client or patient in cash, with no regular invoice, or a greatly underpriced one. However, this is the common way for unincorporated businesses and professionals to avoid both VAT and income tax, and not a specific characteristic of the hidden economy.

[40] The sectors giving the largest contributions to the hidden economy have manifestly changed over the last decades. In the 1970s the most important sector was agriculture, while in the 1980s it was the 'professions'. Broadly speaking, the main reason for the hidden economy in the 1970s was the reaction to the rigidities of the labour market, whereas in the 1980s this was much less the case. In the 1990s new and more numerous causes have emerged, among them the fact that the unions have lost power and that higher income and payroll taxes have made hiding economic transactions more attractive.

[41] Pre-pensioners are people who retire earlier than the compulsory retirement age, after completing a minimum number of working years. Since it is very difficult (indeed impossible in the public sector) to fire workers, in the late 1970s a device was found to reduce employment by encouraging people to anticipate retirement. Essentially, pensions for anticipated retirement were made more generous. Many workers took this opportunity. Once they became pensioners or pre-pensioners, they started a second job: it was quite easy for them to find one in the hidden economy because they were still active and skilled, and their employers no longer paid social security contributions on their earnings.

[42] The average consumption level of pensioners is higher than that of blue-collar workers in industry and agriculture. This cannot be fully explained by the shorter life expectancy.

C4.2 Estimates of Size

The estimates for tax evasion available in the literature are in fact quite high. The evasion of *IRPEF* is estimated to reach 30 per cent, with peaks of 55 per cent self-employed and unincorporated businesses, and that of VAT 20 per cent, with peaks of 30 per cent in commerce.[43]

From the 1980s to the 1990s not only the features of the hidden economy have changed but also public attitudes towards it. While academics and researchers in general show a declining interest in the subject, government agencies seem determined to acquire as accurate an estimate as possible of the size of the hidden economy. Among such institutions SOGEI (an informatics company operating the tax register on behalf of the Ministry of Finance) published in 1992 the results of a study of a random sample of tax returns submitted in 1990 and relative to 1989 incomes, along the lines of the American tax compliance measurement program. The study shows, in line with the common view, that shopkeepers, craftsmen, entrepreneurs, and professionals are the categories which evade the most. While the average annual income of dependent workers is L22.5 million, shopkeepers and entrepreneurs on the one hand and craftsmen on the other report an average income of L19.9 million and L17.6 million respectively (more credible are professionals' reports of an average income of L46.2 million). But it is ISTAT,[44] the agency which has worked more thoroughly on the subject, which has focused on the labour market. For labour supply it uses the information provided by population censuses and sample workforce surveys; for labour demand it uses the information contained in censuses of industry, commerce, handicrafts, services, and agriculture. The main innovation (in the present context) introduced by ISTAT in the system of national accounts is the definition of number of 'working positions' instead of number of employed. The number of individual workers would be equal to the number of 'working positions' when no 'second job' of any kind (part-time or not) exists. It became quite clear in the 1980s that many individuals were engaged in more than one activity. Therefore in the national accounts the amount of labour applied to production is expressed in terms of 'units of labour', which are obtained by transforming working positions into homogeneous units. On the basis of this process ISTAT has produced separate figures for the various categories of working positions. They are reproduced in Table 5.9. As it appears from columns 2 and 3, figures in brackets suggest that the proportion of the irregular economy has not been reduced.

15.1 per cent of GDP can be taken as a plausible estimate of the size of the hidden economy for the period 1970–96. The figures are obtained by applying

---

[43] See Cerea (1992: 158).
[44] ISTAT (Central Statistical Office) completed a general revision of its accounting methods in 1987, which caused substantial revaluations of GNP, namely by 15.4% in 1982, 17.7% in 1985, and 16% in 1986. See ISTAT (1990, 1993).

194   *Italy*

Table 5.9   Total labour units, by category ('000s), 1981–1996

	Total labour units (1)[a]	Regular employm. (2)	Non-regular employm. (3)[b]	Irregular employm. (4)	Secondary jobs (5)	Non-registered employm. (6)	Non-resident foreigners (7)
1981	22,060.3	17,398.3	4,662	2,344.8	1,458.6	537.5	321.1
		(78.9)	(21.1)	(10.6)	(6.6)	(2.4)	(1.4)
1982	22,181.8	17,455.3	4,726.5	2,334.6	1,520.8	482.5	388.6
		(78.7)	(21.3)	(10.5)	(6.8)	(1.9)	(1.7)
1983	22,324.5	17,386.3	4,938.2	2,314.6	1,656.6	532.0	435.0
		(77.9)	(22.1)	(10.4)	(7.4)	(2.4)	(1.9)
1984	22,412.9	17,332.1	5,080.8	2,313.0	1,726.5	576.4	464.9
		(77.3)	(22.7)	(10.3)	(7.7)	(2.6)	(2.1)
1985	22,612.7	17,531.7	5,081.0	2,334.7	1,730.7	520.6	495.0
		(77.5)	(22.5)	(10.3)	(7.7)	(2.3)	(2.2)
1986	22,786.3	17,588.2	5,228.0	2,375.3	1,786.1	511.6	525.1
		(77.2)	(23.0)	(10.4)	(7.8)	(2.2)	(2.3)
1987	22,877.5	17,638.4	5,239.0	2,366.3	1,850.0	472.2	548.6
		(77.1)	(23.0)	(10.3)	(8.1)	(2.1)	(2.4)
1988	23,073	17,795.4	5,277.6	2,391.6	1,878.1	453.3	554.6
		(77.1)	(22.9)	(10.4)	(8.1)	(1.9)	(2.4)
1989	23,087.2	17,835.1	5,225.0	2,376.8	1,860.8	441.7	572.8
		(77.2)	(22.8)	(10.3)	(8.1)	(1.9)	(2.5)
1990	23,344.1	18,013.3	5,330.8	2,416.7	1,923.6	417.2	573.3
		(77.2)	(22.8)	(10.3)	(8.2)	(1.8)	(2.5)
1991	23,522.5	18,138.0	5,384.5	2,470.0	1,942.2	393.1	579.2
		(77.1)	(22.9)	(10.5)	(8.2)	(1.7)	(2.5)
1992	23,271.7	18,006.7	5,265.0	2,478.4	1,774.3	398.2	614.1
		(77.4)	(22.6)	(10.6)	(7.6)	(1.7)	(2.6)
1993	22,603.3	17,490.0	5,113.3	2,366.2	1,764.4	349.0	633.7
		(77.4)	(22.6)	(10.5)	(7.8)	(1.5)	(2.8)
1994	22,290.1	17,255.5	5,034.6	2,285.5	1,798.8	280.7	669.6
		(77.4)	(22.6)	(10.3)	(8.1)	(1.3)	(3.0)
1995	22,234.6	17,229.6	5,005.0	2,254.4	1,788.6	278.6	683.4
		(77.5)	(22.5)	(10.1)	(8.0)	(1.3)	(3.1)
1996	22,273.0	17,298.1	4,974.9	2,240.2	1,776.1	261.5	697.1
		(77.7)	(22.3)	(10.1)	(8.0)	(1.2)	(3.1)

[a] (1) = (2) + (3).
[b] (3) = (4) + (5) + (6) + (7).
In brackets: ratios relative to (1).

Source: ISTAT, *Occupazione e redditi da lavoro dipendente, anni 1980–91*, Rome, 1992. ibid., *Annuario*, various years.

the monetary Tanzi method (Tanzi, 1980) to the Italian data (see Bovi and Castellucci, 1997). Of course different figures may be proposed, claiming to estimate something which is by definition non-measurable, but the very existence of a hidden economy of substantial size is confirmed by many different indicators.[45]

C5 Administrative and Compliance Costs

At the time of the basic tax reform (1973–74) the taxpayers under personal taxation totalled 4.5 million while at the end of the 1980s they had jumped to 24 million and to 27.8 million in 1990. Even an efficient administration (which was not the case) could not manage such a huge increase without substantial changes in its organization. But in fact the organization was never brought up to the new situation and even in the public debate this topic was not given the importance it deserves until very recently. It is now generally recognized that a good tax reform needs a good administration to begin with and therefore some efforts have been made to improve the efficacy and efficiency of public administration in general and of tax administration in particular. Equally, the unsatisfactory functioning of tax administration is widely thought to be responsible for most of tax evasion and avoidance.

It is, however, true that the evolution of the Italian economic system combined with some specific characteristics of the tax system, has contributed to strain the administration. For one thing personal incomes and value added are not generated in a centralized way; and even our large firms have evolved in the direction of reducing their production processes by buying all sorts of goods and services from the outside. Leaving aside social security contributions, of the more than one hundred taxes, 65 per cent of total revenues are provided by personal income tax, value-added tax, and oil production tax (adding just six more, one reaches the 95 per cent of total revenue). The methods of tax collection for these taxes, mainly through 'withholding' (*sostituto d'imposta*) and 'compensation' (*rivalsa*), are not the most suitable ones, in the sense that for a good working of the *sostituto* and *rivalsa* methods would require the structure of the economy to be based on several large firms. However, it must be recognized that a professionally modest staff and its misallocation, both territorially and among agencies, offices, and tax departments, are the main shortcomings of Italy's tax administration. As far as the number of employees is concerned, attention is frequently called to the fact that it is (supposedly) too small.[46] While revenues collected come from the North, the Centre, and the South in the proportion of 59, 25, and 16 per cent respectively, the proportions of employees in those areas are 37, 32, and 31 per cent respectively. Moreover while 10,000 employees administer the registration

---

[45] Information for past years is given in a survey paper by Patrizii (1986).

[46] According to the latest census, from 1974 to 1993 the total (including the military branch, the *Guardia di finanza*) number of employees grew from 97,000 to 127,184, a number slightly smaller than that of the USA. But there is no doubt about their wrong distribution with respect to geographic areas and tax departments.

tax, only one-half of that are assigned to the value-added tax, which provides five times more revenue than the registration tax.[47]

It is generally believed that the costs of overall administration of taxes are excessively high. Not only because the revenue authorities are notoriously inefficient but also because there are a lot of associated costs for taxpayers. According to tentative estimates on 1985 figures, the total cost, considering both the administration and the taxpayer, turns out to be more than 10 per cent of revenue collected. The cost of the tax administration is about 6.5 per cent, 1.8 per cent is the compliance cost for the personal income taxpayer, and 2.6 per cent is the compliance cost for the firms.[48]

D. Tax Reforms

D1 Main Tax Reforms, 1987–97

The following are the main issues considered by the government since 1987:

(1) the local tax system,
(2) the taxation of financial assets,
(3) the introduction of some administrative devices to modernize bureaucratic procedures and to reduce evasion and erosion,
(4) the introduction of a minimum tax,
(5) the taxation of capital gains,
(6) the non-deductibility of ILOR from IRPEG,
(7) the introduction of a wealth tax for firms,
(8) payroll taxes for social security, the revision of the pension system, and the associated introduction and development of pension funds, and
(9) the Eurotax.

D1.1 The Local Tax System

During the last few years there have been great expectations about the reform of the local tax system. Shortly after the 1973–4 tax reform, the difficult financial conditions of municipalities became apparent. Their own taxes had been abolished, and in their place they were entitled to transfers from the central government. Since transfers were always delayed and were smaller than the forgone own revenue, municipalities began stepping up their borrowing from the banking system. The growing interest charges increased expenditures, which were already being pushed upwards by the growing demand for public goods. This produced a 'vicious circle'. In the short run, the way out was to resort to periodic, annual legislation at the national level allowing increases in the rates of whatever municipal taxes still existed, or setting constraints to employment by local authorities to slow down the growth of expenditures. But in the long run a more general reform was needed to stop the growth of local deficits paid by the central government. As explained above (section B7) the idea of linking the responsibility for expenditure with that of taxation gained momentum in the 1993 legislation initiatives which began to reform local taxation.

[47] Ceriani *et al.* (1992: 631).   [48] Ghessi (1980).

D1.2 The Taxation of Financial Assets

A general revision of financial taxation has long since been on the agenda, but only various unconnected regulations have been enacted. First came the taxation of interest income on public bonds in 1986, then the increase in most of the withholding rates in 1988, followed by the introduction of a capital gains tax on financial assets held by individuals in 1991 ('suspended' since 1993). The announced general revision is stil due (law 662/96 empowered the government to legislate on the subject by 1997). The harmonization, or coordination, at the European level is a main concern, as is the reform of the pensions system through 'supplementary private pension schemes'. Such schemes would have implications in terms both of the creation of new financial intermediaries and of the taxation of financial returns of any kind. Finally, although the proposals to reform the taxation of financial assets in the direction of a comprehensive income tax have been advanced (see below), suggestions are more recently for the introduction of dual income tax.

D1.3 Modernizing Bureaucratic Procedures and Reducing Evasion

Some administrative devices have been introduced to (i) enhance efficiency and compliance, and (ii) limit evasion and avoidance. In the 1990s administrative problems were given more importance than in the past, in response to the growing view that for an optimal fiscal system to be effective, it is necessary to have not only well-defined tax bases and tax rates, but also efficient ways of assessing and collecting them. In terms of revenue collected and of equity, more harm might come from the lack of a properly working administrative structure than from imperfections in the tax code design.

(1) In addition to the provision reducing the number of people obliged to fill tax returns (which became effective from 1994), law 413/91 authorizes the constitution of 'Fiscal assistance centres' (*Centri di assistenza fiscale*, CAF). These, very similar to those in France, are of two types, one for dependent workers and one for firms. The first type is intended to help the taxpayers in filling their returns, while the second type should enhance compliance and limit avoidance/evasion in providing the basis for the applications of 'presumptive coefficients' (see below). As for tax collection, a more efficient 'Central service for collection' has been introduced (1990), set up between groups of banks who apply to the Ministry of Finance to get the corresponding licence. Improvements are expected both in terms of managerial qualities and integrity. Another innovation is the introduction of the so-called 'fiscal account' (*Conto fiscale*) sent to the taxpayer who can then automatically compensate his credits and liabilities with respect to the different taxes (IRPEG, VAT, ILOR, taxes of previous years, etc.). This is a big improvement for the Italian taxpayer who has to wait on average more than five years for the reinbursement of taxes overpaid. There is, however, an equity short-coming: the fiscal account has been limited to certain categories of taxpayers.

(2) Two devices have been introduced to limit evasion. One is the 'income-meter' (*redditometro*) and the other is the institute of 'presumptive

coefficients' (*coefficienti presuntivi*). The *redditometro* is device to help revenue authorities in their assessment (*accertamento*) of a physical person's income. The device was introduced in 1983 but only law 413/91 was able to put it into effect. On the basis of ability-to-pay indicators (such as ownership of houses, cars, planes, utilization of domestic servants) that the taxpayer must report in his return, the revenue authorities calculate a synthetic taxpayer's income. If for two consecutive years the reported income is less than that (by a certain amount), then the revenue authorities can levy the tax on such synthetically calculated income. The application is tempered by various qualifications, but the device does encourage more truthful reporting.

'Presumptive coefficients' serve a similar purpose of 'synthetically' determining revenues of professionals and firms with simplified bookkeeping rules. In 1996 these coefficients were replaced by parameters based on so-called 'sectoral studies' to get to estimated revenues.

D1.4 Minimum Tax

Among the initiatives to improve public finance balances, and on the (largely accepted) assumption of high evasion by self-employed people and small businesses, a so-called *minimum tax* was introduced for such sectors by law 438/92 (to be effective until 1994, by which date a general revision of business income taxation was scheduled in vain to be enacted). It was expected to take place during 1997. A new element in the Italian tax system was that the conventionally determined minimum amount of income became effective at the very moment of the taxpayer's self-assessment of his own tax liability, in the sense that if the taxpayer reported an income lower than the minimum, he was charged on this minimum, plus a surcharge on the difference, without any further enquiry. Although the law contained particular provisions for marginal taxpayers, too often the conventional tax basis turned out to be greater than the actual one. After innumerable complaints the tax was in practice, though not formally, repealed by amendments which brought it back into the logic of 'presumptive coefficients'.

D1.5 Capital Gains under the Individual Income Tax

As already mentioned a proper capital gains tax for individuals has been called for ever since the reform of the 1970s in order to close what was regarded as a large loophole in the system. Such a tax was eventually introduced in 1991 by law 102/91. It was supposed to bring a substantial improvement into the system, but it turned out that the loophole closed by it was not as great as had been expected: 0.03 per cent of total revenue in 1991 and slightly more in 1992. And indeed, soon after its introduction the tax was 'suspended', starting with the 1993 fiscal year (see above, B1.2). The importance of taxing in principle all sources of income and therefore also capital gains is a generally and rightly accepted fact. But looking at the Italian tax system as a whole and considering it in its historical perspective and in its connection with the economic system, we believe that other considerations should have prevailed, with no significant losses in terms of equity. It is apparent that the actual tax status of capital gains was not the 'tax-free' one incorrectly described in public debate.

First, the real loophole concerned the *individual taxpayer* only, because capital gains were already in the corporate income tax base.

Second, with the introduction of INVIM in 1973 and its major revision in 1980 all increments of value of land and real estate (whether speculative or not) came under taxation, both for individuals and for corporations.[49] It is true that this way of taxing capital gains did not conform to the idea of a comprehensive income tax,[50] but it was nevertheless a form of taxation. Moreover, revenue expectations were groundless because in Italy the bulk of capital gains came and still comes from land and real estate, as the Italian stock market has so far been fairly marginal and poorly functioning.

Finally, although law 102/1991 aimed at a comprehensive income tax, it introduced in practice two alternative regimes of taxing capital gains: (i) a standard regime that simply puts capital gains under IRPEF and allows for capital loss deductions, and (ii) a *forfait* regime that operates through a final withholding payment of 25 per cent with no deductions for capital losses. This second regime, which was chosen by approximately 97 per cent of taxpayers, was no anomaly. A flat-rate (variable with type of investor, form of finance, etc.) final withholding tax (*imposta sostitutiva*) on nominal interest income exists in the tax system.[51] The extension of such final substitution tax to capital gains is in line with the logic of the system as a whole.

On the whole, it would have been wiser to postpone the introduction of a capital gains tax until the general revision of the tax treatment of financial capital income. This is nowadays one of the most important tax issues and there is unanimity on the need for reform in the area, although for different reasons. The government was expected to submit to Parliament during 1997 a new law reforming the taxation of income from financial capital along the lines of a dual income tax.

---

[49] Corporations were also subjected every ten years to a special INVIM called 'decennial INVIM'.

[50] As a general rule, it is due only if, and when, ownership is transferred (by sale, inheritance, or gift). The tax base is the difference between the sale and acquisition price of the asset (standard INVIM). But for corporations the tax is due every ten years, even if assets do not change hands (decennial INVIM). In this case the tax base is the difference between the current asset value and the value registered the last time the asset was taxed (the initial values were set in 1963). Rates are progressive beginning with 5% for up to a 20% increment in value, and rising to over 30% for increments of over 200%. The tax is assessed and collected by the central government, while municipalities where the assets are located participate in the assessment and receive the revenue.   [51] See Alworth and Castellucci (1993: 218).

D1.6 *Non-deductibility of ILOR from IRPEG*

When the deductibility of ILOR from IRPEG was abolished in 1993 no convincing reasons were given except the need for more revenue. Since the two taxes have practically the same base it would seem fair to allow the deduction.

D1.7 *A Wealth Tax for Firms*

The recent introduction of a tax on net wealth of firms (law 461/92) is another example of the logic underlying the 1990's tax provisions. The tax, which was scheduled to be in existence for only three years, serves only the purpose of increasing tax revenue (for the negative phase of the cycle and the increase in the overall tax rates on firms due to the non-deductibility of ILOR puts an extra burden on firms). It is still there but will disappear with the introduction of the regional tax on economic activities (IRAP).

D1.8 *Payroll Taxes for Social Security and Pension System Revision*

Payroll taxes (*contributi sociali*) are paid directly to social security agencies—by far the most important is the INPS (*Istituto nazionale di previdenza sociale*)—and as they fall far short of total social expenditures other sources of finance are therefore necessary. In 1989 social expenditures (health, pensions, and other social transfers) amounted to 22 per cent of GDP (27.14 per cent in 1994), while social security contributions amounted to 14 per cent of GDP (Tables 5.10 and 5.5). Thus the 'insurance approach' and the 'budget approach' are both at work simultaneously because the financing of social expenditures comes both from social security contributions and transfers from the government. The second source has become more important over the last fifteen years, with the first still contributing at present approximately 85 per cent of total outlays. Social expenditures have been growing without interruption since the Second World War, but with peaks in conjunction with the extension of pension payments and medicare to all citizens who had not paid any social contributions (for instance, agricultural workers in the middle 1960s), with the establishment of the *Cassa integrazione guadagni*,[52] and with the continuous shortening of the 'sliding scale' (*contingenza*) time-interval.[53] The real problem with social security, in particular with pensions, which are its largest component, lies not so much in the growth of social expenditures but in the growing difference between expenditures and contributions. This divergence is the natural consequence of the dynamics of pensions payments and revenues. On the expenditure side, the number of pensioners and the average pension payment have both been growing. Contributions depend on the number of working people and the average

---

[52] A public agency which is, broadly speaking, in charge of paying unemployment benefits to workers temporarily unemployed.

[53] The *scala mobile* or *contingenza* is a supplementary payment added to the base wage, salary, or pension, linked to the cost-of-living index and intended to make adjustment for inflation. The adjustment was originally made every six months.

Table 5.10 Social expenditure: % of GDP, 1987–1994

	1987	1988	1989	1990	1991	1992	1994
Education	5.1	5.2	5.2	5.4	5.2	5.3	5.2
Health	5.7	5.9	5.8	6.3	6.6	6.4	5.8
Pensions & social transfers	16.0	15.9	16.2	16.6	16.7	17.7	18
Total	26.8	27.0	27.2	28.3	28.5	29.4	29

Source: Own calculations on ISAT, *Conti delle amministrazioni pubbliche e della protezione sociale, anni 1987–92*, 1994

contribution, which in turn is a function of payroll tax rates and average pay. The number of working people relative to retired ones has been declining in Italy (as has in all industrial countries). The ageing of population is significant in Italy (as elsewhere), and will become even more so in the future. In addition, with a slow-growing economy, as has been the case in the last few years, the increase in unemployment reduces the payroll tax base.[54]

This well-known dynamics of social security cannot be brought into balance unless the government decides to reduce pensions or increase payroll tax rates, or to rely more on transfers from general revenues to the social security agencies. Contributions have been raised on some categories of self-employed, such as craftsmen and trade dealers, leading to some reduction in current losses, but at the same time there has been a deterioration in the social security balance for agricultural workers. All things considered, it is un-realistic to expect either a further increase in payroll tax rates, which are already high compared to other countries, or a reduction in the average pension. For employees the level of pension payments is not determined on the basis of contributions paid, but as a percentage of the pay received in the three (or five) most favourable years of the last ten. This method is not used for the self-employed, whose pensions are based on the contributions paid. For agricultural workers the reference pay is established by law. On the whole, pensions have become increasingly less tied to contributions and more tied to the rising pay levels of working people and the rising cost of living. Therefore, the share of government transfers in financing social security must be expected to continue to increase in the future. A look at the composition of social expenditures by agencies and by type of services may further clarify the picture. Table 5.11 shows the divergence between expenditures and revenues of social security agencies. It also appears that public social security agencies are in deficit, while private ones exhibit positive balances, reflecting increases in pension reserves set aside by businesses. As to the type of social security services (Table 5.12), the largest expenditure items are pensions (*previdenza*), social welfare provisions (*assistenza*), and health (*sanita*).

---

[54] Payroll tax revenues also decline when, for a given aggregate level of employment, some workers become self-employed.

Table 5.11 Economic accounts of social protection, by agency, 1988–1995 (billion Liras)

Agency		1988	1989	1990	1991	1992	1993	1994	1995
Revenues	Public agencies	229,866	259,903	290,892	327,697	356,334	379,444	404,046	405,616
	Social contributions	149,381	167,472	189,309	210,004	226,358	240,615	244,310	260,833
	Other contributions	75,613	86,601	94,781	110,430	121,855	128,937	150,022	134,468
	Private agencies	25,049	28,397	31,445	34,780	38,041	36,388	36,466	36,772
	Social contributions	22,950	26,241	29,360	32,092	35,033	34,209	32,528	35,170
	Other contributions	2,078	2,134	2,062	2,663	2,978	2,151	3,910	1,573
	Total	254,285	287,541	321,422	361,512	393,336	415,832	440,512	442,388
Expenditures	Public agencies	234,915	260,621	298,118	329,945	360,518	378,162	397,099	411,730
	Social transfers & services	223,476	247,038	282,572	312,147	341,503	358,149	376,287	392,046
	Other contributions	1,571	2,495	2,498	3,262	3,523	3,034	2,812	2,575
	Private agencies	14,919	16,348	18,441	22,188	26,762	25,378	26,262	24,489
	Social transfers & services	13,441	14,918	17,236	20,430	24,755	24,371	24,459	24,093
	Other contributions	1,369	1,312	1,083	1,632	1,872	874	1,684	273
	Total	249,834	276,210	315,644	351,168	386,241	403,540	423,361	436,219
Balances	Public agencies	−5,049	−718	−7,226	−2,248	−4,184	1,282	6,947	−6,114
	Private agencies	10,130	12,049	13,004	12,592	11,279	11,010	10,204	12,283
	Total	5,081	11,331	5,778	10,344	7,095	12,292	17,151	6,169

Figures do not add to total because some revenues and expenditures are not shown.

Source: CEIS, Università di Roma *Tor Vergata*, calculations on ISTAT, *Conti delle amministrazioni pubbliche e della protezione sociale, anni 1987–92*, Rome 1994. ibid., *Annuario*, various years.

Table 5.12 Economic accounts of social protection, by main functions, 1988–1995 (billion Liras)

		1988	1989	1990	1991	1992	1993	1994	1995
Public health	Social contributions (1)	29,591	36,914	42,642	44,860	46,421	48,623	44,626	542
	Other contributions	27,129	23,085	21,651	33,495	36,729	41,308	46,878	34,241
	Total revenues (2)	57,596	61,235	65,673	79,777	85,043	92,531	94,570	85,073
	Social services (3)	57,247	61,895	73,916	83,254	85,707	86,692	86,410	86,382
	Total expenses (4)	62,773	68,269	80,688	91,878	95,021	95,599	95,681	94,715
	(1)–(3)	−27,656	−24,981	−31,274	−38,394	−39,286	−38,069	−41,784	−38,840
	(2)–(4)	−5,177	−7,034	−15,015	−12,101	−9,978	−3,068	−1,111	−9,642
Pensions	Social contributions (5)	140,269	153,755	172,464	192,917	210,486	221,553	227,339	243,441
	Other contributions	36,175	49,171	57,657	61,132	68,229	67,032	83,387	77,611
	Total revenues (6)	180,338	207,415	235,470	259,809	284,862	295,666	317,155	327,851
	Social transfers & services (7)	159,512	177,142	200,413	222,252	251,951	263,614	280,499	295,409
	Total expenses (8)	170,304	180,775	214,513	237,143	267,576	280,671	299,448	312,457
	(5)–(7)	−19,243	−23,387	−27,949	−29,335	−41,465	−42,061	−53,160	−51,968
	(6)–(8)	10,034	26,640	20,957	22,666	17,286	14,995	17,707	15,394
Welfare	Total revenues (9)	20,237	23,268	25,986	27,576	29,163	33,379	35,237	34,563
	Social transfers & services	20,158	22,919	25,479	27,071	28,600	32,214	33,837	34,348
	Total expenses (10)	20,733	23,543	26,150	27,797	29,376	33,014	34,682	35,146
	(9)–(10)	−496	−275	−164	−221	−213	365	555	417

Figures do not add to total because some revenues and expenditures are not shown.

Source: CEIS, Università di Roma *Tor Vergata*, calculations on ISTAT, *Conti delle amministrazioni pubbliche e della protezione sociale, anni 1987–92*, Rome 1994. ibid., *Annuario*, various years

The pension system is among the main causes of Italy's huge public debt. A too generous mechanism for the calculation of pensions, combined with a too small number of working years before being entitled to a pension, together with the adverse demographic evolution, have led to the financial crisis of the largest public pension agency (INPS). The critical situation must be dealt with without delay. The measures adopted so far are of three kinds:

(1) Tightening the rules for calculating pensions. As from January 1993 the entire working life is considered for the calculation instead of the three or five best-salary years. Also the age at which entitlement to pension is reached has been raised to 65 years for men and 60 for women, and the minimum number of working years has been raised to twenty (decree law 503/92).

(2) Social security contributions were raised by 0.2 per cent in 1993, following an increase of 0.6 per cent in 1992. Some other 'temporary provisions' aimed at easing INPS's financial crisis in the very short run have been introduced, such as the delay in pension increases from 1994 to 1995, and the suspension of the entitlement to the pension from September 1992 to December 1993.

(3) The promotion and development of supplementary pension schemes. Such development is called for not only to help to solve the financial crisis of the pension system, but also to help to modernize Italy's financial market through the active presence of new non-bank financial intermediaries, elsewhere known as pension funds. It is a widely held view in Italy that the development of pensions funds in line with the other industrialized countries will substantially contribute to the development of our stock market. So after more than fifteen years of discussions arguing for the necessity of pension funds, a decree law appeared in 1993 (no. 124) to regulate the subject. The decree has been considered a positive step in the right direction, but it does not seem capable of boosting supplementary pensions schemes, and it may be argued that the chosen tax is the main reason for its failure. A withholding tax of 15 per cent is levied on contributions annually paid to the funds and a wealth one of 0.25 per cent is levied on the funds' capital. In addition, the tax treatment of employer, employee, and self-employed is discouraging. While compulsory contributions paid by employers are fully deductible from their profits, only part of the supplementary ones is deductible (the deductible part is 50 per cent of the annual TFR payment). Equally, contributions paid by the employee and the self-employed are not deductible from taxable income; 27 per cent is deductible from gross tax liability, and the amount on which this percentage is calculated cannot exceed L2.5 million. Far from being favourable, the treatment of supplementary pension schemes compares unfavourably with that of the compulsory one.

Finally, mention must be made of another important issue in the controversy over the pension system's reform, namely the 'freeing' of the 'severance funds'. In order to promote the development of supplementary pension funds there is need not only for a favourable tax treatment (which is not the case with the present regime), but also for an increased availability of finance. According to several experts and commentators, the increased finance would come from the freeing of the 'severance funds' (TFR, *Trattamento di fine rapporto*). But even those who are in favour of this change recommend that it should be gradual in order to avoid putting firms into financial difficulties. Predictably, the Confederation of Italian Industries (*Confindustria*) opposes such TFR-freeing. As already mentioned, in a poorly developed financial market, dominated by bank intermediation, severance funds represent a 'cheap' source of finance. There are no simple solutions to this multidimensional problem (financial crisis of current public pension schemes, need for pension funds as new non-bank financial intermediaries, financial disposal of severance funds), but the only viable guideline would seem to be to gradually increase the role of the market and the scope for 'voluntary' behaviour, while providing a minimum of necessary regulations.

D2 Prospective Tax Reforms

D2.1 *Academic and Experts' Proposals*

Several academic and experts' proposals concerning particular aspects of the tax system appear frequently in the media, but no 'organic' ones concerning the tax system as a whole. Both the local tax reform already passed and the prospective one have roots in the academic profession which, having lately rediscovered the benefit principle, has as a result been calling for greater fiscal autonomy of local administrations. Equally widespread in the academic profession is the view favouring a broadening of the income tax base, together with a reduction of its tax rates. Moreover, compensating increases in indirect taxation are now widely looked on favourably, whereas no longer than ten years ago the opposite view was still predominant. There are three main specific proposals.

The first one is about changing the financing of medical care. The proposed change consists in substituting current payroll contributions by general taxes. Suggestions of 'contributions relief' (*fiscalizzazione*) are not new,[55] but have been raised again more recently, supplemented with technical studies on the possible macro-economic effects (on the budget, employment, prices, and the like) of replacing contributions with taxes.[56] Four possibilities of substitution have been studied, namely: (i) supplementary charges to IRPEF and IRPEG; (ii) a single phase consumption tax; (iii) a VAT; and (iv) an energy

---

[55] In 1986 the *Ragioneria Generale dello Stato* published a pamphlet by the title *Hypotheses for Changes in the Financing of the National Medical Care System*. The hypotheses consist in contributions relief (*fiscalizzazione*) financed through IRPEF and VAT. Also in 1986 an official law proposal (1026/86) of contributions relief was submitted by a group of MPs (Visco and others) envisaging the substitution of contributions with the creation of a regional VAT.

[56] *Documentazione per le Commissioni parlamentari*, 384/90.

consumption tax. Of the four possibilities the third seems the most viable. The first possibility would impose yet further taxes or surcharge on IRPEF and IRPEG, but this would be too distortionary, while the fourth would be insufficient. Between the second and the third possibilities, the latter seems preferable because it shifts the burden of medical care from labour input (as is the case with contributions) onto the entire value added and not simply onto consumption (as in case (ii)). Shifting of the burden from labour to value added could incentivate the use of labour input.

The second proposal was recently advanced by Visco, then an academic and now (1997) Minister of Finance, who has been very active in advancing suggestions for tax reform both on specific topics and of a more fundamental nature. He has been pressing for a wealth tax, a broadening of the tax base through (i) the inclusion of financial incomes, (ii) the reduction of tax erosion concentrated (in his view) in agricultural and real estate incomes, (iii) a more accurate definition of incomes and costs,[57] and (iv) a radical revision of 'reliefs granted on taxes and social security contributions'. A further point emphasized by Visco is the different 'time-profile' of tax payments between dependent and pension incomes and other incomes. While the former are subject to a monthly withholding, the latter postpone payments until the compulsory date for filing tax returns. He would consider it fair to charge interest on postponed payments.[58] A tax proportional to the emission of CO_2 or sulphurdioxide is also encouraged, as well as a regional environment tax to replace possible EU required reductions on our excise tax on mineral oil.

The third proposal is by Tremonti and Vitaletti, both academics and the former Finance Minister, who favour a radical reform as easy to summarize in principle as it is difficult to translate into factual terms.[59] In 1994 they suggested shifting the tax burden 'from persons to things' and substituting the present principle of 'centralized sacrifice' with the new one of 'decentralized benefit'. The proposal emphasizes the need to 'simplify' a tax system made up of an enormous number of particular taxes.[60] In practice they seem to share most of the ideas currently prevailing in the debate on tax reform, such as the need to simplify and modernize the tax code, to improve administrative efficiency, to decentralize by giving greater tax autonomy to local administrations, and to shift the tax burden from direct to indirect taxation. They diverge from the more common view with respect to financial incomes taxation. The concern for the stock market, expecially for corporate financing

[57] He refers to such cost items as travel, accommodation, and eating expenses; acquisition or leasing of cars for personal use; bonuses for attending meetings; fringe benefits in general. See law proposal 2991/88 to the Chamber of Deputies by V. Visco and others.

[58] This argument has recently lost weight because in 1991 a tax prepayment of 98% of the previous year tax liability was introduced.

[59] Tremonti and Vitaletti (1991, 1994).

[60] The need for simplification is indisputable, but the system is inherently complex and in many respects aged, and the simple listing and numbering of individual taxes, including the marginal ones, is not particularly meaningful.

through equity capital, leads them to disregard the call for including all financial incomes in the personal income tax base, and to call instead for final withholding taxes on dividends. They also favour tax incentives for the development of private pension funds by eliminating the present 15 per cent withholding tax on annual contributions to such funds.

D2.2 Business Views

The Confederation of Italian Industries has never taken an official position on tax reform, nor has it circulated unofficial reports. One particular view, held unanimously in the business community, is that social security contributions are just too high, especially when compared with competing countries. Requests for fiscal relief of social security contributions are frequently advanced, especially in periods of recession as in the early 1990s. The Confederation has recently declared its opposition to the freeing of severance funds. The provision would greatly damage the financial positions of firms.

D2.3 Trade Union Views

No official position on the reform of the tax system as a whole is attributable to unions. It is known that the unions have been pressing strongly for (i) the introduction of a property tax, (ii) further increasing the (statutory) tax gap between wage and salary income and income from self-employment, on the grounds that the latter has a much larger coefficient of evasion, and (iii) moving from tax allowances to tax credits.

D2.4 Prospects

Substantial changes to the present tax system are in sight, since law 662/96 empowers the government to legislate on business income, returns on financial assets, and regional taxes, as well as revising rates and deductions of the IRPEF. The allowance for corporate equity and the dual income tax appear to be the models for the first two topics. A reduction in income tax rates might be expected, but one might also expect the opposite, due to the imperative need to reduce the deficit. Some decentralization of the tax system on federalist lines is in sight, chiefly because performances by local authorities are so divergent that more fiscal independence and less redistribution through the central government is called for. Finally, some kind of tax amnesty is expected, not only for revenue needs (ever more pressing), but also for reducing the excessive number of overdue legal disputes. If all this were to happen the entire tax system would be substantially transformed.

E. Personal Views on Past and Preferred Future Developments

Except for the extremely numerous and unconnected fiscal provisions of the 1990s, the evolution of the Italian tax code since the reforms of the 1970s and through the 1990s had its own rationale and was not too different from that of other industrialized countries. Furthermore, the increase in tax revenues which the system was capable of generating during the period must be considered high by European standards. This doesn't mean that the system was fully satisfactory. On the contrary many aspects of the tax code had to be improved, or, to put it differently, the reforms of the 1970s have not been completed. The following features were uncontroversially considered in need of revision (while on many others there was no general agreement in the debate): (i) the treatment of financial capital had to be completely revised, (ii) greater fiscal independence had to be granted to the local administrations, (iii) a proper wealth tax should have entered the Italian scene, and (iv) the chaotic and pervasive network of tax expenditures had to be rationalized and reduced to some absolute minimum. While the second and third point have to some degree been addressed (though not to everybody's satisfaction), on the first and fourth revisions have yet to be produced. The rationale underlying the changes made from the 1970s to the 1990s can be summarized as follows: broadening the tax base, conforming to EU common standards as far as VAT and excises were concerned, reducing tax-induced distortions, and simplifying the system as a whole. In fact every industrialized country, at least after the 1986 US tax reform, wants its taxation to be as neutral as possible with respect to resource allocation. But moving towards a neutral tax code does not mean the same things for every country and does not require the same provisions. In every country economic conditions and social and cultural habits have to be considered in their present and historical dimension before attempting to change the tax code.

There are two special constraints in Italy on any intervention in the tax system: the fiscal deficit and the state of public administration in general and tax administration in particular. While much attention has been given to the problems posed by the deficit, the state of tax administration is not treated in practice as a serious concern. In our view, and without underestimating the problems posed by the huge deficit, the state of tax administration is both the main obstacle to successful reforms and what radically distinguishes Italy from most other EU countries. At the time of the main tax reform, recommendations were advanced to improve the administration, and since then and from time to time mention of the administrative problems appears in the debate but without receiving any factual priority. To be sure, something has been done since the 1970s, but *only at the central level* and *without pursuing any well defined long-term design*. We have already mentioned, as an example of the remarkable failures of the administration, the five years a taxpayer must wait on average to be refunded excess tax payments, this waiting period being regarded as normal because the 'fiscal account', introduced to allow for a fast compensation between tax credits and liabilities, has been limited to certain categories of taxpayers and presented as a special concession. The attitude of regarding grave administrative failures as normal is both dangerous and an ominous sign for future prospects. Equally dangerous, although for different reasons, is entrusting tax bureaucrats with too much power in order to reduce avoidance and evasion. The task of reducing these phenomena (common to all tax systems) is a most important one, but we are sceptical about certain ways of dealing with it. For instance, to let the income-meter (*redditometro*) be used as a way of levying taxes rather than as a device for controlling the truthfulness of self-assessments (as is now the case) might impair tax fairness instead of strengthening it. While we favour any device which may help in increasing compliance, we are distrustful of bureaucratic power: between the (honest) taxpayer and the administration it is the former who needs protection. Bureaucratic discretion should be strictly limited if not completely eliminated. This proposition may or may not be applied to all bureaucracies, but it should certainly be applied to the Italian one. The deeply rooted weakness of the citizen–State relationship in Italy reinforces the case against resorting to personal discretion.

For the same reasons, although sharing them in principle, we are worried about the growing pressures to grant substantial fiscal independence to local administrations. At present, the central tax administration is on the whole by far better staffed and more modern in organization and technology then the local tax administrations (of course with exceptions). For this reason we regard it as necessary to first reshape local administration, and then design a new fiscal federalism with an administration capable of coping with it. On the same grounds we distrust the (re)introduction of 'negotiated settlement' (*concordato*). It is proposed mainly as a way of speeding up the process of the final definition of tax liabilities, but it appears to us both as a return to a system of finalizing tax liabilities which has proved to be unjust in the past (as is well known by those who remember the functioning of the 'family tax' of the 1960s), and a confession by the administration of its inability to accomplish its ordinary duty in a reasonable time-span.

We strongly suggest, and would welcome, moves towards the broadening of the tax base and the abolition of tax expenditures (the listing of all tax expenditures, produced in 1991 by a Ministry of Finance committee in view of their abolition, was a good start).

In line with the view that top priority should be given to administrative improvements, the following aspects of more recent fiscal provisions can be singled out as examples of 'bad' interventions. The introduction of a tax shortly (one or two years) followed by its repeal, as has happened with the minimum tax and capital gains tax, harms the tax system by undermining the administration's credibility and the reliability of tax revenue estimates. These two taxes, which are common in the tax systems of industrialized countries, were in principle a coherent completion of the Italian system, but it was proved that they had not been sufficiently studied with respect to the Italian economic and sociological conditions and so produced mainly negative effects. Another harmful habit, which is unlikely to be abandoned, is the resort to supplementary taxes (additionals) in order to increase tax collection.

The abolition of the many existing additionals was among the achievements of the tax reform of the 1970s.

For the time being it would probably be unwise to change the favourable treatment of agricultural and housing incomes. The agricultural sector has long been in a state of crisis, since (i) industrial employment is decreasing and will probably continue to do so and it will not be possible for industry to employ the workforce leaving agriculture, and (ii) environment protection benefits from agricultural care. The alleged tax erosion originating in agriculture is in our view due to a wrong definition of the sector. Industrial processes 'transforming' agricultural products should not be treated as agriculture. We would favour a preferential tax treatment of agriculture but only after a proper redefinition of the sector. Equally there seems no good reason for removing the favourable treatment (already largely reduced by the recent 'cadastral' revision) of housing income. Saving for housing has been encouraged ever since the Second World War, and owner-occupied housing is now the norm in a high percentage of Italian families (around 80 per cent now have owner-occupied houses). Furthermore a contradictory housing policy, characterized by a combination of complicated just-rent regulations and great difficulties in regaining the disposal of rented flats even in the case judicially proved personal need, seems to justify a favourable tax treatment of house ownership. However, with the introduction of ICI this particular issue has lost much of its momentum.

Also, we have reservations about the current popular (and professional) call for fiscal decentralization without a serious, realistic consideration of the state of the local tax administrations. In Italy the call for 'fiscal federalism' has now become a piece of economic conventional wisdom. It is credited with the capacity to solve so many problems as to raise doubts that it will improve anything. It is supposed to solve the national deficit problem, to restore democracy in the political process, to improve the quality of public services, to smooth out contrasts among regions, to reduce evasion, etc. We all know the virtues of fiscal federalism, namely its foundation in the link between expenditure and taxation responsibilities, but personally we fear there is too much confidence in the creation of decentralization through central government decisions. When regional administrations were created in the 1970s by the same sort of centralized decision process, everybody was expecting all sorts of positive effects, which did not come about. A well-functioning fiscal federalism should emerge more out of a gradual growth process from below (at local level) than out of decision processes and handouts at central government level. Moreover, for fiscal federalism to function at its best a structurally dynamic and flexible economy would be needed, and especially highly mobile and flexible labour and housing markets. Unfortunately the Italian social, legal, and economic framework is characterized by substantial rigidities in labour and housing habits and markets, together with substantial tax disincentives to the buying and selling of property. Summing up, we do favour a gradual progress towards fiscal federalism, but only to the extent that certain structural conditions are also secured in the process: (i) a certain administrative standard at the local level, (ii) a recognition and understanding of the many failures of the regional reform, (iii) a satisfactory approach to Italy's 'dualism', and (iv) a move towards a more dynamic economic and social structure.

In our view the evolution of the Italian tax system cannot significantly diverge from the broadly recognizable European model, including capital taxation, VAT and excises, even if the rates and base of personal income taxation, is likely to remain a largely domestic topic. Here the choices will be heavily conditioned by the fiscal deficit and by the socially desired degree of statutory progressivity. Other shortcomings are due to the structural inadequacy of the tax administration, combined with an excessive tax legislation (too many and too frequent tax provisions often contradicting each other and/or being very obscure). Erosion of the tax base is largely due to this excessive and cumbersome legislation, while evasion is largely due to the tax administration's structural inefficiency. It is a common practice in Italy to tax the self-employed and unincorporated businesses more heavily than employees and pensioners (for example through fewer deductions). It is admittedly due to the widely accepted opinion that these categories evade the most, but this is not an insufficient reason for increasing their nominal taxation. Such an approach does more harm than good. The control of the 'hard-to-tax categories' is a challenge that the administration must meet head on, and the government should stop taking tax decisions on the basis of presumed evasion. Equally the government should avoid reverting to the presumptive assessment of tax liability, the analytical determination of tax liability being the objective method generally used by all administratively advanced countries. It is unlikely that Italians are more inclined to evade than others, whereas they probably find it easier and more rewarding. Similarly it is unlikely that they would prefer to work underground if it were not for the fact that otherwise they would face exceedingly restrictive regulations, and that monitoring the 'parallel economy' is very inefficient.

Once a reasonably capable and effective tax administration, comparable to the European average, has been secured, a well-designed reform could be practically implemented. Undoubtedly the many tax provisions of the 1990s have harmed the government's credibility with respect to taxation and have probably spoilt years of effort to simplify and rationalize the system. Such disconnected tax provisions stem from the need to reduce the deficit, but sometimes the search for 'immediate' sources of more revenue (such as, for example, the 1992 wealth tax on bank accounts) reduces future revenues. A look at the deficit return in Fig. 5.1 suggests that not much more can be expected than what the tax system has already done in the recent past, for in 1992 the primary balance actually crossed the surplus line.

Finally, before engaging in any fundamental reform it will be necessary first to define a clear position regarding the role of private saving, investment, and productive work effort in the economy, and then make consistent tax choices.

With a tax burden above 40 per cent it is all the more important to make accurate predictions on how people would react in terms of saving, investment, and work effort, because long-run tax revenues depend largely on such magnitudes.

It is also necessary to study the possible effects of introducing taxes successfully employed abroad, but taking account of the *national system as a whole* in order to avoid hasty conclusions about the real shortcomings of the system itself in comparison with other countries.

The taxation of financial capital income can be cited as an example. The generally held view is that the exclusion of such income from the personal income tax base was among the main factors undermining progressivity. This seems correct, in principle, but for instance the Bernardi–Marenzi–Pozzi microsimulation model shows that such inclusion would not substantially change the distribution of the tax burden. Though the actual validity of such exercises may be qualified and doubted on various grounds, this one does draw attention to the fact that a tax system as a whole can exhibit properties and produce results which escape the assessment of individual issues and provisions in isolation. It is therefore extremely important, in a medium-term and structural perspective, to reduce to an absolute minimum the number of uncoordinated tax provisions, taken without previously placing and assessing them in the context of the tax system as a whole.

References

Alworth, J. S., and Castellucci, L. (1993), 'Italy', in D. W. Jorgenson and R. Landau (eds.), *Tax Reform and the Cost of Capital. An International Comparison*, Brookings Institution, Washington DC.

Ando, A., Guiso, L., and Visco, I. (eds.) (1994), *Savings and the Accumulation of Wealth*, CUP, Cambridge.

Banca d'Italia, *Relazioni Annuali* (various years).

Bernardi L. (1990), 'Recent Analyses on the Distributive Impact of the Public Budget in Italy', in C. Dagum and H. Zenga (eds.), *Income Distribution by Size: Generation, Distribution, Measurement and Application*, Springer-Verlag, Berlin.

—— Marenzi, A., and F. Pozzi (1992), 'L'analisi di microsimulazione delle imposte dirette e dei contributi sociali a carico delle famiglie: modello e risultati', in ISPE, *Bilancio pubblico e redistribuzione*, Il Mulino, Bologna.

Bosi, M., and Castellucci, L. (1997), 'Il sommerso: nuove stime, vecchi resultati', *CEIS Newsletter*, 4–5.

Castellucci, L. (1987), 'Italy', in J. A. Pechman (ed.), *Comparative Tax Systems: Europe, Canada and Japan*, Tax Analysts, Arlington.

Cerea, G. (1992), 'Una stima prudenziale dell'evasione dell'IVA nel commercio', *Rivista di diritto finanziario e scienza delle finanze*, 2.

Ceriani, V. (1981), 'Gli effetti sui prezzi delle manovre del prelievo delle imposte indirette, contributi sociali e tariffe', in *Contributi alla ricerca*, 8, Banca d'Italia.

—— Frasca, F., and Monacelli, D. (1992), 'Il sistema tributario e il disavanzo pubblico: problemi e prospettive', in *Il disavanzo pubblico in Italia: natura strutturale e politiche di rientro*, Ente per gli studi monetari, bancari e finanziari Luigi Einaudi, Il Mulino, Bologna.

Codice Tributario (1993), B. Santamaria (ed.), Maggioli Editore, Rimini.

Contini, B. (1979), *Lo sviluppo di un'economia parallela*, Edizioni comunità, Milano.

—— (1981), 'Labour Market Segmentation and the Development of the Parallel Economy', *Oxford Economic Papers*, 33.

—— (1992), 'The irregular economy of Italy: a survey of contributions', in *Guide-book to Statistics on the Hidden Economy*, Economic Commission for Europe, United Nations, New York.

Das-Gupta, A. (1993), 'A Theory of Hard-to-Tax Groups', paper presented at the IIPF Conference on *Public Finance and Irregular Activities*, Berlin, 23–6 Aug.

Documentazione per le Commissione parliamentari 384/90.

Ghessi, G. (1989), 'I costi gestionali dei tributi', in Pedone, A. (ed.), *La questione tributaria. Analisi e proposte*, Il Mulino, Bologna.

Raccolta legislativa tributaria (1994), Annexe to the journal *Il fisco*, 24th Oct. 1994.

ISTAT (1990), *Nuova contabilità nazionale*, series 9, vol. 9, Rome.

—— (1993), *Annali di statistica*, series 10, vol. 2, Rome.

—— *Annuario statistico*, Rome, various years.

—— (1994), *Conti delle amministrazioni pubbliche e della protezione sociale, anni 1987–92*, Rome.

—— (1992), *Occupazione e redditi da lavoro dipendente, anni 1980–91*, Rome.

Law proposal to the Chamber of Deputies, 2991/88 and 1026/86 (by V. Visco and others).

Marenzi, A. (1989), 'La distribuzione del carico fiscale in Italia: un modello di micro-simulazione', mimeo, Dip.to di economia pubblica e territoriale, Pavia.

OECD Economic Outlook, June 1994.

Pedone, A. (1981), 'Italy', in Aaron (ed.), *The Value-Added Tax: Lessons from Europe*, Brookings Institution, Washington, DC.

Ragioneria Generale dello Stato (1986), *Hypotheses for Changes in the Financing of the National Medical Care System* (mimeo), Rome.

Rossi, N. (ed.) (1993), *La crescita ineguale, 1981–1991. Primo rapporto CNEL sulla distribuzione e redistribuzione del reddito in Italia*, Il Mulino, Bologna.

Tanzi, V. (1980), 'The Underground Economy in the US: Estimates and Implications', *Banca Nazionale del Lavoro Quarterly Review*, 33.

Tremonti, G., and Vitaletti, G. (1991), *La fiera delle tasse*, Il Mulino, Bologna.

—— —— (1994), *Il federalismo fiscale. Autonomia e solidarietà sociale*, Laterza, Bari.

Visco, V. (1995), 'Appunti per una riforma fiscole', *Cespe Materiali*.

Vitaletti, G. *et al.* (1988), 'L'evasione dopo la Visentini ter', IRES, Rome.

6 Japan

HIROMITSU ISHI

A. Overview

The reorganization of Japan's tax system in the post-war period was undertaken on the initiative of the USA by a tax mission headed by Carl S. Shoup. The objective of the Shoup mission was to design a tax system that would ensure a complete overhaul of the Japanese economy. The Shoup mission placed the greatest importance on direct taxes, mainly income tax on individuals and corporations. The entire tax system was completely restructured, leading to a shift from indirect to direct taxes as the major source of government revenue. However, changes initiated by the USA in the tax system were only short-lived since many of the taxes were abolished or modified soon after their enactment. The main features of the post-Shoup tax system are summarized below.

The first and most important change was the replacement of the comprehensive income tax by a combination of a comprehensive and schedular tax. This hybrid system resulted from a modification of the global income tax approach proposed by the Shoup mission. For example, instead of aggregating most income and applying progressive tax rates, some types of income (e.g. capital gains and interest income) are now not subject to global income taxation, but taxed at reduced, flat rates, separate from other incomes.

Second the corporate income tax, which was a split-rate system until 1989, has now become a uniform one in which a single rate is imposed on all corporate income. Furthermore, the introduction of numerous special tax measures have made the corporate income tax very complicated.

Third, a combination of inheritance and gift taxes has replaced the accession tax on the transfer of wealth at death proposed by the Shoup mission.

Fourth, the system of indirect taxes (i.e. the value-added tax) recommended by the Shoup mission was not adopted for a long time. There was no general consumption tax in Japan until April 1989, and selective excise taxes provided most of the consumption tax revenue.

B. The Tax System

This section provides a brief factual account of the provisions of the major taxes over the last decade. (For a more detailed account of the Japanese tax system, see Ishi (1993).)

B1 Personal Income Tax

B1.1 Tax Base

The basic principle of the Japanese tax system is the maintenance of a global system of individual income taxation, even though separate taxation methods have been introduced in exceptional cases.

Taxable income is classified into ten categories: (1) interest income, (2) dividends, (3) real estate income, (4) business income, (5) employment income, (6) retirement income, (7) timber income, (8) capital gains, (9) occasional income, and (10) miscellaneous income. With the exception of interest and dividends, it is possible to claim specific exemptions and deductions from the other categories of income in addition to subtracting necessary expenses from them. Personal exemptions for average households consist of the basic exemption, the exemption for a spouse, and the exemption for dependants. These exemptions equalled ¥350,000 each for the taxpayer, his spouse, and other dependants in 1994.[1]

Besides these personal exemptions, wage and salary workers are permitted to make two special deductions for earned income and social insurance premiums from their employment income. The Ministry of Finance (MOF) includes these five exemptions and deductions in calculating the minimum taxable level (the tax threshold) of each household. Numerous other deductions from different income sources are also allowed. The most important of these are summarized below.

mployment income is given a special deduction in lieu of deductions of actual amounts of personal expenses.[2] The ratio of the amount of this deduction to total earnings was 30.4 per cent in 1986 and 28.6 per cent in 1990.

Generally speaking, net business income is subject to taxation after all necessary expenses are subtracted from gross receipts. Taxpayers filing a blue return[3] are permitted to deduct the cost of preparing tax returns up to a maximum of ¥100,000. A special deduction for wages paid to family employees is also allowed in lieu of deducting them as necessary business expenses from the proprietor's business income. Prior to 1993, even the proprietor's own remuneration was deductible from his business income, and similarly, the special deduction for employment income was applicable if the firm elected to be treated as a quasi-corporation for tax purposes (i.e. as a 'deemed corporation'). However, the tax reform in 1992 abolished this 'deemed corporation' system from 1993. In its place, the special deduction

---

[1] In addition, a special exemption for spouses (¥350,000) was allowed from Sept. 1987 in the case of one-earner couples to balance the tax burden between wage earners and others.

[2] Employment income includes not only wages and salaries, but bonuses, pensions, and other allowances of a similar nature. In 1992, the deduction was 40% of the first ¥1.65 million, 30% of the next ¥1.65 million, 20% of the next ¥2.7 million, 10% of the next ¥4 million, and 5% for amounts in excess of ¥10 million, but the minimum deductible level is set at ¥6.5 million.

[3] The blue return system was introduced for small businesses of self-employed individuals by the Shoup mission, on the condition that proper bookkeeping was required for a tax return. Taxpayers filing blue returns are not inspected by the tax offices.

for filing a blue return was increased from ¥100,000 to ¥350,000 on the condition that good record-keeping is observed.

Besides the special deductions accorded to certain kinds of taxable income, there are nearly 20 deductions involved in the present structure of individual income taxes.[4] To compute final tax liability, several tax credits may also be taken, such as for dividends, foreign taxes, incremental research and experimental expenditure, and for the acquisition of a house. Some of these are linked to the promotion of specific policy goals.

Cash income is taxable, but non-cash benefits given to wage earners and business executives are not taxable at all or are only partially taxable. Although there is no clear boundary between ordinary income and fringe benefits, there are several kinds of tax preferences for fringe benefits, the most important of which is the exclusion of the value of subsidized housing from taxable income. Most large companies, as well as the government, provide housing to many of their employees at much cheaper rents than market prices for comparable facilities. Companies also subsidize loans for the purchase or construction of private residences, so that employees can obtain mortgages at a very low rate of interest over ten or more years. The subsidized portion of such rents and interest payments is excluded from taxable income.

Furthermore, the system of employee compensation includes free or cheap provision of recreational facilities and other welfare benefits. Such payments in kind are not taxable, and greatly benefit Japanese wage earners, particularly those working for large companies.

For the majority of business executives, most of the compensation packages provided by their companies is non-taxable: a car, a large residence, an expense account for entertainment, etc. It is not common, however, for corporate executives in Japan to hold stock in their own companies because of the lack of stock option plans. Of greatest importance is perhaps the expense account, which by and large is used for inviting business customers to expensive restaurants, clubs, and golf facilities. This explains why employers are generous in paying out large sums of money for entertainment purposes; all of these benefits go untaxed in their personal incomes.[5]

B1.2 Tax Rates

All taxable income in excess of the minimum taxable level is subject to tax at progressive income tax rates. Table 6.1 illustrates the schedule of statutory tax rates at all levels of government in 1994.

---

[4] Typical categories of such deductions include deductions for casualty losses, medical expenses, donations, the physically handicapped, etc. For a comprehensive list, *see* MOF Tax Bureau (1994).

[5] At present, total expenditures for entertainment expenses are not deductible from corporate income. However, small firms with ¥10–50 million of capital are permitted to deduct ¥3 million a year, and those with less than ¥10 million are allowed ¥4 million. In the past decade or so, such expenses were taxed more strictly.

Table 6.1 Statutory rates of income taxes at all levels of government, 1994

Taxable income (¥m.)	Tax rates (%)			
	National	Prefecture	Municipal	Total
under 1.6	10	2	3	15
1.6–3.0	10	2	8	20
3.0–3.5	20	2	8	30
5.5–6.0	20	4	11	35
6.0–10.0	30	4	11	45
10.0–20.0	40	4	11	55
20.0 and over	50	4	11	65

Note: Since the exemption levels are different for all three income taxes, the taxable income for any specific taxpayer is not exactly the same in each bracket.

Source: MOF, Tax Bureau, *Primary Statistics of Taxation*, March 1994.

National income tax rates start at 10 per cent of taxable income up to ¥1.6 million, rising to a top rate of 50 per cent above ¥20 million. By contrast, local income tax rates, consisting of both prefectural and municipal rates, are relatively simple. Prefectural income tax rates are 2 per cent on the first ¥5.5 million of taxable income, and 4 per cent above it. The rates for the standard municipal income tax begin at 3 per cent and rise to 11 per cent on taxable income above ¥20 million.

Local income taxes cannot be deducted from the national income tax base. Thus, the combined marginal tax rate seems to have a significant effect on the attitude of taxpayers. At the top income bracket, it reaches a punitive level of 65 per cent.[6] Tax rate structures have varied greatly in Japan throughout the post-war period. Major changes in national income tax rates are shown in Table 6.2. It shows that since 1985, Japan has followed the worldwide trend of lowering marginal rates and reducing the number of brackets.

B1.3 Treatment of Different Kinds of Income

Currently, many kinds of income are taxed separately at reduced rates. These separate taxation methods have been developed mainly to promote policy objectives. The majority of the ten taxable incomes described above are subject to separate forms of taxation. The most important of these is the

[6] When the top rates were 70% for the national income tax and 18% for the local income taxes (i.e. a combined rate of 88% in 1986), a maximum amount of income tax was set to limit the total tax burden on an effective rate of 78%. The adjustment was made in the prefectural and municipal income taxes to maintain that level. This method, however, was repealed after September 1987. In addition to the progressive income tax, there are per capita taxes levied by local governments. For a detailed discussion, *see* Ishi (1993), ch. 14.

Table 6.2   Major changes of tax rates, national income tax, 1984–1994

1984–6		1987		1988		1989–	
Tax rates %	Taxable income classes (¥000)	Tax rates %	Taxable income classes (¥000)	Tax rates %	Taxable income classes (¥000)	Tax rates %	Taxable income classes (¥000)
10.5	500	10.5	1,500				
12	1,200	12	2,000				
14	2,000						
		16	3,000	10	3,000	10	3,000
17	3,000						
		20	5,000				
21	4,000						
25	6,000	25	6,000	20	6,000	20	6,000
30	8,000	30	8,000				
35	10,000	35	10,000	30	10,000	30	10,000
40	12,000	40	12,000	40	20,000	40	20,000
45	15,000	45	15,000				
50	20,000	50	30,000	50	50,000	50	20,000
55	30,000	55	50,000				
60	50,000	60	50,000	60	50,000		
65	80,000						
70	80,000						
No. of income brackets 15		12		6		5	

Source: See Table 6.1.

application of a separate flat tax rate on interest derived from taxable personal savings and dividends.

Retirement income and timber income are also taxed separately under progressive tax rates. Only half of retirement income, after the special deduction for retirement is applied, is subject to taxation, and this is separated from other incomes. Timber income is handled by a sophisticated procedure of averaging: after allowance for the special deduction, taxable income is first divided by five and taxed at the rate applicable for that one-fifth; the tax amount thus computed is multiplied by five to obtain the total tax due. Likewise, capital gains on the sale of real estate are taxed at flat reduced rates favourable to all taxable long-term gains. Fluctuating and extraordinary income, which are usually classified as 'occasional income', are eligible for the 'averaging taxation' method.

The treatment of savings and investment income in Japan is almost the same as that applied to all savings under an expenditure tax until 1987 when the tax-free saving system was repealed. In effect, the Japanese individual income tax has been partially transformed into an expenditure tax. It can therefore be considered a hybrid of a comprehensive income tax and an expenditure tax. However, this hybrid has developed spontaneously, without any special attempt to avoid the double taxation of savings.

B1.4 The Tax Unit

Apart from a few exceptions, the individual has remained the tax unit in the Japanese system, under which two-earner couples are taxed as separate individuals. For one-earner couples with several dependants, the head of the household is treated as a single taxpayer.

If children are recognized as independent earners, they may be taxed separately on their own income. However, few children have incomes large enough to be subject to taxation. Their financial reliance on their parents enables the family to claim exemptions for them as dependants.

Despite the fact that the tax unit is based on the individual, the investment income of the spouse and other dependants used to be taxed as if it was received by the head of the household. The main purpose of aggregating income from investment was to prevent tax avoidance by allocating such income arbitrarily among family members.[7]

The problem of the tax unit in Japan has some bearing on the special treatment of business incomes. As noted earlier, business proprietors are allowed to split their incomes by paying wages and salaries both to other members of their families and to themselves. Obviously, this income-splitting lightens their income tax burden.

B2 Corporation Income Tax

The relative share of the corporate tax in Japan's national tax revenue is the largest among major advanced countries, first, because there has been a growth of economic activities in the corporate sector, reflecting the high growth rate of the Japanese economy throughout the post-war period, and second, because the incorporation of small businesses by self-employed individuals has been accelerated by tax inducements.

B2.1 Tax Base

The corporate tax is levied on the net income earned by both domestic and foreign corporations in each accounting period or in liquidation. Net income

---

[7] The aggregate method of taxing investment income was established as an exception to the individual tax unit in 1950, but it was repealed in 1951. In 1957, this method was re-established and was maintained until 1988. It has since been repealed.

is roughly the excess of gross revenues over expenses incurred doing business. Corporations are required to calculate their net income once during each accounting period (i.e. any one year selected by them), and to file a tax return within two months after the end of the accounting period.

The calculation of corporate net income generally accords with the actual practices of the modern business accounting system, although some adjustments have to be made in arriving at taxable income. Thus, corporate net income for tax purposes conforms to corporate profits before tax in the profit and loss statement of corporate firms. When corporations terminate going concerns by merger or dissolution, the corporate tax is levied on their liquidation income.

The 1994 corporate tax law established the following tax base structure (see MOF Tax Bureau 1994).

First, capital gains of corporations are subject to taxation in full as they are realized. These capital gains are taxed at the same rates as operating profits, although capital gains from short-term transactions involving land owned by corporations are subject to a heavier tax burden.

Second, dividends received from other corporations are fully excluded from taxable income, but the excess of dividends received over those paid is only partially exempted (i.e. 75 per cent of net dividends received).

Third, inventories may be valued at cost or market value, whichever is lower, by using any of eight methods of valuation (e.g. the actual cost method, LIFO, FIFO, etc.).

Fourth, based on original cost and shorter useful lives, depreciation is calculated by the straight-line method or the declining-balance method. Generous provisions have been allowed for accelerated depreciation, increased initial depreciation, and special tax-free reserves to stimulate particular types of investments.

Fifth, corporations filing a blue return may carry back net operating losses so as to offset them against the previous year's taxable income[8] or may carry losses forward for five years. In effect, this provides a six-year period for offsetting losses against gains. These carry-back and carry-forward systems are required to avoid taxing corporations with fluctuating incomes more heavily than those with relatively stable incomes.

Finally, if current outlays for research and development (R&D) exceed the largest amount outlayed for such purposes during any accounting period since 1966, 20 per cent of the increase may be credited against the corporate tax in the year it is made. The maximum amount creditable is 10 per cent of the corporate tax liability. In addition, a tax credit of 7 per cent is available for specific property used for R&D of basic technologies.

---

[8] The carryback of losses was temporarily disallowed between 1 April 1994 and 31 May 1988.

B2.2 Tax Rates

Under the 1994 corporate tax law, the structure of corporate tax rates is as follows.

(1) *Ordinary corporations:* basic rate, 37.5 per cent; lower rates as a concession to small businesses, 28 per cent. (These rates are imposed only on taxable incomes of less than ¥8 million of corporations with less than ¥100 million of paid-in capital. The remainder is taxed at the basic rate.)

(2) *Cooperatives:* 27 per cent.

(3) *Non-profit organizations:* 27 per cent.

In addition to these tax rates on corporate profits, certain portions of income in liquidation are taxed at a rate of 33 per cent.

B2.3 Treatment of Distributed Profits

Japan's corporate tax system during the post-war period has gradually shifted from the integrated scheme proposed by the Shoup mission towards a modified separate system. The main reason for this shift is that the government has introduced into the corporate tax system special treatments in favour of dividends to promote capital accumulation.

B2.4 Small to Medium-Sized Enterprizes

The emergence of 'quasi-corporations' has declined since the 1970s, and their importance as a group of taxpayers has been greatly reduced. One reason is that special tax treatment of 'deemed corporate income' was established in favour of unincorporated, self-employed taxpayers in 1974. Taxpayers filing a blue return could elect to be treated as 'corporations' for tax purposes. Under this 'deemed' method, business proprietors could deduct their own salaries, as well as those of family employees, as a business expense. Furthermore, the deduction for employment income was also applicable to their own salaries. The net income computed for business proprietors was considered 'deemed corporate income' and was taxed at the lower rate of dividend income.[9] Thus, business proprietors no longer needed to become 'quasi-corporations' to mitigate their tax burdens. This 'deemed' system was finally abolished in 1992 to make the income tax burden among taxpayers more equitable.

B3 Social Security Contribution

B3.1 General Features

Social security benefits are classified under three major categories: medical care insurance, pensions, and others (e.g. public assistance). Pensions

---

[9] Business proprietors electing to be 'deemed corporations' for tax purposes totalled 135,597 in 1992. They represent 3.1 per cent of total taxpayers filing blue returns, which has been reduced from 7.3 per cent in 1986.

constitute more than half of total benefits, followed by medical care insurance. In 1991, the relative shares were 51.6 per cent for pensions, 38.6 per cent for medical care, and 9.9 per cent for the remaining benefits. Benefits are provided for by their respective schemes, which historically developed within occupational or regional groups from the pre-war period.

At present, all Japanese citizens are obliged to enter into one of the medical care insurance schemes, from which they can receive insurance benefits for injury and sickness. Broadly speaking, Japan's medical care insurance is divided into two types: one for employees and the other for self-employed workers in agriculture, forestry, and fisheries.

For employees, the dominant share is occupied by Health Insurance, which provides insurance benefits to employees and their dependants for all forms of injury, sickness, childbirth, and death. At the end of fiscal 1992, Health Insurance covered 33.81 million insured persons and 35.52 million dependants, almost 55.8 per cent of the total population in Japan.

Self-employed and other persons not covered under the employees' insurance scheme mentioned above are insured under National Health Insurance, which is managed by the municipalities and which covered 42.62 million persons (i.e. 34.3 per cent of total populaiton) in 1992.

Public pension schemes have existed since the pre-war era. As a result of restructuring and integration of different types of pensions in recent years, the present structure of public pensions is a two-tier scheme covering all residents in Japan.

The first tier is composed of the national pension (the so-called 'basic pension'), under which all Japanese from 20 to 59 years of age are covered. The national pension is subdivided according to three groups of individuals: (i) self-employed workers and others (18.5 million), (ii) wage and salary earners (38.5 million), and (iii) dependent spouses (12.0 million) (figures in parentheses are number of individuals in 1993).

In addition to the first tier, another tier of employee pension supplements the national pension in terms of pension benefits. Broadly speaking, employee pensions are divided into two kinds: (i)Employee Pension Insurance (EPI) and (ii) Mutual Aid Associations (MAA). EPI covers private sector salaried workers; 32.5 million individuals are covered, and EPI holds the largest share of employee pension scheme (84.5 per cent). MAA covers public sector employees and other persons not covered by the above-mentioned categories (e.g. private school teachers and employees).

B3.2 The Mechanism of Social Security Contribution

Table 6.3 summarizes the distribution of financial sources for the social security systems of six major countries. Japan splits relatively evenly the cost of its scheme into three sources: (i) employees' share of contribution, (ii) employers' share of contribution, and (iii) state subsidy from tax revenues.

The most important issue pertinent to public pension schemes is, no doubt,

Table 6.3 Percentage distribution of financial sources for the social security system

Country		Contribution		Subsidy	State[a] operating revenue	Fund- Others	Total (%)
		Employees' Share	Employees' Share				
Japan	1991	28.3	31.8	24.0	12.6	3.3	100.0
US	1989	23.8	31.6	33.1	11.0	0.5[b]	100.0
UK	1989	18.2	26.0	52.0	3.7	0.2	100.0
Germany	1989	36.9	34.3	26.1	0.6	2.1[b]	100.0
France	1986	23.4	50.6	20.9	1.7	3.4[b]	100.0
Sweden	1989	2.8	38.9	49.6	8.7	—	100.0

[a] Including transfers from other public fund, as well as the NT (National Treasury)
[b] Special social security tax is included.
Source: Data from the MOF.

that contribution rates will have to rise sharply to reflect the ageing population. According to current financial projections for EPI by the Ministry of Health and Welfare, based on the 1994 actuarial revaluation, the EPI contribution rate (divided evenly by employer and employee) will have to increase from 14.5 per cent in 1994 to 19.5 per cent in 2000, 24.5 per cent in 2010, and 29.5 per cent in 2020. Likewise the national pension scheme monthly contribution will have to rise from ¥11,700 in 1995 to ¥21,700 in 2020.

These results have taken the Japanese by surprise. Since social security contributions are *de facto* a wage income tax, the combined burden due to the income tax and social security contributions will essentially be much heavier on the working generation due to the ageing society. Obviously, this stimulates arguments in support of switching from direct taxation to indirect taxation (i.e. VAT) as a desirable tax mix in the future.

B4 Value-Added Tax

A kind of value-added tax was introduced in April 1989. Although discussions on the role of VAT in the tax system began in the late 1970s, various attempts to introduce a VAT before 1989 were unsuccessful because of the unfavourable political atmosphere.

Since 1985, the question of introducing a VAT has become the most important political issue for the general public. The tax reform process in Japan began in September 1985, when Prime Minister Nakasone proposed an inquiry to initiate the most sweeping tax reform since the Shoup recommendations in 1950. This was the start of the first stage of the tax reform process (see Ishi (1986*b*)).

In the process of shaping the detailed framework of VAT (i.e. the sales tax proposed by Nakasone) as part of the larger reform, the number of tax-exempted items were greatly expanded from the original plan of seven items. Furthermore, the exemption level of certain firms was raised to ¥100 million in terms of annual sales because of strong political pressure from small traders.[10]

These compromises greatly impaired the advantage of universality inherent in a broad-based indirect tax. Such special considerations cause difficulties and complications in both administering the tax and obtaining compliance from taxpayers. In the end, the contentious implementation issue prevented the government from obtaining general support for introducing the new tax.

Once the legislation reached the Diet in February 1987, dramatic opposition arose from all sides, including even strong supporters of the Liberal Democratic Party (LDP), and Nakasone was forced to withdraw the bill in May 1987. Once again, the VAT proved as unacceptable as it had been in 1979, when Prime Minister Ohira proposed a general consumption tax. Tax increases remained as politically taboo as ever.

The second stage of the tax reform process began with Prime Minister Takeshita's inquiry to the Tax Advisory Commission in November 1987. Tax reform could have been the crowning achievement of Nakasone's term, but Nakasone failed. Thus, when he appointed Takeshita as his successor, he evidently wanted Takeshita to devote all his efforts toward achieving tax reform.

In April 1988, following Nakasone's failed sales tax, another form of broad-based indirect tax was proposed, once again under the name 'consumption tax'. Of the more controversial issues in the tax reform package, the most important concerned this tax. Ultimately, support for the Takeshita tax reform by the general public depended primarily on the pros and cons of introducing the consumption tax, despite the fact that direct tax reductions substantially exceeded the increased indirect tax burden.

Past experience suggested that political considerations rather than economic ones were the decisive factors in obtaining public support for a VAT. The opposition parties strongly opposed the consumption tax bill in the Diet, and as a consequence, the ruling LDP passed the bill on a strict party line vote. Even after the implementation of the consumption tax from 1 April 1989, the opposition parties still promised to repeal it.

There are a couple of major features pertinent to the consumption tax in Japan. First of all, the tax base of the original consumption tax was very broad, as broad as that of New Zealand, because tax-exempted goods and services were limited to only a few items, such as education and medical care.

---

[10] This exemption level was clearly much larger than in other comparable cases, i.e. approximately 10–20 times in comparison with some EU countries and Korea. Even the 'general consumption tax' in 1979 included merely ¥20 million in exemptions for certain firms.

Second, the consumption tax does not use invoices, relying instead on the accounts method of VAT. To compute a firm's value added, total purchases are subtracted from total sales by using bookkeeping records. The balance is then subject to the rate of VAT. Although Nakasone's sales tax was proposed using the invoice-credit method, the Takeshita consumption tax was designed based on the accounts method, without the use of invoices. It is officially stated that, instead of investigating invoices on a transactional basis, this can be accomplished via the audit of accounts that are usually kept for individual and corporate income taxes.

Next, there is a special simplified scheme for computing the tax, a measure that favours small firms. Firms whose annual sales are less than ¥400 million (originally, the limit was ¥500 million, but it was lowered in 1991) are allowed to employ this method to enhance tax compliance. Instead of directly calculating the total value of purchases from other firms, certain fixed percentages (e.g. 10 per cent for wholesalers and 20 per cent for retailers) are multiplied by total sales values and the results deemed to be subject to a 3 per cent rate. For example, tax amounts of retailers can be computed as the total value of sales × 0.2 × 0.03, which is equivalent to the turnover tax with a rate of 0.6 per cent. In 1986, the number of firms liable to these special rules statistically amounted to 96.7 per cent of the total. The special simplified scheme for computation may unduly render the amount of value added smaller than the true amount at each stage.

Furthermore, a vanishing exemption method was introduced to give relief to smaller traders. Those whose annual sales are less than ¥50 million (originally ¥60 million) above the exemption level of ¥30 million can benefit from this method. In this case, the tax due is gradually reduced to zero by a 'marginal deduction' that takes the form of a tax credit. The calculation is as follows:

$$\text{Tax credit} = \frac{\text{¥60 million} - \text{annual sales}}{\text{¥30 million}} \times \text{tax otherwise due}$$

In the case of a much smaller trader, say, with ¥30 million of sales, the tax vanishes at that level because the tax credit is essentially equal to the tax otherwise due. The tax becomes negative at sales below ¥30 million, but there is no refund to the taxpayer.[11]

Taking account of these relief provisions for small and medium-sized firms, various rates of the consumption tax can be applied to different levels of annual sales. Table 6.4 shows four rates applicable to each stage of sales, depending on special tax provisions in favour of smaller firms and traders.

---

[11] On this point, Shoup states that 'so far as I am aware, this type of vanishing exemption is not found in other VATs, coupled with the tax-on-sales option, except, to a degree, in the new Canadian goods and services tax' (Shoup 1990: 438).

B5 Main Excise Taxes

B5.1 *A System of Selective Excise Taxes*

There are a couple of points worth noting to clarify some features unique to excise taxation in Japan. To begin with, taxes on alcoholic beverages and tobacco have traditionally not been conceived in relation to negative externalities. Thus, taxes on alcoholic beverages and tobacco, combined with those on sugar, are defined as taxes on non-essential or luxury items considered proxies for taxpaying capacity. They have long been recognized as being chiefly for revenue purposes.

Second, the commodity tax that was abolished in 1989 was typically given as an example of an excise on luxury consumption, but it is grouped into selective taxes on goods and services with other unrelated taxes. It is noted that admission and travel taxes are two of a very few examples of taxes on the sale of services, although their revenue is minor. The third category consists of three taxes levied on stamps, security transactions, and stocks.

Lastly, excises in motoring and related fields are earmarked for specific appropriations of government-provided services. These taxes were designed as service charges for the use of roads, airports, and power plants. Since the consumption of these services is exclusive to some extent, it seems fair that beneficiaries should pay for them in proportion to their use, even if government does provide services.

B5.2 *Taxes on Alcoholic Beverages*

The alcohol tax is levied on domestic alcoholic beverages shipped from manufacturing premises and on imported ones that are drawn from bonded areas. It is a typical case of a manufacturers' 'excise', which is assumed to be shifted forward onto consumers. Alcoholic beverages are classified into ten categories[12] for tax purposes. In 1988, a specific rate was applied to each type, but if the price of some types (imported whisky, wine, etc.) exceeded a certain amount (i.e. a maximum non-taxable price for an *ad valorem* tax), the *ad valorem* rate was imposed on the full price in place of the specific rate.

In 1988, the alcohol tax still represented the largest share of indirect taxes, generating 16.0 per cent of national indirect taxes and 4.5 per cent of total national taxes. However, the relative weight of the tax has been declining over the long run, and in fact, its relative share of total tax revenues decreased from 18.5 per cent in 1950 to 3.7 per cent in 1994.

The alcohol tax was considerably restructured when the consumption tax was introduced in 1989. The grading system for sake and whisky was repealed, and at the same time, rate structures were simplified. In addition, the *ad*

---

[12] The ten categories of alcoholic beverages are as follows: sake, sake compound, shochu (distilled grain alcohol), mirin (cooking alcohol), beer, wine, whisky, brandy, spirits, and miscellaneous liquors.

Table 6.4 Various tax rates applicable to different sales—the case of non-wholesale firms

Annual sales (¥m.)	Tax rate (%)	Methods
	3	Regular
400		
	0.6	Special simplified scheme
50		
	0–0.6	Vanishing exemption due to 'marginal deduction'
30		
	0	Exemption
0		

Note: Drawn from the explanation of Shoup (1990).

valorem rate was eliminated to adjust for the adoption of the VAT rate on alcoholic beverages.

B5.3 Taxes on Tobacco

Similar to the tax on alcoholic beverages, taxes on tobacco have a very long history, having been a part of the indirect tax system since 1877. Until April 1985, tobacco had been produced and sold exclusively by Japan's Monopolized Public Corporation. Instead of excises on tobacco, a special charge was levied on the monopoly profits of the public corporation. This was equivalent to taxes on tobacco in a quasi-excise form.

When the Monopolized Public Corporation was transformed into the Nippon Tobacco Product Industry in the process of privatization in 1985,[13] a tobacco excise tax was substituted for the special charge on monopoly profits.

The tobacco excise tax is levied on manufacturers of tobacco products, or on imported products withdrawn from bonded areas, in a similar way to the alcohol tax. Tax rates are applied in a combination of *ad valorem* and specific rates, usually in an 80/20 ratio.

The tax base of the *ad valorem* tax is the retail price of tobacco and is subject to the authorization of the MOF. This implies that the MOF can cause revenue under *ad valorem* taxation to rise with the price of tobacco. This is why the *ad valorem* rate is favoured by the MOF for revenue purposes. In addition to being a tax on tobacco, an *ad valorem* rate may be justified as

[13] According to the Nippon Tobacco Product Industry Act, the government should own more than half the new shares of the corporation. However, for the time being, until the business comes into full operation, the government's holding of new shares is required to exceed two-thirds of total.

being a tax on quality, flavour, brand image, packaging, etc. The remainder of the revenue is raised at specific rates.

The ratio of tax to the retail price of the most popular brand ranges from 40 per cent in the USA to 86 per cent in Denmark. Japan is ranked second-lowest next to the USA. The tobacco excise tax has consistently declined as a relative share of national taxes. In 1950, it occupied 20 per cent of the total, but fell to as low as 1.8 per cent in 1994. This declining trend has been caused by both the reallocation of tobacco taxing power to local governments in 1985 and the long-run decrease in tobacco consumption.

B5.4 Taxes on Petrol and Other Related Items

The petrol tax is one of the most important consumption taxes, accounting for 13.2 per cent of indirect taxes and 4.2 per cent of total national taxes in 1992. It is a relatively new tax, having become effective in May 1949 as a national tax for raising general revenue. At an initial stage, local governments requested that the new levy on petrol be made part of their tax structure, but it was decided that the tax could be most conveniently collected at the prime importation and domestic refinery points,[14] and hence, should be administered at the national level.

At present, the petrol tax is collected together with the local road tax when petrol is shipped from refineries or withdrawn from a bonded area. Specific rates are applied with respect to both taxes: ¥48,600 and ¥5,200 per kilolitre of petrol for the petrol and local road taxes, respectively, in 1994. These revenues are allocated to the Special Account for Road Construction and Improvement.

Needless to say, taxes on petrol may be a reasonable proxy for the use of roads. Since they reflect the varying consumption of road services per vehicle-kilometre, they may be regarded as a good measure for determining road-user charges. It is impossible, however, for these taxes to distinguish adequately between types of road services. In view of the variable maintenance charge associated with usage, other car-related taxes have been introduced: a liquefied petroleum gas (LPG) tax in 1965, and a motor vehicle tonnage tax in 1971. In 1994, these specific rates were ¥17.5 per kg. and ¥2,800–6,300 per tonnage of each vehicle, respectively.

B5.5 Taxes on Commodities

The commodity tax was introduced in 1937 as a form of excise tax in wartime for two purposes: (i) to raise wartime revenues and (ii) to discourage consumption of luxury items. Thus, from the outset it was characterized by excises on luxury commodities. During the wartime period, the revenue objective took first priority, and taxable items were greatly expanded (i.e. from 10 in 1937 to 107 at the peak in 1944).

---

[14] At that time, two import and four domestic refinery points were considered for collecting revenue.

The commodity tax was mostly a series of manufacturers' excises levied on a number of specified articles. Taxable commodities were divided into two categories—class 1 and class 2—according to their nature and stage of tax imposition. The tax for commodities in class 1 was levied at the retail stage, while the tax on commodities in class 2 was levied at the manufacturing stage. Different tax rates were applied to each of the retailers' and the manufacturers' prices.

In 1988, ten items, such as jewels and fur products, were being taxed at the retail stage at tax rates of 10 to 15 per cent. On the other hand, at the manufacturing level, seventy-five items, including cars, cosmetics, cameras, and electrical appliances, were being taxed at rates ranging from 5 to 30 per cent.

In 1988, the commodity tax raised the second largest proportion of indirect taxes next to the alcohol tax: 14 per cent of the total. This revenue was collected on eighyt-five taxable items, but three-quarters of it came from taxes on motor cars and electrical home appliances. Table 6.5 illustrates the top ten items by tax amount, accounting for 73.0 per cent of the commodity tax. If the list was extended to cover the top twenty items, these taxes would account for nearly 90 per cent of total revenues. This implies that the major revenue-producing items for commodity excises were relatively few, while the remainder was composed of many miscellaneous commodities, each generating minor revenues.

B5.6 Relation to Existing Indirect Taxes

As seen in Table 6.6, five national excise taxes were repealed as well as three local taxes as part of the 1992 reform. All of these taxes were replaced by the new consumption tax on a nationwide basis. Of most importance was the absorption of the commodity tax into a new tax. The multiple-rate structure of the commodity tax was thus changed into a single rate of 3 per cent on all taxable commodities; as a temporary measure, only passenger cars were taxed at the higher rate of 6 per cent during the transitional period.[15]

In addition, several other excise taxes were adjusted to coexist with the consumption tax. In principle, major commodities such as alcoholic beverages, tobacco, and petroleum are subject to both selective excise and general consumption taxes in VAT countries. The same procedures have been applied in restructuring the indirect tax system in Japan. Alcohol and tobacco taxes initially were applied at specific rates only at the manufacturer's level, and then an *ad valorem* rate of 3 per cent was levied as the consumption tax for distributors and retailers. Despite the combined taxes with different rates,

---

[15] This measure was taken to adjust for too sharp a tax cut on certain commodities, i.e. the commodity tax rate on passenger cars was as high as 23%. Cutting such a high rate suddenly to 3% was regarded as too drastic a change. At first, this temporary measure was intended to expire by the end of fiscal year 1991. However, it was extended for two years at the reduced rate of 4.5% when the budget for fiscal year 1992 showed a deficit. Finally, it was terminated in 1994.

Table 6.5 Commodity tax revenues collected from the top ten major items, 1986

	Tax revenues	
	(¥bn.)	(%)
(1) Passenger cars	675.0	40.9
(2) Air-conditioners	108.4	6.6
(3) Precious stones	77.6	4.7
(4) TV sets	65.6	4.0
(5) Light combined passenger-cargo motor vehicles	51.3	3.1
(6) Video tape recorders	48.1	2.9
(7) Refrigerators	47.4	2.9
(8) Cosmetics	45.5	2.8
(9) Vacuum cleaners	43.7	2.6
(10) Car air-conditioners	41.2	2.5
Total	1,203.8	73.0
Commodity tax	1,650.1	100.0

Source: Data submitted to the Tax Advisory Commission.

Table 6.6 Tax variations in the national and local tax system under the Takeshita tax reform

Item	National	Local
Creation	Consumption tax	Consumption transfer tax
Repeal	Commodity tax, playing-cards tax, sugar excise tax, admission tax, travel tax	Electricity tax, gas tax, timber delivery tax
Amendment	Individual income tax, corporate tax, inheritance tax, liquor tax, tobacco excise tax, petroleum tax, bourse tax, securities transaction tax, stamp tax	Inhabitants' tax, enterprise tax, real property acquisition tax, entertainment tax, tax on consumption at hotels and restaurants

Source: Data from the MOF.

total tax burdens were adjusted to remain unchanged. Taxes on petroleum, however, consisted of both the existing and new taxes, causing a heavier tax burden. Also, the securities transaction tax was reduced because of the increased capital gains tax on the sale of securities.

The introduction of the consumption also had an effect on intergovernmental revenue transfers. Two measures were proposed when the consumption tax was introduced. With respect to local taxes, several excise taxes were repealed or amended, resulting in a substantial loss of revenue. To compensate for this revenue loss, one-fiftieth of the consumption tax was first handed over to local governments as a consumption transfer tax, which in turn was allocated regionally among prefectures and municipalities according to population. Second, 24 per cent of the consumption tax at the national level (exclusive of the consumption transfer tax) was appropriated for tax-sharing grants, which is known as the local allocation tax.

B6 Capital Transfer Taxes

As from 1953, heirs and donees paid their own taxes, based on the value of property left or transferred to them. In 1958, a hybrid system of an estate tax and an inheritance tax was instituted, and this system has remained basically intact up to the present time.

The main aim of combining the two taxes was to balance the tax burden on estates of the same size with the same number and types of heirs, even if the estate was distributed differently among the heirs.

The inheritance tax is levied on the gross estate acquired through inheritance or bequest minus non-taxable property,[16] liability, and funeral expenses; that is, on the net estate. If an heir receives properties by gift from the decedent within three years of his death, the value of such property transfers is included in the tax base. Thereafter, a basic exemption (¥48 million + (¥9.5 million × number of statutory heirs)) is deductible and the remaining property constitutes the amount of taxable inheritance.

B7 The Local Tax System

Local governments levy a variety of taxes to finance their revenue needs. However, due to Japan's centralized fiscal system, they are considerably restricted by the national government in determining the level and nature of their fiscal activities. For example, fewer tax sources are allowed to local governments relative to the scope of services they are responsible for providing.

This imbalance in the allocation of revenue sources necessitates intergovernmental transfers of revenue from national to local governments and a dependence that has been enhanced by various fiscal instruments. Thus, it is often argued that local autonomy (i.e. the ability of local governments to act independently of central control) is greatly impaired in Japan. The main issues regarding local taxation must be considered in the broader context of the interdependence between the national and local governments.

At present, the relationship between the national and local governments is

---

[16] In addition to the non-taxable treatment of life insurance, personal accident insurance, retirement, and similar allowances received by heirs, property transfers through inheritance or bequests to religious, charitable, educational, and scientific organizations are not subject to the inheritance tax.

weighted predominantly in favour of the former in many respects. The extent of authority, the revenue share, and the degree of responsibility of the national government are all greater than those of local governments. Local bureaucrats must heed functional superiors at the national level: since functional lines of authority are dominant, local officials must be responsive to the national officials in each area (e.g. public works, health, agriculture, etc.). It is widely acknowledged that local administration has become vertically fragmented.[17] In Japan, there are several levels of government, each having responsibility for a particular set of public functions. The main levels of the government are national, prefectural, and municipal. The last two are called 'local governments', while the first is referred to as the 'national government'.

On the subnational level, Japan has a two-tier system of local government. There are 3,239 municipalities, consisting of 656 cities and 2,583 towns and villages (in 1991). These numbers have been achieved by constantly reducing the 10,520 municipalities that existed in 1945 through the mergers of cities, towns, and villages. We often refer to prefectures and municipalities jointly as 'local public bodies'.

Fig. 6.1 shows tax shares and fiscal transfers in fiscal 1992 between the national and local governments on the basis of the Local Public Finance Plan (LPFP) and initial national budget data. Total tax revenues were ¥100,121.8 billion, divided into national and local taxes. Before fiscal transfers, local taxes accounted for only 34.7 per cent of total revenues. However, a substantial portion of national taxes is transferred to the local governments.

Major fiscal transfers are of two broad types: unconditional and conditional. Unconditional transfers from the national to local governments are tax-sharing grants on a lump-sum basis financed by the local allocation tax (*chiho-kofuzei*). By contrast, conditional transfers are based on the condition that the recipient government match a certain proportion of the transfer with its own expenditure. Furthermore, these grants are tied to specific types of expenditures (education, social welfare, road construction, etc.), rather than being available for general purposes. Generally, these matching-type categorical grants are called specific-purpose grants (*kokkoshishutsukin*).

In addition to these two types of fiscal transfers between the national and local governments, there are two other types of transfer. One is the local transfer tax, and the other is the transfer from the local to the national government. The latter represents the local government's share in the financing of projects initiated by the national government. As can be seen in Fig. 6.1, these two transfers amount to a much smaller sum than the items mentioned earlier.

After reallocating the tax sources among different levels of the government,

---

[17] In Japanese, the term *tatwari gyosei* (vertical consolidation) is generally used. To obtain more grants from each ministry of the national government, local governments are constantly forced to accede to the priorities of national bureaucrats.

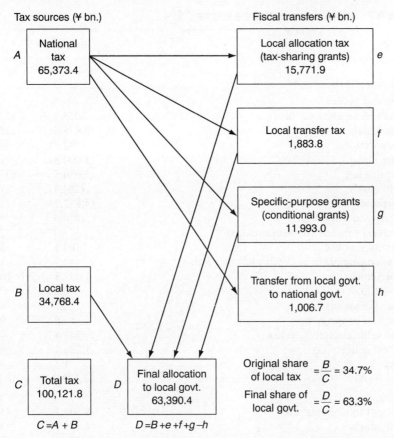

Tax sources (¥ bn.)   Fiscal transfers (¥ bn.)

A | National tax 65,373.4

Local allocation tax (tax-sharing grants) 15,771.9 | e

Local transfer tax 1,883.8 | f

Specific-purpose grants (conditional grants) 11,993.0 | g

Transfer from local govt. to national govt. 1,006.7 | h

B | Local tax 34,768.4

C | Total tax 100,121.8

D | Final allocation to local govt. 63,390.4

$C = A + B$ $D = B + e + f + g - h$

Original share of local tax $= \frac{B}{C} = 34.7\%$

Final share of local govt. $= \frac{D}{C} = 63.3\%$

Figures are based on the initial budget and on local public finance programmes in fiscal 1992.

Fig. 6.1 Tax shares between central and local governments, fiscal 1992
Source: Chiho Jiji Kyokai, Summary of Local Public Finance (Chiho Zaisei Yoran), 1992.

the final share of total tax revenues accruing to local governments increases to 63.3 per cent, as shown by the ratio D: C in Fig. 6.1. The ratio has remained almost unchanged for nearly a decade. This means that one-third of the national tax revenue is used at the local level.

A major part of local government revenues comes from local taxes, which fall into two categories: (i) prefectural taxes, levied by the 47 prefectural governments; and (ii) municipal taxes, imposed by the more than 3,000 municipal governments. Table 6.7 shows the system of local taxes in fiscal year 1994. Nearly half of all local taxes at the municipal level come from the individual and corporate income taxes, while only 30 per cent of prefectural taxes are raised from these income taxes. The inhabitants' tax is another form of local income tax, and the enterprise tax is equivalent to a

Table 6.7   Local tax collection by source, 1994

Sources	Tax revenues[a]	
	¥bn.	%
Prefectural taxes		
Prefectural inhabitants' tax	4058.9	(29.6)
Individuals	(2,475.4)	(18.0)
Corporations	(582.7)	(4.2)
Interests	(1,000.8)	(7.3)
Enterprise tax	5,086.5	(37.0)
Individuals	(264.4)	(1.9)
Corporations	(4,822.1)	(35.1)
Property acquisition tax	690.9	5.0
Prefectural tobacco consumption tax	371.0	2.7
Entertainment tax	100.7	0.7
Tax on consumption at hotels and restaurants	142.7	1.0
Motor vehicle tax	1,473.8	10.8
Mine-lot tax	0.6	0.0
Hunter licence tax	2.1	0.0
Prefectural property tax	14.8	0.1
Motor vehicle acquisition tax	549.4	4.0
Light-oil delivery tax	1,236.3	9.0
Others	1.5	0.0
Subtotal (A)	13,733.7	100.0
Municipal taxes		
Municipal inhabitants' tax	8,507.1	45.1
Individuals	(6,275.9)	(33.3)
Corporations	(2,231.2)	(11.8)
Municipal property tax	7,873.3	41.8
Land	(3,239.4)	(17.2)
Buildings	(3,012.4)	(16.0)
Plant and machinery	(1,621.5)	(8.6)
Small motor vehicle tax	98.2	0.5
Municipal tobacco consumption tax	656.3	3.5
Mineral product tax	2.1	0.0
Special landholding tax	113.4	0.6
Spa tax	20.6	0.1
Business office tax	339.0	1.8
City-planning tax	1,175.3	6.2
Others	61.9	0.3
Subtotal (B)	18,847.2	100.0
Total (A+B)	32,580.9	

[a] Estimated figures.

Source: Ministry of Home Affairs (1994).

tax on the net income of business firms. The structural features of these income taxes are used by both prefectures and municipalities. The remaining taxes produce minor revenues, except for the local property tax, which plays an important role in raising municipal revenues, accounting for 41.8 per cent.

On the working of the present tax system, two points should be made. First, in principle, each level of local government levies its own taxes, separate from the collection of national taxes. In practice, however, all revenue sources are subject to control by the national government under the Local Tax Law (see MOF Tax Bureau (1994: 185–6); Jiji Sogo Centre (1988)). The tax base and rates of major items are legislated by the Diet and can be altered by the proposals of both the Ministry of Home Affairs (MOHA) and the MOF. This implies that a uniform rate is levied on the same tax base in all prefectures and municipalities.

Second, in levying the three levels of taxes, mutual cooperation is established among the municipal, prefectural, and national governments. For instance, when the municipal governments levy their inhabitants' tax on individuals, they collect the prefectural inhabitants' tax, too, using the same tax base. Information on taxable income necessary for computing the local inhabitants' tax is provided by the national government. Although the bases of the individual and corporate income taxes are the same at two (or even three) levels of government, local taxes cannot be deducted from national taxes, except in the case of the enterprise tax. With no deductibility of local taxes in calculating the national tax base, the national government makes adjustments to maintain the proper level of tax burden for each level of government through the allocation of tax sources. In fact, the individual and corporate income taxes at the local level are revised concurrently with revisions in national taxes.

C. Economic and Social Aspects

C1 The Fiscal Deficit

C1.1 Fiscal Deficits and Fiscal Reconstruction

The oil crisis of the 1970s clearly revealed the vulnerability of a country poorly endowed in natural resources. Among the most important effects were the sharp reduction in the country's economic growth rate, large imbalances between domestic saving and investment, a sustained rise in fiscal deficits, and large current account surpluses in the balance of payments (see, for general discussion, Ito (1992); Takenaka (1992)). The most important change was the emergence of huge fiscal deficits after 1973 in an economy that had traditionally followed a balanced-budget policy. Causes of the large fiscal deficits could be attributed to the major burst of new spending on social welfare programmes and the lack of tax revenues due to the slow down of economic growth (see Ishi, 1982, 1986a).

With the emergence of expanding fiscal deficits after the mid-1970s, the MOF began to stress the importance of achieving a balanced budget. Since then, reducing the fiscal deficit has become one of the most crucial objectives of budgetary policy, and even of overall economic policy.[18] Eliminating fiscal deficits is officially called 'fiscal reconstruction'.[19]

C1.2 Tax Increases or Expenditure Cuts?

What approach has the government adopted to reduce the fiscal deficits? Has it sought to reduce spending or raise taxes? At first, the government and the MOF attempted to raise tax revenues in the form of a new VAT, i.e. the general consumption tax, in order to reduce the accumulated debt. Such a bold strategy, however, was completely frustrated when the general consumption tax was politically rejected in the general election of 1979.

Needless to say, the general support for administrative reform has played a vital role in the process of fiscal reconstruction, producing an environment of fiscal austerity. There was an overwhelming concern about the interrelationship between cuts of wasteful expenditures, reductions in the large deficits, and drastic administrative reform during the first half of the 1980s.

As a result of such policies, the growth of government expenditure has indeed been restrained. In particular, non-entitlement government expenditure did not grow at all between 1983 and 1986. Of relevance was the reform of health insurance in 1984 and of the social security system in 1985, which contributed considerably to reducing social welfare spending, although it evoked a great deal of criticism from the general beneficiaries. Likewise, the rising trend of fiscal deficits was reversed from around 1980 in terms of the bond dependency ratio (the percentage of bond issues to total expenditures). Overall, the whole process of fiscal austerity under the administrative reform

---

[18] The MOF used four arguments to counter those who favoured expansionary fiscal policies, following the Keynesian principle: (i) the sharp rise of debt service costs (redemption and interest payments), (ii) the crowding-out effect in capital markets, (iii) the debt burden on future generations, and (iv) the increase of inefficient and wasteful expenditures (*see* e.g. the MOF's documents collected in the pamphlet, *Considering Fiscal Reform*, Feb. 1983).

[19] The exact definition of 'fiscal reconstruction' refers to the reduction of the amount of 'deficit-covering bonds', not 'construction bonds' in the general account of the national government by the targeted fiscal year. The Suzuki administration set a specific deadline of fiscal 1984 at the outset, but the date had to be postponed because of big revenue shortages after the second oil shock. Following this failure, the Nakasone administration set a target of fiscal year 1990 for curtailing deficits, a target that was finally attained in 1991 due to expanded revenues caused by the 'bubble economy' (*see* Ishi and Ihori, 1992).

movement is worth assessing if we focus only on the specific aspect of fiscal reconstruction.[20]

C1.3 Current and Future Trends

The target of fiscal reconstruction was successfully achieved in 1991, as evidenced by the disappearance of debt-covering bonds in the initial budget at that time. Ironically, the main cause of this success story was due to huge tax increases that had automatically been generated during a period of a 'bubble economy' in 1987–9. Compared to the previous years, national tax revenues expanded by 13.6 per cent in 1987, 12.7 per cent in 1988, and 7.7 per cent in 1989. These tax increases were derived mainly from the corporate tax, the self-assessed personal income tax, the security transaction tax, etc., which reflected a large expansion of the tax base, such as corporate profits, capital gains, and capital transfers.

In 1989, the Bank of Japan (BOJ) started to adopt a restrictive monetary policy, partly triggered by social criticism over the sharp increase in land prices. Particular attention was paid to a complaint among the general public that rising land prices destroyed people's desire to purchase their own lands and dwellings. The BOJ raised the discount rate five times, from 2.5 to 6 per cent, within about one year, and in addition imposed a regulation on loans related to real estate transactions.

The sharp drop in land and stock prices brought the bubble economy to a final collapse in the early 1990s. After the collapse of the bubble economy, the Japanese economy entered into recession or depression for about three years. By mid-1994, the economy had not fully recovered from the trough of depression (at the time of writing), although it is widely acknowledged that there have been some improvements, albeit at a very slow tempo. Such prolonged recession after the collapse of the bubble is considered the greatest economic hardship in post-war Japan, except for the oil shock.

Particular attention is paid to the damage done to tax revenues. The recession caused a shortfall in revenue from national taxes between 1991 and 1993, and to make up for the expenditure–revenue gap, the government has been compelled, once again, to increase the issuance of national bonds. In practice, this implies that budgetary behaviour has returned to the emergence of fiscal deficits. As a matter of fact, the bond dependency ratio (i.e. the ratio of national bond issuance to government expenditure in the central government general account) has risen from the lowest value of 9.5 per cent in 1991 to 20.9 per cent in 1993.

---

[20] Of course, a variety of criticisms has been raised against fiscal austerity. Of greatest importance is the MOF's usual failure to generate a macroeconomic policy response. The MOF's continued concern for austerity has induced both irritating debate over stimulating domestic demand and foreign criticism of Japan's macroeconomic policy, when the economy was weakening and current account surpluses were accumulating sharply (*see* Ishi, 1986a; Yashiro, 1987).

C2 Savings and Investment Incentives

C2.1 Special Tax Measures

Table 6.8 summarizes the percentage distribution of the revenue costs of special tax measures, dating back to 1980, for which the relevant data are available. Of utmost importance are the following two categories.

The first category, incentives to promote individual saving and housing, is tied exclusively to the individual income tax. The other category is related mainly to the corporate income tax. Over each time period, the first category cost more in terms of forgone revenue. The second largest share of revenue loss arising from tax incentives is related to the promotion of business saving and investment. The tax devices used to promote these activities include tax exemptions and credits, accelerated depreciation, and tax-free reserves. These devices generally are used for particular industries or specific activities, and in many cases, two or three measures are employed to promote the same objective.

C2.2 Tax Incentives for Personal Savings

Japan's high savings rate during the post-war period has received worldwide attention as a contributing factor to the country's notable economic performance. There has been a general belief that the high rate of personal savings has been stimulated by government tax policy. The most salient feature of these special tax measures is the substantial amount of revenue losses that have been sustained in order to stimulate personal savings (see Table 6.8. It is often pointed out that the special tax measures were initiated to implement specific policy goals—in particular, capital accumulation, i.e. the promotion of savings and equity investments during the process of rapid economic growth.

Although some special provisions were phasesd out, tax preferences for savings remained intact until 1987. Needless to say, special measures applicable to specific sources of income are a clear deviation from the global tax system proposed by the Shoup mission. There were several forms of savings that received exemption or highly favourable tax treatment. Thus, a major effect of the Japanese tax system has been its impact on saving behaviour, although the nature of its impact is difficult to pin down.

As regards tax preferences for specific personal savings prior to March 1987, income earned from interest, up to a specific limit of total principal (or total face value) of personal savings (or public bonds), was exempt from income taxation. In April 1988, these special treatments were replaced by a flat tax rate of 20 per cent at source.

Currently, capital gains on the sale of stocks are treated more favourably for tax purposes than other investment incomes. Between 1953 and 1988, individuals' capital gains on securities in practice were exempt from tax, a treatment that had become a symbol of unfairness of the income tax. Although capital

Table 6.8 Percentage distribution of the estimated revenue loss from special tax measures, by type of incentive, 1958–1991 (%)

Fiscal year	Promotion of individual saving and housing (1)	Promotion of business saving and investment (2)	Promotion of export and foreign investment (3)	Promotion of environment quality (4)	Others (5)
1980	53.6	20.6	1.9	3.6	20.4
1981	57.4	20.2	1.7	4.2	16.5
1982	58.0	21.1	2.3	4.3	14.4
1983	57.3	23.4	1.6	4.1	13.7
1984	54.6	26.0	2.4	4.2	12.7
1985	59.0	24.2	2.2	4.1	10.6
1986	59.8	24.2	1.7	4.1	10.2
1987	57.4	29.1	1.9	2.9	8.7
1988	59.3	26.4	1.4	3.2	9.7
1989	58.2	28.7	1.0	2.8	9.3
1990[a]	60.3	22.8	0.8	3.5	12.7
1991[b]	61.8	21.2	0.6	4.0	12.4

[a] Preliminary figures.
[b] Estimated on the basis of budget data.
Note: The official classification was rearranged into five items as listed above.
Source: Data presented to the Budget Committee, National Diet by the Tax Bureau, MOF.

gains had once been fully taxed (losses fully deductible) in accordance with the Shoup tax proposals, they were exempted from taxation in 1953 because the administration of the tax was too difficult to enforce. Subsequently, capital gains were, in principle, tax-exempt, although those who dealt continuously with stocks in large volumes (30 transactions a year, involving more than 120,000 shares in 1988) were required to include capital gains in their tax base, which was then subject to aggregate taxation.

In response to criticism of the non-taxable status of capital gains, the Takeshita tax reform in 1988 introduced two alternative capital gains taxes. Under the first method, taxpayers' self-assessment realized capital gains, separate from other incomes, at a rate of 20 per cent (plus 6 per cent for the local inhabitants' tax). Under the second method, a 20 per cent tax is imposed on capital gains at source. For this purpose, capital gains are deemed as 5 per cent of gross proceeds derived from the stock sales price. Consequently, the taxpayer is required to pay 1 per cent (0.2 × 0.05) of the stock sales price as a deemed capital gains tax under the withholding system. This amount is exactly the same as the securities transaction tax. The taxpayer may choose between the self-assessment or withholding methods. Taxation of capital gains from the sale of stocks became effective from April 1989.

C2.3   Investment Incentives for Firms

There were several steps in the development of tax incentives for the promotion of specific policy goals for business activities. First, earlier in the post-war period, both the promotion of exports and the encouragement of certain key industries (e.g. petrochemicals) formed a major consideration in tax policy. In the main, tax exemptions were used to achieve these objectives. Today, however, these provisions are of very minor significance. Second, a more important goal was to stimulate business saving and investment among targeted industries. Targeted industries were authorized to use various types of tax devices, such as special depreciations, tax-free reserves, and tax credits. In particular, we should note the interaction between investment and exports.

Third, tax incentives were directed towards developing technological innovation. Tax devices also were used to stimulate such innovation indirectly by generating the growth of capital formation in important, selected industries. Major beneficiaries of such special measures were the steel and machinery industries, which may have thereby developed international competitiveness to a great degree. Lastly, as time went by, the benefits of special tax measures were extended from key industries to cover a wide variety of policy objectives, such as pollution control and the enhancement of social welfare. The use of tax incentives was diversified to advance various economic and social policy goals.

Since the late 1970s, however, tax benefits for business investment, corporate savings, and industrial production began to be phased out because of the large fiscal deficit. The scope of tax incentive policies thus became narrower.

More detailed information on recent special tax measures for corporations is given in Table 6.9. There are three broad types of tax incentives: (i) special depreciation, (ii) reserves, and (iii) tax credits and allowances. In 1991, the third type accounted for the largest tax expenditure among the three (61.3 per cent of the total), having greatly expanded from 16.2 per cent in 1977. In addition to a big increase in credits for research and experimental expenditures, three new items (3(b), 3(c), and 3(e)) to promote specific investments were added.

C3   Distribution of the Tax Burden

The Japanese income tax system has violated the principles of both vertical and horizontal equity to a considerable degree, mainly because many special provisions have been introduced to benefit selected groups of taxpayers. For instance, the application of reduced tax rates to specific types of investment income favours higher-income classes, impairing vertical equity. Likewise, a number of special exclusions, deductions, and tax credits reduce the income tax base and create large differences in tax burdens among people with equal incomes. They also generate the phenomenon of income tax erosion.

Table 6.9 Revenue losses of special tax measures of corporations, by type, 1977, 1987, and 1991

	1977		1991	
	¥bn.	%	¥bn.	%
1. Special measures for depreciation	128	56.1	162	25.7
(a) Special depreciation qualified equipment (e.g. machinery and equipment for reducing pollution, saving energy, recycling etc.)	34	14.9	29	4.6
(b) Special depreciation on manufacturing machinery used in underdeveloped regions	14	6.1	24	3.8
(c) Special depreciation on machinery and equipment acquired by small and medium-sized firms	43	18.9	45	7.1
(d) Others	37	16.2	64	10.2
2. Reserves	63	27.6	82	13.0
(a) Reserve for overseas investment loss	12	5.3	10.2	
(b) Reserve for losses caused by repurchase of computer	1	0.4	—	—
(c) Others	50	21.9	81	12.9
3. Tax credits and allowances	37	16.2	386	61.3
(a) Credit for research and experimental expenditures	17	7.5	110	17.5
(b) Tax measures to promote investments for efficient use of energy	0	0.0	—	—
(c) Tax measures to promote investments by small and medium-sized firms on equipment utilizing electronic devices	0	0.0	55	8.7
(d) Special deduction for income derived from overseas technial service transactions	12	5.2	13	2.1
(e) Tax measures to improve managerial fundamentals of small and medium-sized enterprises	0	0.0	39	6.2
(f) Others	8	3.5	169	26.8
Total	228	100.0	630	100.0

Source: MOF, Tax Bureau (1977, 1987, 1991).

Tax erosion is analysed in terms of the effective rate of tax by income class. The 'effective rate of tax' is here defined as the ratio of tax liability to the comprehensive tax base. Comparison is made between the effective rate of tax under a comprehensive income tax base (after eliminating all special provisions) and the actual effective rate of tax (the ratio of actual taxes to comprehensive income). This comparison reveals the extent of erosion caused by the special provisions of the income tax law. Since the effective burden of statutory tax rates is altered by the existence of tax-eroding provisions, the usual practice of examining the movement of nominal tax rates by income class does not reveal the true distribution of the tax burden. An examination of the difference between comprehensive and actual effective rates of tax over income classes reveals the distribution of the benefits of tax preferences, and provides a better tool for judging the equity of the tax system.

It is generally believed that tax-eroding provisions have greater impact at higher income levels. In particular, it is expected that the exclusion of interest and dividends and the separate taxation of capital gains primarily affects taxpayers in the highest brackets. Thus, tax erosion is assumed to benefit higher-income individuals more than taxpayers in the lower brackets, and the entire tax system is thought to be much less progressive than the statutory tax rates imply.

Fig. 6.2 shows the comprehensive tax base and yield for 1991. Using these estimates, two effective rates of tax can be derived. The results presented in Fig. 6.2 to some extent confirm these expectations.

C4 Administrative Costs

C4.1 Patterns of Administrative Costs: An International Comparison

We now turn to the relative size of administrative costs compared to tax revenue. In general, administrative costs are officially calculated by the

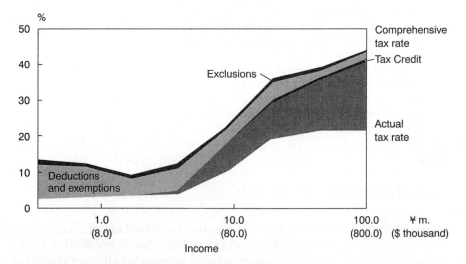

Figures in parentheses on the income scale are in US dollars, converted at $1 = ¥125.
The horizontal axis is drawn to a logarithmic scale.

Fig. 6.2 Income tax erosion by income class, 1991

revenue department of a country, such as the Internal Revenue Service (IRS) in the USA. Therefore, based on official data, an approximate international comparison becomes feasible in terms of administrative costs as a percentage of tax revenue. Fig. 6.3 shows the movements of such a ratio at the central government level in the USA, the UK, Canada, and Japan, mainly during the period 1960–90.

In view of the possible different coverage of costs in each country, a strict comparison is not possible, but two interesting points are worth noting in the case of Japan. First, the ratio of costs to revenue until the early 1970s was higher in Japan than in the other countries. In particular, it was much higher than in the USA, where the ratio has been kept very low. On this point, it seems that Japan's tax system was administered less efficiently in terms of the cost/revenue ratio. Second, the ratio in Japan declined sharply

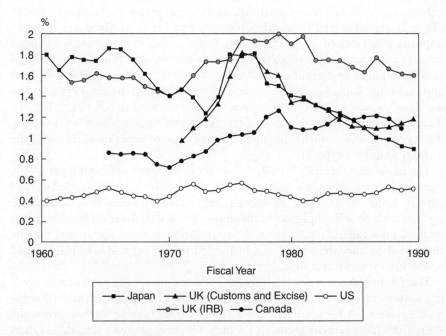

Fig. 6.3 Administrative cost as a percentage of tax revenue, selected countries, 1960–1990

Note: Each figure is calculated as a percentage of costs per $100, £100 or ¥100.

Sources: USA: Internal Revenue Service, *Annual Report*, 1989 and 1990. Canada: Revenue Canada Taxation, *Inside Taxation*, 1975 and 1989; Supply and Service Canada, *Report of the Department of National Revenue Customs Excise and Taxation*, 1977–9 and 1981. UK: Board of Inland Revenue, *Report of the Year* 1970, 1972–5 and 1987–90; Customs and Excise, *Report of the Commissioners of Her Majesty's Customs and Excise*, each year. Japan: National Tax Administration, *Annual Report of Statistics*, 1970, 1985, and 1990.

in the mid-1970s, and was lower than that of Canada. Thus, Japan now seems to lie between the USA and Canada.

C4.2 A Well-Established Withholding Tax System

One of the factors explaining the current efficiency of tax administration in Japan is the withholding tax system, which is firmly built into the basic structure of the individual income tax.

At present, taxable income under the individual income tax is divided into ten categories, which are in turn classified into four types, depending on tax collection methods. The relationship between taxable income and different types of collection are summarized in Table 6.9.

Tax on employment and retirement incomes (Type 1, see B1.1 above) is collected from payers on the basis of withholding on behalf of taxpayers. Such income is first computed comprehensively and progressive tax rates are strictly applied.

Interest, dividends (some portion), and capital gains on the sale of stocks (Type 2) are separated from other incomes and tax is withheld at source by applying a flat rate of 20 or 35 per cent.[21] Moreover, such income is excluded from the tax base when taxpayers file their tax returns. Another method of taxation applies to certain other dividends, capital gains on the sale of land and buildings, some business income, and miscellaneous income (Type 3). Tax on these incomes is withheld separately at a lower rate of tax,[22] but the incomes then must be reported later as taxable income in a final return. The need for final returns distinguishes one type of separate taxation (Type 2) from another (Type 3).

The remaining income (Type 4)—from other categories of capital gains (e.g. from the sale of valuable assets, paintings, or jewels) or a self-assessed part of capital gains on the sale of stocks, real estate, timber, and occasional, agricultural, or self-employment incomes—are taxed under a self-assessment method on a calendar-year basis. A tax return is required for annual income to be filed no later than 15 March of the following year and tax must be paid to the tax office at that time.

The relative share of taxable income collected under the present withholding system in 1991 is calculated in Table 6.10. The pure method of withholding accounts for about three-quarters of total taxable income, while the share from filing returns accounts for only 4.9 per cent. Since sepaate taxation can be grouped into a withholding category (Type 2), the importance in the

---

[21] All interest income and capital gains on the sale of stocks are withheld at source at a rate of 20% (including 5% of local tax), while dividends attract 35% tax.

[22] In Type 3, dividends may alternatively be subject to the rate of 20% at the taxpayer's option, but the taxpayer must file a final return. Capital gains on the sale of land and buildings are taxed separately on a self-assessed basis, depending on the holding period of the relevant assets. Some portions of business income and miscellaneous income, which are mainly composed of fees, royalties, and remuneration paid to professionals, are withheld, usually at the rate of 10%, as an advance taxation.

Table 6.10   Tax collection methods by taxable income in 1991 (¥bn)

| Income | Withholding (Type 1) | Separate taxation at source | | Filing returns (Type 4) |
		without final returns (Type 2)	without final returns (Type 3)	
Employment	212,617			
Retirement	9,301			
Interest		33,096		
Dividends		850	4,837	
Capital gains Stock, etc.		2,330		909
Others			17,676	254
Real estate				4,395
Timber				71
Business Agricultural and Self-employed				8,839
Others			3,382	
Occasional				216
Miscellaneous			2,778	
Subtotals	221,918 (73.6)	36,276 (12.0)	28,673 (9.5)	14,684 (4.9)
Total	301,551 (100.0)			

Note: Figures in parentheses are percentage distribution. Interest and dividends contain some amounts that corporations have earned as well as individuals.

Source: Calculated from NTA (1992).

tax system of non-filing returns increases further. Is is difficult to estimate corresponding figures for other countries, but the use of withholding for tax collection in Japan seems much broader than in any other country.

D. Tax Reforms

D1 Main Tax Reforms, 1987–93

An understanding of recent tax developments should start with a complete picture of the tax reform movement that began in the mid-1980s, because the results obtained from those reforms, as well as the remaining issues, have considerably affected the workings of the contemporary tax system. After the tax reforms that ended with the adoption of a VAT in April 1989, greater attention has been paid to two tax policy issues: amendments to the consumption tax and land tax reform.

D1.1 The Emergence of Sweeping Tax Reforms

The history of the first and second tax reforms began with special reference to the process of introducing the consumption tax (Japan's VAT). The basic characteristics of the reform are evident from Nakasone's inquiry to the Tax Advisory Commission on 20 September 1985. In October 1986, the final plan for the first sweeping tax reform was presented to him by the commission, and the next step of the legislative process was embarked on. However, this reform plan failed, like Ohira's proposal for a general consumption tax in 1979, chiefly because Nakasone made a big political mistake in the 1986 general election campaign. As a result of political turmoil, Nakasone was finally obliged to withdraw the bill in May 1987.

The second stage of the tax reform was initiated by Prime Minister Takeshita in his inquiry to the Tax Advisory Commission in November 1987. In his inquiry, Takeshita placed emphasis on the following two points:

- the current tax system should be thoroughly restructured to secure stable revenues for an ageing society; and
- for this purpose, a well-balanced tax system should be achieved through an appropriate mix of taxation of income, consumption, and property.

The Takeshita administration's tax reform was intended to revive the postponed part of Nakasone's first tax package. After the original Nakasone tax reform was shelved in May 1987, the government introduced a limited package consisting of individual income tax reductions and repeal of the *Maruyu* tax-free saving system. As a result of a political compromise between the LDP and the opposition parties in September 1987, tax reform was partially effected beginning in fiscal 1988 (see Aoki, 1988; Nagano, 1988). Two proposed reforms, however, were postponed: (i) the introduction of a broad-based indirect tax, and (ii) a cut in the corporate tax rate.

These two reforms were taken up by the Takeshita administration. Obviously, the Takeshita tax reform was extremely important in the history of the Japanese tax system as it resulted in the adoption of Japan's VAT.

Along with the transition from the first stage to the second, the fundamental conditions for achieving tax reform changed during the years 1987–88. Land and stock prices soared rapidly during the short time of the 'bubble economy', widening the gulf between rich and poor. Continued economic expansion yielded large revenue increases in 1988. Even the target of 'fiscal reconstruction' (i.e. no issuance of deficit-covering bonds in the general account of the national government) no longer looked unattainable. If tax revenues had been falling and no other means were available for raising needed revenues, the population might have agreed that higher tax burdens were required. However, this was not the case. Abundant revenue sources prevented the government from proposing the prompt adoption of a new broad-based indirect tax for collecting revenues.

As a consequence, to make the tax reform debate more palatable, emphasis had to be shifted away from recovering the revenue lost due to income tax cuts and towards the elimination of unfair tax burdens. Accordingly, the perceived lack of fairness among taxpayers became a decisive factor in promoting the need for tax reform. In particular, wage and salary workers had long criticized the income tax in view of its unfavourable treatment of their employment income compared to other incomes (e.g. business or capital income), and had always complained that their income tax burden was too heavy. This view was constantly expressed by labour unions on behalf of their members. Thus, relieving such a perception of unfairness among working groups became an important goal of tax reform.

The government had two aims for the second tax reform. One was to correct inequities in the existing tax system; the other was to create a new broad-based consumption tax in order to rebuild the indirect tax system and to secure long-term, stable revenue sources. To mitigate the strong resistance to the latter aim, the government reduced income and corporate tax burdens substantially. Great efforts were made to design the least objectionable package of tax reform (see Ishi, 1988).

In July 1988, a new tax reform plan was sent to the Diet incorporating a ¥2,400 billion net tax reduction (see Table 6.11). This plan formed a striking contrast to the Nakasone tax reform, which was to remain 'revenue-neutral'.

The choice of a net reduction in tax amounts was unexpected, considering the MOF's traditional goal of raising revenue while maintaining fiscal austerity. There are two special reasons, however, why the reduction of tax revenues became feasible at that time. First, the failure of the Nakasone tax reform forced the government to make tax reform more attractive by offering a large-scale cut in direct taxes. Second, the government could afford to cut taxes to some extent without creating new tax sources, given the ample revenue derived from the economic expansion.

The main feature of the reform plan was a mixture of individual income tax reductions and indirect tax increases via the introduction of a new consumption tax. Great emphasis should be placed on this mixed reform package, which resulted in a change in the tax mix towards indirect taxes. Thus, the ¥5,600 billion reduction of direct taxes came from cuts in the individual income tax, the corporate tax, and the inheritance tax combined, while tax increases were derived mostly from the introduction of a consumption tax. As a result, the net amount of the tax cut was ¥2,400 billion.

D1.2 Individual Income Tax Reform

The main objective of the individual income tax reform was to reduce the tax burden at both the national and local levels by reducing progressive tax rates

Table 6.11 Reform package of tax increases and reductions: [a] tax bill proposed in July 1988 (¥bn.)

Tax reduction		Tax increases	
Direct tax reduction	5,600	Creation of a new consumption tax	5,400
Individual income tax	3,100		
Corporate income tax	1,800		
Inheritance tax	700	Others (repeal of the reduced tax rate on dividends, amendment of foreign tax credit, etc.)	1,200
Repeal of certain selective excise taxes	3,400		
Total	9,000	Total	6,600

[a] Includes both national and local taxes.

Source: Data submitted to the Tax Advisory Commission.

drastically. It was widely acknowledged that individual income tax reform should be based on the reduction of marginal tax rates through a broadening of the income tax base. This goal was very important, given the necessity of reforming the income tax system in terms of fairness, neutrality, and simplicity.

Obviously, broadening the income tax base has a close bearing on the correction of inequitable tax burdens. The narrowly defined tax base often resulted in an unequal treatment of two taxpayers with equal incomes, simply because one received income in ways that were tax-favoured.

The primary goal of the Takeshita tax reform was to correct the unfairness of the existing income tax system. Accordingly, the income tax base should have been widened by removing exclusions, special exemptions, deductions, etc. Unfortunately, this did not happen.

Instead, the planners of the tax reform left the tax base intact, placing greater emphasis on achieving substantial rate reductions for individual taxpayers. This choice was made primarily because no one opposed a reduction in rates, whereas vested interests and specific beneficiaries strongly resisted the elimination of eroding provisions that would widen the tax base. Broadening the tax base entails a heavy political cost, and so far, no Japanese politician has been willing to take the risk.

In September 1987, a part of the Nakasone tax plan was put into effect in which individual income tax cuts were achieved by widening income brackets. From the outset, however, this reform was considered a temporary measure before the final tax rates were determined; thus, it was expected that an even flatter rate structure would be proposed during the second stage of the tax reform process (see Table 6.2).

Given the state of the Japanese economy and society, a flatter progressive rate structure has several advantages over a steeply progressive income tax. If base-broadening is accompanied by a flatter rate structure, such a tax would reduce the inequality of tax treatment of taxpayers with equal incomes, would abate possible distortions of economic decisions (such as those determining the labour supply, saving, and risk-taking), and would alleviate some of the complexities that result from steep progressivity. Furthermore, the reduction of income brackets and the widening of income bands would mitigate problems inherent to a progressive rates structure, e.g. bracket creep, bunching of income, and incentives to avoid or evade taxes.

D1.3 Corporate and Inheritance Tax Reform

In the Takeshita tax reform package, the major goal of corporate tax reform was to reduce the tax burden by decreasing the basic rate on retained earnings. A lowering of these tax rates aimed to establish a corporate tax system in harmony with the international environment. Among advanced industrialized nations, Japan's effective corporate tax rates (combined national and local tax rates) were the second highest in 1988, at 52 per cent. To attain parity with other countries, both the first and second stages of tax reform proposed that effective rates be lowered to less than 50 per cent in the near future.

The basic rate levied on ordinary corporations was gradually reduced, from 42 per cent in 1988 to 37.5 per cent after 1990. On the other hand, lower tax rates on small and medium-sized corporations were only reduced from 30 to 28 per cent. The tax rate of cooperatives remained unchanged, even though all other basic rates were reduced to some extent. Consequently, the difference between ordinary corporations and other firms was substantially narrowed in terms of the tax rates on retained earnings.

In addition, several adjustments were planned to rationalize the corporate tax burden. They involved tax increases through broadening the tax base. First, the tax on intercorporate dividends was increased, and dividends paid by one corporation to another were subject to an additional corporate tax. Corporations previously were allowed to deduct 100 per cent of the dividends they received from other corporations, but this percentage was reduced to 90 per cent in 1989 and to 80 per cent after 1990. Second, corporations were restricted as to the amount of deductions they could take on interest payments for land purchases when computing their tax base. This measure made it impossible for them to deduct interest payments on loans for land purchases as business expenses for four years. Third, the generous treatment of foreign tax credits, a practice that was much criticized, was corrected to prevent an excessive amount of credits from being taken.

It was relatively easy to lower corporate tax rates, despite the repeal of measures that had enabled corporations to reduce the rate they paid on dividends. The base-broadening measures, however, were insufficient to allow a substantial reduction of corporate tax rates. This posed practically the same problem as with the individual income tax. In addition, no attempts were made to eliminate other tax-free reserves, such as the bonus reserve, so as to widen the tax base.

D1.4 Amendments to the Consumption Tax

Contrary to earlier fears, the new consumption tax was incorporated smoothly in the Japanese tax system only a year after it was enacted. Politically, however, arguments continued between the left-wing opposition parties and the ruling LDP before both parties were merged into a coalition in 1994. The former persisted in demanding repeal of the VAT from the beginning of its implementation, while the latter gradually had to respond to such political attacks by amending some parts of the tax.

The three points in dispute were as follows: (i) the regressive tax burden on lower income-earners; (ii) the cash-flow benefits for businesses during the period before tax revenues are handed over to the tax authorities; and (iii) the windfall revenue gains under the special simplified scheme of deemed value added.

The first point, concerning regressivity, remained predominant for a long time among the opposition parties, which were supported politically by the anti-VAT movement. Each time a VAT was proposed, the most criticism centred on its basic nature as a regressive tax and the distributional consequences. This was the reason the number of exempted items in the Nakasone sales tax was increased from the original seven to fifty-one. Needless to say, a large number of exempted items distort the fundamental structure of the VAT, impairing uniformity and scope, which are of great advantage to tax neutrality. The government persistently maintained that distributional issues could be better served by progressive income taxation and by carefully targeted transfer payments to the poorer households. Politically, however, the increased use of exemptions from VAT has been getting more popular support from consumers.

The second point of contention was the cash-flow advantages granted to traders, who have the use of VAT revenues before passing them on to the tax authorities. Originally, traders were allowed to file a return and pay the tax due twice a year (including once for interim payment). This 'grace period' thus was substantial, covering more than several months. Consumers were highly critical of the benefits that traders derived during the grace period on equity grounds.

As a third point, great emphasis was placed on the inequitable aspects of the windfall revenue gains caused by the application of the special simplified scheme and the vanishing exemption. In particular, the deemed value-added rule (i.e. 10 per cent for wholesalers and 20 per cent for retailers) underestimated the tax base. Big differences can be observed between the approximate ratio and the actual ratio of value added by type of industry.

The process of rectifying the structure of the consumption tax was divided into two stages. The first stage was a 'Tax bill for the amendment of the consumption tax' approved by the cabinet in March 1990, but it was not successful. The second stage was based on an 'Amended tax bill of the consumption tax' presented by the Joint Committee in April 1991, which led to the revised form of the current consumption tax. During this period, the opposition parties twice submitted bills to repeal the consumption tax.

The first amendment plan was mainly composed of three features, as follows.

First, food was to be fully exempted only at the retail level, while half VAT rates (i.e. 1.5 per cent) were to be applied to interfirm transactions on the same product.

Second, the scope of exemptions was to be expanded to cover (i) birth expenses, (ii) cremation and burial costs, (iii) certain goods and services for disabled persons, (iv) certain welfare services, (v) education, and (vi) housing rents.

Third, the annual number of tax returns and payments was to be increased from once a year to four times for larger traders to shorten the 'grace period'.

This amended scheme of VAT did not come into effect as the tax bill was withdrawn at the 118th Extraordinary Diet in June 1990. We must conclude that this was a good decision. If the revised form had passed the Diet, a very strange style of VAT would have been created. The next amendment, which was successful, was derived from a joint agreement between the ruling and opposition parties. As a consequence, the consumption tax was altered to a considerable extent on the basis of the fundamental direction mentioned above.

The main features of the new VAT are as follows. First, the 'grace period' was shortened by increasing the annual number of tax returns and payments from twice a year to four times a year. This rule applies only to large traders whose tax due exceeds more than ¥5 million.

Second, windfall revenue gains were lessened by establishing new requirements. Different deemed ratios of value added were established for different types of businesses as follows: (i) 10 per cent for wholesale; (ii) 20 per cent for retail; (iii) 30 per cent for agriculture, forestry, fisheries, mining, construction, and manufacturing; and (iv) 40 per cent for others, such as transport, telecommunications, real estate, restaurants, etc. Also, the maximum amount of taxable sales for purposes of the special simplified scheme was reduced from ¥500 million to ¥400 million. Likewise, the maximum amount for purposes of the vanishing exemption was reduced from ¥60 million to ¥50 million. However, the exemption level remained unchanged at ¥30 million, although many asserted that it should be reduced to as low as ¥10–20 million.

Third, exempted goods and services were expanded in a way similar to the first amendment plan listed above.

As a result of these changes, the new consumption tax had two side effects. No doubt the first and second set of changes contributed to the improvement of the VAT, but the tax was worsened by the third set of changes, which eroded the tax base. The new tax became effective in October 1991.

D1.5 Land Tax Reform

A sharp rise in land prices began in the late 1980s, causing a number of land-related problems within the Japanese economy and society. In 1990, heated arguments occurred in the government and the private sector over an effective policy with respect to reducing land prices. From the expectation that land taxes could play a substantial role in slowing down the increase of land prices, particularly in urban areas, land tax reform emerged as an important measure.

On 30 October 1990, the Tax Advisory Commission submitted to Prime Minister Toshiki Kaifu a tax report entitled 'Basic Recommendations on the Ideal Framework of Land Taxation', based on the seven months of intensive deliberations by the Subcommittee on Land Taxation. These recommendations had the ambitious target of restructuring the land tax system as a whole and giving it basic direction for the coming decade or so. Following deliberations in the LDP Tax Council, during which several political compromises were made, the proposal was presented to the 120th Diet session as the Land Tax Bill, and became effective from 1991 to 1992. The six major provisions of the land tax reform are summarized below.

(1) *Introduction of the land value tax.* The Land Tax Bill imposed a new national landholding tax on the ownership or leasehold of lands throughout the entire country. Both individuals and corporations had to pay the tax based on a uniform level of assessment corresponding to the inheritance tax land value.

(2) *Increased land values for property tax purposes.* To remedy the extremely low land assessment values under the property tax, a new system of periodic revaluation was introduced from fiscal year 1994. However, the planned revaluation for fiscal year 1991 was implemented as usual. The basic aim of the new revaluation was to bring the valuation for tax purposes to within a certain margin of the official valuation price.[23] A specific relief programme eased the effect of a sudden tax increase on individual residential land.

(3) *Increase in land value and property taxes.* The special land value tax and the property tax were generally increased to promote the efficient utilization of land and to prevent speculative land transactions.

(4) *Increased land valuation for inheritance tax.* Land valuation for the inheritance tax was raised in 1992 to weaken the preference for land as an asset. The target rate was approximately 80 per cent of the official valuation price, compared with the rate of 60–70 per cent in the past. To compensate for the increased tax burden that accompanies the higher valuation of land, an

---

[23] Implicitly, it is expected that the revaluation of land for the property tax assessment should reach a target of approximately 70% of the official valuation price.

inheritance tax reduction was implemented in 1992 that reduced progressive tax rates and raised the tax threshold.

(5) *Tax increases on capital gains for individuals and corporations.* The individual income tax rates for long-term capital gains from the transfer of land or buildings owned by individuals for more than five years were raised from 20 per cent (plus 6 per cent local inhabitants' tax) below ¥40 million and 25 per cent (plus 7.5 per cent inhabitants' tax) above ¥40 million to flat rates of 30 per cent (plus 9 per cent local inhabitants' tax) on a uniform basis (percentage figures in parentheses are the inhabitants' tax rates). Likewise, the corporate tax on capital gains from land sales was substantially changed from the former system. Short-term capital gains on land held no longer than two years were taxed separately from other income at a 30 per cent rate in addition to the basic rate, and even deficit-operating firms had to pay taxes under this method of separate taxation. As for long-term capital gains on land held more than five years, a rate of 10 per cent was levied in addition to the ordinary corporate taxes. The additional tax was also applicable to deficit-operating firms in an effort to curtail tax avoidance.

(6) *Improvement of taxation of agricultural land within urbanization promotion areas.* The special treatment of agricultural land for both inheritance tax and property tax purposes was abolished in an effort to promote tax equity and promote an increase in the land supply. For this purpose, not later than the end of 1992, agricultural land to be preserved within Urbanization Promotion Areas in the three metropolitan areas had to be designated in city planning under the Productive Green Tract Area System. At the same time, the conversion of this agricultural land into other uses was restricted by law.

D2 Recent and Prospective Tax Reform

D2.1 Direction of Future Reforms

In terms of future reforms, the first thing to be done is to broaden the tax base of the individual income tax as much as possible. There is wide agreement that an inequitable tax system is unlikely to be remedied without a comprehensive tax base. If certain types of income are omitted from the tax base, or if particular uses of income are treated more favourably than others, taxpayers with similar economic situations will not be taxed equally. In addition, since deviations from a comprehensive tax base tend to accrue to higher-income earners, it is absolutely necessary to broaden the tax base to achieve vertical equity.

The two tax reforms were very incomplete in broadening the income tax base. The repeal of tax-free interest on small savings accounts is one successful example of base-broadening, but other measures remain to be taken. Two points in particular are worth noting relating to the individual income tax.

First, there are still too many unnecessary and unimportant exemptions, deductions, and credits. If some of these were eliminated or merged so as to obtain a broader tax base, a more uniform treatment of all sources and uses of income would be achieved and would lead to a more complete reform of the tax system. Some of the exemptions and credits that could be eliminated are: exemptions for aged persons, widows, widowers, or working students; special exemptions for spouses; additional exemptions for dependants aged 16–22; deductions for fire and other casualty insurance premiums; deduction for life insurance; and so on.

Second, the tax treatment of capital gains from the sale of securities has become very controversial among general taxpayers in relation to the elimination of unfair tax burdens. Clearly, such capital gains should be taxed more heavily and should be combined with other income sources and subject to progressive rates. The present provisions do not constitute a genuine income tax reform that incorporates a comprehensive definition of income. Left-wing parties and labour unions have agreed to a change from the present separate tax on capital gains with a flat rate to a system whereby capital gains are combined with ordinary income. Since political compromises have been made to strengthen taxes on capital gains, future reform should move towards a comprehensive income tax, on condition that tax rates should be further flattened.

Similarly, the reforms to date have not sufficiently broadened the base of corporate taxes. In 1994, the basic rate of the national corporate tax was reduced from 42 to 37.5 per cent, but no major efforts have been made to broaden the corporate tax base. However, repeal of the provision applying a lower tax rate on dividends may be of help as a base-broadening measure, because dividends are fully taxed as a part of corporate taxable income in addition to retained earnings.

With regard to the full taxation of capital gains from the sale of securities, the tax identification number (TIN), like the US social security number, is intended to assess such gains accurately. If the TIN is successfully adopted by the government, other investment income, such as interest and dividends, could be treated equally, as ordinary income, in a fashion similar to capital gains. Aggregate income taxation would be restored, as opposed to separate taxation at a flat rate, and such a reform would reflect a return to the Shoup proposals.

Rather than addressing these basic issues, tax changes since 1993 have reflected the conflict between fiscal consolidation and stimulating the economy. Thus, there were temporary personal income tax cuts from 1994 to 1996, not renewed in 1997 where there was a significant tightening of the fiscal stance. As signs of recession spread, a supplementary 1997 budget provided another temporary personal income tax cut of about ¥2 trillion, to be implemented in the first half of 1998, together with an increase in personal allowances and a further reduction of the corporate tax rate by 3 percentage points.

In addition, there have been increases in October 1996 to employers' and employees' social security contributions, with further increase planned for 1999. Finally, there have been recent increases in the tabacco tax.

D2.2 Further Amendments to Japan's VAT

Japan's VAT has been amended, but there still remain a number of areas that need to be improved. In comparison with the most common type of VAT used in EU countries today,[24] the consumption tax in Japan contains several special measures that are likely to impair the possible merits of such a tax. These measures are acknowledged as falling short of the full standard treatment under the usual type of VAT, but are justified by the existence of administrative and compliance problems. No doubt, political considerations were also involved, since it was necessary to obtain support from opposing groups in the retail and wholesale industries, who played a major role in the sales tax controversy as noted previously. Special treatments should be phased out more in favour of the normal scheme of VAT.

First of all, the special simplified procedures for measuring the tax base impair the advantages of broad-based indirect taxes. This special scheme may be justified to some extent in simplifying the procedure for charging the tax, but the current scheme applies too broadly for a special rule. Taxable traders whose annual sales are less than ¥400 million are eligible to apply the simplified procedures, and these firms make up as much as two thirds of total firms. Thus, the coverage of eligible taxable traders should be narrowed to a great extent, say to those with less than ¥100 million in annual sales.

Second, the consumption tax does not employ the tax-credit method, which is used almost universally nowadays. The account method has many disadvantages as compared to the tax-credit method. For instance, without the aid of invoices, there is no means to ascertain the chain of transactions from one stage to another. Thus, it is very difficult to assess the value of the tax base accurately because a strong incentive for cheating exists. Thus, the current form of consumption tax should be replaced by a tax-credit, invoice VAT.

Third, one of the unique features of the consumption tax is its extremely low rate. In fact, the original 3 per cent standard tax rate was by far the lowest among major VAT countries. The 3 per cent rate was lower than the 5 per cent sales tax that was proposed in the Nakasone tax reform, and was chosen so that it would be accepted more readily by taxpayers. However, while it proved successful in achieving acceptance, it could cause other troubles. For instance, in theory, VAT should be passed on to the ultimate consumers, but taxable traders may find it difficult to increase their prices by such a small amount. Thus, the tax may not be forward-shifted at each stage of transactions.

Lastly, attention should be paid to expanding the exemption of smaller undertakings from the consumption tax. All VAT countries admit problems in applying the normal tax scheme to small traders because of their specific business structure or activities. Thus, some exemption system is usually devised to free certain taxpayers from VAT. At present, the consumption

---

[24] Shoup (1990) points out that the most common—indeed, almost universal-type of VAT contains the following characteristics: consumption type, destination principle, tax-credit method, multiple rates that are tax-exclusive, and exemptions rather than zero-rating.

tax fixes the exemption level at ¥30 million in terms of annual sales, but this is an extremely high threshold by international standards.

It is apparent that the Japanese consumption tax departs from the standard type of VAT in several respects. In fact, it may be called an intermediate or imperfect form of VAT. Since the consumption tax was introduced in such an incomplete form, further reform is necessary to achieve greater economic fairness.

In fact, the Murayama Cabinet in 1996 decided to make several amendments to the VAT that will at least partially address the above concerns. These amendments became effective from April 1997.

First, the rate of the consumption tax was raised from 3 to 5 per cent.

Second, the maximum level of annual taxable sales for purposes of the special simplified scheme was reduced from ¥400 million to ¥200 million.

Third, the vanishing exemption system was abolished.

Fourth, a so-called 'Japanese invoice system' was introduced on the condition that the keeping of certain trade documents (e.g. receipts, delivery statements, and other forms of book records) to prove the amount of purchases needed to allow traders to deduct taxes on their purchases from those on their sales. This treatment is obviously different from the conventional use of invoices in European countries.

The ¥30 million exemption level will remain unchanged, however.

In summary, the Japanese system may be called an intermediate or imperfect form of VAT and further reform will be necessary to achieve greater economic fairness.

D2.3 An Ideal Tax Mix?

The tax system in Japan has been reformulated significantly in recent years with consequences that are likely to be far-reaching. However, the ultimate goal of tax reform should be to alter the relative shares of major tax sources to secure an ideal tax mix. As a result of recent reforms, the relative reliance on revenue sources was expected to be considerably shifted from an income base to a consumption base, resulting in a new mix of direct and indirect taxes. However, in the four years since the adoption of the consumption tax, there has been no observable shift from an income base to a consumption base in national and local taxes. Indeed, the relative share of direct taxes to the total (including local taxes) was 76.6 per cent in 1992, 76.7 per cent in 1993, and 76.0 per cent in 1994 (the 1993 and 1994 figures depend on those of the supplementary budget and initial budget). The present tax mix is far from ideal.

However, to the extent that consumption taxes are substituted for income taxes and progressive tax rates are mitigated in favour of higher-income classes, there is likely to be a corresponding need for strengthening the tax burdens on wealth, in order to maintain distributional equity and to avoid an excessive concentration of wealth. Indeed, in light of the past trends of sharp rises in land and stock prices, many believe that wealth taxation should be used for redistributional considerations. For this purpose, the tax burdens on wealth and capital transfers (e.g. gift and inheritance taxes, property tax, landholding tax, etc.) should have been increased more heavily than in the Takeshita tax plan. A response to this criticism was the introduction of the land value tax as a new landholding tax in 1992 as noted above.

There is widespread criticism that the heavier use of consumption taxes is regressive by nature; that is, the poor thereby pay relatively more of their income in taxes than the rich. If we follow this reasoning, the basic direction of recent tax reforms cannot be supported on the grounds that distributional equity can be achieved only by means of a progressive income tax. However, the problem of regressive tax burdens stemming from consumption taxes can substantially be resolved by combining two other approaches.

The first of these is designed to establish overall progressivity of the tax system by changes in the structure of tax sources, placing heavier burdens on wealth and capital transfers as well as creating a broad-based indirect tax. In addition, base-broadening measures in the individual income tax must be used to this end. The second approach is directed towards obtaining greater distributional equity via the expenditure side of government budgets, in particular, by means of welfare benefits to individuals with low incomes. A combination of these two approaches might achieve better results than a steeply progressive income tax. The reason for preferring such a combination to the existing heavy reliance on a progressive income tax is that the former measures can be implemented in such a way to improve distributional effects and neutrality. The proposed tax mix should thus be further biased towards taxes on consumption and wealth, although there is no way of attaining an ideal combination of these three sources.

References

Aoki, T. (1988), 'Tax Reform in Japan', *Bulletin for International Fiscal Documentation*, March.

Ishi, H. (1982), 'Causes and Cures of Tax Shortfalls', *Economic Eye*, 3 (Sept.).

—— (1986a), 'Overview of Fiscal Deficits in Japan with Special Reference to the Fiscal Policy Debate', *Hitosubashi Journal of Economics*, 27 (Dec.).

—— (1986b), 'Moving toward Tax Reform', *Sumitomo Quarterly* (Spring).

—— (1988), 'Tax Reform: The Takeshita Bill—Changes in Store', *Look Japan*, 34 (Oct.).

—— (1993), *The Japanese Tax System*, 2nd edn., Oxford University Press.

Ishi, H., and Ihori, H. (1992), 'How Have Fiscal Deficits been Reduced in Japan?', paper presented to the Tokyo Conference of International Seminar in Public Economics, 31 Aug–1 Sept.

Ito, T. (1992), *The Japanese Economy*, MIT Press, Cambridge, Mass.

Jichi Sogo Centre (1983), (1988), (1992). *Local Public Finance in Japan*, March.

Ministry of Finance, Tax Bureau (1977a, 1986, 1987, 1991, 1994), Tax Bureau, *An Outline of Japanese Taxes*, Tokyo.

Nagano, A. (1988), 'Japan', in J. A. Pechman (ed.), *World Tax Reform*, Brookings Institution, Washington, D.C.

Shoup, C. (1990), 'Choosing among Types of Value-Added Tax', in M. Gillis, C. S. Shoup, and G. P. Sicat (eds.), *Value-Added Taxation in Developing Countries*, World Bank, Washington, D.C.

Shoup Mission (1949), *The Report on Japanese Taxation by the Shoup Mission*, Tokyo.

Takenaka, H. (1992), *The Japanese Economy*, University of Michigan Press, Ann Arbor.

US Treasury (1984), *Tax Reform for Fairness, Simplicity and Economic Growth*, 1–3 (Nov.).

Yashiro, N. (1987), 'Japan's Fiscal Policy—An International Comparison', *Japanese Economic Studies*, 61 (Autumn).

7 The Netherlands

FLIP DE KAM

A. Overview

In 1994, public expenditure in the Netherlands amounted to Gld348 billion, or 58.5 per cent of GDP. Between the mid-1950s and the mid-1980s, the claim of the public sector on national income nearly doubled. This strong expansion of public outlays was not caused by increasing exhaustive expenditures. In fact, these have for many years been on a level comparable to that in the USA. The expansion of the public sector in the Netherlands was caused almost solely by strongly rising transfer payments to families, and growing interest payments on public debt.

Table 7.1 outlines recent trends in outlays, tax revenue, and the net public sector borrowing requirement.

Over three-quarters of public outlays are financed by taxes and social security contributions.[1] Non-tax revenues of the public sector and new debt cover the gap that remains. Over the period 1987–94, the total tax level fluctuated between 48.6 and 45.1 per cent of GDP.

Table 7.2 shows the tax mix, both in 1987 and 1994. The characteristics of these different levies are discussed in Sect. B below. Over the seven-year period considered here, aggregate tax revenue increased by 32 per cent, from Gld205 billion to Gld270 billion. Central government taxes account for over 50 per cent of total revenue, the combined tax share of local and provincial government is less than 3 per cent. Clearly, in quantitative terms, local and provincial taxes are of limited importance (Sect. B7). On the other hand, between 1987 and 1994, local tax revenues increased by 60 per cent, as against 30 per cent for central government taxes. Taxes to finance social insurance—including mandatory health-care insurance—account for over 40 per cent of total tax revenues.

Table 7.2 shows that after 1987, revenue from central and local government 'green' taxes increased the most, by 750 and 242 per cent respectively, reflecting environmental concerns of policy-makers and the population at large. Proceeds from import duties (index = 179), the motor vehicle tax (index = 156), and various excise taxes (index = 152) also grew above average. The

The author is most grateful to Ken Messere, whose valuable comments greatly helped to improve a preliminary draft of this chapter.
[1] Social security contributions will be treated as taxes.

Table 7.1   The public sector, 1987–1994 (% of GDP)

	1987	1990	1993	1994[a]
Outlays	64.6	58.0	58.6	58.1
Taxes	48.6	45.1	47.5	46.2
Non-tax revenues	8.3	8.1	8.1	8.0
Net borrowing requirement	7.7	4.8	3.0	3.9

[a] Estimates, due to be revised.

Source: Central Economic Planning Bureau (1994: 225).

recent boom in stock and real estate prices is reflected in higher revenues from the net wealth tax, and the estate and gift tax respectively (index = 150). The economic slowdown of 1992–3 is the major reason that revenue from the corporate income tax hardly increased between 1987 and 1994 (index = 101).

Revenue from the health-insurance *Ziekenfonds* tax fell by 15 per cent, reflecting a reduction of the insured package.[2]

In 1994, total tax revenues, as shown in Table 7.2, amount to Gld270 billion, or 45.5 per cent of GDP.[3] In revenue terms, the personal income tax is the most important tax (Gld53.5 billion), accounting for nearly 20 per cent of total tax revenue.[4] Less than 10 per cent of income tax due is collected by assessment, the remainder being collected by withholding the tax at source (wage withholding tax).

The value-added tax (VAT) is the second most important tax levied by the central government, followed by the corporation income tax. A company that distributes profits must withhold 25 per cent on dividends paid out to its shareholders (dividend withholding tax).

In 1994, contributions to finance the general social insurances (hereafter, 'general' social insurance taxes) generated over Gld77 billion in revenue. All residents are covered by four such programmes, the most important one being the general old-age pension programme.

Contributions to finance the employee social insurances (hereafter, 'employee' social insurance taxes) grossed nearly Gld28 billion. Participation in these programmes is mandatory for all workers in the market sector. Insured workers are entitled to benefits in case of unemployment, sickness, and disability.

About 60 per cent of the population is collectively insured against health-care expenses under the *Ziekenfonds* programme. Participation in the

[2] In 1989–91, several risks were lifted out of the *Ziekenfonds* health-insurance programme to be included in the package that is insured under the AWBZ general social insurance programme.

[3] For year 1994, Table 7.1 mentions a tax/GDP ratio of slightly over 46%. The difference with the ratio mentioned here (equivalent to Gld3 billion) mainly consists of several producer levies and will not be detailed here.

[4] Unless indicated otherwise, all revenue data and the description of the tax system refer to the situation in 1994.

Table 7.2 Taxes by revenue, 1987 and 1994[a,b]

	Gld billion		%-share		
	1987	1994	1987	1994	index[c]
Central government taxes	113.0	145.6			130
Personal income tax	39.2	53.5	19.1	19.8	136
Value-added tax	34.2	40.2	16.7	14.9	118
Corporate income tax	16.0	16.2	7.8	6.0	101
Excise taxes	9.0	13.7	4.4	5.1	152
Motor vehicle tax	3.2	5.0	1.6	1.8	156
Consumption tax on cars	2.7	3.7	1.3	1.4	137
Taxes on transactions	2.6	3.4	1.3	1.3	131
Import duties	1.9	3.4	0.9	1.3	179
Dividend tax	1.8	2.0	0.9	0.7	111
Green energy taxes	0.2	1.5	0.1	0.7	750
Net wealth tax	1.0	1.5	0.5	0.6	150
Estate and gift tax	1.1	1.5	0.5	0.6	136
Other central government taxes	0.1	0.1	0.0	0.0	100
Other government taxes	5.0	8.0			160
Local property taxes	2.9	3.8	1.4	1.4	131
Other local government taxes	0.1	0.2	0.0	0.1	150
Various green taxes (user fees)	1.2	2.9	0.6	1.1	242
Water board tax	0.6	0.8	0.3	0.3	133
Provincial tax	0.2	0.3	0.1	0.1	150
Taxes to finance social insurance	87.4	116.7			134
General social insurance taxes	54.0	77.4	26.3	28.6	143
Employee social insurance taxes	19.8	27.7	9.6	10.2	140
Ziekenfonds tax	13.6	11.6	6.6	4.3	85
Total	205.4	270.3	100	100	132

[a] 1987: National Accounts data (transactions basis); 1994: Estimates, taken from various sources (cash basis). The national currency is the guilder (Gld). In 1994, one US dollar was worth nearly two guilders.
[b] Taxes ranked by type, and in order of decreasing revenue (in 1994).
[c] 1987 = 100.

Sources: Central Bureau of Statistics (1991: 128–9, 131, 146); Ministry of Finance (1993: 111); Ministry of Social Affairs (1993: 155); Council for Local Finances (1994: 72).

programme is mandatory for market sector employees and benefit recipients with gross earnings under Gld54,400 per year. All other households must privately insure against health-care expenses. Sect. B describes the various levies that constitute the Dutch tax system.[5] Sect. C discusses economic and social aspects. Sect. D looks at tax reform, and its prospects.

[5] See also Te Spenke and Lier (1992).

B. The Tax System

B1   Personal Income Tax

The personal income tax is levied on the basis of the Income Tax Act of 1964 (ITA 1964). Taxpayers are either resident or non-resident individuals. The residence of an individual is determined according to circumstances. In this respect, a number of facts may be relevant, such as whether an individual has (permanent) personal ties with the Netherlands. Resident taxpayers are, in principle, subject to income tax on their worldwide income. Non-resident taxpayers are liable only to Dutch income tax for income that is derived from a limited number of domestic sources (Sect. B1.6).

To protect its resident taxpayers from double taxation, which may result if foreign income is also taxed in another jurisdiction, the Netherlands has concluded over 50 tax treaties with other States. If no treaty applies, unilateral double taxation relief may be obtained under national tax law.

Income tax is collected in two ways: either by assessment or by withholding tax at source. In the case of assessment, the tax inspector issues a tax return form to individuals who, in his opinion, are liable to the tax. Taxpayers are obliged to file their completed tax return with the tax inspector. If a qualifying individual does not receive a form, he is obliged to ask for one. Generally, the tax return has to be filed within three months after expiration of the calendar year. In most cases, the taxpayer will receive a provisional assessment during the calendar year concerned, or immediately after sending in his tax return. The final assessment follows after examination of the tax return by the tax office.

B1.1   Tax Base

The ITA 1964 defines income as aggregate income flowing from five 'sources'. Resident taxpayers are subject to the tax on income they have received within a given calendar year. Worldwide income from the following five sources is relevant here:

- net income from employment;
- business income of the self-employed;
- net investment income;
- income in the form of periodic payments, and certain income transfers from the public sector; and
- gains from disposing of a substantial interest in a company with limited liability.

As a rule, capital gains are *not* taxed, unless they are realized within an enterprise, qualify as income from independently performed economic activities, or are derived from the sale of a 'substantial interest' (in a company).

Proceeds from the five sources mentioned add up to *aggregate income*. To determine the tax base, a number of exemptions and deductions can be taken into account, such as (limited) exemptions for interest and dividend income and a special deduction for the self-employed. After such deductions and exemptions have been taken into account, we have *income*.

Negative income incurred in a given year may—in certain conditions—be compensated with positive income of other years. Losses can be carried forward (eight years) as well as carried back (three years). Subtraction of losses incurred in other years—if any—from income finally results in the tax base: *income subject to tax*.

This section discusses each of the five sources of income, and lists some major deductions (see Table 7.3).

Income from labour. Income from labour includes wages and salaries of employees and income derived from independently performed services.

Generally speaking, expenses are deductible if costs are incurred to acquire or to keep income from employment. As from 1990, some expenses are no longer, or only partly, deductible. For example, expenses related to educational travel, office space in a private home, personal care, food, and drinks are no longer deductible. Employee social insurance taxes constitute the largest single deduction for wage earners. Employee contributions to fund private pension schemes (that supplement the general old-age pension) form another major deduction.

Travelling expenses between home and a place of work are only partially deductible. The law sets fixed amounts that are based on the distance the employee must cover daily. As a direct consequence of the tax reform of 1990, those who live within 10 km. from their work can no longer claim any deduction. Several other restrictions apply. In 1994, the maximum deduction is Gld1,950 (distance of 30 km. and over).[6]

The standard deduction for general expenses is 8 per cent of gross income from labour, with a minimum of Gld231 and a maximum of Gld2,086. If, however, the employee actually incurs higher expenses, those higher actual expenses may be deducted. The tax authorities may judge whether costs claimed by taxpayers are 'reasonable'. Moreover, as from 1990, several explicit restrictions have been enacted. Notably, expenses for which a deduction is claimed must be 'common', *i.e.* in line with expenses of taxpayers who are in a comparable position.

Allowances to compensate employees for costs that are necessitated by their job are not taxed, except to the extent that the tax inspector finds such allowances to be excessive. Also, certain limitations apply after the tax reform of 1990.

Proceeds from labour activity that does not qualify as employment are

---

[6] For employees who use the public transport system the maximum annual deduction is Gld4,390, when travelling 80 km. or more.

taxed as income from independently performed services. Examples are fees, income received from copyrights, and so on.

Benefit recipients can claim a standard deduction of Gld569.

In addition to social insurance taxes (Sect. B3), a *wage tax* is withheld at source from wages, salaries, and other benefits in cash or kind arising from present or former employment. The wage tax is levied on the employee, that is, any individual who is employed by a wage withholding agent. Whether an employment situation exists is primarily judged on the basis of civil law. Recipients of private pension income and public social security benefits are deemed 'employees'. Likewise, pension funds, insurance companies, and public agencies that administer and pay social security benefits are all deemed 'employers'.

The wage tax can be credited against personal income tax. If certain conditions are met, the wage withholding tax will function as final tax for the employee. In 1990, some 10 million individuals had income and were therefore liable for income tax. For 4.7 million taxpayers, the wage tax was the final tax, *i.e.* these taxpayers did not need to file a tax return and they did not receive an assessment, because approximately the right amount of (wage) tax had been withheld at source. The other 5.3 million taxpayers had to file a return.[7]

The tax base of the wage withholding tax is net wage. Net wage is defined as gross earnings from employment less relevant deductible expenses and personal exemptions. Rates and personal exemptions of the wage withholding tax mirror those of the personal income tax.

The wage tax is levied by self-assessment of the employer. Employers pay the wage tax monthly or quarterly to the tax collector.

Business income. Annual business income of self-employed individuals is calculated in accordance with rules of sound business practice. Business operating profits are defined as turnover less operating costs, including administrative and selling expenses. The tax authorities are not allowed to test whether outlays made are reasonable or necessary to run the business. However, as from 1989, several limitations apply. Certain costs are no longer deductible at all, or only 75 per cent of the costs are deductible (for example, business entertaining expenses).

Inventories can be valued at the lower of historical cost or market value. LIFO may be applied. Under sound business practice, various depreciation methods are allowed.

The ITA 1964 also provides for a number of exemptions. Some apply to the calculation of taxable profit in general and, consequently, are also relevant for corporate income taxpayers. Self-employed individuals may annually set aside a certain amount to add to their 'old-age reserve'. This deduction is calculated

---

[7] See Ministry of Finance (1992: 53).

as 11.5 per cent of the first Gld66,955 of taxable profit, plus 10 per cent of the excess, with a ceiling of Gld19,008. Over the years, the total amount of the old-age reserve may not exceed the net worth of the business, as listed in the balance sheet. Self-employed individuals can at any time decide to convert their old-age reserve into an annuity right. Annuity payments received in later years are then taxed.

Entrepreneurs may also claim a special deduction for the self-employed that is targeted to help smaller businesses. If annual profits remain below Gld85,560, this deduction is worth Gld6,635. Self-employed individuals with higher profits may claim Gld4,275.

Investment income. Investment income consists of all income from immovable and intangible property. Income from immovable property includes rent and any other compensation received from tenants and lessees of land and buildings, less all expenses (local property tax, costs of maintenance, depreciation).

Special rules apply for determining the imputed rent of owner-occupied housing. The ITA 1964 fixes *net* imputed rent at 1.68 per cent of the market value of the property. Moreover, (mortgage) interest paid remains deductible in full. Given that most homeowners initially loan-finance their homes, this explains why, in 1990, aggregate *negative* income from owner-occupied housing amounted to Gld12.7 billion, or over 2 per cent of GDP.

Income from intangible property includes a wide range of investment income, such as interest, dividends, and other distributions of company profits. Any distribution of profit by a company, whether or not in the form of dividends, will be considered taxable income derived from the holding of shares.

In principle, interest included in capital payments under a life insurance policy is treated as taxable investment income.[8] However, under certain conditions, such interest can be received tax-free. Since 1992, interest included in capital payments received *at death* is tax-exempt if the claimant dies before the age of 72 years. Interest included in capital payments received *during life* is taxed at the special rate of 45 per cent. However, an amount of Gld220,000 (couple: Gld440,000) is exempt from tax if premiums have been paid during at least twenty years. Before 1992, these restrictions did not apply.

To counter tax avoidance, the bare owner of rights on claims and securities, of which the temporary usufruct is divided, must annually include 6 per cent of the full economic value of those rights in his taxable income. This requirement was introduced in 1990.

Also, resident taxpayers can be taxed on a deemed annual income if they own shares in certain qualifying foreign investment companies.

The first Gld1,000 of interest received is exempt from tax. This interest

---

[8] Here, interest is defined as the difference of the capital payment over the aggregate of premiums previously paid.

exemption is doubled to Gld2,000 if the spouse does not file a tax return of his or her own. Generally speaking, dividends received from Netherlands companies are exempt up to Gld1,000 per year. The dividend exemption is Gld2,000 if the spouse does not file his or her own tax return. Under Dutch tax laws, corporate income is taxed both at the level of the company (corporate income tax) and at the level of shareholders (personal income tax). Some defend the dividend exemption as a way of reducing this 'double taxation' of shareholders.

Income in the form of periodic payments. Apart from taxable periodic income that can be claimed because of the earlier payment of premiums or a lump sum, such as annuity payments, the ITA 1964 recognizes several other taxable payments of a periodic character. Major examples are certain government grants and alimony received. However, child benefit and rent subsidy are tax-exempt.

Gain from substantial interest. The capital gain realized on the sale of qualifying shares is considered a separate source of income under Dutch income tax law. A taxpayer has a 'substantial interest' in a company if he owns (or owned during the last five years), either directly or indirectly, alone or together with certain relatives, at least one-third of the shares of a company and, in addition, together with his spouse, owns more than 7 per cent of the nominal paid-in share capital. Not only will gains from the sale of such shares be taxed, but also those realized by disposing of the shares in other ways. Profit is calculated by subtracting the original acquisition price of the shares from the transfer price.

Some major deductions. The ITA 1964 provides for several deductions of expenses that are *not related* to any particular *source of income*. The most important deductions under this heading are the following:

- Life annuity premiums paid to an insurance company (a ceiling applies) and premiums for private insurance against the risk of income loss due to disablement, sickness, and so on. As of 1992, a taxpayer may annually deduct at least Gld5,496 (couple: Gld10,991) for annuity premiums paid. The maximum deduction for older contracts (dating from before 1992) is Gld19,190. Although the deductibility of annuity premiums has thus been tightened, much higher deductions are now allowed if other financial provisions for old age are deficient.
- Interest paid on debts, without limit.
- Extraordinary expenses, if not reimbursed through private insurance, notably for health-care expenses, training or study costs, and financial support of certain categories of relatives. Such expenses must exceed a threshold amount as specified by law, and sometimes a ceiling applies. The tax reform of 1990 has substantially restricted the deduction of medical expenses.
- Charitable gifts to qualifying domestic institutions, with a cap.

Table 7.3 details the composition of aggregate income and income subject to tax by major components in both 1989 and 1990.

B1.2 Tax Rates

The personal income tax in the Netherlands is characterized by steeply progressive rates that are applied to taxable income (that is, income subject to tax less personal exemptions). The tax reform of 1990 replaced the previous nine-bracket rate schedule with a three-bracket schedule. Also, former top rates of 61, 67, 70, and 72 per cent were all cut back to 60 per cent.

After relevant personal exemptions (see Sect. B1.4) have been subtracted from income subject to tax, the following rate schedule applies to taxable income:

On the first	Gld43,267	7.05%
On the next	Gld43,265	50%
On the excess		60%

Moreover, the income tax has two proportional rates that apply to certain types of income only:

- a flat 20 per cent rate that applies, for instance, to gains from the sale of a substantial interest; and
- a flat 45 per cent rate that applies, for instance, to profit derived from the sale or termination of a private enterprise and interest included in capital payments under certain life insurance policies.

Table 7.3 Composition of aggregate (taxable) income in 1989 and 1990 (Gld billion)

	1989	1990	index
Net labour income	206.2	220.3	107
Business income	26.9	26.9	100
Net investment income	11.2	12.7	113
Income owner-occupied housing	−12.5	−12.7	102
Periodical payments	86.6	91.2	105
Other (unknown)	2.4	3.5	146
Aggregate income	320.8	342.8	107
Income subject to tax	254.5	305.0	120
Some major deductions/exemptions			
Annuity premiums	3.4	4.1	121
Extraordinary expenses	2.9	1.7	59
Interest paid	2.3	2.6	113

Source: De Kam and Sturm (1994: 1263).

In general, income subject to this reduced rate is not received annually. The flat rate is intended to smooth the effects of progressive rates that would otherwise be applicable.

B1.3 Tax Unit

Every taxpayer is taxed on his or her own income. There are two exceptions to this rule, regarding certain income components of (i) married couples, and (ii) minor children.

A spouse will be individually taxed on:

- profits from his/her own business;
- a limited part of his/her spouse's business income that is related to the time he/she has worked in the spouse's enterprise;
- net income from employment;
- most social security benefits; and
- pensions, annuities, and other periodic payments related to former business or labour activities.

From his/her income, he/she can deduct two items: (i) additions to the old-age reserve, and (ii) premiums paid for future (taxable) periodic payments.

Any other income or deductions are allocated to the partner (husband or wife) with the highest 'personal income'. Such other income may consist of, for example, investment income or profits from a substantial interest. Deductions may include charitable contributions, interest paid, and so on.

Since 1972, the treatment of singles and (un)married couples for income tax and general social insurance tax purposes has been revised regularly. As a result, spouses are now mostly taxed on an individual basis. Moreover, between 1990 and 1993, the former additional personal exemption for single taxpayers was gradually abolished. Quite remarkably, however, over the whole 1970–90 period, the relative tax burden of various household types hardly changed, largely because successive revisions of the tax regime tended to neutralize the consequences of previous policy measures (De Kam and Van Herwaarden 1990).

Minor children are individually taxed if their income consists of:

- profits from an enterprise;
- profits from a substantial interest; and
- net income from employment and other economic activities.

Investment income of children under 18, as well as their personal liabilities, are always included in the income of their parents.

As a rule, every taxpayer is entitled to the same basic personal exemption of Gld5,925. If a partner in the household (married or unmarried) earns less than this amount, he or she is allowed to transfer his or her basic exemption to the other partner, who may then claim the double exemption (Gld11,850).

In this case, the low- or no-income partner is liable to tax on the first guilder of his or her taxable income.

Depending on personal circumstances, two additional exemptions may be claimed: (i) the one-parent exemption (Gld4,741) for single-parent families if the household has dependent children under 27 years of age, and (ii) an additional one-parent exemption if the head of a single-parent family works outside the home and the household has dependent children under 12 years of age. The additional one-parent exemption amounts to one-quarter of earnings, with a maximum of Gld4,741. In the latter case, a total exemption of Gld15,407 applies.

B1.4 Indexing for Inflation

Personal exemptions, income brackets, and certain other amounts mentioned in ITA 1964 are automatically adjusted for inflation every year unless parliament explicitly legislates otherwise. Over the period 1985–94, personal exemptions were fully indexed every year. Tax brackets were not, or were only partially adjusted for inflation in 1992–4. Table 7.4 shows the annual adjustments.

In recent years, the centre-left cabinet has opted for a combination of protecting personal exemptions, while allowing bracket creep. This option was motivated by the income-political goals of reducing the statutory tax burden for low-income groups, while increasing the tax burden on middle- and higher-income groups through bracket creep.

A direct consequence of freezing the first bracket is that the tax base of the general social insurance taxes shrinks, relative to GDP (Sect. B3.3). At the same time, outlays for the insurance against exceptional health expenses have recently increased dramatically.[9] This accounts for about one-third of the steep rise in the combined rate of the four general social insurance taxes from 22.1 per cent (1990) to 31.07 per cent (1994).[10]

B1.5 Non-resident Taxpayers

Under Dutch law, non-residents are subject to personal income tax only if they receive income from certain well-defined domestic sources; namely:

- income from a permanent business establishment;
- income from employment within the Netherlands (including pensions);
- income from real estate located in the Netherlands (as a rule, private capital gains will not be taxed);

[9] Not only do prices of medical services outpace the average rate of inflation, but also the package insured under the AWBZ programme has been considerably extended (see note 2).

[10] The remaining two-thirds of the 9-percentage point increase in the general social insurance tax rate is attributable to the following: after the tax reform of 1990, some Gld14 billion. in general social insurance outlays was financed via a surcharge of 6 points on the basic rate (7%) of the personal income tax. As from 1994, this surcharge was replaced by a 6-point increase in general social insurance tax rates, while the basic income tax rate was set at 7.05%.

Table 7.4   Indexing for inflation, 1985–1994 (%)

Year	Reference inflation rate		Adjustment of	
			Personal exemptions	Bracket length
1985	2.4		2.4	2.4
1986	1.8		2.4	2.4
1987	−1.1	(etc.)	1.8	1.8
1988	0.3		−1.1	−1.1
1989	1.5		0.3	0.3
1990	2.0		1.5	1.5
1991	3.0		2.0	2.0
1992	3.9		3.0	0.0
1993	2.7		3.9	0.7
1994	n.a.		2.7	0.0

Source: Private communication Ministry of Finance.

- interest on debts that are secured by a mortgage on Dutch real estate;
- income from shares, bonds issued, or debts incurred by a domestic corporation that accrues to a foreign shareholder who owns a substantial interest in that company; and
- social security benefits and other periodic payments under public transfer programmes.

Non-resident taxpayers can claim a deduction only for interest on loans secured by a mortgage on real estate located in the Netherlands.

B1.6 Small to Medium Enterprizes

Several tax incentives are explicitly targeted to help small and medium-sized enterprizes. The schedule for donations to the old-age reserve and the structure of the deduction for self-employed individuals clearly favour smaller enterprizes. Moreover, a starting entrepreneur may for three successive years claim an additional deduction for self-employed individuals of Gld2,415 (per year). As a result, his total deduction increases to Gld9,050. The schedule of the investment deduction also benefits smaller enterprizes most. If annual investment does not exceed Gld56,000, the deduction is equal to 18 per cent of the amount invested (with a ceiling of Gld10,080). The percentage of the deduction is stepwise reduced as total annual investment rises. The deduction can never exceed Gld27,900. If investment in any year surpasses half a million guilders, no deduction can be claimed at all.

B1.7 Tax Expenditures

In practice, all OECD countries invariably use a mix of tax and direct expenditure programmes to achieve their policy goals, whether to encourage economic activity or redistribute income (OECD 1984: 13). *Tax expenditures* are special provisions in tax laws that limit tax revenue and give rise to public outlays through the tax system so as to achieve economic and social policy objectives.

There is no widely accepted definition of what exactly constitutes the general or 'normal' tax structure against which tax expenditures can be measured. Twice, the Ministry of Finance (1987; 1994) produced a tax expenditures list. Departing from a pragmatic income concept, the list was drawn up by applying a rather narrow definition of legal provisions that give rise to tax expenditures. For example, it was assumed that the favourable tax treatment of owner-occupied housing does not result in a tax expenditure.

Table 7.5 specifies the revenue forgone through the quantitatively most important items on the income tax expenditure list. Items that imply a revenue loss of less than Gld200 million. (in 1994) are not included. Generally speaking, the number of tax expenditure programmes has grown over the past ten years, reflecting an increased tendency among policy-makers to use tax breaks to achieve various policy goals. Also, over the last few years a number of relatively small tax expenditure programmes have been incorporated into the ITA 1964, largely as a result of initiatives taken by Members of Parliament (not shown). Such trends clearly have contributed to making the personal income tax code still more complicated.

Table 7.5 shows that—with only one exception—between 1984 and 1994, the growth of tax expenditures outpaced the increase of total direct central government spending. The amounts involved with the dividend exemption (index = 666), the standard deduction for benefit recipients (index = 470), and the interest exemption (index = 378) grew particularly dramatically, reflecting both changes in tax legislation and the dynamics of economic fundamentals, like the rising number of benefit recipients and higher interest receipts reported to the tax authorities (see also Sect. C5).

B2 Corporation Income Tax

Corporate income tax is levied on the basis of the Corporate Income Tax Act of 1969 (CITA 1969). The tax is due from all resident and certain non-resident legal entities. Such entities are considered to be resident taxpayers if incorporated under Dutch law or actually established in the Netherlands. Whether this is, in fact, the case will depend on the specific circumstances. The following entities established in the Netherlands are subject to corporate income tax: (i) corporations (limited liability companies), (ii) cooperatives, and (iii) certain other, less important categories as enumerated in CITA (1969).

The basic idea is that any entity that carries on a business (except individuals and associations of individuals, such as partnerships) should be subject to the tax. Pension funds and hospitals, among several other entities, are tax-exempt, provided certain conditions are met. Some non-resident entities are

Table 7.5 Tax expenditures in personal income tax (Gld million)[a]

	1984	1994	index[b]
Interest exemption	275	1,040	378
Deduction for self-employed	700	1,020	146
Exemption of rent subsidy, assistance	650	1,020	157
Exemption for investment tax credit	525	—	—
Deduction for benefit recipients	115	540	470
Exemption employee profit-sharing	—	525	—
Old age reserve of self-employed	225	495	220
Investment deduction	—	395	—
Deduction charitable donations	250	350	140
Special rates	150	345	230
Exempted interest capital insurance	125	295	236
Various exemptions for self-employed	185	230	124
Wage subsidies for R&D firms	—	210	—
Dividend exemption	30	200	666
Memorandum items			
Total outlays central government	168,678	231,605	137
Revenue from personal income tax	37,200	53,550	144

[a] Items ranked in order of decreasing magnitude (in 1994).
[b] 1984 = 100.

Sources: Ministry of Finance (1984: 136 and 179); Ministry of Finance (1993: 111 and 330); Ministry of Finance (1994: annexe 8).

also subject to Netherlands corporate income tax, provided such entities have domestic income.

Taxable entities must file tax accounts together with their annual tax return.

B2.1 Tax Base

The tax is levied on the basis of taxable profit, which must be calculated in accordance with sound business practice, based on consistent principles. Profit consists of all types of income of whatever nature, derived from undertakings in the Netherlands or abroad. No distinction is made here between 'ordinary' profits and capital gains, which are both taxed on the same basis.

In the Netherlands, rules for depreciation of assets and the valuation of inventories are fairly generous, as it is sufficient that depreciation and valuation methods are in accordance with sound business practice (as interpreted by the tax courts).

Corporate taxpayers enjoy several exemptions, of which the participation exemption is by far the most important. This exemption has been introduced to avoid double taxation. All proceeds (profits, capital gains) derived from participation in the share capital of another company that has been held without interruption since the beginning of the book year are excluded from the taxable profit of the 'holding' company. To qualify for the exemption, the participation must be equal to at least 5 per cent of the par value of the paid-up capital of the company invested in.

A participation in a foreign company qualifies only if that company is subject to a state tax on its profits. However, the rate of this profit tax is irrelevant. Moreover, it is not required that the foreign profit tax should actually have been imposed or collected.

B2.2 Tax Rates

The standard rate of the corporate income tax is 35 per cent, or 25 points below the top rate of the personal income tax. To limit the incentive for self-employed individuals to incorporate their business, the first Gld250,000 of taxable profit of limited liability companies are taxed at 40 per cent.[11]

B2.3 Treatment of Distributed Profits

Under Dutch tax law, corporate income is taxed both at the level of the company (corporate income tax) and at the level of shareholders (personal income tax). Resident taxpayers subject to personal income tax may claim the dividend exemption of Gld1,000 (couple: Gld2,000). Resident parent and holding companies that collect dividends from other companies may in many cases enjoy the participation exemption (Sect. B2.1).

B3 Social Insurance Taxes

In the Netherlands, the distribution branch of the public sector is highly developed. All in all, public income transfers to households absorb over 25 per cent of GDP. Apart from transfers out of the government budget, social insurance benefits are an important vehicle to redistribute personal incomes. Such benefits are nearly financed in full from 'contributions', which are channelled into separate funds. These funds also receive supplementing grants from central government.

Social insurance programmes fall into two categories: (i) *general* social insurances, which cover all residents; and (ii) *employee* social insurances, which are restricted to market sector workers and their families.

All residents are covered by four general social insurance programmes and are liable to four separate taxes that finance these programmes. Table 7.6 specifies general social insurances by programme, and identifies tax rates and aggregate revenues for 1994. Individuals aged 65 years and over pay only 10.4 per cent (in AWW and AWBZ taxes).

Table 7.6 suggests that employees pay all general social insurance taxes. In fact, after the tax reform of 1990 (Sect. D1), employees are partially

---

[11] As of 1 July 1994, this threshold was lowered to Gld100,000.

Table 7.6 Social insurance programmes, 1994

	Tax rates (%)		Revenue (Gld.bn.)
	Employer	Employee	
General social insurances[a]			
Old-age pension (AOW)	—	14.12	32,450
Widow and orphan pension (AWW)	—	1.85	4,830
Disablement pension (AAW)	—	6.55	14,900
Exc. medical expenses (AWBZ)	—	8.55	25,200
Total	—	31.07	77,380
Employee social insurances			
Unemployment (WW)	1.62	2.30	8,880
Sickness (ZW)	2.05	1.00	9,450
Disability (WAO)	—	5.15	9,360
Total	3.67	8.45	27,690
Ziekenfonds (health insurance)	5.15	1.20	11,600

[a] Employees are partially compensated by employers. See sections B3 and D1.

Source: Central Economic Planning Bureau (1994: 134); Ministry of Social Affairs (1993: 155).

compensated for these taxes, because—in addition to normal wages—employers must pay to their employees an allowance (*overhevelingstoeslag*). This (taxable) allowance equals 11.64 per cent of gross wage less deductions, with a ceiling of Gld8,971. The arrangement similarly applies to certain groups of benefit recipients.

General social insurance taxes are levied together with personal income tax, both by way of assessment and through withholding (in combination with the wage tax).

Participation in the employee social insurances is mandatory for all workers in the market sector. Employee social insurances entitle covered workers to benefits in cases of unemployment, illness, and disability. Civil servants have income maintenance programmes of their own, which are financed out of general revenue. In addition to possible benefits from general social insurances, the self-employed must rely on private insurance against the risk of income loss due to illness and disability.

Table 7.6 specifies employee insurances by programme. The table also indicates, for each programme, which rates are paid by employers and by employees respectively. Employers withhold taxes due by their employees from gross wage. Employee social insurance taxes are levied by self-assessment. Employers pay these taxes to the Industrial Boards entrusted with the administration of the programmes concerned.

B3.1 Tax Base

As a direct consequence of the tax reform of 1990, since that year personal income tax and the *general* social insurance taxes have a common tax base: *taxable income* (Sect. B1.1). The general social insurance taxes are due on income in the first income tax bracket only.

The tax base of the *employee* social insurance taxes and the *Ziekenfonds* tax is the *gross wage* of individual employees (after deduction of the employees' contribution to their pension scheme). Part of these taxes is withheld from employee wages, and part is directly paid by employers.

B3.2 Tax Rates

When calculating the amount of general social insurance tax due, the personal exemptions of the income tax apply. Only income in the first bracket of the personal income tax rate structure is liable to 31.07 per cent of *general* social insurance taxes. Including the 7.05 per cent income tax, the combined (flat) rate reaches 38.12 per cent.

Employee social insurance taxes have a flat rate and no personal exemption. These taxes are subject to a ceiling of Gld74,360 (the maximum insured wage). Disability insurance is the exception. No contribution is due on the first Gld25,740 of wages, since this wage income is already covered by general disability insurance. The ceiling of Gld74,360 applies.

The maximum amount of wage earnings (benefits) subject to *Ziekenfonds* tax amounts to Gld49,400.

B4 Value-Added Tax

In 1969, the Netherlands introduced a turnover tax based on the value-added tax system. The Value-Added Tax Act of 1968 (VATA 1968) stipulates that any entrepreneur who sells goods and renders services is liable to the tax. Taxpayers are liable for value-added tax (VAT) on their turnover, but they may subtract from the tax due VAT that has been charged to them on their inputs (purchases, expenses, investments). As regards general principles, the Dutch VAT system follows those of other European VAT systems. Accordingly, the following paragraphs refer only to some specific provisions in the Netherlands regarding the tax base and tax rates.

B4.1 Tax Base

Two types of economic activity give rise to tax liability: (i) delivery of goods and supply of services within the Netherlands by entrepreneurs, and (ii) import of goods by entrepreneurs.

The delivery and import of a number of goods and services is exempted from VAT. In such cases the entrepreneur cannot deduct the pre-paid VAT that has been charged to him on his inputs. Exempted goods and services include, among others:

- transfer, or rental of real estate;
- medical services;
- education and public broadcast services; and
- most services provided by banks.

B4.2 Tax Rates

The value-added tax has three rates:

- the general or standard rate is 17.5 per cent;
- a reduced rate of 6 per cent applies to certain goods and services as enumerated in VATA 1968; for instance, to various foodstuffs, drinking water, books, and works of art; and
- the zero rate applies to goods that are exported.

B5 Excises and Other Consumption Taxes

Apart from the three main taxes (personal and corporate income tax and VAT), the central government levies a number of smaller taxes. Among these taxes, excises are by far the most important in revenue terms (Table 7.2). Various consumption taxes of the central government are briefly discussed in this section.

B5.1 Excise Taxes

Excise taxes are due in case of production and import of certain goods. The European Union has limited the number of excise goods to three categories: (i) mineral oil products; (ii) alcohol as well as products and drinks containing alcohol; and (iii) tobacco products. Some illustrative tax rates are:

- unleaded petrol: Gld1.08 per litre;
- leaded petrol: Gld1.22 per litre;
- beer: Gld46.90 per 100 litres;
- wine: Gld107.50 per 100 litres; and
- cigarettes (standard pack of 25): Gld3.14.

B5.2 Specific Consumption Taxes

If a car or motorcycle is registered for the first time in the Netherlands under its permanent licence number, a one-time tax is due. The person or legal entity that has been awarded the licence number is liable to the tax. For cars, the tax rate is 45.2 per cent of the net list price, less Gld3,394. In the case of a used car, rate reductions apply.

The production and import of fruit juices, mineral water, and lemonades are subject to a specific consumption tax.

B5.3 Motor Vehicle Tax

Car owners and motorists pay an annual tax ('road charge'). The amount of tax due depends on the type of fuel used and the weight of the vehicle. The tax must have been paid (through self-assessment) before the car is used on public roads.

B5.4 Green Taxes

Since the early 1970s, an air pollution charge has been levied on traffic and industry. By 1987, this charge still grossed only Gld130 million in revenues. A charge on undue 'noise' generated Gld110 million. In the early 1990s, both charges were transformed into a 'green tax' on energy use, while tax rates were substantially increased. Presently, the energy tax produces Gld1.5 billion in revenues.

The tax base is related to the energy content of various fuels (petrol, natural gas, coal). Rates include a tax of Gld25.10 per 1,000 litres of (un)leaded petrol, which is levied together with the excise tax.

B5.5 Import Duties

Import duties are levied on the basis of EU regulations if goods are imported from non-EU countries. Generally, the tax base is import value, which is established in accordance with the customs valuation code of the former GATT (presently the WTO). The tax rate may vary from 0 to 20 per cent. All revenue from import duties is remitted to the European Union. [Note by Editor: this treatment of import duties applies to all EU countries.]

B6 Capital Taxes

This section briefly discusses the central government taxes on net wealth, estates and gifts, and certain types of economic and financial transactions. In 1994, the net wealth tax and the estates and gift tax each produced Gld1.5 billion in revenue. Taxes on economic and financial transactions grossed Gld3.4 billion.

B6.1 Net Wealth Tax

Only resident individuals are subject to a tax on their net wealth (assets minus liabilities). Non-residents are subject to the tax only if they own certain assets located in the country.

The tax authorities establish taxable net wealth on the basis of a return that qualifying taxpayers have to file together with their income tax return.[12] A wife is subject to the wealth tax herself, but her assets and liabilities are added to those of her husband, regardless of how they have established their matrimonial property rights. Children are taxed separately.

The tax is levied on total net wealth at the beginning of the calendar year.

---

[12] Actually, both returns are on one form.

Assets are defined as any assets that have a market value or for which a market value can be estimated. There exists, however, an important exception for owner-occupied property: the taxpayers' residence is valued at 60 per cent of the freehold market value. Goodwill, pension rights, and the value of life insurance policies (under certain conditions) are exempt. Works of art are also tax-exempt and offer a 'tax shelter' for well-to-do taxpayers who want to evade the wealth tax.

The tax rate is 0.8 per cent of net wealth, after personal exemptions have been taken into account. The exemption varies from Gld68,000 (single persons under 27 years) to Gld136,000 (one- and two-earner families). There is an additional exemption of Gld7,000 for each child under 18 years. Self-employed individuals may claim a special exemption, which is calculated as 50 per cent of the capital invested in their enterprise, with minimum (Gld135,000) and maximum (Gld1,541,000) amounts.

The wealthy are often advised to use the provision of article 14, paragraph 5, of the Wealth Tax Act 1964 as a device in strategic tax-planning. Under this provision, no taxpayer has to pay in combined income tax and wealth tax more than 68 (until 1994: 80) per cent of the gap between his taxable income and general social insurance taxes (over the previous tax year). So any wealthy taxpayer who succeeds in bringing down his taxable income (and there are several ways to achieve this outcome) can substantially reduce the tax on his personal wealth.[13]

B6.2 Estate Tax and Gift Tax

The estate and gift taxes are levied on the basis of the Estate Tax Act of 1956. The estate tax is levied on the (net) value of assets that are acquired through inheritance from a resident of the Netherlands. The gift tax is levied on the (net) value of assets that the donee receives as a gift from a donor who is a resident of the Netherlands. Residence is decided on the basis of actual circumstances. Main exemptions under the estate tax include benefits from a pension scheme and acquisitions by husband or wife, not exceeding Gld522,790. The value of pension rights is subtracted, but the exemption remains at least Gld149,368. There is an additional exemption for children that depends on the child's age and varies between Gld171,764 (zero years) and Gld14,936 (22 years).

The rate structure is highly progressive. The amount of tax due depends both on the value of the acquired assets (after the relevant exemptions have been applied) and the relationship of the heir (donee) towards the deceased

---

[13] This provision can be illustrated with the following example. Assume taxable net wealth (after personal exemptions) amounts to Gld10 million. Net wealth tax due is Gld80,000. Taxable income (after personal exemptions) amounts to Gld10,000. The maximum amount of income and wealth tax due is: $0.68 \times (10,000 - 3,107$ general social insurance taxes$) = 4,687$. Personal income tax is Gld705. The assessment for net wealth tax is now reduced from Gld80,000 to Gld3,982.

(donor). The top rate applies if acquisitions exceed Gld1.5 million, and varies between 27 per cent (husband or wife) and 68 per cent (non-relatives).

B6.3 Taxes on Economic or Financial Transactions

The central government levies three taxes on the following types of transactions.

The *transfer tax* is levied on buyers who acquire real estate situated in the Netherlands. Certain exemptions apply. The tax base is the market value of immovable property. The tax rate is 6 per cent.

The *insurance tax* is payable by holders of insurance policies if the insured risk is located within the Netherlands. The tax base is the insurance premium. Certain exemptions apply, for example, for life insurance. The tax rate is 7 per cent.

The *capital tax* is levied on corporations and other legal entities of which the capital is divided into shares, on attracting or expanding their capital. The tax base is the nominal amount or market value of capital contributed. The tax rate is 1 per cent.

B7 Local and Provincial Taxes

The Netherlands is a unitary state with three levels of government: state, provincial, and municipal. Provinces and municipalities (local government) spend about one-third of total public outlays. However, local and provincial authorities are limited in their spending decisions, as a consequence of detailed regulation and in circumstances of extremely strict supervision by central government agencies.

The 636 municipalities mainly act as agents of the central government, especially in the areas of housing, payment of welfare benefits, and education. Spending of local authorities is controlled through 'block grants' and 'specific purpose grants' from the central government, which taken together finance about 88 per cent of total current local expenditure. The remaining 12 per cent of current local spending is financed from proceeds of local taxes and user fees, and from profits generated by municipally owned public utilities.

Although local governments are allowed to borrow for capital expenditure, the central government can restrict local borrowing.

With revenue of Gld3.8 billion, property taxes dominate the local tax structure. All other local taxes combined produce only Gld0.2 billion. The property tax actually consists of two levies, based on the *use* and the *ownership* of property respectively. The tax base is assessed (market) value of land and buildings. The tax base is eroded because of several important exemptions, notably for farm land, railroads, and other infrastructure. The local council annually decides upon the rates. Property taxes must be flat rate. Rates for owners may be set at 1.25 times the rates for users of property. Nationwide, the combined average rate of both property taxes is about 0.3 per cent of the assessed market value of land and buildings.

Municipalities also charge user fees, especially to finance waste disposal (Gld1.9 billion) and the sewer system (Gld0.9 billion). Such fees, although not taxes proper, have been included in Tables 7.2 and 7.8.

The twelve provinces levy just one tax in the form of a surcharge on the central government motor vehicle tax. The rates vary across provinces. Total revenue amounts to Gld0.3 billion.

C. Economic and Social Aspects

C1 The Fiscal Deficit

In the Netherlands, the rise of the welfare state has been reflected in the particularly strong growth of public spending and taxation levels after the mid-1950s. In the 1960s and early 1970s, the expansion of the public sector was greatly facilitated by relatively high rates of economic growth. The decline in national economic performance during the later 1970s and early 1980s triggered a financial 'crisis' of the Dutch welfare state.

The proportion of the population of working age (15–64 years) actively involved in the production of goods and services is relatively small (59 per cent) if compared to the participation rate in most OECD countries. In a welfare state, such as the Netherlands undoubtedly is,[14] relatively low participation rates translate into massive claims upon public sector programmes. Over the years, the number of benefit recipients (B) has continually grown relative to the labour force (L). Between 1960 and 1990, the B/L ratio exploded from 0.36 to 0.86. This ratio is expected to further deteriorate as a consequence of demographic trends.

During the 1960s and 1970s, the relative 'price' of transfers also went up. In 1960, average benefits (b) amounted to 25 per cent of average wage income (w), whereas by 1980 the b/w ratio had climbed to 0.43. Since policy-makers could not stem the rising tide of benefit recipients, they were forced to cut back the relative price of transfers. By the early 1990s, successive reductions of benefit levels during the previous decade had brought the b/w ratio down again to 0.37.

Over the years, increasing outlays were not fully matched by higher taxes and social insurance contributions. Especially since 1975, annual budget deficits have been large in historical terms, which was reflected in the subsequent upsweep of the central government debt/GDP ratio from 0.21 in the

---

[14] 'Among OECD countries the Netherlands is one of those which have gone furthest in their sustained efforts to promote a tolerant, caring, and supportive society through the action of government' (OECD 1991a: 57).

mid-1970s to 0.68 in 1994. The growth of public debt, combined with higher interest rates, led to rapidly rising interest payments that have tended to crowd out other categories of public spending.

By 1982, the deficit had grown to 7 per cent of GDP. From then on, successive governments have forcefully tried to rein in the share of public outlays and the deficit in GDP, holding the level of taxes and other public sector revenues more or less constant. After ten years of restraint, the process of public sector consolidation has clearly met with some success. Improved macroeconomic performance during the second half of the 1980s, and prolonged efforts to effectively curb public spending, enabled policy-makers to gradually reduce the level of public outlays by about six points of GDP.

During the first half of the 1990s, the level of public spending more or less stabilized. Still, the government succeeded in further reducing its net borrowing requirement, because between 1990 and 1993 the tax level was raised by two points of GDP. As a result of these trends, the deficit has been halved to about 3 per cent of GDP in the 1990s (Table 7.1 and Fig. 7.1).

The recession of the 1990s made itself felt in the Netherlands rather late, since initially the reunification of Germany boosted exports to the large eastern neighbour. Between 1991 and 1993, the general stance of macroeconomic policy further depressed the level of economic activity. Late in 1993, with national elections coming up, fiscal discipline weakened and public spending as a proportion of GDP tended to rise again. The incoming government agreed upon tight norms for fiscal policy. The economy strongly recovered in 1994 and later years. For the immediate future, further deficit reductions are envisaged.[15]

Fig. 7.1 summarizes trends in both public debt and the deficit of the public sector over the period 1982–97.

C2 Taxes, Savings, and Investment

The extent to which taxes on capital income reduce savings is controversial (OECD 1994). Partly motivated by the wish to correct for possible disincentives, the Dutch tax system has a number of provisions that are intended to promote saving and investment. Moreover, as a consequence of the different tax treatment of various saving and investment vehicles, the tax system is not neutral as regards saving and investment decisions.

[15] As noted in Ch. 1 Sect. D, the European Union set certain preconditions for member countries to enter the Economic and Monetary Union.

Although in the Netherlands the deficit has dropped to well below 3% of GDP, projections produced by the Ministry of Finance also illustrate that it will take a number of years to bring the public debt down to under 60% of GDP.

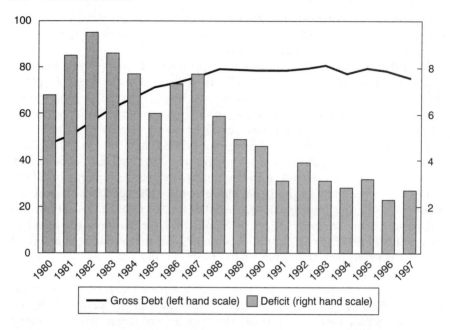

Fig. 7.1 Public sector debt and deficit as percentage of GDP, 1982–1997
Source: Central Economic Planning Bureau (1996: 140–1).

C2.1 Income Tax and Personal Savings

Returns on household savings are generally subject to personal income tax. On average, investment income is taxed heavily. However, notably taxpayers with small savings may profit from the dividend exemption and the intrest exemption. More importantly, most private capital gains of individual investors are not taxed in the Netherlands, although with some notable exeptions. Therefore, many taxpayers have channelled part of their savings into incorporated capital investment funds, which retain all income earned. Although such funds pay 35 per cent of investment income earned in corporate income tax, participants receive the remaining 65 per cent net of tax, in the form of untaxed capital gains. By 1994, capital investment funds already had accumulated assets to the tune of over Gld20 billion.[16]

The tax treatment of private pension plans may seriously distort capital markets. Unlike the general old-age pension, all private pension plans in the Netherlands are fully funded. Employer contributions to pension funds are exempt from income tax (and deductible under the corporate income tax), while employees may fully deduct their contributions. Pensions drawn from these funds will be taxed in the future. In the meantime, the value of pension

---

[16] Lower House, Parliamentary Documents, 1993–1994, 23071, 15, 4.

rights is not taxed under the net wealth tax. Moreover, pension funds themselves are exempt from tax as they accumulate the returns on assets they hold. As these funds have an investment policy which tries to minimize risks, the tax system discriminates against venture capital for industry and starting entrepreneurs.

The lenient tax treatment of pension plans moreover discriminates against individuals who prefer or have to rely on their own savings to provide for old age. In this regard, it is relevant that self-employed individuals may create an old-age reserve; amounts added to this reserve are deductible within rather generous limits.

Taxpayers may also deduct annuity premiums, if these are paid to an insurance company. An annual ceiling of Gld5,496 to Gld274,770 applies, depending on taxable income and other old-age provisions to which the taxpayer is entitled.

Possibly as a consequence of the favourable tax treatment of contractual saving (pension plans, annuities), the pattern of household saving in the Netherlands has fundamentally changed over the past twenty-five years. Whereas the level of total household saving has remained more or less stable (some 9–11 per cent of GDP), contractual saving has increased considerably, at the expense of saving channelled through banks and in the form of personal investment in shares, bonds, and so on (Fig. 7.2).

Although the drop in non-contractual saving has often been blamed on tax-favoured contractual saving, Bakker (1993: ch. 5) suggests that lower non-contractual saving is mainly due to the slower growth of labour income (in the 1980s) and the large rise of housing prices (in the 1970s).

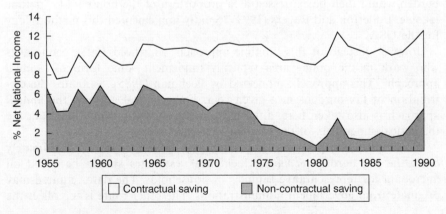

Fig. 7.2 Breakdown of personal saving, 1955–1990

Source: Bakker (1993: 129).

C2.2 Income Tax and Investment

Both the personal and the corporate income tax have several provisions to foster business investment. For instance, although in 1988 the investment tax credit (WIR premiums) was suspended, as from 1990 self-employed individuals and firms may claim a—limited—investment deduction (Sect. B1.7). Also, self-employed individuals and firms may set aside profits realized on the sale of business assets if such profits are reinvested within four years (replacement reserve). Finally, private investors can often realize capital gains, which are left untaxed.

Under the current tax system, the effective tax rate on returns from investment may differ widely, depending on the assets involved, the source of finance, and type of ownership (OECD, 1991*b* 97–117; Cnossenn 1994: 16–21). For instance, investment financed from the proceeds of new share issues is relatively heavily taxed in the Netherlands. Because corporate income is taxed both at the level of the company (35 per cent) and the shareholder, investors in the 60 per cent income tax bracket net only 26 cents of each guilder of company profits before tax.[17] If investors use the vehicle of a capital investment fund, they will realize a net return of 65 cents. On the other hand, investment in owner-occupied housing is tax-subsidized, because net imputed rent is low (1.68 per cent of the freehold value), while nominal interest payments are deductible in full.

C3 Distribution of the Tax Burden

To measure tax distributions, relevant income units first must be identified. Usually, households are the preferred income unit. Next, many economists would consider using a general equilibrium model to calculate the present value of tax burdens imposed upon each household over its lifetime. This burden would then be expressed as a proportion of the household's lifetime income. Fullerton and Rogers (1993) recently implemented this methodology for the USA.

However, instead of this 'lifetime approach' (Barthold 1993), economists who work in the policy area typically implement some form of 'annual approach'. This approach, pioneered by Pechman (1985), estimates the distribution of tax burdens in a given year. For practical reasons, the annual approach is also taken here, although some economists would maintain the theoretical superiority of the lifetime approach.

To establish who pays the taxes (*statutory* incidence) and who ultimately *bears* the tax burden (*economic* incidence), estimates should be based on microdata for representative samples of households. The data required may originate from government administrations. The other route is to collect the

---

[17] After-tax investment income amounts to: 100 less 35% corporate income tax (35) = 65; 65 less 60% personal income tax (39) = 26.

data needed by way of surveys among households. De Kam (1990) discusses data sets and micromodels available in the Netherlands to simulate the distribution of tax burdens. The most reliable source of information concerning personal income distribution in the Netherlands is the Panel Survey of Income, which is published annually by the Central Bureau of Statistics (CBS). For a representative sample of 75,000 households, CBS collects demographic and income data from various government administrations. Most income data in the sample originate from the Tax Administration. The Panel Survey of Income has directly observed data on the statutory incidence of:

- personal income tax (including wage withholding tax);
- net wealth tax; and
- general social insurance taxes.

In addition, using data available in the Panel Survey, CBS has microsimulated the statutory incidence of employee social insurance taxes. The most recent Panel Survey available is for year 1994.

CBS also organizes an annual Consumer Survey, which offers detailed information on patterns of household spending. The number of households in this representative sample is about 2,000. In the Consumer Survey, some tax payments are directly observed; for example, motor vehicle tax paid. The burden of most consumption taxes, notably VAT and various excise taxes, can be microsimulated by applying relevant tax rates to taxable items consumed, as reported by households in the sample. The most recent Consumer Survey available is for year 1995.

Although some progress has been made in recent years in improving the methodology of tax analysis, economists still disagree about the economic incidence of taxes. Therefore, once the statutory incidence of (most) taxes has been determined, estimates of their economic incidence have to be based on a set of assumptions. Following Pechman (1985: ch. 3), a set of eclectic incidence assumptions underpins the results presented in this section.

It is assumed that personal income tax and the net wealth tax are not shifted, and that VAT and other consumption taxes are borne by consumers of the taxed commodities. Social insurance taxes paid by employees, self-employed individuals, and benefit recipients are assumed not to be shifted, while such taxes imposed on employers are assumed to be borne by employees (3/4) and consumers (1/4). Corporation income tax is allocated to shareholders (1/3), recipients of property income (1/3), and consumers (1/3). Property tax and a number of other taxes paid by firms and the government are assumed to be shifted to consumers in proportion to their total consumption.

For the presentation of tax distributions, all households are ranked in ten 'deciles' by increasing net disposable income. Roughly, this concept measures household income net of income tax, wealth tax, and social insurance taxes. Net income may be consumed or saved. The first decile contains the 10 per cent of households with the lowest net incomes, the tenth decile comprises the 10 per cent of households with highest net incomes.

As a final step, the share of (households in) each decile in total tax revenue is calculated. Economic incidence of all taxes analysed is found by weighing distributions of individual taxes by their share in total revenue collected. Table 7.7 shows the economic incidence of taxes (distribution of tax shares by decile) in 1991–2.

In the early 1990s, one-quarter of all taxes covered were paid by the top decile, and 40 per cent were paid by the next 30 per cent of the households. The bottom half of the distribution contributed only 24 per cent of total tax revenue. Income tax and net wealth tax, being the most progressive levies, are skewed most strongly to richer households.

Distributions of taxes paid by households in different deciles can present a misleading picture of the progressivity of the tax system, because such a presentation takes no account of the different income level in each decile.

Table 7.7 Distribution of tax shares by decile, 1991/1992[a]

Deciles	1	2	3	4	5	6	7	8	9	10
Taxes										
Personal income tax	1	2	3	4	5	7	9	12	17	39
Value-added tax	4	5	6	8	9	10	12	13	15	19
Corporation income tax[b]	3	2	4	5	6	7	10	12	16	36
Excise taxes	2	4	6	9	10	11	13	13	15	17
Motor vehicle tax	2	3	6	10	11	11	11	13	15	18
Special tax on cars	0	0	4	3	3	6	21	13	23	26
Import duties	5	5	7	8	9	10	12	13	14	18
Green energy taxes	4	6	7	9	10	11	12	12	14	16
Net wealth tax	12	1	1	1	2	5	6	10	14	48
Transfer tax	2	2	3	5	8	7	11	14	22	26
Local property taxes	5	5	6	7	10	10	11	12	15	21
Local waste disposal tax	9	9	9	10	10	10	10	11	11	11
Local sewer tax	6	8	9	9	12	9	12	12	11	12
Water pollution tax	5	6	9	10	10	11	12	12	12	12
Water board tax	2	3	5	7	11	11	13	13	16	20
General social insurance taxes	2	3	5	7	9	11	13	14	16	19
Employee social insurance taxes										
employees	2	3	6	8	10	11	13	14	16	17
employers	2	4	6	8	10	11	13	14	15	17
Total all taxes	**2**	**3**	**5**	**6**	**8**	**9**	**11**	**13**	**16**	**25**
Memorandum items										
Labour income	1	1	3	5	8	10	13	15	19	25
Property income	2	2	3	5	7	9	10	13	17	33
Dividend income	2	0	1	1	2	4	7	10	16	57
Consumption	5	5	7	8	9	10	12	13	14	18

[a] Due to rounding, row totals do not always add up to 100.
[b] Includes dividend withholding tax.

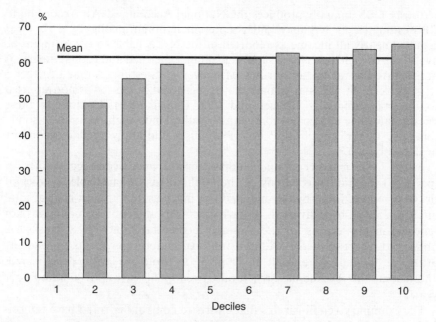

Fig. 7.3 Average burden of all taxes, 1991/1992[a]

[a] Taxes paid as proportion of gross household income, per decile.

Therefore, Fig. 7.3 shows total tax paid in each decile as a proportion of total gross household income in that decile. On average, households handed over 61 per cent of their gross income to the taxman. The top two deciles paid only a few percentage points more. The bottom two deciles clearly had somewhat lighter tax burdens, which makes the overall distribution of tax burdens slightly progressive. Still, even the poorest households on average contribute half of their gross income to the Treasury.

C4 The Hidden Economy

By its very nature, the size of the 'hidden economy' is not known. The hidden economy may be defined as comprising all income received, sales made, and wealth holdings that go untaxed because the economic transactions and wealth concerned are, in violation of the law, not properly reported to the tax authorities. Hidden economic activity may consist of both illegal (drug traffic) and legal transactions. Many in the Netherlands firmly believe that the hidden economy has grown in importance over the past twenty years because tax levels went up and public morals were eroded.

As yet, however, there is no firm empirical evidence on the relationship between tax levels and the amount of unreported income and wealth, since data on the past and present size of the hidden economy are simply not available. Several macroeconomic estimates of the hidden economy have been published. Only those of the Central Bureau of Statistics can be taken seriously. CBS annually produces the National Accounts (NA). According to CBS estimates, its NA may under-represent national income by 3 to 4 per cent. As nearly all income as reported in the NA is liable to tax, it might be hypothesized that at least the same percentage of earned and capital income is not reported to the tax authorities. Moreover, CBS estimates that a further 5 to 10 per cent of national income that is registered in the NA is not reported to the tax authorities (Begeer and Van Tuinen 1986). Combining these guesstimates, the hidden economy in the Netherlands might amount to something like 10 per cent of GDP. For 1994, this would imply a hidden economy of Gld60 billion.

Apart from macroeconomic studies, several microeconomic studies of (parts of) the hidden economy of the Netherlands are available. Studies of the CBS reported that by the mid-1970s as much as 40 to 50 per cent of total interest received by individuals on saving deposits and bank accounts was not reported in tax returns for the personal income tax. Since 1988, banks are obliged to report to the Tax Administration all interest payments to residents of the Netherlands. As a result, this type of tax fraud has largely disappeared, and income tax revenue has structurally risen by at least Gld700 million per year.[18]

The example given illustrates that efforts to combat tax fraud have intensified, starting from the mid-1980s. In 1985, a 'tax number' to identify taxpayers was introduced, which, in combination with the introduction of data-crunching computers, has improved the efficiency of the drive against tax fraud. In the early 1990s, the tax number was broadened to a combined tax/social security number. Also, powers of the Tax Administration have been extended through legislative changes, and its efficiency has improved as a consequence of automation and a major internal reorganization. Recently, observers of the Tax Administration have taken to the streets, and they report back to their office economic activity that might otherwise escape the paper world of the tax bureaucracy.

All in all, it seems that the battle waged by government to reconquer part of the domain of the hidden economy has met with a certain degree of success. On the other hand, it must be concluded that both the administration and law enforcement agencies still lack sufficient qualified manpower in the fight against fraud.

C5 Administrative and Compliance Costs

The costs of operating a national tax-benefit system are divided between the public and the private sectors of the economy. Only recently has the issue of administrative and compliance costs of tax and benefit programmes begun to receive the attention it deserves, both in the Netherlands and in a number of other OECD countries.

---

[18] Lower House, Parliamentary Documents, 1990–1, 21800 IXB, 50, 4.

Allers (1994) has estimated the total costs of operating the tax-benefit system in the Netherlands. Data on administrative costs of the public sector apparatus have been taken from official documents and, whenever necessary, supplemented with directly acquired information from the government agencies involved. Data on compliance costs of the business community and family households have been collected by way of two representative, nationwide surveys, covering over 1,000 firms and 11,000 households.

According to the study by Allers, in 1990, total operating costs of the Dutch tax-benefit system amounted to at least Gld15.3 billion, or 3 per cent of GDP. Since the costs involved could be quantified only partially, true operating costs are more likely to be in the order of 4 per cent of GDP. Table 7.8 summarizes operating costs of the tax system.

In Table 7.8, the costs of levying general and employee social insurance taxes are combined with those of the personal income tax since these levies are largely collected jointly. In 1990, less than one-quarter of total operating costs of the tax system (Gld10.6 billion) were incurred by government (Gld2.3 billion). The business sector (Gld6.8 billion) and family households (Gld1.5 billion) were confronted with the lion's share of all identifiable operating costs.

Total costs amount to slightly over 5 per cent of total revenue from taxes considered here. However, the cost ratio per tax varies widely, from 26.4 per

Table 7.8 Operating costs of major taxes, around 1990[a]

	Revenues Gld billion	Costs (Gld million)		Cost ratio
		Administration	Taxpayers	
Wealth tax	1.2	70	250	26.4
Import duties	2.7	250	220	17.6
Green energy taxes	0.6	40	na	7.1
Value added tax	38.0	250	2,100	6.2
Corporation income tax	17.0	210	670	5.1
Personal income tax, plus payroll taxes	130.0	1,200	4,900	4.8
Local property taxes	3.1	70	60	4.3
Motor vehicle tax	3.7	88	na	2.4
Estate tax	1.2	25	na	2.2
Dividend tax	2.3	12	30	1.9
Excise taxes	9.7	82	70	1.5
Transfer tax	1.7	11	na	0.7
Special car tax	2.6	6	na	0.2
All taxes	209.1	2,300	8,300	5.1

[a] Taxes ranked by decreasing cost ratio.

Source: Allers (1994: 178).

cent for the net wealth tax to only 0.2 per cent for the special consumption tax on cars and motorcycles.

Policy-makers should seriously consider such diverging cost ratios, since they imply that important cost savings for society as a whole might be achieved. But clearly, potential efficiency gains must be traded off against other policy goals, such as limiting the inequality of the personal income and wealth distribution and the diverse revenue-raising capacity of different kinds of taxes.

C6 Taxes and Labour Supply

Taxes drive a 'wedge' between pre-tax and after-tax labour income and capital returns. Employer taxes on labour inputs may restrict *demand* for workers. Because taxes on income cut into earnings, labour *supply* may fall. Indeed, many policy analysts in the Netherlands believe that current high average and marginal rates of taxes on income reduce labour supply. However, the evidence is rather mixed. After discussing various recent estimates of behavioural responses to marginal changes in tax levels, the Central Planning Bureau concluded that the elasticity of aggregate labour supply (measured in hours) is somewhere between -0.15 and 0.25 if net wages change by 1 per cent (CPB 1988: 187). On the other hand, analysts are unanimous that existing wedges limit the demand for labour, thus contributing to current unemployment levels. This conclusion is corroborated by recent economic research (Gelauff 1992).

Table 7.9 details the average and the marginal wedge for minimum wage earners, the average production worker (APW) with annual gross wage of Gld48,960, and of salaried individuals and managers, earning two and four times the APW wage respectively.

Table 7.9 Average and marginal wedge, 1994[a]

	Minimum wage	APW[b]	2×APW	4×APW
Average wedge				
Employee	7.4	19.9	32.4	43.3
Employer	19.0	21.7	20.6	15.7
Total	26.4	41.6	53.0	59.0
Marginal wedge				
Employee	35.3	35.3	47.4	55.9
Employer	25.0	25.0	10.2	10.2
Total	60.3	60.3	57.6	66.1

[a] Per cent of total labour costs.
[b] APW = average production worker.

Source: Ministry of Finance (1994: annexe 1).

Average wedges increase rapidly, notably reflecting the progressive rate structure of the personal income tax. The marginal wedge is a stunning 60.3 per cent for all workers at the lower end of the income distribution, and is nearly exclusively accounted for by social insurance taxes.

D. Tax Reforms

D1 Main Tax Reforms, 1987–1994

Following the lead of a number of other countries, tax reform efforts in the Netherlands have primarily concentrated—at least until now—on the personal and the corporate income tax. Initially, tax reformers intended to tackle the complexity of the personal income tax. Later on, growing awareness of the damage that high tax rates might cause to national economic performance in the longer run increasingly dominated the tax reform debate.

Since 1985, the rate of the corporation income tax has been lowered in two steps, from 43 per cent to the present 35 per cent. In 1988, a rate reduction by 7 points was combined with scrapping the investment tax credit. Also, deductibility of certain categories of expenses was restricted.

In line with trends elsewhere, the major reform of the personal income tax in 1990 sought to broaden the tax base, while at the same time reducing the level and flattening the structure of rates. Following the lead of the first Tax Reform Commission chaired by Dr Oort (1986), personal income tax and general social insurance taxes were integrated, with a uniform tax base and combined rate. Until 1990, general social insurance taxes were fully deductible for income tax purposes. By absorbing the deductibility into a lower rate of the combined levy, by far the largest deduction (of some Gld28 billion) was eliminated.

Formerly, employees and benefit recipients paid only two general social insurance taxes (for the AOW and the AWW programme), whereas three such taxes were directly paid by withholding agents. As from 1989, the child benefit programme (AKW) is no longer financed through a separate social insurance tax, but out of general revenue. Moreover, in 1990, the AAW and AWBZ social insurance taxes were shifted from employers to wage earners and benefit recipients. At the same time, to ensure that their after-tax incomes underwent no substantial change, these groups received a (taxable) compensation (*overhevelingstoeslag*). Although a large sum is involved (Gld26 billion), this part of the tax reform was essentially a paper operation, since total labour costs of employers and after-tax income of workers were hardly affected.

Also, the value of personal exemptions was considerably reduced, broadening the tax base by another Gld39 billion. Notably, the additional exemption for single taxpayers was phased out. Including the effect of several other—in quantitative terms, less important—base-broadening measures, the tax reform has increased aggregate taxable income from Gld153 billion to Gld250 billion.[19]

The number of tax brackets was cut back from nine to three. The top rates were reduced considerably, to 60 per cent.

Over the 1986 to 1990 period, tax revenues were Gld18 billion higher than previously expected. Although over half of this tax bonus was used to compensate for net spending overruns (Gld10 billion), most of the remainder was used to reduce taxes (OECD 1991*a*: 47). The personal income tax reform package resulted in a net aggregate tax reduction for households amounting to over Gld4 billion, or nearly 1.5 per cent of aggregate disposable household income.

The Ministry of Finance has microsimulated the distributional impacts of the tax reform, and found that the 4 per cent of tax payers in the third bracket had obtained 8 per cent of the aggregate tax reduction, whereas the 62 per cent of tax payers in the first bracket received 49 per cent. Fig. 7.4, which is based on aggregate data from the Tax Administration for 1989 and 1990 shows what may really have happened.[20]

The combined burden of income tax and general social insurance taxes actually increased for most taxpayers earning between Gld10,000 and Gld25,000. As a group, taxpayers in the first bracket received only 7 per cent of the total tax break, the main reason probably being the substantial reduction of personal exemptions that was part of the tax reform. On average, the effective burden for taxpayers from higher-income groups fell by 4 to 5 points. Taxpayers in the third bracket received one-quarter of the total tax break, mainly because marginal top rates were reduced by up to 12 points. With the benefit of hindsight, it is clear that the tax reform provided the greatest gains for middle- and high-income groups (Table 7.10). Overall, the tax reform of 1990 has increased after-tax income inequality.

Other major changes of the personal income tax code included tightening the deduction of annuity premiums and extending the taxation of the interest component of capital payments based on life insurance policies.

Over the past ten years, the tax base of VAT has been marginally adjusted, so as to conform to successive EU Directives. During the 1980s, the standard VAT-rate (1980: 16 per cent) was repeatedly increased, reflecting urgent budgetary needs. Booming tax receipts then allowed for a gradual reduction of the standard rate in the late 1980s and the early 1990s to the present rate of 17.5 per cent.

---

[19] Since income subject to tax amounted to Gld305 billion. (Table 7.3), it follows that in 1990 personal exemptions totalled Gld55 billion.

[20] Both the microsimulations done by the Ministry of Finance (1994) and the approach of De Kam and Sturm (1994) have some methodological weaknesses. While indeed strong indications exist that the microsimulations seriously underestimate the tax advantage of taxpayers from higher-income groups, the results of De Kam and Sturm must also be interpreted as rough approximations only.

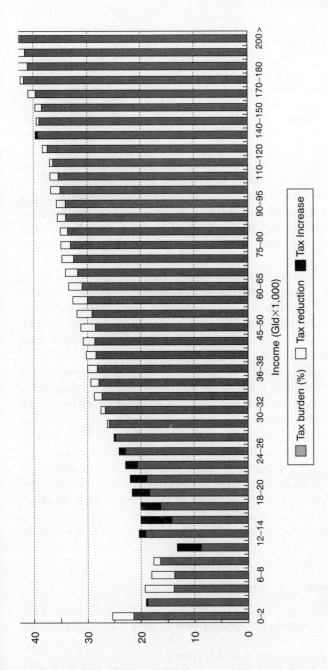

Fig. 7.4 Level of personal income tax and general social insurance taxes, before and after the tax reform of 1990 (%)

Source: De Kam and Sturm (1994).

Table 7.10   Income effects of the tax reform of 1990

Income class (Gld)	Taxpayers (%)	Tax reduction (%)	
		Ministry of Finance (1994)	De Kam and Sturm (1994)
First bracket	62	49	7
Second bracket	34	43	69
Third bracket	4	8	24
Total	100	100	100

Policy-makers have advocated reductions of the (top) rates of major taxes (see Fig. 7.5), pointing to increasing competition in the European tax 'theatre'. For the same reason, the former stock exchange tax was abolished in July 1990 so as to reinforce the competitive position of the Amsterdam Stock Exchange.

The net wealth tax is increasingly under attack from tax advisers, and tax professors as well.[21] It is believed that wealthy taxpayers massively move to tax jurisdictions without a wealth tax, notably neighbouring Belgium. In fact, over the whole 1983 to 1988 period, some 350 millionaires left the country, and not always for tax reasons too (Juch *et al.* 1990), while in 1990, over 50,000 millionaires still lived in the Netherlands.

Policy-makers nevertheless appear to have become extremely sensitive to the argument of an impeding tax flight of the rich, especially of entrepreneurs. Therefore, the ceiling on the exemption for capital invested by self-employed individuals in their business and for directors with a substantial interest in their company (of Gld1.54 million) was eliminated as of 1995.[22] Of course, this tax concession implies an additional distortion of capital markets.

Over the past five years, green taxes have become more important in revenue terms. Rates of taxes on energy consumption went up; by 1994, energy taxes produced some Gld1.5 billion in revenue. New taxes, based on the volume of solid waste treated, and groundwater consumption, have been enacted and been implemented as from 1995. Their joint revenue is estimated at Gld0.5 billion.

D2   Recent and Prospective Tax Reforms

At present, the relatively high rates of major taxes in the Netherlands are a direct consequence of voluminous government spending and, especially, an

---

[21] In nearly all cases, the professors are tax advisers as well.

[22] The exemption amounts to 50% (1995: 68%) of capital invested. So the effective tax rate is (more than) halved, from 0.8 to 0.4 per cent (1995: 0.256%) of net wealth invested in a business enterprise.

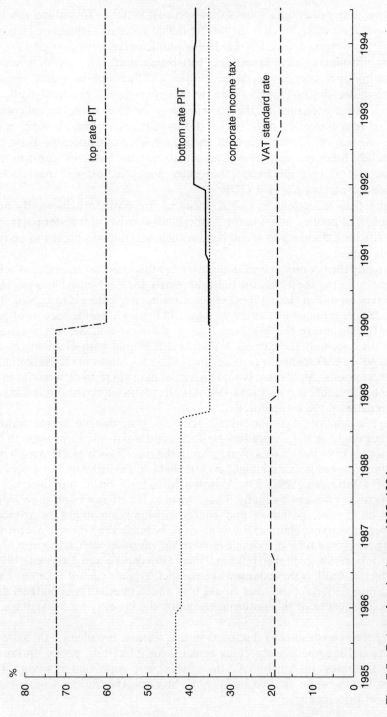

Fig. 7.5 Rates of major taxes, 1985–1994

extensive and rather generous social security system. To reduce rates of existing taxes—while holding the budget deficit constant—there are basically three policy options available: (i) reducing public outlays; (ii) changing the tax mix by introducing new taxes; and (iii) broadening the base of taxes by eliminating or restricting existing exemptions, deductions, or special rates.

Only under the first option can the macroeconomic tax level really be reduced. After a change of the tax mix, a given level of public revenue is collected only through a different set of tax instruments that show up in the wedge one way or another, since all taxes diminish real disposable income of households. Likewise, simplifying and broadening tax bases will contribute to revenue-neutral rate reductions, but such policy action will not directly produce a lower tax share in GDP.

In practice, reductions in public spending are hard to achieve. By now, almost half of public outlays in the Netherlands consists of transfer payments. For politicians, deciding to spend less on such programmes proves to be very difficult indeed.

Changing the tax mix, the second option for fundamental reform, has other drawbacks. In the short run, the only alternative for the Netherlands is a shift from taxes on income to higher taxes on consumer spending and capital. The VAT rates are more or less at the average EU level. Given the success of past efforts to harmonize the VAT tax base in the Common Market area, and taking into account the current VAT rate differential with Germany of 2.5 points, policy-makers might consider increasing VAT rates in the Netherlands by several points. Also, there is some room of manœuvre to raise excise taxes on alcohol and tobacco products. Petrol is already taxed to the limits dictated by international tax competition.

The taxation of pollution or of activities that deplete scarce natural resources might in the longer run produce substantial revenues. Some in the Netherlands have high hopes of expanding the role of such green taxes. Their maximum revenue potential might eventually be in the order of 3 to 4 per cent of GDP (Witteveen, 1992: 53). A switch from taxes on labour (income) to green taxes is favoured by many. Thus, demand for labour might grow, while at the same time, pollution and energy consumption might be reduced. However, if workers claim extra wage rises, because they do not accept the ensuing erosion of their disposable income, the proposed switch to green taxes would only result in higher inflation rates (Bovenberg and Cnossen, 1991). Moreover, a small, open economy like the Netherlands cannot take this road alone, since national producers would lose out in international markets as a direct consequence of this government-imposed competitive disadvantage.

Given policy constraints as discussed in this section, broadening the base of the personal income tax especially remains an interesting policy option to reduce tax rates. In April 1990, the government appointed a second Tax Reform Commission, chaired by W. F. C. Stevens. The Stevens Commission (1991) set three goals:

(1) achieving further reductions of the combined rate of the personal income tax and general social insurance taxes;

(2) broadening the tax base by another Gld22 billion, mainly by eliminating the present deduction of employee social insurance taxes; and

(3) simplifying the tax system, notably by harmonizing the base of all taxes that employers withhold from gross wages.

Extra revenues due to the broader tax base would enable the introduction of a two-bracket rate structure. The first bracket could be extended to Gld57,000 (and be taxed at 1.5 points below the current rate), with the top rate further reduced from the present 60 per cent to 55 per cent. The Stevens Commission has also proposed a tax credit of Gld2,175 to replace the basic personal exemptions.

These proposals have met with strong resistance from various pressure groups. Partly for that reason, the government has not been willing to implement them. However, any future attempt to reform the personal income tax must consider the Stevens proposals.

By now, the Netherlands is one of the few OECD countries without a capital gains tax. Apart from horizontal equity arguments, the main reason for their adoption in almost all OECD countries—especially in recent years— is that, in their absence, the tax avoidance industry can thrive by 'transforming' (taxable) income into (untaxed) capital gains. Until now, policy-makers in the Netherlands have taken recourse to complicated legislation and the tax courts to repair and to fight the most glaring loopholes in the current income tax system. Indeed, the goal of a more equitable tax system would greatly be served by taxing realized capital gains of private investors, with deemed realization in the event of death. This option, which if enacted would certainly further complicate the tax system, has stout defenders (Van Dijck, 1988), but its support in circles of policy-makers is, as yet, decidedly weak.

The tax treatment of the family is a recurring issue in tax reform debates. The Scientific Council for Government Policy (1990: 217–29) has suggested abolishing the current option for non-earning partners to transfer their basic personal exemption to the breadwinner (Sect. B1.4) so as to give non-earners an incentive to enter the labour market. This suggestion has the support of a majority in parliament, but until now no satisfactory solution has been found to compensate one-earner families in low-income groups for the resulting higher tax burden.

Other problems of the labour market have also been linked to tax reform. Spokesmen of major political parties, as well as representatives of employer organizations and the unions, have recently stressed that the wide gap between labour costs and net wages (the 'wedge') should be narrowed. Policy-makers are now actively considering substantial rate reductions for the lower paid, whereas interest in lowering the top rates has—perhaps temporarily—waned.

Two proposals for reducing the wedge for lower-paid workers stand out. One option is to reduce the rate of the first (basic) income tax bracket (including general social insurance taxes). After-tax income of employees and most benefit recipients would not rise, however, because the *overhevelings-toeslag* that employers currently pay to their employees would be slashed by the exact amount of the tax reduction. As a result, labour costs could fall substantially. Self-employed individuals and pensioners would see their after-tax income rise.

The Andriessen Commission (1994) has advocated a second option, i.e. introducing an earned income tax credit of Gld2,400 per annum. Thus, the current negligible difference between net minimum wage and net minimum benefits (of only Gld25 per month) would increase to Gld225 per month. As a consequence, reservation wages would drop,[23] with the resulting growing labour supply depressing the overall level of labour costs.

Both options are expected to generate some 150,000 additional jobs (after four years) at comparable cost to the public budget. Spokesmen of all major political parties have agreed that a reduction of the wedge along these lines would, in any event, require substantial cuts in social security spending.

To recoup part of the resulting revenue losses, it has also been suggested that the low, combined rate of income and general social insurance taxes for senior citizens be abolished. As noted in Sect. B3, for taxpayers aged 65 years and over, a reduced combined rate of only 17.45 per cent applies, instead of 38.12 per cent. If the elderly would be fully taxed, revenue would expand by Gld4.5 billion, of 0.8 per cent of GDP.[24]

Although the current corporation income tax rate is internationally competitive, representatives of the business community have pressed for an extension of several existing tax facilities, so as to reinforce the position of the Netherlands as a home country for international investors and financial institutions. The Ministry of Finance (1992b) seems to be inclined to lend such pleas a willing ear, perhaps sometimes hesitantly so. To reaffirm the position of the Netherlands as a home base for both holding and manufacturing companies, several measures to accommodate internationally operating firms are under discussion now. For the near future, it may be expected that policy-makers in the Netherlands will cling to a continuation of the classical system, under which corporate profits are doubly taxed.

A final word on the future of local taxes seems to be in order here. A government-appointed Commission chaired by Dr De Kam (1992) recom-

---

[23] This concept refers to the wage that benefit recipients minimally demand when accepting a job offer. The reservation wage is equal to the sum of present benefit received, plus all costs associated with the job on offer, plus the value of leisure foregone.

[24] Growing enthusiasm for this option has rather dampened in political circles, when after the elections of May 1994, two new 'granny power parties' entered Parliament and (together) took seven out of its 150 seats.

mended substantially increasing the local tax share, while at the same time reducing central government grants and taxes so as to prevent the overall tax level from increasing. However, proposals of the De Kam Commission to enlarge the role of local taxation and bring it more in line with the situation in other countries got a cold shoulder. Although some participants in the current tax reform debate advocate a larger role for local taxation, the central government seems reluctant to hand over tax capacity to local authorities. The government has followed up on one recommendation of the De Kam Commission, i.e. to double the role of the provincial tax (Sect. B7).

Since 1995, the overall tax level has dropped by several points. By 1998, the tax take-out of GDP amounted to 43 per cent. The net borrowing requirement of the government had fallen to 1.5 per cent of GDP; the debt/GDP ratio to 75 per cent. Partly, all these ratios shrank because the denominator (GDP) reflects the strong economic performance of the Dutch economy during the 1995–1998 period.

In 1996, the regime for shareholders with a substantial interest was fundamentally overhauled. A 'substantial interest' is now defined as a stake of 5 per cent or more in the share capital of the company. As from 1997, all profits earned by shareholders with a substantial interest (in the form of dividends, capital gains, and so on) are taxed at a flat rate of 25 per cent (final tax). This move constituted a small but significant step towards a schedular (or 'dual') personal income tax system. The corporation income tax now has a flat rate of 35 per cent, because the higher rate applicable to the first Gld100,000 of taxable profit (Sect. B2.2) was annulled starting in 1998. Also, as from 1 January 1998, the rate of the net wealth tax has been reduced from 0.8 per cent to 0.7 per cent. Personal exemptions of the wealth tax have been raised substantially.

The social security system underwent major revisions. The general disability insurance programme (AAW) has been abolished as of 1998. In tandem, coverage of the employee disability programme (WAO) was extended (see Sect. B3). Contributions to finance the WAO programme have been shifted from employees to employers. In return, by far the largest part of the *over-hevelingstoeslag* (Sect. D1) has been scrapped.

In December 1997, the government published a Green paper with a blueprint for tax reform in the next century (Ministry of Finance, 1997). The option that will probably be adopted by the incoming government (after the general elections held in May 1998) includes full integration of the personal income tax and the contributions to finance the remaining three general social insurances, while the rates will be reduced. The new top rate is expected to be in the 50–55 per cent range. Personal exemptions will be replaced by tax credits. The net wealth tax will be abolished. For the taxation of most forms of capital income the Green paper envisages a unique system: interest and dividend income earned would no longer be taxed. Instead, a deemed return equal to 4 per cent of a tax payer's net wealth would be taxed at a flat rate of 25 per cent. In fact, this of course works out as a net wealth tax of 1 per cent.

The total cost of this tax reform package—estimated at some Gld12–15 billion (slightly less than 2 per cent of GDP)—would be covered by increasing the standard rate of the value-added tax from 17.5 to 19 per cent (additional revenue Gld4 billion), further greening of the tax system (Gld3.5 billion), some broadening of the personal income tax base (Gld2.5 billion), and Gld3–5 billion which the new government has earmarked for a reduction of the overall tax level.

This major tax reform, if enacted, clearly reflects problems increasingly encountered by the Dutch fiscal system when it tries to effectively tax capital income and private wealth. Major explanations for 'leakage' of the tax base are growing 'tax competition' within the European Union, and immensely popular tax planning devices that transform taxed capital income into untaxed capital gains. Remarkably, the Dutch government has declined to introduce as a remedy capital gains taxation. Instead, it opts for taxation of a deemed return on net wealth.

Unmistakably, the tax reform—at the moment of writing still on the drawing board—would (further) reduce the redistributive potential of the Dutch tax system.

References

Allers, M. A. (1994), *Administrative and Compliance Costs of Taxation and Public Transfers in the Netherlands*, Ph.D. thesis, Groningen.

Andriessen Commission (1994), *De onderste baan boven*, The Hague.

Bakker, Bas B. (1993), *Saving in the Netherlands*, Ph.D. thesis, Groningen.

Barthold, Thomas A. (1993), 'How Should We Measure Distribution?', *National Tax Journal*, 46: 291–9.

Begeer, W., and van Tuinen, H. K. (1986), 'The Statistical Representation of the Informal Economy', *Netherlands Official Statistics* 3: 5–25.

Bovenberg, A. L., and Cnossenn, S. (1991), Fiscaal fata morgana, *Economisch Statistische Berichten*, 766, 3837, 1200–3.

Central Bureau of Statistics (1991), *Nationale Rekeningen 1990*, The Hague.

Central Economic Planning Bureau (1988), *Centraal Economisch Plan 1988*, The Hague.

—— (1994), *Centraal Economisch Plan 1994*, The Hague.

—— (1996), *Macro Economische Verkenning 1997*, The Hague.

Cnossenn, S. (1994), *Werken aan de wig*, Rotterdam.

Council for Local Finances (1994), *Jaarboek Gemeentefinanciën 1994*, The Hague.

De Kam Commission (1992), *Belastingen omlaag*, The Hague.

Dijck, J. E. A. M. van (1988), Vermogenswinstbelasting, *Weekblad voor fiscaal recht*, 117/5850: 1661–81.

Fullerton, Don, and Rogers, Diana Lim (1993), *Who Bears the Lifetime Tax Burden?*, Washington, DC.

Gelauff, G. M. M. (1992), *Taxation, Social Security and the Labour Market*, Tilburg.

Juch, D., van der Geld, J., and Serail, S. (1990), *De invloed van de vermogensbelasting op de fiscale emigratie*, Tilburg.

Kam, Flip de (1987), 'Netherlands', in Joseph A. Pechman (ed.), *Comparative Tax Systems*, Arlington: 91–149.

—— (1990), 'An Overview of Microanalytical Models and Datasets in the Netherlands for Simulation of Changes in Tax-Transfer Programs', in Johann Kurt Brunner and Hans-Georg Petersen (eds.), *Simulation Models in Tax and Transfer Policy*, New York, 323–46.

Kam, C. A. de, and van Herwaarden, F. G. De fiscale behandeling van leefvormen, 1970–1990, *Weekblad voor fiscaal recht*, 119/5905: 321–8.

—— (1993), 'Tax Policies in the 1980s and the 1990s: The Case of the Netherlands', in Anthonie Knoester (ed.), *Taxation in the United States and Europe*, London: 355–77.

—— and Sturm, J. E. (1994), De Effectieve Druk van Inkomensheffingen en Vermogensbelasting, voor en na de operatie Oort, *Weekblad voor fiscaal recht*, 123/6117: 1261–75.

Ministry of Finance (1984), *Miljoenennota 1985*, The Hague.

—— (1987), *Belastinguitgaven in de Nederlandse inkomstenbelasting en de loonbelasting*, Lower House, Parliamentary Documents, 1986/1987.

—— (1992a), *Jaarverslag Belastingdienst 1991*, The Hague.

—— (1992b), *Fiscaal vestigingsklimaat*, Lower House, Parliamentary Documents, 1992–1993.

—— (1993), *Miljoenennota 1994*, The Hague.

—— (1994), *Bouwstenennotitie*, The Hague.

—— (1997), *Belastingen in de 21e eeuw*, The Hague.

Ministry of Social Affairs (1993), *Sociale Nota 1994*, The Hague.

OECD (1984), *Tax Expenditures. A Review of the Issues and Country Practices*, Paris.

—— (1991a), *Economic Surveys 1991/1992: Netherlands*, Paris.

—— (1991b), *Taxing Profits in a Global Economy*, Paris.

—— (1994), *Taxation and Household Saving*, Paris.

Oort Commission (1986), *Zicht op eenvoud*, The Hague.

Pechman, Joseph A. (1985), *Who Paid the Taxes, 1965–1985*, Washington, DC.

Scientific Council for Government Policy (1990), *Een werkend perspectief*, The Hague.

Spenke, G. te, and Lier, A. P. (1992), *Taxation in the Netherlands*, Deventer.

Stevens Commission (1991), *Graag of niet*, The Hague.

Stevens, L. G. M. (1993), Fiscale beleidsnotities, *Weekblad voor fiscaal recht*, 122/6073: 1477–92.

Witteveen, D. E. (1992), De kleine gereedschapskist van de milieufiscalist, in K. L. Bangma and H. de Groot (eds.), *Milieubeleid en overheidsfinanciën*, The Hague: 51–6.

8 Spain

MIGUEL A. LASHERAS AND ISABEL MENENDEZ

A. Overview

Until the end of the 1970s, Spain's tax system was based on indirect taxation, with a cumulative and cascade sales tax, and a set of direct taxes that represented a poorly generalized tax system with few formal obligations that applied to few taxpayers. Individual taxation played a complementary role and consisted of source-based taxes (minimum taxes paid against a general income tax). Almost all the revenue collected from the income tax was in the form of withholding taxes, and the tax administration was simple. However, by the end of the 1970s, the tax system was unable to provide sufficient funds to meet the increasing demand for public services, and it was widely criticized, not only for its failure to produce sufficient revenue, but also for the lack of equity in the distribution of the tax burden among the population.[1]

Coinciding with the Democratic Constitution, a fiscal reform was introduced in 1978 that transformed the Spanish tax system. The reform was based on the introduction of a small number of highly generalized tax concepts rather than on a large number of taxes with a narrow range of application. The first step in the reform of the tax system was to implement a personal income tax (PIT), with only one comprehensive tax base per taxpayer unit (the family) and a progressive rate schedule. The system of self-assessment became generalized and there was a spectacular increase in both the number of taxpayers and the number of returns filed. In 1986, when Spain joined the European Union, consumption taxes were adapted to EU directives, with the introduction of a value-added tax (VAT) similar to those existing in the rest of Europe. The VAT replaced a cumulative tax on the sales of manufacturers and wholesalers. Finally, the tax administration was reformed, and during the 1980s, there was a process of computerization and development of tax offices.

As a result of this process, Spain increased the ratio of total tax receipts to GDP by more than 10 percentage points between 1982 and 1992. However, due to a slowdown in economic growth and the maturation of the tax system, the rate of growth of revenues declined significantly between 1992 and 1994, thus widening the gap between expenditures and taxes in the budget. The

---

[1] See Fuentes (1980) for a summary of this criticism.

consolidated fiscal deficit for all levels of government in 1993 was the highest since the 1978 tax reform. During 1994, 1995, and 1996 the deficit has been progressively reduced in order to achieve the target of Maastricht Treaty for European single currency (3 per cent) by the end of 1997.

This chapter describes the main features of Spain's tax system, their effects, and the prospects for further reform. Sect. B describes the tax system. Sect. C deals with the consequences of the tax system both for the government and on taxpayers' behaviour. The huge acceleration in the rate of growth of tax revenues has had two effects that deserve special attention: the adaptation of the tax administration and the distribution of compliance and the tax burden.

The tax administration has had to adapt to accommodate a tax system that in 1996 generated approximately 15 million annual tax returns, compared to approximately 1 million at the end of the 1970s. Meanwhile, the primary problem facing tax policy-makers has been the unequal distribution of the tax burden, mainly due to the unequal distribution of fiscal compliance. In Sect. D, we consider the suggestions of different groups for further reforms to address these and other problems.

B. The Tax System

B1 Personal Income Tax

The present personal income tax was introduced in Law 44/78, which came into force on 1 January 1979. As introduced in 1979, the PIT was a progressive tax levied on all income attributable to individuals. In 1985, treatment of income from financial assets was substantially modified; specifically, income paid as a difference between the issue price and the reimbursement value of bonds began to be treated as interest instead of capital gains, and consequently subject to withholding tax. A new PIT (Law 18/92) came into force on 1 January 1992, and included a new definition of the 'taxpaying unit'. In response to a Constitutional Court decision in February 1989, the new law is based on individual taxation instead of the family unit. However, it provides an option for joint taxation for those families who find that system more beneficial. The taxpayer is allowed to choose between filing a single return for himself only or filing a joint return for the whole family. Different tax rate schedules apply depending on the filing status chosen. In election year 1996, the new Government proposed and the Parliament approved a new Tax Law modifying the treatment of capital gains under PIT. According to such a new law, capital gains are taxed at a single tax rate of 20 per cent. In 1998, the Popular Party government presented a reform of the PIT to Parliament. The major changes were lowering the tax schedules and modifying the personal deductions from the tax due, transforming some of them to only one deduction from the tax base.

Income from capital (dividends and interest) and from compensation for personal work (labour and self-employed professionals) is subject to with-holding at source as a prepayment against final tax liability. Certain items (use of houses, vehicles, loans of money at interest rates lower than the market) are classified as compensation-in-kind to employees and are included in the tax base. Companies are required to withhold tax from such income under special rules for valuation. The withholding tax at source is fully creditable against the final tax due and is refundable if it exceeds the final liability. An individual's final tax liability is determined on an annual basis and reported in a return that covers the whole year. This return is presented to the tax admin-istration (directly or through the bank system) during the months of May and June following the year to which the return refers. When the return results in a credit for reimbursement (i.e. tax withheld exceeds the final tax due), the tax administration refunds the amount due to the taxpayer. The refund usually takes place during the last period of the year in which the return is presented.

The PIT base is yearly net income defined as yearly gross income reduced by only those expenditures that are considered by the tax law as absolutely necessary to obtain income. The rules, and consequently the importance of the reductions, depend on whether the income is from labour, business or professional activities, or financial assets. These rules are described below.

B1.1 Income from Labour

The main deductions allowed from salary income are for social security taxes, contributions to registered pension plans up to certain limits, and 5 per cent of gross income, with a maximum limit of Ptas 250,000 (around $US 1,800 in 1995).

Income from labour provides a greater degree of effective tax burden than other types of income as a consequence of its high transparency and controllability. Therefore, this kind of income has a special treatment with two main allowances. The first reduces the tax base (2 per cent of gross income from labour) and the second reduces the effective tax rate (reducing a fixed amount that is adjusted each year). The tax base also is subject to several adjustments to reflect situations involving periodic income, such as in the case of professional athletes, or reimbursements of pension funds. When income is perceived in just one year but generated during a longer period of time, only a part of the income is considered to determine the bracket and the correspond-ing tax rate, although once obtained, the tax rate is applied to the whole income.

B1.2 Income from Business and Professional Activities

There are two methods of determining the tax base for income from business and professional activities: the direct method and the objective method. Under the first method, the tax base is determined by means of accounting information; under the second method, the tax base is determined by means of indices and some linear relationships established by statistical methods.

Use of the direct method has required the introduction into the PIT of concepts used in the corporate income tax. This coordination facilitates unified criteria for both taxes and allows for neutrality in determining taxable income from each economic activity, regardless of the legal nature of the taxpayer.

Taxpayers may opt to use the simpler objective method instead of the direct method. The objective method employs indices to determine the implied income of an economic activity as a function of its sales. Indices or modules characteristic of each business sector are applied to determine the income of the business activity. The objective method is optional, and taxpayers who choose not to use it are subject to the direct method. The objective method also can be used as a minimum return when accounting requirements are not complied with for purposes of the direct method.

B1.3 Income from Financial Assets

There are three kinds of income from financial assets under the PIT: dividends, interest, and capital gains. Dividends are subject to withholding when they are distributed by the company. They are included in the tax base of the individual at their gross value (net payment plus withholding tax, without including corporate tax) and no deduction is allowed in determining the base. Taxpayers may, however, claim a credit of 10 per cent of the gross dividend against their tax due as compensation for double taxation. This system of compensating for double income taxation does not add the tax paid by the company to the tax base of the individual. It has been criticized for being insufficient and regressive (Gonzalez-Paramo, 1992 and Garcia Sobrino, 1992). The treatment of interest income is very similar to the treatment of dividends but there is no deduction for double taxation. Interest also is subject to withholding tax.

Capital gains derived from financial assets or from real estate have to be added to the other components of the tax base only when such assets are sold by the taxpayer. The amount included in the tax base is the difference between the sale value and the historical cost of the asset, modified by a coefficient according to the year in which the asset was acquired and, until 1992 when the law was amended, to take into account accumulated inflation. The 1992 reform introduced a new way to determine the capital gains tax base, with a coefficient to multiply directly the difference between the sale and the cost prices and whose value depends on the year of acquisition and on the kind of asset and not on accumulated inflation. In 1996 the law was again amended establishing new coefficients to actualize the costs of acquisitions of the transmitted assets.

The 1992 law also established an allowance of Ptas 25,000 ($US 190) for interest income and dividends. Further, capital gains are exempt from the PIT when the sales value does not exceed Ptas 500,000 ($US 3,900). From 1996, capital gains are taxed at a single rate of 20 per cent when the capital gains are higher than Ptas 200,000 ($US 1,500). Up to Ptas 200,000, the tax rate is 0 per cent (see Table 8.1).

Table 8.1 Tax rates schedules,[a] 1997

Individual taxation			Joint taxation		
Tax base (Ptas)	General tax rate (%)	AC tax rate[b] (%)	Tax base (Ptas)	General tax rate (%)	AC tax rate[b] (%)
442,000	0,00	0,00	882,000	0,00	0,00
1. 136,000	10,38	1,83	2,198,000	10,18	1,80
2. 305,000	15,03	2,65	3,100,000	13,28	2,34
3. 474,000	17,98	3,17	4,300,000	16,45	2,90
4. 643,000	20,30	3,58	5,550,000	19,24	3,36
5. 812,000	22,37	3,95	6,850,000	21,41	3,78
6. 981,000	24,32	4,29	8,150,000	23,56	4,16
8. 150,000	26,32	4,64	9,950,000	25,58	4,51
9. 319,000	28,24	4,98	10,750,000	27,62	4,87
10. 488,000	30,12	5,31	12,100,000	29,57	5,22
Excess over	47,60	8,40	Excess over	47,60	8,40

[a] These schedules are simplifications of the legal tax rates schedules which have a first column with the lower limit of the bracket, a second with the initial tax for such a limit, a third with the difference between the tax base and the upper limit of the bracket, a fourth with the marginal tax rate to apply to the difference between the tax base and the lower limit.
[b] From 1.997 the Autonomous Communities may legislate on their own tax rate schedule. If they don't, the tax rate to apply is the one included in the table.

B1.4 Tax Rate Schedules and Deductions

Once the tax base from all kinds of income of different capital gains is added up, one of the two tax rate schedules is applied and an initial tax amount is obtained. There are two tax rate schedules, one for taxpayers who file individual returns and the other for joint (family) returns. The top marginal tax rate is 56 per cent in both schedules, and for the 1996 tax year it applied to income above Ptas 13,836,550 for single filers and Ptas 15,872,030 for joint returns (respectively, $US 108,000 and $US 124,000). The bottom rate is 20 per cent and applies to incomes of Ptas 430,000 and Ptas 857,000. There are seventeen brackets between the upper and lower limits.

After the initial tax amount is obtained, a set of tax credits is applied. These include personal credits, which vary according to family situation, and investment credits, the primary one being a credit of 15 per cent of the amounts applied to the amortization of mortgages or the acquisition of housing.

B2 Corporate Income Tax

Spain's corporate income tax (CIT), which was introduced on 1 January 1979 and reformed in 1995, is levied on the net profit of business corporations. Non-business corporations, like trade unions, charitable and religious organizations, and political parties, are exempt from the tax. However, in the case of exempted entities, withholding taxes on interest and dividends operated as a minimum tax up to the 1995 reform, because they were not reimbursed. For not exempted legal entities, resident or with a permanent establishment in Spanish territory, the CIT is levied on the business and non-business income accruing to it.

B2.1 Taxation of Resident Entities

Resident corporations are taxable on their worldwide income. Taxable income includes all the profits from operations, income from investments not relating to the corporation's regular business purpose, and capital gains. Spain's treaties with other countries may influence the determination of income subject to tax in Spain. Before the 1995 reform, 'taxable income' was defined as the difference between revenues and expenses during the period. The principles for allocating revenues and expenses to determine taxable income roughly followed accounting principles. The 1995 law identifies the tax base with the balance of profit and loss account. The accrual method is generally applicable for revenue and expense-recognition purposes, provided the accounting records reflect the true net worth position of the company. For certain transactions, companies are permitted to use special allocation methods.

Inventory valuation. The generally applicable method for valuing inventories for tax purposes is the acquisition cost or weighted average cost for homogeneous groups of goods. If inventories are valued by methods other than weighted cost average, the related adjustment must be made for tax purposes. The LIFO (last in, first out) method has been generally disallowed, although it could be used for accounting purposes provided the appropriate adjustments were reported in the tax return. The 1995 reform of CIT law allows for this method of valuation from 1995 on.

Valuation of transactions between related companies. For corporate income tax purposes, revenues and expenses arising from transactions between companies and their shareholders, or between companies and their directors must be valued at market prices. Two companies are related for tax purposes if one directly or indirectly owns at least 25 per cent of the capital of the other, or exercises functions at the other signifying the power to influence decisions, or if the same shareholders own at least 25 per cent of the capital of the other or own at least 25 per cent of the capital stock of both. Also, companies that are members of a group are deemed to be related for income tax purposes.

Depreciation and amortization. Depreciation qualifies as a deductible expense only if it is effective and is recorded in the accounts. The basis for depreciation is the acquisition cost of the asset. There are official depreciation rate tables, which, if complied with, relieve the company of the need to prove the effectiveness of the depreciation. The standard method of depreciation is the straight-line method. Taxpayers may, however, use the declining balance method for certain assets (industrial machinery, data-processing equipment, hotel installations, etc., but not for buildings or furniture). Under this method, depreciation can be shifted to the early years of the asset's useful life, when the effective depreciation may be greater. Companies that want to depreciate at faster rates can get prior approval from the administration for special depreciation plans with higher annual rates of depreciation.

According to the 1978 law intangible assets and rights that can be given an economic value that are acquired for consideration and recorded as intangibles in the balance sheet could only be depreciated if they had a finite life that could not be extended or if they suffered continuous diminution in value. The 1995 law has eliminated those special conditions for qualification as deductible expenses.

Financial lease arrangements. Lease payments (interest plus the portion of the payment relating to the cost of the asset) are deductible with some exceptions. In the case of land, only the interest portion is deductible. Under Spanish law, there is a minimum term of two years for lease contracts for movable assets and ten years for real estate.

Loss carry forwards. A company can carry forward its tax losses to offset taxable income of the following five fiscal years. Loss carry-backs are not permitted neither in the 1978 law nor in the 1995 amended law.

Capital gains and losses. Capital gains are added to and losses deducted from regular business income to determine the amount of taxable income. In the 1978 law a gain on the sale of an operating, tangible fixed asset was exempt from tax if the total proceeds of the sale were reinvested in a new operating, tangible fixed asset within two years. The company must retain the new asset in which the reinvestment was made for a minimum of two years in the case of movable property and ten years in the case of real estate. In 1995 this exemption was reformed and maintained for corporations below a certain amount of turnover and eliminated for the others.

B2.2 Taxation of Non-Resident Entities

The tax regime for non-resident entities varies depending on whether they have a permanent establishment (PE) in Spain. Further, the taxation of income of permanent establishments also varies depending on the circumstances of the PE.

In the case of a PE with continuous activity, taxable income is determined under the same rules applicable to Spanish-resident companies. There is a special regime for PEs whose activities are not carried out in a continuous fashion in Spain. Special rules also apply to PEs that have a place of work in Spain but use the goods produced or the services provided therein for their own purposes. They do not obtain revenues but reimbursement for costs incurred. These PEs under the 1978 law were taxed at a 35 per cent rate on 15 per cent of their expenses and at 35 per cent on capital gains and non-operating revenues. The 1995 reform establishes the arm's-length principle to evaluate their revenues, but maintains as a subsidiary method the percentage on expenses method.

As regards income obtained other than through a PE, non-resident entities are taxable on their Spanish-source income as defined under Spanish law.

B2.3 Tax Rates

The standard corporate tax rate is 35 per cent. Special tax rates apply to entities such as credit cooperatives and insurance institutions (26 per cent up to 1995 and 25 per cent from 1995 on), other cooperatives (20 per cent), investment institutions (1 per cent), and pension funds (zero per cent). From financial year 1997 on, there exists a specific tax rate of 30 per cent for small and medium enterprises, such a tax rate to apply to the portion of the tax base below Ptas 15 million ($US 115,000).

B2.4 Tax Credits

(i) *Foreign tax credits.* Spain has adopted the ordinary allocation method for determining foreign tax credits to counteract the effect of international double taxation. The gross income earned abroad is added to all other income for purposes of calculating Spanish tax. A credit can be taken against the tax so calculated for the lower of the following two amounts: the Spanish tax that would be payable if the income had been earned in Spain or the tax of a similar nature paid abroad.

(ii) *Dividend tax credit.* Resident corporations receiving a dividend may claim a credit for 100 per cent of the tax paid on the underlying profits when the recipient company owns more than 5 per cent (25 per cent before 1995) of the resident company paying the dividend and had its holding during the preceding year to the one in which the dividend was distributed. If these requirements are not met, only 50 per cent of the tax paid on the income underlying the dividend received is creditable.

(iii) *Withholdings and prepayments.* Non-operating income such as interest, rent, and dividends is subject to a 25 per cent withholding tax at source as a prepayment against final tax. Taxpayers may claim a credit for withholding taxes and prepayments in their annual tax returns, and if the credits available exceed the final tax payable, they are entitled to a refund of the excess.

B2.5 The Main Characteristics of the 1995 Reform of the CIT

In December 1995, Parliament passed a new law reforming the 1978 law of the CIT. The reform was defended and supported by the majority coalition of socialist and Catalonian parties, arguing the necessity of reducing some negative effects of the tax on industrial activities. The new law tried to cover three main objectives: to reduce the compliance costs, to act as an incentive for the investment of the small and medium-sized enterprises, and to correct some shortcomings of the 1978 law. Taking into account such objectives, the main innovations of the 1995 reform were:

- The tax base was defined to coincide with the balance of the profit and loss account.
- Intangible assets as goodwill, trade marks, or rights to transfer, were allowed to be depreciated.
- There was an allowance of free depreciation for investments up to Ptas. 15m. by newly hired worker and by year. Out-of-limit investments were allowed to accelerate depreciation rules.
- The capital gains obtained for the sale of assets were exempted in corporations with turnover lower than Ptas 250 million. Those with higher turnover were allowed to pay the tax on capital gains following the depreciation of the new asset, actually postponing the payment of the tax.
- The incentives to R&D activities were widened.
- The correction for international double taxation was applied to corporations owning 5 per cent of the capital of foreign companies (instead of the 25 per cent limit contained in the 1978 law).

Despite the pressures of the opposition to reduce the tax burden, neither the rate of the tax (35 per cent) nor the disallowance to adapt the accounting values to inflation changed. In the 1995 reform the rate of tax stayed at the same level as was established in the 1978 law and the depreciation allowance based on historical values of assets was maintained. When the Popular Party formed the government in 1996, Parliament approved a law allowing for this adaptation to the inflation rate of previous years.

B3 Payroll Taxes

Spain's social security system relies heavily on payroll taxes and contributions. Under the Spanish social security system, social contributions (for contributory and non-contributory pensions and some medical services for the elderly) are partly paid by the employer, partly by the employee, and partly by the State from general revenues.

Personnel are classified under a series of professional and labour categories for the purpose of determining the taxable base of their social security tax. Each category has a maximum and a minimum contribution base, usually revised annually. Employees whose total compensation exceeds the maximum base, or does not reach the minimum base for their respective category, pay social security tax according to either the maximum or minimum base respectively.

To alleviate the burden on labour as a production input, the possibility of reducing payroll taxes and increasing other taxes instead has been debated extensively in Europe in recent years (i.e. Commission de las Comunidades Europeas (1993). It is argued that a reduction in the cost of labour through a decrease in payroll tax would increase employment, due to a fall in the relative price of labour.

This debate has been even more important in Spain, where the unemployment rate is very high (23 per cent in 1995) and there is a need to improve the competitiveness of Spanish enterprises. Payroll tax accounts for about 25 per cent of tax revenue in Spain, while in other EU countries, these taxes represent only 15 per cent of total tax revenue.[2] The desire to reduce the payroll tax has been tempered, however, by the realization that the current small surplus in the social security accounts will not last much beyond the end of this century and that a deficit is expected by the first decade of the next century.

After extensive debate about which tax should be increased to offset any reduction in the payroll tax, the government decided in September 1994 to reduce the payroll tax by one percentage point from January 1995 and to offset the revenue loss with a one point increase in VAT rates. It was argued that shifting the tax burden from labour to consumption would improve the international competitiveness of the Spanish economy, as there is a reimbursement of VAT on exports.

The 1994 government's decision revived the fear of inflation, however. The payroll tax cut reduced revenues by Ptas 175,000 billion (around $US 1.3 billion), which had to be offset with an increase in VAT. The effect of such an offset on the consumer price index (CPI) was around 0.8 percentage points in the month of January (nearly one-quarter of the total CPI for 1995).

In 1995 an agreement was signed in the city of Toledo by all the political parties who agreed not to introduce substantial reforms in the system, to defend the indexation of the public pension with CPI, to increase the proportionality of the system, and to improve the control and management of the system. When in 1996 the Popular Party won the elections it confirmed the guidelines of the social security system according to the Toledo Agreement.

B4 Value-Added Tax

Spain adopted VAT on its entry to the EU in January 1986. Spain's first VAT was virtually identical in form and function to the VAT defined in the EU's Sixth Directive. That VAT law replaced an assortment of approximately twenty-five other consumption taxes that included a general cumulative turnover tax ('IGTE').

A new VAT law came into force on 1 January 1993. The purpose of the new law was to adapt the Spanish legislation to EU directives and regulations related to the implementation of the objectives of the 1992 White Paper for a Single Market. For 1993 and 1994, the standard VAT rate was 15 per cent, applicable to most sales of goods and services. The standard rate was increased to 16 per cent on 1 January 1995. Similarly, the reduced rate of 6 per cent rose to 7 per cent and the superreduced rate rose from 3 to 4 per cent. Following the EU model, some transactions (services and supplies of goods

---

[2] Both percentages refer to 1990. In 1980, the percentage in Spain was nearly 50.

relating to financial activities, health, insurance, education, and rents of residential property) are VAT-exempt.

VAT is not applicable in the Canary Islands, Ceuta, and Melilla. Ceuta and Melilla have no consumption tax. With respect to the Canary Islands, there is an indirect general tax similar to VAT that is levied on goods and services supplied in the islands by entrepreneurs and professionals and on imports of goods. Its standard rate is 4 per cent.

B5 Excises and Other Consumption Taxes

As in the case of VAT, Spain has had to adapt its legislation on excise taxes to several EU directives. Harmonization has been needed to suppress distortionary excise taxes and approximate both tax rates and the tax bases to EU averages. Although Spain has made significant progress with respect to its excise on tobacco, hydrocarbons, and alcoholic beverages, it still has a long way to go to reach the level of harmonization that has been reached with VAT.

Spain's specific consumption taxes are levied on products (alcohol, alcoholic beverages, beer, hydrocarbons, and manufactured tobacco) at the manufacturing, processing, or import phases. In general, these taxes are not applicable in the Canary Islands (except taxes on alcohol and beer), and Ceuta and Melilla (except the tax on manufactured tobacco). Under the provision of an EU directive that allows the creation of special taxes (other than taxes on alcohol, alcoholic beverages, beer, hydrocarbons, and manufactured tobacco), and following the abolition of the higher tax rate of the old VAT law, a 13 per cent consumption tax on certain vehicles was introduced on 1 January 1993. The purpose of this tax was not only to collect taxes from the automobile sector to compensate for the revenue lost from the reduction of the top VAT rate from 33 to 15 per cent, but also to defray the social cost derived from the damage caused by vehicles to the environment and public health. This tax also applies at special rates in the Canary Islands (11 per cent) and Ceuta and Melilla (zero per cent).

With effect from 1997, a new tax on insurance premiums came into force. The tax rate is 4 per cent and the tax base the premium paid by the subscribers. The tax is collected from insurance companies which pass it on to the subscribers.

B6 Capital Taxes

B6.1 Net Wealth Taxes

The 1978 reform of direct taxation of individuals gave rise to the enactment of a net wealth tax. Like the PIT, this tax was reformed in 1992. Resident individuals pay net worth tax on their worldwide assets, valued in accordance with tax rules, as of 31 December each year. Non-residents are taxable on property. The same treatment applies to rights on real estates (i.e. time-sharing) exercisable in Spanish territory. The revenue raised is not a significant amount, as compared to the whole net worth tax, but it compensates for the hard-to-tax income associated with non-resident property assets. Certain assets are exempt from the net worth tax. The tax rules establish different valuation methods for each asset item. Resident individuals are granted an exemption of Ptas 17 million of their taxable base. The expected revision of estate cadastral values will probably lead to an increase in the minimum tax-exempt amount to Ptas 20 million. Non-residents do not qualify for any tax-exempt amount.

B6.2 Capital Transfer Tax

There is an inheritance tax on bequests, the rates varying according to the relationship between donor and donee.

B7 The Local Tax System

Taxes are levied at three levels of government in Spain: the central government level, the autonomous community (AC) level, and the local authority level. The autonomous communities obtain revenue from two primary sources: their own taxes (mainly the tax on the transfer of properties) and a share of the revenue from central government taxes. The ACs' revenue share is determined using a formula that takes into account such variables as population, area, tax effort, and other secondary variables on a five-year basis. The formula is negotiated and approved by the ACs and the central administration. From 1993 on, 15 per cent of the PIT collected in each AC is considered a resource of the AC budget. From 1996 this percentage was raised to 30 per cent and each AC establishes by law its own tax rate schedule to apply on such a percentage. These measures have been recently approved in the financial law for 1997. They were initially proposed by the Popular Party government and were supported by nationalist parties (Basques and Catalonians). Both measures tried to answer two main problems with the AC-financing system. One is the lack of correlation between decisions on expenditures and decisions on revenues. The AC administrations decide how to spend, but the political cost of raising revenue is paid mostly by the central government administration. The other is the lack of tax competition among the AC governments in order to achieve the efficiency of ACs' tax systems. Despite this problem, the evolution of the AC financing system has enabled the regional governments to achieve considerable financial autonomy in a very short period of time. Between 1980 and 1994, the ACs were given control over more than 20 per cent of total public expenditure, reflecting an unprecedented process of decentralization.

With respect to taxes administered and collected by local authorities, Law 39/1988 on local finance introduced a new scheme to rationalize the local taxation system and facilitate the activity of local entities. That legislation allows local authorities to modify some aspects of their taxes. The primary local taxes levied by all municipal governments are listed below.

Real property tax. This tax is levied annually on the ownership of real property and based on the cadastral value established by the tax administration and the municipality.

Opening licence tax. This tax is levied on the inception of a business. Its amount varies depending on factors such as type of activity and location.

Business activity tax. Effective from 1 January 1992, this tax is levied annually on any business activity conducted within the municipality. The tax is based on the type of activity, location, and number of employees. The tax applies to all businesses owned by corporations or individuals and to professionals and artists. It is an annual tax and a deductible expense for corporate and individual income tax purposes.

Motor vehicle tax. This tax is levied annually on the basis of the horsepower of the vehicle.

In addition to the above-mentioned taxes, the local authorities may also levy several other local taxes. These optional taxes are listed below.

Tax on increase in urban land value. This tax is levied on the increase in the value of urban land when the land is transferred. The tax base is calculated as an annual percentage of the cadastral value at the moment of the transfer.

Licence tax on installation and construction works. This tax is levied on the cost of any work or construction activity that requires previous municipal permission. Its rates vary between 2 and 4 per cent on the actual cost of construction.

C. Economic and Social Aspects

C1   The Fiscal Deficit

The level of social welfare expenditure in Spain during the 1980s was similar to those maintained by other European countries with a comparable level of income per capita. Between 1980 and 1990, social expenditure increased by more than 4 percentage points of GDP, rising from 21.7 to 25.5 per cent. The development of a welfare system with universal coverage in the areas of health care, pensions, education, and unemployment benefits was one of the main causes of the rise in public expenditure that took place during the 1980s. Other reasons were the increase in the cost of the national debt, which increased from 1 to 5 per cent of GDP between 1982 and 1993, the rise in public investment, and, to a lesser extent, the expenditures of other levels of government and the transfers to public enterprises. The 1993 fiscal deficit was the highest in recent Spanish history, amounting to 7.2 per cent of GDP.

The tax reforms implemented during the 1980s have been unable to guarantee coverage of the expenditures fixed by the budget since 1989. The Spanish economy suffered a contractive phase of the cycle between 1990 and 1993 that has been extremely harmful to employment (the unemployment rate was 24 per cent in 1993) and production (GDP fell by 1.2 percentage points in 1993). To a great extent, the expenditures (mainly transfers to families) required by the crisis worsened the problem of the deficit. Assuming that the deficit can be broken down into three parts—structural, cyclical, and discretionary—it is argued (Gonzalez-Paramo, 1994) that the problems of the Spanish deficit in 1993 came from its discretionary component during 1989, 1990, and 1991.

Three causes contributed to the increase in the discretionary component of the deficit at the beginning of the 1990s, making the fiscal policy anticyclical: (i) the public investment necessary to finance the 1992 Olympic Games and Seville's World Exhibition projects; (ii) the increasing cost of the national debt once the Bank of Spain was committed to applying an orthodox monetary policy; and (iii) the increasing cost of social security pensions resulting from a 1985 law that generalized the pension system.

The possibility that the rate of growth of interest payments on the public debt may exceed the growth rate of GDP, the difficulties in reducing long-term interest rates, and the necessity of fulfilling the Maastricht Treaty conditions in order to achieve the European Monetary Union are tough constraints that limit the government's choices and require a tight fiscal policy. The government has decided to try to reduce the deficit in the coming years, setting a deficit target of 3.5 per cent of GDP by the end of 1997. But the main problem in achieving this target is making it acceptable to the voters. The difficulties in complying with deficit targets in the past caused an erosion of the Socialist government's credibility. The authorization of expenditures, according to modifications of the initial budget, have greatly changed the figures initially passed by Parliament. The budgetary process and the control procedures need to be changed to allow a credibility gain among economic agents (Perez Campanero, 1992). During 1994 and at the beginning of 1995, the government approved different measures with the aim of keeping expenditures under control. As a result, the execution of the 1995 budget has reduced the discrepancies between actual and planned expenditures and so improved the credibility of fiscal policy.

By March 1996 the Socialist government was removed and a new government led by the Popular Party was nominated. The new government was strongly committed to reduce the fiscal deficit, which coinciding with a reduction in interest rates and an economic recovery during 1996 allowed an important reduction in the fiscal deficit for that and the following year. By the end of 1998 the level of public deficit had largely achieved the target of the Maastricht Treaty.

C2 Savings and Investment Incentives

During the years that followed the USA and UK tax reforms of 1986, there was a lively debate in Spain on the effects of tax incentives on saving and investment (Moneda and Credito, 1991). The facts are that in the second part of the 1980s, whlie the tax burden increased, the saving rate of families decreased sharply. Calls followed for reducing marginal PIT rates and introducing tax incentives to stimulate family saving (Fuentes Quintana *et al.*, 1990 and Montoro, 1992).

Mainly because of government concerns connected with the abolition of barriers to capital flows, the 1992 PIT reform introduced some incentives for saving. Those incentives were deemed to have no effect on the rate of saving, but rather, on the allocation of funds (Libro Blanco, 1990). The fact is that the rate of saving of families increased considerably in the early 1990s, but probably more because of a fall in consumption (due to the greater uncertainty associated with the economic crisis) than because of tax incentives.

The savings incentives introduced in the 1992 PIT reform are described below.

C2.1 Pension Funds

The 1992 law established a system of tax-preferred pension funds. Under this system, pension fund contributions are deductible and tax is deferred until the taxpayer is eligible by law to make withdrawals from the fund. If a taxpayer makes an early withdrawal, all the tax deductions associated with the fund have to be repaid to the government in a complementary return. At the beginning of 1994, more than 1 million taxpayers reported having a pension fund, while in 1986 such funds did not exist. The development of these funds, however slow, has been constant from the time the law came into effect.

C2.2 Investment Funds

Investment funds have been the preferred way of savings for Spanish families in recent years. The reduced tax rate on income earned within the funds (0.3 per cent) and the treatment of the income as capital gains (instead of as interest or dividend income), with the consequent tax-free allowance, have contributed to a huge increase in saving resources being allocated to these kind of funds. It is clear that the high interest rates of financial markets during those years also played a significant role in explaining the success of investment funds in Spain.

The effect of the tax system on the saving rate is uncertain and difficult to assess, but it is clearly identifiable in the movements observed in Spain in the allocation of existing funds during the early 1990s.

C2.3 Investment Tax Credit and Depreciation Allowance

The influence of investment incentives on investment decisions is also difficult to evaluate. There is no doubt about the distortionary effect on marginal tax rates of this kind of incentive. The work done by Cuervo-Arango and Trujillo (1986) and Espitia *et al.* (1988), following the King–Fullerton procedure, shows a great disparity in the marginal tax rate (MTR) depending on the kind of asset in which investment is made and how it is financed. The main conclusions of those papers were:

- the special rules for depreciation allowances, in particular the free depreciation allowance in 1985, were responsible for the greatest variance in MTR;
- the difference between economic and fiscal depreciation is not very high, and the rates of depreciation allowances, on average, are not significantly different from economic depreciation rates; and
- instead of eliminating the investment tax credit, whose uniformity across the assets contributes also to the variance in MTR, adjusting the rate of the credit according to the economic life of the asset could provide better results.

Otherwise, the incentives to invest in real estate, and in particular in the acquisition of family houses, seem not to have had much influence on taxpayers' behaviour. Lasheras *et al* (1993) found that the 1985 reform did not have much effect on the behaviour of taxpayers in respect of home purchases. That reform temporarily (for two years) extended the tax credit under the PIT for housing acquisitions from only one residence per family to any number of acquisitions of houses per family.

C3 Distribution of the Burden

The distribution of taxes can be analysed according to different divisions of the collectives that support the tax burden. First, we can consider the incidence of taxes on the return to capital and labour as production inputs, or on consumption and saving, as part of national value added (GDP). Second, we can analyse the distribution of the burden among different taxpayers according to their level of income or among different kinds of income within the income tax. Whatever method is chosen, the conclusion is that the main part of the tax revenue is supported by labour income and, within the income tax, by labour incomes above Ptas 3 million.

C3.1 Functional Distribution

Although according to Herrera (1990), in the composition of PIT revenue it is possible to observe, between 1980 and 1990, a slight increase in the part attributable to capital income. For the whole tax system in 1989, the 33.82 percentage points of fiscal burden (revenue as percentage of GDP) broke down as follows: 5.5 percentage points were directly attributable to labour income within the PIT, 12 percentage points to payroll contributions, 6.5 to capital income, and the rest, 9.8 percentage points, to consumption taxes. Under the assumption that both payroll taxes and indirect taxes are supported by labour—the latter by impacting real wages through prices—it is clear that the main part of fiscal burden is supported by labour income (around 80 per cent of the entire 1989 burden). According to Herrera (1990), under such assumptions it is possible to observe a slight increase in the part of the fiscal burden supported by capital income between 1980 and 1990.

C3.2 Personal Distribution

With respect to the PIT, the effective tax rates paid by the 25 per cent of taxpayers with highest income increased between 1982 and 1991 from 12.3 to 13.6 per cent, while the effective rate on 10 per cent of taxpayers with the lowest income fell from 0.6 to zero per cent. Without a doubt, the PIT was more redistributed at the beginning of the 1990s than it was ten years before, even if incomes declared are more unequally distributed (as the evolution of Gini's coefficient shows).

The redistributive capacity of income tax expanded considerably in the period between 1982 and 1990 (it has nearly doubled under the Reynold–Smolensky index). The causes, as analysed in Lasheras *et al.* (1993), are the increase in the average income (explaining 52.5 per cent of the total change), the changes in the distribution of pre-tax income (36.6 per cent of total change), and the results of the tax reforms during those years (10.9 per cent of total change).

Indirect taxation, in particular VAT, has a regressive effect on the distribution of the tax burden, as Mayo and Salas (1993) have analysed. But in some deciles of taxpayers (the lowest six), the tax represents a progressive distribution, due mainly to the incidence of the higher rate of VAT on motor vehicles.

C4 The Hidden Economy

Since the 1970s, public finance analysts have generally considered that the hidden economy is a very important problem in Spain. At the beginning of the 1980s, an official commission was set up to produce reports and figures of tax evasion. The Tax Evasion Commission (TEC) produced several reports between 1980 and 1987. The Commission's conclusions were that although PIT evasion during those years was decreasing, the level of evasion was very high. According to the TEC's report, only 58.4 per cent of taxpayers due to file a return did so in 1987, and only 56.5 per cent of taxable income was declared.

There are at least two problems with the TEC's findings. First, it is difficult to identify an accurate method to measure tax evasion. Very often what the Commission observed were statistical discrepancies between national accounts and tax data files rather than delinquent behaviour of citizens. Second, even assuming the possibility of measuring tax evasion, the effect of officially announcing the figures (being such high numbers) could worsen voluntary compliance instead of improving it.

For these two reasons, between 1988 and 1993, no official Commission dealt with tax evasion. However, different studies of the problem of tax evasion were developed during that period by the Spanish Institute of Fiscal Studies. The main conclusions of such studies are as follows.

First, tax evasion on labour income tax was around 6 per cent for salaries and 3 per cent for pensions for 1990, instead of the 27 per cent for 1987 found by the TEC. The study by Diaz and Fernandez (1993) is methodologically similar to the TEC study, but the former takes into account the effect of exempted minimum income on returns.

Second, income from business and corporate income seem to have higher levels of evasion. According to Melis (1992) and Truyols (1993), undeclared income could be around 35 per cent.

Third, with respect to VAT, tax evasion could be around 26 per cent (actual revenue was 74 per cent of potential revenue), according to Diaz and Herrera (1990). In VAT, there has been an alarming development of enterprises issuing false invoices in order to claim a tax refund. The response of administration and courts to the observed cases, however, has been sufficiently firm for this problem to be considered under control.

Fourth, estimating the black economy by equations of monetary demand (following the methods of Feige, 1989 and Tanzi, 1982), Mauleon and Escobedo (1991) found that the black economy due to tax causes increased between 1980 and 1989, growing at an accumulated rate slightly higher than the rate of growth of observed GDP. The black economy was around 13 to 15 per cent of GDP in 1989.

Finally, micromodels on survey data show that Spanish taxpayers behave according to classical variables of tax-evasion models (probability of detection and penalty rate) although marginal tax rates may not be a major determinant. The results reported by De Juan *et al.* (1993) point out that there is statistical evidence that those taxpayers who are socially oriented, those who have a negative attitude towards tax evasion, and those who are not acquainted with tax evaders are less inclined to evade taxes.

In 1994, an official commission on tax fraud and evasion issued a special report to the government that contained a set of proposals to improve the co-ordination of information systems with respect to tax, contributions, and benefits, to organize the information on tax evasion, and to analyse not only figures and measuring methods but also social acceptance and institutional behaviour towards tax evasion.

According to all available studies, there are reasons to think that the problem of tax evasion in Spain and Spanish citizens' behaviour is not much different from that in other parts of Europe. We have a similar tax system (supported mainly by a VAT and a progressive PIT) and a similar proportion of revenue to GDP as other European countries. Consequently, tax evasion should not be very different measured as a percentage of GDP, even though, as noted earlier, it could be that evasion does not distribute uniformly among income groups.

Whatever portion of the whole economy the hidden economy represents, a social consensus is emerging about requiring greater efficacy of government expenditures and punishment of tax evaders. According to a recent survey, De Juan (1992) reports that 76.3 per cent of Spanish taxpayers believe that the tax administration is improving the detection of tax evasion. Around 64 per cent of the persons questioned by the Sociological Research Centre in 1992 believed that the tax administration acted effectively and correctly managed the fight against tax fraud. But around half of taxpayers questioned (52.3 per cent) thought that they were not paying their fair share, 67.4 per cent thought that taxes were difficult to comply with, and around 67 per cent thought that they received less from the administration than what they paid for.

C5 Administrative Costs

During the 1980s, as the number of PIT returns grew to 10 million, the tax administration focused on computerizing administrative tasks. The computerization process started in 1984 as a response to the need to modernize following the implementation of the new tax system passed by Parliament in 1978. This process has been very rapid and has been politically backed to maintain the required rate of investment in equipment and personnel. The main effects of the process have been the standardization of tax procedures (in a new tax management procedure called *Nuevo Procedimiento de Gestion Tributaria*) and the design and building up of a single database for tax purposes.

Despite the administration's success in computerizing tasks and processes, tax administrative techniques remain deficient in certain respects.[3] For example: (i) the procedures to obtain information have not evolved in the same way as the capacity to store it; (ii) the functional character of the organizational structure of the tax administration has not changed since the 1970s; and (iii) the tax-auditing methods in cases of fiscal fraud under the criminal law do not differ from methods and processes used for administrative offences.

Under such conditions, the administrative costs of the Spanish tax system are not very high. According to data published by the State Tax Administration Agency (Diaz and Martinez, 1991), the number of employees in the tax administration per 1,000 inhabitants is 0.52 in Spain, fewer than the 0.92 in the USA, the 1.79 in France, or the 2.36 in the UK. These data, although possibly not very accurate, give an idea of the relative size of the Spanish tax administration.

The administrative costs of managing the tax system in Spain are not higher than those of other countries. In 1991, the Spanish taxpayer devoted an average of 6.8 hours per year to complying with the PIT. These hours were

---

[3] For a full description and evaluation of the computerization process, see Lasheras and Menendez (1992).

employed in compiling documents, meetings with tax advisers, and filling out the tax return (Diaz and Delgado, 1992).

The average fee paid to tax advisers was Ptas 5,500 (around $US 40) for a simplified return (with a tax base constituted mainly of income from labour) and Ptas 11,500 (around $US 82) for an ordinary return.

D. Prospects for Tax Reform

D1 Government Proposals

At the beginning of the 1990s, there were no expectations of dramatic reforms to the PIT in the near future. Only those features related to the improvement of corporate taxation (for example, rising the excise taxes or introducing ecological taxes) or the prospective adoption of new regulations in specific areas (for example, in the indices used for the objective method or in the fines to tax evaders) were on the government's agenda of tax reforms.

The Socialist government tried to reduce the marginal tax rates from 56 to 50 per cent in the 1992 reform. However, because the economic recession caused a reduction in PIT revenue, the reduction of marginal tax rates was dropped during the discussion of the draft law in Parliament.

In November 1994, the government introduced an important reform regarding the definition of 'tax fraud' under the criminal law. Under the new provision, social security fraud falls within the criminal law. The argument for this provision is that an illegal enjoyment of benefits or the undue receipt of reimbursements from the social security system undermines the Treasury to the same extent as tax fraud. The government also has proposed that individuals who facilitate or organize tax fraud by third persons, whether they commit fraud by themselves or not, be punished under the new law.

In 1996 a new government, from the Popular Party, was elected. Its main aim has been to achieve the Maastricht objectives, particularly in regard to the fiscal deficit. If the economic recovery of 1994 and 1995 continues and the fiscal deficit is kept under control, a reduction in marginal tax rates could reappear on the government's political agenda. The main measures related to taxation adopted by 1996's government have been: (i) the new tax on insurance premiums; (ii) the new flat tax rate on capital gains, in the personal income tax; (iii) the new reduced tax rate in CIT for small and medium enterprises; and (iv) the indexation of asset values.

The reform of the PIT in 1998 basically consisted of lowering the tax schedules (for example, reducing the marginal tax rate from 56 per cent to 48 per cent). The reform also modified deductions and eliminated the obligation to declare for the vast majority of low-income taxpayers.

D2 Proposals of the Parliamentary Opposition

During the first half of the 1990s, the main proposals of the PP political opposition to the Socialist government in the tax reform area related to the

PIT rate schedule. According to the Popular Party, the schedule had two main drawbacks. First, marginal tax rates were too high (56 per cent on incomes above Ptas 10 million, or around $US 70,000 of taxable income). Second, the rate schedule is too progressive; that is, the shape of the tax rate schedule is quite vertical, with the highest marginal tax rate being reached too early. Both problems distort economic behaviour and act as a disincentive. Taxpayers observe that a large piece of the cake goes to the government and that every small effort to increase the cake ends with a higher portion of it in the hands of the government.

Other proposals of the Popular Party when in opposition involved corporate and income tax incentives to foster productive activity and simplification of the tax rate schedule by reducing the present number of brackets.

A recently published report financed by the Institute of Family Enterprises (Albi, 1994) proposes making changes in the tax system to improve the competitiveness of family assets employed in businesses and enterprises. The proposals include changes in the imputation system for dividends, in a deduction to correct for double taxation, and in the net worth taxation of family business assets. Most of these proposals were included in tax reforms proposed during 1994 and 1995, as they were adopted and defended by Convergencia i Unio, a political party that in those years supported the Socialist government.

The indexation of the assets, allowing for tax depreciation calculated on market values of the assets, has been a demand of the PP during its opposition period. Once in government the PP in 1996 approved the indexation of balance sheets, in order to eliminate the effects of inflation on corporate and business taxation.

With the change of government in 1996, the main measures adopted by the Popular Party have been those above mentioned related to capital gains, the ACs' revenue share, and the new tax on insurance premiums. The main arguments argued by the Socialist opposition in 1996 have been the regressivity of such measures and the rupture of the solidarity principle (both among territories and among levels and sources of income) associated with them. The socialist opposition criticised the reform of PIT presented by the government to Parliament in 1998 using the same assumptions that criticised the 1996 reforms. The main criticisms were the regressive nature of lowering the tax schedule and changing the deductions system, and the lack of information about the reduction in revenues due to the reform.

D3 Academic Proposals

During the 1980s, the academic profession criticized the tax system because of its lack of neutrality and its disincentive effects on economic decisions. According to the optimal taxation theory, progressive rate schedules and corporate taxation give rise to high efficiency costs. Critics of the tax system focused on issues of tax neutrality, the effets of high marginal tax rates, and double taxation. They argued that the system's highly progressive tax schedule adversely affected the savings rate of families, the propensity to evade taxes, and the inclusion of women in the labour market. For these reasons, some academics argued for a less progressive, flatter rate schedule, with fewer brackets and lower rates (Fuentes Quintana, 1990).

In the run up to the PIT reform of 1992, academics argued for a splitting system to tax the family. Under this system, the income received by each member of the family would be added up and then divided by the number of family members. The tax schedule then would be applied to each part of the total income. Parliament instead adopted a dual tax rate schedule, one for single individuals and another one for families. Under the dual schedule, the highest marginal tax rate (56 per cent) was maintained and critics of the system thought that a good opportunity to reduce the top marginal tax rate had been lost.

At the beginning of the 1990s, the PIT was criticized for being a huge disincentive to family saving (Montoro, 1992). Concerns over the effects of the free movement of capital in Europe also led to arguments against the taxation of capital income. As Europe abandoned efforts to achieve harmonized tax systems, the possibility of effectively taxing capital income vanished and several university professors argued for a reduction in the taxation of capital gains and other income from capital.

Some voices have demanded a radical change in the corporation tax to make it more like a cash-flow tax. On the other hand, a paper prepared by a group of public finance professors recommended a more 'conservative' reform based on the reduction of double taxation, depreciation allowances based on present values, and a greater approximation between accounting and tax rules (Fuentes Quintana, 1990). Most of these proposals were included in the 1995 corporate tax reform.

As far as indirect taxation and payroll taxes are concerned, the question has been raised of the negative impact of high payroll taxes on international trade and, therefore, on the international competitiveness of Spanish economy. Payroll taxes can be supported mostly by labour, via lower wages, or by consumers, via higher prices. Given the rate of unemployment in the Spanish economy and the rigidities in the labour market, a reduction in payroll taxes would probably imply lower prices more than higher wages. Since payroll taxes are not adjusted at the border, assuming they are shifted into prices, it is reasonable to believe that the burden of social security contributions is negatively affecting the competitive position of companies that export to other countries. Under such reasoning, Spain exports less than it would if the same tax revenue was raised from VAT instead of payroll taxes. Therefore, it can be argued that a reduction in payroll taxes and an increase in VAT would improve the trade balance through a decrease in the domestic costs of exports, since exporters could recover VAT on input, and, consequently, exports would increase. As far as the European Monetary System makes difficult the adjustments of the exchange rates to compensate for the deficits of trade, this substitution of VAT for payroll taxes could balance such a reduction in the use of exchange rates as a policy instrument, as it is argued by the defenders of this substitution.

Zabalza (1988) analyses the effects of VAT substitution on the Spanish economy, concluding that a reform such as the one described above would increase prices and real wages and, consequently, that the initial reduction in the cost of labour would be largely offset. The final effect would be an increase in the relative prices of the products of capital-intensive industries: since payroll taxes are a labour cost, a reduction in them would result in an increase in the price of capital relative to the price of labour.

In any case, the debate on a reduction in payroll taxes has to be included in a general discussion of the social security model and its financial equilibrium considering demographic evolution. To promote employment, it would probably be more effective to introduce discrimination in payroll payments, establishing higher rates for skilled workers and lower ones for unskilled workers. Such a plan would introduce a certain level of progressivity to social security contributions, which thus far have been characterized in Spain by their proportionality or, in some cases, regressivity.

E. Conclusion

Taking into account the above opinions, it is possible to maintain that the main focus of tax reforms during the coming years should be on tax administration. The need to modernize the administration and to adapt it to the changes that have occurred in recent years overshadows the need for other tax changes.

The possibility of reducing marginal PIT rates, avidly sought by those segments of the population who would be most affected, is limited by the necessity of controlling the fiscal deficit. A reduction of the tax schedule was approved in 1998, but it does not seem plausible that taxes can be dramatically reduced in the near future.

As far as social security contributions are concerned, the payroll tax reduction that went into effect on 1 January 1995 (accompanied by the VAT increase) will have to satisfy those who have demanded payroll tax cuts. The need to secure the future financial balance of the social security system, while maintaining the present level of benefits, makes any further tax reductions highly improbable. Only to the extent that revenues increase due to improvements in compliance is the possibility of tax reductions likely to appear on the political agenda. Meanwhile, the objective of controlling the deficit leaves little room for loosening tax policy.

References

Albi, E. (1994) 'Fiscalidad y Empresa Familiar', Instituto de la Empresa Familiar.
Comision de las Comunidades Europeas (1993) 'Crecimiento competitividad y empleo. Retos y pistas para entrar en el siglo XXI' COM (93) 700 final, BOCE, suppl. 6/1993.

Cuervo-Arango, C., and Trujillo, J. A. (1986) 'Estructura fiscal e incentivos a la inversion', FEDEA.

De Juan, A. (1992) 'La percepcion de la realidad fiscal por los declarantes de IRPF', Instituto de Estudios Fiscales, Papeles de Trabajo, 24/92.

—— Lasheras, M., and Mayo, R. (1993) 'Voluntary Compliance and Behaviour of Spanish Taxpayers,' International Institute of Public Finance, Berlin Annual Meeting.

Diaz, C., and Delgado, M. (1992) 'Aspectos Psicosociales de la Tributacion: Los Costes del Cumplimiento en el IRPF', Instituto de Estudios Fiscales, Papeles de Trabajo, 13/92.

—— and Fernandez (1993), 'El fraude en las rentas del trabajo. Salarios y pensiones', Instituto de Estudios Fiscales, Papeles de Trabajo, 6193.

—— and Herrera, C. (1990), 'El fraude en el Impuesto sobre el Valor Anadido', Instituto de Estudios Fiscales. Cuadernos de Actualidad, 7/90.

—— and Martinez, J. (1991), 'La Agencia Estatal de Administracion Tributaria. Un Avance en la Modernizacion de las Administraciones Publicas', Cuadernos de Actualidad, 1/91.

Espitia, M., Huerta, C., and Salas, V. (1988), 'Estimulos fiscales a la inversion', Instituto de Estudios Fiscales, monograph 69.

Feige, E. L. (1989), 'The Underground Economies: Tax Evasion and Information Distortion', Cambridge University Press.

Fuentes Quintana, E. (1980), 'Los Principios de la Imposicion Espanola y los Problemas de su Reforma', in *Crecimiento Economico y Crisis Estructural en Espana (1959–80)*, Akal/Textos Publications.

—— *et al.* (1990), 'La Reforma Fiscal los Problemas de la Hacienda Publica Espanola', (ed.) Fuentets Quintana. Civitas.

Garcia Sobrino, E. (1992), 'Comparacion de productos financieros de la nueva ley del IRPF', Instituto de Estudios Fiscales, Papeles de Trabajo, 21/92.

Gonzales-Paramo, J. M. (1992), 'En cuanto corregimos la doble imposicion de los dividendos? Comentarios sobre el uso de medidas de atenuacion', Hacienda Publica Espanola, 2192. Impuesto sobre Sociedades.

—— (1994), 'Política fiscal, competitividad y convergencia el caso de Espana', Instituto de Estudios Fiscales, Papeles de Trabajo, 1/94.

Herrera, C. (1990), 'Distribucion de la Presion Fiscal entre Trabajo y Capital 1982–89', Cuadernos de Actualidad, 6/90.

Lasheras, M., Salas, R., and Perez-Villacastin, E. (1993), 'Efectos de los Incentivos Fiscales en Espana sobre la Adquisicion de Vivienda', Instituto de Estudios Fiscales, Papeles de Trabajo, 5/93.

—— Rabadan, I., and Salas, R. (1993), 'Politica Redistributiva en el IRPF entre 1982 y 1990', Cuadernos de Actualidad, 5/93.

—— and Menendez, I. (1992), 'Tax Administration and Information Systems. The Case of Spain', Workshop on Computerising Tax Administration, Harvard International Tax Program.

Libro Blanco (1990), 'Informe sobre la Reforma de la Imposicion Personal sobre la Renta y el Patrimonio', Ministerio de Economia y Hacienda.

Mauleon, I., and Escobedo, M. (1991), 'Demanda de dinero y economia sumergida', Hacienda Publica Espanola no. 119, Instituto de Estudios Fiscales.

Mayo, R., and Salas, S. (1993), 'La progresividad de la imposicion indirecta. Incidencia de las pautas de gasto de los hogares', Cuadernos de Actualidad, 5/93.

Melis, F. (1992), 'Notas sobre el Fraude Fiscal de las Empresas Espanolas', Instituto de Estudios Fiscales, Moneda and Credito (1991), 192 (mimeo).

Moneda y Credito (1991), Fundación Banco Hispano Americano, 192.

Montoro, C. (1992), 'La armonizacion de la fiscalidad europea en un entorno competitivo', Actualidad Tributaria, 5, Semana 3.

Perez Campanero, J. (1992), 'La perdida de credibilidad de la economia espanola', FEDEA. Informe Tecnico 92–19.

Tanzi, V. (1982), *The Underground Economy in the United States and Abroad*, Lexington Books.

Truyols, A. (1993), 'El Impuesto sobre Sociedades en Terminos de Contabilidad Nacional', Instituto de Estudios Fiscales, Papeles de Trabajo, 2/93.

Zabalza, A. (1988), 'Los Efectos Economicos de la Cotizaciones a la Seguridad Social', En la Fiscalidad de la Empresa, Colecciones Debates, 2, FEDEA.

9 Sweden

KRISTER ANDERSSON AND LEIF MUTÉN

A. Overview

Following the 1986 US tax reform, Sweden, like so many other countries, remodelled its tax system in 1990 according to the principle of lower rates and broader bases. The repeal of special reserves and relief provisions was accompanied by a considerable reduction in corporate and individual income tax rates. Another major change was the abolition of the traditional global (or synthetic) income tax in favour of a dual tax, with lower nominal rates on income from capital. In the area of taxes on goods and services, the base was likewise broadened, although the general VAT rate was kept at its high 25-percent level.

The general thrust of the reform did not include a lowering of the overall tax ratio. Nevertheless, part of the compensation for the reduced rates was accounted for under expected dynamic effects of the reform. The recession of the early 1990s implied that these dynamic effects hardly materialized, and the general tax ratio fell, whereas unemployment compensation and interest on the public debt caused upward pressure on public expenditures.

With a change in government to a non-Socialist coalition in September 1991, the stage was set for further tax adjustments, particularly in the field of capital taxes. Some of these measures, such as the complete abolition of the net wealth tax and the reduction from 30 to 25 percent of the tax rate on income from capital, were postponed until 1995 in the framework of bipartisan crisis programmes. Thus, they would never see the light of day, since the September 1994 election brought the Social Democratic government back.

Other measures were the result of bipartisan political pressure, such as the introduction of lower VAT rates on food and tourist services. There also was a follow-up to the tax reform to introduce better, more corporation-like tax conditions for proprietary firms and partnerships. Finally, in a legislative rush during the last year of its three-year mandate, the government pushed through legislation making dividends of Swedish corporations tax-exempt in the hands of resident shareholders and replacing the former partial dividend deduction system (see B2.3 below for details). The classical double taxation was quickly restored in 1994.

Future tax developments were affected by the victory of Social Democrats in the 18 September 1994 general election and the positive outcome of the 13

November 1994 referendum on joining the European Union. References are made later in this chapter to what has happened in this context.

B. The Tax System

B1 Personal Income Tax

B1.1 Tax Rates

Income taxation has a long history in Sweden, beginning, after some abandoned efforts, in 1862. The modern era started in 1910 or at its very latest in 1928, when the present municipal income tax law and a corresponding act on state (i.e. central government) income tax were adopted. Much has changed since, however. The original concept, under which municipal income tax (payable at the provincial and municipal government levels as well as to the church) was a relatively small addition to the general state income tax, has changed. The municipal income tax has risen to an average (between districts) compound (adding all three government levels) of slightly above 31 percent of income above the personal exemption of SEK8,600 ($1,300).

Under the 1990 reform, the classes of income were reduced to three: business (including income from agriculture and renting property other than private homes), employment, and capital (including income from renting private homes and capital gains). The municipal income tax on property and business income earned by those not resident in the local government district has been abolished (they pay all their tax in the district where they are resident), and income from capital is now not subject to municipal tax.

Meanwhile, the central government income tax has been split into a schedular tax on income from capital (including, in principle, capital gains, although gains on shares and homes get special treatment) at a 30 percent proportional rate with no basic exemption, and a tax on income from other sources of revenue, notably employment and business income in the widest sense. This latter tax is levied only on incomes above a breaking point, indexed and presently set at SEK209,100 ($31,680), making more than half of Swedes exempt. There is only one rate, 20 percent (plus a token SEK200 for all taxpayers), so that the maximum marginal tax on earned income, assuming a 31 percent municipal tax, is 51 percent, much below the approximately 80 percent rate once applied to the top bracket. A provisional increase of the state income tax rate to 25 percent (cf. below, Sect. D2) presently increases the total to 56 percent.

Non-residents of Sweden obtaining income from employment in Sweden do not pay municipal income tax; rather, they pay a proportional withholding tax to the central government of 25 percent (for artists, the rate is 15 percent, but on the gross). On income from capital, non-residents pay tax only on capital gains on real property (or shares in real property corporations) and, by withholding, on dividends. The latter tax is basically 30 percent, but reduced in all tax treaties.

B1.2 Tax Base[1]

The original concept of taxable income excluded capital gains in the proper sense. A deeming provision characterized short-term gains on property acquired through purchase or exchange as speculative gains, and these were subject to tax, albeit on a sliding scale depending on the time since the purchase. Gradually, the attitude towards capital gains taxation changed, and gains are now taxable without time restriction. Reliefs for homeowners have been tried in different forms. Indexation of the cost price was part of the first legislative package but was dropped in favour of a 'maximum' rule, under which a portion of the proceeds was taxed at a 30 percent rate: specifically, a maximum of 30 percent of the proceeds on sales of a principal residence and 60 percent on sales of a vacation home. This treatment resulted in a net tax payment of 9 and 18 percent of the proceeds respectively. A roll-over provision was tried but dropped. In 1993, the roll-over provision came back, but the maximum rule disappeared in favour of a general 50 percent reduction.

As to capital gains on shares, no indexation but several maximum rules were applied. The enterprise-friendly attitude of the 1991 cabinet was reflected in a reduction from 30 to 25 percent of the effective tax rate applied to gains on shares. With the abolition of the individual income tax on dividends, some adjustment was needed on the capital gains tax side. Pending a further study of the Norwegian system for adjusting the capital gains tax base with the amount of retained corporate profits, a provisional reduction by half of the taxable share gains was introduced, making the effective rate 12.5 percent. Both reductions were abolished as the classical system of taxing corporate dividends was reintroduced in 1994.

The concept of income has been widened with respect to benefits in kind. Sweden has never tried the system of taxing the employer, but the comprehensive taxation of company cars and employer-provided meals has been brought close to perfection. Employee parking and employer-paid travel to and from work constitute less of a problem, given the basic attitude of such travel being an income-related, hence deductible, expense. The tide is turning on that one as well, however. In the context of tax simplification, a basic amount for travel to and from work of SEK4,000 is non-deductible. Only an excess is a valid deduction.

The most important development, and one that has been strongly reflected in the savings behaviour of households, has been in the treatment of homes and mortgage interest payments. The original concept was one under which the imputed income of the taxpayer's home was taxable. All interest expenses,

---

[1] Here, it is not intended to give a full description of the system, but rather to highlight a couple of controversial areas. Table 9.1. describes in brief developments 1988–96.

regardless of whether they referred to income-yielding investments or private consumption loans, were deductible in full, including mortgage interest payments.

The imputed income, originally the result of a detailed assessment of rental value on the one hand and expenses for upkeep and financing on the other, was standardized as a percentage, later progressive, of the assessed value of the property. The deductibility of interest, combined with extremely high progressive tax rates and the absence of inflation adjustment of the loans, made homeowners profit by increasing their mortgage loans. A first step to remedy this situation was splitting up the tax between normal tax and surtax and allowing a deduction for the interest-caused deficit only from the base of the former tax. Thus, the tax reduction caused by loan interest was reduced from—in many cases—80 percent to a maximum of around 50 percent.

With the 1990 reform the figure came down further, to 30 and sometimes even 21 percent. This was brought about, first, by abolishing the tax on imputed income from the taxpayer's home in favour of a 1.5 percent (state) property tax and, second, by making non-business interest expenses deductible from interest income only. A net deficit was not deductible from income, but a proportion of it—30 percent on the first SEK100,000, 21 percent on the excess—could be taken as a credit against income tax. There is no tracing of loans. Thus interest on consumption credits gets the same treatment as mortgage interest.

Another area where the tax base has been made more comprehensive is with respect to hobby income. Hobby farms, of course, have always been regarded as income sources, and the deficit problem had to be tackled by a proper evaluation of the benefits in kind derived from the estate. In the case of a horse kept for leisure-time riding, the rule of thumb accepts one horse, but regards several of them as a source of income. Other hobbies were deemed income sources depending on whether there was a realistic prospect that they would bring positive income—a taxpayer could not, however, ensure a deduction for regular deficits by showing a profit in one single year. The post-1990 rule is now quite clear: if the result is negative, the activity is a hobby, if positive, it is a source of income, yet with the right to carry forward losses from the previous five years. As a compromise with nature-loving voters, those picking berries and fungi in the woods would enjoy a basic exemption of SEK5,000 before being taxed on the proceeds.

The 1990 reform was not complete with respect to the treatment of proprietary firms and partnerships. Only in December 1993 was legislation implemented to achieve a certain approximation between the rules for such business income and those applied to corporations. The legislation contains two elements.

One is a subdivision of business income into income from business activity and from capital yield respectively. A positive adjustment is made, when the business capital is positive (and above a certain limit). In this case, an amount corresponding to the net invested capital multiplied by the 'government credit rate' plus one percentage point is deemed the capital yield and is subject to the 30 percent proportional tax that applies to income from capital. If the capital is negative, a corresponding negative adjustment may be made, referring to deficit (negative) income from capital with the imputed negative interest being treated under the 30(21) percent rule for negative income from capital, and the business profit increased (or loss reduced) by the corresponding amount.

The other measure is the introduction of a so-called 'expansion fund', allowing a set-aside of profits against payment of a 28 percent tax (which corresponds to the corporate income tax rate). By this method, capital retained in the business will not be subject to higher tax than profits retained in a corporation. If the set-aside is brought back to account, typically if used for financing investments or to be taken out of the business by the owner, the regular tax applies, but the expansion fund tax is refunded.

B1.3 *Treatment of Family*

The traditional approach to income taxation was the joint assessment of husband and wife, albeit with each spouse filling out his or her return. To stop tax-motivated divorces, the law was amended so that individuals who divorced but still lived together were treated the same as spouses; in addition, the new rules treated couples living together as spouses if they had (or had had) common children. The steep progressivity of the tax made household taxation a strongly negative factor in the other spouse's choice to enter the labour market. A splitting system in accordance with the US model was considered to remedy the 'penalty tax on marriage', but the negative incentive towards joining the labour market had to be removed by a full system of separate taxation. Initially, at the end of the 1960s, this was implemented for earned income only. Later on, separate taxation was consistently made the rule, except with respect to the net wealth tax.

The issue naturally arose whether one spouse could employ the other in his or her business. The solution was not to repeal the prohibition against a deduction for wages and benefits paid to the employer's spouse. Instead, spouses may share the income from the business, provided that the other spouse makes a substantial contribution, although the other spouse's share is limited to a market-conforming salary.

A deduction may be claimed with respect to the hiring of children only if the child is above the age of 16 and is paid at a normal wage rate. The tax treatment of children in some cases includes joint taxation of net wealth but not of other income. There have been a number of court cases concerning the use of a partnership to split income between parents and children. The most abusive of such constructions have, in practice, been stopped.

The general tax relief (exemption) for children was abolished in 1947 in favour of a general child subsidy, payable to the guardian, normally the mother, of a resident child up to the age of 16 (other subsidies supplement this general one for older children and students). The reason for this reform was a comparison between the net value of the child exemption to a top-bracket taxpayer and to a taxpayer with low income or insufficient income even to make full use of the exemption. Needless to say, this system tends to increase the tax ratio to GDP, and a refundable tax credit with the same economic implication would reduce the amount of tax collections and government expenditure without any real difference in distributive effect.

There was for a long time some relief for one-parent families, but not any more. The payment of child support is non-deductible and not taxable for the recipient, this in contrast to the treatment of alimony to the ex-spouse. Although gradually becoming more rare with the increased activity of women in the labour market, alimony remains deductible to the payor and taxable to the payee.

With respect to the net wealth tax, joint taxation is still the rule, although each spouse declares his or her wealth and each pays his or her share of the total tax assessed on the basis of the joint net wealth. (The net wealth tax was abolished in 1991, but the coming into force of the law repealing it was postponed, most recently in 1994, when the decision was taken, in principle, to restore the tax permanently.)

B1.4 Indexation for Inflation

The traditional conflict with respect to the indexation of brackets and exemptions is between those who want indexation to prevent fiscal drag and invisible tax increases, and those who want tax increases to remain invisible so that compensatory measures to limit them or maintain the status quo will, politically, stand out as tax reductions. With the help of inflation, Swedish ministers of finance have at times been able to achieve a long-term increase of the effective total tax ratio, while in the meantime introducing one bill after the other ostensibly aimed at reducing the tax.

The inflation rate came tumbling down in the course of the recession, and, accordingly, indexation is not a very hot topic any more. The 1990 reform package was presented with a study from a committee entitled in English 'Inflation-adjusted income taxation' in which a system of indexation was proposed, both of the exemptions and bracket limits (as had been done before), and of the tax base (largely a novelty). The government, both the outgoing one in 1990–1 and the following ones, felt, however, that the present modest inflation rate did not provide sufficient reason for a full indexation of the system. The current indexation rules only affect exemption limits, and those adjustments have, at times, been less than the inflation rate.

Nevertheless, it is an indexation argument that lies behind the choice of the 30 percent tax rate on income from capital. The fundamental calculation governing this choice is simple: assuming a 10 percent interest rate and a 4 percent inflation rate, a 30 percent tax on gross interest will correspond to a 50 percent tax on net interest. It is noteworthy that the same choice of capital income rate in Norway was based on the totally different argument that capital is also hit by net wealth tax, making the cumulative net wealth and capital income taxation comparable to the regular taxation of employment income.

As mentioned earlier, the indexation of capital gains from real property was largely abolished in the 1990 reform and has now been totally abandoned.[2] The 50 percent reduction of the base for homes is obviously not an adequate compensation if the gain does no more than cover the loss in purchasing power of the money, yet, a reduced rate has often been regarded as a second-best solution when the political will or the administrative resources are insufficient for proper indexation. Reflecting the same measures on the liability side, there is no tax on debtors' gains on nominal debts, an argument often used as a defence for the failure to index capital gains on real property.

With respect to income from capital, there is no exemption of the part of interest income that merely corresponds to the price level change. According to a decision from 1943, index compensation on a loan, guaranteed to be repaid in index-adjusted money, was deemed to be interest and thus taxable even at a time when most capital gains on securities were exempt. The development of new financial instruments has slowly caught up with this otherwise slightly awkward decision. The rules provide for the taxation as interest of the real yield on zero-interest bonds and the like as interest. Moreover, gains and losses on foreign exchange are dealt with as capital gains and losses (including, in the case of the latter, a reduction to 70 percent of the loss before 30 (21) percent of it is used as a reduction of tax).

B2 Corporation Income Tax

B2.1 Tax Base

Sweden never had a separate corporate income tax law, but rather included corporations and other entities among persons liable to income tax, albeit in many respects under different rules.[3] Since 1938, the corporate tax has been proportional, and this, in turn, made the lawmaker somewhat less observant with respect to the opportunities of moving profits between the tax years. In

[2] There is a small compensation in the form of a minimum base for properties acquired before 1952. For such properties, there is an option to set the base at 150% of the assessed value in 1952 (plus improvements after that time). There has been a good deal of inflation after 1952, however.
[3] Partnerships were always liable to file tax returns, but their profits are nevertheless taxed as part of the income of the partners. This, however, does not exclude them from being treated as legal entities, for instance with respect to the treatment of the sale of a share in a partnership. Here, the seller is considered to have sold his share of the partnership, rather than a share in the assets and liabilities of the partnership. In other words, on the partnership's balance sheet, which forms the base of the income tax assessment of all partners, the same residual values of the partnership's assets will apply even after the sale, whereas any additional price above book value paid by the purchaser will be taxed as a capital gain of the seller and enter as a new capital gains tax base of the purchaser.

1938, new legislation went as far as to authorize free depreciation for corporations, a flagrant disregard of the time-value of money. This provision was retracted thirteen years later, when experience had shown shipowners ready to write down newly built tonnage to SEK1 from the first year.

With free depreciation came the need to treat gains and losses on depreciable assets as profit-relevant rather than as normally tax-exempt capital gains (and non-deductible capital losses). This came, accordingly, first in the context of corporate profits taxation, but was later extended to proprietary firms and partnerships. Thus, while Sweden has never formally applied the German pattern of treating all gains and losses on business assets as profit-relevant, the concept of capital gains inside a business has shrunk to insignificance, and the odd capital loss (the latest case an insufficiently insured loss of cash in a supermarket robbery) is seen more or less as irrelevant.

It is, moreover, fair to say that the tradition in Swedish tax law has been to show more understanding of the needs of business enterprises than of those of taxpaying individuals. The free depreciation was, of course, discarded as too far-reaching, but the steady use of the full-year convention for new assets, the disregarding of scrap values for depreciation purposes, and the use of the declining-balance method of depreciation with an accompanying right to full write-off of movables within a five-year period are cases in point.

The valuation of inventories for tax purposes was, up to the 1990 reform, another example of legislative largesse. The new rules are far from liberal, however. No LIFO rule is applied, only cost or market, whichever is the lower, combined with a niggardly 3 percent for obsolescence that is applied to the cost price but not to the market price if that price is lower.

Whereas the concept of capital gain and loss has an extremely minor role in the taxation of corporations, there is, on one point, a distinction between current income and capital loss, namely with regard to shares not dealt with as stock-in-trade, not representing a 25 percent or greater share, and not otherwise held for business purposes. Losses on such shares are deductible from similar gains only, and any net loss might be carried forward to the next year but used against share gains only.

It is relevant to note that in the course of the 1990 reform, while the nominal tax rate was reduced from 52 to 30 percent, it was found that to prevent the effective tax rate from increasing, a special reserve had to be instituted, the so-called 'tax equalization reserve' (SURV). Only by that means was it possible to keep the effective tax rate below 24 percent, the level where it had been under the previous regime. The SURV was eventually abolished from 1994 on, yet the accompanying reduction of the rate to 28 percent necessitated a new reserve, the 'period equalization reserve', so that the effective rate would not exceed slightly more than 25 percent.[4]

---

[4] The SURV, in principle, had to be clawed back and made part of taxable profits at the time it was abolished. However, since the original intention had been for the SURV to be retained

The reserve allows a tax-exempt set-aside of up to 25 percent of profits with the obligation of bringing the amount back to tax by the sixth year after the set-aside. This reserve was primarily conceived to ensure that firms would have sufficient taxable profits to make use of the liberal depreciation rules in a period of expected heavy investment.

It is worth noting, in light of the somewhat comparable role played by the period equalization reserve, that there was no strong need felt for a provision on loss carry-backs. The loss carry-forward provision, in contrast, was liberalized in 1990 to be open-ended rather than limited to five years, as before. Several restrictions on the carry-forward provisions were added in 1993, mainly with a view to prevent commercial dealing in loss corporations.

One of these restrictions implied a prohibition against a corporation using taxable subsidy payments from a new affiliate corporation to cover losses carried forward from years before the acquisition that established the affiliation. Lacking a provision on consolidated returns, Sweden has for a long time permitted open subsidy payments between affiliated corporations, but this restriction on the use of such subsidies should be seen in the context of the general reluctance to recognize the transferability of deductions for earlier years' losses.

As to international activities, Sweden has traditionally applied worldwide taxation, although very much modified by a great number of tax treaties, at present more than seventy. Unilateral adjustment of international double taxation came late, but a foreign tax credit rule as well as the alternative right of deducting foreign tax from the base, is in place. Intercorporate foreign dividends are exemp, provided there is a 25 percent ownership or a business-motivated holding and provided that the foreign tax is comparable to (in practice, not less than half) the Swedish tax. If there is insufficient tax on the foreign corporation, the Swedish parent will be taxable, but will enjoy a 13 percent foreign tax credit corresponding to assumed underlying foreign tax.

There is a provision on controlled foreign corporations (CFCs) denying treatment as a foreign corporation to Swedish-controlled corporations that do not pay foreign tax comparable to the Swedish tax, and that are not included under tax treaties concluded with a number of listed countries.[5] If there is domestic control, direct and indirect shareholders having at least a 10 percent share in such an entity are taxable on that share under the rules normally applied to partnerships.

Most Swedish tax treaties apply the credit method rather than the exemption method to deal with double taxation. This was not always the case;

without time limitation, a compromise was struck, under which half the SURV was brought back without tax, the other half with tax but spread over five years. In 1994, the new government introduced a rule under which, in principle, the whole SURV would be taxed except the fraction that had already been brought back tax exempt.

[5] The Swedish action against CFCs came a quarter of a century later than the US Subpart F legislation. Until then, foreign exchange restrictions were relied on.

however, since the introduction of the rule under which a deduction for losses incurred abroad is denied if corresponding profits are exempt in Sweden, it has been seen as being in the interest of business enterprises to have the credit method applied, and recent tax treaties have been drafted accordingly.

Developments in the EU member countries are of particular interest to Sweden now that the country has gained membership, effective 1 January 1995. Sweden had already gone a long way to satisfy the parent–subsidiary directive before joining and has duly implemented the directive thereafter. With respect to the merger directive, there was a considerable body of precedence pointing mainly in the same way as the directive. Some polishing of the rules was made, however, to harmonize the Swedish legislation fully with the directive. Finally, the arbitration convention, if opened to the new members, should cause no troubles, especially since, in its recent revised tax treaty with Germany, Sweden has accepted a more far-reaching arbitration clause.

B2.2 Tax Rates

The abolition of the corporate municipal income tax was accompanied by a corresponding increase of the central government nominal tax rate to 52 percent. With the 1990 reform, as mentioned earlier, the nominal rate was brought down to 30 percent, yet the effective rate of some 24 percent would have risen as a consequence of the abolition of a number of reserves and other tax-saving opportunities, but for the introduction of the SURV. The same consideration lies behind the successor to the SURV, the period equalization reserve, introduced at the same time that the nominal corporate income tax rate was reduced to 28 percent.

One half of capital gains on shares were taxable 1994, and for individuals the effective rate on that half was reduced to 25 percent. Since 1995, all these gains are taxed in full at 30 percent.

B2.3 Treatment of Distributed Profits

Sweden always used to apply the classical system of double taxation of corporations and shareholders. There have been some exceptions to this rule, however.

One such exception had to do with closely held corporations that were engaged in business activities. In this case, the managing shareholder could, in practice, use his own salary as a means of deciding the level of corporate profit. There was no effective check with respect to those actively working in their corporations as to whether their remuneration was excessive or not, and many closely held corporations were accordingly steadily realizing zero profits, thus effectively achieving the partnership treatment that, for instance, in the USA is provided for under sub-chapter S.

Another exception came in the context of the 1967 legislation, which restricted tax exemption for intercorporate dividends to include substantial

(25 percent) or business-related holdings only. The idea behind the so-called 'Annell deduction' (named after its originator, a high-ranking tax official) was to facilitate share issues by making the price of capital acquired through such issues cheaper than it was under the classical double tax system that normally applied. At the time the deduction was abolished, effective from 1994 (it had undergone several permutations since enactment), it allowed dividends declared on newly issued shares to be deductible up to a cumulative maximum of 100 percent of the paid-up amount, but not more than 10 percent in any one year, and not over a period longer than twenty years after the issue of the new shares.

When, in December 1993, the drastic step was taken to abolish the income tax on dividends paid by Swedish corporations to resident shareholders, the Annell deduction was likewise abolished.[6] There were some limitations to the exemption. First of all, it did not apply to dividends paid on shares held as stock-in-trade. Second, the exemption was limited to dividends paid by Swedish corporations to residents of Sweden; this limitation basically was to serve as a bargaining chip in the hope of achieving similar relief from other treaty countries. Third, in December 1993 and in the first half of 1994, limitations were introduced to prevent abuses in the form of excessive dividends. This risk was perceived as imminent, since a new government was (rightly) expected to make the tax-exempt dividend a one-time affair.

Finally, the special rules concerning closely held corporations were retained, with the result that dividends above a percentage of invested capital (increased, after the 1993 modification, by 10 percent of payroll) were still dealt with as remuneration for work rather than as dividends.

In the context of the introduction of the dividend exemption, there was extensive discussion of what this meant with respect to capital gains taxation. Obviously, it could be argued that once double taxation was abolished, corporate income tax would be enough. Capital gains on shares, to the extent they represented accumulated retained after-tax profits, would require no further taxation as capital gains once dividends were exempted from income tax.

On the other hand, it was argued that capital gains normally include not just retained profits but also expectations for the future. The simple solution—and the one adopted—was to reduce the tax base of capital gains on shares by half, assuming that only half of the gains represented retained profits. For a while the government kept its eyes on the sophisticated Norwegian system for adjusting the capital gains tax base with the amount of retained profits. This system was, however, not regarded as sufficiently

---

[6] There was, of course, a slight discrepancy between the limitation to the tax exemption and the deduction being abolished. Those shareholders, who as non-residents had benefited from dividends deductible under the Annell law, would not be better off than before, with respect to their tax on dividends, whereas the corporations would be denied their deductions.

studied to take the risk of its implementation. Expert witness from Norway had testified both that the system there was in chaos and that it worked well.

B2.4 *Concessions to Small Enterprises*

Sweden offers few privileges to small and medium-sized enterprises. Apart from the now obsolete system of allowing high salaries to managing shareholders, outright concessions are basically found only in the context of wealth and transfer taxes. Instead, legislation has been introduced and gradually sharpened to limit abuses involving closely held corporations. The deeming of excessive dividends and capital gains as remuneration is just one case in point. Another is the set of rules prohibiting the spending of corporate means to purchase assets for the use of a principal shareholder or his relatives (by way of taxing the owner in full on the amount), as well as the prohibition against loans to shareholders. Although, arguably, some of these rules might have been rendered obsolete with the abolition of the system of double taxation, there were no signs of such a review taking place at the time double taxation was suspended.

Soon after the reintroduction of the classical system, however, a study was initiated with the purpose of finding some form of relief for smaller corporations, preferably on the corporation's side, but if that would not be practical, on the side of the shareholders.

B3 Payroll Taxes

B3.1 *Earmarked for Social Security*

Payroll taxes to pay for social benefits have been introduced gradually. One of the most significant changes was the introduction in 1960, on top of the basic 'people's pension', of an additional pension that is related both to the number of years the individual has been enrolled and to his or her income in the fifteen best years. Under the motto 'employers pay', the system was introduced and expanded. At the time, nothing was heard of the arguments, often made in the USA, that high social security contributions impair the employers' ability to give their staff a raise, so that, in fact, it is the employee who pays, rather than the employer.

Payroll taxes traditionally are paid in entirely by employers, but self-employed individuals have to pay a corresponding contribution on their own. The bulk of the contributions are earmarked for social security, in particular for pension purposes, but also for health insurance and the income-related sick pay benefits. Interestingly, whereas the income-related benefits have a ceiling provision, whereby income above the ceiling does not affect the amount of the benefit, the contributions are paid on employment income and personal business income without any limit provision. Since the total employer contribution is 33.06 percent and the own contribution (i.e. the contribution made by self-employed individuals) is 31.25 percent of net income (although both are deductible from the income tax base) these contributions represent a very important element in the 'tax wedge'.

B3.2 Not Earmarked for Social Security

Passive income as well as income earned by those who have passed the pension age (65 years) carries a 'special wage tax', representing the tax element of the social security contributions. The rate of this tax is 21.39 percent of wages or net enterprise income, and like all other social security contributions, it is deductible from the income tax base if paid by the income-earner himself.

B3.3 Trends

Two developments are discernible in this area. One is the discussion whether employees should be informed about their gross salary before payroll taxes, so as to better appreciate the importance of the tax wedge. With both the income taxes and the VAT openly accounted for, it seems to run against good principles to establish as important a levy as the social security tax as a hidden tax.

The other development is the gradual introduction of own contributions not just for the self-employed, but for all taxpayers. The theory, as it was tried in the 1920s and up to 1960, was that a special item on the tax bill named for the people's pension would be one of those rare taxes taxpayers like to pay. The official cynicism about this is probably total, but the 1991–4 government had a preference for open taxes—politically motivated or founded on democratic principles. The upshot was the social security fees paid as own contributions, presently at 4.95 percent. They have a ceiling at an income of presently SEK176,000, they are deductible from taxable income, and they are not paid by those above retirement age (65).

Another element was the introduction of employee contributions to unemployment insurance, long a jealously guarded preserve of the trade unions but for a while about to be made independent of them. The initial rate was 1 percent, heading for 4 percent, but the charge is now part of the above-mentioned employee-paid social security fee, payable to the health insurance programme.

B4 Value-Added and Sales Taxes

Sweden tried a retail sales tax (at 5 percent of the tax-inclusive price, and with important exemptions) during the Second World War. The tax was then seen as an emergency measure, running against the principles of the social state by being regressive. It was abolished soon after the War, only to be reintroduced again a couple of years later. The rate was gradually increased to 10 percent.

At that rate, serious erosion developed. The cascading when business inputs had to be purchased at retail prices was difficult to remedy. The tax exemption for wholesalers tempted many wholesalers, particularly in the cash-and-carry trade, to compete with the retailers by illegally selling tax-free to what effectively were consumers. Border adjustments in observation of the destination principle were made, but there was no effective relief for input taxes.

Therefore, in 1968, Sweden unilaterally, without being in any way pressed to do so by the European Common Market, decided to introduce a VAT. The VAT law was thoroughly redrafted in 1994, although with rather limited material change.

To begin with the VAT rate was expressed as 10 percent of the price including the tax itself (equals 11.1 per cent of the price exclusive of the tax). At the time of the 1990 reform, the rate was expressed at 25 percent of the tax-exclusive price, which is now the base used by all other EU countries. Sweden was not quite a one-rate country, however, since the VAT base for restaurant services was reduced by 30 percent and the base for some contracting work was reduced by 80 percent, with the 25 percent rate applied to the reduced amount.

In 1992, the rate on food was reduced to 18 percent, but it was later adjusted again to 21 percent (and from 1996 it is down at 12 percent). In 1993, the tax on tourist services, such as hotel rooms, was reduced to 12 percent, and restaurant meals were made subject to the 21 percent food rate (now again 25 percent). Although the 1990 reform went very far in including all services in the tax base, discussions are going on about extending the lower tax rate at least to some services. The advantage of a single rate, long regarded as extremely important and still very much an ideal to tax technicians, has a tendency to sink into oblivion among makers of tax policy.

The EU's sixth directive on VAT has influenced Swedish legislation, although not in an absolute sense. There is little zero-rating—only for exports and, until 1995, for newspapers, who now pay at 7 percent. An intricate system has been introduced to achieve neutrality in the competition between independent suppliers of goods and services to government and the production of goods and services by government itself. With respect to the central government, this is achieved by having all VAT on deliveries to central government (even VAT on bills supporting civil servants' travel claims) charged to a separate budget account, so as not to affect the budget appropriations of the administrative unit paying VAT.

In the case of local governments, the somewhat more complicated route has been taken of granting local governments a refund of input taxes.

B5 Excises and Other Important Consumption Taxes

Sweden is using the excise weapon to a considerable extent. There has been a reduction in the number of items subject to excise—gone are the taxes on sweets, toothpaste, hygiene products, perfume, video tapes, etc. Left are the traditional excises on automobiles, petroleum products, tobacco, and alcoholic beverages.

The petroleum taxes have been modified, first to accommodate the inclusion of petroleum products under the VAT, and later with respect to environmental policies. Lead-free petrol and low-sulphur diesel and fuel oil have been given preferences.

Another environmental tax measure has been directed towards emissions of carbon dioxide, but here ambitions have been modified by the inability of the EU, internally as well as in discussion with the USA, to come to terms with the problem by setting general, international standards. This has been seen as particularly important given the well-founded assumption that this type of tax is not subject to border tax adjustments under the GATT. An unresolved problem here is whether Sweden can impose an excise on electricity from which there is substantial relief for high-energy consumers in the manufacturing industry. Another development is the introduction of special duties on nuclear power (with no border tax adjustments), seen as preparing for the closing-down of nuclear power plants officially foreseen, as well as to a lesser extent on hydroelectric power.

With respect to tobacco, the relatively high VAT rate and the traditionally rather high mark-up in the distribution chain raises the problem that Sweden, if it wants to increase the relative share of specific tax on tobacco products to EU standards, will have to raise total taxation to a point where the products would be more expensive than anywhere else in Europe.

A somewhat similar situation would occur with respect to beer, partly because Sweden imposes no tax other than VAT on light beer (this in the interest of keeping alcohol consumption down), whereas the EU has a definition that includes light beer under the excise. Sweden's relatively high excise duty on beer with higher alcohol content would, accordingly, necessitate a much higher price for light beer as well. Alternatively, the tax would have to be reduced, a development possibly necessitated by the increasing importance of private border trade, particularly in the area close to Denmark.

In other respects, Sweden, while keeping its alcohol taxation at a very high level, has modified the structure somewhat. There is no other *ad valorem* tax besides VAT, and tax is charged at specific rates applied in relation to alcohol content. This strategy is necessitated by the fact that an *ad valorem* tax on the cheaper variants of hard liquor, to be sufficiently high to keep consumption of such products down, would price better brands out of the market.

B6 Net Wealth and Capital Transfer Taxes

The net wealth tax was initially a surcharge levied by a percentage of net wealth being added to the taxable income of individuals for purposes of the progressive state tax. In that respect, it was very close to the British surtax on 'unearned income', albeit based on the stock of wealth rather than on the yield. Later on, from 1947, the net wealth tax was charged as a seperate, progressive tax on net wealth, but still with one connection to the income tax: a ceiling rule was intended to guarantee that total income and net wealth tax did not exceed 80 percent, later 85 percent, of income. The ceiling was, however, not absolute. At least as much net wealth tax as applied to half of a taxpayer's net wealth was in all cases payable. Thus, there would always be some tax, even if the net wealth was invested in assets that did not yield annual income.

The net wealth tax was abolished in principle once the non-Socialist government took over in 1991, but, partly as a result of political compromises in the context of the 1992 crisis programmes to defend the exchange rate, the effective date of the abolition was postponed. Therefore, the old tax, although at a rate of 1.5 percent (earlier the top marginal rate was 3 percent), is still payable under the transitional provisions to the law once intended as abolishing it. Under the new government the decision in principle has been taken to restore it permanently.

Apart from the (rather insignificant) yield of the net wealth tax, the tax was seen as having some merit in facilitating the control of individual tax returns. For net wealth tax purposes, all taxpayers with gross assets above a very modest amount had to complete their income tax return with a net wealth return. Compared with the same return for the previous year, this could occasionally be used by the tax authorities as a means of estimating whether a taxpayer's declared income in conjunction with movements on capital account had provided the taxpayer with sufficient means to keep up his standard of living. Present assessment methods have rendered this use of the net wealth tax return obsolete, however.

The base of the net wealth tax never included furniture, antiques, pieces of art, etc., and while jewellery was in principle taxable, tax on jewellery was normally paid only by those who had it stolen and reported the value to the police. Automobiles, sailboats, and other similar assets kept outside the home were taxable.

The valuation of property, while not posing great problems with respect to cash, bank accounts, and stock quoted on the Stock Exchange, leaves much to be desired in the case of real property, and has caused serious problems with respect to unquoted shares, partnerships, and proprietary firms. The tendency in recent years of the net wealth tax has been to introduce special reliefs in these cases. In the latest round of such modifications (1996), the net value of proprietary firms and partnerships was not taxable, quoted shares taxable at 100 percent of the quoted value (earlier 75 percent), and over-the-counter-quoted shares not taxable.

Taxable net wealth does not include the value of pensions or life insurance (if it has no repurchase value). For trusts, there are provisions for taxation of the beneficiary in many cases. In 1995, however, the previous exemption rule for foreign insurance was changed for insurance taken up or expanded after 30 June 1995.[7]

Transfer taxes on inheritance and gifts are in principle applied to the donee, legatee, etc. but for practical purposes in the case of death duties the estate pays the duty. The marital law provides, according to the choice of the spouses, either a separation of assets or a right for each spouse, at the time of one spouse's death or at the time of separation, to take one half of the other spouse's property (provided that property has not been separated as his or her own). Thus, in normal cases, half the common estate goes to the surviving spouse without any tax, and as for the rest, there is a SEK280,000 exemption; the exemption for children and other close relatives is SEK70,000.

Gift tax is levied on the donee's acquisition. There is a cumulation between gifts received within ten years before the death of the donor and inheritance or legacy from the same donor. Both gifts and inheritances from a married couple are normally regarded as coming separately, one half each, from the spouses, provided the legal arrangement is set up that way.

It is noteworthy that while the Swedes never adopted rules providing for an income tax deduction for charitable gifts, both the income tax laws, the net wealth tax law, and the law on taxation of inheritance and gifts exempt charitable foundations and associations. The detailed classification will not be described here, but it is worth mentioning that the charities that enjoy an exemption from gift tax are defined somewhat more widely than those exempted from inheritance tax. Therefore, there is some motive for charities affected to try to influence prospective donors not to postpone showing their generosity until they die.

The 1991 government cut the inheritance and gift tax rates by half at an early stage. It is yet somewhat early in the day to analyse the effects of this. It is noteworthy, however, that Professor Edward Andersson of Finland has observed that in the other Nordic countries, where tax rates before this change were approximately half those of Sweden, the ratio of inheritance and gift tax collected in proportion to GDP was approximately the same in all countries.[8]

B7 The Local Tax System

Mention has already been made of the municipal income tax being the most important tax on individuals' incomes. The prerogative of the municipalities and provincial councils, as well as parishes of the Church of Sweden, to

---

[7] A premium tax on foreign insurance, introduced with the tax reform, compensating for the yield tax payable by Swedish insurance institutions, was repealed in 1996 in favour of a system of yield tax payable by the insured.

[8] Edward Andersson, *Arvsskattens avkastning i de nordiska länderna* (The Yield of the Inheritance Tax in the Nordic Countries), *Skattenytt*, 1991: 505.

establish the municipal income tax rate on those liable to tax in their areas has existed for a very long time. The freedom of the municipalities in this regard is, however, limited to setting the rate. Provisions on the tax base are made in laws made by the Riksdag.

Initially, the municipal income tax was deductible from income for purposes of the progressive state income tax. Based on the argument that this deduction was of greater value to high-bracket individuals than to those in lower brackets, this deduction was abolished. If this had been the real reason, the problem could have been solved by an adjustment of the rate schedule. The real reason underlying the reform was a different one, however. The minister of finance felt that the steep and steady upward movement of the municipal tax rates might be explained by the attitude of municipal voters, who felt that with the deduction from the income tax base the municipal tax was, to a large extent, effectively paid by the central Treasury.

Later, continued increases in the municipal tax rates up to the present average of some 31 percent moved the government to establish more far-reaching measures to stem the tide. A halt to further local government tax increases was declared, succeeded in 1994 by a provision making any local government that increased its tax rate face an almost matching cut in government subsidies. The constitutionality of this legislation was doubtful, to say the least, and even the cutting of subsidies, while not unconstitutional in form, was at least a limitation of local government sovereignty that was rather far from the intentions of the writers of the Constitution.

Finally, it has always been an issue to what extent there should be compensation for the very considerable differences in income levels between different local government districts. Obviously, if central government subsidies could always be counted on to make up for all such differences, nothing much would be left of local financial responsibility and the rights of local governments to establish their own standards for municipal public services. If the differences were allowed to stay altogether uncompensated, there would be an exodus from the poorest districts, where tax rates would be the highest and public services the lowest.

The present government feels that an equalization tax levied on the richest communities in favour of the poorest ones might do the trick. It has been temporarily tried before, but a constitutional problem is raised by the fact that municipalities have the right to levy taxes only to cover their own expenses. It should come as no surprise that the proposal, enacted in 1995, has caused an outcry among the intended victims of such a 'Robin Hood levy', e.g. the high income suburban areas of Stockholm. The problem of dealing with intergovernmental fiscal relations remains as vexed as ever.

C. Economic and Social Aspects

C1 The Fiscal Deficit

The tradition of the Stockholm School, in the views of many scholars a forerunner to the Keynesian revolution, prescribed limited deficit financing in recession periods followed by compensatory budget surpluses in better times. The budget did not need to be balanced every year as long as the intention was to establish a balance over the whole cycle.

Meanwhile, the size of the budget deficits has grown over time, and the picture has been blurred by the multitude of deficit concepts being thrown around. There was, for instance, a period during which social security funds for financing pensions were in an accretion stage, making their operation a considerable part of government savings, thus turning the consolidated government sector balance into an overall surplus. With the ageing of the population and increasing unemployment figures, this wealth accumulation is no longer taking place. Furthermore, the size of contingent liabilities in the form of pension rights has grown, and these liabilities now exceed assets several times over. Some estimates point to a net liability in the pension system of between two and four times the size of the gross national product.

The Swedish economy was severely overheated at the end of the 1980s. Credit grew rapidly, and in 1989, households spent as much as 5 percent more than they earned. Unemployment was below 2 percent of the labour force despite the highest female labour participation rate of any country. The overconsumption resulted in extraordinarily large tax revenues from indirect taxes (with a VAT rate of 25 percent), but despite an increase in the overall tax ratio to GDP from around 50 percent to above 56 percent, public finances only registered a surplus of a mere percentage point. However, the surplus, albeit small, led some politicians to believe that state finances were in good order, and therefore no attention was paid to the underlying structural deficit.

In the early 1990s, the Swedish economy went into recession. When overconsumption became obvious and asset prices started falling, excessive borrowing resulted in credit losses. At the same time, the long overdue 1990 tax reform had been put in place, making borrowing considerably less favourable, and thus exacerbating the adjustment in the financial sector by rightly increasing the incentives to work and save. Tax revenues fell and social outlays rose as unemployment increased to unprecedented levels (in the period 1994–6, the unemployment was around 8 percent of the workforce with an additional 5 percent being engaged in labour market programmes).

A consequence of having had the most rapidly deteriorating public finances among the industrialized countries of the world was an increase in the gross national debt from 45 percent of GDP in 1991 to some 80 percent in 1995–6. A substantial part of the debt is held by foreigners—some 45 percent—and a third of the debt is in foreign currency, up from only 8 percent in 1991.

The necessary abolition of foreign exchange controls, the liberalization of credit markets, and ongoing international integration have made effective room for Keynesian deficit-financing much narrower. To add to the troubles, interest rates have continued to be relatively high compared to other European countries. Despite a depreciation of the krona by some 15 percent since November 1992 (at times as much as 30 percent), when the Central Bank had to abandon the unilateral peg of the krona to the ECU, investors demand several percentage-points higher return on Swedish government bonds than on German bonds. The increase in interest rates adds greatly to a large central government budget deficit. The primary deficit, i.e. income minus spending other than interest payments on the debt, was around 11 percent of GDP in 1993. At the same time, the consistent deficit in the central government budget was some 17 percent, while the deficit in the consolidated government sector was lower, around 13 percent of GDP. These figures obviously served as a warning signal to both foreign and domestic investors. As a consequence, a rapid consolidation programme was enacted, and for 1996 the public sector deficit was expected to be 4 percent.

One result of the very large public deficits is that households tend to save more in anticipation of future tax increases and cuts in transfer payments. Most Swedes seem to expect that taxes will go up from the very high levels they have remained at despite the 1990 tax reform. The tax ratio to GDP had, according to OECD revenue statistics, fallen to 55.4 percent in 1991, and national estimates indicated a further decline in 1992 and 1993 to around 51 percent. The ratio had risen to some 54–5 percent in 1995. Public sector spending reached 73 percent of GDP in 1993, and closing the gap by tax increases would completely have stifled the economy. The uncertainty about the magnitude of future tax changes may to some extent explain why households and businesses have not considered the outcome of the tax reform as viable, and, therefore, they have not fully adjusted to the new rules.

C2 Savings and Investment Incentives

With the 1990 reform, many, if not all, tax incentives were abolished. Sweden had once been a pioneer in cyclical tax incentives and a growth-oriented system of corporate taxation.[9] Now was the time to retract.

Still, some of the incentives just waited to be reinvented. To take the most striking example, Parliament introduced and enacted an initiative under which homeowners and condominium owners could claim a tax credit if they took the opportunity of high unemployment in the construction industry to undertake repair and improvement work and use taxpaying craftsmen to do the job. Another similar initiative currently under discussion is a limited

---

[9] Cf. e.g. L. Mutén and K.-O. Faxén, 'Sweden' in *Foreign Tax Policies and Economic Growth*, NBER, New York 1966.

tax relief for buying domestic services. The reduction of the VAT rate on tourist services has been followed by a discussion in which the generally beneficial effect of a lower VAT on services has been stressed. It is not a general opinion, however, that the programme of broadening the bases and lowering the rates has been ill-conceived, and it would be too early to call what is now happening a turning of the tide.

By adopting a cost-of-capital approach the effects of the tax rules and various incentive schemes on the marginal effective tax rate may be calculated.[10] A study of the Swedish tax system after the 1990 tax reform revealed that the marginal effective tax rate was low in an international comparison for investments in machinery.[11] The Swedish corporate tax system was found to be highly competitive while the total marginal effective tax rate, including the taxes paid by the investor, was among the highest of any OECD member country. The relatively high taxes on nominal capital returns (dividends, capital gains, and interest payments) were the primary cause of this.

C3 Distribution of the Tax Burden

The general effect of the 1990 tax reform was rather similar to the 1986 US reform, inasmuch as both the base-broadening and the rate reduction were disproportionately affecting those in the highest-income brackets. These were the ones who had been best in a position to reduce their income by interest expense deductions as well as by tax-avoidance schemes made less inviting after the reform. As a consequence of the old tax system, the household savings ratio was very low and even became negative, measured in relation to disposable income. In 1989, the household savings ratio was −5 percent. Partly as a consequence of the tax reform of 1990, the savings ratio increased and reached a level of 8 percent in 1994. Another outcome of the pre-reform tax system had been extensive accumulation of debt by high-income households. Even the highest-income decile reported on average larger interest expenses than taxable capital income. It was only in the highest percentile that net tax revenues were collected as a result of the taxation of net capital income. After 1990, high-income earners began to readjust their portfolios so that they held a larger proportion of financial assets.

[10] This approach was first presented in *Bolagsbeskattning och kapitalkostnader* (The Corporation Income Tax and the Cost of Capital) by L. Mutén in 1968 and was later on formalized in M. King and D. Fullerton (eds.), *The Taxation of Income from Capital—A Comparative Study of the United States, the United Kingdom, Sweden, and West Germany*, Chicago University Press 1984. An extension for open economies was published by L. Bovenberg, K. Andersson, K. Aramaki, and S. Chand in A. Ràzin and J. Slemrod (eds.), *Taxation in the Global Economy* in 1990.
[11] See Annexe 2 to the Swedish Medium Term Survey, *Svensk beskattning i ett integrerat Europa* (Swedish Taxation in an Integrated Europe), by K. Andersson, Ministry of Finance, Stockholm, 1992.

Tightening the rules on company cars, as well as other fringe benefits, likewise hit the upper brackets. The token reduction of the 25 percent VAT on food, first to 18 percent, later on to 21 percent (and from 1996 a more than token reduction to 12 percent), did not make very much difference to the total tax burden but is likely to have been of more importance to lower-bracket taxpayers.

A comprehensive official study evaluating the effects of the 1990–1 tax reform has been published.[12] The study concluded that labour supply has risen by a couple of percentage points. This is a slightly lower level than international studies suggested, but fairly closely in line with the assessments made by the tax commission prior to the reform. Even if the effects are not especially extensive, they are none the less important in light of the fact that tax wedges were wide before the reform, and still are for certain groups. Even modest changes in the supply of labour result in significant efficiency gains.

The study also attributes some 15 percentage points of the reduction in the price of private homes to the tax reform. This represents roughly half of the total fall in real house prices between 1990 and 1993. However, the tax reform is not considered to be the main factor behind the reduction in private consumption in the early 1990s. On the other hand, it is quite clear that the reform has led to a changed portfolio mix, with an increase in nominal assets and less investment in housing and a reduction in the level of borrowing.

The report also concludes that high-income earners pay roughly the same amount in taxes as before the tax reform. However, actual tax payments by individuals earning a given income have been significantly equalized. The broader tax base is considered to be the main factor behind this outcome. The evaluation also shows that there is nothing to indicate any increase in tax evasion during the 1980–92 period. Insofar as the tax reform as such had any effect on tax evasion, it went, according to the report, probably in the direction of reducing it.

At present, there are conflicting views on the net effect of the reform. Officially, all parties still support the reform as it was originally conceived. Yet there is a clear difference between those on the present opposition side, who believe that the reform should be supplemented by further reliefs, especially on the enterprise side, and those on the Social Democrat side, who feel that the present fiscal crisis calls for sacrifices, particularly by those who have the best ability to pay.

C4 The Hidden Economy

Studies of the size of the grey sector in Sweden's economy have, with few exceptions, ended up with a rather low figure for the grey sector, perhaps as

---

[12] *Skattereformen 1990–1991, En utvärdering* (An Evaluation of the 1990–91 Tax Reform), *SOU* 1995: 104, Stockholm, 1995.

low as 5 percent of GNP or slightly more.[13] There are, of course, also those who describe the Swedes as 'a people of tricksters' (Gunnar Myrdal), but most studies, regardless of method, have brought the estimates down to this level.

It should be noted, however, that these estimates do not include estimates of incomes made in the illegal sector, such as by smuggling, moonshining, prostitution, and the like. Moreover, few analyses have been made of the interplay between welfare benefits, in particular unemployment benefits, and the willingness of recipients to take jobs offered in the white sector as compared to continued benefits supplemented by grey-sector work.

Finally, there is a trend towards discovering more VAT fraud cases than before. There is a conflict between the wish to offer quick refund service to VAT taxpayers who because of exports or because of temporarily important inputs—normally investments—find themselves entitled to a refund, and the need to check before paying refund claims that rest on fraudulent documentation. The solution must be found in spot audits, which, in turn, require staffing to an extent unforeseen at the time VAT was introduced as a 'self-controlling' tax.

C5 Administrative and Compliance Costs

In Sweden, as elsewhere, the compliance cost aspect has received increased attention lately. The study mentioned above showed that the majority of taxpayers found the 1990 tax reform to have clearly simplified the task of filling out the tax return form and estimating tax.[14]

The study computed administrative and compliance costs of the tax system and found that the total corresponded to SEK14 billion, i.e. 1 percent of GDP, or 2 percent of tax collected. Of these, two-thirds were compliance costs and one-third administrative costs. The compliance costs for income tax were estimated at SEK4.5 billion, VAT at SEK3.2 billion, and handling employees' taxes and payroll taxes at SEK1.2 billion. In relation to the tax revenues collected, VAT was the most expensive of the major taxes, underlining, so says the study, the importance of having simple VAT rules and few rates of tax.

A further simplification was implemented in 1995. Most taxpayers then received a preprinted tax return form, including a computation of tax payable, based on the information returns received by the tax authorities and fed into the computerized taxpayer file. There was still a requirement for the taxpayer to sign the return, and before signing, the taxpayer was required to adjust the return for items not included. With the present information returns system, it

---

[13] The most recent study is one by Åke Tengblad, 'Beräkning av svart ekonomi och skatteundandragandet i Sverige 1980–1991', Part II of Håkan Malmer, Annika Persson, and Åke Tengblad, *Århundradets skattereform*, Stockholm (Fritzes), 1994.

[14] Malmer *et al. Århundradets skattereform*. There is an English summary on pp. 25–39.

was not expected that more than a minority of typical taxpayers would have to report any adjustments.

Whereas this reform will obviously further reduce compliance costs for the great number of taxpayers, it will not be costless to the tax authorities. Particularly in times when tax reform implies substantial extraordinary work (preparing new manuals, forms, taxpayer instruction leaflets, etc.), keeping the cost of tax administration down may imply a considerable reduction in regular audit activities. The observation has been made that in the years after the 1990 reform, the number of tax cases reaching the tax appeals courts fell significantly. It is a reasonable guess that, if not the whole decline, at least much of it may be explained by the fact that fewer returns are being audited and hence less discrepancies are being discovered.

D. Tax Reforms

D1 Main Tax Reforms, 1987–1993

In the foregoing, a good deal has been said about the 1990 tax reform and its aftermath. The reform was brought about in a joint effort by the then-governing Social Democrats and the Liberals. The Liberals, after the 1991 election, joined forces with three other non-Socialist parties, and whereas the coalition government certainly modified the 1991 system more than its original instigators had foreseen, it is fair to say that the main thrust of the 1990 tax reform was respected by the non-Socialist government.

Nevertheless, the government was criticized by the opposition Social Democrats for having abandoned the principles of the tax reform, e.g. by exempting dividends from individual income tax, by reducing the tax rate on income from capital, particularly on capital gains on shares, and by abolishing the net wealth tax.

D2 Continuing Tax Reforms, 1994–

The Social Democrats, back in power through the September 1994 elections, saw the need to strengthen the revenue side, and did so by reintroducing the classical system of taxation of corporations and shareholders, as well as by again increasing the tax on capital gains on shares. On the side of personal income taxation, they introduced a provisional 5 percent addition to the state income tax on earned income (a so-called 'defence tax'), making the new top marginal tax rate 56 to 57 percent, and cancelled the reductions of the tax on capital income and the abolition of the net wealth tax.

Investment activity in Sweden picked up somewhat after the positive outcome of the EU membership referendum, but it is still low, and the unemployment figures remain disturbingly high. To increase taxes on shareholders at such a moment was seen by the opposition as counter-productive, and in 1995, signals were perceived that the new government might be ready to test new forms of double taxation relief, albeit preferably placed on the corporation side.

It might be of some importance that well-known economic spokesmen for the party have been heard ridiculing the government debt problem, referring to the net debt rather than the gross debt as the relevant figure to be taken into account. If this attitude were to prevail, the need to get rid of most of the budget deficit might not rate as high on the priority list of the new Social Democratic government as on that of its predecessor. The development on the interest market and the inability of government to regulate interest rates the way it could in the first three decades after the War, might, however, cause some rethinking on this score.

In the academic world, there is, of course, a panoply of different ideas. Some academics who specialize in the effects of taxation, like Professor Jan Södersten, originally came out strongly against the 1993 reform of the taxation of corporations and shareholders, stressing that the reform would have no effect on those major foreign investors the country needs most. Others, like Professor Assar Lindbeck, take a different position, the most extreme being that of Professor Sven-Olof Lodin, who was instrumental in all reform activities in 1990 and onwards, and particularly involved in his capacity as the spokesman on taxation for Swedish industry. Interestingly, both Lodin and Södersten together came up with a common proposal for a corporation-based relief measure, implying a tax credit to corporations for income tax paid by shareholders on dividends received.[15] A study of the proposal rejected it, mainly on the ground that it would discriminate corporations with a low share of resident individual owners and make corporate financial planning complicated.[16]

The business community was reasonably happy with the reform work, both that of 1990 and the reforms instigated by the 1991 government. There was, however, some criticism against the last part of the reform package, namely the abolition of the classical system. The haste with which the reform was undertaken made for some unfortunate complications of the law. The abolition of the Annell deduction was criticized in some quarters as retrospective, if not in the sense of the Constitution (it would then be forbidden), at least in an economic sense. The measures taken to avoid excessive dividend pay-outs,

---

[15] Jan Södersten, *Bör utdelningarna förbli skattefria?* (Should Dividends Remain Tax Exempt?), *Skattenytt*, 1994: 596–602; Sven-Olof Lodin, 'Behåll enkelbeskattningen av bolagsinkomsterna— en replik' (Keep the Single Taxation of Corporate Profits—a Reply), *Skattenytt*, 1994: 683–6; id. *The Nordic Reforms of Company and Shareholder Taxation: a Comparison*, Stockholm, 1994; Assar Lindbeck (ed.), 'Nya villkor för ekonomi och politik. Betänkande av ekonomikommissionen' (New Conditions for Economy and Politics. Report by the Economy Commission), *SOU* 1993: 16; Mutén, 'Sweden Considers New Corporate Income Tax Integration', *Tax Notes International*, 11: 978 (9 Oct. 1995).
[16] 1992 års företagsskatteutredning, Lättnad i dubbelbeskattningen av mindre företags inkomster (Relief in the double taxation of the profits of small enterprises), *SOU*, 1996: 119.

Table 9.1   The Swedish tax system, 1988–1996

	1988	1989	1990	1991	1992	1993	1994	1995	1996
Personal income tax									
Average local tax rate	30.56	30.44	31.16	31.15	31.04	31.04	31.05	31.50	31.65
Top marginal tax rate (%)	75.56	72.44	66.16	51.15	51.04	51.04	51.05	56.50	56.65
at incomes in excess of SEK	190,000	190,000	190,000	170,000	186,700	190,700	198,800	204,000	209,100
Zero bracket, SEK	10,000	10,000	10,000	10,300[g]	10,700[h]	11,000[k]	0/8,800[o]	8,900[q]	8,600[w]
Social security fees paid by employee (%)	0.00	0.00	0.00	0.00	0.00	0.95[n]	1.95	3.95[s]	4.95[v]
Individual wealth tax rate									
Top marginal tax rate (%)	3.00	3.00	3.00	2.50	1.50	1.50	1.50	1.50	1.50
at wealth in excess of SEK	1,800,000	1,800,000	3,600,000	1,600,000	800,000	800,000	800,000	800,000	900,000
Zero bracket, SEK	400,000	400,000	800,000	800,000	800,000	800,000	800,000	800,000	900,000
Corporate income tax									
tax rate (%)	57.00	[a]	57.00	[a]	57.00	[a]	30.00	[c]	30.00
Social security fees paid by employer (%)	37.07	37.47	[b]	38.97	39.19	[d]	34.83	[i]	31.00[j]
Self-employed	33.97	34.19	34.19	34.19	[e]	33.85	29.55[l]	29.75	31.25[r]
Standard VAT tax rate	23.46	23.46	23.46	25.00	25.00	[t]	25.00[m]	25.00	25.00

[a] A 52% corporate income tax plus 20% real income based employee investment fund contribution, both levies mutually deductible.

[b] From Sept. 1989, 38.97%.

[c] The reduction was accompanied by a significant broadening of the tax base, in fact as important as to give rise to a new 'tax equalization reserve' to keep the effective tax rate at about 24%, as before.

[d] From July 1991, 37.29%. For persons over 65 years of age, 22.2%.

[e] From July 1991, 34.01%.

[f] As of 1 January 1992, food, hotel, and restaurant services received preferential tax treatment, at a rate of 18%.

[g] The zero bracket increases with higher income, up to a maximum of SEK18,500 which is reached at an income of SEK98,800. It is then gradually reduced to SEK10,300 which is reached at an income of SEK179,900.

[h] The zero bracket increases with higher income, up to a maximum of SEK 19,400 which is reached at an income of SEK97,200. At an income of 103,100 it is gradually reduced to SEK10,700 which is reached at an income of SEK197,400.

[i] For persons over 65 years of age, 21.85%.

[j] For persons over 65 years of age, 17.69%.

[k] The zero bracket increases with higher income, up to a maximum of SEK19,800 which is reached at an income of SEK99,200. At an income of 105,300 it is gradually reduced to SEK11,000 which is reached at an income of SEK201,700.

[l] For persons over 65 years of age, 17.89%.

[m] The reduced rate on food and restaurant services was increased from 18 to 21% 1 January 1993. Only 6 months later, on 1 July 1993, the tax rate on hotel services and tourism was lowered to 12%.

[n] The tax is applicable to incomes up to SEK258,000.

[o] The zero bracket increases with higher income, up to a maximum of SEK17,800 which is reached at an income of SEK101,500. At an income of 107,700 it is gradually reduced to SEK8,800 which is reached at an income of SEK198,800. Unlike earlier years, the zero bracket is only valid when calculating the local income tax.

[p] The 'tax equalization reserve' was abolished, half the reserves to be clawed back during a five-year period. Instead the 'period equalization reserve' was introduced. In 1994, dividends from the Swedish corporations to Swedish shareholders were exempted, and the limited deduction for dividends on newly emitted shares abolished. 90% of the old tax equalization reserves was to be clawed back.

Table 9.1 Continued

---

[q] The zero bracket increases with higher income, up to a maximum of SEK18,100 which is reached at an income of SEK103,200. At an income of 108,800 it is gradually reduced to SEK8,900 which is reached at an income of SEK212,900. The zero bracket is again applicable both to local taxes and central government taxes.

[r] For persons over 65 years of age, 21.39%.

[s] The tax is applicable to incomes up to SEK270,000.

[t] In 1995, the tax exemption for dividends received was again abolished, but the limited deduction for dividends on new shares was not restored.

[u] The tax rate on food is reduced to 12%.

[v] The tax is applicable to incomes up to SEK276,000.

[w] The zero bracket increases with higher income, up to a maximum of SEK18,000 which is reached at an income of SEK104,600. At an income of 110,100 it is gradually reduced to SEK8,600 which is reached at an income of SEK203,200.

feared not least because of the Social Democrats' threat to reintroduce individual income tax on dividends after the election, left corporations in limbo, not knowing exactly what rules would apply on dividends being decided on in the spring of 1994. The capital gains tax rules, in particular the adjustment of the base method that was contemplated but postponed, provoked a good deal of professional criticism.

As to the unions, they stick to the traditional view of the Social Democrats: that the tax climate should be kept reasonably pleasant for the corporations themselves, but that there is no need for feathering the nests of the owners of corporate stock.

10 The United Kingdom

ANDREW DILNOT AND GARY STEARS

A. Overview

A1 Purpose

This chapter aims to give a general outline of the tax system in the UK, how each of the main taxes works, and some sense of recent and prospective reform. We begin with a disaggregation of total revenue which shows that in the UK, as in many other countries, public discussion about taxation focuses more heavily on income tax than is justified by its contribution to total revenue. We move on to discuss personal income tax, taxes on companies, the national insurance contribution (social security tax) system, indirect taxes, capital taxes, and local taxes. We then discuss a number of economic and social issues, broadly following the topics discussed in the other chapters.

Sect. D4.1 describes and assesses the main tax reforms which occurred between 1987 and 1993, concluding that there has been a great deal of change, but little in the way of a coherent strategy. There is much to be welcomed, but also much to criticize. Finally, in section D4.2 we discuss the prospects for tax reform in the future, and repeat the call for a clear set of objectives, without which we may see much change without great improvement.

A2 Revenue Raised by UK Taxes

Total government receipts amounted to £271.9 billion in 1995–6, or 38.25 per cent of UK GDP. Table 10.1 summarizes the breakdown of UK government revenue.

In 1995–6 the largest single source of revenue for the government was taxes on income. £68.9 billion was raised from income tax and £9.9 billion from advance corporation tax (a tax on dividends), with a further £44.4 billion from national insurance contributions. These three sources accounted for some 45% of government revenue. Mainstream corporation tax raised around £14.8 billion, while business rates yielded £13.6 billion. £89.5 billion, or 33% of revenue was raised by taxes on expenditure of which VAT raised £44.0 billion and council tax £9.2 billion. The remainder was raised by excise duties on petrol, alcohol, and tobacco, (£28.3 billion) and vehicle

Table 10.1 Sources of government revenue, 1995–1996

Source of revenue	£bn.	% of total
Income tax	68.9	25.3
National insurance contributions	44.4	16.3
Corporation taxes		
Corporation tax[a]	24.7	9.1
Petroleum revenue tax	0.9	0.3
National non-domestic rates	13.6	5.0
Capital taxes		
Capital gains tax[b]	0.9	0.3
Inheritance tax	1.5	0.6
Stamp duty	2.0	0.7
Value-added tax	44.0	16.2
Other indirect taxes		
Petrol duties	15.5	5.7
Tobacco duties	7.2	2.6
Alcohol duties	5.6	2.1
Betting and gaming duties	1.6	0.6
Vehicle excise duties	4.1	1.5
Custom duties	2.3	0.8
Council tax	9.2	3.4
Other	25.5	9.4
General government receipts	271.9	100.0

[a] includes advance corporation tax (ACT). [b] Though classified here as a capital tax, capital gains is treated as part of the income tax in the text, as in other countries (Section B1.1).

Source: HM Treasury Financial Statement and Budget Report, 1996–7.

excise duty (£4.1 billion). Taxes on capital provided a further £4.4 billion for the Exchequer.

B. The Tax System

B1 Individual Income Tax

B1.1 Tax Base

Over 25 million individuals pay income tax in the UK but not all income incurs tax. The main kinds of income upon which income tax is levied are pay, pension payments upon retirement, unemployment benefit, profits from business, income from property, bank and building society interest, and dividends on shares. Incomes from certain social security benefits are not liable to income tax; these exempt benefits are listed in Table 10.2 along with the cost of these reliefs in 1994–5. Income tax is also not paid on certain privileged savings products such as national savings certificates.

Table 10.2   Revenue forgone in untaxed benefits, 1995–1996

Benefit	Estimated no. of recipients (000s)	Estimated cost of tax relief (£m.)
Child and one parent benefit	7,000[a]	700
Industrial disablement benefits	240	70
Attendance allowance	1,130	240
Disability living allowance	1,690	275
War disablement benefits	195[b]	130

[a] no. of families receiving child benefit
[b] figure for 1991

Sources: Social Security Statistics, 1996; Inland Revenue Statistics.

Table 10.3   Allowances and thresholds for 1996–1997

Allowance	(£)
Personal	3,765
Married couple	1,790
Personal (aged 65–74)	4,910
Married couple (aged 65–74)	3,115
Personal (aged 75+)	5,090
Married couple (aged 75+)	3,155
Income limit for age-related allowances	15,200
Basic rate limit	25,500
Lower rate limit	3,900

Capital gains tax was introduced in 1965 and is levied on gains arising from the disposal of assets. The first £6,300 of an individual's capital gain is exempt from tax, as is the first £3,150 of capital gains made by trusts. Gains are taxed at the individual's income tax rate, while corporation tax is charged on capital gains made by a company. The current system only taxes non-inflationary gains that have arisen since March 1982, while gains arising from the sale of certain assets are exempt, the most important being owner-occupied housing and pensions. Tax relief from capital gains tax is available for entrepreneurs who sell up on retirement. In addition a capital gains charge can be deferred indefinitely by reinvesting the gain in an unquoted trading company.

B1.2 Tax Rates

The structure of income tax in the UK operates via a system of allowances and bands. All individuals have a personal allowance which is deducted from total pre-tax income in order to derive taxable income. Taxpayers under 65 years old

Table 10.4 Tax rates and bands

Taxable income per year (£) 1996–7	Rate of tax (%)
0–3,000 (Lower rate band)	20
3,901–25,500 (Basic rate band)	24
Over 25,500 (Higher rate band)	40

Table 10.5 Income tax liabilities of lower, basic, and higher rate taxpayers, 1994–1995

Taxpayers liable at:	No. of taxpayers (000s)	Total amount of tax (£m.)
Lower rate only	4,940	1,270
Basic rate only	18,410	40,680
Higher rate only	2,000	27,360
Total	25,350	69,310

Source: *Inland Revenue Statistics.*

receive a personal allowance of £3,765, while older persons are entitled to higher personal allowances as shown in Table 10.3. If income for the over 65s exceeds a certain limit, known as the 'income limit for age-related allowances', then the excess income becomes subject to a taper of 50% which reduces the allowance down to a minimum level equal to the allowance for the under 65s.

Taxable income is subject to different tax rates depending upon the 'tax band' that income falls within. For 1996–7 the first £3,900 of taxable income is taxed at the 'lower rate' of 20%, the next £21,600 is subject to the 'basic rate' of 24%. All taxable income above this ceiling of £25,500, known as the 'basic rate limit', is taxed at the 'higher rate' of 40%. Table 10.4 summarizes the tax rates and bands. In addition to their personal allowances a married couple is eligible to a 'married couple's allowance'. The married couple's allowance is presently £1,790 for those under 65 years old, while over 65s are entitled to higher allowances as shown in Table 10.3. The married couple's allowance can be appropriated between the couple in two ways. The total amount can be allocated to one person or it can be split equally, although in the event of a disagreement it is split automatically.

Before April 1994 the married couple's allowance was simply an addition to the personal allowance. This reduced taxable income and benefited higher rate taxpayers more than lower or basic rate tax payers as relief to higher rate taxpayers was received at 40% of the allowance. Now the relief is restricted to 15%, effectively making the allowance a tax credit and equalizing the cash value to all couples.

Inflation Adjustment   The bands and allowances of individual income tax are subject to statutory indexation provisions, announced at the time of the annual Budget in late November, unless Parliament otherwise decrees. The increase is in line with the percentage increase in the retail price index in the year to September. Changes in allowances have to be rounded up to the nearest multiple of £10 and threshold and bands to the nearest multiple of £100.

Payments Systems   Most income tax on earned income is deducted at source by employers. The main unusual feature of UK payment systems is that the calculation of tax by employers is cumulative as opposed to the non-cumulative systems operated almost everywhere else. When calculating tax due each week or month the employer considers not simply the income for the period in question, but for the whole of the tax year to date. The tax due on the total cumulative income is calculated, tax paid thus far is deducted, and the remainder is due. For those with stable incomes this produces a pattern of payments much like that in a non-cumulative system, but for those with volatile incomes it still achieves the result that at the end of the tax year the correct amount of tax should have been deducted. The Inland Revenue supplies employers with a 'tax code', which describes the level of tax allowances or credits available over the year; if individual circumstances change, for example because of marriage, the Revenue issues a new code to employers.

It is this cumulative system that allows so few tax returns to be issued (see below), since for those with relatively simple affairs there will be no adjustment necessary to the amount of tax already paid.

For the self-employed the system is much more complex, although about to be reformed (see Macdonald and Whitehouse, 1993; Inland Revenue, 1991, 1992 for details). The difficulties of charging tax before final accounts are available, and adjustments at the beginning and end of a business enterprise's life make for a system which has been little understood. The proposed reforms, which move towards self-assessment, should improve this.

B1.3 Tax Returns

The cumulative deduction of income tax has meant that in the past fewer than 10% of the adult population have filled in tax returns each year, with tax returns concentrated on those with higher incomes and a greater probability of multiple income sources. The proposed move to self-assessment, alongside growing affluence and a tendency towards more self-employment, contract work, and part-time work will lead to more people filling in returns. The return used in the past has been fairly complicated and there is now a debate about the way forward. Two principal options are discussed. The first would be to send out a very simple return quite widely, with those with more complex affairs requesting a fuller return. The second would be based on an Australian-type model with a substantial 'tax-pack' which would lead individuals through a very detailed return. In the near future it seems unlikely that we will see substantial changes made to the form of the tax return, but extension of returns to a much larger public might make reform essential.

B2 Corporate Income Tax

Corporation tax is charged on profits made by UK resident companies, public corporations, and unincorporated associations. The 'profit' upon which corporation tax is charged is made up of income from trading and/or investments and capital gains. If a company makes a trading loss, then the loss can be carried back for three years to be set against profits in that period or it may be carried forward indefinitely. The standard rate of corporation tax is currently 33%, although there is a reduced rate for small companies. The reduced rate is 24% and is levied on companies with profits of less than £300,000. For firms with profits between £300,001 and £1,500,000 a marginal rate of 35.25% is applied so that by £1,500,000 the average rate is 33%. Table 10.6 summarizes.

When a dividend is paid the company makes a payment of advance corporation tax which is currently 20% of the gross dividend. Advance corporation tax can be set off against the corporation tax liability of the accounting period. A company that cannot set off the whole of the advance corporation tax against the tax charged on its profits has surplus advance corporation tax. Surplus advance corporation tax can be carried back for up to six years to offset tax liabilities in earlier accounting periods, or it may be carried forward without time limit.

Relief against corporation tax is offered by capital allowances for the depreciation of capital assets incurred in the carrying on of trade. Capital allowances may be claimed in the year that they accrue and any unused capital allowances can be set against future profits or carried back up to three years. Different classes of capital expenditure are offset in different ways. Plant and machinery is calculated on a 25% reducing balance basis, while for industrial buildings, hotels, and other commercial buildings it is on a straight-line basis of 4% per year.

B2.1 National Non-Domestic Rates

National non-domestic rates were transferred from local control to national control in 1990. Companies pay a tax bill based on the national uniform rate poundage multiplied by the rateable value of the properties they occupy. The

Table 10.6 Rates of corporation tax, 1996–1997

Profits (per year) (£)	Marginal tax rate (%)	Average tax rate (%)
<300,000	24	24
300,001–1,500,000	35.25	24–33
>1,500,000	33	33

rateable value is an official estimate of the market rent for the property. The rates bills paid by businesses with properties of similar value should be the same wherever they are located.

B2.2 Petroleum Revenue Tax

Petroleum revenue tax raised around £900 million in 1996–7. Companies involved in the extraction of oil and gas from the UK and its continental shelf (mainly the North Sea) are liable to petroleum revenue tax as well as corporation tax. Petroleum revenue tax is assessed for each separate oil and gas field and then charged on the cash flow arising in each chargeable period. Since July 1993 the petroleum revenue tax rate has been 50% on existing fields but new fields are exempt.

B3 Social Security Contributions and Earmarked Payroll Taxes

The only payroll tax in the United Kingdom is the national insurance system. Payment of national insurance contributions entitles individuals to receipt of certain social security benefits and, in principle, contributions pay exactly for benefits from the national insurance fund. In practice payments from and receipts into the fund bear little relation to each other. In the national insurance system current contributions finance current benefits with the fund merely being a device to prevent cash-flow problems. Officially the fund should not fall below one-sixth of national insurance expenditure. Historically this has been achieved through a grant from central taxation, although during the mid-1980s the high level of economic activity expanded contribution levels resulting in the grant being abolished in 1990. The subsequent recession reduced contributions and raised the costs of benefits so that the grant had to be reintroduced in 1993–4.

In 1995–6 national insurance contributions raised some £44.4 billion of which around 95% was raised by Class 1 contributions. Class 1 contributions are paid by two groups, employees as a tax on their earnings, and employers as secondary contributions on those they employ. Since 1975 Class 1 contributions for both employers and employees have been earnings-related subject to an earnings floor, known as the 'lower earnings limit' (LEL). Employees only pay national insurance contributions if their weekly earnings exceed the LEL, which in 1996–7 was £61. Those earning between the LEL and the 'upper earnings limit' (UEL), £455 in 1996–7, pay a rate of 2% on the slice of earnings up to the LEL and a rate of 10% on all other earnings up to the UEL. For income above the UEL no contributions are paid. A summary of employees' Class 1 contributions structure for 1996–7 is given in Table 10.7. Employers also pay national insurance contributions, known as secondary Class 1 contributions, for each employee who earns over the LEL. Employer contributions are structured differently and there is no UEL. The rates at which these contributions are made are shown in Table 10.8.

Table 10.7 Employees' rates of Class 1 contributions for 1996–1997

Weekly earnings (£)	Contracted-in rates (weekly)	Contracted-out rates (weekly)
0–60.99	zero	zero
61 (LEL)	2% of £61 = £1.22	2% of £61 = £1.22
61.01–454.99	£1.22 plus 10% of earnings over £61	£1.22 plus 8.2% of earnings over £61
455 (UEL) and over	£40.42	£33.53

Table 10.8 Employers' rates of NI contributions for 1996–1997

Weekly earnings {£}	Contracted-in rates (weekly)	Contracted-out rates (weekly)
0–60.99	zero	zero
61 (LEL)	3.0% of all earnings	3.0% of all earnings
61.01–109.99	3.0% of all earnings	3.0% of the LEL
110–154.99	5.0% of all earnings	3.0% of the LEL plus 2% of earnings in excess of the LEL
155–209.99	7.0% of all earnings	3.0% of the LEL plus 4% of earnings in excess of the LEL
210–455 (UEL)	10.2% of all earnings	3.0% of the LEL plus 7.2% of earnings in excess of the LEL
455+	10.2% of all earnings	3.0% of the LEL plus 7.2% of earnings between the LEL and the UEL plus 10.2% of earnings in excess of the UEL

National Insurance contributions are lower for those who have 'contracted out' of the state earnings-related pension scheme (SERPS) and instead belong to a 'recognized' pension scheme. The percentage levied on the earnings between the LEL and the UEL is currently reduced by 1.8% for employee contributions and by 3% for employer contributions.

The self-employed pay two different classes of national insurance contributions, Class 2 and Class 4. Class 2 contributions are paid at a flat rate which for 1996–7 is £6.05 per week. It is paid by those whose income exceeds a 'small earnings exception' which is presently £3,260 a year. Class 4 contributions are payable by self-employed individuals whose profits exceed the lower profits limit, which for 1996–7 is £6,860 per annum. Class 4 contributions are a proportionate profits tax of 6.0% on that part of profits above the lower-profits limit and below the upper-profits limit. The upper-profits limit is currently equal to UEL. Half of any Class 4 contributions are allowable against an individual's income tax liability. Class 3 national insurance contributions are voluntary and are usually made by UK citizens living abroad in order to maintain their entitlement to benefits when they return. Class 3 contributions are £5.95 per week for 1996–7.

B4 Value-Added Tax

The standard rate of value-added tax (VAT) in the UK is 17.5%, although a lower rate of 8% is applied to domestic fuel. Various categories of goods are either 'zero-rated' or 'exempt'. Zero-rated goods have no VAT levied upon the final good or upon the inputs used in its creation. Exempt goods have no VAT levied on the final good sold to the consumer, but firms cannot reclaim the VAT paid on inputs, thus exempt goods are effectively liable to lower rates of VAT (between 4 and 7% depending upon the firm's cost structure and the nature of suppliers). Approximately 25% of consumer expenditure is on zero-rated goods and about 15% upon exempt goods. Table 10.9 lists the main categories of goods that are zero-rated or exempt.

B5 Excises and Other Taxes

B5.1 Excises

Excise duties are flat-rate taxes (per pint, per litre, per packet, etc.) levied upon alcoholic drinks, tobacco, and petrol. Tobacco products are subject to an additional *ad valorem* tax of 20% on the total retail price including the duty. The Government announced a commitment to raising the real value of the duties on petrol and diesel by at least 5% and on tobacco by at least 3% per annum. These announced changes arise partly from budgetary and partly from health and environmental considerations. Table 10.10 shows the rates of duties levied in 1996–7.

B5.2 Licences and Other Taxes

In addition to VAT and duties revenue is raised through a system of licences. The main licence is the vehicle excise duty which is levied annually at £140 per

Table 10.9 Zero-rated and VAT exempt goods

Zero-rated goods	VAT exempt goods
Most food (not alcohol, soft drinks, confectionery and crisps and meals out)	Rents
	Private education
Construction of new dwellings	Health services
Passenger transport	Postal services
Books, newspapers and magazines	Finance and insurance
Medicines on prescription	Burial and cremation
Children's clothing	

Table 10.10 Excise duties for 1994–1995

Good	Duty (pence)	Total duty as a percentage of price
Pint of beer	24	15.6
Packet of cigarettes (20)		
Duty	125	
Ad valorem	58	63.3
Wine (75 cl bottle)	105	0.35
Spirits (75 cl bottle)	554	49.7
Petrol (litre)	39	61.9
Unleaded petrol (litre)	34	59.6
Diesel (litre)	34	59.6

car, with higher duties for commerical vehicles. In 1995–6 vehicle excise duty raised some £4.1 billion. There are also duties on betting and gaming which raise some £1.6 billion a year.

In 1994 two new taxes were implemented. The insurance premium tax came into effect in October of that year and applies to most general insurance where the risk insured is located in the UK. The tax is levied at 2.5% of the gross premium and in 1995–6 raised around £600 million. Long-term insurance, such as life insurance, is exempt. In addition an excise duty on air travel from UK airports was implemented. Called the air passenger duty, passengers are charged £5 for flights to UK and European Community destinations and £10 elsewhere. In 1995–6 air passenger duty raised some £300 million.

B6 Capital Taxes

B6.1 Inheritance Taxes

Inheritance tax was introduced in 1986 replacing capital transfer tax. The tax is applied to transfers of wealth after or shortly before death that exceed a threshold (£200,000 in 1996–7). The tax is charged at a single rate of 40% on the amount above the threshold for transfers on death, with reductions in this rate if the transfer occurred during the seven-year period before the death of the donor. These reductions for lifetime transfers are shown in Table 10.11. Certain transfers of wealth are exempt from inheritance tax, the main exemptions being transfers between spouses, transfers to charities, and transfers to political parties. Certain assets, particularly those associated with farms and small businesses, are eligible to relief. The relief reduces by 50 or 100%, depending on the nature of the interest transferred, the value of the asset upon which inheritance tax is calculated. The number of estates paying inheritance tax is only around 3% of all deaths.

B6.2 Stamp Duty

Stamp duty is payable upon many legal and commerical documents and its payment is indicated by 'stamps' put on the documents following their presentation to the Stamp Office, unless an arrangement operates whereby the document has a printed indication of the amount of duty payable. The main stamp duties are levied on stock and share transactions and upon conveyances and transfers of land and property. For land and property transactions there is a threshold below which no stampt duty is paid. In 1996–7 the threshold was £60,000. Transfers that exceed this threshold are subject to a duty of 1% on the entire purchase price. For stocks and shares there is no threshold and stamp duty is levied at 0.5% on the price of the shares. Table 10.12 summarizes the current rates of stamp duty.

B7 The Local Tax System

In 1993 the community charge system of local taxation, otherwise known as the 'poll tax', was replaced by the council tax. The council tax raised some £9.2 billion in 1995–6 providing around 20% of local authority revenue. Properties are banded according to an assessment of their valuation (as at April 1991), with local authorities individually determining the rate levels levied on these bands. Table 10.13 shows the value bands for England, Scotland, and Wales. Reductions on the council tax bill are available for properties with only one resident adult or if the property is empty. The reliefs are reductions of 25 and 50% respectively.

C. Economic and Social Aspects

C1 The Fiscal Deficit

In 1995–6 general government expenditure exceeded receipts by £31.7 billion, some 4.5% of GDP. This deficit is known as the public sector borrowing requirement (PSBR). 1993–4 represented a peak in the PSBR which had until then been a cause of concern due to its growth as a result of the recession and increased real government expenditure. The PSBR is now on a downward trend falling to £26.4 billion in 1996–7, or 3.5% or GDP, with the expectation of public sector finances returning to balance by the end of the decade. The reduction in the PSBR is due to nominal public spending reductions and strong government revenue growth caused by the tightening of fiscal policy by nearly 3% of GDP in 1993 and rapid economic growth. For 1996–7 the stock of government debt is forecast to rise to £350 billion or 45.5% of GDP.

C2 Savings and Investment Incentives

Currently investors pay tax at their marginal rate on income invested in banks and building societies. Therefore, savings of this kind are effectively taxed

Table 10.11 Inheritance tax reductions for transfers before death

Years between transfer and death	Reduction in tax rate (%)	Actual tax rate (%)
0–3	0	40
3–4	20	32
4–5	40	24
5–6	60	16
6–7	80	8

Table 10.12 Rates of stamp duty, 1994–1995

Rates of stamp duty	Rate
Land and buildings:	
up to £60,000	zero
above £60,000	1% of total
Stocks and shares	0.5%

Table 10.13 Value bands for England, Scotland, and Wales

Band	Tax rate relative to band D	England	Scotland	Wales
A	$\frac{2}{3}$	up to £40,000	up to £27,000	up to £30,000
B	$\frac{7}{9}$	£40,000 to £52,000	£27,000 to £35,000	£30,000 to £39,000
C	$\frac{8}{9}$	£52,000 to £68,000	£35,000 to 45,000	£39,000 to £51,000
D	1	£68,000 to £88,000	£45,000 to £58,000	£51,000 to £66,000
E	$1\frac{2}{9}$	£88,000 to £120,000	£58,000 to £80,000	£66,000 to £90,000
F	$1\frac{4}{9}$	£120,000 to £160,000	£80,000 to £106,000	£90,000 to £120,000
G	$1\frac{2}{3}$	£160,000 to £320,000	£106,000 to £212,000	£120,000 to £240,000
H	2	£320,000	£212,000	£240,000

twice as they are made out of taxed income, although non-taxpayers are excluded from paying tax provided they inform their bank/building society of their status. The UK tax system does, however, contain a number of ways in which various forms of savings are treated preferentially. The two most important are owner-occupied housing and pensions which account for a high proportion of personal savings due to their fiscal advantage.

C2.1 *Owner-Occupied Housing and Pensions*

Owner-occupied housing enjoys considerable fiscal privilege. First, any increase in value of the property, provided it is the individual's main residence, is free from capital gains tax. Second, the owner-occupier receives 'mortgage interest relief at source' (MIRAS) which reduces the amount of interest payments on a mortgage. As the name suggests the relief is at source, that is the mortgage lender is refunded the relief by the Exchequer and they in turn reduce the mortgage payment. Therefore, while MIRAS is technically an income tax relief, it has the effect of reducing mortgage repayments rather than the amount of tax borrowers have to pay. Indeed, borrowers still receive MIRAS even if they have no tax liability. The relief is presently 15% of the interest payable on the first £30,000 of the mortgage. The ceiling for MIRAS has been fixed in nominal terms at £30,000 since 1983, therefore the real value of the relief has fallen. The reduction in the real value of the ceiling, coupled with the restrictions, has diminished the attractiveness of saving through owner-occupied housing.

Tax relief is applied at the marginal rate on contributions to 'tax-approved' personal or occupational pension plans. This effectively makes pension contributions tax-free. Income generated by pension funds from the accumulation of the returns on assets is also exempt from tax. When a pension is paid, it is treated as part of earned income and taxed accordingly, although part of an individual's pension rights can be paid out as a tax-free lump sum. The limit on the size of the tax-free lump sum is at present defined as 25% of the value of the accumulated fund for personal pensions and 1.5 times final earnings for company pension. Pension tax relief is restricted to a maximum level of rearnings which is currently £82,200. This limit is known as the pensions earnings cap. If the salary on which an occupational pension is calculated exceeds the ceiling, there is no tax relief on the excess and the employer's contributions are counted as income. With personal pensions relief is given on contributions up to certain limits. These limits are expressed as a percentage of eligible earnings and vary with age as shown in Table 10.15.

C2.2 *Other Incentives to Save and Invest*

During the late 1980s and early 1990s a number of initiatives with favourable tax treatment were implemented with the aim of increasing personal savings. The major schemes that presently exist are tax-exempt special savings accounts (TESSAs), personal equity plans (PEPs), and the enterprise investment scheme.

Table 10.14 Income tax rates on earned income, 1978–1997

	1978–9	1979–80	1980–1 to 1985–6	1986–7	1987–8	1988–9	1989–90	1990–1	1991–2	1992–3 to 1995–6	1996–7
Lower rate	25	25								20	20
Basic rate	33	30	30	29	27	25	25	25	25	25	24
Top rate	83	60	60	60	60	40	40	40	40	40	40

Table 10.15 Contribution limits for personal pensions

Age	Percentage of qualifying earnings which may be contributed per tax year
16–35	17.5
36–45	20
46–50	25
51–55	30
56–60	35
61 and over	40

TESSAs provide tax relief to encourage small savers. From January 1991 taxpayers over 18 years of age can open a TESSA account with an approved bank or building society. The interest upon a TESSA account is not liable to tax provided the capital is not withdrawn during a five-year period. Interest on the capital may be withdrawn at any time, although this is liable to the basic rate of tax. A maximum of £3,000 may be saved in the first year and up to £1,800 a year thereafter until an overall limit of £9,000 is reached. At the end of five years the account will automatically cease to be exempt from tax, and interest on the account will become liable for tax. An investor could open another account, but would be able to contribute only £3,000 in the first year. In December 1995 an amount of £28 billion was invested in some 4.5 million live TESSAs.

Personal equity plans were introduced in the 1986 Budget as an initiative to widen share ownership. Investors in personal equity plans are exempt from income tax on dividends and capital gains tax arising on shares held in a plan. Administration of the scheme is undertaken by approved plan managers, while indirect investment via a unit or investment trust is permitted. In January 1992 personal equity plans were extended to include other European Community shares. Individuals can invest a maximum of £6,000 per tax year in a general personal equity plan. However, an additional £3,000 can be invested in a single-company personal equity plan, which as its name suggests is a plan that holds ordinary shares in a single UK or European Community company. By 1995–6 a total of some 7.2 million general plans and 0.9 million single-company plans had been taken out, with total amounts invested of £26 billion and £2.2 billion respectively.

The enterprise investment scheme provides tax relief for new equity investment in 'qualifying' unquoted UK trading companies. The relief is currently 20% on qualifying investments of up to £100,000 in any tax year. Losses on investments qualify for income tax and capital gains tax relief, while all capital gains within the scheme are entirely free of capital gains tax. The enterprise investment scheme also allows an investor to become a paid director and still qualify for relief, provided the investor was previously unconnected with the company or its trade. The enterprise investment scheme was implemented in January 1994 and replaced the business expansion scheme with which it shares the same objective, namely the expansion of investment in unquoted companies. The business expansion scheme allowed investment in private rented housing which resulted in a large proportion of investment in this relatively safe sector.

C3 Distribution of the Tax Burden

Distribution of income is affected by the tax and benefit system. Tables 10.16 and 10.17 summarize this impact upon household income in the UK. It should be noted that equivalence scales are used to allow for different household compositions.

From Tables 10.16 and 10.17 the following trends are evident. The dispersion of income is reduced by the tax and benefit system. This is shown by the richest quintile of households having final income of around four times greater than the bottom quintiles, when the top fifth's original income was some twenty-one times larger. This redistribution is also illustrated by the income share of the bottom quintile of households increasing from 2.1 to 6.5% after taxes and benefits have been taken into account, while the top fifth of households experience a reduction from 50 to 44%. This redistribution would have been greater, i.e. 7.4% for the bottom quintile and 42% for top quintile, had it not been for the regressive effects of indirect taxation. The compression of the income distribution is caused mainly by the payment of cash benefits. Cash benefits decline in importance as gross income increases, for the bottom quintile of households about 70% of gross income is made up of cash benefits, while for the top fifth cash benefits account for less than 3% of gross income. Benefits in kind also decline in importance with rising incomes. The bottom quintile pays around 13% of its gross income in direct taxation, while the top quintile pays about 22%. For indirect taxation however the poorer fifth are regressively affected as they pay about 30% of their disposable income in indirect taxes compared with the richest fifth's 15%.

Table 10.16 Summary of the effects of taxes and benefits on households 1992

Average per household (£pa)	Quintile groups of households ranked by equivalized disposable income					
	Bottom	2nd	3rd	4th	Top	All house-holds
Original income	1,770	5,380	13,210	21,330	37,060	15,750
plus cash benefits	4,320	4,080	2,720	1,570	1,020	2,740
Gross income	6,090	9,470	15,930	22,900	38,080	18,490
less direct taxes	780	1,290	2,810	4,540	8,480	3,580
Disposal income	5,300	8,180	13,120	18,360	29,600	14,910
less indirect tax	1,620	1,920	3,010	3,660	4,550	2,950
Post-tax income	3,690	6,260	10,110	14,690	25,050	11,960
plus benefits in kind	3,320	2,830	2,710	2,330	1,850	2,610
Final income	7,000	9,100	12,820	17,030	26,900	14,570
Equivalized disposable income	5,144	7,941	11,315	15,926	28,810	13,828

Note: Equivalized income has only been used in the ranking process to produce the quintile groups. The monetary values are unequivalized unless indicated.

Source: CSO *Economic Trends*, Jan. 1994.

C4 The Hidden Economy

All estimates of tax evasion, that is illegal failure to report income to the tax authorities, are by their nature inexact, and certainly in the UK there is a tendency to exaggerate the scale of this problem: one good anecdote goes a very long way. With the general reduction in marginal direct tax rates the incentives to evade and avoid at the margin have fallen over the last fifteen years. Average tax rates have also fallen for those with high incomes, but not for those lower down the income scale. For those receiving social security benefits the financial incentive to fail to declare income is little changed. Prosecutions for either tax or social security fraud are still quite rare, but penalties and repayments are far more common than prosecutions, and arguably more cost-effective.

There is no convincing evidence for the wilder claims that the hidden economy is burgeoning. The evidence of Dilnot and Morris (1981), Smith (1986), Pissarides and Weber (1989), and Baker (1993), all points to a plausible figure for the size of unreported income between 2 and 5 per cent of GDP.

C5 Administrative and Compliance Costs

Sandford *et al.* (1989) estimate that the combined administrative and compliance cost of operating the UK tax system in 1986–7 was over £5 billion.

Table 10.17   Percentage shares of total household income, 1992

Quintile group	Percentage shares of total equivalized income for households ranked by equivalized disposable income			
	Original income	Gross income	Disposable income	Post-tax income
Bottom	2.1	6.9	7.4	6.5
2nd	6.0	11.0	11.0	11.0
3rd	15.0	16.0	16.0	16.0
4th	26.0	23.0	23.0	23.0
Top	50.0	43.0	42.0	44.0
All households	100.0	100.0	100.0	100.0

Source: CSO, *Economic Trends*, Jan. 1994.

This represented nearly 4% of total UK tax revenue, or approximately 1.5% of the UK's GDP for that period. Table 10.18 gives a breakdown of the UK's administrative and compliance costs in 1986–7 by individual taxes. The total cost of compliance was more than twice the size of total administrative costs, although by individual taxes this ratio varied, e.g. the compliance cost of excise duties was less than the administrative cost. Total cost as a proportion of tax revenue also varied between individual taxes, with the most expensive taxes to operate being direct taxes and VAT, with excise duties being the cheapest.

The operating cost of the UK tax system is not evenly distributed. The burden of administrative costs is distributed by the government's policy on taxation because administrative costs are paid for out of tax revenues. The burden of compliance costs on the other hand is not dependent on the tax system and many commentators have noted that it is regressive in its distribution. The inequality in the distribution of compliance costs is most notable in the UK with taxes on businesses where smaller firms bear a disproportionate cost of compliance. This is illustrated in Table 10.19 which shows estimates by Sandford *et al.* (1989) of compliance costs for firms of different size. From the figures it can clearly be seen that as a percentage of taxable turnover average compliance cost decreases as a firm's sales increase.

Businesses in the UK can use tax receipts for a period of time before such taxes are given over to the revenue authorities. This cash-flow benefit is a major offset to compliance costs for firms. Sandford *et al.* estimate that the cash-flow benefits exceed the compliance costs, but the regressiveness of compliance costs upon businesses remains unchanged. For large firms net compliance costs are often negative as a result of cash-flow benefits; for small firms however they remain positive and significant.

Table 10.18 Tax operating costs, United Kingdom, 1986–1987

Tax or group	Revenue (£bn.)	Administrative costs		Compliance costs		Operating costs	
		£m.	%	£m.	%	£m.	%
Income tax, CGT & NICs	65.1	997	1.53	2,212	3.40	3,209	4.93
VAT	21.4	220	1.03	791	3.69	1,011	4.72
Corporation tax	13.5	70	0.52	300	2.22	370	2.74
Petroleum revenue tax	1.2	1	0.12	5	0.44	7	0.56
Excise duties	16.5	42	0.25	33	0.20	75	0.45
Minor taxes[a]	4.6	39	0.85	68	1.48	107	2.33
Total central government	122.3	1,369	1.12	3,409	2.79	4,778	3.91
Local rates	15.5	236	1.52	58	0.37	294	1.89
Total	137.8	1,605	1.16	3,467	2.52	5,072	3.68

[a] Includes stamp duty, inheritance tax, VED, betting and gaming.
Note: Lines and columns may not sum due to rounding.
Source: C. Sandford *et al.* (1989).

C6 Taxes and Labour Supply[1]

The impact of taxation on labour supply has without doubt been a central element in the UK debate on tax reform since the late 1970s. The large reductions in top-income tax rates were in large part motivated by labour supply concerns, as were the reduction in lower rates of income tax. Somewhat depressingly, the discussion of these issues continues to be rather narrowly focused, and based on a number of simplifying and often misleading assumptions. The first common mistake is to assume that direct taxes on earnings will affect labour supply but that indirect taxes on consumption will not. The trade-off being made in choosing how hard to work in the standard economic model is between hours of leisure and consumption of goods financed by income from work. Consumption of goods can be reduced either by reducing net income through higher direct tax or by raising the price of goods through higher indirect tax. The argument that shifting from direct to indirect tax will necessarily improve labour supply incentives is wrong.

A second common problem is that economist's models of labour supply typically focus on hours of work as the measure of effort to the exclusion of alternatives such as intensity of effort or willingness to take risks. The latter, in particular, can be much affected by changes in very high rates of income tax on those with high earnings.

[1] See Blundell (1992) and Dilnot and Duncan (1992) for general discussion.

Table 10.19   Compliance costs as a percentage of taxable turnover for UK firms, 1986–1987

Turnover (£)	Compliance costs as a percentage of taxable turnover
0–100,000	3.66
100,001–1,000,000	0.62
1,000,001+	0.17

Source: See Table 10.18.

For the UK, there is little evidence that reducing top-income tax rates increases labour supply,[2] but there is evidence of important effects of the social security system. The two groups for whom social security disincentives are greatest are lone-parent families and women married to unemployed men. For these groups the combination of low pay if in paid work, heavy unpaid domestic responsibilities and a heavily means-tested social security system make work unlikely to be financially rewarding.[3]

For other groups there is little persuasive evidence of powerful effects, although as Blundell (1992) shows, we do find that married women in general tend to be more responsive than men, something yielding surprising results. In particular reductions in income tax rates yield increases in the net income of married couples through their effect on the largely stable incomes of men, and these income effects can offset most of, or in some cases more than offset, the incentive for married women to work harder generated by the reduction in marginal tax rates.

Here, as in other areas of tax analysis, careful work using large and representative datasets is likely to be the only way of arriving at reliable answers. The common and seductive practice of trying to deduce results from hypothetical or typical families simply will not work.

D. Tax Reforms

D1 Main Tax Reforms 1987–1996

The later years of the 1980s were rich ones for tax changes. Public finances were in surplus, which always makes change easier, and the Conservative Party had won a third successive election in 1987. It is striking that the 1992–7 government saw little that could claim to be substantial reform.

---

[2] See Dilnot and Kell (1988) and Brown (1988) for discussion.
[3] See Blundell *et al.* (1992) for further discussion of lone parents, Dilnot and Kell (1987) for women married to unemployed men.

Without doubt the most remembered tax reform of the 1980s and 1990s came in 1988, when the basic rate of income tax was cut to 25%, and the top rate from 60 to 40%. The basic rate has since been cut to 24%.[4] Whether changes in tax rates in general merit the description of reform is questionable, but these changes were in a sense the culmination of a long-held aim of the government, to reduce income tax rates. The new lower rate of 20% for the first small slice of income came in 1992, just before an election, and is best thought of as an attempt to emphasize the government's tax-cutting agenda. The declared aim of the government is now a basic rate of 20%.

Eighteen years ago the top income tax rate in the UK was 98%. This was plainly absurd, and was cut to 75%, or 60% on earned income from 1979. Whether cutting from 60 to 40% was so necessary is certainly open for debate. What is clear, is that the desire to cut the basic rate of income tax to 20% is hard to understand in economic terms. The reductions we have seen in income tax have typically been bought by increases elsewhere. It is hard to believe that a marginal income tax rate of 24% does great damage to incentives, and the introduction of the 20% band has made the system more complex. The reductions in tax rates other than the top rate must be understood in political terms.

The move to taxing husbands and wives separately came in 1990. We retain a special allowance, the Married Couple's Allowance (MCA) which reduces the tax bill of such households, but it has been first frozen and then cut, and seems destined for fairly rapid removal. The move to independence has been well received, but there continues to be confusion about the extent to which the State should give special treatment to certain types of household.

In the taxation of savings the introduction and expansion of PEPs and TESSAs, conferring an exenditure tax-type treatment, has been significant. With housing and pension saving already at least as generously taxed, the UK is now in practice very close to an expenditure tax at the personal level, although the institutional arrangements are still somewhat complex. The steady reduction in mortgage interest relief has been welcome, although to the extent that it was capitalized into house prices has penalized those who entered the market since it was last increased in 1983.

One of the taxes that has been increased to pay for income tax reduction is national insurance contributions, most recently increased from 9% for employees to 10% in March 1993. The NIC system was reformed in 1989 to reduce liabilities for low-paid employees, and employer liabilities for low-paid employees have been cut in several recent budgets. The tax base for income tax and NICs has been aligned more closely, reducing the scope for avoidance of NIC liability by using imaginative payment means.

Value-added tax has also helped to fund tax reductions. In 1991 the VAT rate was raised from 15 to 17.5% to pay for a large reduction in the ill-fated

---

[4] A cut in the basic rate to 23% was proposed in the November 1996 budget.

Table 10.20   Summary of main reforms

Personal income taxes	Basic rate 29% down to 24%
	Top rate 60% down to 40%
	New lower rate of 20%
	Independent taxation of husbands and wives
	New tax-relieved savings regimes (PEPs + TESSAs)
	Capital gains changed at income tax rates
	Mortgage interest relief cutback
National insurance	Restructured to reduce liabilities for low paid
	Employee rate up from 9 to 10%
	Base extended to cover some benefits in kind
VAT	Main rate up from 15 to 17.5%
	Base extended to domestic fuel
Excises	Big increases for tobacco and road fuels
Corporate income tax	Main rate 35% down to 33%
	ACT rate cut from 25 to 20%
Local tax	Poll tax abolished, replaced by council tax
	Locally varying business rate abolished, replaced by national business rate

poll tax. In 1993 a decision was taken to impose VAT on demostic fuel and energy which was previously zero-rated. The proposal was to impose an initial rate of 8% and one year later move to the full 17.5%. But despite a generous compensation package, particularly for the elderly, and the fact that the real cost of fuel had been falling, the government lost a vote in December 1994 on the second stage of the increase. This emphasized again the difficulty of extending the VAT base, even with generous compensation. We are still left in the UK with large amounts of consumption zero-rated, which cannot be an effective way of assisting those on low incomes. Any attempt to extend the VAT base though, seems set to face great difficulties on the grounds that it appears to hit the poor.

There has been no major structural reform of excise duties, but we have seen substantial increases in the real level of tax on tabocco products and road fuels. The tobacco increases are mainly defended on health grounds, the petrol increases on environmental grounds. We have also seen the introduction and widening of a tax differential in favour of unleaded petrol, which has certainly coincided with a large increase in its use.

On company taxation we have seen a decade of remarkable stability for corporation tax. The main rate has been cut from 35 to 33% and the rate of advance corporation tax from 25 to 20%. The most significant change to company taxation was the replacement of locally varying business rates with a national business rate.

The saga of the poll tax is by now well known. The intent was to increase local accountability but it was highly unpopular, much higher than intended because of loss of control of local spending, and politically disastrous. The new council tax is a function both of property value and of the number of adults in the household. The underlying problem of local authority finance, that local spending outstrips locally determined fundraising by a ratio of around six to one, remains entirely unresolved.

Looking back over the period since 1986 there has been change, but few coherent themes. The development of the taxation of savings is to be welcomed, the independent taxation of husband and wife was overdue, and the reduction in NIC liabilities at low earnings has reduced labour market distortions. The changes in tax burden have involved a shift from income tax to other taxes, both direct and indirect, to no obvious efficiency gain. The idea that income tax is somehow in general more distortionary than other taxes is economically absurd. The failure to achieve widening of the VAT base is another reminder of the difficulty of changing tax structures.

D2 Recent and Prospective Tax Reforms[5]

Looking to the future the prospects are uncertain, especially given the lack of clarity about tax from both main political parties in the UK. This lack of clarity at least in part flows from the failure to face the trade-off between the level of tax and the level of public spending. Despite being elected to cut back the size of the State, the share of public spending in national income is just as high now as it was when the Conservative government came to power in 1979. This will be no surprise to those who have given the matter much thought since it is true across the world that public spending has tended to rise as a share of the economy, reflecting the nature of the goods it provides. Unless far tougher decisions are made on public spending than Conservative politicians seem prepared to make, tax burdens will not fall, and their tax strategy seems to be to cut income tax rates and find the money by raising other taxes. For Labour this trend is just as uncompromising, since it means that to offer better public services in the end means offering higher taxes. Faced with this, the Labour Party is at present still vague about tax reform, since they have no desire to admit to being in favour of higher taxes, except on the very rich (undefined) and those avoiding tax.

At an academic level, there is a growing consensus that the effects of

[5] This section was drafted in early 1997, and no attempt is made to evaluate tax changes made by the Labour Government in 1997 and 1998 after the Labour election victory of June 1997. The main changes have been the introduction of an earmarked windfall tax on the profits of privatized utilities; increases in excises and stamp duties; the abolition of ACT and a widening of the corporate tax base, which increased revenues, despite a reduction in nominal rates; an increase in social security (national insurance) contributions, including abolition of UEL for employers. In accordance with a pre-election pledge, no change was made to the personal income tax rates.

globalization are becoming ever more important, which makes taxing capital, whether at the personal or corporate level, more difficult, and will tend to lead to a reduction in taxes on these factors. There is also growing interest in the use of taxation to achieve environmental goals. The recently announced landfill levy, the existing differential in favour of unleaded petrol, and the prospects of road-charging, are all part of this trend.

What is most lacking is a clear statement of objectives for the tax system as a whole, and its relationship to public spending, from either government or main opposition. Without such a statement, the prospects for coherent reform are gloomy.

References

Baker, P. (1993), 'Taxpayer Compliance of the Self-Employed: Estimates from Household Spending Data', IFS Working Paper, 93/14.

Blundell, R. W. (1992), 'Labour Supply and Taxation: A Survey', *Fiscal Studies*, 13/3: 15–40.

——— Duncan, A., and Meghir, C. (1992), 'Taxation and Empirical Labour Supply Models: Lone Parents in the UK', *Economic Journal*, 102: 265–78.

Central Statistical Office (1994), *The Effects of Taxes and Benefits upon Household Income 1990, Economic Trends*, no. 483.

Brown, C. (1988), 'Will the 1988 Income Tax Cuts either Increase Work Incentives or Raise More Revenue?', *Fiscal Studies*, 9/4: 93–107.

Dilnot, A. W., and Duncan, A. (1992), 'Thinking about Labour Supply', *Journal of Economic Psychology*, 13/4: 687–713.

——— and Kell, M. (1987), 'Male Unemployment and Women's Work' *Fiscal Studies*, 8/13: 1–16.

——— (1988), 'Top-rate Tax Cuts and Incentives: Some Empirical Evidence', *Fiscal Studies*, 9/4: 70–92.

——— and Morris, C. N. (1981), 'The Exchequer Costs of Unemployment', *Fiscal Studies*, 2/3: 10–19.

——— and Webb, S. (1988), 'Reforming National Insurance Contributions', *Fiscal Studies*, 9/4: 1–24.

Financial Statement and Budget Report 1996–97 (1994), London, HMSO.

IFS BBC Budget Guide 1996–97 (1996), London, Institute for Fiscal Studies

Inland Revenue (1991), *A Simpler System for Taxing the Self-Employed: A Consultative Document*, London, Inland Revenue.

——— (1992), *A Simpler System for Assessing Personal Tax: A Consultative Document*, London, Inland Revenue.

——— (1995), *Inland Revenue Statistics, 1996*, London, HMSO.

Macdonald, G., and Whitehouse, E. (1993), Changing Tax for the Self-Employed, *Fiscal Studies*, 14/1: 107–26.

Pisarides, C. A., and Weber, G. (1989), 'An Expenditure-Based Estimate of Britain's Black Economy', *Journal of Public Economics*, 39: 17–32.

Sandford, C., and Godwin, M., and Hardwick, P. (1989), *Administrative and Compliance Costs of Taxation*, Bath, Fiscal Publications.

Social Security Statistics (1996), Dept. of Social Security, London, Stationery Office.

Smith, S. (1986), *Britain's Shadow Economy*, Oxford, Oxford University Press.

11 The United States

EMIL M. SUNLEY AND JANET G. STOTSKY

A. Overview

Taxes are levied in the USA by the federal, state, and local governments. Each government imposes its own taxes. There are no shared taxes, although more than one government may exploit the major revenue sources. In addition, there is considerable shifting of money through shared expenditure programmes from higher to lower levels of government. The federal government, most state governments, and some local governments impose income taxes. The most important revenue sources are income and payroll taxes at the federal level, sales and income taxes at the state level, and property taxes at the local level.

Total taxes in the USA in 1992 were 29.4 per cent of GDP, the lowest relative to GDP of all OECD countries other than Turkey and Australia and the same as Japan.[1] Federal taxes (excluding social insurance contributions) were 11.1 per cent of GDP in 1992, falling from 12.0 per cent in 1975. State taxes were 5.5 per cent of GDP in 1992, rising from 5.1 per cent in 1975, and local taxes were 3.8 per cent of GDP in 1992, falling from 3.9 per cent in 1975. Federal and state social insurance contributions were 9.0 per cent of GDP in 1992, rising from 6.8 per cent of GDP in 1975. At the federal level, the personal income tax is the most important revenue source, comprising 8.0 per cent of GDP in 1992, rising from 7.7 per cent in 1975. Over this same period, the corporate income tax decreased from 2.6 per cent of GDP in 1975 to a low of 1.5 per cent in 1985 and 1986, increasing to 1.7 per cent in 1992.[2] Unlike every other industrialized country, there is no broad-based consumption tax at the federal level.[3]

At the state level, the general retail sales tax has traditionally been the largest source of revenue, increasing to 1.8 per cent of GDP in 1992 from 1.6 per cent in 1975. The personal income tax has, however, now essentially reached parity with the general sales tax, increasing to 1.8 per cent of GDP in 1992 from 1.2 per cent in 1975. Over this period, the state corporate income tax and selective sales taxes diminished in importance. At the local level, the property tax remains the predominant form of tax revenue, although it has

[1] *Revenue Statistics of OECD Member Countries, 1965–93*, Paris: OECD, 1994: 73.
[2] Advisory Commission on Intergovernmental Relations (1994): 68–9.
[3] Ken Messere (1993).

diminished in importance in recent years, dropping from 3.2 per cent of GDP in 1975 to 2.9 per cent in 1992. Over this period, the gap was filled by increases in both sales and income taxes.[4]

B. The Tax System

B1 The Federal Tax System

In the USA, income tax applies to every individual and entity having taxable income. Taxpayers are classified by the type of return they are required to file. Individuals file the individual tax return, and in calendar year 1993, 114 million of these forms were filed, making them the best-known and least-liked government forms. Corporations, trusts and estates, and partnerships file another form.

The base of the income tax falls far short of a comprehensive notion of income. The starting point is 'gross income', defined broadly as 'all income from whatever source derived'. Taxable income is determined for both individuals and corporations by subtracting allowable exclusions, exemptions, and deductions from gross income.

B1.1 Personal Income Tax

For individuals, gross income includes wages and salaries, taxable interest, dividends, capital gains, rents, royalties, pension income including distributions of individual retirement accounts (IRAs), business income from sole proprietorships, income from partnerships, income from estates and trusts, farm income, refunds of state and local income taxes (if they were previously deducted), alimony received, unemployment benefits, social security benefits over certain dollar limits, and other income. US residents are in general taxed on worldwide income, although they may receive credit for taxes paid to foreign countries.

Gross income is a misnomer in two important ways. First, certain items are specifically excluded from gross income. These include gifts and bequests, death benefits, interest on tax-exempt state and local bonds, compensation for injuries or sickness, amounts received on accident and health plans, certain fringe benefits (the most important are pension contributions and health care benefits), and certain income transfers. Second, gross income is in some cases a net concept because certain expenses relating to earning income are netted out (for example, from partnerships and sub-chapter S corporations).

Taxpayers are allowed to deduct certain amounts, termed 'adjustments', from gross income to arrive at adjusted gross income (AGI). The most important of these adjustments are one-half of self-employment taxes paid

---

[4] Advisory Commission on Intergovernmental Relations (1994): 68–9.

by the self-employed, qualified contributions to certain tax-deferred retirement accounts (IRAs and Keogh retirement plans), and alimony paid.

Taxable income is defined as AGI minus personal exemptions and either a standard deduction or allowable itemized deductions. Taxpayers could claim a personal exemption of $2,550 in 1996, which is adjusted annually for inflation, for each taxpayer and dependant included on the tax return, although these exemptions are phased out for high-income taxpayers. Individuals can choose to itemize personal deductions or to claim the standard deduction—$4,000 for single individuals and $6,700 for married couples filing jointly in 1996. Itemized deductions consist of medical expenses over 7.5 per cent of AGI; mortgage interest (with some restrictions); charitable contributions; state and local income and property taxes (but not sales or excise taxes or fees paid to state and local governments); casualty or theft losses over 10 per cent of AGI; and unreimbursed employee business expenses, expenses incurred in earning investment income, and other miscellaneous expenses over 2 per cent of AGI. Middle- and higher-income families and individuals are more likely to itemize their personal deductions because they tend to pay high state and local taxes and have larger home mortgage interest deductions. Overall less than 28 per cent of individual taxpayers itemize.[5] In 1994, taxpayers reported taxable income of $2,594 billion.[6]

The US personal income tax has a rate schedule with five marginal tax rates—15, 28, 31, 36, and 39.6 per cent. In 1996, the top marginal tax rate took the form of a 10 per cent surcharge on the tax liability on taxable income over $263,750. In addition, various phase-out provisions for personal exemptions and itemized deductions can increase the effective marginal tax rate for many taxpayers. The combination of five brackets, phase-outs of personal exemptions and itemized deductions as well as a maximum tax rate on long-term capital gains, floors on specified itemized deductions, social security and Medicare payroll taxes, the earned-income tax credit, and the tax on social security benefits has resulted in a marginal tax rate schedule that varies in a complicated fashion with income.[7]

Individuals may file under four different rate schedules, applying to different forms of household composition. The most widely used schedules are for married couples filing jointly and for single individuals. The widths of the tax brackets are wider for the joint filers than for single filers. There is a rate schedule for married couples filing separately, but it is little used as it is seldom advantageous on tax grounds for married couples to file separately. The final rate schedule applies to heads of households, which generally is used by unmarried individuals with a dependent child. It provides brackets that are wider than the rate schedule for single filers but narrower than the rate schedule for joint filers (see Table 11.1).

[5] Internal Revenue Service (1996): 10.   [6] Ibid. 7.
[7] Manning and Andress (1996): 1585–1614.

Table 11.1   1996 Tax rate schedules for federal personal income tax ($)

Single

If taxable income is:		Tax is:	
over	but not over	of the amount over	
0	24,000	15%	0
24,000	58,150	3,600.00 + 28%	24,000
58,150	121,300	13,162.00 + 31%	58,150
121,300	263,750	32,738.50 + 36%	121,300
263,750	—	84,020.50 + 39.6%	263,750

Head of household

If taxable income is:		Tax is:	
over	but not over	of the amount over	
0	32,150	15%	0
32,150	83,050	4,822.50 + 28%	32,150
83,050	134,500	19,074.50 + 31%	83,050
134,500	263,750	35,024.00 + 36%	134,500
263,750	—	81,554.00 + 39.6%	263,750

Married filing jointly or qualifying widow(er)

If taxable income is:		Tax is:	
over	but not over	of the amount over	
0	40,100	15%	0
40,100	96,900	6,015.00 + 28%	40,100
96,900	147,700	21,919.00 + 31%	96,900
147,700	263,750	37,667.00 + 36%	147,700
263,750	—	79,445.00 + 39.6%	263,750

Married filing separately

If taxable income is:		Tax is:	
over	but not over	of the amount over	
0	20,050	15%	0
20,050	48,450	3,007.50 + 28%	20,050
48,450	73,850	10,959.50 + 31%	48,450
73,850	131,875	18,833.50 + 36%	73,850
131,875	—	39,772.50 + 39.6%	131,875

By permitting joint filing, the US personal income tax imposes the same tax on married couples with the same income regardless of how the total income is split between the spouses, but imposes a different tax on a married couple and a single individual with the same income. One result of permitting joint filing is that the personal income tax results in both marriage penalties and marriage subsidies. If two individuals with about the same income marry, their tax burden under the joint rate schedule will be higher than it would be if they were both permitted to continue to file as single individuals. On the other hand, if two individuals with highly uneven incomes marry, the combined tax burden will be lower under joint filing. The introduction in recent years of higher marginal tax rates and the narrowing of tax brackets have increased the marriage penalty for couples with similar incomes.

For developments since 1997, see the last paragraph of Sect. D2.1 below, but between 1986 and 1996, realized capital gains were included in full in taxable income, though long-term capital gains were subject to a maximum rate of 28 per cent. Thus for higher-income taxpayers, there was a significant difference between the tax rates on ordinary income and capital gains. Capital losses could be offset against capital gains and then against ordinary income, but no more than $3,000 per year in losses may be offset against ordinary income, with the remainder carried forward indefinitely. Taxpayers could defer capital gains tax on a principal residence if they purchase a principal residence within two years. In addition, taxpayers aged 55 or older get a one-time exclusion from tax of $125,000 of capital gains on the sale of their principal residence.

Individuals who derive income from sole proprietorships may claim their income and expenses related to their business activities on a separate schedule, which is then integrated with the rest of the personal income tax.

After computing tax on taxable income, the individual taxpayer is allowed to claim certain tax credits. The most important of these are the earned-income credit (a variable, vanishing credit targeted to low-income filers who work), credit for care of child or dependant, the credit for the elderly or disabled, the foreign tax credit, and the low-income housing tax credit. Of these, only the earned-income credit is refundable (the excess of the credit over the tax liability is returned to the taxpayer). Many low-income households are not liable to tax (if their AGI is less than the total of their deductions and personal exemptions) but may still receive a tax credit refund through the earned-income credit.

Individuals are also subject to the alternative minimum tax. The tax is computed by taking AGI, making adjustments and additions for tax preferences, and then subtracting certain itemized deductions and the personal exemption. The rate is 26 and 28 per cent for individuals. Taxpayers pay the alternative minimum tax if it exceeds their regular tax.

The personal income tax is partly indexed to inflation. The personal exemption, the standard deduction, the maximum earned income, and the phase-out base amounts of the earned-income credit, and the bracket widths are all indexed to the overall change in the Consumer Price Index. Indexing of fixed dollar amounts was first enacted in 1981 for tax years after 1984, but frequent changes in the tax law since then have resulted in a number of discretionary changes in the indexed parameters. There is no indexing of depreciation, capital gains, or interest income and expense.

The main form of tax collection is based on withholding of employee earnings, instituted in 1943 with the dramatic expansion of the income tax to finance the Second World War. There is only very limited withholding of capital income. However, individuals with significant income outside the withholding system must estimate their tax liability and pay it in quarterly instalments during the year. On their final tax return, taxpayers reconcile their final tax liability with amounts already paid.

B1.2 Corporation Income Tax

Taxable income for corporations and other entities required to file the corporation income tax return is defined as gross income less allowable deductions. Domestic corporations are, in general, taxed on worldwide income, although they may receive credit for tax paid to foreign countries. Most businesses use the accrual method of accounting, and businesses that have inventories are required to do so. Reserves typically are not allowed for tax purposes, although small banks can maintain tax-deductible reserves for bad debts and insurance companies can maintain reserves for future liabilities. Businesses may use either the last-in, first-out (LIFO) or first-in, first-out (FIFO) methods of inventory accounting. They depreciate machinery and equipment under accelerated methods and real estate using the straight-line method over lifetimes set to approximate the economic usefulness of the asset. They also can write off as an expense $10,000 of machinery and equipment each year. State and local taxes paid by a business generally are deductible business expenses for income tax purposes. Net operating losses typically can be carried back three years and forward fifteen years.

The USA adheres to the classical system of a separate corporate tax with no tax relief for dividends paid by corporations or dividends received by individuals. Double taxation, however, is mitigated for Subchapter S corporations (small corporations taxed like partnerships), cooperatives, regulated investment companies, real estate investment trusts, and real estate mortgage investment conduits. In addition, domestic corporations are allowed a deduction of 70, 80, or 100 per cent of dividends received from taxable domestic corporations, with the amount of the deduction dependent on the degree of ownership.

The formal tax rate schedule for corporations has progressive marginal rates of 15, 25, 34, and 35 per cent, with the top rate applying to corporations with taxable income in excess of $10 million. The benefit of the lower tax rates, however, is phased out or recaptured over certain income ranges by imposing additional taxes of 3 or 5 per cent. As a result, the marginal tax rate schedule for corporations can be said to have eight marginal rates of 15, 25,

34, 39, 34, 35, 38, and 35 per cent with the 39 and 38 per cent rates being the marginal rates for taxable income in the income range over which the benefits of the lower marginal rates are phased out.

Corporations can claim certain tax credits, including the foreign tax credit and the general business credit. The latter credit is an umbrella covering eight separate tax credits for investment, targeted jobs (for individuals in certain groups with high unemployment rates), alcohol used as fuel, research and development, and so forth.

Corporations pay tax on income from the sale of capital assets at the same rate as other income. Certain tax benefits, such as depreciation, are subject to recapture at ordinary income tax rates. Unlike individuals, corporations can only offset capital losses against capital gains. The remaining losses may be carried back three years and carried forward five years against capital gains.

Certain non-profit organizations, including charitable, religious, educational, and medical organizations, trade associations, labour unions, and fraternal organizations, are exempt from corporate income taxes. These organizations are, however, subject to tax on business income derived from activities unrelated to their exempt purposes.

There is no indexing of business income for inflation. Depreciation allowances are based on historical cost. Accelerated depreciation is sometimes justified on the grounds that this compensates businesses for the use of historical cost basis in an inflationary environment. Though inventories are based on historical costs, businesses may choose whether to use LIFO- or FIFO-inventory accounting. LIFO offers some advantages in an inflationary environment. Financial assets are not indexed to inflation. There is no adjustment to the stock of debt based on changes in its value from inflation fluctuations. Nominal capital gains and nominal interest income are taxable, while nominal interest payments are deductible.

Corporations are also subject to an alternative minimum tax (AMT), which was designed to ensure that all corporations pay tax, even those benefiting from extensive tax preferences. The base of this tax is computed by recalculating taxable income, making adjustments, and adding back certain tax preference items. The rate of tax is 20 per cent for corporations. In 1992, 28,002 corporations reported an AMT liability of $4.9 billion, equal to 3.7 per cent of total corporate income tax liability. This liability was over and above their regular tax liability, although much of this may be credited against regular tax liability in later years.[8] In addition to the alternative minimum tax, corporations are subject to an environmental tax. The base for this tax is alternative minimum taxable income in excess of $2 million. The tax rate is 0.12 per cent.

There is no withholding system for corporations. Instead, they are required to pay estimated taxes in quarterly instalments, based on their estimated

---

[8] Internal Revenue Service (1995*a*): 33.

current earnings or, in some cases, previous earnings. On their final tax return, taxpayers reconcile their final tax liability with amounts already paid.

B1.3 Payroll Taxes

The USA uses payroll taxes to finance social insurance programmes. The major US payroll tax is the social security tax, which applies to both employees and employers, and to the self-employed. The tax consists of two components. The largest component is the old-age, survivors, and disability insurance (OASDI) tax, which is levied on gross wages at the rate of 6.2 per cent on employees and 6.2 per cent on employers. The second component is the hospital insurance (HI) tax, with a rate of 1.45 per cent on both employees and employers. The self-employed pay both the employee and employer components of the tax but on only 92.35 per cent of self-employment earnings, effectively excluding the 'employer' portion from tax. In 1996, the OASDI tax applied to the first $62,700 of wages (the limit is indexed to changes in average wages) and the HI tax applies to all wages. Many workers pay more in social security taxes (employer and employee contribution combined) than in personal income tax, although the employee's contribution is often less than the personal income tax. Consider a typical worker earning a wage of $40,000 who has a spouse and two dependants and who claims four exemptions and the standard deduction. The worker would have paid $3,465 in personal income taxes and the employer and employee would have paid $6,120 in social security taxes. The other two US payroll taxes are the relatively small unemployment tax—a tax applying only to employers—and the railroad retirement tax—a tax similar to the social security tax.

B1.4 Sales and Excise Taxes

The USA does not have a broad-based federal sales or consumption tax, although there are a variety of excise taxes. In 1995, the federal government collected $57.5 billion (or 0.8 per cent of GDP) in excise taxes. The major federal excise taxes are taxes on alcohol and tobacco, petrol and other fuel taxes, mostly dedicated to the highway and airport trust funds, and the telephone tax. The telephone excise tax is the most widespread federal tax as 94 per cent of households have telephones. The tax reaches more households than the income tax or the social security tax.

The USA makes only limited use of environmental excise taxes. It imposes excises on petroleum to fund the Hazardous Substance Superfund. The USA also taxes certain chemicals to fund the Superfund and taxes certain ozone-depleting chemicals. These environmental taxes produce a negligible amount of revenue. The USA imposes no excises on pollutants such as carbon or sulphur emissions.

The US government imposes both specific and *ad valorem* excises. Examples of specific excises include the petrol tax of 18.4 cents per gallon (which is low by international standards), cigarette tax of 24 cents per pack, distilled spirits tax of $13.50 per proof gallon, and the international departure tax of $6 per person. Examples of *ad valorem* taxes include the 3 per cent telephone tax, a 10 per cent tax on domestic air fares, a 12 per cent tax on truck trailers and semitrailers, and an 11 per cent tax on bows and arrows.

B1.5 Net Wealth and Capital Transfer Taxes

The principal federal wealth tax is the unified estate and gift tax, a tax on the transfer of wealth. In 1993, 60,211 federal estate tax returns were filed with gross estates of at least $600,000. These returns reported combined gross estates of almost $104 billion.[9] Under this tax, a single rate schedule with rates from 37 to 55 per cent applies to taxable lifetime gifts and transfers occurring at death. In the case of gifts, the tax is applied on a tax-exclusive basis, while in the case of transfers at death, it is applied on a tax-inclusive basis, providing a tax incentive to make lifetime gifts. As the tax is cumulative, a credit is given for the tax paid in prior years. A credit for a limited amount of state death taxes paid and a unified credit of $192,800 are also available. The unified credit permits transfer of $600,000 by gift or death, before incurring either an estate or gift tax liability. In addition to the unified credit, donors are permitted an annual exclusion from the gift tax of $10,000 per donee ($20,000 for married couples). Gifts and bequests from one spouse to another or to charity are not taxable.

To protect the estate tax base, the USA imposes a 55 per cent tax on transfers in trust and outright transfers that skip a generation, such as a transfer from a grandparent to a grandchild. Transfers up to $1 million per grantor are exempt from this tax.

B2 The State and Local Tax System

Most states impose their own personal and corporate income taxes, sales taxes, and wealth transfer taxes. Broad-based state personal income taxes are imposed by forty-three states, while corporate income taxes are imposed by forty-four states. Michigan replaced its corporate income tax with a value-added tax. Texas added an income component to its corporate franchise tax, making it a quasi-corporate income tax. General sales taxes are imposed by forty-five states. Both Alaska and New Hampshire impose no broad-based personal income taxes or general sales taxes. The principal wealth tax imposed in the USA is the local property tax, primarily a tax on real property.

State income taxes generally follow the federal income tax base with modifications. In the case of the personal income tax, most states conform to federal AGI and federal itemized deductions with certain adjustments. These states make their own provision for the standard deduction, personal exemption, and tax rate schedule. Some states, however, use a broader defini-

---

[9] Internal Revenue Service (1995*b*): 101.

tion of income than the federal one. For states with a broad-based personal income tax, the marginal tax rates and brackets vary widely across states. The deductibility of state income taxes for federal income tax purposes by taxpayers who itemize lowers the effective rate of state income taxes for these taxpayers.

Many states provide their own rules for tax depreciation. The most critical issue for state corporate income taxes is the allocation and apportionment of interstate income. The most common apportionment formula is a three-factor formula of sales, property, and payroll with sales on a destination basis double-weighted. But some states equal weight the three factors, use only two factors, or use only sales to apportion income. Also important is whether separate accounting or a unitary domestic or worldwide business is the basis for apportioning income. Most states use unitary domestic apportionment. For the forty-four states that impose a corporate income tax, the marginal tax rates and schedules exhibit a great deal of variance.

Sixteen states allow some cities to levy a personal income tax. Most of these local income taxes apply to earned income only. Counties in Maryland and school districts in Iowa piggyback on the state income tax by imposing a local tax equal to a percentage of the state tax liability. New York City imposes a progressive tax on New York City income with a top marginal tax rate of 3.4 per cent.

State sales taxes generally apply to retail sales of goods and selected services. The rates of tax range from 3 per cent in Colorado to 7 per cent in Mississippi and Rhode Island, with the median, 5 per cent (though cascading of tax through taxation of some business inputs may result in a higher effective tax rate on final consumption). Many states exempt food and most states exempt prescription drugs. States may also exempt a variety of other goods. Many local governments impose their own sales taxes (sometimes by piggybacking them on state sales taxes). The combined state and local sales tax rate is 9 per cent in a few jurisdictions. In addition to sales taxes, states impose excises on cigarettes and alcohol, often at rates in excess of the federal excises. They also impose taxes and fees on automobiles and motor fuels.

All states impose taxes on the transfer of wealth at death, and seven states impose gift taxes. The most common state death tax is the so-called 'pick-up' tax, which is equal to the maximum state death tax credit allowed under the federal estate tax. In addition to the 'pick-up' tax, some states impose separate estate or inheritance taxes. Some states also levy a tax on real and personal property, on intangibles (primarily financial assets), and on real estate transfers.

The primary tax at the local level is the property tax on real property. The base of the property tax is assessed value, although the relationship between assessed and market value varies greatly by jurisdiction and type of property. Assessed value is typically well under market value. The effective property tax rate generally ranges from 1 to 2 per cent, although nominal rates might be higher as a result of underassessment of property. Property may also be categorized into different classes, depending on its use, with residential property typically taxed at a lower rate than commercial or industrial property. Many localities have provisions, often termed 'circuit breakers', in the property tax to provide credits or otherwise reduce the burden of the tax on low-income taxpayers or renters. In addition, many localities impose a tax on tangible personal property, primarily automobiles. The tax rate is typically the same as on real property. Since property taxes are deductible for federal income tax purposes by taxpayers who itemize, this lowers the effective rate of property taxes for these taxpayers. This deductibility is unusual among OECD countries.[10]

C. Economic and Social Aspects

C1 The Fiscal Deficit

The federal deficit was \$163.8 billion (2.3 per cent of GDP) in 1995.[11] Although the federal deficit has fallen relative to GDP in recent years, health care reform is essential to prevent deficits from exploding again.

For the purpose of examining trends, the deficit is typically measured in absolute terms and relative to GDP. Table 11.2 indicates the size of the deficit and the stock of debt in absolute terms in recent decades. Table 11.3 indicates the size of the deficit and the stock of debt relative to GDP in recent decades. In every decade from the 1950s to the 1980s, the annual deficit relative to GDP (averaged over the decade) rose. The stock of debt was quite large following the Second World War, but shrank steadily relative to GDP until 1974 when it began an upward trend. Reflecting this increase in debt, interest payments on debt have also risen rapidly over this period.

Most tax bills since 1981 (with the marked exception of the Tax Reform Act of 1986) have been driven by the budget deficit. Recently, the US Congress rejected adopting a balanced budget amendment to the Constitution, which would have required a balanced budget by the year 2001 and a two-thirds majority in both chambers of the Congress to run a deficit and increase the debt limit. Nevertheless, the deficit has continued to generate debate and held up the 1996 budget and the increase in the statutory debt limit. Despite all of the attention paid to the deficit in recent decades, even such basic issues as how to measure the deficit and the consequences of a large deficit are still controversial matters. On one side, some argue that a large federal deficit is the most serious problem facing the federal government and the national economy, while on the other side some argue that this problem is greatly exaggerated.

The main argument against high deficits is that they may lead to a decline in

---

[10] Messere (1993): 441.   [11] Economic Report of the President (1996): 367.

overall saving in the economy. US saving is low compared to historical norms and other industrialized countries. The concern over low saving stems from the belief that it may lead to a low level of investment or large capital inflows. If the deficit absorbs a significant part of the net savings of the private sector, then domestic saving may be insufficient to finance investment. This may result in the USA depending on flows of foreign capital to finance this gap. Ultimately, foreign financing leads to the acquisition of wealth by foreigners to whom accrues the return to capital. While foreign financing may raise the capital stock of the USA (and thus the amount of capital per worker), many of the benefits of the productive investments flow abroad. The deficit may also lead to higher interest rates, crowding out private investment and thus leading to a lower long-run capital stock.

The main argument against excess concern over the deficit is the traditional Keynesian notion that deficits stimulate demand through higher government spending or lower taxes and hence have a beneficial effect on the economy, particularly when economic activity is slack. In addition, it is argued that mismeasurement of the deficit ignores the component of debt that is used for public capital investments, which may lead to higher output in the long run.

From a distributional perspective, it is argued that since most of the debt is held by Americans, it is largely a transfer from one to the other. The inter-generational aspects of this redistribution have received more attention in recent years, however.

The most common measure of the federal deficit is the difference between federal government expenditures and revenues. The federal government's unified budget measures the cash deficit, and the budget's annual surplus or deficit reflects the combined expenditures and revenues of the general fund and the trust funds.[12] Within the conventional measure of the deficit, there are many ways to distort its size. In any fiscal year, the government can accelerate revenues or slow down payments. In addition, the government can sell assets, move agencies or expenditures and revenues off budget, or redefine the general fund.

Some economists have criticized the conventional measurement of the deficit and debt. Eisner (1986) argues that conventional measures are mis-leading for several important reasons. First, the measurement of the deficit is flawed because the federal budget, unlike state budgets, does not separate capital and current expenditures. Capital expenditures are typically financed by debt because they finance investments that lead to an increase in the wealth-generating capacity of the economy. The conventional measurement of the deficit thus may create a bias against capital investments. Second, the measurement of the deficit is flawed because it does not account for changes in the stock of outstanding debt as a result of inflation, which reduces the value

---

[12] US Postal Service and the Tennessee Valley Authority are part of the budget even though they are quasi-government activities.

Table 11.2 Federal receipts, outlays, surplus or deficit, and debt, fiscal years 1950–1995 ($bn.; fiscal years)

Fiscal year or period	Receipts	Outlays	Surplus or deficit (−)	Gross federal debt (end of period)	GDP
1950	39.4	42.6	−3.1	256.9	265.8
1951	51.6	45.5	6.1	255.3	313.5
1952	66.2	67.7	−1.5	259.1	340.5
1953	69.6	76.1	−6.5	266.0	363.8
1954	69.7	70.9	−1.2	270.8	368.0
1955	65.5	68.4	−3.0	274.4	384.7
1956	74.6	70.6	3.9	272.7	416.3
1957	80.0	76.6	3.4	272.3	438.3
1958	79.6	82.4	−2.8	279.7	448.1
1959	79.2	92.1	−12.8	287.5	480.2
1960	92.5	92.2	0.3	290.5	504.6
1961	94.4	97.7	−3.3	292.6	517.0
1962	99.7	106.8	−7.1	302.9	555.2
1963	106.6	111.3	−4.8	310.3	584.5
1964	112.6	118.5	−5.9	316.1	625.3
1965	116.8	118.2	−1.4	322.3	671.0
1966	130.8	134.5	−3.7	328.5	735.4
1967	148.8	157.5	−8.6	340.4	793.3
1968	153.0	178.1	−25.2	368.7	847.2
1969	186.9	183.6	3.2	365.8	925.7
1970	192.8	195.6	−2.8	380.9	985.4
1971	187.1	210.2	−23.0	408.2	1,050.9
1972	207.3	230.7	−23.4	435.9	1,147.8
1973	230.8	245.7	−14.9	466.3	1,274.0
1974	263.2	269.4	−6.1	483.9	1,403.6
1975	279.1	332.3	−53.2	541.9	1,509.8
1976	298.1	371.8	−73.7	629.0	1,684.2
trans. quarter	81.2	96.0	−14.7	643.6	445.0
1977	355.6	409.2	−53.7	706.4	1,917.2
1978	399.6	458.7	−59.2	776.6	2,155.0
1979	463.3	503.5	−40.2	828.9	2,429.5
1980	517.1	590.9	−73.8	908.5	2,644.1
1981	599.3	678.2	−79.0	994.3	2,964.4
1982	617.8	745.8	−128.0	1,136.8	3,122.2
1983	600.6	808.4	−207.8	1,371.2	3,316.5
1984	666.5	851.8	−185.4	1,564.1	3,695.0
1985	734.1	946.4	−212.3	1,817.0	3,967.7
1986	769.1	990.3	−221.2	2,120.1	4,219.0
1987	854.1	1,003.9	−149.8	2,345.6	4,452.4
1988	909.0	1,064.1	−155.2	2,600.8	4,808.4

Table 11.2   Continued

Fiscal year or period	Receipts	Outlays	Surplus or deficit (−)	Gross federal debt (end of period)	GDP
1989	990.7	1,143.2	−152.5	2,867.5	5,173.3
1990	1,031.3	1,252.7	−221.4	3,206.2	5,481.5
1991	1,054.3	1,323.8	−269.5	3,598.3	5,673.3
1992	1,090.5	1,380.9	−290.4	4,001.9	5,937.2
1993	1,153.5	1,408.7	−255.1	4,351.4	6,258.6
1994	1,257.7	1,460.9	−203.2	4,643.7	6,633.6
1995	1,350.6	1,514.4	−163.8	4,921.0	7,004.5

Note: Through fiscal year 1976, the fiscal year was on a 1 July–30 June basis; beginning October 1976 (fiscal year 1977), the fiscal year is on a 1 October–30 September basis. The 3-month period from 1 July 1976, through 30 September 1976, is a separate fiscal period known as the transition quarter. Refunds of receipts are excluded from receipts and outlays.

Source: Economic Report of the President (1996) Table B–74: 367.

of this debt relative to GDP. Third, the changes in the value of government debt should be offset by changes in the value of government assets to get a true measure of the net debt of the government, defined as federal liabilities minus financial assets.

In addition, conventional measures of the budget deficit have been criticized for focusing only on cash issues not commitments, such as loan guarantees and potential social security insurance claims. These loan guarantees and potential insurance claims can result in large expenditures for the government, as in the savings and loan crisis, and it is therefore argued that some account of potential expenditures should be included in the measure of the deficit.

Auerbach *et al.* (1994) argue that the conventional measure of the deficit is misleading because it ignores future taxes and transfers, thereby neglecting the intergenerational aspects of the deficit. They recommend using generational accounts, which comprise a set of numbers, one for each generation, indicating the net amount members of that generation will, on average, pay the government over their remaining lifetime. They argue that shifting of fiscal burdens can occur even leaving the conventional measure of the budget deficit unchanged. Nevertheless, Haveman (1994) suggests some limitations of this analysis, including the important problem that the measure ignores the benefits from the non-transfer component of government spending.

Modifying the simple cash deficit to account for these additional considerations raises a whole host of measurement and conceptual issues. As a result, most measures of the deficit are still limited to the conventional definition, although there is more awareness nowadays of the arbitrary nature of this definition.

Table 11.3 Federal receipts, outlays, surplus or deficit, and debt, as a percentage of gross domestic product, fiscal years 1950–1995 (%; fiscal years)

Fiscal year or period	Receipts	Outlays	Surplus or deficit (−)	Gross federal debt (end of period)
1950	14.8	16.0	−1.2	96.6
1951	16.5	14.5	1.9	81.4
1952	19.4	19.9	−0.4	76.1
1953	19.1	20.9	−1.8	73.1
1954	18.9	19.3	−0.3	73.6
1955	17.0	17.8	−0.8	71.3
1956	17.9	17.0	0.9	65.5
1957	18.3	17.5	0.8	62.1
1958	17.8	18.4	−0.6	62.4
1959	16.5	19.2	−2.7	59.9
1960	18.3	18.3	0.1	57.6
1961	18.3	18.9	−0.6	56.6
1962	18.0	19.2	−1.3	54.6
1963	18.2	19.0	−0.8	53.1
1964	18.0	19.0	−0.9	50.5
1965	17.4	17.6	−0.2	48.0
1966	17.8	18.3	−0.5	44.7
1967	18.8	19.8	−1.1	42.9
1968	18.1	21.0	−3.0	43.5
1969	20.2	19.8	0.4	39.5
1970	19.6	19.9	−0.3	38.7
1971	17.8	20.0	−2.2	38.8
1972	18.1	20.1	−2.0	38.0
1973	18.1	19.3	−1.2	36.6
1974	18.8	19.2	−0.4	34.5
1975	18.5	22.0	−3.5	35.9
1976	17.7	22.1	−4.4	37.3
trans. quarter	18.3	21.6	−3.3	36.2
1977	18.5	21.3	−2.8	36.8
1978	18.5	21.3	−2.7	36.0
1979	19.1	20.7	−1.7	34.1
1980	19.6	22.3	−2.8	34.4
1981	20.2	22.9	−2.7	33.5
1982	19.8	23.9	−4.1	36.4
1983	18.1	24.4	−6.3	41.3
1984	18.0	23.1	−5.0	42.3
1985	18.5	23.9	−5.4	45.8
1986	18.2	23.5	−5.2	50.3
1987	19.2	22.5	−3.4	52.7
1988	18.9	22.1	−3.2	54.1

Table 11.3   Continued

Fiscal year or period	Receipts	Outlays	Surplus or deficit (−)	Gross federal debt (end of period)
1989	19.2	22.1	−2.9	55.4
1990	18.8	22.9	−4.0	58.5
1991	18.6	23.3	−4.8	63.4
1992	18.4	23.3	−4.9	67.4
1993	18.4	22.5	−4.1	69.5
1994	19.0	22.0	−3.1	70.0
1995	19.3	21.6	−2.3	70.3

Note: Through fiscal year 1976, the fiscal year was on a 1 July–30 June basis; beginning October 1976 (fiscal year 1977), the fiscal year is on a 1 October–30 September basis. The 3-month period from 1 July 1976 through 1 September 1976, is a separate fiscal period known as the transition quarter. Refunds of receipts are excluded from receipts and outlays.

Source: Economic Report of the President (1996), Table B–75: 368.

The federal budget process is a complicated undertaking, consisting of several distinct stages.[13] First, the Congress must authorize a programme to spend funds. The authorization sets the limit on the amount that can be spent on a programme. Second, the Congress must appropriate funds. An entitlement is a type of authorization that does not need a specific appropriation because it requires the federal government to pay benefits to any person or unit of government that qualifies. It requires an appropriation but it is often permanent from year to year with no specific amount allocated. Examples are the largest programmes of the federal government, including social security and Medicare. Authorization and appropriation bills list amounts in terms of 'budget authority'.

Outlays are actual spending measured on a cash basis. In some cases, many activities take place over more than one year, so budget authority is given beyond the current fiscal year. Spending in any year consists of outlays from new authorizations and outlays from previous authorizations.

Expenditures are divided in the budget act into those termed 'discretionary' and 'mandatory'. Discretionary expenditures are those for which the government must pass an appropriation, while mandatory expenditures are those for which it does not need to pass a specific appropriation. Nevertheless, mandatory expenditures are not really outside of legislative control because they may be altered through legislation. A large part of the federal budget is classified as mandatory expenditures, especially entitlements and interest on the national debt.

The federal government has passed various legislation in recent years to

[13] Collender (1994).

provide a framework for limiting the deficit. The Balanced Budget and Emergency Deficit Control Act of 1985, also known as Gramm–Rudman–Hollings (GRH), set declining annual deficit targets to produce a balanced budget and created a provision for automatic across-the-board cuts, termed sequestration, in the event that the Office of Management and Budget estimated the regular spending and revenue legislation did not achieve that year's deficit target. This sequestration feature set limits for discretionary and mandatory spending and required sequestration when the limits for either were exceeded, although many mandatory programmes were exempted. The Budget Enforcement Act of 1990 (BEA) subsequently revised this sequestration and the Omnibus Budget Reconciliation Act of 1993 extended its most important provisions through fiscal year 1998. BEA, in contrast to GRH, does not force the federal government to limit the deficit. Instead, it sets out sequestration procedures to limit spending to current levels for mandatory programmes and at or below a cap for discretionary programmes, and to maintain expected revenues at or above an expected baseline. The Pay-as-you-go (PAYGO) sequester sets a baseline that is the amount of mandatory spending and revenue that will be raised under existing law. The PAYGO rules require that the net effect of all congressional legislation dealing with mandatory spending and tax legislation does not increase the deficit in any year. If it does, then the government is required to cut eligible mandatory programmes so as to offset the increase.

The upshot of all this legislation has been that the federal government budget process has become complicated and unwieldy. The debate over limiting the budget deficit has led to sensible efforts to contain the deficit. But it has also spawned a whole host of misleading and unnecessary budget practices, further complicating attempts to formulate a sensible budget strategy and obscuring the meaning of the deficit.

There are several important trends in federal revenues and expenditures underlying measures of the deficit. In recent years, the overall share of federal taxes in GDP has not changed much, but an increasing share has come from the trust fund taxes, primarily social security, and a diminishing share from general revenues, primarily in corporate income tax and excise taxes.

Federal expenditures for both the general fund and trust funds have increased, with the general fund rising more rapidly in recent years. By the late 1970s, it became clear that the social security trust fund would become insolvent when the baby boom generation retired because of the lower birth rate, the lower rate of growth of productivity, the generous level of benefits, and the overindexing of initial benefit levels. As a result, the federal government reformed the social security system in 1977 and 1983, significantly increasing the payroll tax, modestly increasing the retirement age for full benefits, taxing some benefits for the first time, and eliminating of the over-indexation of initial benefit levels in 1977. Under current law, the social insurance trust funds would be sufficient to pay timely benefits for the next thirty-three years or so.[14] At the same time, the government took steps toward fuller funding of civilian and military retirement programmes, producing surpluses in those trust funds as well. The trust fund surpluses are invested in Treasury bonds that finance the general fund deficit, so in net, the trust funds are financing a significant part of the deficit. In the 1980s, expenditures for defence and health care grew rapidly along with interest on the public debt. While defence spending has slowed in recent years, health care continues to absorb an increasing share of the budget.

There are many options for limiting any budget problems, which involve a combination of increasing revenues and cutting spending. On the revenue side, the federal government could increase personal income, corporate income, payroll, or excise tax rates; it could broaden the base of the personal or corporate income taxes or it could reduce tax expenditures; it could introduce a broad-based consumption or energy tax; or it could undertake some mixture of these revenue measures. On the expenditure side, it has many options, of which the most promising is curtailing the growth of health-care expenditures.

C2 Savings and Investment Incentives

C2.1 Savings

Private savings relative to income has declined since the early 1950s. The factors underlying this decline in the savings rate are complex, and give rise to public policy concern. Private savings is undertaken by private corporations in the form of retained earnings and by individuals in many forms, including homeownership and other consumer durables, pensions, and financial instruments. The concern over the low rate of savings in the USA has spawned many attempts to influence this rate through savings incentives built into the tax code. Steuerle (1985) estimates that about 80 per cent of all individual assets qualify for some form of tax incentive.

Economic theory suggests that saving is linked to its after-tax return. Despite extensive research on this issue, it is an open empirical question whether saving is responsive to its after-tax return. Bovenberg (1989) finds in a survey of the literature that there is little link between saving and rates of return, while other factors are more critical.

Even if tax policy does not affect the overall level of savings, another important issue is whether tax policy influences the composition of savings. The evidence is more compelling that tax incentives can alter the composition of savings. The tax system may lead to distortions in the allocation of savings between housing and financial assets, and among corporate assets, other

---

[14] Congress of the United States (1996): 25.

business assets, and personal assets, and so on. These tax-induced shifts in the composition of savings can potentially lead to significant efficiency losses.[15]

The tax treatment of capital income through capital gains taxes and taxes on interest and dividends has varied over time. Preferential taxation of capital gains realizations, exclusion of gains upon death, and the deferral of taxation on unrealized gains offer incentives to save in the form of capital assets likely to appreciate in value, although these incentives are offset by the tax on purely inflationary gains because the measure of gains is not indexed to inflation. The degree of integration of the individual and corporate income taxes also influences the taxation of capital income. These issues are discussed in more detail later.

Incentives to save in the form of homeownership exist because of the advantages to homeowners through the continuing non-taxation of imputed income from homeownership. In the absence of taxation of imputed income, mortgage and home equity interest should not be allowed as a deduction. As a result, there is a considerable tax advantage to homeownership, although the extent of this advantage has changed over time.[16]

The tax code also has incentives for savings through pensions and life insurance vehicles, although life insurance savings must have a significant insurance component to gain the tax advantages. There are various incentives in the tax code intended to increase retirement savings. The Revenue Act of 1942 made employer pension contributions tax-deductible. In addition, income on investments is deferred until the pension is paid out. There are two main types of pension plans. Defined benefit plans prescribe a specific benefit to retirees based on their income and years of employment with the enterprise and the pay-out depends in part on the continued survival and health of the enterprise. Defined contribution plans prescribe a certain contribution to the fund and the pay-out depends on the investment performance of the fund. The Internal Revenue Service limits the deductibility of employer contributions to defined benefit plans, depending on the level of funding of the plan. Hence, higher returns on the investments of these funds may actually lead to a decline in contributions, thus resulting in an inverse relationship between return on savings and contributions. Nevertheless, the overall tax advantages to pension savings have led to enormous growth in pension funds, particularly defined contribution plans, although this growth has slowed recently. In 1990, defined benefit plans accounted for 57 per cent of pension assets.[17] Tax advantages for life insurance exist because only life insurance companies can offer certain products, such as tax-deferred annuities, and the inside build-up on life insurance policies with a significant investment component is tax-deferred.

Many employees are not, however, covered by employer-provided pension

[15] Fullerton *et al.* (1983): 3–23.   [16] Poterba (1990): 141–60.
[17] US House of Representatives Committee on Ways and Means (1994): 735.

arrangements. To provide savings incentives to these employees, there are several alternatives. The Congress created the individual retirement account (IRA) in 1974. Under the original IRA, employees without employer-provided pension plans could put up to $1,500 each year in an IRA. As with pensions, contributions are tax-deductible and the investment earnings are untaxed until withdrawn. The income was then taxed on withdrawal. Self-employed taxpayers obtained a similar benefit in 1962 with the introduction of Keogh plans.

The 401(k) programme is another form of pension arrangement. It was created in 1978 but was not widely used until 1981. Only employees of firms that offer these plans may participate and employers may match employee contributions to these plans. As with qualified pensions, contributions are tax-deductible and the investment earnings are untaxed until withdrawn.

Legislation in 1981 extended IRAs to all employees, leading to a rapid increase in their use. The Tax Reform Act of 1986 restricted IRA benefits by eliminating the deduction for contributions for higher-income individuals covered by employee pension plans. Nevertheless, non-deductible IRAs, like individual annuities, still have tax advantages because the income earned by the IRA is not subject to tax until withdrawal. New IRA savings declined precipitously after 1986 because of the loss of tax privileges to higher-income taxpayers and the reduced promotion of IRAs by financial institutions. Proposals to enhance the appeal of IRAs include restoring the up-front deduction, eliminating penalties for early withdrawals or if withdrawals are used for certain purposes such as home purchases, and introducing back-loaded plans (no deductibility of contributions and no tax upon withdrawal). The last option defers the revenue costs for the government (and the tax savings to individuals) to the future. In 1996, Congress increased the avail-ability of spousal IRAs.

In contrast to IRAs, 401(k) plan contributions have grown in recent years. Contributions were $49 billion in 1990 compared to IRA contributions of $10 billion. Taken together, individual contributions to IRAs and 401(k) plans have grown relative to employer contributions to pension plans in recent years.

The importance of encouraging private savings has led to considerable research on the extent to which these IRAs and similar plans stimulate private savings. Gravelle (1991) argues that the tax difference is the only difference between saving in the form of IRAs and other forms of saving, and since IRAs can be financed from tax savings, shifting, borrowing, diverting new savings, or reducing consumption, the key issue is how much comes from reduced consumption. Gravelle maintains that theory and evidence suggest not much. The theoretical case against IRAs is that savings are unresponsive to the change in the after-tax rate of return, the dollar cap limits the substitution effect at the margin for individuals whose assets or new savings exceed the limit, and the overall low savings rate leaves little room for IRAs to play a role. Gale and Scholz (1994) suggest that IRAs do not largely represent a net addition to personal saving, though Venti and Wise (1992) suggest the contrary. Poterba *et al.* (1995) conclude that 401(k) saving largely represents a net addition to personal saving.

Although the evidence is mixed, many observers have questioned the effectiveness of personal savings incentives and instead suggest that reduction of the public sector deficit is more important for promoting national savings.

C2.2 Investment

The decline in saving has been accompanied by a decline in domestic investment. This decline was, however, smaller than the decline in domestic saving because flows of financing from abroad compensated for some of the decline in the latter. In the standard neoclassical model of the firm, firms invest until the real marginal product of capital is equal to the marginal user cost of capital. Investment demand is inversely related to the cost of capital. Taxes alter the cost of capital, creating a divergence between actual returns and returns investors receive on investments.[18] By altering the cost of capital, taxes may alter investment demand. Many areas of the tax code influence the cost of capital, including the treatment of debt and equity, corporate and personal income tax rates, the treatment of capital gains, depreciation allowances, investment tax credits, special tax preferences, the lack of inflation adjustment, and the classical system of taxation.

The user cost of capital is difficult to measure because it depends in a complicated way on the provisions of both corporate and personal income taxes, as well as assumptions about inflation rates and other economic variables. A recent study compared marginal effective tax rates on corporate capital, non-corporate capital, and owner-occupied housing and also by type of asset, industry, source of finance, and form of ownership, using the methodology developed in King and Fullerton (1984).[19] This study compared the marginal effective tax rates for nine countries (the G7 countries, Australia, and Sweden) for the years 1980, 1985, and 1990.

Under one set of assumptions, in 1990, the overall marginal effective tax rate on corporate-source income in the USA was 38.5 per cent; only Australia, Canada, and France had higher overall tax rates. The US effective tax rate increased from 26.2 per cent in 1985. The overall marginal effective tax rate on non-corporate-source income was 21.7 per cent in 1990, rising from 12.7 per cent in 1985. The overall marginal effective tax rate on housing was 11.2 per cent in 1990, falling slightly from 11.8 per cent in 1985. Both the tax rates on non-corporate and housing capital were considerably lower than the tax rate on corporate-source income over this period, thus leading to significant incentives to invest outside of the corporate sector. In addition, the gap between corporate and other forms of investment widened over this period.

[18] Sinn (1991): 25–54.   [19] Jorgenson and Landau (1993): 16–23.

There was considerable variation in the tax rate across asset, industry, source of finance, and owner. The tax on different corporate assets ranged from 34.1 per cent for machinery to 39.6 per cent on buildings and 40.3 per cent on inventories in 1990, but this variation was considerably less than in 1985 when the tax rates were 3.8 per cent on machinery, 28.7 per cent on buildings, and 41.8 per cent on inventories. The tax rate was higher for manufacturing compared to other industries and for equity compared to debt in 1990, but again these gaps narrowed over the 1985–90 period.

Various tax measures have been proposed to stimulate investment, including reducing the capital gains or ordinary income tax rates, corporate tax integration, providing more generous depreciation allowances, establishing special enterprise zones, and providing either investment tax credits or allowances. In addition, some economists have long advocated shifting to a consumption-based tax system from an income-based system. As a result of the interest in stimulating investment, there have been frequent changes in the provisions of the tax law that apply to corporate investment. The 1986 Act eliminated the investment tax credit and lengthened depreciation for most assets, increasing the cost of capital but reducing the differences in effective tax rates between machinery and buildings. Despite its elimination in 1986, the investment tax credit in one form or another has been a recurring proposal. Most research has found, however, that the increase in the cost of capital—at least in the range found in the USA—has not had a strong impact on investment,[20] although conflicting evidence is available.[21]

C3 Distribution of the Tax Burden

Distributional analysis in the tax policy process assesses the effect of the tax system on different taxpayers, generally taking as given the underlying pattern of income distribution. Distributional analysis has taken on more importance in the federal tax policy process in recent years because of the concern over the changing distribution of income. This concern manifested itself during the debate over the 1986 Act. To focus on horizontal equity and efficiency issues, the intention then was to leave roughly unchanged the overall distribution of tax burdens on different groups. This intention changed under the Clinton administration with President Clinton making it clear in the 1993 Budget Act that he intended to raise tax burdens only on the wealthy.

Under the assumption that after-tax income is a measure of well-being, the critical issue is the extent to which the tax system offsets or accentuates any inequality in pre-tax income. It is widely believed that income distribution in the USA has grown more unequal in recent years. This growing inequality has been attributed to various causes. It has been argued that the changing demands of the workplace have led to an increase in the demand for highly

---

[20] Gravelle (1993): 275–90.   [21] Auerbach and Hassett (1990): 13–40.

skilled workers, a reduction in the demand for less-educated workers in well-paid blue-collar jobs, as well as an increase in the supply of less-educated workers through large-scale immigration. Several commentators have suggested that a disproportionate share of the increases in real income in recent years accrued to a relatively small group of the highest-income tax-payers.[22] Nevertheless, since there is a significant degree of income mobility, the highest-income taxpayers are not the same in each year.

Feenberg and Poterba (1993) investigated the rising share of AGI reported by high-income taxpayers using tax return data from 1951 to 1990. They found that most of the increase was owing to a rise in reported income for the richest one-quarter of 1 per cent of taxpayers, with this pattern sharpest in 1987 and 1988. They attribute some of this change to a reduced incentive to avoid taxes following the reduction in the highest marginal tax rates in the 1986 Act. This line of research emphasizes the importance of examining not only the effect of taxes on after-tax income but also how pre-tax income is changing.

The Congressional Budget Office regularly presents data on trends in income tax progressivity. Table 11.4 shows the federal effective tax rate for all families categorized by income group in quintiles. The effective tax rate on the poorest fifth went up and down during the 1977–94 period, falling quite substantially by 1994. In this same period, the tax burden on the highest income quintile fell slightly, although rising from its low in the 1980s. Families with the highest 1 per cent of income experienced the largest overall drop in the effective tax rate from 35.4 to 28.8 per cent. In this same period, the tax burden on the middle income quintiles remained roughly the same.[23]

Fullerton and Rogers (1993) also examined the incidence of the US tax system, taking a lifetime approach to measuring incidence. They term a tax as progressive if the lifetime tax burden as a fraction of lifetime income rises and vice versa. They found that the personal income tax is progressive while sales, excise, and payroll taxes are regressive. The results are thus similar to existing studies using an annual burden measure.[24] With respect to a tax on capital, Fullerton and Rogers found, in contrast to previous research, a u-shaped pattern of incidence, with the lowest burden on middle-income taxpayers. They also found that the corporate tax has a regressive incidence. Overall, they concluded that the US tax system is roughly proportional across middle-income groups but progressive at the very bottom and very top of the income distribution. Their assessment of the effect of the 1986 Act was that all groups gained through improved resource allocation but that the Act did not significantly alter the progressivity of the tax system.

Metcalf (1994) computed the lifetime tax incidence of major state and local

[22] Congress of the United States Congressional Budget Office (1992).
[23] US House of Representatives Committee on Ways and Means (1993): 1497.
[24] Pechman (1985).

Table 11.4 Total federal effective tax rates for all families

All families (by income group)	1977	1980	1985	1988	1990	1994[a]	Per cent change	
							1977–94	1985–94
Lowest quintile	9.2	8.1	10.4	9.3	8.9	7.1	−23.2	−32.0
Second quintile	15.5	15.6	15.9	15.9	15.8	15.1	−2.3	−4.9
Middle quintile	19.5	19.8	19.2	19.8	19.5	19.4	−0.7	0.8
Fourth quintile	21.9	22.9	21.7	22.4	22.1	22.1	1.1	1.8
81 to 90%	24.0	25.3	23.5	24.6	24.4	24.6	2.5	4.7
91 to 95%	25.4	26.5	24.3	26.0	25.6	25.9	2.2	6.5
96 to 99%	27.1	28.1	24.3	26.5	26.1	27.0	−0.4	11.0
Top 1%	35.4	31.9	24.5	26.9	26.3	28.8	−18.8	17.2
Overall	22.8	23.3	21.8	22.9	22.6	23.0	1.0	5.8
Highest quintile	27.2	27.6	24.1	26.0	25.5	26.5	−2.7	9.9
Top 10%	28.9	28.7	24.4	26.5	26.0	27.3	−5.5	11.9
Top 5%	30.6	29.7	24.4	26.7	26.2	27.9	−9.0	14.1

[a] Projected.
Note: Quintiles are weighted by families.
Source: Congressional Budget Office.

taxes in the USA during the 1980s. He found that, over the life cycle, general sales taxes are progressive—as progressive as state and local income taxes—which is a surprising conclusion. He also found that state income taxes became less progressive over the 1984–9 period and property taxes more progressive. He concluded that the overall state and local tax system is mildly progressive over the life cycle and became slightly more so over the 1984–9 period.

There are many important methodological issues involved in distributional analysis,[25] including what taxes to consider, how to define income, how to measure the tax burden, what assumptions to use about the incidence of each tax, and the manner of presenting the results. Agencies of the federal government responsible for analysing tax policy (as well as academic researchers) have expended considerable effort in using economic theory, empirical findings, and high-quality tax data to derive measures of the distributional effect of taxes. These agencies—the Congressional Budget Office (CBO), the Joint Committee on Taxation (JCT), and the Office of Tax Analysis in the US Treasury Department (OTA)—employ similar, although not identical, methods.

The best source of data for analysing the distributional impact of federal taxes is provided in Statistics of Income (SOI), compiled by the Internal

[25] Hubbard (1993): 527–37 and Congress of the United States Joint Committee on Taxation (1993).

Revenue Service (IRS) from tax records. The IRS generates statistically representative samples from taxpayers on an annual basis, providing a highly accurate source of data on information contained in tax returns. Nevertheless, SOI data still have certain problems. The most important problem is that AGI lacks certain key components of income that taxpayers are not required to include on their returns. Another problem is that the definition of AGI changes from year to year depending on tax legislation. Therefore, for purposes of accurate distributional analysis, it is necessary to augment AGI by components missing from the tax data and to use a constant definition of income.

Another problem with the tax data is that they provide information only on tax filers. Many low-income taxpayers do not file if they have no tax liability. Given the importance of low-income taxpayers in distributional concerns, the federal agencies have augmented the tax data by merging information from other sources, primarily the Current Population Survey (CPS), based on a 'statistical match' using common core variables, to construct the overall distribution of income.[26] Another problem stems from taxpayers who simply do not file or present highly inaccurate information. The SOI data also ignore state and local taxes and some foreign taxes, leaving a less than comprehensive picture of taxes. In addition, tax records yield little information on demographic characteristics of taxpayers. The CPS data present an appealing supplement to SOI data but are also limited in that high incomes are top-coded (only the lower bound of the top range is indicated) and the information on specific components of income, such as capital income, are relatively poor compared to SOI data.

With respect to which taxes to include, the most complete analysis would include taxes at all levels of government, although the federal agencies typically focus only on federal taxes, excluding customs duties (which are negligible).

There are many possible ways to define income for purposes of this analysis. The federal agencies use different annual income measures that attempt to capture economic income. The income measure found on tax returns is AGI, but for purposes of distributional analysis, this measure is typically expanded to account for other forms of income, such as tax-exempt interest, workers' compensation, non-taxable social security benefits, the value of Medicare benefits in excess of premiums paid, minimum tax preferences, employer contributions for health plans and life insurance, cash transfers, and so on. The precise additions to income vary across the federal agencies.

Income must also be measured relative to some unit of analysis, such as the family or the individual, the filing unit, or households. There is no uniformity among the federal agencies in their unit of analysis. JCT uses tax returns as the unit of analysis, while CBO and OTA use families as the unit of analysis.

[26] Cilke and Wyscarver (1987): 43–75.

A related issue is the time-period over which to measure income. Typically, the analysis is based on current annual income, while permanent income is another possibility. One fundamental criticism of the use of current income to measure distributional outcomes is that it may not reflect well-being as well as consumption because current income contains large transitory elements. The life-cycle hypothesis postulates that income starts low in the early stages of life, increases over the life cycle, peaks and then declines in old age, while consumption is smoothed. Some measure of permanent or average lifetime income, which may be more highly correlated to consumption, may thus provide a better measure than annual income. In part, whether a permanent income measure is a better measure than annual income depends on the availability of accurate data on saving and borrowing. Unfortunately, basing distributional analysis on a permanent income measure considerably increases the information needed on each unit of analysis because the unit must be tracked over time. To avoid problems with annual income, some research has suggested using annual consumption rather than income as the measure for distributional analysis. But then there are problems related to the absence of accurate data on consumption and the absence of an explicit link of consumption data to tax data.

The time frame also matters when taxpayers behave strategically with respect to taxes and when tax changes are phased in or out or carry over several periods.

A critical issue is how to measure the incidence of taxes. Most analysis does not rely on constructing measures derived from formal economic concepts, but instead relies on measuring the effective tax rate on families or households with different pre-tax incomes.

Underlying the calculation of the effective tax rates are assumptions regarding the incidence of each tax. For some taxes, there is widespread agreement as to the economic incidence, while for others, there is less argument. Typically, it is assumed that the burden of the individual income tax falls on individual taxpayers, the burden of payroll taxes falls on labour, and the burden of excise taxes falls on consumers. The most controversial assumption regards the burden of the corporate income tax: the agencies diverge on whether the burden falls on owners of capital or on owners of capital and also on labour and purchasers of corporate goods.

If tax incidence is measured under the assumption that there are no behavioural changes in response to a change in taxes, ignoring substitution possibilities, this tends to overestimate the loss from tax increases and underestimates the gains from tax reductions. The federal agencies differ with respect to their behavioural assumptions as well.

Another issue is the means by which to present the results. Generally, the distribution is summarized by subgroups of the population. The choice of breakpoints for the analysis is thus an important issue. Some analyses break the distribution down according to nominal classes of expanded income, while others break the distribution down by income decile. These latter analyses may convey more information because the same number of entities are represented in each class and decile represent a standardized group rather than a group whose size relative to the population is unknown.

Graetz (1995) contrasts and critiques the different measures the federal agencies use in arriving at measurements of distributional outcomes. He suggests that given the inherent complexity and differences in the underlying methodologies, these measurements create an illusion of precision and are more misleading than helpful to the political process. He recommends discontinuing them and instead relying on qualitative judgements about the distributional impacts of tax changes. Nevertheless, policy-makers need quantitative information on the effects of tax changes. Hence, it is likely that these distributional analyses will continue to play an important role in the federal tax process.

C4 Tax Compliance and Administration

Tax evasion takes many different forms, including the failure to report income; underreporting of income, sales, or wealth; over-reporting of deductible expenses, exemptions, or exclusions; claiming of false credits; and so on.[27] Tax evasion is difficult to measure, in part because of ambiguities in the notion of evasion. Academic interest in this topic first emerged in the 1970s, with reports of a large underground economy in the USA and elsewhere.[28]

The IRS periodically measures the tax gap, defined as the difference between what taxpayers owe and what they voluntarily pay. The tax gap is $150 billion per year in taxes for all federal taxes, including income taxes, payroll taxes, and excise taxes, and is $119 billion for income taxes alone, according to recent IRS estimates. Voluntary compliance is 82 per cent of tax liability, according to these estimates. This measure represents the so-called underground economy, but not illegal activities, which would add to measures of non-compliance.[29]

The theoretical literature on tax compliance has linked compliance to the probability that non-compliance will be detected, the penalties and penalty structure for non-compliance, tax rates and the tax rate structure, and income. Empirical research, summarized in Roth *et al.* (1989), has reached some straightforward conclusions. First, income that is more visible to the IRS is more likely to be reported than other income; second, experiencing an audit may slightly increase future compliance, at least if the audit discovers all unreported taxes and the taxpayer feels the outcome is fair; third, for at least some taxpayers, higher audit rates in local geographic areas may increase compliance; and fourth, the IRS succeeds to some extent in concentrating audit resources on the least compliant taxpayers.

[27] Tanzi and Shome (1993): 807–28.   [28] Tanzi (1982).   [29] Hershey (1993).

This research has also reached some surprising conclusions. First, the evidence linking higher compliance to higher penalties is relatively weak, and second, lower tax rates do not necessarily lead to more compliance by reducing the rewards of evasion. It thus appears that a simple economic explanation for tax evasion is not sufficient. In addition to financial self-interest, there may be many other factors influencing compliance. Certainly public attitudes towards social responsibility are important determinants of tax compliance.

In calendar year 1993, 153 million tax returns were filed, including 114 million for individual income taxes and 4.4 million for corporations.[30] For returns filed in calendar year 1993, the IRS examined 1.08 per cent of individual returns and 2.31 per cent of corporate returns, although it examines a greater proportion of returns from high-income taxpayers and large corporations. In 1993, it examined 55.14 per cent of returns for corporations with assets of $250 million or more.[31]

Compliance is integrally linked to the system of tax administration. The IRS pursues several tacks to increase compliance. The most effective tool for maintaining a high degree of compliance is the withholding system in place for wage earners. Set up during the Second World War, this system enabled the enormous increase in the personal income tax. Although Congress has debated the merits of extending the withholding system to non-labour income, as is found in some other industrialized nations, interest and dividend income are not generally subject to withholding.

To supplement the withholding system for individual filers, the IRS relies upon its information returns programme to ensure compliance. Information reports are filed for income from which tax has been withheld, as well as some income not subject to withholding, such as interest and dividends. Other reports provide information on deductions, such as mortgage interest. These reports also go to the taxpayers, easing their compliance burden, since much of the information taxpayers need for filing their return is contained in these reports. The IRS then matches these information reports with the returns filed by taxpayers to ensure that this income does not escape tax.

Greater difficulties in ensuring high levels of compliance arise with business and corporate taxpayers and partnerships and sole proprietorships, which have neither a withholding system nor information reporting.

To enhance its compliance efforts, the IRS has several programmes. First, it audits taxpayers through the general examination programme to determine compliance across all types of taxpayers. Second, it audits specific types of taxpayers, such as sole proprietors, through a special examination programme. Third, it has undertaken research as part of the Taxpayer Compliance Measurement Program (TCMP), which uses detailed examinations of a random sample of taxpayers of various types taken on a regular

---

[30] Internal Revenue Service (1995): 92.   [31] Ibid.

basis to measure non-compliance. In 1996, the IRS postponed its TCMP effort on 1994 individual returns owing to Congressional concerns that the audits were too invasive.

In 1987, the IRS studied in detail sources of non-compliance among several important groups of taxpayers. The IRS based its estimates of the tax gap for sole proprietors and small businesses on the results of its TCMP study. The IRS based its estimates for large corporations on detailed examinations in its Coordinated Examination Program, which uses teams of examiners and specialists. The IRS could not use detailed examinations to estimate informal suppliers' non-compliance since there is little documentation on those operating on a cash basis.

The 1987 study showed that sole proprietors have extensive amounts of unreported income and also overstate business deductions. The IRS also finds that small corporations tend to have unreported income and to overstate deductions, while large corporations generally report their income but improperly allocate it among their foreign and domestic operations.

Across components, the IRS concludes that the factors responsible for non-compliance include the absence of third-party reporting and withholding on business transactions of small businesses, and the complexity and vagueness of the nation's tax law.[32, 33]

For sole proprietors and small corporations, the IRS concludes that non-compliance is both intentional, reflecting a competitive business environment, and unintentional, reflecting the inability of taxpayers to understand the tax law. It also concludes that the absence of withholding and information reporting contributes to non-compliance. For large corporations, it concludes non-compliance results from vagueness in the tax law. For informal suppliers, it finds that non-compliance stems from the use of cash, and the absence of documentation on transactions and third-party controls.

The General Accounting Office, the IRS, and others have recommended ways to improve compliance. For example, they have recommended using information returns to identify other types of non-compliance, such as mis-classifying employees as independent contractors. In addition, they have recommended expanding information reporting to cover payments made by households and corporations, withholding on certain payments, such as dividends and interest, and other means. For many years, the IRS has been engaged in a programme to improve its computer system to allow it to expand its tax-compliance capabilities. The IRS's computing capabilities have seriously lagged in recent years.

One difficulty the IRS confronts in enhancing compliance is the complexity of the tax code, particularly the income tax. The US tax code and regulations

[32] US General Accounting Office (1990a).
[33] At times, the US tax system has been criticized for being too specific, rather than too vague, and insufficiently based on broad principles.

take up volumes. Adding to this complexity is the frequency of changes in the tax laws. The Internal Revenue Code has been amended more than 100 times since 1980.[34] To increase compliance and reduce the opportunities for evasion, the IRS has made efforts to simplify the tax-filing process for tax-payers. These efforts include new and simpler forms, town meetings, safe harbours for complicated rules, and so on.

Nevertheless, the costs of complying with the tax code remain substantial. Taxpayers face high monetary and time costs in record-keeping, research, preparing and filing of returns, the purchase of professional assistance, and tax-related litigation. There are also costs associated with third parties, such as employers and financial institutions, and costs associated with taxpayers rearranging their activities to reduce taxes. Slemrod (1992) estimated that the costs of collecting the personal income tax is between 5 and 10 per cent of tax revenue.

Tax policy interacts with compliance as well. Many of the reforms of the 1986 Act should have contributed to increased tax compliance. For instance, a flatter rate structure should improve compliance since taxpayers cannot benefit from shifting income from one bracket to another. Raising the floor on certain itemized deductions should increase compliance by limiting the number of taxpayers who can claim these deductions. Limiting tax shelters should increase compliance by affording taxpayers fewer opportunities to shelter income. A tax system that is perceived as fair is also likely to improve compliance. Nevertheless, the 1986 Act failed to simplify many critical parts of the tax code, leaving high compliance costs for certain types of taxpayers. Blumenthal and Slemrod (1992) found that contrary to expectations that the 1986 Act would reduce the compliance costs of the tax system, it made the corporate tax and part of the individual tax much more complicated. Compliance costs rose in real terms between 1982 and 1989, although they argue that not all of this increase should be attributed to the 1986 Act. In part, they argue that this increased cost could stem from changes in characteristics of taxpayers, for instance, a larger proportion of taxpayers with self-employment, capital gains, dividends or pension income, who normally face higher compliance costs.

Similar work has examined the business costs of complying with the tax system. Businesses face many similar costs to individuals in complying with the tax code. A study by Arthur D. Little, Inc. (1988), commissioned by the IRS, finds that business compliance costs are substantial and that the 1986 reforms failed to reduce these costs. Slemrod and Blumenthal (1993) found further evidence of this in a study that focuses on big businesses. They concluded that Fortune 500 companies spend over $1 billion annually complying with the tax laws. The largest share of their tax compliance costs is for filing returns. Capital cost recovery (depreciation and inventory

---

[34] Internal Revenue Service (1991): 7.

capitalization rules), the alternative minimum tax, and foreign-source income were the areas that the businesses in their study most frequently cited as leading to high compliance costs. Hall (1994) found that businesses have economies of scale in compliance costs, with costs relative to sales declining across businesses as sales increase. He estimated that businesses with annual sales of $50 million or less face a compliance cost to sales ratio of 0.5 per cent, while for businesses with annual sales greater than $10 billion, this ratio drops to 0.05 per cent. He concluded that the total business cost of compliance in 1993 was $123 billion, including corporations, partnerships, and non-farm sole proprietors.

D. Tax Reforms

D1 Main Tax Reforms, 1986–1996

The Tax Reform Act of 1986 was the most sweeping federal tax legislation since the wartime Revenue Act of 1942, which converted the income tax from a tax applying to only a few taxpayers to a mass tax applying to the many. The 1986 Act capped ten years of almost continuous major income tax legislation. It dramatically lowered marginal tax rates: for individuals, it cut the top marginal tax rate from 50 to 28 per cent, and for corporations, it reduced the top tax rate from 46 to 34 per cent, while retaining graduated tax rates for small businesses. For the first time in the history of US income tax, the top corporate tax rate was higher than the top marginal tax rate for individuals. This reduction in marginal tax rates was viewed as leading to potentially large efficiency gains in the economy through reduced distortions in labour supply, personal saving and investment, and other forms of economic behaviour.

One novel feature of the 1986 Act was the use of various income-related phase-outs to eliminate otherwise available benefits. These phase-outs produced effective marginal tax rates well in excess of the advertised top 28 per cent rate for individuals. For example, the phase-out of lower-bracket benefits and personal exemptions pushed many high-income taxpayers into a 33 per cent marginal tax bracket, the phase-out of real estate passive losses could have resulted in a 49.5 per cent marginal rate, and the phase-out of the IRA deductions could have resulted in a 33.6 per cent, or even a 39.2 per cent, marginal rate.

To achieve a revenue-neutral outcome in the face of reduced marginal tax rates, the 1986 Act significantly broadened the bases of the individual and corporate income taxes. The most important base-broadening provisions included full taxation of capital gains, curtailment of deductions for IRAs for moderate- or high-income taxpayers covered by a qualified retirement plan (or whose spouses are covered by a plan), new passive loss rules to curtail tax shelters, lengthening the depreciation period for real estate, and repeal of the two-earner deduction, the sales tax deduction, income averaging, and the investment tax credit. The 1986 Act also elevated the minimum tax from a back-stop for the regular tax to an integral part of the tax system. For corporations, the 1986 Act converted the minimum tax from a 15 per cent add-on tax to a 20 per cent alternative tax with an expanded list of tax preferences. As a result, a sizeable portion of corporate taxpayers now pay the minimum tax on a regular basis.

Although the 1986 Act was intended to be revenue-neutral, it did shift the burden of the income tax away from individuals and towards corporations. Individual income taxes were expected to decrease by $122 billion through 1991, or by about 5 per cent from expected levels under prior law, while corporate income taxes were expected to increase by $120 billion over the same period, or by about 22 per cent.[35] This increase in the taxation of corporate income led some to question whether the overall reform would improve the efficiency of the tax system.

Although the overall reduction in individual income taxes averaged 5 per cent, taxpayers at the lower end of the income scale had above average tax decreases, owing primarily to the increases in the personal exemption and the standard deduction. About one-fifth of all individual taxpayers had a tax increase. Two-earner families who had no dependants and lost the IRA deduction and high earners who made heavy use of tax shelters or realized large capital gains were likely to have tax increases.

The 1986 Act eliminated, or rapidly phased out, tax benefits for investments entered into prior to enactment of the legislation, whereas Congress had historically been liberal in granting transitional relief to taxpayers whose taxes increased as a result of changes in the tax law. By being tough on transition rules, Congress was able to phase in the tax rate reductions over only two years, thus ensuring that the rate cuts would be fully effective before President Reagan left office. Many taxpayers who had invested heavily in tax shelters suffered windfall losses as a result of the harsh transition rules.

The 1986 Act simplified the income tax for many taxpayers who lead fairly simple economic lives. It removed approximately 6 million low-income taxpayers from the tax rolls. The increase in the standard deduction shifted many taxpayers from itemizing deductions to claiming the standard deduction. Taxing capital gains at the same rate as ordinary income simplified transactional planning as it generally made little difference whether a gain was classified as ordinary or capital.

For most businesses, the 1986 Act increased the complexity of the tax law. It contained complex accounting rule changes that moved tax accounting farther away from financial accounting for income. The strengthened minimum tax, with its own accounting rules, made it difficult for many businesses to know just what tax they would be subject to in any one year.

---

[35] Congress of the United States Joint Committee on Taxation (1987): 1378.

The 1986 Act also contained complex foreign tax provisions with separate limitations on the foreign tax credit for particular kinds of foreign income.

In summary, the Tax Reform Act of 1986 was revolutionary in the depth of the rate cuts, the extent of its base broadening, and the increase in business taxes. It also set the stage for the income tax legislation enacted since 1986. But while the 1986 Act was designed to address fundamental issues of tax efficiency in a revenue-neutral manner, the post-1986 tax legislation was budget-driven and much less concerned with the fundamentals of taxation.

The Revenue Act of 1987, enacted as part of the Omnibus Reconciliation Act of 1987, made a small downpayment on reducing the $200 billion annual gap between federal spending and revenue. That bill contained an ad hoc assortment of tax increases chosen so that the vast majority of Americans would not be directly affected. Congress accelerated the collections of some taxes, extended the telephone excise tax, corrected a technical drafting error in the 1986 Act that threatened to reduce estate tax revenues significantly, and adopted a number of fairly technical changes primarily affecting business taxpayers. Overall, the 1987 Act was expected to increase tax revenues by $9 billion in fiscal year 1988 and $14 billion in fiscal year 1989.

A modest tax bill, the Technical and Miscellaneous Revenue Act of 1988, was enacted in an election year during which then-Vice-President Bush campaigned on the pledge of no new taxes if he were elected President. The 1988 Act was revenue neutral over the three-year period, fiscal years 1989–91. The revenue loss from extending certain expiring provisions was offset by speeding up corporate estimated tax payments, tightening the completed contract method of accounting for long-term contracts, and repealing the special rules relating to loss transfers by Alaska Native Corporations, which had allowed certain tax practitioners to generate tax savings in the form of transferable tax losses almost without limit.

In early 1989, President Bush proposed a 45 per cent exclusion for long-term capital gains realized by individuals. This proposal, discussed in greater detail below, became the centrepiece of the President's domestic programme. The President did not push for significant deficit reduction, and Congress enacted another modest tax bill as part of the Omnibus Budget Reconciliation Act of 1989. This Act raised about $6 billion in fiscal year 1990 and about $5 billion in the next two years. Again, there were some extensions of expiring provisions and speed-ups of tax collections. Two modest tax reforms were the repeal of the completed contract method of accounting for long-term contracts and repeal of the exclusion of interest on employee stock-ownership plan (ESOP) loans. The 1989 Act provided some simplification of the corporate alternative minimum tax, including the elimination of the requirement that the cost recovery allowance for purposes of this alternative tax be determined by reference to the present value of the company's financial statement cost recovery allowance.

In 1990, President Bush and the Congress finally came to grips with deficit reduction. President Bush began the year by renewing his proposal to cut the tax rate on long-term capital gains realized by individuals. Congress and the President debated the possibility of tax increases until the President indicated that he would break his pledge of no tax increases. By mid-year, the President and the Congress had agreed on a $500 billion deficit reduction package over five years. The so-called budget compromise, enacted as part of the Omnibus Budget Reconciliation Act of 1990, included the most significant tax legislation since 1986.

The 1990 Act did not contain much that could be labelled true tax reform; indeed there were several new tax incentives for energy and small business that represented a retreat from the Tax Reform Act of 1986. Major revenue raisers included increases in alcohol and tobacco excise taxes, changes in the tax treatment of insurance companies, and an increase in the amount of wages subject to the 1.45 per cent Medicare payroll tax from $53,400 to $125,000. The 1990 Act again extended certain expiring tax provisions.

The 1990 legislation rekindled the debate over tax equity and progressivity, in part, as a result of President Bush's push for capital gains relief. At the lower end of the income distribution, Congress liberalized the earned-income tax credit available for individuals who maintain a home for one or more children. The 1990 legislation increased the rate of the credit and provided an adjustment for family size. It also included an additional credit for young children and a supplemental credit for certain health insurance premium expenses. Finally, it increased the phase-out rates for the credit, based on income, increasing the effective marginal tax rates for taxpayers in the phase-out range. As a result of these changes, the earned-income credit had become incredibly complex, particularly given its target population.

At the upper end of the income distribution, the 1990 legislation repealed the 5 per cent surcharge, the so-called bubble, that had resulted in a 33 per cent marginal tax rate for many upper-income taxpayers. This surcharge had phased out the benefits of personal exemptions and the 15 per cent lower rate. In its place, Congress imposed a top marginal tax rate of 31 per cent so that the individual rate schedule now had three marginal rates of 15, 28, and 31 per cent. Although the final legislation did not include the capital gains cuts sought by the President, it did provide a maximum 28 per cent tax rate on long-term capital gains. This maximum rate provided a small capital gains differential for high-income taxpayers subject to the 31 per cent marginal tax rate. Under prior law, capital gains were subject to the 33 per cent bubble rate.

In addition to the new rate schedule, Congress reduced certain itemized deductions by 3 per cent of AGI in excess of $100,000. For a taxpayer in the new 31 per cent tax bracket, this reduction increased the marginal tax rate on income by 0.93 percentage points. To complete the picture, Congress decided to adopt a new phase-out for personal exemptions, but the phase-out rate now depended on the number of personal exemptions. This phase-out increased the marginal tax rate on income by 0.53 percentage points per exemption over the phase-out range. Thus, for a four-person family subject to the limit on itemized deductions and the phase-out of personal exemptions, the top marginal income tax rate on ordinary income would be 34.1 per cent, 1.1 percentage points higher than the 33 per cent bubble rate. In the case of capital gains, the top marginal rate would be 30.8 per cent.

In 1991, President Bush again proposed cuts in the taxation of capital gains for individuals. However, in the end, Congress simply extended twelve expiring provisions and 'paid' for them by further accelerating estimated income tax payments by large corporations.

In the last year of the Bush administration, the President again proposed a capital gains cut for individuals plus some additional tax incentives to jump-start the faltering economy. Before the year was over, the President had vetoed two tax bills. The March bill contained a schedule of capital gains rates, tied to the marginal tax rates on ordinary income. These rates would have ranged from zero to 28 per cent. It also included a 36 per cent marginal tax rate for individuals and a 10 per cent surtax on millionaires, which the President found unacceptable. The President vetoed the November bill the day after the election, even though this bill contained six of the seven tax breaks he had proposed in January. The President did sign an energy bill, which contained some tax breaks for the oil and gas industry. Thus, 1992 ended with no major tax legislation enacted for over two years.

Taxes figured prominently in the political debates leading up to the presidential election in November. After apologizing for signing the budget agreement, President Bush renewed his pledge for no tax increase. Clinton made fairness an issue. He claimed that the tax cuts during the Reagan/Bush years had favoured the rich and he would, if elected, make the wealthiest Americans pay their fair share in taxes. With the election of Clinton, the stage was set for a new administration and a new direction in tax policy.

In 1993, the first year of the Clinton administration, Congress enacted the most significant tax legislation since 1986. The Omnibus Budget Reconciliation Act of 1993 intended to reduce the deficit relative to its level under prior law by almost $500 billion over five years. This deficit reduction was to be accomplished, in part, by $241 billion of tax increases that follow the broad outline of the tax proposals made by President Clinton in February 1993. The tax increases will fall primarily on higher-income individuals. The 1993 Act included some business tax increases, primarily on international business, and some relief for the working poor. The 1993 Act departed from the President's plan by rejecting his proposal for a broad-based energy tax and instead included a modest 4.3-cents-per-gallon increase in the petrol tax.

The 1993 Act created two new marginal tax rates for individuals—36 and 39.6 per cent. The top rate was in the form of a 10 per cent surcharge on taxable incomes over $250,000 (indexed to annual inflation). The top marginal rate on long-term capital gains remains at 28 per cent and the new surtax does not apply to these capital gains. By raising the tax rate on ordinary income and retaining the 28 per cent rate for long-term capital gains, the 1993 Act further rolled back one of the most significant reforms of the 1986 Act. By opening up a significant rate differential between ordinary income and capital gains, the Act will increase transactional planning, as taxpayers will seek to characterize income as ordinary instead of capital gains. The 1993 Act does contain some anti-abuse rules aimed at limiting the conversion of ordinary income into capital gains, but most seasoned tax practitioners believe that ways will be found to work around these rules.

The 1993 Act made permanent the 3 per cent reduction in itemized deductions and the phase-out of personal exemptions. These hidden tax rates increase marginal tax rates on income. For example, the 3 per cent reduction in itemized deductions increases the 39.6 per cent tax rate to 40.8 per cent (1.03 × 39.6). Most taxpayers subject to the 39.6 per cent rate will, at the margin, not be subject to the phase-out of personal exemptions. For a taxpayer in the 39.6 per cent bracket, her marginal tax rate on capital gains will be 28.84 per cent (1.03 × 28).

In 1993, only the first $135,000 of wages were subject to the 1.45 per cent Medicare tax (2.9 per cent in the case of the self-employed). The 1993 Act removed this wage cap beginning in 1994. This change increases the statutory top effective marginal rate on earned income from 40.8 to 42.2 per cent (43.7 per cent in the case of the self-employed).

The rate of the alternative minimum tax (AMT) for individuals was increased to mirror the increase in ordinary income tax rates. The AMT now has two rates of 26 and 28 per cent. The 1993 Act also increased the taxation of social security benefits for single individuals with incomes over $34,000 and married couples with incomes over $44,000.

The 1993 Act modified the earned-income credit, increasing the maximum credit and for the first time including a limited credit for low-income workers without children. By 1996, the maximum credit for a family with two or more children was $3,556, compared to $1,995 in 1994 under prior law. The 1993 Act eliminated the additional credit for young children and the health insurance credit.

The 1993 legislation is unusual in that it included only a few significant changes that affect corporations. The top corporate tax rate was increased from 34 to 35 per cent. (President Clinton had proposed a 36 per cent rate coupled with a temporary investment tax credit that Congress rejected.) The 1993 Act reduced the deduction for business meals and entertainment from 80 to 50 per cent. Few expect this change to curtail business lunches noticeably. The 1993 Act also eliminated the deduction for certain cash compensation in excess of $1 million per year. An exception applies to compensation linked to productivity, and tax planners are using this exception to find ways around the new limitation. Finally, the 1993 Act targeted certain industries for tax increases and simplified the corporate alternative minimum tax by eliminating the special depreciation system used to calculate adjusted current earnings.

In 1994, only one tax bill emerged from Congress—a bill to reform the social security treatment of domestic workers—the so-called 'nanny tax'. The bill increased the threshold for wages subject to social security from $50 per quarter to $1,000 per year.

In 1995, the Republicans gained control of both the House and Senate for the first time since 1953. The House Republicans promised sweeping tax changes, including a balanced budget amendment to the Constitution, a $500 per child tax credit for families, a 50 per cent exclusion for capital gains, and indexed depreciation for business. Although tax reform was centre stage in the 1995–6 debates over domestic policy, only a few minor tax bills emerged from Congress and were signed into law.

During the 1996 Presidential election, former Senator Dole promised a 15 per cent tax reduction for individuals, but this proposal received little support from the electorate. President Clinton was re-elected easily, promising only targeted tax cuts for individuals and business.

In summary, the legislation enacted since the Tax Reform Act of 1986 was primarily budget-driven.[36] The election of Clinton restored Executive Branch concern for progressivity. The resulting 1993 legislation raised taxes on the wealthy and lowered taxes on the working poor.

D2 Prospective Tax Reforms

The most likely large-scale tax changes in the future will address: (*a*) capital gains, (*b*) corporate integration, (*c*) the value-added tax and other consumption tax proposals, (*d*) health care, and (*e*) state-local financing of education.

D2.1 Capital Gains

Tax reformers hailed the Tax Reform Act of 1986 for eliminating the differential in tax rates between ordinary income and capital gains. This was viewed as a major improvement in the equity, efficiency, and simplicity of the tax system. It was achieved primarily by lowering the tax rate on ordinary income instead of increasing the tax rate on long-term capital gains. But, as we have seen, the Tax Reform Act of 1986 did not put the capital gains issue to rest. At the beginning of each year of his administration, President Bush proposed cutting the tax on capital gains. Congress rejected the President's call, but when Congress increased the top marginal tax rates first in 1990 and again in 1993, Congress adopted a 28 per cent maximum tax rate on capital gains, reintroducing the rate differential of pre-1986 law.

The debate over capital gains was fairly predictable as the arguments are well known.[37] President Bush stressed that a capital gains tax cut 'will

---

[36] Steuerle (1992).   [37] Hoerner (1992).

increase revenues, help savings, and create new jobs. We won't be competitive if we leave whole sectors of America behind.'[38] In addition, the capital gains tax cut would provide a rough adjustment for taxing inflationary gains that do not represent any increase in real income. Opponents stressed that a tax cut for capital gains would primarily benefit high-income individuals, and if inflation is the problem, the basis of capital assets could be adjusted to reflect inflation. This would be somewhat complex, but the UK has adopted a scheme for inflation adjustment for capital gains. Proponents wanted nothing to do with a basis adjustment for inflation, an implicit admission that this adjustment would be of little benefit for many investors holding low-basis assets.

The most critical issue in the capital gains debate was whether the proposals would be scored as increasing or decreasing federal revenues. If the proposals were scored as increasing revenues, the political opposition to any capital gains cut would be reduced, and, in fact, the revenue gain could have been used to pay for other tax reductions or to meet any deficit reduction target. The Treasury estimated that the administration's 1990 capital gains proposal would increase federal tax receipts by $12.5 billion for fiscal years 1990–5. The Joint Committee on Taxation estimated that the same proposal would reduce tax receipts by $11.4 billion over the same period.[39]

Cutting the tax rate on capital gains will increase realizations in the short run, and there is no disagreement that this behavioural response is significant and must be taken into account when preparing a revenue estimate. If realizations increase sufficiently, then a cut in the tax on capital gains will increase revenues in the short run. The initial question then is, how responsive are realizations to changes in the tax on capital gains? A second question is whether this behavioural response will be significant in the long run as well.

It turns out that Treasury and the Joint Committee both assumed a significant short-run behavioural response to a cut in capital gains. The Joint Committee found that a static estimate—that is, an estimate ignoring any possible behavioural response—for a proposal very similar to the administration's capital gains proposal would lose $100.2 billion of revenue over the five-year period.[40] Thus, according to the Joint Committee, the behavioural response would offset about 89 per cent of the static revenue loss. The Treasury believed that the behavioural response would offset 112 per cent of the static revenue loss. When viewed this way, the Treasury and the Joint Committee differed only by about 23 per cent, and this may be understandable and acceptable given that empirical work on the responsiveness of capital gains realizations to cuts in the tax rate are not sufficiently robust to distinguish between the elasticity assumptions used by the US Treasury

---

[38] President George Bush, Address on Administration Goals Before a Joint Session of Congress, 9 February 1989.
[39] Congress of the United States Joint Committee on Taxation (1990): 10.   [40] Ibid. 11.

Department and those used by the Joint Committee.[41] Nevertheless, the debate over the revenue estimates for the various capital gains proposals demonstrates that revenue estimates have significant legislative implications, particularly when tax bills are budget-driven.[42]

In the event, in 1997, the maximum rate for taxpayers was reduced to 20 per cent for assets held more than 18 months, remaining at 28 per cent for assets held 12 to 18 months, except where taxpayers fall in the 15 per cent bracket, whose maximum rates are lower.

D2.2 Corporate Integration

The issue of whether to integrate the corporate and individual income taxes has been long debated in the USA and remains controversial. The US corporate income tax is now almost ninety years old, and except for a two-year period during 1936 and 1937, when a graduated surtax was imposed on undistributed profits, the USA generally has adhered to the classical system of a separate corporate tax.

Although the USA continues to hold fast to the classical system of separate taxes on corporations and individuals, one of the most significant trends in tax policy over the last thirty years in the rest of the industrial world has been the movement in national tax structures towards some form of integration of corporate and shareholder taxation with respect to distributed corporate profits. It is not clear whether this trend grew out of a concern over the impact of the double tax burden that the classical system places on income from capital in the corporate sector. Many countries were concerned about encouraging domestic investment in local companies. Integration can be used to discourage both outbound and inbound investment.

In January 1992, at the end of the Bush administration, the Treasury Department released a study of the integration of corporate and individual income taxes.[43] In addition to the familiar integration methods (which include excluding distributed dividends from tax and imputing a credit to taxpayers for tax on dividends at the corporate level), the Treasury report outlined a new prototype, the Comprehensive Business Income Tax (CBIT), which would apply to both corporations and unincorporated businesses. CBIT would tax enterprises on the annual income of the incorporated or unincorporated business, with no deduction allowed for interest or dividends.

CBIT seeks to equalize the treatment of debt and equity by taxing interest and dividends only once at the company level, at a flat rate of 31 per cent. This would lower the effective tax rate on some equity income that is now double taxed and increase the effective tax rate on most interest income. Treasury estimated that once CBIT was fully phased in and behavioural changes were taken into account, it would increase revenues by $3.2 billion a year at 1991 levels of income (with no taxation of capital gains).[44] Thus, it would be

---

[41] Burman and Randolph (1994): 794–809 and Feldstein (1995).
[42] Sunley and Weiss (1992): 261–306.   [43] US Treasury Department (1992).
[44] Ibid. 151.

possible to eliminate the individual tax on dividends, eliminate the capital gains tax on CBIT assets, and reduce the corporate tax rate from 34 to 31 per cent without a revenue loss if no deduction is allowed for interest expense and interest income is not included in the income of the recipient.

CBIT is not the only way that debt and equity could be treated equally. An alternative would be to allow no deduction for interest or dividends at the company level and to provide an imputation credit for the recipients of interest and dividend income. This would ensure that the returns on debt and equity are taxed only once, but at the recipients' marginal tax rate, not the company tax rate.

Sunley (1992) argues that CBIT, while reducing the tension between debt and equity, would create a whole new set of tensions in the tax system. A major tension would arise because not all interest would be CBIT interest. For example, mortgage interest would continue to be deductible by the borrower and includable in the income of the recipient. Interest received on debt issued by foreign entities would be taxable. In addition, CBIT would put pressure on distinguishing non-deductible interest from deductible rental and royalty payments, particularly when the recipient is a tax-exempt entity or a CBIT entity with a net operating loss. CBIT would put increased pressure on distinguishing true leases (with deductible rental payments) from finance leases (with non-deductible interest payments.)

The Treasury report generated little political or business support for integration. The business community in the USA generally has favoured a cut in the corporate tax rate or faster capital recovery over corporate integration. Business opposition to corporate integration largely derives from concern that it would lead to increased pressure to distribute funds and that the benefits of integration would be spread unevenly across industries and across firms within an industry. Integration would provide little or no current benefit to small companies controlled by a few individuals or rapidly growing companies that pay little in dividends.

One reason the USA has not adopted corporate integration is that there is considerable uncertainty as to whether the benefits are worth the costs. For example, a revenue-neutral tax change that eliminated the distortion between distributed and retained earnings would increase the pressure on corporations to pay out dividends. This by itself would reduce business savings. Unless individuals increased personal savings, dollar for dollar, total savings in the economy would decrease. Indeed, it was just this concern over the impact of corporate integration on corporate distributions that led the UK to flip-flop on integration in 1965 and France to impose a higher tax on distributed profits than retained profits in 1989. Another concern is that proposals for corporate integration may involve windfalls to owners of old equity.

D2.3 Value-Added Tax and Other Consumption Tax Proposals

Interest in VAT has waxed and waned in the USA over the last twenty-five years. In 1969 and 1970, President Nixon considered proposing a federal VAT to permit a reduction in local property taxes or the federal corporate income tax. Then in 1978 and 1979, Chairman Al Ullman of the House Ways and Means Committee proposed a VAT as the centrepiece of his 'Tax Restructuring Act'. This bill would have imposed a VAT, generally at a 10 per cent rate, and the $130 billion of annual revenues from this tax would have been used to reduce both social security taxes and income taxes on corporations and on individuals. Many believe that this proposal led to Mr Ullman's 1980 defeat for re-election.

At this time, there is no groundswell of support in the USA for a VAT. Many in the business community oppose this tax because they fear it will be a money machine, raising $25 billion to $30 billion of revenue a year for each percentage point in the tax rate. If the government is given a new lever to pull, the government will surely pull it, or so the argument goes. There is some evidence to suggest that the VAT has led to an increase in the size of government, although this evidence is mixed.[45] Others oppose the VAT because it is generally believed to be regressive, putting an unfair burden on lower-income households. The state governments also oppose the VAT because the sales tax is viewed as the domain of state and local governments alone, although some state governments view the revenue-sharing possibilities under a federal VAT as potentially appealing. Still others argue that a VAT is inflationary because when a VAT is introduced, prices will go up, although there is little evidence to suggest that a VAT has serious inflationary consequences.[46]

The proponents of the VAT also come in different stripes. Some favour this tax because it could lead to a significant reduction in federal deficits. Some supporters argue that by shifting the US tax system towards one based on consumption rather than income, a VAT would increase the rate of economic growth and lead to a higher level of national income. Related to this is the argument that a portion of the revenues could be used to provide new incentives for investment under the income tax. Others favour the VAT because accepting this tax would be better than having to cut domestic spending programmes that benefit low-income families; alternatively, it could be used to eliminate low-income families from the income tax. Many business proponents of a VAT believe that its adoption would provide the USA with a trade advantage because under the General Agreement on Tariffs and Trade, the VAT can be imposed on imports and rebated on exports. Economists generally doubt the trade benefits of a VAT.

Unlike most European countries that have adopted a VAT, the USA has not had any experience with multistage turnover taxes. A VAT would, therefore, be a totally new tax, requiring new returns, new regulations, and an expanded staff at the Internal Revenue Service. Nevertheless, the administration of the tax overlaps to some extent with the administration of the corporate income tax, reducing the additional administrative demands.

More recently, there has been interest in other types of consumption taxes.

[45] Messere (1993): 391–2.   [46] Tait (1988): 212–13.

Senator Lugar, R-Ind., has recently proposed a 17 per cent retail sales tax on all consumption expenditures except food and medicine. This tax, however, would suffer from the problems that gave rise to the VAT as a revenue source elsewhere. Hall and Rabushka (1995) proposed a flat tax plan which would assess a 19 per cent tax on all business and individual income. Businesses would pay tax as under a subtraction-method VAT except wage and pension contributions would be deducted. Individuals would pay a 19 per cent tax on wage and pension benefits above an exemption of $25,500 for a family of four. Rep. Armey, R-Tex. and Sen. Shelby, R-Ala., have proposed another variant of flat tax with a different exemption and tax rate. Bradford (1986) proposed a tax similar to the Hall and Rabushka flat tax but it would tax individual wage income in a progressive manner, with the business tax rate set equal to the highest tax rate on wage income. Sens. Domenici, R-NM., and Nunn, D-Ga., have proposed a flat-rate subtraction method VAT at 11 per cent (the 'business tax' in the proposal) and a graduated cash-flow tax on personal consumption (the 'individual tax' in the proposal). In addition to deducting net savings, individuals also would be allowed a standard exemption and certain deductions and tax preferences.

Although there is little political support in the USA for a broad-based consumption tax, this could change if a consensus develops that a new federal revenue source is needed to reduce the federal budget deficit, to finance increased domestic spending for health or education, or to reduce income or social security taxes. Indeed, the one of the most critical issues regarding a future VAT (or other broad-based consumption tax) is how the revenues would be used.

D2.4 Health Care

The USA does not have a national health insurance plan covering all citizens and residents for a broad range of health-care services, but in September 1993, President Clinton unveiled his plan to provide universal health insurance coverage. Action on the President's plan was the major legislative issue for Congress in 1994.

The President did not propose an increase in the social security tax to finance the new entitlement programme. Instead, he proposed that all employers be required to pay health insurance premiums on behalf of their employees in an amount equal to 80 per cent of the average per capita premium cost. Employed persons, through payroll withholding, would pay the portion of their insurance cost not paid by their employers. Subsidies would be available for some employers and for low-income families.

The first issue raised by the President's plan was whether these mandatory premiums are scored (counted) as 'taxes'. This issue is important given the political difficulty in the USA of raising taxes for any purpose. The scoring issue, although quite political, is not clear-cut because the premiums would not be paid to the federal government but to regional health alliances established and overseen by states or to corporate alliances. The Congressional Budget Office concluded that the system of mandatory payments to finance health benefits represents an exercise of sovereign power. The premiums should be on budget and shown as government 'receipts'.[47]

Second, the plan would have limited the employee's exclusion from income of employer-paid premiums for health insurance, but this provision would not have had a major effect until 2004, when employees would no longer be able to exclude employer-paid premiums for coverage of health services not included in the Comprehensive Benefit Plan. Even then, the proposals would have made only a small dent in reducing the $51 billion tax expenditure for the employee exclusion. The argument for a limit on the exclusion is that the exclusion reduces the price employees pay for health insurance and is likely to increase the demand for coverage under health insurance. In addition, its incidence is regressive since employer-provided health insurance is disproportionately provided to more highly compensated employees. Since the tax rates are higher in higher-income brackets, the price reduction—and the price incentive to increase the quantity and quality of service demanded—increases with income.

Third, the plan would have expanded the tax subsidy for health insurance purchased by the self-employed. When phased in, the self-employed would have been allowed to deduct 100 per cent of premiums paid for the Standard Benefit Plan. There were a number of other tax proposals but they were of lesser significance than these three.

Many observers believe that any comprehensive national health insurance plan will need an infusion of general revenues. This is particularly true if the growth in health care expenses is not contained. Possibilities include a VAT, a much higher petrol tax (raising $1 billion a cent per gallon), or a comprehensive energy tax. If additional tax revenues are not acceptable politically, then health services will have to be scaled back or phased in over a number of years or the national health insurance plan will not be able to cover all citizens and residents.

Congress in 1994 failed to agree on a comprehensive health reform plan. Over the course of the legislative year, many alternatives to the Clinton plan were proposed. No plan with universal coverage and employer mandates could command majority support. By the end of the legislative session, there were several unsuccessful efforts to enact scaled-down versions of health reform. The tax provisions in the various reform packages varied widely, although many of the plans contained increases in the excise tax on cigarettes and limits on the exclusion for employer-provided health insurance benefits. Health reform and the related financing issues will remain high on the nation's agenda. The near term focus will be on cutting entitlements under Medicare and Medicaid and not on adopting a national insurance plan with comprehensive coverage of health services.

---

[47] Congress of the United States Congressional Budget Office (1994*b*).

D2.5 State and Local Tax Reform

State and local tax systems vary greatly from state to state, making it more difficult to predict the possible areas of reform. Nevertheless, there are several common issues.[48]

The local property tax has come under fire in recent decades, starting with Proposition 13 in California in 1978. At one time, most funding for public primary and secondary education came from local governments through the local property tax. In recent decades, however, the states have assumed a more important role in this funding. Since the 1970s, state governments have financed a larger share of public primary and secondary education than local governments. The main reason for this change is the demand for equalization in spending on public primary and secondary education across communities.

Since the local property tax is the main source of tax revenue for localities, the variation in wealth across communities in the USA, reflected in property values, leads to similar variation in the ability to fund local public services. State governments have reduced this variation through intergovernmental grants to the local governments for funding public primary and secondary education. Nevertheless, these efforts have been inadequate.

Since the 1971 Serrano vs. Priest decision in California, under which the state supreme court ordered the state to devise a grant programme to equalize per-pupil spending across California school districts, courts in the majority of states have ordered state governments to reform their public education financing system, leading to far-reaching changes in state tax systems to finance the additional responsibilities. Nevertheless, twenty years after Serrano, there are still many inequalities in public education financing and the court cases continue. Ultimately, in most states, state governments will have to assume a greater role of funding public primary and secondary education, requiring stronger taxing powers.

Strengthening the taxing powers of the state governments generally entails reforming both the general sales tax and the personal income tax. The main problem with the general sales tax is that it often taxes business inputs while exempting a significant fraction of personal consumption. Although this taxation of business inputs is not inherent in a sales tax, it is easier to eliminate in a VAT than a retail sales tax. Most general sales taxes do not tax consumer services in any significant or comprehensive way, and efforts on the part of state governments to extend the sales tax to services have at times met with significant opposition, such as in Florida, during the 1980s. Nevertheless, states are incrementally extending the sales tax to services. Personal income taxes are the brightest hope for enabling state governments to expand their taxing powers in a sensible way. This tax has grown rapidly in recent decades as a share of state government revenues and is best suited to meet the demands for increased redistribution between communities in a state.

[48] Break (1994): 1–5.

Table 11.5   Major federal, state, and local tax revenues, by source, 1950–1992[a] ($m.)

Fiscal year	Federal state and local	Federal					
		Total	Individual income	Corporation income	Sales gross receipts and customs	Gift and death	All other
1950	51,100	35,186	15,745	10,488	7,843	698	412
1951	63,585	46,032	21,643	14,106	9,143	708	432
1952	79,066	59,744	27,921	21,226	9,332	818	446
1953	83,704	62,796	29,816	21,238	10,352	881	508
1954	84,476	62,409	29,542	21,101	10,367	934	465
1955	81,072	57,589	28,747	17,861	9,578	924	478
1956	91,593	65,226	32,188	20,880	10,469	1,161	528
1957	98,632	69,815	35,620	21,167	11,127	1,365	537
1958	98,387	68,007	34,724	20,074	11,273	1,393	543
1959	99,636	67,257	36,719	17,309	11,332	1,333	563
1960	113,120	77,003	40,715	21,494	12,603	1,606	585
1961	116,331	77,470	41,338	20,954	12,649	1,896	633
1962	123,816	82,262	45,571	20,523	13,428	2,016	724
1963	130,811	86,797	47,588	21,579	14,215	2,167	1,248
1964	138,292	90,507	48,697	23,493	14,776	2,394	1,148
1965	144,953	93,710	48,792	25,461	15,786	2,716	954
1966	160,742	104,095	55,446	30,073	14,641	3,066	869
1967	176,121	115,121	61,526	33,971	15,806	2,978	840
1968	185,126	117,554	68,726	28,665	16,275	3,051	838
1969	222,708	145,996	87,249	36,678	17,826	3,491	753
1970	232,877	146,082	90,412	32,829	18,297	3,644	900
1971	232,252	137,277	86,320	26,785	19,427	3,735	1,100
1972	263,342	153,733	94,737	32,166	20,101	5,436	1,293
1973	286,132	165,030	103,246	36,153	19,722	4,917	992
1974	314,785	184,112	118,952	38,620	20,534	5,035	971
1975	331,435	189,970	122,386	40,621	21,090	4,611	1,262
1976	358,227	201,414	131,603	41,409	21,718	5,216	1,468
1977	419,778	243,842	156,725	54,892	23,180	7,327	1,718
1978	468,161	274,519	180,988	59,952	25,453	5,285	2,841
1979	524,446	318,932	217,841	65,677	26,714	5,411	3,289
1980	574,243	350,781	244,069	64,600	32,034	6,389	3,689
1981	650,228	405,714	285,551	61,137	48,561	6,787	3,678
1982	671,424	405,125	298,111	49,207	45,675	7,991	4,141
1983	665,764	381,179	288,938	37,022	44,471	6,053	4,695
1984	735,023	414,829	295,955	56,893	49,459	6,010	6,512
1985	803,404	454,037	330,918	61,331	49,159	6,422	6,207
1986	844,977	471,898	348,959	63,143	47,046	6,958	5,792
1987	944,203	539,400	392,557	83,926	48,423	7,493	7,001

Table 11.5   Continued

Fiscal year	Federal state and local	Federal					
		Total	Individual income	Corpor-ation income	Sales gross receipts and customs	Gift and death	All other
1988	998,347	562,600	401,181	94,195	52,604	7,594	7,026
1989	1,084,500	615,853	445,690	103,291	52,527	8,745	5,600
1990	1,133,886	632,267	466,884	93,507	53,970	11,500	6,406
1991	1,167,272	641,982	467,827	98,086	58,495	11,138	6,436
1992	1,214,530	659,041	476,465	100,270	64,282	11,143	6,881

Fiscal year	State and local	State		
		Total	Individual income	Corpora-tion
1950	15,914	7,930	724	586
1951	17,554	8,933	805	687
1952	19,323	9,857	913	838
1953	20,908	10,552	969	810
1954	22,067	11,089	1,004	772
1955	23,483	11,597	1,094	737
1956	26,368	13,375	1,374	890
1957	28,817	14,531	1,563	984
1958	30,380	14,919	1,544	1,018
1959	32,379	15,848	1,764	1,001
1960	36,117	18,036	2,209	1,180
1961	38,861	19,057	2,355	1,266
1962	41,554	20,561	2,728	1,308
1963	44,014	22,117	2,956	1,505
1964	47,785	24,243	3,415	1,695
1965	51,243	26,126	3,657	1,929
1966	56,471	29,380	4,288	2,038
1967	61,000	31,926	4,909	2,227
1968	67,572	36,400	6,231	2,518
1969	76,712	41,931	7,527	3,181
1970	86,795	47,962	9,183	3,738
1971	94,975	51,541	10,153	3,424
1972	109,609	59,870	12,996	4,416
1973	121,102	68,069	15,587	5,425
1974	130,673	74,207	17,078	6,015
1975	141,465	80,155	18,819	6,642
1976	156,813	89,256	21,448	7,273
1977	175,936	101,085	25,493	9,174

Table 11.5 Continued

Fiscal year	State and local	State		
		Total	Individual income	Corpora-tion
1978	193,642	113,261	29,105	10,738
1979	205,514	124,908	32,622	12,128
1980	223,462	137,075	37,089	13,321
1981	244,514	149,738	40,875	14,143
1982	266,299	162,658	45,708	14,006
1983	284,585	171,440	49,789	13,153
1984	320,194	196,795	58,942	15,511
1985	350,366	215,893	63,908	17,631
1986	373,051	228,054	67,469	18,363
1987	405,149	246,933	75,965	20,724
1988	435,675	264,080	80,133	21,685
1989	468,647	284,169	88,819	23,861
1990	501,619	300,489	96,076	21,751
1991	525,290	310,561	99,279	20,357
1992	555,479	327,822	104,401	21,566

Fiscal year	State				
	General sales and gross	Selective sales and gross receipts	Motor vehicle and operators' licences	Gift and death	All other
1950	1,670	3,000	755	168	1,027
1951	2,000	3,268	840	196	1,137
1952	2,229	3,501	924	211	1,241
1953	2,433	3,776	949	222	1,393
1954	2,540	4,033	1,098	247	1,395
1955	2,637	4,227	1,184	249	1,469
1956	3,036	4,765	1,295	310	1,705
1957	3,373	5,063	1,368	338	1,842
1958	3,507	5,243	1,415	351	1,841
1959	3,697	5,590	1,492	347	1,957
1960	4,302	6,208	1,573	420	2,144
1961	4,510	6,521	1,641	501	2,263
1962	5,111	6,927	1,667	516	2,304
1963	5,539	7,314	1,780	595	2,428
1964	6,084	7,873	1,917	658	2,601
1965	6,711	8,348	2,021	731	2,729
1966	7,873	9,171	2,236	808	2,966

Table 11.5   Continued

Fiscal year	State				
	General sales and gross	Selective sales and gross receipts	Motor vehicle and operators' licences	Gift and death	All other
1967	8,923	9,652	2,311	795	3,109
1968	10,441	10,538	2,485	872	3,315
1969	12,443	11,607	2,685	996	3,492
1970	14,177	13,077	2,728	996	4,063
1971	15,478	14,092	2,953	1,104	4,337
1972	17,619	15,631	3,340	1,294	4,574
1973	19,793	17,330	3,636	1,431	4,867
1974	22,612	17,944	3,755	1,425	5,378
1975	24,780	18,566	3,941	1,418	5,989
1976	27,333	20,058	4,356	1,513	7,275
1977	30,896	21,466	4,587	1,805	7,664
1978	35,280	22,990	4,836	1,842	8,470
1979	39,505	24,163	5,155	1,973	9,362
1980	43,168	24,687	5,325	2,035	11,450
1981	46,412	6,339	5,695	2,229	14,025
1982	50,343	28,458	6,051	2,300	15,742
1983	53,639	30,255	6,289	2,545	15,770
1984	62,564	33,238	6,921	2,226	17,393
1985	69,633	35,787	7,780	2,328	18,826
1986	74,821	37,522	8,374	2,534	18,971
1987	79,638	40,200	9,037	3,035	18,334
1988	87,010	43,126	9,644	3,241	19,241
1989	93,414	44,834	10,145	3,486	19,609
1990	99,702	47,367	10,675	3,832	21,086
1991	103,165	50,369	10,996	4,284	22,111
1992	107,757	54,964	10,660	4,456	24,048

Fiscal year	Local				
	Total	Property	General and selective sales and gross receipts	Local income	All other
1950	7,984	7,042	484	64	394
1951	8,621	7,580	551	68	422

Table 11.5 Continued

Fiscal year	Local				
	Total	Property	General and selective sales and gross receipts	Local income	All other
1952	9,466	8,282	627	85	473
1953	10,356	9,010	718	96	530
1954	10,978	9,577	703	122	576
1955	11,886	10,323	779	143	641
1956	12,992	11,282	889	164	657
1957	14,286	12,385	1,031	191	679
1958	15,461	13,514	1,079	215	653
1959	16,531	14,417	1,150	230	734
1960	18,081	15,798	1,339	254	692
1961	19,804	17,370	1,432	258	744
1962	20,993	18,414	1,456	309	815
1963	21,897	19,145	1,574	311	867
1964	23,542	20,519	1,806	376	841
1965	25,116	21,817	2,059	433	807
1966	27,361	23,836	2,041	472	1,012
1967	29,074	25,186	1,956	916	1,016
1968	31,171	26,835	1,932	1,077	1,327
1969	34,781	29,692	2,470	1,381	1,239
1970	38,833	32,963	3,068	1,630	1,173
1971	43,434	36,726	3,662	1,747	1,298
1972	49,739	41,620	4,268	2,230	1,621
1973	53,032	43,970	4,924	2,406	1,731
1974	56,466	46,404	5,542	2,413	2,108
1975	61,310	50,040	6,468	2,635	2,166
1976	67,557	54,884	7,156	3,127	2,390
1977	74,852	60,267	8,278	3,754	2,552
1978	80,381	64,058	9,326	4,071	2,926
1979	80,606	62,453	10,579	4,309	3,265
1980	86,387	65,607	12,072	4,990	3,718
1981	94,776	72,020	13,220	5,531	4,005
1982	103,641	78,805	14,836	6,105	3,895
1983	113,145	85,973	16,352	6,445	4,375
1984	128,399	92,595	18,296	7,215	5,293
1985	134,473	99,772	20,956	7,974	5,771
1986	144,997	107,356	22,628	8,536	6,477
1987	158,216	116,618	24,455	9,663	7,480
1988	171,595	127,191	26,122	10,272	8,010

Table 11.5 Continued

Fiscal year	Local				
	Total	Property	General and selective sales and gross receipts	Local income	All other
1989	184,478	137,107	27,767	11,048	9,248
1990	201,130	149,765	30,815	11,379	9,170
1991	214,728	161,706	32,036	11,947	9,039
1992	227,099	171,723	33,429	12,591	9,356

[a] Excludes social insurance taxes and contributions

Sources: US Dept. of Commerce, Bureau of the Census, Government Finances; State Government Finances.

E. Conclusion

The Tax Reform Act of 1986 broadened the income tax base and lowered the marginal tax rate on high incomes to 28 per cent for individuals and 34 per cent for corporations. Overall, this watershed legislation was expected to be revenue-neutral.

Since 1986, federal tax legislation has been budget-driven and much less concerned with the fundamentals of taxation. The USA has increased marginal tax rates to nearly 40 per cent for individuals and 35 per cent for corporations, and it has rolled back a few of the most significant reforms enacted in 1986. The 1990 legislation reintroduced a capital gains rate differential and the 1993 legislation expanded it. Beginning with the 1986 legislation, the individual income tax was made less transparent by increased use of income-related phase-outs of tax benefits. In contrast to the tax legislation of the 1980s, tax equity and progressivity were primary concerns in shaping the 1993 legislation.

Compared to other industrial countries, the USA has not integrated its personal and corporate income taxes nor has it adopted a value-added tax. These reforms are discussed in tax circles, but there appears to be little political support for them.

There will probably be continuing need to reform state and local taxes, specifically, strengthening the taxing powers of state governments to meet increased demands for assistance from local governments.

References

Advisory Commission on Intergovernmental Relations (1994), *Significant Features of Fiscal Federalism*, ii, Washington, DC: US Advisory Commission on Intergovernmental Relations.

Arthur D. Little, Inc. (1998), Development of Methodology for Estimating the Taxpayer Paperwork Burden, Final Report to the Department of Treasury, Internal Revenue Service, Washington, DC.

Auerbach, Alan J., Gokhale, Jagadeesh, and Kotlikoff Laurence J. (1994), 'Generational Accounting: A Meaningful Way to Evaluate Fiscal Policy', *Journal of Economic Perspectives*, 8/1: 73–94.

—— and Hassett, Kevin (1990), 'Investment, Tax Policy and the Tax Reform Act of 1986', in Joel Slemrod (ed), *Do Taxes Matter?*, Cambridge, Mass: MIT Press: 13–14.

Blumenthal, Marsha, and Slemrod, Joel (1992), 'The Compliance Cost of the U.S. Individual Income Tax System: A Second Look After Tax Reform', *National Tax Journal*, 45/2: 185–202.

Bovenberg, A. Lans (1489), 'Tax Policy and National Saving in the United States: A Survey', *National Tax Journal*, 42/2: 123–138.

Bradford, David E. (1986), *Untangling the Income Tax*, Cambridge, Mass: Harvard University Press.

Break, George F. (1994), 'The Big Four of State-Local Tax Finance: Under Siege in a Changing World', NTA Forum, Spring/Summer 1994: 1–5.

Burman, Leonard E., and. Randolph, William C. (1994), 'Measuring Permanent Responses to Capital-Gains Tax Changes in Panel Data', *American Economic Review*, 84/4: 794–809.

Cilke, James M., and. Wyscarver, Roy A. (1987), 'The Individual Income Tax Simulation Model', in *Office of Tax Analysis*, Dept. of The Treasury, Compendium of Tax Research: 43–75.

Collender, Stanley E. (1994), *The Guide to the Federal Budget*, Washington, DC: Urban Institute Press.

Congress of the United States (1996), Annual Report of the Board of Trustees of the Federal Old-Age and Survivors Insurance and Disability Insurance Trust Funds, Washington, DC: US Government Printing Office.

Congress of the United States Congressional Budget Office (1992), Measuring the Distribution of Income Gains, Memorandum, March 1992.

—— (1994*a*) *The Economic and Budget Outlook*: *Fiscal Years 1995–1999*, Washington, DC: US Government Printing Office.

—— (1994*b*). *An Analysis of the Administration's Health Proposal*, Washington, DC: US Government Printing Office.

Congress of the United States Joint Committee on Taxation (1987), *General Explanation of the Tax Reform Act of 1986*, Washington DC: US Government Printing Office, 4 May 1987.

—— (1990), *Explanation of the Methodology Used to Estimate Proposals Affecting the Taxation of Capital Gains*, Washington, DC: US Government Printing Office.

—— (1993), *Methodology and Issues in Measuring Changes in the Distribution of Tax Burdens* (JCS-&-93), Washington, DC: US Government Printing Office.

Economic Report of the President (1996), Washington, DC: US Government Printing Office, Feb. 1996.

Eisner, Robert (1986), *How Real Is the Federal Deficit*, New York: Free Press.

Feenberg, Daniel R., and Poterba, James M. (1993), 'Income Inequality and the Incomes of Very High-Income Taxpayers: Evidence from Tax Returns', in *Tax Policy and the Economy*, vii, Cambridge, Mass: MIT Press for National Bureau of Economic Research: 145–77.

Feldstein, Martin (1995), ' The Effect of Marginal Tax Rates on Taxable Income: A Panel Study of the 1986 Tax Reform Act', *Journal of Political Economy*, 103/3: 551–72.

Fullerton, Don, Shoven, John B., and Whalley, John (1983), 'Replacing the U.S. Income Tax with a Progressive Consumption Tax: A Sequenced General Equilibrium Approach', *Journal of Public Economics*, 20/1: 3–23.

—— and Rogers, Diane Lim (1993), *Who Bears the Lifetime Tax Burden*, Washington, DC: Brookings Institution.

Gale, William G., and Scholz, John Karl (1994), 'IRAs and Household Savings', *American Economic Review*, 84/5: 1233–1260.

Graetz, Michael J. (1995), 'Illusions of Precision: Distribution Tables and the Politics of Taxation', in David F. Bradford (ed), *Distributional Analysis of Tax Policy*, Washington DC: AEI Press: 15–78.

Gravelle, Jane G. (1991), 'Do Individual Retirement Accounts Increase Saving?' *Journal of Economic Perspectives*, 5/2: 133–149.

—— (1993) ' What Can Private Investment Incentives Accomplish? The Case of the Investment Tax Credit', *National Tax Journal*, 66/3: 275–290.

Hall, Arthur. (1994), 'The High Cost of Tax Compliance for U.S. Business', *Tax Notes*: 887–893.

Hall, Robert E., and Rabushka, Albin (1995), *The Flat Tax*, 2nd Edn., Stanford, Calif.: Hoover Insititution Press.

Haveman, Robert (1994), 'Should Generational Accounts Replace Public Budgets and Deficits? '*Journal of Economics Perspectives*, 8/1: 95–111.

Hershey, Robert D. Jr. (1993), 'IRS Raises Its Estimate of Tax Cheating', *Washington Post*, 29 Dec. 1993.

Hoerner, J. Andrew (ed.) (1992), *The Capital Gains Controversy: a Tax Analysts Reader* Arlington, VA. Tax Analysts.

Hubbard, R. Glenn (1993), 'On the Use of "Distribution Tables" in the Tax Policy Process', *National Tax Journal*, 66/4: 527–537.

Internal Revenue Service (1991), *Annual Report 1990*, DC: US Government Printing Office.

—— (1995*a*), *Data Book 1993/94*, Washington, DC: US Governemnt Printing Office.

—— (1995*b*), *Statistics of Income Bulletin, 1992*, Corporate Income Tax Returns, Washington, DC: US Government Printing Office.

—— (1995*c*), *Statistics of Income Bulletin*, Washington, DC: US Government Printing Office.

—— (1996), *Statistics of Income Bulletin*, Washington, Dc: US Government Printing Office.

Jorgenson, Dale W., and Landau, Ralph (eds.), (1993), *Tax Reform and the Cost of Capital: An International Comparison*, Washington, DC: Brookings Institution.

King, Mervyn A., and Fullerton, Don (1984), *The Taxation of Income From Capital*, Chicago: University of Chicago Press.

Manning, Elliot, and Andress, Laurence M. (1996), 'The 1996 Marginal Federal Income Tax Rates: The Image and the Reality', *Tax Notes*, 30 Dec.:1585–614.

Messere, Ken (1993), *Tax Policy in OECD Countries*, Amsterdam: IBFD Publications BV.

Metcalf, Gilbert E. (1994), ' The Lifetime Incidence of State and Local Taxes: Measuring Changes During the 1980's, *State Tax Notes*, 24 Jan.: 221–236.

OECD (1996), *Revenue Statistics of OECD Member Countries, 1965–95*, Paris: OECD.

Pechman, Joseph A. (1985), *Who Paid the Taxes, 1966-1985*, Washington, DC: Brookings Institution.

—— (1987), 'Pechman's Tax Incidence Study: A Response', American Economic Review, 77/1: 232–234.

Poterba, James M. (1990), 'Taxation and Housing Markets: Preliminary Evidence on the Effect of Recent Tax Reforms', in Joel Slemrod (ed), *Do Taxes Matter?*, Cambridge, Mass.: MIT Press: 141–160.

—— Venti, Steven F., and Wise David A. (1995), Do 401 (k) Contributions Crowd Out Other Personal Saving?' *Journal of Public Economics*, 58/1: 1–32.

Roth, Jeffrey A., Scholz, John T., and Witte, Ann Dryden (eds.) (1989), *Taxpayer Compliance*, i, Philadelphia: University of Pennsylvania Press.

Sinn, Hans-Werner (1991), ' Taxation and the Cost of Capital: The "Old" View, the "New" View, and Another View', in *Tax Policy and the Economy*, v, Cambridge, Mass: MIT Press for National Bureau for Economic Research: 25–52.

Slemrod, Joel (1992), 'Did the Tax Reform Act of 1986 Simplify Tax Matters?', *Journal of Economic Perspectives*, 6/1: 42–57.

—— and Blumenthal, Marsha (1993), '*The Income Tax Compliance Costs of Big Business*', Report to the Tax Foundation.

Steuerle, C. Eugene (1985), *Taxes, Loans, and Inflation*, Washington, DC: Brookings Institution.

—— (1992), *The Tax Decade*, Washington, DC: Urban Institute Press.

Sunley, Emil M. (1992), 'Corporate Integration: An Economic Perspective', *Tax Law Review*, 47/3: 621–43.

—— and Weiss, Randall D. (1992), 'The Revenue Estimating Process', *American Journal of Tax Policy*, 10/2: 261–306.

Tait, Alan A. (1988), *Value-Added Tax: Practice and Problems*, Washington, DC: International Monetary Fund.

Tanzi, Vito (ed.) (1982), *The Underground Economy in the United States and Abroad*, Lexington, Mass. Heath & Co.

—— and Shome, Parthasarathi (1993), 'Primer on Tax Evasion', Staff Papers, International Monetary Fund, 40/4:807–828.

US General Accounting Office (1990a), *Tax Administration: Profiles of Major Components of the Tax Gap*, GAO/GGD-90-53BR, Washington, DC: US Government Printing Office.

—— (1999b), *The Budget Deficit: Outlook, Implications, and Choices*, GAO/OCG-90-5, Washington, DC: US Government Printing Office.

United States House of Representives Committee in Ways and Means (1993), *1993 Green Book: Overview of Entitlement Programs*, Washington, DC: US Government Printing Office.

—— *1994 Green Book: Overview of Entitlement Programs*, Washington, DC: US Government Printing Office.

Venti, Steven F., and Wise, David A. (1992), 'Government Policy and Personal Retirement Saving', in James M. Poterba (ed.), *Tax Policy and the Economy*, Cambridge, Mass.: MIT Press for National Bureau of Economic Research.